COLETTE

Colette is volume 3 of *Female Genius: Life, Madness, Words—*
Hannah Arendt, Melanie Klein, Colette, a trilogy by Julia Kristeva.

EUROPEAN PERSPECTIVES

EUROPEAN PERSPECTIVES

A Series in Social Thought and Cultural Criticism
Lawrence D. Kritzman, Editor

European Perspectives presents outstanding books by leading European thinkers. With both classic and contemporary works, the series aims to shape the major intellectual controversies of our day and to facilitate the tasks of historical understanding.

For a complete list of books in the series, see pages 523–525.

'Colette,

by

Julia Kristeva

Translated by Jane Marie Todd

COLUMBIA UNIVERSITY PRESS   NEW YORK

Columbia University Press wishes to express its appreciation
for assistance given by the government of France through the
Ministère de la Culture in the preparation of this translation.

COLUMBIA UNIVERSITY PRESS

Publishers Since 1893

New York   Chichester, West Sussex

Copyright © 2004 Columbia University Press

Le Génie féminin, Colette © Librairie Arthème Fayard, 2002

All rights reserved

Library of Congress Cataloging-in-Publication Data

Kristeva, Julia, 1941–

[Colette. English]

Colette / by Julia Kristeva ; translated by Jane Marie Todd.

p.   cm. — (European perspectives)

Translation of: Le Génie féminin, t. 3, Colette.

Includes bibliographical references and index.

ISBN 0–231–12896–7 (cloth : alk. paper)

1. Colette, 1873–1954. 2. Authors, French—20th century—Biography.

I. Todd, Jane Marie. II. Title. III. Series.

PQ2605.O28Z6927   2004

848'.91209—dc22

2003068812

Columbia University Press books
are printed on permanent and durable acid-free paper.

Printed in the United States of America

c 10 9 8 7 6 5 4 3 2 1

CONTENTS

ACKNOWLEDGMENT

My thanks, for their careful readings, to Yannick Resch and J. F. Rabain; and, for their collaboration, to Elisabeth Bélorgey-Kalogerpoulos, Frédéric Bensaïd, Raymonde Coudert, Marie-Noëlle Demarre, Valentine Leys, and Catherine Joubaud.

Words

Colette
or the world's flesh

Colette [. . .] Believe me, it's an arcanum, the study of which is forbidden to most contemporaries! There one finds beauties of the first order that are nothing but thrilling frissons of the flesh.

—Guillaume Apollinaire, "La littérature féminine" (1909)

The seen world is not "in" my body and my body is not ultimately "in" the visible world: flesh applied to a flesh, the world does not surround it, nor is it surrounded by it. [. . .] There is reciprocal insertion and intertwining of one with the other [. . .] such that viewer and visible reciprocate each other and one no longer knows who sees and who is seen. It is that Visibility, that generality of the Sensory in itself, that innate anonymity of Myself that we called flesh [. . .] and we know there is no name in traditional philosophy to designate that. [. . .] It would require [. . .] the old term "element," in the sense that it was used to refer to water, air, earth, and fire [. . .] midway between the spatiotemporal individual and the idea, a sort of principle incarnate that imports a style of being everywhere a parcel of it is to be found. Flesh is [. . .] an "element" of Being.

—Maurice Merleau-Ponty, *Le visible et l'invisible* (1964)

FIGURE I. Colette in 1912. "Female I was, and female I again find myself, to derive suffering and jouissance from it [. . .] What to do? . . . write, briefly, since time is running short, and tell lies." (*La Vagabonde*)

WHY COLETTE?

SHE INVENTED AN ALPHABET

It is only in a century or two that we will be able to determine
with some chance of precision Colette's contribution to French
literature. No women prose writers who preceded her, from
Marguerite de Navarre to Mme de Staël and George Sand,
wrote differently from men. Colette created a style.

—Benjamin Crémieux, *NRF* (December 1920)

"Finally, a Frenchwoman, after Hannah Arendt and Melanie
Klein!" some of my readers exclaim approvingly, relieved to hear
Colette's name announced. "A genius, Colette?" others protest.
"Well then, it's the genius of an outdated and bygone France, and
one we prefer to forget!"

I love that woman's writing: it is an immediate pleasure, without
"why"; nevertheless, I want to hazard an explanation. Colette
found a language to express a strange osmosis between her sensations, her desires, her anxieties—those "pleasures thoughtlessly
called physical"[1]—and the infiniteness of the world, the blossoming of flowers, the rippling of beasts, sublime apparitions, contagious monsters. That language transcends her presence as a woman
of her century—vagabond or shackled, free, cruel, or compassionate. The style embraces her rural roots and her Burgundian accent,

while at the same time giving them a lightness through an alchemy that still remains mysterious to us. She herself calls it a "new alphabet."[2] What alphabet?

As she often does, Colette offers us a condensed narrative whose center, not always named, is the mother, Sido, and whose horizon is a sort of love. The last letter from Sido, elliptical and gleaming with joyous light, addresses Colette as "my love." But the daughter, who has just broken free of the gravity of love to celebrate only its "frivolity," "far from passionate nights and comparable to the mere break of day," is no dupe: "This time I have the scruples to claim that burning word for myself alone. It holds its place among traits, the interlaced design of a swallow, plant whorls, among the messages of a hand that was trying to transmit a new alphabet to me, or the sketch of a site glimpsed at dawn under rays that would never reach the gloomy zenith."[3]

Let us make no mistake: the alphabet transmitted by Sido is an evocation of writing as Colette herself practices it: a love letter, if you like, but one whose addressee, "my love," is no one in particular, not even a beloved child. That love disseminates itself in the interlacing of cosmic lines, of natural folds traced by the swallows and the flowers, and in which the traits of a man's or woman's face are incorporated, having finally escaped the ordeal of erotic love, having been restored to the clarity of a style. Writing, therefore, has no autonomous existence; it is part of the monogram of the world, embroidered by the "tendrils of the vine," by the pure and the impure, and by animals at peace. The alphabet writes the world, and the world comes to pass through the alphabet: writing and world coexist as the two aspects of a single experience, for this woman who writes in a state of feverish rapture that defies language ("Fever is the beginning of what one does not name")[4] but that Sido's daughter nevertheless manages to inscribe.

Opposite that solar alphabet is another alphabet, this one monstrous: a nocturnal Colette explores the depths of our identities, which she calls a "nauseous chaos without beginning or end" but of which "certain arabesques can be read like characters of an alphabet."[5] Colette's writing, an integral part of the realm of the senses and of female sexuality, which she defines as "more dispersed than a spasm and hotter than it,"[6] formulates these depths with an intensity and a restraint that transform her texts themselves into a "powerful arabesque of flesh, a cipher of tangled members, a symbolic monogram of the Inexorable."[7]

On several occasions throughout her books, Colette returns to an idea I find central in her work: writing is an interpenetration of language and the world, style and flesh, which reveals the universe and bodies to her as an "arabesque." Language is heard like a "savage chant," working its seduction on fruit, tools, and fabrics: "For me, a particular word is enough to recreate the odor, the color of the hours lived, it is sonorous and full and mysterious, like a shell in which the sea is singing."[8] Conversely, the gesture of writing involves a metamorphosis of signs into things: "To write! To be able to write! That means [. . .] *unconscious scrawls,* pen doodles around an ink spot that *nibbles at the imperfect word,* claws at it, surrounds it with darts, adorns it with antennae, with paws, until it loses its *readable word shape* and, transformed into a fantastic insect, takes flight as a fairy-butterfly."[9] Even more savory are the alphabets of frost or of thirst: "When I repeat the sparkling word ["frost"], it seems to me I am biting into a crunchy snowball, a beautiful winter apple fashioned by my hands."[10] "Harsh: now there is a good plastic word, fashioned like a rasp. It makes you thirsty. Harsh—I'll have something frosty to drink."[11]

In that sensual experience, metaphors are seasoned with sounds from somewhere else: "When words are not beautiful enough, langue d'oc embellishes them."[12] To give flavor to her dishes, Colette livens them up with a great deal of garlic, a condiment prized in the south. The taste of words and that of food set in motion the same secret alchemy: "If you're not capable of a little witchcraft, it's not worthwhile getting mixed up in cookery."[13]

Is Colette a witch—or rather a modest (male) gardener of the world's alphabet? She contemplates her handwriting: "I went to take up my post at the edge of a table desk, from which point my woman's eyes followed, on the turquoise vellum, the short, hard [male] gardener's hand that was writing."[14]

It never seemed enough to her to be defined as a "writer." Was this false modesty? Inordinate pride? Neither one: she knew from the outset that her tongue relished the universe in order to remake it.

Colette was engaged in a pitched battle to impose her freedom as a woman and her signature as a writer, and, before being crowned with a most academic success, she imposed on French letters a sensuality that defied the more or less chaste repression of respectable people. Yet she did not lay claim to a triumphal eroticism, at which her so-called liberated sisters would distinguish themselves; nor, at the opposite extreme, did she embrace a more conventional dolorous decency. Provocative, scandalous in the audacity of her mores and in her life choices, that engaging woman refused to confine herself to any manner of militantism and did not preach transgression of any kind. She managed to render her experience of freedom without neurosis, in a profuse language disciplined by classical rhetoric that returns modern readers to the serenity of the Greek miracle.

Was it necessary to be a foreigner, as I am, to be fascinated by her witchcraft, which would therefore be not just French but perhaps—one never knows—universal? As for alphabets, I remember the twenty-fourths of May of my childhood, the holiday celebrating the Cyrillic alphabet. At each parade, loaded down with roses and peonies, drunk on their beauty in full bloom and on their fragrance, which blurred my vision until I no longer knew where I began and where I ended, I held up a different letter of the Slavic alphabet. I was one mark among others, inserted into a "rule [that] cures everything"[15]—even communism— and nevertheless disseminated among all these young bodies stripped bare by springtime, interwoven with the voices offered up in ancient song, the silkiness of shirts and of hair, in the ocher wind that, in Byzantium or what remains of it, grows heavy with a stubborn fragrance of flowers. The alphabet, engraved within me, got the better of me; all around me was the alphabet, yet there was neither all nor alphabet—nothing but a jubilant memory, a call to writing specific to no literature, a sort of surplus life, "refreshing and pink," as Marcel Proust would have said.

The twentieth century will forever bear the stigmata of war and of madness: that is what the geniuses Hannah Arendt and Melanie Klein, respectively, analyzed, with an unparalleled radicality. Because it decreed the "superfluity" of certain human beings and attempted to destroy thought by "banalizing evil," that century of extravagant technological progress will remain in the collective memory as that of the Shoah. Hannah Arendt, wresting unexpected political judgments from the most demanding philosophical tradition, denounced Nazism and Stalinism, paired together as a single totalitarianism that destroyed human life and the world, that pulverized singular *love* and social *relationships* based on *taste, forgiveness,* and the *promise.*

The twentieth century also confronted, again with unprecedented lucidity, the madness inherent in the human mind. With the discovery of the Freudian unconscious, madness became, for the first time in history, an object of knowledge. But it was also recognized as a disorder that could be treated, modulated, dealt with, and creatively managed. In listening to children and to the child within us, Melanie Klein discovered the anxiety underlying desire and shed new light on the impact of the "death drives" identified by Freud. In detecting the "schizoparanoid" substructure of the human mind, she attributed all our aptitude for reparation and symbolic creation to the so-called depressive position that follows it—that is, our capacity to lose the other and, in moving beyond the mourning of that dispossession, to imagine and think it. We can imagine the other only on the condition that we lose it; and, as a result, thought is a capacity to absent others from oneself and to reconstruct them, to make them exist in representation, beyond the mourning of that abandonment.

Each in her singular and incomparable way, Arendt and Klein, two rootless women tested by the upheavals of their age, meditated on horror in order to consolidate the possibilities of thinking and living through the creation of productive relationships: political relationships for Arendt, relationships of the psyche and of thought for Klein.

To their nomadism, their abrasive reflections that found peace only by navigating tragedy, Colette adds another experience, which is also an aspect of that century. Her art, "meticulous like [that of] a primitive" (Paul Morand), imposes and demonstrates the idea that pleasure itself is possible if and only if it understands voluptuousness and at the same time its prolongation in an alphabet written as part of the world's flesh. These values asserted themselves, in Colette's life and works, as a "gay science," enchanting some and disheartening others.

As for me, I receive her experience like a very precious legacy of tradition, particularly the French tradition. Nevertheless, naïve about the Debacle, blind to politics, far from an example of historical lucidity, she preferred not to know: under the Occupation, rather than resist, she used her imaginative pen to aid her contemporaries, suffering from rationing and penury, to nourish themselves better. It is only by identifying her limitations and dead ends, her contradictions and paradoxes, that we will see her affirmative genius emerge, in the strange contribution it made within the human tragedy as it was exhibited in the twentieth century.

The firmly rooted Colette, the amorous Colette, the hedonist Colette, who demands her right to happiness at any cost—these images are not merely fraudulent imitations produced by public opinion, they are also those she herself delighted in cultivating. Perfidious detractors and fervent admirers lay claim to the same writings of the Idol of the Palais-Royal. Submitting to a pleasure that does not waver before perversion of any kind, not even that of the "maternal instinct" (Jeannie Malige), confined to the realm of sensations and the cult of the native soil, the reflection of "a certain France [. . .] as complicated as an old China" (Marguerite Yourcenar), Colette's works may exude the odor of an "infernal wickedness" (Liane de Pougy), or even of "the armpit" (François Mauriac). Indeed. . . . With and against that, her life and works—indistinguishable from each other and yet subtly distinct—offer contemporary readers powerful pleasures and pertinent meditations, the details of which appear in the course of the journey through her books. At the risk of chipping away at the "old France" image suprimposed on that "peasant girl" who "raised a scandal" before ending up priestess of the Palais-Royal and of the Goncourt prize jury, I propose the following interpretive summation:

Against the frustrations of her love life, against the ordeals imposed by social reality and especially the war, Colette clung to the pleasure of living, which was, for her, indiscriminately a pleasure of the senses and a pleasure of words. Her gourmandise and strong appetite privilege taste—at the basis of every civilization—all the while tirelessly contaminating it with vision, hearing, smell, touch, and all the variants of sexuality—with Eros and Thanatos blending together in a shamelessness purified by style. That hymn to jouissance—whose pagan accents some have praised—exuding the aroma of Rabelais's feasts and reviving Villon's insolence, is articulated for the first time in the voice and by the pen of a woman, a Frenchwoman.

Just as Freud (1856–1939) was discovering psychoanalysis through an analysis of his dreams (*The Interpretation of Dreams* dates from 1900), Colette (1873–1954) published *Claudine at School* (1900) under Willy's name. The *Claudine* series would follow (*Claudine in Paris*, 1901; *Claudine Married*, 1902; *Claudine Takes Off*, 1903). In the guise of an easy commercial success, these texts do not simply forge a new literary "type," that of the mischievous and rather daring young girl who would bequeath her "Claudine collar" to several generations thanks to Colette's theatrical double, the young actress Polaire. Above all, they reveal another image of female eroticism, a solar sister to the Freudian hysteric, who confessed, to the ear of the very attentive Viennese doctor, a traumatized and somewhat shameful sexuality. In vigorous counterpoint, Colette imposes the uninhibited words of a woman pleased to formulate her pleasures but without denying her anxieties. We would be underestimating the emancipatory and creative scope of these revelations of intimate and social truths if we confined ourselves to calling the author "perverse." From the precocious sensuality of the little provincial girl to the escapades of the Belle Epoque actress—and Colette shared the crazes of that age without balking—her pleasures awaken the memory of peasant women of easy virtue and the courtesans of French kings. Fortified by that corporeal memory, a new sexual experience was played out in the writer's life and texts, on the cusp of two centuries. It stands in contrast to that of Freud's neurotics, defies repression and a certain rigidity of divine and moral prohibitions, as well as the rigidity of the social norm itself. Atheism and amoralism were to be the two faces of that exploration, as pleasurable as it was risky, laden with metaphysical import behind an off-hand manner and a scandalous nature, not to mention the seductiveness of a "media event" before the term was even invented, and which Colette knew how to exploit. The sadomasochistic foundations of such an eroticism escaped neither its actors—Sade is the ringing proof of that in the French tradition—nor more distant observers, nor Colette herself who, beginning with the *Claudine* series but even more so when she moved on to other things, became its complacent and nonetheless lucid investigator. Through a knowledge more unconscious than analytical, she accorded complete trust in French civilization, to which she was proud to belong, a civilization founded less on repression than on seduction and its logic of masquerade, mime, artifice, denial, perversity, lies—in short, on imagination at once acerbic and salutary, imparting both poison and jouissance.

Caught in the trap of Belle Epoque morality and wounded by the repeated infidelity of her husband Willy, Colette spent a brief season in a depressive hell, an experience she would not disavow but, on the contrary, would distill, excavate, then pass through. This entailed not extinguishing the pain but, rather, reviving it in order to better express it, think it, and transmit it. With an insatiable voracity that began with an (oral) appetite and in the end mobilized all her curiosity and her physical and mental endurance, the betrayed spouse became involved with her inconstant husband's mistresses, joined the glittering milieu of wealthy Parisian lesbians, and, as much as possible, provided provocation in the world of the spectacle by displaying herself—to the delight and scandal of the bourgeoisie—naked in *The Flesh* (performed for the first time at the Apollo in 1907). The voracious Colette choked back her tears to better bite into life—the life of her lovers, male and female, of her husbands and mistresses, cheating or faithful. In 1910 she divorced Willy (he died in 1931); in 1923 she divorced Henry de Jouvenel (he died in 1935); in 1905 she met the marquise de Morny, known as Missy, then separated from her in 1910–11, keeping, however, the beautiful villa of Rozven in Brittany, which Missy had offered her. Missy would commit suicide in 1944, abandoned and nearly bankrupt: Colette had not seen her in nearly two years. Was Colette cruel, a "plump bee" (Mauriac) or a praying mantis "unencumbered by scruples"?[16] Or was she oblivious to all affection, attached solely to her pleasure, and increasingly subject only to the "rule that cures everything," the rule of her writing?

What a strange body Colette's was—so French!—taking its place onstage to show its suffering and its jouissance, dissociated, spasmodic, and, above all, rhetorical. It was a body that enjoyed exhibiting its peculiarities by creating no less strange harmonies in music, poetry, and philosophy—like Rameau's Nephew dear to Diderot, in whom sad Hegel thought he recognized the very epitome of culture: not the "absolute spirit" to which the German philosopher aspired but quite simply *culture,* defined as a "rending apart," an "impudence in expressing itself," an avoidance of "abstraction," a "trivial way" of knowing how to condense spirit in language. At this point Hegel perceived what he nevertheless refrained from developing: if the "impudence in expressing itself" that distinguishes the carnivalesque body is a "culture," it is because it is a verbal technique. Transmute the feverish sensation of a passion into the pleasure of mouth and ear, where spirit is incarnated in the words of the mother tongue. Such is the threshold where speaking humanity seeks its truth; and Colette never deviates from the sensual precision of that truth. It is truly the Bacchante Colette to whom we are indebted for that sober definition of culture as cult of the word: "Between the real and the imagined, there is always the place of the word, the magnificent word, larger than the object."[17] And she allows herself this tender mockery of Frenchness, which she considers fully chiseled in the jewel of language: "It is a very difficult language, French is. Barely have you written for forty-five years and you begin to realize it."[18]

Might culture, understood as a happy rending apart and as an impudence in expressing oneself—if we are to believe Hegel—be specifically French? Unbeknownst to him, in the naïveté of Colette's embroidery between flesh and words, her "alphabet" reopens that question. The least one can say is that the early twenty-first century, in search of the proper use for a "national" feeling submerged in the anonymity of "globalization," obviously demonstrates the pertinence of the question. Can I still feel, if to feel is to articulate? And in what language can impudence be spoken? A national language? Which one? A "crossbreed" language? How so?

Similarly, we all observe that what is bluntly called "perversion" is currently invading our mores and even the political institutions of democracies; that it is challenging the juridical space, which is more or less powerless to contain it; that contemporary art, in its own way, continually makes itself the explorer and consoler of transgressive experiences, for better or for worse. Can it lay claim to them? Ought it to lay claim to them? Are there limits not to be crossed in the race toward beauty and ugliness? In the already long history of that question, Colette's alphabet occupies a brilliant place.

The fact that this cult of jouissance was celebrated by a woman is not the least of the singularities in the adventure that holds our attention here. Where the great literary works of her European and American sisters excel at melancholy—from Emily Dickinson to Anna Akhmatova to Virginia Woolf—the French Colette, had she been able to become "the favorite at Versailles, would have governed the king and the kingdom." So jokes François Nourissier. It is through her hymn to feminine jouissance that she dominated the literature of the first half of the twentieth century. Although she despised feminists, frequented homosexual women, refused to let herself be confined within the sour and insipid charms of Gommorhean chapels, she imposed a female pride that, deep down, is not alien to the revolution of consciousness through which women's economic and sexual emancipation would slowly get under way. She says so explicitly in *Music-Hall Sidelights* (1913) and in many journalistic texts. Bravely facing the need to earn a living, as money-grubbing as she was extravagant, Colette managed to acquire her economic independence, knowing instinctively that it is the precondition for any other form of freedom: "I am guided by the mad ambition to earn my own living, both in theater and in literature, and my response to you is that one needs persistence for that."[19]

A certain kind of feminism, making its just cause into a rigid platform, confined the struggle for the improvement of the female condition solely to the political and sociological demands of the suffragettes. One sees the effects of that tendency in *The Second Sex* as well, even though in that book Simone de Beauvoir champions sexual freedom. Conversely, Colette, who knew nothing of politics, dreamt only of revealing feminine jouissance. In fact, her alphabet of the world is an alphabet of feminine pleasure, subject to the pleasure of men but marked by an incommensurable difference from it. There is no emancipation of women without a liberation of women's sexuality, which is fundamentally a bisexuality[20] and a polyphonic sensuality: that is what Colette continually proclaims throughout her life and works, in a constant dialogue between what she calls "the pure" and "the impure," describing herself from the outset as a "mental hermaphrodite."

Moreover, contrary to another simplistic image that has been created of Colette, that gourmand of sexual pleasures was also a woman whose works are a perpetual evasion of the love relationship and a constant tearing away from the life of the couple (heterosexual or homosexual) in favor of an immersion in the infiniteness of the world. No one grasped better than Colette to what extent erotic life is dominated by drives on one hand and by relationships to the object and to the partner on the other. No one knew better than she how to write that a woman's freedom is achieved only on the condition that she wrest herself both from her drives and from the other, less in order to accede to a mystic fusion with the Great Other than to immerse herself in a singular orgasm with the world's flesh. That orgasm fragments her, maroons her, sublimates her. In it there is no longer ego or sex but, rather, plants, beasts, monsters, and marvels. These are so many bursts of freedom, never beyond sex but always through sexuality, through an orgasmic exaltation of the ego whose sovereignty finds fulfillment in a joy at the limits of the extraordinary, the monstrous. Such is Colette's jouissance, continuous and scattered, scrupulous and sensual: it includes the man's phallic discharge without being limited to its pulsing; it is prolonged in rhythmic vibrations in the recesses of Being, which it appropriates through the musical precision of her style, thereby rendered physical. Indissolubly sense, sound, and sensation, Mme Colette's decretal simplicity is a true transubstantiation of her body.

In quest of voluptuousness, the writer stubbornly applies herself to *naming* it, coming as close to its truth as possible: her eroticism, filtered through sexuality and her drives and culminating in verbal pleasure, is, for that very reason, something other than a "perversion." Startled by the sudden dazzlement, that woman convinced herself that her continuous, hypersensitive jouissance, both organic and formulaic, shared something inhuman, cosmic, and, in that sense, monstrous—a challenge to the universe of civilized mastery attributed to humans. The metaphor of beasts and plants then imposed itself on her as a way of translating that refined brutishness, that overactive vegetation experienced in a pulverized but living ego, that is, an ego whose jouissance comes from its words and phrases and occurs in unison with the elements. The first *Dialogues of Beasts*, published in 1904, is in no way a sentimental anthropomorphism of the only beings—animals—that supposedly remained faithful after Willy's betrayals. In projecting herself into the "Four-footed Ones," the narrator domesticates the refinement and cruelty of her own sensual existence, which is perceived as radically inhuman.

The written flora and fauna thus become the true and only metamorphoses of jouissance, and trace the metaphorical alphabet of ecstasy that brings her into being and confers her ultimate reality on her. That is what will convince her that she is not writing literature. But what is she doing then? "I don't like to write.

Not only do I not like to write, but I especially like not to write."[21] Literature is merely a pretext for being astonished: "Where, in my career, could I have drawn on anything but astonishment?"[22] When the literary critic André Billy praises her to the skies after seeing *The Hidden Woman* (1924), she replies: "The greatest French prose writer alive, me? Even if that were true, *I don't feel it*, you understand, *inside of me*."[23] Is this the writer's false modesty or the conviction of a woman who knows she is completely identified with an extravagant sensibility regulated by the written word?

In an ingenious intuition, Colette guesses that it is by appropriating her mother, by creating the mythical figure of Sido, that she will be able definitively to transmute perversion—*père-version*, turning toward the father—into *mère-version*, turning toward the mother, to reconcile herself with her always somewhat humiliated femininity and to finally install herself in the oblatory sensuality of a henceforth fateful writing. Claudine is motherless, and the author's own mother appears only gradually in her writing. In 1913, nine months after Sido's death in 1912, Colette (who had married Henry de Jouvenel) became a mother herself; but the marriage to that second husband—nicknamed Sidi, not to be confused with Sido!—foundered in its turn. The incestuous relationship with her stepson, Bertrand de Jouvenel, looked like a revenge that, in actuality and at a profound level, would lead the writer to return once more to childhood memories. In *My Mother's House* (1922), the narrator's mother is belatedly introduced, through the evocation of time regained; she would be celebrated for the first time in all her importance in *Break of Day* (1928), which opens with the famous so-called pink cactus letter, signed "Sidonie Colette, née Landoy." Then, in 1929—reprinted in a bound volume in 1930 under the title *Sido*—the vibrant tribute finally appeared: to "the one whom a single being in the world— my father—called 'Sido.' "[24] "I am the daughter of a woman who, in a shamefaced, miserly, narrow-minded little region, opened her village home to stray cats, tramps, and pregnant servant girls."[25]

Was Sido a woman, then? Or rather a world, space itself: a "glorious garden face" on one hand, an "anxious house face" on the other.[26] She was a woman if you like, but, more likely, an original model reconstructed through the projections of the narrator, who in the end identifies her with the cosmic cycle: "rising at daybreak, sometimes before daybreak," in harmony with "the cardinal points, their gifts and their misdeeds."[27] An emblem of Being, which she humanizes and feminizes in return, Sido is the bull's-eye of the imaginary, according to Colette: the magical, impossible, precious place where the jealous and melancholic fascination a woman feels in her love for another woman finally manages to be appeased by winning over her own mother; only then, as a consoled explorer, does she open herself to the inhuman universe— men, women, flowers, beasts, and monsters. Henceforth, and with an enigmatic precision, Colette would consider "pure" any passion that fed on a similar *mère-version,* and "impure" the relationships (particularly heterosexual ones) that knew nothing of it.[28] Defensive—and clear-sighted—Colette!

But it is from her one-legged father, a very good swimmer, an excellent singer, an impotent writer and failed politician, that Colette borrows her patronymic, a woman's first name, and makes it her nom de plume (beginning in 1904, she signs "Colette Willy"; as of 1923, quite simply "Colette"), thus immortalizing the daughter and father in equal measure: "It was he, let there be no doubt, it was he who dominated me when music, a dance spectacle—and not words, never words!—brought tears to my eyes. It was he who wanted to come to light, and to live again, when I began, dimly, to write, and who won me the most acerbic conjugal praise—definitely the most useful: 'Could I have married the last of the lyric poets?'"[29]

A bold experiment, at once cruel and soothing, would be carried out by the writer Colette throughout her life: namely, the transmutation of love into style. At thirty-six, when she published under the name Colette Willy, she was already seeking "a love, different from Love, [which] can thrive in the very shadow of Love."[30] At fifty-five, under the name Colette, she added that "a woman [. . .] is born under every sky where she recovers from the pain of loving,"[31] and that, though she appreciates "the intelligent joy of the flesh," she prefers those "depths to which love, surface foam, does not always have access."[32] In the end she expresses the conviction that would scandalize our postmodern poets in love with Love: "One of the great banalities of existence, love, takes its leave from mine. [. . .] Having come out of it, we perceive that all the rest is gay, varied, multiple."[33]

According to Colette, that writing connection, a substitute for love, is, in fact, lyrical, poetic and, though it takes narrative paths, it does not remain on them. What is one to recount if nothing is forbidden, considering that narrative, since the mists of time, has only retraced the ordeals necessary to the quest—transgression, questioning, punishment? Immersed in the instant of pleasure, Colette labors to tell stories: her shattered stories overwhelm us, by virtue, above all, of their sensual flashes and the meditations on the war between the sexes and very little, or not at all, by their plots, which are repetitive and rather commonplace. Narrative time is eclipsed in Colette's books, her antiquated farces have grown tired, have not aged well, but the poetry of pure incorporated time remains, like that invented by Proust, which Colette reshapes in her way: hers is less metaphysical, brighter, with a sensuality that fills the mouth, that fills language. That Balzac fanatic ("I was born in Balzac"—she read him when she was six, and Labiche at seven) inherited from him a talent for depicting the excesses of love's passion and not for telling tragic tales about money. But it is in the journey to the end of the passionate night that she inscribes the mark of her true genius, and in that sense escapes it. Her path is free from the scatological or blasphemous ruts into which Céline and Proust sink. If Colette shares with the masters of the contemporary novel the poetic art of capturing sensory time, she does so in her own incomparable manner, with the inhuman serenity that marries man's jouissance to woman's, when they are in harmony with the world's flesh. Indeed, if "I" reconcile myself with the "object" (the primordial object, the maternal object, the object of love), there is no longer any "subject" or "object," and the "ego" is disseminated, incorporated, into the writing of Being.

"You are on the whole an upstanding woman, but of a particular kind. [. . .] You have the talent to write and to interest the reader in things . . . I can't say in nothings, since, at bottom, they are not nothings, far from it, and I even have to acknowledge that you are two centuries ahead in many respects."[34] What better guide than these words of Sido—tender without being overly kind and prophetic for that very reason—could accompany us in our reading of these "nothings," thanks to which the writer was able to re-create her life?

LIFE OR WORKS?

She had chosen neither time nor the world.

—Louis Aragon, "Madame Colette,"
in *Les Lettres Françaises* (August 12–19, 1954)

Whether coquettishly or in all sincerity, Colette said she regretted Claudine's fame.[1] She did not want her body of work to be reduced to the character she had created under Willy's influence or herself to be remembered only for that literary type.[2]

Nevertheless, more than the "type" of the mischievous seductress, and in a different way, it is the "new alphabet" woven from sensations and words that would turn out to be the most formidable trap involved in evaluating her works. Of course, Colette is the priestess of the mot juste, and never has the simplicity of the French language captured so tastefully the nuances of pleasure. Gide was enchanted: "A savory language, almost excessively so. [. . .] What sureness in the choice of words! What a delicate feeling for nuance! And all done so easily, like La Fontaine, without seeming to tamper with it, the result of assiduous labor, and an exquisite result!"[3] But is it simply a language, in the sense of a means of expression, a form of being, albeit an exquisite one? Or is it a language in the absolute sense, indistinguishable from the perpetual rebirth of Being itself?

Reading that "alphabet" invented by Colette is an emotional shock, which most of us receive like an immersion in life—ineffable. Recount Colette? Interpret her? It is not easy, and may even be impossible: the memory of what you have read slips away from you. Try: you have become an impersonal "one" without memory; have you really read, or *simply*—let us rather say *strongly*—felt? But felt what? Whom? Obviously, there is no dearth of plots in Colette's works, and they repeat themselves: threesomes, adultery, jealousy. But the originality of her writing does not really lie in this repetitiveness. How to define it? As an intersection between the flesh of a woman and the world's flesh: Colette interrupts her narrative with reveries, states of mind, ordinary or extreme bodily sensations. She unfurls flora and pomona, scrutinizes cats and dogs—"nothings," says Sido graciously. But the palette of colors, the fragrances, are woven in the music of the words, always excellently chosen, smooth, savory, scented, and that break forth in private within the reader. Seduced by that pleasure of the senses, accompanied by an irrational but scrupulous reason, with the precision of a dream, you believe you are awake, present, and yet what is at issue is lost time, which slips away once the book is closed. And you forget Colette's text; or, rather, the memory you keep of it is as vague as it is powerful, as inexpressible as it is moving. Indeed, how could one name differently what she formulated with a precision so definitive that changing a single syllable would destroy the palpitating flesh of the world? In addition, you have the impression that this text is only a passageway toward—the lived, life? What to call it?—toward an experience? Let us allow the word to resonate. Then, when someone declares that Colette is a second-rate writer, that she is French, too French, feminine, too feminine, you don't know what to retort. After reading Colette, you're left with a sense of self-evidence that the usual literary criteria fail to capture—she was the first to say so. It's regrettable, but that's the way it is.

Nevertheless, some have not relinquished the fight: consider how many biographies of Colette have appeared in recent years.[4] Charm is like that: at the shock of the metamorphic alphabet invented by Colette, you either fall silent or you come back to life—to her life, naturally. Her friend Germaine Beaumont gave a superb and very inspired evocation of it, adding something of her own existence, and thus inaugurated the quasi-hagiographical genre of Colette worshippers, who admire the enigma of her vitality, as intensely amoral and animalistic as it is sharp. "My life came in contact with her life," the projective biographer says in essence: "I once saw life only through poorly adjusted opera glasses, but, having encountered Colette's, suddenly, I see clearly."[5]

Colette leads the way, acknowledging she recounted nothing but her life: "Man, my friend, you are happy to make fun of the works of woman, inevitably autobiographical";[6] "I have no imagination";[7] "I'm sure I've never written a novel, a real one, a work of pure imagination, free of all alluvium of memory and egoism, relieved of the weight of myself, of my worst and my best, of resemblance, in short." There is no whimsy either, she proclaims, but a "regular, obstinate labor, which extracts its joy only out of the springs it draws from. Mine run no risk of running dry, and I will die on their banks before I have used them up."[8]

Yes, but it would be wrong to trust such declarations: Colette covers her tracks, makes little adjustments to the truth, as all writers do, and perhaps even more so. In fact, with insolent pride she extols and loves lying, one of the most seductive resources of the imaginary and of narration: "People who do not lie spontaneously [. . .] are lazybones who don't even take the trouble to arrange the truth a little, if only out of politeness, or to be intriguing."[9] Similarly, "there is a pleasure in attaching ourselves to those who deceive us, who wear lies like a very ornate gown and set them aside only out of a voluptuous desire for nudity."[10] Even when one shares confidences, one does so only in part: "One speaks of one lover and keeps quiet about the rest."[11]

Hence, serious minds need to untangle the real from the imaginary, to reestablish the facts, the pure biographical truth—

and who could complain? A superb erudition gives substance to the Pléiade editions of literary works: as we know, they devote more than a third of each volume to scholarly "notes" explaining the circumstances and presenting variants of each piece of writing. For Colette, there are also detailed "notices," which are true literary analyses. Could it be anxiety about the biographical "recuperation" of a body of writing that lends itself to such recuperation but also rejects it, which inspired such an editorial labor? Could it be the abundance of such commentary that has stood in the way of a finally complete edition of Colette's works, which we have awaited in vain and that is still lacking? Nevertheless, these critics attempt to synthesize the complex life of the times, of the author, and her stylistic development at the time of each publication, in order to point out the writer's exaggerations or omissions. Interpretations of the writing itself are proposed; in contrast, a number of biographical works, too focused on lived experience, generally overlooked them. That rigorous research, placed modestly at the end of the volume and in tiny print, constitutes a sort of overview of scholarship, which enriches the works with new material and makes possible a new guided rereading from back to front.

It is a different matter when Colette's life, absorbed and restored by biographers, is posited as supreme truth. Despite the precautions taken by the authors, the necessarily subjective reconstitution of the writer's existential adventures takes precedence over readings of the works. The moral, ideological, and political considerations of commentators prevail and, in the end, often efface Colette's text, of which one retains only references to the lived events as they are perceived and judged by the biographer or essayist.

Another side of Colette criticism, marked by deep ambivalence, simultaneously condemns and venerates the author. Hence the unhappy consciousness can declare itself "politically correct" by displaying outrage at the moral and political errors of a victim of "Frenchness," while at the same time confessing it is overcome by the witchcraft of that magician of taste and French style. Naturally, when it excels at its precious ambivalence, that biographical-style criticism is found appealing by literary juries, especially female ones. Definitively, and at the expense of her writing, it is *images* of a mythical Colette that a good number of biographers are pleased to serve up to the readers of women's magazines: a provincial woman surrounded by her animals, embodying old France and imbued with its tastes, who resists the barbarism of technology and globalization but who, in truth, might conceal a stingy bourgeois woman with a petty mind, one who dominates males and weaklings.

Critics of all stripes pretend to forget that this body they are spying on exists if and only if it is written—if it incarnates itself in writing, if writing takes root in it. As we move through her books, we will try to extricate Colette from the populist and psychological clichés that assail her. Because she writes, Sido's daughter cannot be reduced to a certain listless, even Vichyist France. Of course, through her sure and spicy writing, she also shares that identity and so many others. Nevertheless, in spite of the acts of cowardice and the crimes of Vichy, which she supposedly witnessed without objecting or resisting, she manages to reveal a completely different France. Her art of living participates in a French and European civilization that it is up to us to rehabilitate, to reinvent, without insolence but without neurosis as well. From that perspective Colette stands as a precursor.

In the best of cases the moral objections raised by her detractors in the course of their biographical reconstructions can be traced back to Mauriac. Having hailed Colette's "human courage" "for never giving in to the fascination of death," for avoiding, in essence, the melancholy of the moderns, and for taking on an "animality" that has never been "less base or more intelligent in a human creature," Mauriac congratulates her, quite simply, for having known how to live—before letting fly, in conclusion, the accusatory "whether to live is to be happy in your way. That's the whole question."[12]

Happiness at any price, with no moral sense other than that of following her desires and writing them down: this is an art of living that goes against the teachings of the Church and of its secular successors. It would take a great deal of indulgence, after the pleasure produced by reading Colette, not to place in doubt the legitimacy of happiness in Colette's sense. Or, on the contrary, it would take a true revolution in our conceptions of morality, of the human, of animality, and, consequently, of the happiness of living—in short, a revolution in the very experience of what one calls "a life." It would take a great deal of blindness as well not to detect in her a bold exploration of the "perfumed paradises" that Baudelaire experienced as a profanation and that Colette, not familiar with Freud and intransigent toward psychoanalysis, deposited—but without guilt—in the henceforth open dossier of knowledge of the human soul, which is essentially rebellious and in love with sublimation.

Indeed, Colette's experience is situated on an exquisite borderline and takes its distance from the Way of the Cross. For her, Body and Word, desire and meaning do not intersect only to diverge but meet and accompany each other continuously, at a certain distance but nonetheless in complicity, in order, yes, to assure Life, but a strange life, which *is* only because it *imagines*. In other words, in experience according to Colette, fantasy remakes the body and attaches it to the world's flesh, itself nestled in the flesh of language. Mauriac, who knew that experience well, undoubtedly saw his fellow writer as one far along on that path of sublimation: much too far? In her way, the atheist Colette was also a mystic, whose happiness in the glorious body of writing is purchased at the price of transgressions morality perceives as an evil.[13] Because we have experienced jouissance with her, we feel guilt, which plays a role in erasing the emotional shock produced by the writer's texts and in attempting to cover it with the biographical events gleaned from the woman's life.

In chorus with an ecstatic Colette, J.-M. G. Le Clézio moves beyond the work and, like a Robinson Crusoe of French letters, believes he can detect a nature without culture, which would be the secret of the alphabet according to Colette. It is, as a result, an alphabet doomed to mutism or to biographical inflation: "Colette is life. One reads Colette and one forgets the words, one forgets the barrier of written language, the author, culture."[14] Could there be a writing without words and without author, a writing that would be "life"? If a Colette exists somewhere without the "barrier of written language," then, in fact, *Colette is life*. And since *Colette is life*, Colette would be unthinkable—like Balzac and Proust, not to mention Céline, Duras, and a few others? We thought we could finally hold onto the singular Colette in the Colette who is entirely identified with life, whereas, in reality, we see her dissolve once and for all in the vitalist myth.

It is therefore not enough for Colette to *tell her life* in order for the reader to have the sensation of *being* with her in *life* in general. She would also have to write with a *style* inseparable from a *way of being,* in such a way that the sentences, no sooner read, would be transformed into things felt, and that the book would realize its own metamorphosis into sensory reality. That alchemy, which wrongly brings to mind irrationalism or some pagan cult, in fact rests on a particular *experience* of Colette as "subject of the utterance," with her desire and her history, and for whom the *formality* of style is only an aspect of her *participation in Being*.

We will see that, by seizing hold of childhood—in reality, a remembrance of the latency period—Colette chooses, as her position of writing, a specific phase in human life, the one, curiously, also chosen by Proust to create "time regained" in *In Search of Lost Time*. That subjective position, which calls upon the reader to join the narrator and to plunge back into his or her own latency period, is the place where sexuality, still immature, pours itself into sensuality, at once jubilatory and anxious, free and shackled, needing to secure itself to the ideal power of language to counterbalance the troubles of adolescence and to grapple with reality.[15]

That experience can become a source of failure at school, of childhood psychosis, and of social bungling of various kinds. In the optimal hypothesis, on the contrary, it inscribes *ek-stasis,* that is, the decentering of self, the cleavage from and osmosis with the prepsychic at the heart of the human maturation process. It is not surprising that many authors have found, in the return to the latency period, a major source of aesthetic inspiration, either through the intervention of child characters or through a remembrance by adult heroes meditating on the hazards of temporality. A suspension of linear time, pursued and haunted by birth and death, takes shape in that imaginary centered on childhood, which celebrates the ecstatic instant, at the juncture between sensuality and symbolization, senses and signs. It is therefore clear that the advent of sexuality, if and when it comes about, can take place on the horizon of the ecstatic experience that encompasses it, favoring the *joy* and, at the same time, the obliviousness, of the person experiencing it and of the person receiving it, the writer and the reader. To stabilize it, the writer continually returns to her alphabet, tirelessly beginning the same text over again, which becomes her repetitive style, a sort of immortality. The reader, when she does not repress the shock of reading, seeks to reassure herself by inquiring into the author's biography, which supposedly holds the answer to the riddle of what must be called the *miracle of the imaginary*; or she rereads indefinitely, to return to the experience and include herself in the alphabet.

Let us therefore attempt to read Colette in the text, but without ignoring the meticulous labor accomplished by biographers, to which the reader is invited to refer. We will confine ourselves at this point to recalling a few major moments in that life, entirely remade by and in writing. We will see that everyday existence takes on an extreme importance in that writing dominated by the sensory—contrary to its role in the fates of Arendt and Klein who, though passionate about the concrete details of history and the psyche, had the aim of extracting from them the general import, the concept, or the analytical key. Much more than I have done with the two other "female geniuses," I will first need to trace, with the help of the biographers, the framework of these events, to better appreciate the specific alchemy Colette's writing instills in them.

In broad strokes, let us focus on the key moments of the life as they intersect the works, before pausing at more length on the latter to better detect the difference between life and works, the contradictions that set them apart, the complicity that connects them. This is particularly true in that Colette's writing—and this is not the least of its originality—challenges the dichotomies of life and works, content and form, by working with the literality of language, not to isolate it in its formal autonomy, not to "forget" it in some sort of naturalist denial, but to immerse it in the flesh of her womanly desire and in the world's flesh.

FROM SAINT-SAUVEUR TO WILLY:
AN INITIATION

In *1900*, Paul Morand draws a succinct and incisive portrait, tinged with caustic affection, of the Belle Epoque, which witnessed Colette's beginnings. How can we, along with Michel del Castillo, not see it as something like a wellspring, if not a mirror of the writer who would not be long in making her mark? Paris amuses itself, disguises itself; Paris makes itself beautiful for the Universal Exposition. "Europe was on the move to see merchandise," wrote Ernest Renan ironically. From Maurice Barrès to Nini-pattes-en-l'air,[16] from the pope to Kaiser Wilhelm, everyone is—socialist? The French want to be both believers and anticlerical; religious education is replaced by a "gorging on general ideas." The blame falls on the French Revolution, which "destroyed everything intervening between the isolation of the individual and the omnipotence of the State," as Ferdinand Brunetière has not failed to diagnose it. It is not surprising that all political parties lay claim to Nietzsche, who is dying in Weimar, and that puns reappear on the far left and in Freud's clinical practice. France is governed by a center left bourgeoisie, "a race of clear-sighted prefects and advisers," "reading little, rereading the classics"; despite or because of that, "people had never written so pretentiously badly." From that literary disaster a few elect writers emerge, however, whose style "*pète sec.*"[17] There is Claudel, who "is saved from all purification by the thin air of China"; Mallarmé, who, when Zola told him, "For me, everything has the same value, diamonds and sh—," quietly replied "Diamond are rarer nonetheless"; and Colette, who "pays her readers in strong currency."[18]

Born on January 28, 1873, in Saint-Sauveur-en-Puisaye, in the department of Yonne in Burgundy, Sidonie-Gabrielle was not baptized until August 11. Her parents, Catholic but not observant, were instead free thinkers and rarely went to church: the writer's mother attended mass like everyone else, but accompanied by her dog and concealing Corneille in her missal. "Nothing is commonplace in your existence,"[19] she would write her daughter much later. In fact, nothing was commonplace in the existence of our heroine's two parents, and the biographers have not failed to make the comparison.

Her father, Jules-Joseph Colette, known as "the Captain" in his daughter's mentions of him, was born in Toulon in 1829. Of Italian and Lorrainian extraction, the son of a captain as well, he chose a military career. A student at Saint-Cyr, a soldier in Algeria, then in the Crimea, he was wounded in the battle of Alma; he was promoted to lieutenant and then to captain; finally, during the war in Italy, he lost his left leg and retired at age thirty. In 1860 he was named tax collector for Saint-Sauveur.

There he met Sidonie, wife of Jules Robineau-Duclos. She had been born in Paris in 1835, and her family and personal history are better known and more thoroughly discussed by biographers than those of the Captain. The daughter of Sophie Chatenay, who died a few weeks after her birth (let us keep in mind that it is on a dead mother, the future Colette's grandmother, that the statue of Sido as absolute mother is erected), and of Henry Landoy, the little motherless girl was put out to nurse in Yonne. When her father died in turn—she was only nine— Sidonie was taken in by her brothers, Eugène and Paul. The nomadic and rather extraordinary destiny of the Colette and Landoy families[20] takes on added spice given that Henry Landoy, nicknamed "the Gorilla," was a mulatto, a dealer in coffee and other exotic foodstuffs.[21]

Sido owed her education to her brother Eugène, twenty years her elder, an editor at *Le Figaro,* then a journalist in Brussels. She benefited from the free atmosphere of the Belgian capital, enlivened by intellectual debates, and from the open-mindedness of an anticlerical, even antireligious milieu associated with Freemasonry.[22] But—perhaps because she had no dowry?—the brothers arranged a marriage between their younger sister and a rich land-owner of Saint-Sauveur-en-Puisaye, who was twenty years older than she. That village nobleman, alcoholic and bizarre, abused his young wife, who, nevertheless, two months after the marriage, would not be taken in: by "hurling everything at hand at him," she "gave [him] a beautiful scar on his face."[23] All the same, the couple would have two children, Juliette (born in 1860) and Achille (born in 1863), the writer's half-brother and half-sister. Then Jules Robineau-Duclos died of a sudden stroke after eight years of marriage, in 1865. It was also whispered that he had been poisoned by Sido—or by Captain Colette?

Certain rumors insinuated that Achille was in fact the Captain's son. In any case, the widowed Sidonie married Captain Jules-Joseph Colette in December 1865; Léopold, known as Léo, the musician brother, whimsical and hard to pin down, was born in 1866. On January 28, 1873, Sidonie-Gabrielle Colette, "Minet-Chéri," "my solid-gold jewel" to her mother, came into the world.

The residence inherited from Robineau-Duclos, and especially its gardens, the Upper Garden and the Lower Garden, "a world of which I have ceased to be worthy,"[24] would be glorified and immortalized by the writer in texts that have become famous. They profoundly marked Colette and, alongside Sido, constituted the center of gravity of her childhood memory. No other writer, not Baudelaire, though captivated by his "perfumed paradises," nor Proust, though the initiator of "the search for lost time," was able to give so many precise and spell-binding details about a childhood proclaimed uniquely and indisputably happy and that was lived on the margins of the ordinary.

Hence, though enriched by an inheritance, the Colette family did not put their daughter in Catholic school but, rather, in the secular public school; indeed, amid the schisms still shaking late-nineteenth-century Burgundian France, the Colettes were more "red" than "white." Jules-Joseph Colette, a sincere Republican, as if to remedy his early state of disability as an amputated zouave, ran for election after retiring as tax collector: he aspired to the post of general councillor, then mayor. But, though his daughter, his "best electoral representative," helped him on his tours (before Sido put an end to these outings too awash in alcohol), Captain Colette proved to be a wretched politician: he was defeated twice. He was a wretched writer as well. Indeed, our heroine's father pretended to write, shut himself up in his office, installed himself at his table covered with pens and inkwells, lined up bound notebooks with high-sounding titles that supposedly celebrated his military adventures and impressed the entire family; until it was discovered upon his death in 1905 that Jules Colette's records were blank. The one-legged father was in reality a sham writer.

Minet-Chéri lived in a climate of freedom and joy that contrasted sharply with the upbringing of the other young girls of her social milieu: nocturnal escapades in the woods, permission to witness the "break of day," but also trips to Brussels and Paris. In public school she had the benefit of a serious education where she excelled in French, not surprisingly, under the supervision of Mlle Terrain and her assistant, Mlle Duchemin. They would be transformed into the "flagrantly ugly" Mlle Sergent and her subordinate, Aimée, who form a homosexual couple in *Claudine at School*—a caricature that would produce confusion and indignation in the two spinsters. They inculcated the art of composition into her and appreciated the "mischievous" student and her sense for uncommon words. Those who witnessed the prime of Colette's youth describe her as in love with her own image, contemplating at length her nude body in the mirror every evening, a sort of female Narcissus. Conversely, she depicted herself as a *girl-and-boy*: " 'I'll be a sailor!' Because she sometimes dreams of being a boy and of wearing blue trousers and a beret."[25] "I was twelve years old, with the language and manner of an intelligent boy, a bit gruff, but my strange appearance was not mannish, because of a body already femininely shaped, and above all two long braids, whistling like whips around me."[26] A sulfurous reputation began to attach itself to our heroine: could she ever be married off in her native region?

Whereupon the Colette family encountered financial difficulties. Not only did Jules and Sido manage their budget poorly, but Juliette, the older half-sister, "my sister with the long hair," "appealingly ugly," "with the sarcastic mouth of a pretty Kalmuck,"[27] had a falling-out with her family after her marriage to Dr. Charles Roché and demanded her share of the Robineau-Duclos inheritance, which was divided up. The Colettes, who received only a third of it, emerged from that ordeal considerably impoverished: they had to leave the beautiful house, which went to Achille,[28] and their furniture was sold. Sido, who wanted to remain with her favorite son, Achille, a doctor settled in Châtillon-sur-Loing (which would become Châtillon-Coligny), joined him with the Captain, Léo, and Gabrielle. It was 1891; the future writer had spent eighteen years in Saint-Sauveur and everything was already inscribed in what would now be her lost paradise. She would continually return there to glorify it in writing and, on the basis of that time regained, to appropriate, beyond her love affairs, the world itself.

Captain Colette counted among his acquaintances Jean-Albert Gauthier-Villars,[29] the son and grandson of printers, a graduate of the Ecole Polytechnique, then the founder of the Editions Gauthier-Villars, which would make its mark as the first French publishing house for scientific works. His eldest son, Henri Gauthier-Villars, born in 1859, was on his way to a career in literature: he wrote sonnets, then devoted himself to music criticism, signing breezy reviews with the pseudonyms "Willy," "Usherette of the Cirque d'Eté," or "Maugis." He frequented freethinking intellectual and aesthetic milieus, notably the decadents and symbolists, from Mallarmé and Zola, whom he attacked, to Joseph de Maistre and Louis Veuillot, of whom he approved, as well as musicians such as Debussy, Stravinksi, and Poulenc, whom he defended.

A rebellious and contradictory soul, a lover of scandal and a provocateur, Henri Gauthier-Villars, known as Willy, was an alert and appealing writer, endowed with a sense for language that would make him a very good editor. He lived on the fringes of his Catholic and conservative milieu, but without breaking away from it, maintaining relations of ironic and obliging submission to his family. A sex life that good families call "turbulent" went hand in hand with that bohemian comportment: in

1892 he found himself the father of a little boy, Jacques, whose mother, Marie-Louise Servat, wife of the draftsman Emile Cohl and adored mistress of Willy, had just died. The Gauthier-Villars undertook to place little Jacques with a nurse in Châtillon, "under the protection of Achille."[30]

With little enthusiasm on either side, a plan was hatched to make Gabri Willy's wife and the adoptive mother of Jacques.[31] The dual advantage for the families was only too obvious: the Colettes would marry off their daughter without a dowry, and the Gauthier-Villars would normalize their skirt-chasing son and their grandson.

Gabri, however, became infatuated with the bohemian writer, to the point, according to her future husband, of throwing herself, while tipsy, at him during a visit to Paris in 1892.[32] The journalist's Parisian fame seduced the little nineteen-year-old provincial, who, moreover, expected a sexual initiation from the already mature man of thirty-four. It proved to be brilliant on the expert pedagogue's part, and well understood by his apparently very gifted student: "With the help of youth and ignorance, I had had a good start with intoxication—a guilty intoxication, a horrible and impure adolescent fervor. There are many such girls, scarcely nubile, who dream of being the spectacle, the plaything, the libertine masterpiece of a mature man."[33]

The wedding was held in Châtillon on May 15, 1893, in the absence of the Gauthier-Villars family and with no other banquet than a meal for close friends. The next day the newlyweds left for Paris. They first settled in Willy's "Vénusberg"—as he called his top floor bachelor pad at 55, quai des Grands-Augustins, in the family-owned building. In June they moved to 28, rue Jacob, three dark rooms on the fourth floor, between two courtyards.

Thus began the future Colette's Parisian life. The libertine Willy, who prized adolescent girls with an androgynous look, played the incestuous father to them; Gabri slipped into the role of "tender shoot" without too much difficulty,[34] it appears, despite what she would later say in *My Apprenticeships* (1936). They frequented "Tout-Paris," which was gravitating around the literary luminaries of the fin-de-siècle: Anatole France, Jules Renard,

Pierre Louÿs, Marcel Schwob, Catulle Mendès, and others, not to mention Marcel Proust, whose importance would appear only much later. A few prestigious salons vied with one another for these celebrities: that of Mme Arman de Caillavet, Anatole France's Egeria; that of Jeanne and Lucien Muhlfeld, which was associated with *La Revue Blanche;* and that of the woman writer Rachilde and her husband, Alfred Vallette, who ran *Le Mercure de France.* The freshness of the Burgundian girl, her accent, her rolling r's, but also the cleverness of her repartees and her stories about public school, with which these ladies raised among nuns were unfamiliar, fascinated the salons, where high society and the demimonde rubbed shoulders. The immutable Sido, who received daily letters from our little provincial, followed from afar the adventures of her daughter, who was increasingly torn between the charms of society and the more corrosive charms of being Willy's prisoner.

Anonymous letters did not neglect to inform Colette of her husband's affairs: first it was Louise Willy, she of the fateful name, then Charlotte Kinceler, whom Gabri caught with him in 1894. She would give an account of that adventure in *My Apprenticeships,* paying tribute to a rival who would put an end to her "intransigent, beautiful, absurd character of a young lady" and who taught her "the idea of tolerance and dissimulation, of consenting to pacts with an enemy."[35]

Although the young wife immediately proved herself very complicitous with Willy's mistresses, and though her good sense, which did not require the writings of Dr. Freud, led her to set free her homosexual tendencies with these ladies rather than suffer from an incurable jealousy, that remedy (was it discovered intuitively or prompted by her husband's desires?) and her perversity do not seem at first to have been truly effective.

In fact, Gabri, "a child no sooner married than betrayed,"[36] fell physically and emotionally ill: for two months, Dr. Julien could make no sense of things, and the Captain grew anxious in Châtillon. Finally, Sido was called to Paris. Syphilis, whispered the scandalmongers; psychosomatic illness, recent biographical research has pronounced—and I agree. It was within the context of that sexual ordeal, in response to the shock of Willy's infidelities and the suffering in which his inconstancy immersed her, that Colette first discovered writing.

There are many young girls—and I know their bewilderment—who, arriving from *out there,* from the provinces or abroad, in a Paris long glorified for its culture and daring, endure the unexpected wounds that these free ways, heretofore admired from afar in the abstract, inflict on them, which they abruptly experience, when they truly suffer from them, as sadistic insults to their dignity or quite simply to their identity. Indeed, our bodies and souls are so made that the adolescent and the young adult need, after the family shelter, a faithful welcome, in order to receive from their loving mirror the assurance that they exist. Without it, they fall sick with one of those lovesicknesses mistaken for jaundice or—why not?—syphilis, from which one recovers only by breaking things off (but rare is the man or woman who possesses the insolence to fall out of love or enjoys an economic situation that allows it). Some find their salvation in writing, which is always—but in such different ways for each individual—an unlearning of obedience (that of love, all things considered), its transubstantiation into an insatiable curiosity.

Forced, therefore, to distinguish between "the presence—at the least the illusion—of happiness" and "its absence," "between love" (for which she was searching) and "laborious, exhausting sensual diversion"[37] (which she found), Gabri at first faltered: "There is always a moment in the life of young persons when dying is just as normal and seductive to them as living."[38] Her unconscious nevertheless avoided suicide and chose the symptom, a psychosomatic illness that had the advantage, one might say, of sparing her too great an emotional suffering, as Colette seemed to understand: a "grave illness" is a "surprising state [which] did not leave me enough strength to suffer a great deal."[39] As luck would have it, and thanks to our heroine's astonishing unsuspected talent, another symptom, more social and more valorizing, would replace it: writing. Writing would entirely absorb the woman, as we will see, and would leave no reserve available to devote to suffering. Did not Colette consider her *Claudine* books something excessive, a mask, a farce from which a "free tone" would gradually emerge? "It is unusual for young women (old ones too) to have a concern for moderation while writing. In addition, nothing is so reassuring as a mask. The birth and anonymity of 'Claudine' amused me like a slightly indelicate farce, which I docilely nudged toward a free tone."[40]

We read the account of that discovery of writing as a remedy for lovesickness in *My Apprenticeships* (1936) and in the preface to the *Claudine* series that accompanied the Fleuron edition of the complete works (1948). That discovery, unconscious, imperceptible, and at first denied, would gradually assert itself, both as a battle weapon and as the continual experience of a rebirth of self.

In autumn 1894, or perhaps 1895 (Colette is unsure), Willy, between escapades and always short of money ("Funds are running low!" was, at the time, the refrain of a man who would become an inveterate gambler by the end of his life), recommended that his young wife set down on paper her memories of primary school: "Don't be afraid of the spicy details, I might be able to make something of them." The result disappointed him—"I was wrong, it's of no possible use"—and the novice's notebooks would lie forgotten at the bottom of a drawer. During the same period, between 1894 and 1898, Willy, who had become a novelist—in collaboration with coauthors—published three novels on the theme of the femme fatale and man's impotence. Willy's studio or factory dates from that era: obsessed with impotence, he surrounded himself with ghostwriters whom he oversaw, whose talents spurred his productivity, and whom he liked to dominate. The newspapers did not neglect to speak ironically of that odd team.[41] Pierre Veber, Auguste Germain, Curnonsky, Marcel Boulestin, Paul Acker, Henri Albert, and, above all, the shrewd Jean de Tinan and even Carco were part of it, and the future Colette established affectionate friendships with them before becoming in turn the principal laborer in the factory.

As it happened, two years after the first rejection (in 1896 or 1897, therefore), Willy rediscovered the previously scorned notebooks, which now seemed "nice" to him; he regretted his initial blindness and, after enduring a few rejections from editors, secured the publication of *Claudine at School* by Ollendorff in 1900, under the name "Willy." In the preface, using a classic literary technique (used in *Adolphe, Armance,* and many other works), the author Willy presented himself as the editor of a handwritten, pseudopersonal journal of "disconcerting confessions" that had supposedly been sent him by a "young lady."

At the time, Colette did not seem impressed by that publication. Nevertheless, Charles Maurras was the first to hail the novel's "maturity of language and style." Rachilde praised Claudine as a "living, breathing person, a terror": "it's all womankind, howling, in mid-puberty, her instincts, her desires, her will." And Willy himself boasted, almost confessing he was not its author: "Don't you know that child was precious to me? So, so precious! She told me delightful things about her 'secular school'!"[42] Despite the warm reception of the critics, the big event for Colette in 1900 was less the publication of her text, signed by Willy, than the purchase of the property of Monts-Boucons, near Besançon, whose grounds she adored and where she treated herself to long horse rides.[43] It was only after breaking up with Willy, and later, when she became aware she was an author, that she would instigate a bitter lawsuit against Willy's illegitimate claim of authorship for the four *Claudine* novels.

Contemporary criticism is divided: many (like Michèle Sarde) put their trust in Colette's statements, her accusation that Willy was a jailer who locked up his wife and exploited her literary labor when he did not abuse her physically. Others regret the loss of the manuscripts for the first two *Claudine* books (*Claudine at School* [1900] and *Claudine in Paris* [1901]), probably destroyed on Willy's order by his secretary Paul Barlet, without which it is impossible to form an idea of the corrections made by Colette herself and those attributable to her husband. The manuscripts of *Claudine Married* (1902) and *Claudine Takes Off* (1903) attest to Willy's intervention; he livened up the Sapphic episodes, made stylistic corrections (tightening descriptions, disciplining the adjectives) or added salacious puns, and, in an entirely different register, polished up erudite remarks on Wagner.

"My name is Claudine, I live in Montigny; I was born there in 1884; I will probably not die there." So began Colette's career in literature, and the text surprised all the connoisseurs by its authenticity, which contrasted with the decadence of the age, then made an impression on the general public with its heroine's mischievous libertinage. "A twentieth-century *Liaisons dangereuses* by a modern style Laclos," Jean Lorrain hailed it in *Le Journal* of May 29, 1902. Within a few years, the four *Claudine* books sold at "best-seller" levels: respectively, 54,000, 55,000, 60,000, and 40,000 copies for 1907 and 1908. It was *Claudine Married* that sold the most copies, certainly because of its bawdy stories: people decoded in it the affair between Mme Willy and Georgie Raoul-Duval, Mr. Willy's mistress, who became "Rézi" in the novel. Translations began to appear, especially in Germany, which prompted this disapproving remark from Romain Rolland: "*Claudine in Paris* is, I believe—along with Rostand's *L'aiglon* [The eaglet]—the French book that has had the most editions in Europe in the last ten years."[44] In the shadows, however, working intensely, an eternally young man, Marcel Proust (he was twenty-nine in 1900), had already set in motion what he would later call an "involuntary memory," which Colette, masked as Willy, had just discovered without knowing it: he himself had begun "the transmutation of memory into a directly experienced reality" in his fragments of *Jean Santeuil*.[45]

For the moment, however, it was the theatrical stage that assured the popular success of the *Claudine* books. And it was, on the contrary, within the intimacy of her circle of friends that Colette found the resources to pursue her writing.

Apart from his talents as an editor, Willy's unprecedented flair for dealing with the "media," before the term even existed, must be recognized: attuned to the always somewhat hysterical desires of the general public, the husband perceived the seductiveness he could extract from a couple formed of two women, in the first place, the "doubles" or "twins" Colette and Polaire, then the homosexual couple Colette and Missy.

Polaire, born in Algeria of French parents, "ugly" to some people because of her mixed-race features, was a short woman with a "painfully thin" waist; very free with her young lovers, she imposed her vivacity and her working-class vulgarity on stage, to the point of bewitching her contemporaries. Childlike, masculine, Colette's twin: Willy the publicity hound made use of her, throwing his "twins" in the faces of spectators and posing as their father. Colette and Polaire were dressed alike and given the same hairstyle; Willy went so far as to get Colette to cut her long serpentine braids, to Sido's great chagrin.

As for friends, in these first years of her Paris initiation, Colette managed to make extraordinary ones, sufficient to belie or at least nuance her image as a cruel and calculating woman. During her mysterious illness in 1894, Marcel Schwob read Oscar Wilde's "The Nightingale and the Rose" to her, which she would transform into *Tendrils of the Vine* in 1908. Marguerite Moreno, Schwob's wife and a remarkable actress, would remain faithful to her until her own death in 1948. She was close to Pierre Louÿs and, curiously, to Alfred Jarry, whom that young woman of twenty-three appreciated a great deal, even though she would never have any feeling for the surrealists, Picasso, or most of the innovators. She was also close to the Muhlfelds, Lucien and Jeanne, who associated with Apollinaire, Verlaine, Mallarmé, Claudel, and Barrès; to the painter Jacques-Emile Blanche, "who painted three portraits of me, which he destroyed with his own hands"; but also to Jean Lorrain, Comtesse Mirabeau-Martel (alias Gyp), Liane de Pougy, and Mme Arman de Caillavet, at whose Wednesday salons on avenue Hoche Colette met Proust; and, of course, to a galaxy of composers and musicians with whom Willy kept company. She would prefer Debussy, would collaborate with Maurice Ravel on *The Child and the Enchantments,* and would be the friend of Francis Poulenc.

In 1896 the Willys moved to the Right Bank, to the seventh floor of 93, rue de Courcelles; then, in late 1902 they settled at 177 bis, rue de Courcelles, their last conjugal domicile, which occupied a mansion's third floor, above which Colette set up a gymnastics room. The salons vied for the striking little savage, many appreciating her musical gifts—she played Schumann's *Walnut Tree* without a false note—but they were already sneering at her provocative immorality, nicknaming her Colette-"Culotte" ("Colette wears the trousers"), a "woman of genius and of vice."[46] There would later be other dear acquaintances who accompanied her throughout her life and left traces in her texts: Caroline Otéro, whose artifice Colette admired; Wague, her faithful companion on theatrical tours, and his wife; the writers Claude Farrère and Louis de Robert; the valuable confidant Léon Hamel, who followed her from 1908 till his death in 1917; but also Octave Mirbeau, Musidora, and many others, the list and merits of whom biographers have not neglected to reconstruct.

In the crucible of that intense activity, an alchemy was occurring in secret, which would transform Willy's female ghostwriter into a writer without peer. One can follow that journey in the progressive detachment that finally separated Colette from Willy. He found a new passion in the young actress Marguerite Maniez, one of the many "aspiring Claudines." She would take the pseudonym Meg Villars, would become for a time Willy's wife, and would remain Colette's friend to the end. But, above all, Colette's style, already consolidated in the four *Claudine* books, clearly marked itself off from the literary extravagance— not devoid of originality, however—that Willy continued to pursue. She reached a new stage with the publication of the working draft *Dialogues of Beasts,* published by Le Mercure de France in 1904 under a new name: Colette Willy. Francis Jammes hailed her with a memorable preface dated 1905: "Mme Colette Willy is a living woman, an *honest to goodness* woman, who has dared to be natural and who resembles a little village bride much more than a perverse woman of letters. [. . .] A woman who sings, with the voice of a pure French brook, the sad tenderness that makes the hearts of beasts beat so quickly."[47] There would be a great deal to say about this praise; and the essence of the animal revolution in Colette, whom Jammes is pleased to contrast to the "more backward symbolists," may not lie where the poet sees it. But, through that preface Mme Colette Willy is more than brilliantly rehabilitated, she is enthroned, she has achieved her standing in literature. She has only to continue, and she will not hesitate—always amid scandal and with an extravagant firmness.

The beasts, for their part, will continue ever afterward to accompany her: from *Peace Among the Beasts* (1916) to *From Paw to Wing* (1943), not to mention the novel *The Cat* (1933), in which the feline who gives it its title rises to the stature of a character.

On September 17, 1905, Jules-Joseph Colette died; his loved ones then discovered the blank pages of his so-called memoirs. Colette and Willy arrived late to the funeral, and the daughter's feelings about her father's death are unknown. How can we not notice, however, that the narrowing of her life in the "retreat from love" is situated at the time of that loss, along with her abreactions onstage, the more or less calculated provocations of high society, and the various acts that elicited the blame of right-thinking people? The portrait of the Captain and the daughter's debt to her father would not be committed to writing for another twenty-five years, in *Sido* (1930).[48]

Henceforth the "life" and "works" become confused: they journey along together, nourish each other, and, more and more clearly, the writing influences the existence, anticipates it and modulates it. Colette herself would call that ascendancy of "works" over "life" a "premonitory" writing. In the meantime her style became purer under the influence of an intense concentration of sensuality and a stubborn intellectual discipline: she arrived at a new stage of that experiment, which still strikes us as inseparably sexual *and* stylistic.

After *Dialogues of Beasts* Colette returned to the task of wresting herself from the dependency on love that *Claudine Takes Off* had sketched out, a task that was still far from accomplished. She patiently pursued the same theme in *Minne* (1904) and in *The Error of Minne's Ways* (1905, published under Willy's name); repeated and reworked it in *The Innocent Libertine* (1909), signed Colette Willy; and asserted it almost as a "feminist" credo in *The Retreat from Love* (1907), again signed Colette Willy. That veritable work of self-analysis, conducted through the intermediary of the novel,[49] would be followed by a second stage of stylistic autonomy, masterfully marked by *Tendrils of the Vine* (published in the review *La Vie Parisienne* in 1980, again under the name Colette Willy): that text finally imposed the inimitable style of the Colette comet in the firmament of French letters.[50] *The Shackle* (1913) introduced the hybrid signature "Colette (Colette Willy)." She would publish under "Colette Willy" until October 30, 1913 (subsequently using "C. de Jouvenel" for her correspondence, until her divorce), before the name "Colette" appeared by itself as of 1923.

The crystallization of the working drafts *Dialogues of Beasts* and *Tendrils of the Vine* was accompanied in Colette's life by two new passions: the stage and Missy.

VAGABONDAGE AND SOCIAL SUCCESS: MISSY, SIDI, BEL-GAZOU

It was certainly Willy who immersed his young wife in the Parisian milieu of the spectacle, with the Polaire/Claudine duo representing in turn a fascinating example of stage competition, which mobilized Colette, still a novice and the inexperienced "twin" of the much better-trained Polaire. With Lugné-Poe and Charles Vayre (under the composite pseudonym "Luvey"), Willy produced the play *Claudine in Paris,* which was an enormous success, first performed at the Bouffes-Parisiens on January 22, 1902; it would be reprised with Polaire or with Colette, in Paris and in the provinces. Willy himself got involved, sparking the reprobation of conservative Catholic circles. It should be mentioned that Colette was always drawn to the theater, then to film, and that the experience onstage, the tours, as exhausting as they were exhilarating, the universe of the music hall with its dramas, its masks, its illusions, its suffering, its benefits and losses, its drugs, and its flaunting of everything, seem to have suited her perfectly. It was as if the stage was indispensable in her escape from her increasingly morose marriage and, above all, in the consolidation of a style that was never formal, that was always and immediately incarnated, if she was to remain in continuous contact with that bodily writing, engaged with the physical rhythm of her words.

Colette took lessons from Georges Wague and from Etienne Decroux, who had revived the pantomime; she first performed in

private, exhibiting a compact, muscular body that she had subjected to conscientious gymnastic exercises. Her debut on the
stage took place on February 6, 1906, at the Mathurins theater,
where she played the role of a faun in the mime *Desire, Love, and
Chimera*. Then, this time as an actress and not a mime, in *Be-
ginners Have All the Luck* at the Théâtre Royal, she took on the
role of a male seducer who exchanges a long kiss with a lady
picked up in a bar. She played a faun and a transvestite, played
at being herself or against type, showed the unknown part of herself. Colette's monsters were beginning to surface, and this was
only the beginning. In spring 1906 Lugné-Poe gave her the role
of Paniska in *Pan* at the Marigny theater, for the Théâtre de
l'Oeuvre: nearly naked in the last scene, Colette-Paniska feted
the old god Pan, who was decidedly not dead, contrary to what
Plutarch had claimed. With the breakup from Willy under way,
it was Mathilde de Morny, called Missy, who entered Colette's
life in spring 1906 and sometimes accompanied her in her appearances onstage.[51]

After the flirtation with Georgie Raoul-Duval ("Rézi" in *Claudine Married*) in 1901, Colette's relations with the Gommorhean
milieu in Paris intensified. She kept company with one of its
most eminent Egerias, Natalie Clifford-Barney (a "semi-affair,"
the American would say), whom Colette nicknamed "Flossie" in
her torrid letters and at whose home she performed in tableaux
vivants and pantomimes. There Colette met—with Willy's complicity—other homosexual stars, including Eva Palmer, Lucie
Delarue-Mardrus, and the melancholic poet Renée Vivien (the
pseudonym of Pauline Tarn). When Willy moved in with Meg
Villars near place de l'Alma, Colette settled in at 44, rue de Ville-
just (now rue Paul-Valéry), often residing, however, at the home
of the marquise de Morny, at 2, rue Georges-Ville. The daughter of the duc de Morny (half-brother of Napoleon III) and of
the comtesse Troubetskoy, Missy, who bore the title "marquise
de Belbeuf" after a brief marriage, was a woman for whom nobility was painful. Unloved in her childhood, she experienced her
marginality as an aristocracy—or vice versa—finally dedicating
herself to her passion for women with a generosity she lavished

quite particularly on Colette and that in the end ruined her. Cultivating a masculine appearance to the point of caricature, Missy was nonetheless maternal toward Colette, who sought refuge in her, living out that relationship as a consolation for both of their latent or explicit depressive tendencies.[52]

Willy and Colette finally separated after thirteen years together. Even though Colette, still attached to her ex-husband, hoped to win him back from Meg and sent passionate letters to the man she still called "My Sweetie Pie," her independence grew as the authority of her style asserted itself. The couple's relationship, therefore, continued to be rather stormy despite the separation, and included a stint onstage. The theater gossip columns did not neglect to sneer at the romantic foursome formed by Willy, Meg, Missy, and Colette. Braving the attacks with a courage no other woman had at the time, Colette showed herself off in the lesbian clubs and replied as follows to the *Cri de Paris:* "I read your items with pleasure, a frequent pleasure, since for some time you've been pampering me. What a shame you entitled one of the wittiest ones 'All in the Family'! It makes us, Willy, who is my friend, the marquise and me, and that calm and kind English dancer Willy calls Meg, sound like a shady phalanstery. . . . You have surely distressed three of us. Do not intimately join together, in the minds of your many readers, two couples who have arranged their lives in the most normal way I know, which is to say, just as they please."[53] In effect, although female homosexuality had been in fashion in Paris since 1900 and the complaisance between Sodom and Gomorrah proliferated in the best neighborhoods after taking over artistic bohemia, these lines of Colette attest to a much more radical freedom. Beyond the worldliness and the aesthetic provocation, the writer was asserting a true anarchistic spirit that disputed the legitimacy of the family and marriage by demanding, as the only criterion for normality, the individual recognition of pleasure— a theme she would also develop throughout her works. Without subscribing to any militant, political, or sexist group, she showed herself to be, with that thoroughly modern firmness in her behavior and in her writings—with all due respect to the prudent—an original pioneer, to whom certain libertarian feminists have rightly laid claim.

The major scandal erupted on January 3, 1906, at the Moulin-Rouge, during the performance of the pantomime *Egyptian Dream,* composed by the marquise and performed by herself and Colette. An Egyptologist scholar named Yssim (the anagram of Missy's name is easily decipherable) revives a mummy who rises from its sarcophagus and mimes a love scene with the scientist, up to the kiss that is to bring said mummy back to life. As one might expect, the tumultuous show degenerated into a storm: Bonapartists were indignant to see one of their own "prostitute herself"; they became even angrier upon noticing Willy in the hall, accompanied by Meg, who, it seems, had participated in the preparations for the show. The couple was driven off with canes.

Colette, who remained not only calm but "indifferent" about the whole matter,[54] seemed already to be elsewhere, intent in her desire to acquire her independence, to defend her economic interests against Willy, who had kept all the rights to the *Claudine* books, and already prepared to take her revenge. A legal separation was decreed on February 13, 1907; Monts-Boucons was sold on January 7, 1908. But it was only in 1909 that Colette realized she had been robbed by Willy, if not in legal terms, then at least morally speaking, as a result of a contract with Ollendorff he alone had negotiated and that deprived her of all annual royalties for the *Claudine* books. "At the bottom of both contracts, I signed my signature as a married person. That relinquishment is truly the most inexcusable gesture that fear extracted from me, and I have not forgiven myself for it."[55]

How can we not be struck by the fact that that realization occurred as her career as a mime or nomadic actress was unfolding: *Music-Hall Sidelights* (1913) would bear witness to it in a tone if not of revolt then at least of social compassion. The postcards sent to her mother[56] retrace her itinerary with a mixture of modesty and narcissism, whereas the letters from Sido from that same period offer an anxious and unsparing commentary: "You are going to appear in theater again, and that pains me for a thousand reasons. The first is that you do not have what it takes to succeed onstage. What I'm telling you may make you angry, but I am convinced I'm telling you the truth. You'll tell me again that you need to earn your living."[57] Sido undoubtedly wanted to protect her daughter from the attacks she was enduring, rescue her from a bohemian life that was too difficult, and channel her talent toward writing, which Sido herself held in high esteem and at which her daughter excelled. That did not prevent her, however, from also approving of the vagabond's life: "You seem to me enchanted with the life you are leading, you're using the need you've got inside you to be active."[58] Sido urged her daughter to defend herself against Willy: "My treasure, I'd like you to be able to smash him with a work of your own."[59] "Ask for your divorce then! You'll be free at least!"[60] She proved to be very grateful to Missy, whom she often thanked for the attention lavished on "[her] sorrowful sweetheart"[61] and to whom she sent farm eggs or chickens.

Colette and Willy's divorce was granted on June 21, 1910. Shortly before that, in late February, the young François Mauriac, who had appreciated the author of *Retreat from Love*, discovered Colette onstage in Brussels in *The Flesh*, the object of the "laughter" and "ignoble comments" of a "boisterous crowd [that] was drinking beer and smoking." Outraged, he thought first only of protecting her, before adding: "As I thought of Colette, my heart broken [. . .] the thing I am sure of is that I was not returning to France as blind as I had left."[62]

Colette's writing was thus part of a frenetic context of activities leading in every direction, a veritable orgy punctuated by theatrical performances, including the famous and still scandalous *Flesh*, which was reprised in Paris in 1911 with her in it.[63] She also gave lectures at the Centre Femina in the Théâtre des Arts. She composed many newspaper articles: despite the initial reluctance of certain serious journalists at *Le Matin*, who, like Stéphane Lauzanne, did not want to hire an acrobat at such a prestigious newspaper, she contributed various columns to the daily—as the author of stories, as reporter, drama critic, literary editor, etc.—which allowed her to be in direct contact with the social, political, legal, and cultural life of the country. She found the time to take boxing (!) lessons in order to acquire, according to a friend's statement,[64] the most vicious punch possible. All to make a name for herself? To make people talk about her? To earn money, preoccupied as she was by her precarious position, anxious to assure her economic independence? Or, equally and more imperiously, because she was moved by an insatiable desire that "sensual consumption" (as she said of Renée Vivien) did not satisfy but that was fulfilled only in symbolic acts, in sublimations?

Juliette, her elder half-sister, committed suicide in 1911 and would be commemorated only later by a poignant portrait in *Sido* (1930): "My half-sister, the eldest of us all—the outsider, the agreeably ugly woman with Tibetan eyes—became engaged just before her twenty-fifth birthday, on the brink of becoming an old maid."[65]

In 1910 a new lover appeared in Colette's life: Auguste Hériot, son of the superrich owners of the Grands Magasins du Louvre, a beautiful athletic male with a military career. Did Missy introduce him to Colette to bring a man into the twosome of women who were beginning to tire of each other? He was thirteen years younger than Colette, seemed to be in love with her, and wanted to marry her. She behaved like a domineering mistress, calling him "kid," "twit," or "little idiot." Nevertheless, Colette and Missy drifted apart in 1911. The relationship resumed amicably in 1928 and ended in 1940: the marquise did not appreciate Colette's portrait of her as "The Lady Knight" in *The Pure and the Impure* (1932; 1941). She would die by gas, abandoned, in a second suicide attempt during the Occupation (in 1944), at age eighty-six.

But in 1911 Colette, while performing in *Nightbird* or *The Flesh* and contributing to *Paris-Journal* and *Le Matin,* began an affair with Henry de Jouvenel, one of the two editors-in-chief of *Le Matin.* Born in 1876, from a Corrèze family ennobled in 1817, he was in no way related to the illustrious Juvénal des Ursins, who was himself connected to the Orsini princes. In 1917 he would be named private secretary to his friend Anatole de Monzie, undersecretary of maritime transport and of the merchant marine in the Painlevé cabinet; he would become senator from Corrèze in 1921. His brilliant career would lead him, among other places, to Geneva in 1922, as head of the French delegation to the Commission on Disarmament. According to some vicious gossip about Colette, the Germans rejected his nomination to the post of ambassador to Berlin because an illustrated newspaper published a photo of Colette dancing nude at the music hall, with the caption: "The Future Ambassadress of France."[66]

Although he belonged to no party, Jouvenel was a radical-socialist in his ideas. His friend Monzie and he were considered republicans and freethinking democrats, men of independent ideas more than politicians. Jouvenel would be compared to Lamartine because of his idealism and his art as an orator.[67] In 1924 he would be named minister of public education, the fine arts, and technical education in the Poincaré cabinet.

In September-October Colette moved with him to Passy, at 57, rue Cortambert, and remained there until 1916. After their Passy chalet collapsed in the rain, they moved to 69, boulevard Suchet, within the confines of the Bois de Boulogne. "Sidi" or "the Sultaness," as she called him, had been married to Claire Boas—who had the rather unusual peculiarity of irritating Colette—with whom he already had a son, Bertrand, born in 1903. He also had a mistress, the beautiful Isabelle de Comminges, known as "the Panther," who gave him another son, Renaud, born in 1907. The Panther, ferociously jealous, threatened to kill her new rival; Colette triumphed, tearing Sidi away from her; a sexual entente, which could be called "erotic gymnastics," was established between the baron and the writer. Such were the three key melodramatic moments that temporarily united the couple. They were married on December 19, 1912, at the town hall of the sixteenth arrondissement, without the blessing of the Church, since both spouses were divorced and, in any case, not particularly set on it.

In the meantime, Sido was dying: Colette visited her in August 1912, but, preoccupied with her new vagabondage, refused to believe in her imminent demise, which would take place in September. Colette missed the funeral and did not wear any signs of mourning. Is that the reason the family of her brother

Achille destroyed the letters from Colette to Sido? Or was it "simply" that these letters displayed no affection for her sister-in-law Jane de La Fare? Yet Colette admitted to her friend Hamel: "Right now things are going all right. But I am tormented by the stupid idea that I'll no longer be able to write to Mama as I so often used to do. [. . .] I have, as I do every time a sorrow is worth the trouble, an attack of an internal inflammation, which is very painful."[68] That apparent off-handedness veiled the pain that, for Colette, only rarely took the form of psychic expression proper, but was converted either into a bodily symptom ("internal inflammation") or into writing. Nevertheless, the conditions were not yet right for her to do her mother's portrait: that would take the birth of Bel-Gazou, the affair with Bertrand, and a new search for lost time in *My Mother's House* in 1922. Then, finally, only in 1929–30, would the hymn to her mother be written, in *Sido*.

For the moment, the new baroness de Jouvenel, pregnant a month after her mother's death (and to give birth to "little Colette," nicknamed Bel-Gazou, on July 3, 1913), increased her activities, crowning her achievement with her ascent to the most prestigious Parisian circles. Having barely slipped out of her costume for *Nightbird*, did she not attend the ceremony celebrating the election of Raymond Poincaré to the presidency of the Republic?

Achille died on December 31, 1913, and he too would be commemorated only in 1930, in the chapter "The Savages" in *Sido*, along with the younger brother, Léo.[69]

Life with Sidi was eventful. When the Great War broke out, he was mobilized in the twenty-third regiment. Colette joined up as a nurse for the military hospital at the Janson-de-Sailly high school, then became a journalist again and quickly departed—for Verdun, to lead "a harem life" near her man, whom she did not want to abandon at any cost. In 1915 *Le Matin* sent her as a reporter to Rome, which made her "gag"; with the exception of "the adorable little secret church" Santa Maria in Cosmedin, all the basilicas (Saint Peter's, Santa Maria Maggiore, and Saint John of Lateran) prompted tart criticism from her.[70] In July 1915 she was in Venice, which disappointed her,[71] and contributed to the review *Le Film,* directed by Diamant-Berget, thus making her debut in film criticism.

By 1916 the Jouvenel marriage was struggling to survive. In January 1917 Colette and her husband were in Rome, where he was a delegate to the conference of what would become, in 1920, the Little Entente, bringing together the Balkan countries favorable to the Allies.

Upon her return in 1917 Colette developed a passion for film: she composed the screenplay for *The Hidden Flame,* now regrettably lost, for which Musidora did the shooting script and the film adaptation. Her perspicacity in immediately understanding the importance of cinema would earn her the praise of Louis Delluc: "Mme Colette discovered (with all the secrets of her enthusiasm) the art of cinema at a time when very few French people were thinking about it."[72] She also enthusiastically reviewed Abel Gance's *Mater dolorosa.* And, beginning in 1918, she became a drama critic for *L'Eclair,* run by Annie de Pène; she reviewed Sacha Guitry's *Deburau* and there found Francis Carco. After Annie de Pène died in 1918, she was replaced in Colette's heart by a friend just as dear, Annie's daughter, Germaine Beaumont.

In that whirlwind there was not much time left to devote to Bel-Gazou who, initially left behind in Rozven, would spend most of the war on the Jouvenel property in Castel-Novel, entrusted to a nanny, Miss Draper, for seven years. Motherhood was not really Colette's "vocation": she would first have to appropriate all the facets of her femininity, beginning with the other woman, the rival, would have to overcome jealousy, get her homosexuality under control, then return to her own mother—and above all write, without, as she claimed, any "vocation" in that area either. All the same, what fulguration over the long term, what perseverance! A few months after *Chéri* (1920), *The Bright Room* (1921) brought together unusual texts, where we will go in search of the Colettian version of maternal love.[73] Colette had difficulty devoting herself to her family life, particularly since Henry de Jouvenel took the couturiere Germaine Patat as his official mistress upon his return from the war. Colette once more fell into depression, invisible, as always, to the author herself, if one can call "invisible" the spectacular expansion of her silhouette, due to an immoderate taste for good food—preferably raw garlic and chocolate, to be shocking in public, of course, but also to give herself pleasure and to stave off the feeling of emptiness.

Publications, prestigious and always warmly received, followed in quick succession. *The Long Hours* (1917) was a collection of her war reporting, published between 1914 and 1917 in *Le Matin, Le Flambeau, Excelsior,* and *La Vie Parisienne,* and devoted less to the battles or political aspects of World War I than to the daily life of the soldiers and women, including the impression the deprivation made on the innocent Bel-Gazou. *In the Crowd* (1918) was a selection of articles published in *Le Matin* from 1911 to 1914, under the rubric "Tales of a Thousand and One Mornings." In them Colette points out, beneath the frivolity of high society, salient moments of modern life: various trials, the capture of the Bonnot gang, dirigible flights, Russian ballets, women in politics, and so on. *Mitsou,* first published in *La Vie Parisienne* in 1917, came to the bookstores in 1919: that overpowering sketch of a female passion doomed by the inequity in the lovers' social conditions and by the war, earned her praise from Proust, who was moved to tears on reading Mitsou's farewell letter.[74]

Parallel to that literary ascent, new friendships—with Hélène Picard and Léopold Marchand in particular—brightened that period, which was both a crisis and a new beginning.

A peculiar adventure then came to mark Colette's life and works, an adventure on which I shall insist more than others have, since it seems to have deeply affected the woman and writer, changing once again—this time, definitively—her passionate love into a cult of memory and language.

FROM MOTHER-SON INCEST TO THE CONSECRATION OF THE MOTHER: BERTRAND DE JOUVENEL AND SIDO

The novel *Chéri* would take time to mature: the title character first appeared, in his listless version as Clouk, in "tales" published in *Le Matin* in 1912; then the writer tried to write it as a play, but without success. It was only in June 1920 that the novel would be published in *La Vie Parisienne*. Léopold Marchand, in collaboration with the author, would do a theatrical adaptation in which Colette would play the role of Léa. But the actress would be much less convincing than the novelist.

Whether as obsessive idea or as tenacious unconscious fantasy, the love affair between a mature woman and a young man was at the heart of Colette's imaginary. The incestuous, or incestual, relations our French Lolita had had with Willy were reversed in fiction: Léa de Lonval, a middle-aged demimondaine, lavishes protective tenderness and sexual attentions on Chéri, the adolescent son of her friend Charlotte Peloux. In the end Chéri marries the young and dynamic Edmée, while an aging Léa abandons that condemned love affair, leaving the spoiled child Chéri, weak and listless, at a sordid dead end. *The End of Chéri* (1926) accentuates that atmosphere of utter defeat in which the hero founders. Transformed into a man-object, the "naughty nursling," who is not lacking in animal charm, breaks down and becomes a sinister "lover devastated by a unique love."[75]

Could Colette's former lover Auguste Hériot, thirteen years her junior, whom she met in 1910, have been the prototype for Chéri? The novel's imaginary drew from literary sources such as Racine's *Phaedra*, Stendhal's *The Red and the Black*, and Flaubert's *Sentimental Education*. Nevertheless, traditional criticism has hesitated to add, to the couples Mme de Rénal and Julien Sorel, or Mme Arnoux and Frédéric Moreau, that of Jocasta and Oedipus. In fact, the love between a maternal character and a very young man inevitably evokes the incest presented in Sophocles's play. All the same, until Oedipus learns that Jocasta is his own mother, whom he won by killing his father, Laius, the tragedy depicts their affair as an ordinary relationship between a mature woman and a young hero, as in many texts and fables of world literature. Clinical analysis has taught us that perverse behavior comes into being through a transgression of both the difference between the *sexes* and that between *generations*. Not to be confused with the *reality* of incest and the psychic wounds it inflicts on the children who are its victims, the *uncon-scious incestuous fantasy* participates in our essentially perverse sexuality, which can even determine the choice of partners and fix them in archaic relationships of the parent-child type (*inces-tual,* in other words), which exert an influence over the couple that is as jubilant as it is risky and inexorable.[76]

The writing of *Chéri* began in August 1919. Colette spent her vacation with her daughter in Rozven, as she would do until 1924. From time to time her husband Henry de Jouvenel joined her there, when he managed to tear himself away from his mistress Germaine Patat. His two sons, Bertrand and Renaud, along with friends, stayed at Colette's house. The family had fun posing: "tritons" surrounded Sidi-Neptune (Henry) and the writer took on the role of a fat "tritoness"—she would weigh nearly a hundred and eighty pounds in 1922. Her correspondence does not reveal melancholic moods at that time, though Jouvenel's Don Juanism and his many political responsibilities, which always left Colette feeling like an outsider ("Politics? Opera!" she decreed), often deprived her of his presence. But is not solitude indispensable if one is to write? As usual her states of mind *were incarnated,* expressed in bodily terms, and were allowed to be resolved in voracity: she displayed a solid appetite and manifested a hyperactivity that compensated for that relative frustration. Her contributions to the *Excelsior, L'Eclair,* and *Le Matin,* for example, led our "serious reporter" to take the maiden voyage of the airbus Chaudron, one of the first airplanes to take passengers. Given her duties as "short story editor" at *Le Matin,* she found herself placed in the center of the delicate relations and complicated networks of the Parisian literary milieu. At the same daily paper she was responsible for drama criticism, which did not prevent her from also contributing to the *Revue de Paris,* to *Le Figaro* for a few months, then to *Le Quotidien, Cyrano, Demain, Les Annales Politiques et Littéraires, Vogue, Les Quatre Saisons,* and so on, not to mention her participation in the Conservatoire competition, as a juror for the Renaissance political, literary, and artistic award. And, always greedy for relationships, she forged new friendships for herself: Hélène Picard, a subtle but careless poet, entered her life in 1919 and would become her secretary; then there was Germaine Beaumont, daughter of Annie de Pène, and, of course, Léopold Marchand, son of the director of Eldorado, La Scala, and the Folies-Bergères. What an odd solitude! Under such conditions, cobbled together by Colette herself, she ran no risk of being bored and even less of being depressed.

As for writing, it was not a labor, since in that case she would have detested it: "Man is not made to labor, and the proof is that it tires him."[77] Although she sometimes complained of being a "bureaucrat"[78] of the pen because of her beginnings under Willy's domination, it was decidedly not writing that bored her.

Did she feel abandoned or jealous? Don't believe it. The dedications in the books she sent her husband's mistress are, it is true, rather cold in 1918, but they would become exuberant in the 1930s: at that later stage in the writer's life, the question of the "other woman" would be worked out. For the moment, in 1919, Colette displayed a bit more tolerance toward the irritating Claire Boas, the other baroness de Jouvenel, whose visit to Rome had so annoyed her. But can appearances be trusted? Might not the circumstantial affability have been another ruse for attaching Sidi to herself?

Colette's stepson Bertrand de Jouvenel, a youngster of seventeen (she was forty-seven at the time), "particularly childlike and timid"[79] as he described himself, attended Hoche high school. He had previously resided in Versailles at the home of a Protestant old maid, whose scrupulous coolness can easily be imagined. Claire Boas, Bertrand's mother, was worried: when she picked him up on Sundays, he was interested only in history, did not want to hear about golf or boxing, and, as for his young English girlfriend, Pam, well. . . .

So he was in Rozven for Easter vacation 1920, then again in July and August. "She [Claire Boas] entrusted her son to me," Colette claimed. "My father, who had wanted me to come . . ." added Bertrand. During the summer, Colette was surrounded by her daughter, Germaine Beaumont, and Hélène Picard. "And Colette gave me a copy of *Chéri,* which had just been published—and with the dedication 'To my *Cheri*shed son. . . . ' It was unexpected, I was not her son, I barely knew her, but she had already exerted her power over me."[80]

Bertrand de Jouvenel's text, published in 1986 in volume 2 of the Pléiade edition of Colette's works, put an end to years of silence, embarrassment, indiscretions, and revelations of every kind. Bertrand is not the hero of *Chéri*. In that novel the *imaginary* depiction of the incestual relationship between Fred, known as the Peloux boy, and Léa, occurs prior to the *real* affair between Henry de Jouvenel's son and his stepmother, Colette. The fantasy truly preceded the act.

Colette's whole familial and personal history nonetheless pushed her toward it: she took her revenge on her mother and Achille, whose relationship had eclipsed Sido's love for her daughter. She took revenge on the "depraved father" Willy by reversing the roles: it is not a father but a mother who will possess the "tender shoot," and Colette will play the role of the adult. She was also reacting to the infidelity of her second husband, Sidi, settling accounts with the overly seductive Germaine Parat and the unapproachable Claire Boas. Let us also not rule out the hypothesis that Claire, also to take revenge on Sidi, might have thrown her own son into Colette's arms.[81]

The "thing" was not yet acted on or even thought of, but only nursed as a fantasy. It may have crystallized and been incarnated in a writing as direct as a boxer's uppercuts; it may also have procured the beginnings of relief, and never the one without the other, since, even when it is not realized, a fantasy is effective. Dreams and fantasies are "the true powers of our psychic life," Freud observed at nearly the same moment in time.[82] The imaginary insinuates itself into reality, contaminates it, and, in the end, creates it. At Rozven, Colette offered Bertrand the choice of a lover from among the "young attractive women" who surrounded him. In face of the adolescent's incomprehension, she "undertook [his] sentimental education."[83]

Following this curious vacation, Bertrand's suspicious mother imposed a separation: no more luncheons at Colette's house! But the relationship between the two lovers resumed the next summer, in 1921. Colette taught Bertrand to swim, pampered him: "I rub him down, force feed him, buff him with sand, brown him in the sun," she exulted.[84] She evokes her childhood, but the revenge that shows through in *Chéri* is transformed here into an idyll: the mature Colette is metamorphosed into a dynamic and enterprising young woman, even a young androgyne, through her identification with her lover. Had she not already explored that sexual ambivalence when, in writing *Chéri,* she had abandoned the first-person novel to let Léa express herself in an internal monologue while, for the first time in her writing, the main character was a man, Fred, and not a woman, not woman in general? A reversal of sexual identities, then, a mingling of generations, an appropriation of youth and libertine fantasies: the entire phantasmal process, which the affair with Bertrand would enact, was already under way.

That enactment, which plunged deep into the incestuous unconscious of childhood, led the two protagonists back to Claudine, who had already experienced the nostalgia for lost time. But now what was at stake was to rewrite the infantile in an entirely different way, since the mischievousness of the early writings gave way to the gravity of celebration. The cult of the past, of its spaces and sensations, does more than satisfy the heroine, it allows her to be reborn, by resuscitating, in the center of that temple of time regained, the mother goddess herself, forgotten until now: Sido. "I believe it was at my insistence that she wrote her book, *My Mother's House,* in 1922,"[85] suggested Bertrand de Jouvenel. How right he was. The *Claudine* books produced "the indiscreet child and the little fool,"[86] added Colette. In counterpoint, *My Mother's House* recognized the permanence, at the center of pleasure, of a mother always started afresh, and, at the heart of writing, of an exquisite guilt toward "a world of which I have ceased to be worthy."[87] The affair with Bertrand and the self-analytical novels surrounding it mark that shift.

In fact, *The Ripening Seed,* published in part in *Le Matin,* and by Flammarion in 1923, relates the adventures of the young Phil and Mme Dalleray, a "Lady in White" who comes between the adolescent and his love for Vinca. That story is a transposition of the affair under way between Colette and Bertrand: in 1922–23 the writer lodged her young lover on rue d'Alleray (which sounds the same as the name of the female character of *The Ripening Seed,* Mme Dalleray). After their trip to Algeria, they stayed in Gstaad, where Colette discovered skiing and tobogganing, then in Montreux, where she devoted herself to bobsledding and took rejuvenation treatments. *The Ripening Seed* stands as the happy version of *Chéri,* undoubtedly modified by the real experience with Bertrand. Where *Chéri* presents the relationship between the two lovers, founded on an incestuous fantasy, as an aggressive and culpable union, *The Ripening Seed* relieves that guilt and shows the adventure as a necessary maturation and transition toward the love for Vinca, in a tone closer to a pastoral such as *Daphnis and Chloe* than to an Oedipal tragedy. The decomposition of a world of love is now replaced by a love conscious of its incompleteness but radiating serene generosity: the love between Vinca and Phil, which the Lady in White is content to initiate.

In counterpoint to *The Ripening Seed* (1923), and for the time of the unconscious, it is *My Mother's House* (1922) that materializes the esoteric face of that adventure. Through the worldly topicality of *The Ripening Seed,* and through the erotic initiation Colette freely gave Bertrand, the writer provided herself with a valorizing identification with virile youth. Through that play of mirrors, she managed to constitute a new identity for herself, polymorphous and contented, into which she transposed the still living memory of Saint-Sauveur. What some accomplish in psychoanalysis, Colette realized in an erotic acting out, accompanied by a rewriting of her childhood and adolescent memory. In that strange anamorphosis, in that fountain of youth, in these various reflections of overlapping mirrors, Bertrand did not really play the role of the analyst—no more, in fact, than Colette herself. Their unconscious fantasies remained preconscious, covered by a hypnotic, defensive idealization. But the son-lover occupied the role of what could be called an "analyzer": in innocently and genuinely consenting to that transgression, he stimulated Colette's reconstruction, and she turned out to be, in that adventure, at once her own *patient* and the *analyst of herself.* Her unspeakable wounds as a betrayed wife, and the fantasies of a seductive and virile mother intended to dress them, crystallized in a superb appropriation not only of her past but of her entire world, and finally of the world itself. Colette now anchored it, in an absolute and impregnable manner, in what she imagined as a model: Sido—Sido, the cosmic mother, Sido, the cosmos-mother, so aptly called *Sido, or, the cardinal points*.[88]

Claudine was motherless. Now Sido was dead; Colette had given birth to her own daughter, Colette de Jouvenel, and, above all, had experienced the erotic triumph of the mother over and with Bertrand. Her mourning for her own mother—which she did not manifest externally—may have been accomplished only now, and authoritatively, in reality and through the text, thanks to the pathway cut by the unconscious matricidal fantasy, reversed and glorified as an incestuous relationship. The mother is dead, finally defeated: I am henceforth the mother who has every right because she has every pleasure, because *I* have every pleasure. Yes, long live the *Mother* who is nothing other than *my world*!

A CONTINUAL REBIRTH

The splitting in two of the writer would never be so explicit and would accompany her throughout her life: on one side the rebirth of the phoenix Colette through a writing that is less the equivalent of a perpetual analysis than, more intensely and beyond any analysis, a transubstantiation of her being into a poetic prose, to the glory of pure incorporated time; on the other the anxiety of everyday life, emotional and material difficulties, and the account, endlessly reiterated, of the impossibility of love, of the war between the sexes, of wounds, betrayals, and jealousies.

The affair with Bertrand lasted until 1924–25. After a fruitless attempt at marriage with Mlle de Ricqlès, he would marry, at his mother's insistence, a young lady, Marcelle Prat, and would have a brilliant career as an economist. But in 1923 Henry de Jouvenel had a new mistress, the beautiful Romanian princess Marthe Bibesco. This would be one of the rare affairs by her husbands that Colette would not manage to rein in. The princess directed a vigorous hatred toward the plebeian Colette.[89]

In 1924 Colette lost her job at *Le Matin*. Her breakup with Henry seems to have been complete in 1923. She herself would return to these moments of distress only in 1941, in *Julie de Carneilhan*. For the moment, scarcely regenerated by her adventure with the young Bertrand, she detached herself from him, just as she knew how to liberate herself from everything. And then she met Maurice Goudeket.

Born in 1889, he was sixteen years younger than she. A broker in pearls and diamonds, the son of a Dutch Jewish father and a French mother, Maurice would be her last love, her "best friend." They met at the home of mutual friends, the Bloch-Levalois. By some ordinary combination of circumstances, Maurice brought her back to Paris from Cap d'Ail in his car. Very quickly, they were full of devilment: "Do you want to know what that boy Maurice is? He's a bastard, and a so-and-so, and even a great guy, and a satin-skin. That's the point I've reached."[90] The letters from Maurice Goudeket, recently published by Jean Chalon, attest to the reciprocity of that ardent sensuality and the indestructible friendship that would unite them until Colette's death.[91]

Colette had an extraordinary vitality, an iron discipline, an art of living her passions completely—and it was only in that way that she could dominate them, while dominating others by the same means. That power over self was unusually violent: hence some have seen it as an animality and a cruelty. In challenging sentimentality and humanism, Colette defied the shared values of "love" and "happiness."[92] Even her proverbial love for animals was not really love but, rather, an identification with the states of war and détente characteristic of animal instincts. Colette tamed their desire like an animal trainer and stopped play when that desire was eradicated, that is, on the verge of death, which she did not attend to in any way. Rather, monstrous or supremely complicitous as she was, she did not hesitate to precipitate it.[93]

Although she fully acknowledged her bisexuality, Colette finally posited herself as equally monstrous and sublime, of no sex.

It was not that she ignored or transcended sexuality but that she stood at the crossroads of all sexes, which is also that of all differences, so that she could write in unison with the elements of Being.

Everything was now in place, completed and solidified in a style that is indiscriminately a style of life-*and*-writing. She had only to amplify it, expand upon it, and consolidate it. That path would be strewn with battles, financial difficulties, and the hard knocks of war, error, and acts of ingenuity. But, in 1925, at age fifty-two, Colette possessed all the logic of her being and was mastering all the advantages in her immediate environment, in order to impose on everyone, and increasingly well, what was already there: a writing that, through the intermediary of Sido, was indistinguishable from the world's flesh.

TWO SIDES: MONEY AND WRITING

From that moment on and until World War II, Colette's existence unfolded on two fronts. First and foremost, supported by Maurice Goudeket, there was a life of pleasures and travel marked by the rhythm of writing and dominated by it. Second, there were material worries, accentuated by the crisis of 1929.

"Little Colette" de Jouvenel went to boarding school in Saint-Germain-en-Laye from 1922 to 1924 and was sent to England in 1925. Colette, who had never been intimately involved in her care, but who devoted beautiful pages to motherhood and to her child, now found herself free of both. Bel-Gazou suffered from that separation and envied the close emotional ties that her schoolmates maintained with their parents.[94] Believing it was her friends' Jewishness that ensured their family happiness, she wanted her mother to become a Jew.[95] In her way Colette was sensitive to childhood: in that same year, 1925, she probably attended the production of the little comic opera *The Child and the Enchantments*, a lyrical fantasia in two parts for which Maurice Ravel wrote the music and she the libretto. Then she traveled with Goudeket to Morocco and purchased the house in Saint-Tropez that she would name "La Treille Muscate" [The Muscat Arbor]. The shores of the Mediterranean in the company of Goudeket replaced Rozven with Missy and Sidi, just as Brittany had replaced Monts-Boucons, in the Jura, with Willy. She left boulevard Suchet and moved to the Palais-Royal, into a narrow and dark room on a mezzanine at 9, rue de Beaujolais. She contributed to *Vogue* and *Le Regard,* then moved again, in late December 1930-early January 1931, to the seventh floor of the Claridge Hotel. The whole staff was careful not to bother "the lady who writes." In 1935, following the decline of that establishment, she would move for a time to the ninth floor of the Marignan building and finally, in 1938, would find her definitive and long-coveted lodgings: the second floor, again at 9, rue de Beaujolais, where she would relish her apotheosis as "priestess of the Palais-Royal."

Willy died in 1931, Sidi in 1935. Colette continued to travel: to Berlin in 1929; to Austria, Romania, Tunisia, and Algeria in 1931—though she had broken her fibula that same "rotten year." In the following years the travels continued: Geneva, Zurich, Luxembourg, Amiens, Brussels, Toulon, Cannes. She wrote journalism, gave lectures, and adapted her novels, such as *The Vagabond,* into screenplays. Her fame raised her to the national and international firmament: Paul Reboux devoted a first book of criticism to her in 1925: *Colette ou le génie du style* [Colette, or, The genius of style]. Francis Ducharne, a silk merchant from Lyons and a great admirer of Colette, purchased the house in Saint-Sauveur from Dr. Achille Robineau-Duclos's heirs and offered it to Colette in usufruct, beautifully realizing the imaginary of *My Mother's House,* which, once more, had preceded the real events. And, as the ultimate glory, a plaque was erected. An unexpected visitor showed up at the Palais-Royal: Walter Benjamin. Colette, like her contemporaries, still knew nothing of his keenness of thought, fashioned from melancholy and political ordeals. He asked the provocative question of the day: "Should women participate in political life?" Colette gave a nuanced response: she of course praised the capacities of women but not without insisting on menstruation, which made them unpredictable, something that did not exactly bode well for their entry into politics. Even in literature, the struggle was not yet over: the Académie Goncourt was already wondering whether it ought to co-opt Colette as one of its members, but it would not do so. In 1929 it was still too soon; she would have to wait until 1945. Already, in December 1910, *The Vagabond* had been supported, before that jury, by Paul Margueritte and Gustave Geffroy, but had gotten only three votes in the first rounds—like Apollinaire's *L'hérésiarque et Cie.*[96] Thirty-five years separated that episode from the apotheosis of "our Colette" within that same academy.

Colette's life was now indistinguishable from her travels and her countless professional relationships: Dunoyer de Segonzac, Courteline, Coco Chanel, Maurice Chevalier, Sacha Guitry, Henri Mondor, Paul Valéry, Claudel, Gide, Mauriac, and many others. Not to mention the stars of Parisian Sapphism, with whom she continued to consort: Natalie Clifford-Barney, Winnie de Polignac, Elisabeth de Gramont, the duchesse de Clermont-Tonnerre, among other celebrities. And, no doubt, there was a final lesbian affair with the painter Emilie Charmy. But the feeling of insecurity was still there, and Colette kept running, because her being was incarnated and reborn in that way, as we have seen, but also because she felt truly threatened in that life of pleasures: hers was a life of war, exposed and difficult to win; and it was a livelihood difficult to earn.

The word "earn" implies the word "money." Was Colette greedy? This has been claimed many times. Perhaps. But she also possessed a Balzacian, some would say a Marxist, intuition: experience depends on existence, which is fundamentally economical. That constant financial anxiety produced a grammatical error—unless it is a slang expression or a wicked pun: "Elle est dure à gagner, l'argent." "She's hard to earn, money is."[97] Is it (masculine) money or one's (feminine) livelihood that must be earned? It comes down to the same thing, all things considered. It may be the same thing: "Elle est dure . . . l'argent," "She's hard . . . money is."

The Wall Street crash, which did not affect the writer, proved disastrous for Goudeket, a diamond and pearl dealer. But never mind: Colette threw herself into creating a beauty parlor, which opened at 6, rue de Miromesnil, on June 1, 1932, with the support of the pasha of Marrakech and the princesse de Polignac. Despite her inexperience, she insisted on trying her hand. The result: clients came out somewhat uglier than when they went in. The establishment was short-lived, closing the next year. That did not prevent her, in 1933, from writing the dialogue for the film *Ladies Lake* by Marc Allégret, based on the novel by Vicki Baum. During the summer of 1934 she devoted herself to writing the screenplay and dialogue for Max Ophuls's *Divine;* Ophuls would flee Germany after Hitler came to power.

Then there was a cruise aboard the *Normandie* to New York. It was an opportunity to marry Maurice Goudeket in 1935, to be in conformity with American law, which allotted shared quarters only to married couples. New York and Harlem offered little to inspire her: her accounts, published in part in *My Notebooks* (1941), fell far short of Paul Morand's and Céline's texts on the capital of the New World. But she remained on the lookout for monsters: in Fez she attended the trial of Oum el-Hassen, who was accused of murdering prostitutes. At a more banal level, her regular contributions to *Marie-Claire* began in January 1939.

For this woman, who had become a wanderer, the purchase of the villa Le Parc in Méré, near Montfort-l'Amaury, and the sale of La Treille Muscate in 1938 were notable events. Colette was getting old, was eating far too much for her sixty-six years, walked only with great difficulty, then not at all. Arthritis had set in.

It was always in writing that she pursued the most intense experiences, distilled into poetic fragments and usually buried in novels whose farcical plots allowed the writer to settle accounts with her two ex-husbands: *The Hidden Woman* (1924) and *The End of Chéri* (1926). Then came *Break of Day* (1928): like a "nouveau roman," that text abandoned narrative continuity and excelled at rendering the alluvium of sensorial memory, at transubstantiating childhood and adolescence, of which Colette was now the recognized master. She returned to the problem of the ménage à trois in *The Other One* (1929), then, once more, drew sublimely from the resources of Being for the work that, as one

might expect, would bear the title *Sido* (1929–30). Many consider-
er *The Cat* (1933) her most accomplished text. That precise and
searing novel reaches the same level of finesse as her previous successes, with an analysis of the impasses of living as a couple and
of an animal sensibility assimilated to that of humans. It depicts
the savage jealousy of Camille: her husband, Alain, moved by a
passion as subtle as it is unspeakable and also very attached to his
mother, prefers a cat to her. *Duo* (1934) embroiders anew on the
impossibility of love between two people, but the precision of
words and the evocation of sensations prevails over the plot. *My
Apprenticeships* (1936) attests to the fact that the war declared on
Willy in 1909–10 was still not over. In 1934 she also began publishing theater news under the title *The Black Opera Glass*. In the
manner of the impressionists, Colette's flesh, her veritable alphabet, was disseminated into a series of moody and meditative
texts, collections of fragments, brief narratives, and résumés of
poetry and moral lessons, which followed *Sido*: *Stories for Bel-
Gazou* (1930), *Twelve Dialogues of Beasts* (1930), *Earthly Paradises*
(1932), and *Those Pleasures . . .* (1932), which would later be giv-
en the definitive title *The Pure and the Impure* (in 1941).

There was also an abundance of tributes: she was named
chevalier of the Legion of Honor in 1920, officer in 1928, com-
mander in 1936, and would be a senior officer in 1953. Chosen
over Paul Claudel, who had been ambassador to Belgium since
1933, she was named a member of the Académie Royale de
Langue et Littérature Française in Belgium on April 4, 1936, succeeding Anna de Noailles. In a perfidious echo of the bargaining
that had preceded that selection, *Allô Paris* commented on February 9, 1934: "The members of the academy wavered between
an ambassador and a perfume maker."

In 1934 neither the Front Populaire nor the war in Spain interested her. In hindsight, critics such as Jean Chalon have diagnosed her as "politically naïve." She published the four short stories of *Bella-Vista* in *Gringoire* and *Candide* (1936–37), which
were far right weeklies, but was she even aware of it? The publishing houses Ferenczi and Grasset fought over her; she was
most concerned about her royalties, the price of her manuscripts.

Nevertheless, the caricature she traced of Hitler is more incisive than many supposedly serious political commentaries: "A vegetarian gentlemen who eats only oat flakes at noon and sometimes an egg in the evening . . . a gentleman who does not make love, not even with men. . . . A fine comedienne!"[98] But it ended there: Colette made no political judgment. She who loved to dream with pythonesses and seers believed herself sheltered from History.

THE IDOL CORNERED BY HISTORY

The younger brother, Léo, died on March 7, 1940, and the only inheritance he left Colette was his stamp collection. On June 14 the German army entered Paris. Colette and Goudeket took refuge on Bel-Gazou's property in Curemonte. Then, after the French defeat and the installation of the Vichy government, the couple returned to Paris, as her *Backward-Looking Journal* (1941) indicates. Colette was very ill: she was suffering from arthritis, added to bronchitis and food poisoning. Drs. Raymond Leibovici and Marthe Lamy did their best. They were great admirers of her work and would care for her with devotion and friendship until her death.

During the Occupation, Colette nonetheless continued to publish her novels and to contribute to the official press. The editor of the May 24, 1940, issue of *Marie-Claire* rather than merely a contributor, she emphasized the role of women during the war, spoke of love and seduction, offered Burgundian recipes, and annotated fashion sketches.[99] In 1941 she wrote a review of the Michel theater, which would have several performances in the occupied capital: but she explained that she did so "with an incomparable repugnance" and that the fatigue that followed prompted a false heart attack.[100] Instead of resisting, the writer took on various "little remunerative jobs," while continuing to publish in the collaborationist press and with publishing houses. Maurice Goudeket, having quit the diamond business, could no longer practice his profession as a journalist at *Marie-Claire* and *Match* because he was Jewish.

Not only *L'Officiel de la Couture,* whose off-hand style was not always appreciated by the proponents of the National Revolution, but also far right newspapers such as *La Gerbe,* run by Alphonse de Châteaubriant, and the Pétainist and collaborationist *Le Petit Parisien,*[101] as well as *Candide* and *Gringoire,* prided themselves on publishing Colette's work.[102] Although her texts were politically innocent, the context was not. Hence, in the issue of *La Gerbe* dated November 12, 1942, she published "My Burgundy," an article celebrating the two faces of her native region: the "Burgundy of vintage wines" and "my beloved, poverty-stricken Burgundy." Unfortunately, in the same issue, another article presents that same Burgundy as a steppingstone toward Hitler's Germany, to which, it was argued, the region ought to be returned.[103]

Les Lettres Françaises, an underground publication, did not fail to attack "a writer [who] is playing her part in the concert of enemy propaganda orchestrated by Goebbels"; was it not "painful to see the heretofore respected name of Colette put to such a use"?[104] Aragon would rectify that blast from the Resistance by offering the beautiful pages from *The Blue Lantern,* published in *Les Lettres Françaises* on May 5, 1949, under the title: "The Memories of the Greatest French Writer: Colette."[105] And, after Colette's death, he would write a long laudatory poem to her.[106]

In *Le Petit Parisien* Colette was content to evoke the cold, the difficulties getting food, the impossible workload of mothers. It was a matter of maintaining hope, she thought, and of setting a French art of living against the annihilation that was crashing down from abroad and from the war.[107] But perhaps she did not believe in Germany's defeat—unlike Maurice who, after Hitler broke the German-Soviet pact and attacked the USSR, judged that the war would soon be over. In a few years, he asserted, the German soldiers who crossed by his windows would be only ghosts.[108]

The same ambiguity or the same blindness manifested itself when, on March 3, 1942, Colette agreed to compose a *dictée* on national solidarity for the schoolchildren of France, at the request of Secours National. That rather mediocre text, published in *La Semaine* on March 5, exalts "the field of grain" that, "when the wind assails it, lies down flat, all on the same side," and praises the "great republics of insects" that show "a solidarity pushed to total abnegation"—which, the author laments, is not always the case for human society. Jacques Doriot congratulated the writer for having given the Marshal pleasure.[109] As for Sacha Guitry, who intervened to get Goudeket released from an internment camp,[110] he would have no difficulty persuading Colette to contribute to the volume *De Jeanne d'Arc à Philippe Pétain* [From Joan of Arc to Philippe Pétain] (April 1944), with a superb text on Balzac.[111]

That indirect and naïve collaboration occurred in the context of the persecution of the Jews, of which Colette was not the least unaware. Erna Redtenbacher, her Austrian Jewish translator, who had taken refuge in France, was interned in a camp in the Basses-Pyrénées. For fear of drawing the attention of the authorities to Maurice, Colette refused to sign the petition protesting the arrest of Julien Cain, director of the Bibliothèque Nationale. That did not prevent Goudeket from easily blending into the elegant society entertained by Florence Gould: in her salons the influential American patron of the arts brought together everyone who counted at the time, including Germans and collaborationists, such as the director of *Gringoire*, Horace de Carbuccia. Under the pressure of persecution, Léopold Marchand's wife, Misz, committed suicide; Pierre Lazareff and the Kessel brothers emigrated to the United States; Winnie de Polignac, who had offered Colette a secretary so that she could write in bed, sought refuge in England. Colette, for her part, was embroidering and "waiting," like many French people. *Julie de Carneilhan*, which first appeared between June 13 and August 22, 1941, in installments in *Gringoire*, would be published by the Arthème Fayard publishing house with, on the back cover, an advertisement for Adolf Hitler's *Mein Kampf*.[112] A pragmatic Colette strengthened her ties with her friends living in the countryside, to ensure she would "not starve to death." Alice in Var, Renée Hamon in Brittany, and Yvonne Brochard and Thérèse Sourisse, known as the two "Petites Fermières" [little farmer girls] from Normandy, would do their best to supply the writer with provisions and to honor French taste.

Colette kept a low profile, not only out of heedlessness but also in the hope of saving her husband. But it was in vain: Maurice was arrested on December 12, 1941, and transferred to the Royallieu camp near Compiègne. She then mobilized all her friends in a position to influence the German authorities, including Drieu La Rochelle, Robert Brasillach, Jacques Chardonne, Sacha Guitry, Bertrand de Jouvenel,[113] José-Maria Sert—Franco's ambassador to the Vatican at the time—and even the wife of Otto Abetz. Two months later, on February 6, 1942, Goudeket was freed. In the spring Colette and her husband were invited to tea by Ambassador Abetz and his wife—just two months before the Jews began to be deported to the death camps, as a rightly outraged Herbert Lottman has pointed out.[114] All the same, Goudeket thought it wise to seek refuge with the Van der Hensts in Saint-Tropez, in the free zone, then in Tarn at the home of the graphologist Lecerf (Colette, as Sido had done, became intensely interested in graphology). Maurice would spend the last two years of the Occupation in Paris, at the Palais-Royal, content to hide in the servants' quarters in the evening, without troubling himself further.

During that time Colette de Jouvenel joined the Resistance— yet another reason to distance herself from her mother, whose marriage to Goudeket she did not appreciate. Upon Liberation, she was elected mayor of Curement and would be among the first French journalists to give an eyewitness account of the concentration camps, which the Allies had just liberated, for the far left review *Fraternité,* whose publication she backed.[115] On that occasion Colette finally realized that her daughter bore the same first and last names as she. The writer was astonished that her daughter could sign her name "Colette de Jouvenel," though she admitted that, after all, it was perfectly legitimate. It was as if she was not able to discover her daughter until the latter had asserted herself somewhat—as a writer.

Renaud de Jouvenel, the son of Isabelle de Comminges and one of Colette's "marginal children," followed a life course similar to that of his half-sister Colette. He defined himself as a "left-ist and antifascist," joined the Resistance, then became deputy mayor of Brive upon Liberation. A Communist, dramatic author, and politically engaged novelist, he received encouragement from Colette, though she did not embrace his social ideology, which promised a better future for the poor and whose totalitarian illusion he subsequently denounced.[116] At the other end of the political chessboard, his half-brother, Bertrand de Jouvenel, was granted an interview with Hitler for *Paris-Soir-Dimanche* in 1936—an interview he would later disavow.[117] In 1942 the French authorities forced Jews to wear the yellow star. Colette wrote: "Maurice, who day after tomorrow will wear his star of David for the first time, is perfectly serene, or appears so. He is a good companion, decidedly."[118] She commented elsewhere on that discrimination measure: "The question of the star is unfolding in an excellent atmosphere. Only those who don't want to wear it expose themselves to any unpleasantness."[119] Was it blindness? Ingenuity and ruse in the face of censorship? When Maurice lived in the free zone, the couple corresponded cautiously, in code. Or was it fatalism? After Pierre Moreno, active in the Resistance, was arrested in February 1944, Colette very often wrote to Marguerite: "What are you eating? I beg of you, don't forget to eat! God keep me from telling you what is happening around us, very close by—too close? *Who [sic] supports us, if not a fatalism that is content to be increasingly blind?* Afterward, when we are busy catching our breath, getting caught up on our sleep, we will tell each other everything."[120]

Finally, the Allies were approaching. The Palais-Royal building was trembling under the bombing; people went down into their cellars, or no longer went down, and continued to bide their time. Colette's enthusiasm at Liberation was moderate, to say the least. It was just the end of a waiting period, which she hailed with a brief phrase: "And then, yesterday, the excitement of the landing."[121] The purges of collaborators revolted her; she judged them "disgusting." But at first she refused to sign the petition Mauriac circulated calling for a pardon for Brasillach, whom she had known well and who had intervened in Goudeket's favor during his internment. "Forgetful," Brasillach lamented. "No courage," added his lawyer, Maître Isorni. Under pressure from Cocteau, the shackled woman finally signed. De Gaulle, let us remind ourselves, would reject the appeal.

Céline, who was prosecuted after the Liberation, was furious at Colette, who was guilty in his eyes of having escaped judgment, "even though it was Mme Abetz who got Colette's husband through Drancy customs straightaway! [. . .] I'm the one who paid for that whole bit of nonsense in the end!" He vituperated against that "Beauce [for Burgundy] [. . .] meatball," that "half-nigger," who, he recognized, had had "an ingenious idea, *The Cat,* a little idea, but a real find, rehashed, it's academic shit."[122]

The ambiguities of Colette's attitude elicited real embarrassment for all parties concerned. The friends of her own generation vanished one by one: Hélène Picard, one of the most beloved, died in 1945, Marguerite Moreno in 1948. Now a "literary monument," but afflicted with ailments that were cured neither by radiation nor by hormone injections, Novocain, electric shock, or even the treatment of a miracle worker in Switzerland, Colette went through a phase of depression.

Old age, which she had not anticipated, confined her to a wheelchair. Pauline, her faithful governess, tended to the impotent but fleshy priestess: two robust men were needed to get her down the stairs. In reality, the discomfort of that "old Chinese empress with bound feet"[123] was very relative. Colette contributed to *Elle,* founded by Hélène Gordon-Lazareff in 1945, publishing the beginning of *The Evening Star* in the first issue. As her crowning glory, she was finally selected as a member of the Académie Goncourt in 1945, and in 1949 replaced the late president Lucien Descaves. And Tout-Paris thronged around her.

Her neighbor Jean Marais visited her often: Cocteau was a faithful friend and introduced her to Jean Genet. Mauriac offered her a black missal: did she really consider returning to the faith, reestablishing ties with the catechism of her childhood, or did she simply wish to win the support of the Catholics *as well?* Aragon, who was influenced by *The End of Chéri* (1926) for his

Aurélien (1945), would pay her a posthumous tribute.[124] Elsa Triolet, to whom Colette awarded "her" first Prix Goncourt in 1945, devoted an article to the writer in 1943. Sartre, who had sent her *Nausea* in 1938 with "admiration" and "friendship," later came to possess the entire Fleuron edition. The actress Simone Berriau, whom Colette admired and who ran the Antoine theater, joined Sartre for dinner with the author of *The Ripening Seed* on the occasion of the performance of *The Dirty Hands* on March 5, 1948.

Simone de Beauvoir, for her part, wrote Nelson Algren: "[Colette] is the only great woman writer in France, I mean a truly great writer."[125] To her lover she described her meeting with a seventy-five-year old Colette, who had "conserved a fascinating gaze, a charming triangular face, but had become very fat, impotent, a bit deaf. [. . .] What a mystery, an old woman who has lived so full, so ardent, so free a life, who knows so much about it and who is detached from everything because, for her, it's all over."[126] Much later, Beauvoir would return to that conversation in *Force of Circumstance* (1963)—or was it another? Sartre was present, and the encounter between the two sacred monsters held all her attention at the time. Beauvoir's enthusiasm for the author of *Sido* had cooled; she criticized "her complacence," "her contempt for other women," and "her respect for safe values." Nevertheless, in the epilogue she judged that, despite the ideological differences that separated them, they were both "the same" in their struggle to relieve the weight of tradition that was stifling the second sex.[127]

More than other contemporary writers, the author of *The Second Sex* (1949) paid particular attention to Colette's works, in which she discovered a precise portrait of women's condition and of sexual liberation that intersected her own analyses. Although Colette was, in the first place, a great writer, she was also a fighting woman who knew how to make "a living from her pen." Beauvoir admired her for knowing how to depict "the harsh death struggle of a little music-hall dancer," Gribiche; she showed Colette was sensitive to female masochism and to the miseries of young wives (Sido's first marriage, and Colette's as well, "uprooted" the bride). Colette's sensual daring and the truths about women's sexuality, which she did not hesitate to write down, also appealed to the philosopher: for example, the "diffuse and precise caresses" of the young girls in *Claudine at School;* the voluptuousness of the Vagabond (which was nevertheless not "a solid foundation on which to build the enterprise of a lifetime"); and the fearlessness of the innocent libertine, who "sought to complete her education in strangers' beds."

The Colettian vision of female homosexuality and of its consolatory role also garnered Beauvoir's full approval. The awakening of the woman in Vinca, her "youthful orgies," her "rather brutal defloration," and her domestication were discussed at length. Similarly, she was interested in Léa the courtesan, who was as fulfilled by Chéri's docility as Mme de Warens was by Rousseau's, since Léa proved to be more virile than her lover and rejected a cover profession (here, Beauvoir enjoyed underscoring Léa-Colette's humor in response to a friend who called her a "dear artist": "Artist? Now really, my lovers are quite indiscreet!"). She also noted Colette's happy pregnancy, "a man's pregnancy" nevertheless, and the fact that she did not breastfeed her daughter. Without suspecting the daughter-writer's projection onto her mother "model," the existentialist hailed the exceptional harmony between Colette and Sido, "a well-balanced and generous mother." And she was full of compliments for the pride of the amorous women in Colette's writing, whose desire would not be shattered by disappointment: for example, Renée Néré, and also Sido, who was proud to know her daughter was not just an amorous woman.

There are few remarks about Colette's art, except that Beauvoir appreciates "her spontaneity, which is not found in any male writer," and the gift for exploring passion or for showing "an attentive love" for nature, which leads Beauvoir to compare the writer to Katherine Mansfield. Nevertheless, like women in general, Colette is supposedly incapable of capturing nature in its "inhuman freedom" and does not really contest the "human condition" because she scarcely takes cognizance of it. Although an extremely attentive reading, it limits Colette's works to certain of its emancipatory themes and does not take into account the writer's art, its complexities, its depths. Yet Beauvoir was able to courageously underscore Colette's libertarian message and to transmit her aura to a female and feminist public that, in the years to come, would take to examining much more attentively the polyphonic genius of the woman who impressed the author of *The Second Sex*.[128]

At the other end of the social spectrum stood another admirer: François Mauriac. Finding he had been awarded the Nobel Prize for literature in 1951, he immediately telephoned Colette to tell her that she was the one who ought to have received it.

Naturally, there were some unyielding people who did not like her: Léautaud, for example, accused her of producing "commercial literature." In the meantime, visitors, often young readers and writers, thronged to rue de Beaujolais to be received by "our Colette." They met with only relative success, however, for although the Idol sometimes allowed herself to be admired, she also knew how to keep the door shut.

Her literary verve had faded somewhat but was nevertheless plentiful in the last period of her life. *Julie de Carneilhan* (1941) upset the Jouvenel family, particularly Bel-Gazou, who was shocked by the attacks on her father. Monzie, Henry de Jouvenel's old friend, was himself so outraged that Colette hastened to assure him that the character of Herbert d'Espivant had nothing to do with her ex-husband. Nevertheless, a personal settling of accounts does feed the novel and prevails over a supposedly collaborationist and anti-Semitic ideological message, which creeps in only between the lines.[129] The *Julie de Carneilhan* affair definitively estranged Colette from her daughter.

After her 1935 marriage to Dr. Dausse, who was much older than she, and whom she left after a few weeks of living together, Colette de Jouvenel accepted the fact that she was homosexual. The same year, her mother married Goudeket. Her father, Henry de Jouvenel, died shortly thereafter. The relationship she had with her mother would remain very strained until the end.[130]

Many witnesses hailed Colette's courage in her old age: she continued to write on her now famous blue sheets, by the light of her bedside lamp, which she called her "blue lantern." The

Backward-Looking Journal (1941) collected her reflections on war—from Sido's war in 1870 until Colette's last—along with hymns to beasts and tributes to France. *From My Window* (1942) championed resistance through physical well-being: was it a denial of the disaster, or, on the contrary, a cult of the *dolce vita,* which preferred to laugh at frustration rather than resist the tormentors? *Flowers and Fruit* (1943) paid a poetic tribute to French gardens and dissected admired contemporaries.[131] *Nudity* (1943) rediscovered the body; *The Kepi* (1943; initially published in *Candide* in 1942) traced an unsparing portrait of passion in an aging woman. In *Gigi* (1944) vaudeville gave way to a warm fascination with the character of a young lady, astonishingly mature in her chaste love, who manages to marry the heir to "Lachaille Sugar Works." The writer projected into it her innocent and depraved youth—an ultimate variation on the theme of the *Claudine* books. Colette had decidedly not yet said everything or, rather, she had reached her cruising speed, which she would define this way two years before her death: "What I would like: 1) to begin again; 2) to begin again; 3) to begin again."[132]

Nevertheless, some of her texts did not refrain from analyzing the less joyful facets of life: depression, illness, and fever for example, other recesses of the flesh, monstrosities that Colette was happy to explore after so many others in "The Photographer's Lady" and "The Sick Child" (reprinted in *Gigi,* 1945). But the sick child gets well: can he be seen as a symbol for a sick France, which is being reborn? She quickly rediscovered her favorite themes in a new avalanche of flowers and beasts: *Fine Seasons* (1945), *For a Herbarium* (1949), *Line by Line* (1949), *Intermittent Journal* (1949), *The Prime of Life* (1949), *In Familiar Country* (1949), *Within Reach, Miscellanea* (1950). Finally, there were the last major novels, *Evening Star* (1946) and *The Blue Lantern* (1949), which indicate a talent that, yes, repeats itself but that is marked by a searing sensuality.

Beginning in 1945, however, Colette's pace slowed, and many so-called original texts now appear, upon examination by specialists, "to be the result of manipulations carried out by Goudeket,"[133] who in late 1945 conceived the plan to publish

Colette's complete works and founded the Fleuron publishing house, in association with Flammarion (volume 15, the last, would appear in late 1950). The silk-skinned lover who became her "best friend" was not content to take care of the old lady and to push her around in her wheelchair; he also attended to the legacy of her works.

Many stage adaptations of her novels reinforced her popular fame as her creative capacities diminished: late 1949 marked the success of the film *Gigi*; then there would be a revival of *Chéri* on stage, and finally, in 1954, the film *The Ripening Seed* by Claude Autant-Lara, taken from the novel of the same name.[134] Cinema, to which Colette was drawn from World War I to the 1940s, continued to excite her. Was it not, for that artist in search of sensory signs, another way to incorporate words, as well as a re-placement for her adventure as a mime and actress? Colette pre-ferred silent films but was not in the least out-of-date: if Holly-wood irritated her, it was because she was calling for French cinema to rise again. In Monte Carlo, where she and Maurice had been invited annually by Prince Rainier beginning in 1951, Colette noticed a young actress whom she immediately designat-ed to play Gigi for America: Audrey Hepburn.[135] In 1948 there was even talk of Marlene Dietrich playing Colette in a film: the rumor would remain without substance, but what more could one wish for in a world now wholly designed to end up on screen?[136] It was Colette herself who would play Colette in the film shot by the young filmmaker Yannick Bellon in 1950. Also in 1950 André Parinaud recorded radio interviews in which Co-lette revealed her Burgundian accent but few secrets: the latter found their way into her written work, not into her voice. The old lady never tired of preening her image, her press and radio interviews, her publications. The pythoness of the Palais-Royal was already a national monument; she knew it and she polished up the details for posterity. The party given for her eightieth birthday turned into a formal tribute.

There was nothing more to write; Colette's strength was de-clining perceptibly; she lapsed into obliviousness, silence, torpor. She was not even mean anymore, smiled sweetly at nothing and at no one, and would die smiling. She no longer left her bed/ writing desk. Did she think of the amputee Captain, whom she honored much more discreetly than Sido? She had transformed his patronymic into a nom de plume, and his impotence at writing into a work of genius.

Not without difficulty and despite significant opposition, Colette was promoted to the rank of senior officer in the order of the Legion of Honor on March 3, 1953. "Look"—Sido's word—would be the last word spoken to her "best friend" before she died, on August 3, 1954, at age eighty-one.

The Church refused her a religious funeral. Graham Greene protested in *Le Figaro,* since the party in question had, in fact, been baptized. Monseigneur Feltin persisted in his refusal, since the writer had not lived in accordance with the faith. It was the state that took things in hand: Colette was the first woman in the history of the Republic—and the only one to this day—to have had a national funeral. A crowd of 6,240 official guests formed a procession for her. In the court of honor of the Palais-Royal, taken over by wreaths of flowers, including a spray of dahlias from her compatriots in Saint-Sauveur-en-Puisaye, she was given military honors. Then she was buried in Père Lachaise cemetery in the midst of one of the century's most violent storms.

She had written: "Perhaps it is only the two of us who understood something of death, you out of serenity, and I out of indifference, since I cannot be interested in what is not life."[137]

WRITING:

TENDRILS OF THE VINE

A gourmet style, which takes words only when they're nice and juicy,
but also a gymnast style, with lithe rebounds, nicely controlled leaps.

—Ramón Fernandez, *NRF,* March 1, 1942

I work very honestly, as well as I can, with strictness [. . .]
yes, with strictness, that may be the most suitable word.

—Colette, interview in *Nouvelles Littéraires,* March 27, 1926

THE "LARGE-LIMBED" NEED TO WRITE

In her *Backward-Looking Journal,* at the height of her literary glory, the aging writer remembered the little six-year-old who, though she loved to read, hated to write: "Was not the repugnance that the gesture of writing inspired in me providential advice? [. . .] Because I felt, more and more every day, I felt I was made precisely *not* to write."[1]

Throughout her life Colette always said writing was alien to her and adamantly denied any literary vocation. "I became a writer without paying attention, and without anyone suspecting it."[2] "I do not like to write. Not only do I not like to write, but I especially like not to write. [. . .]—But, Colette, if you didn't write, what would you do?—Anything! Anything but write!"[3] And, at the end of one of her best books, *The Pure and the Impure,* she declares:

"My book is finished. It makes me sick to my stomach, needless to say."[4] The literary critics mock her: "It's all a pose! She's just being provocative!" The psychoanalysts go one better: "It's a denial of writing!" But what if we took Colette at her word?

In *My Apprenticeships* (1936), a late text that retraces her life's journey, the writer briefly recounts how, after the *Claudine* series, her writing and themes changed. Without shedding light on the circumstances of that shift, or describing her mental state at the time, or detailing the stylistic aspirations that spurred her on, she states that *Dialogues of Beasts* required that she "wrest" herself from lived experience. A "duty" was imposed on her, to make reality "exude" a few "images" and to compose them into a "bouquet": "I was vaguely awakening to a duty toward myself to write something other than the *Claudine* books. And, drop by drop, I was exuding the *Dialogues of Beasts,* in which I gave myself the pleasure—not keen, but respectable—of not speaking of love. [. . .] We cling to vanished possessions by an image, but it is the act of *wresting away* that forms the image, that *assembles,* ties up the *bouquet.* What would I have kept of Monts-Boucons if M. Willy had not taken it away from me? Perhaps less than I have of it at present."[5]

Let us try to follow closely that "rhythmic labor" that "wrests a smile" from her and that she would also call an "insurrection,"[6] an "instigation,"[7] and even, with an almost psychoanalytic lucidity, a "large-limbed" need to write.[8] As an example, let us turn to *Tendrils of the Vine*: In it Colette's writing changes as her desires are modified, and the metaphors used are condensations of a new way of holding onto the world and others.

The year 1905 was a period of crisis, to which *The Retreat from Love* (1906) bears explicit witness. Colette was less and less amused by Willy's infidelities and by the amorous conquest of "Rézi." Colette stole her for a time from her own husband to wreak revenge for his betrayal and to discover new pleasures, just as the last *Claudine* books had narrated, and, as it were, programmed, them. *My Apprenticeships* (1936) gave a retrospective accounting of that turning point: "But I was changing. What does it matter that it happened slowly! The whole thing is to change." She added this perspicacious remark: "While I was writing *The*

Retreat from Love, . . . I was developing strengths that had nothing to do with literature."[9] Prior to any literary choice, she was reevaluating her life, her pleasures, and the meaning the writer gave them. The slow dissolution of the marital relationship with Willy led to a detachment from love itself. Colette lost respect for male sexuality and sought refuge with the maternal Missy, her new love affair.[10] On several occasions, she would inquire into the foundation of the written work, namely, the love relationship, in order to make and remake it: "All my novels after that hark back to love, and I have not tired of it. But I began to put love back into novels, to enjoy doing so, only when my respect for it—and for myself—was restored."[11]

In reality, however, it was the very meaning of the love relationship that was modified over the course of that inquiry: what remains of love when the writer detaches herself from the "object" of love, from any "other," whatever its sex, in order to merge, alone and exclusively, with the rhythm of the world? To marry a cat, or a flower:[12] Colette not only dreams of it, she *really* does it, by *writing the cat, the flower.* That psychic and corporeal alchemy comes about gradually and hesitantly, since she would produce many facile pages in which searing epiphanies stand beside tiresome variations on the ménage à trois. But "change" matters more to her than the literary creations resulting from it: to say it has "nothing to do with literature" does not necessarily point to a devalorization of writing on the writer's part but, rather, the inclusion of the total literary experience in that of Being as a whole, for a subject named Colette.

The first sections of *Tendrils of the Vine* to be published appeared in the *Mercure Musical*.[13] They open with the song of the nightingale (1), then veer toward a few anecdotal scenes with the characters from the last *Claudine* books (Rézi, Maugis, and Renaud), with Claudine herself meditating on classical and popular music, on Bayreuth and on music societies, on love compared to the music drug. Some echoes of plots reminiscent of the earlier novels in the first version of the text (articles 2, 3, 5, and 11 in the *Mercure Musical*) would be suppressed when *Tendrils of the Vine* was published in book form (La vie parisienne, 1908). Similarly, everything

referring to the initiation received from Willy would disappear—
all signs of the discipline of pleasure and speech induced by that
"change." With the successive editions of *Tendrils* (1908, 1923,
1930, 1934, 1950), Colette would constantly refine and tighten the
composition and style of what she called, at the time of its first
publication, "my last-born, made up of bits and pieces." A new
style emerged through later reworking and increasingly asserted itself. In abandoning the linearity of the earlier novels, which, despite the many lyrical digressions, respected the rule of narrative
progression, and in renouncing the thematic unity secured by the
recurrence of established characters in *Dialogues of Beasts* (1904),
Tendrils of the Vine offered a kaleidoscope of fragments.

The 1908 book comprises eighteen texts, each constructed on
a musical or poetic model of juxtaposed "phrases" or "pieces,"
repeated and modulated but without the motley text obeying any
precise narrative logic. The fragmentation and discipline of the
composition reveal a growing vigilance and mark a decisive stage
in the birth of the author Colette.

That mastery of relationships to others and to the elements is
expressed in an economical style, surrounded by silences, which
confirms a relation to the world based less on reverie than on
seizure or shock: not *per via di porre* (as Leonardo da Vinci described painting), but *per via di levare* (as he defined sculpture).
Freud used that formula of Leonardo's to conceptualize psychoanalytic interpretation as an entirely negative act of extraction,
composed of frustrations and disappointments, which drags the
representation out of the complacent patient and inflicts on him
the wound of a lucid word.[14] Even in the *Claudine* books, Colette's apparent exuberance was cognizant of that need for precision; but now it tended to submit even more to the art of condensation. With her new way of being and writing, she acceded
to figuration through *subtraction,* which was, in very different
ways, both Leonardo's and Freud's aim. Like a gash or a bite, her
sparkling, succinct style, in which opulence itself is filled with the
unspoken, makes its claim on negativity, which swallows up the
prolix. Similarly, in her life, Colette adopts a form of cruelty by
persisting—since the stakes are existential—in privileging her

writer's solitude, though she is certainly surrounded by solid, gratifying, and demanding friendships. Later, the experienced author would describe her art in negative terms, as "the knowledge of what it is advisable not to write. [. . .] One becomes a great writer [. . .] as much by what one refuses one's pen as by what one grants it; . . . the honor of the writer is renunciation."[15]

In *Letter from Claudine to Renaud,* published in the review *Le Damier* in April 1905, the author reveals her scheme to escape a certain, now intolerable, style of life-and-writing, in order to accede to the concision of *Tendrils.* Implicitly picking up on Willy's mocking remarks, she speaks ironically of her propensities as a wife, then as the author of the *Claudine* books under the charm of Mme Millet-Robinet's *La maison rustique des dames* [The country house of ladies], a book famous at the time, which Francis Jammes mentions in his preface to *Seven Dialogues of Beasts* (1905). Although she concurs with the sarcasm of Willy-Renaud, who is exasperated by his wife's possessiveness, by her "monogamous blood,"[16] she "discourses" briefly on that forbidden subject, to "brave it, and to laugh, and dance nervously." But Colette does not refrain from evoking Renaud's own jealousy: he cannot stand Claudine's love for another woman, his mistress Rézi, whom Claudine admits she desired to the point of wishing for her death. Nevertheless, that passion was already dying out: "I no longer love her." The description of the lover's body is followed by a cosmic fragment that condenses into a few lines the best pages of the *Claudine* books.

Let us recall that, within the framework of schoolgirl plots strewn with criticism of the public schools, filled with Mlle Sergent's Gommorhean love for Mlle Aimée, with the later discoveries and disappointments of Paris in *Claudine Married,* and finally with her desire to take off, to attempt, against the attachment of desire, a retreat from love, Colette revealed herself above all a poet of rural life. Although the public became infatuated with the little pest Claudine, reminiscent of characters in certain novels by Gyp, and though the fashion for Claudine collars and socks eclipsed that for the book, lovers of the French language discovered a lyrical work and author. Colette's prose and sensibility, immersed in the French landscape as filtered through classical writers and eighteenth-century painters, marking the beat of the *rigodon*[17] and painted in the light-filled palette of the impressionists, are evocative of Poussin, Watteau, or Manet:

The charm, the delight of that region composed of hills and of valleys so narrow that some are ravines, it is the woods, the profound and invasive woods, that break like waves and undulate out in the distance, as far as one can see. [. . .] Dear woods! I know them all; I have combed them so often. There is brushwood, shrubs that spitefully cling to your face as you pass, they are full of sun, of strawberries, of lilies of the valley, and also of snakes. I have started there with suffocating fright, seeing those atrocious smooth and cold little bodies slip in front of my feet; twenty times I have stopped, gasping for breath, finding under my hand, near the *passe-rose,* the hollyhock, a very docile grass snake, rolled into a regular little snail, his head on top, his little golden eyes looking at me; it was not dangerous, but what terror! Never mind, I always end up returning there alone or with friends; preferably alone, because the little big girls annoy me, they're afraid of getting scratched up on brambles, they're afraid of bugs, of fuzzy caterpillars, and of the spiders in the heather, so pretty, round and pink as pearls; they yell, they get tired—unbearable, in short.[18]

I feel so alone there, my eyes wandering far into the trees in the green and mysterious day, I am at once deliciously calm and a little anxious, because of the solitude and the indistinct darkness. . . . No bugs in these great woods, no high grass, the ground well-trod, everything by turns dry, sonorous, or soft, because of the springs.[19]

And she repeats, a hundred pages later, the same hymn to the shade of the rustling and fragrant woods:

Ah, the woods, the dear woods of Montigny! At this hour, I know it well, how they hum! The wasps and flies sucking from the lime blossoms and elder trees make the whole forest vibrate like an organ; and the birds do not sing, because at noon they stand on the branches, seek the shade, preen their feathers, and look at the undergrowth with shifting and brilliant eyes. I would be lying down beside the Sapinière, from which you can see the whole city below you, with the hot wind on my face, half dead from relaxation and laziness.[20]

There is a bit of Rameau in that gaiety, and a female body that remembered Fragonard, and offered itself, more sensual then Cézanne's bathers, more agile than Degas's dancers:

Back there, barely do the thornbush hedges veil themselves in that green fog, a long distance away, which seems to hang from their branches, and which is woven from the tiny tender leaves. At the Luxembourg, I wanted to eat the shoots of trees, as in Montigny; but here, they crunch between your teeth, powdered with coal dust. And never, never again will I smell the wet odor of the rotted leaves and the pools strewn with rushes, or the slight pungency of the wind that has passed over the woods where coal cinders were burning. Back there, the first violets have come up, I see them. The hedge near the garden wall, the one facing west, is in bloom with little violets, stunted, ugly, and sickly, but with a supreme odor. How sad I am! The excessive mildness of this Paris spring, and its listlessness, make me nothing more than a poor beast of the woods condemned to live in a menagerie. [. . .] Happily, my body is doing well; I take frequent note of it, with kindness, squatting in the hot water of my washtub. It is all elastic and supple, long, not very fat, but muscular enough not to seem too skinny.[21]

The plant and animal worlds continue to leave their mark in the bitter love affairs of the abandoned, and no less enterprising, wife:

In the red glow of evening, I listen to the kindly garden fall asleep. Above my head, a fickle little rat zigzags in its mute and dark flight. . . . A Saint John's pear tree, eager and generous, drops its round fruit one by one, overripe as soon as mature, and which brings down tenacious wasps as it comes. . . . Five, six, ten wasps in the hole of a little pear. . . . They fall while continuing to eat, simply beating the air with their blond wings. [. . .] Under my lips, the golden eyelashes of Rézi once beat in the same way.[22]

Is this an evocation of the body of a female lover, of Rézi's irresistible seductiveness? Or of the loving body of Claudine, who never makes love better than she does with her "dear woods"?

How beautiful the woods are! How soft the light! On the edge of the grassy ditches, how cold the dew! If, under the copse and in the meadows, I no longer found the charming populace of thin little flowers, forget-me-nots and campions, narcissuses and spring daisies . . . , if the Solomon's seals and the lilies of the valleys had long since lost their blossoms, their hanging bells, I was at least able to bathe my bare hands, my shivering legs, in deep and even grass, sprawl my fatigue in the dry velvet of the moss and pine needles, bake my repose without thinking in the harsh and rising sun . . . I am penetrated by rays, traversed by gusts, resounding with cicadas and the cries of birds, like a room that looks out on a garden.[23]

In the series of novels from her early period, such evocations of the world's flesh were subordinated to the mischievous heroine's intrigues and to those of her free or shackled successors: first, the various stages of Claudine's sexual initiation, then Annie, Minne, Renée Néré. And the narrator hesitated: should the hymn to Being be included in the desire to write to the lover, or, on the contrary, was it only in the desire to *write* (intransitive verb) that the joy in Being could be expressed?

Should the hour pass, should the sun turn, should the delicate butterflies, already nocturnal and uncertain in their flight, come out of the woods, should a little timid, sociable, and dazzled barn owl show itself too early on the edge of the wood and blink, should the copse come to life at nightfall with a thousand anxious noises, with tiny cries, I grant them only distracted ears, absent and tender eyes. . . . Now I am standing, stretching my numb arms, my stiff knee joints, then fleeing toward Montigny spurred on by the hour . . . the hour for the mail to be delivered, of course! I want to write, to write to Renaud. My resolution is made. . . . Ah, how little it cost me![24]

The scents of mushrooms, vanilla, and orange trees seem to offer themselves not as protection, but as a prolongation of loveless desire:

I fear no one—not even myself! Temptation? I know it. I live with it, and it becomes familiar and inoffensive. It is the sun in which I bathe, the mortal coolness of evenings whose caress falls on my surprised shoulders, an ardent thirst, so that I run to the dark water where the image of my lips joined to my lips trembles—a vigorous hunger that is faint from impatience.

The *other* temptation, flesh, fresh or not? . . . Anything is possible, I expect it. A loveless desire, that must not be so terrible. It can be contained, castigated, dispersed. No, I do not fear it. I am no longer a child it can catch off guard, or an old virgin inflamed at its mere approach. . . . With all the unused force that beats so peacefully in my arteries, I will arm myself against that vulgar enemy. At each victory, I will take as my witness the man leaning on his elbows on the stone behind me, invisible, and whom I see without turning around—I will tell him: "You see? It's so easy."

Night falls, quick to close over that garden whose lush greenery remains dark in the sun. The humidity of the earth rises to my nostrils: the odor of mushrooms and vanilla and orange tree [. . .] it's as if an invisible gardenia, feverish and white, were spreading its petals in the darkness, it's the aroma of that night itself dripping with dew.[25]

Colette's direct contact with sensory time, present from her early texts, becomes diluted in a youthful reverie that shatters the retreat from love, however courageously sketched. Hesitations of the heart and syntactical overloads weigh down that sensorial vibration.

By contrast, in the prefatory texts of *Tendrils of the Vine*, and especially in the *Letter from Claudine to Renaud* (1905), where everything is elliptical and left in suspense, the rosy tints of her bucolic childhood are jotted down at a hurried pace, which oscillates between an oneiric mood and self-control, and they acquire the accents of a self-assured song with no purpose outside itself:

But in the garden this morning a white iris blossomed beside me, suddenly; I heard the slight tearing of its silk. . . . But on the espalier, against the warm wall embroidered with lizards, a peach is ripening, inexplicably early, and its down tempts my fingers. . . . But in the wind the cornfield shakes a thousand golden tasseled heads turning green.

Farewell, then, to the beautiful Rézi's scent of peach and iris, mentioned in the previous paragraph; farewell to the comet tail hair of that mistress, shared by husband and wife: henceforth, the world at large is an object of desire. Nevertheless, that detachment is far from absolute and never will be. For the moment, revenge is at stake, a "wicked game of a woman in love," an appeal the letter-writer addresses to her "tyrannical master": "Suffer, my dear, suffer a good knock! [. . .] Come back." The certainty that a different path is possible emerges: the prisoner whom Willy locked up, according to *My Apprenticeships*—a fact disputed by other statements: was she not the captive of a voluntary servitude?—persuades herself of the benefits of another, apparently solitary world. It is the solitude of her jouissance in Being, which she has just distinguished from her pleasures with a man (Renaud) or with a woman (Rézi); it is the solitude of writing as well. In breaking her romantic connections, Colette thus disengages herself from any exclusive relationship, in order to give herself, beyond that very relative and provisional crossing of the desert, to a multitude of connections with others and the world, with an intensity as exuberant as it is disciplined. The letter does not make quite so explicit the orientation that diverts love into writing, but the cry for help—"Come back"—shouted at Renaud, is tinged with a different and entirely new jubilation: that of *writing the recollection*. "You have locked up the wolf in the sheep pen! [. . .] Fear that the *memory of the past* will come back to your Claudine in her enchanted house, O cautious, incautious husband."[26]

Who is the wolf locked up by Willy? Colette or her memory? *Memory*, in fact, will be the principal wellspring, now consciously chosen as the Archimedean point for that rebirth of body and style that Colette had attempted from the beginning in Willy's "jail." These few flashes of "pure incorporated time" in the early writings just quoted form a foundation on which she will continue to rely with each new development. A stylistic metamorphosis is nevertheless already under way, contemporary to the dawning awareness of childhood memory, which would now be the "big bad wolf," the sacred monster guiding the pen of the "great Colette." It is 1905. The first notebook of Proust's *In Search of Lost Time* dates only from 1908.[27]

The fragments from issues 2, 3, 5, and 11 of the *Mercure Musical* recapitulate the details of that already old but still fresh threesome, though Colette later judged them superfluous and eliminated them from the 1908 collection: without being hasty, the author lets a new body and a new writing mature. In fact, almost simultaneously with the *Letter from Claudine* of April 1905, she published, in May, "The Nightingale's Song,"[28] which would be the introductory text to *Tendrils of the Vine*.[29]

Dialogues of Beasts, hailed by Francis Jammes, had already opened the way for that radical shift we follow in *Tendrils of the Vine,* by replacing the human point of view on the world with that of a sensibility supposedly belonging to a dog and a cat, Toby-Chien and Kiki-la-Doucette. Is this an anthropomorphic projection that appropriates animals, utterly domesticates them? Not really, because Colette wants to describe the extreme destitution of her own sensibility, pushed to the limits of animality. Savage intuitions and brutalities dwell within her. She immerses herself in that universe, unknown or repressed by most of us, in that archaic dimension of the psyche of us "Two-legged Ones," with our "soft furless skin."[30] Thanks to these beasts, Colette succeeds in taming and *excusing the paroxysms* of the psyche that, in other people, dig hells and promise paradises. For her, the animal brings a touch of simplicity and humor, which, like a modest grace, saves speaking beings both from Gehenna and from ecstasy. Even though the human reveals its inhumanity in exquisite or monstrous excess, Colette does not call for hatred, as in a journey to the end of the night. There are no violent catastrophes in that Colettian Being when it expands to the limits of the sensory. Her ecstasy is not an anguished transition pushed to the point of anger, or even an insolent escape route: the complicit smiles shared with Kiki-la-Doucette and Toby-Chien brush against her, swallow her up, and, in fact, nullify her. Faced with the untenable strangeness of self and other, the writer tames extreme perceptions and desires as if they were those of a beast—both a formidable stranger and a beloved companion. Hence, through the "Four-legged Ones," the night of the sensory slips away from vindictive rage, and its strangeness, which brings me jouissance and death, is called *my* animality. That is also my humor, my irony, my way of not becoming fixed as an écorché,[31] and even less as something sublime, a way of laughing about it with unlikely and, when all is said and done, probable accomplices. That animality, the *figure for a sense of humor* about oneself, therefore attests to a beautiful optimism. The other is not only my enemy, his beastly jouissance is inside me: I am that beast, O animal, my soulmate, my brother!

Tendrils of the Vine IN SEVEN MOVEMENTS

In hindsight, *Tendrils of the Vine* looks to us like the masterly working drawing for the movement that detaches the writer

Colette from Mme Willy. There is no longer any story: exeunt Claudine, Rézi, Renaud, Maugis; no more vagabond, no more captive, not even a recluse from love. Or rather, various stories connected to that psychological context withdraw into the unspoken and weave the intertext of a concise fable, which, in the style of a bucolic meditation, brings two protagonists face to face: "the nightingale" and "me." The text, itself a fragment of some vanished myth by some immemorial La Fontaine, unfolds in seven movements.

First Movement

There is an immediate return to the past, since the beginning is a memory: nothing begins without an antecedent; memory makes every beginning undecidable. When? Where? "Formerly." The speech act that begins in this way will certainly not be a story in the discursive sense of the term. From the outset it presents itself as haunted by passing time: how to come to it in order to come into being anew? With that temporal adverb, the hero immediately appears: it's a nightingale.

It is an astonishing choice. The reader does not know it yet, but will learn in Colette's later texts, that the author does not like birds: "Birds are distant. [. . .] I prefer beasts with four feet or paws. Birds always have their arms crossed behind their backs, and use them only to fly. They intrigue me, they escape me, they excite me less than quadrupeds."[32] In one of Colette's detective stories, as the ultimate perversity, one of her monstrous characters, the very proper M. Daste, amuses himself killing parakeets by the dozen: "I did not stay long to contemplate, scattered at my feet, the work accomplished by the civilized monster rigged out in human guise, lover of the deaths of birds."[33] As for Landru, the famous murderer on whose trial Colette wrote disconcerting texts (an article in *Le Matin* on November 8, 1921, then two more pieces),[34] she find his eyes "shining like the eyes of birds, like them devoid of language, of pity, and of melancholy."[35] Are birds monstrous—like a murderer, or like a writer-nightingale?

Or like a woman who knows how to feign jouissance and, in that extreme generosity, gives her lover, preferably very young, the impression of virile omnipotence, of a "reward like those found in novels," a "public pleasure"? Hence Charlotte, in *The Pure and the Impure* (1932–41), a false lover and oblatory partner, drugs her "poor little guy" in an opium den with a "melodious and merciful lie." It is certainly that true-false song of Charlotte's that, twenty-eight years after *Tendrils of the Vine,* brings the figure of the nightingale once more to Colette's writing: "the lament of the nightingale, the full notes, reiterated, identical, one extending into the other, racing to the breaking point of their trembling equilibrium at the height of a torrential sob."[36]

In contrast, butterflies, even though they fly, will not be relegated to the distance: as the friends of flowers, as flowers themselves with their vibrant splendor and delicate palette, they will find a sincere admirer in Colette, well before Nabokov.[37]

In *Tendrils of the Vine,* then, it is not the inaccessible fowl but the king of song that, through its voice, fills Colette with wonder: the nightingale is an artist. Moreover, the alliteration in the French title, *Les vrilles de la vigne,* full of resonant and palatalized labials (*v, r, illi, gne*) suggests as much—it is in its music that a nightingale truly takes flight. All the same that assertion has to be nuanced, since certain conditions are required for that flight to occur. Gifted with a "gentle wisp of a voice," that carefree bird, lost in the crowd of its "comrades," "formerly" would go to bed anywhere, "often in the vines," simply to sleep—naïve or stunned—until the next day.

Let us listen again to the French title— *Les vrilles de la vigne:* VR/ILLE/ V/IGNE. In the writer's secret life, vibrations of the mouth and the humming of ears, teeth, and lips, joined together in *vvv,* are associated with a loss of self, of ravaging fever, and yet are propitious for writing: "The fever is running its course, which is not troublesome. It sends greats gusts of *vvou* around me, with a profusion of *v*'s; it seems to have borrowed all the *v*'s possessed by vast airy words like *vent, vortex, vol.*"[38] Might *Tendrils of the Vine* have been written in that feverish state, where the limits of self are effaced in the wind [*vent*], the vortex, in flight [*vol*]?

The nightingale, a rare figure in Colette's bestiary, is no doubt too closely tied to the first sorrows of the young Mme Gauthier-Villars in Paris. In 1894, when Colette, unhappy with Willy's infidelity, was suffering from a psychosomatic illness, chance sent her friend Maurice Schwob to her bedside, and he "faithfully opened a volume of American or English short stories."[39] In 1891 Schwob had translated four stories by Oscar Wilde, one of which was called "The Nightingale and the Rose." Could he have read his young friend that story of impossible love, which depicts the lack of understanding between the sexes?

To win the heart of his beloved, a student wishes to offer her a rose, which can be obtained only on one condition: a nightingale must press his heart against its thorns until it dies. Despite the poignant sacrifice of the bird musician, the young lady turns up her nose at the flower and prefers a jewel. That suffices to scandalize the young man, who abandons the beautiful girl and turns back to his studies. Since wisdom follows that realization of the gap separating the two sexes, the nightingale symbolizes for Oscar Wilde the heart pierced by the lover, who dies as lover of the opposite sex but who continues to sing as a scholar alone with his books.

Somewhat later, in August 1902, a lyric drama was performed, based on a piece of music by Camille Saint-Saëns, and it unleashed Maugis-Willy's wrath.[40] The work is drawn from *Parysatis,* a novel by Jeanne Dieulafoy, the wife of the archaeologist who discovered the palace of Darius and Ataxerxes. Here again it is a drama of love: Ataxerxes loves the beautiful Greek slave Aspasia, who is also loved by the crown prince, Darius, supported in that adventure by his grandmother Parysatis. To avoid war between father and son, who become rivals in love, Aspasia kills herself. The soprano solo that precedes her suicide is an adaptation of "The Nightingale and the Rose": here a woman plays the role of the sacrificed nightingale.

That tragic romanticism, which permeated the culture of her time and did not spare Colette's marital life despite Willy's libertine denial, remains implicit in *Tendrils of the Vine*. Modestly, the author avoids the account of her painful love affairs and records only the traces of aesthetic sublimation that followed them.

Finally, one ought to add to these romantic resonances the unconscious symbolism of fowl and its phallic connotation: in many languages, birds are associated with the erection of the male member. We will return to Colette's claim of psychic bisexuality.[41] Let us note for the moment, keeping the male symbol in mind, that, although in the second movement of the text the nightingale is afraid of being a prisoner to the vine, it does not fail to form a couple with it: do we not hear the same liquid palatal consonant *gn* in the French word for nightingale, *rossignol,* and in *vigne*—as if they corresponded to each other like an echo or a mirror reflection, a duo bound together by the same pleasure of the mouth, by a drowsy voracity? The second movement, precisely, will hasten to awaken and to change that intoxication of love. But from the outset the music of words suggests that the nightingale does not simply symbolize *man* or even his desire: the musician bird evokes the *artist* who holds the pen, and her fluid being leads her to identify with her partners and to make a world from them—the world of her song.

Second Movement

The "horns of the vine, those brittle and clinging tendrils," grow so thick one spring night that "the nightingale awoke tied down, its feet entangled in forked bonds, its wings powerless." Next to the *writer,* the subject of the utterance, who protects herself in the shadow of the intertext, and the *nightingale,* which plays the lead role, a third character makes its entrance here, announced in the title and now deploying its extreme noxiousness: the *vine.*

That attribute of Bacchus is evoked at least twice by Colette: in *Claudine Married* (1902), the author describes Rézi's voluptuousness, insisting on her "pointed fingers" and the arabesques of her "hardy hands."[42] Then, in *My Apprenticeships,* recalling her "guilty intoxication," that is, her discovery of eroticism in marriage, she presents Willy surrounded by a bewitching "shade of Priapus" (another god of the vine) and "in the end unmasks the shadow of an already aging man who has troubled, unreadable bluish eyes, a gift of tears to make you shudder, a marvelously veiled voice, an agility strange in an obese man, and the hardness of an eiderdown quilt stuffed with pebbles."[43]

The image of a captivating and maleficent voluptuousness, the nightingale's vine is not unrelated to Captain Colette: his little girl, his favorite "electoral representative," enjoyed the intoxication of wine to such excess that Sido had to intervene to stop their—political—closeness. "The first times, when we got back, my open-mouthed prostration astonished my mother, who quickly put me to bed, reproaching my father for my fatigue. Then, one evening, she discovered in my eyes a little very Burgundian gaiety, and on my breath the secret of that sarcasm, alas!"[44]

After her rediscovery of Sido in 1930 and the reconciliation with cosmic space-time that Sido would incarnate, Colette stopped feeling guilty about Bacchic pleasures. In *Prisons and Paradises* (1932), she savored wine as the most delicious of nectars:

> I was very well brought up. As the first piece of evidence for such a categorical assertion, I will say that I was no more than three when my father gave me a full liqueur glass of a bronze-colored wine to drink, sent from his native Midi: Frontignan muscatel. Sunstroke, a voluptuous shock, illumination of brand-new taste buds! That rite made me forever worthy of wine.[45]

> In the plant kingdom, only the vine makes intelligible to us the true flavor of the earth. What fidelity in the translation! The vine experiences and expresses through the grape the secrets of the soil. The flint, through it, lets us know it is living, fusible, nourishing. The barren chalk, in wine, weeps golden tears.[46]

For the moment, however, in 1905–8, tendrils are threatening. Sexual intoxication is experienced as a morbid magic: the spells of desire—Rézi's spells as well as Willy's—are "forked bonds" that tie you down and make your "wings powerless." Therefore, after suffering "a thousand pains," to the point of believing it will die of them, our nightingale promises itself not to sleep again so long as the tendrils of the vine are growing. But will vigilance alone suffice to protect it from that poison of others' desire, of the desire for others?

Third Movement

As a technique for staying awake in the first place, or as an exercise in lucidity, the nightingale begins to sing rather than fall asleep as it "formerly" did, as an innocent child, around "seven o'clock, seven thirty" in the evening. To protect itself from the tendrils of the vine, it sings, sings, sings:

> So long as the vine grows, grows, grows
> I will not sleep again!
> So long as the vine grows, grows, grows.

In that way, forgetting the dangers of the vine, the nightingale in the end falls in love with its own voice, and its repetitions are transformed into "variations." But that "desperate" self-intoxication metamorphoses our Narcissus-artist into an object of fascination for others. *One* (for the moment, the narrator conceals herself behind that impersonal pronoun) imputes a new and "unbearable desire" to it: to *see* it sing—or to be *seen* singing.

"Look," Sido's motto, will also become Colette's. Her career as a mime and actress led her to expose herself—when not her art—to the public and preceded the nightingale's adventures. Does not that desire to offer to view—to show, make seen—the nightingale's vocal jouissance anticipate our pleasure as modern voyeurs, optical consumers of media events? See and be seen: from her first forays into the Parisian salons, from her first novels, from her first roles on the stage, Colette was completely aware of that French taste for the spectacle. Belle Epoque France, a culture of display, of apparition and of appearance, invented a modernity that is somewhat reminiscent both of the gilded pomp of the royal courts and of the ribald exhibitions of fairground theater and other Carnaval farces.[47] Colette fully belonged to that culture of appearance and did not reject any of its acidulous charms. Does not *one* believe one is capturing the jouissance of unique creators by exhibiting them for everyone to see? Formerly through the music hall, now on the small screen? "It varied its theme, garlanded it with vocalizations, fell in love with its voice, became that desperate singer, drunk and gasping, to which *one* listens with the unbearable desire to *see* it sing" (my emphasis).

Fourth Movement

Let us now abandon the *one* of the anonymous public, since it is "I" at issue in that brief fable introduced by the nightingale. It is time for that first person to make herself seen, to speak up: "I saw a nightingale singing under the moon."

Nevertheless, that *I* is no longer solely that of the *look*: it is an *I* that immerses itself in the *voice* and that brings the singer back to itself. *I* is a split and reflexive consciousness that observes itself, analyzes itself, transforms itself. A brief face-to-face encounter follows between *I* and *it*. Henceforth, *it* and *I* are not opposites except in appearance, and it is the artist's internal dialogue with herself that is being staged, by Colette (*I*) who listens to herself (*it*) write (I/it): "It sometimes breaks off, its head cocked, as if to listen within itself for the prolongation of a faint note. . . . Then it resumes with all its might, puffed up, head thrown back, with a look of loving despair. It sings to sing, it sings such beautiful things that it no longer knows what they mean."

That objectless song has no other significance than its internal beauty. The *me-I* hears it, hears itself, and identifies with that act which has no finality outside itself: "But I, I still hear in the golden notes the sounds of grave flutes, tremulous and crystalline trills." The threatening tendrils, *vrilles,* are replaced by trills, *trilles,* grave gold and tremulous crystal. *Me,* I intone the nightingale's song, I am the nightingale: "So long as the vine grows, grows, grows."

Fifth Moment

Indeed, it is truly "me" the tendrils of desire had bound—the reader has guessed as much based on the intertext. Only here can the narrator say so in her oneiric cantilena, with all her wordplay, sound play, and intersecting identities: her undefiant youth was abused by "twisted strands" that did not leave her indifferent, "that already held to [her] flesh." If the *Claudine* books recount their delights and impasses, *The Retreat from Love* (1907) and *The Innocent Libertine* (1909) try to break free of them. Now, under the cover of a fable, *I* can admit it without rancor and with the certainty that I possess a voice that is *my* new way of being. Yes, priapic intoxication is still frightening, I still fear it, and only my suffering, finally expressed, can ground the truth of my words: "I feared the tendrils of the vine and I raised up a plaint that revealed my voice to me!" In melancholy, sadness has no chance of being transcended unless it first manifests itself in tears, then makes itself explicit in words: similarly, the writing of sorrow breaks away from the maniacal excitation of puerile flirtation and brings forth a promise of renewal.

Sixth Movement

Colette does not like to be weighed down by depression and evokes its suffering only to move beyond it. A single sentence, left hanging, depicts her "all alone," looking at the "voluptuous and morose star." The black sun of melancholy overlooks the horizon of that change of desires and of the world, which she is in the process of living and writing: the journey through melancholy is evoked with maximum economy, as a word to the wise. The writer will not fall back into the child's naïve innocence but also will not wallow in sadness. Another mode of being appears to her, similar in every respect to that of the nightingale and not yet assured, hesitating between the excess of sorrow—"I weep frantically"—and phobic shame—"I dare not go on."

Seventh Movement

Beyond that hesitancy—but does she not also reveal a surplus of severe lucidity?—her style becomes lighter and her language absorbs the trills of the nightingale in its concise lines. The ternary world of Claudine-Renaud-Rézi is gone, the triplets of the trills remain: nothing but a threefold pattern that transfers what was an erotic love story into the rhythm of a sentence, the music of words. Let us listen to the triads of that incantation, the triple repetition of words and the replication by threes of syntactic turns of phrase. What we are witnessing is not Colette moving beyond desire-driven plots but, rather, transubstantiating them: "I would like to say, to say, to say, everything I know, everything I think, everything I discern, everything that enchants me and wounds me and astonishes me."

That act of wresting herself from psychology, that hard-won autonomy in which our nightingale-author is engaged, is nevertheless not autarkic. Unexpectedly, in the exhausting program of seduction-betrayal set in place by man's phallic sexuality, help is offered her. "The wise fresh hand placed over my mouth" in that new "sonorous night" is Missy's hand, and three texts in the original collection will contain dedications alluding to her maternal protection.[48]

In opposition to the toxic night of the vine, our nightingale puts forth her own sonorous night. Colette has not yet uncovered the lethal traps of female homosexual friendships, as she would do in *The Pure and the Impure*.[49] For the moment she pacifies herself with extraordinary lucidity by entrusting herself to the hands of a replacement mother, in search of that polyphonic ego, which will be realized only in the solitude of her works. She does not fail to perceive that, from now on, the calming embrace of her friend bears the weight of a regression that

pushes her "toward moderate verbiage" when not to "the volubility of a child [. . .] trying to forget." No matter: a new sublimation is under way, which comes about through Missy and
makes it possible to mourn a certain venomous desire, that of the
tendrils of the vine. But Colette also knows to acknowledge her
debt toward the Dionysian world of desire: always beyond it,
never on the near side of it, provided she has done with it.
Farewell, happy sleep! The finality of an *other* jouissance remains.
But which one?

Nothing spells it out for the moment. The multiple facets of
Colette's texts invite us to decipher it between the lines. Could it
be Agape that our transformed nightingale will sing, against
Eros? Cybele and Attis, that he/she might celebrate, against Bacchus and his bacchantes? Or fertility, against sadomasochistic
pleasure? Not at all: love and motherhood are not values for Colette; and her adherence to sublimation does not lead her to dis-
regard the cruelties of phallic desire, those "twisted strands"—
those "tendrils of the vine"—where the ravages of love and the
consolations of friendship mingle together. The author also does
not renounce her own virility, that of a nightingale following its
path pen in hand. But she increases her intoxication by constantly resorting to an ever-incomplete femininity, concealed,
enigmatic: turning to female homosexuality in the first place,
then capturing and devouring the incestuous mother, before being appeased with a new version of her rediscovered flesh in the
now triumphal song that is neither cry nor murmur but a true
pagan hymn to serenity. That hymn begins with *My Mother's
House*, triumphs with *Sido, Break of Day, The Pure and the Impure*, and is disseminated into all the other writings.

METAPHORS? NO, METAMORPHOSES

We read *Tendrils of the Vine* as a parable, a coded and elliptical evocation of the stylistic shift under way, with the nightingale and the
vine as the two polymorphic and intersecting metaphors for the
writer herself, for her desires and her sublimating transcendence.

Nevertheless, the precision and oneiric conciseness of Colette's writing make them more than mere rhetorical images: they are the *very realization* of the change under way. They are better than metaphors, they are metamorphoses: the nightingale's imagined trills are those of Colette herself. These metamorphoses reveal imaginary, provisional postures—and, in that sense, necessarily impostures—but they also form its only reality today, in the process of change: body-soul-and-music confused in the writing of a reality so real in its simplicity that it cannot be experienced, nor can it simply be read as a *piece of literature*. Thanks to the stinging intensity of its physical and psychic movements, inseparable from their formulation, the "ego" does not *compare* itself to the nightingale or *take itself* for it, my "ego" *is* the nightingale, my "ego" *is* the sonorous night.

How, in that shift so particular to Colette, which she is in the process of living-and-writing, can we fail to recall Baudelaire, the "assassin" (*haschiscin*) of *Paradis artificiels*: "Your eye fixes on a tree [. . .] what would be, in a poet's brain, only a very natural comparison will become a reality in yours. You first attribute to the tree your passions, your desire, or your melancholy; its moans and oscillations become your own, and soon you are the tree." "Cause and effect, subject and object, mesmerist and somnambulist."[50]

The subject and the object, the nightingale and the vine, the writing and the pretext identify with each other in an indivisible osmosis. But, unlike Baudelaire, for Colette drunkenness is not at issue. And, contrary to what some have said, it is also not a *domestication* of the world—that word reduces it to banality—but an *innocence,* a refusal to do harm. Might sublimation therefore be the maximum, ideal protection against aggressive violence, its supreme absolution? That appropriation of the other, of the external, of the outsider, compensates for the pain of loving and suspends vengeful cruelty into appeasement; only the concision and fulguration betray the scar of the wounds endured.

It cannot be repeated enough: Colette's allegories, like her metaphors, are metamorphoses because they grasp the object named (the nightingale, the vine) in its sensory impact on the subject and communicate that acute, unique, revealing sensibility to the reader, who slips from words to things. The most frequent logic behind the verbalization of these metamorphoses is *analogy* and *contrast*. The Colettian metaphor proceeds by suddenly seizing on an "inexpressible relation" tracing circles and spirals between two things, two sensations, and two words. Curiously, the "tendrils" of that "inexpressible relation" prick the "object's" heart like darts, the same way the object excites the "subject": "I grope timidly, I invent an *inexpressible relation* between the milky drop of lilies of the valley, the tear of warm rain, the crystalline bubble that rises from the toad."[51] Invention lies in the relationship of analogy and opposition governing desire, not in the dream that relaxes logical constraints: Colette does not dream, never loses her footing; she tells lies or modifies, but the real is always there.

Is she a poet? Yes, but one diametrically opposed to the nominalist Mallarmé. Whereas the master of *Un coup de dés* celebrates "the one absent from any bouquet," Colette bites into the toxic vine and slips into the nightingale's throat. Her tendrils are more evocative of the "rings" of Proustian metaphors,[52] except that Proust's metaphorical "rings" are linked ad infinitum, whereas Colette's "hooked" tendrils are not oblivious to the fact that they originate in the flavor of the vine. And even though, with a click of the tongue, the writer escapes, keeping only the drunkenness of the "tremulous and crystalline trills [that] sing to sing," that musical cohesion to words has the ultimate aim of returning, through the pleasure of the rhythm of sound, to the sap of the plant, the vigorous cry of the bird.

Colette's metaphors can also be differentiated from the surrealist use of that trope. In *Le paysan de Paris,* Louis Aragon fancied himself a "kleptomaniac of voluptuousness," whose metaphors would bring into being "the vagabondage of uncertainty": "Error with radium fingers, my singing mistress, my pathetic shadow." The oneiric play of surrealist metaphors defied the constraints of language and identities: "Neither face nor sighs find the mirror or the echo sought." The word's vocation was to corrupt through a subjective flood the land of meaning itself: "I call style the tone taken, on the occasion of a given man, the flood, reflected back by him, of the symbolic ocean that universally mines the earth through metaphor."[53] There is nothing like that in Colette: the surprise she causes is that of opposition added to analogy, which, through the shock of paradox, "hits the bull's eye." She does not concern herself with opening the ocean of infinite associations, but captures and fixes the instant of pleasure.

Antithetical, disjointed terms unite into oxymorons, and Colettian metaphors frequently rely on "oppositeness," which, according to Roland Barthes, is "structural, or tragic, jouissance strictly speaking."[54] It is, in fact, through structural opposition that metaphor in Colette's writing is incarnated as metamorphoses.

So it is with the *rose*, which, like the writer's style, is only a "prodigious [. . .] inexhaustible gift of metamorphosis [. . .] you, ebony roses, odor confiture."[55] The rose, usually red, pink, or tea yellow, here darkens to black. In conjunction with that contrast, which extracts it from the world of flowers and transports it (the first effect of metaphor) to the world of culture (of artifice) or of melancholy (like the black sun), is a second metaphoric movement, spun from the logic of sensorial inversions and displacements. The eyes eat the rose, sight has become taste, I savor the flower like jam. Finally, a third displacement will lead from the palate and tongue to the nose. It is now scents that become confections, the rose cooks its fragrance: "you, ebony roses, odor confiture." In this series of shifts, the words weave tendrils and the spirals of that embroidery mingle the interlacing sensations with the music of semantic fields that magnetize words with their pleasant tones: "ebony roses, odor confiture," *roses noires, confiture d'odeur*, ro:z/ nwa:r/kõfity:r/dɔdœ:r.

That is how Colette's metaphorical *invention* proceeds: less through an oneiric act of flight that, for its part, breathes sexual connotations into innocent objects (such as Breton's and Aragon's "soluble fish,"[56] which turn out to be metaphors for masturbation) than by the "inexpressible establishment of a relationship" that pairs objects, twists perceptions together, and leads the author, along with the reader, to project herself into the plenitude of the senses, to metamorphose herself into the sensory world through vibrations of her tongue.

Even the discovery of the mot juste, which one imagines is immediate, aiming straight for the heart of the passionate relationship that envelops the author and her objects, seems to result from that "tendrils of the vine" movement specific to Colette's thought: simultaneously analogy, contrast, and identification of the resonant word with its sensory referent. Let us read on: the metaphor of *fire* changes peacocks into elusive birds before transferring its heat to the cold clarity of their blue plumage. "For a short moment, the unstable fire [*feu*] that envelops them [*eux*] becomes motionless and maintains itself in the fixed blue [*bleu*]" *Eux, feu, bleu*: do you believe this "blue" is an absolute sign, an inexorable, immediate monogram? Don't be fooled: the very choice of this word resulted from many "tendrils," which led it to take a detour through its synonyms and antonyms, tendrils that passed from the optical to the mental, from the spoken to the sensed to the intuited, before "abolishing" the word in the series of greens. The metaphor-metamorphosis is spun out in a little sequence of sentences that compose a short short story of the "tendrils of the vine" variety:

> I say "blue"; but what name are we to give that color that *surpasses blue*, pushes back the limits of *violet,* evokes *purple* in a realm more *mental* than *optical,* since, though I call purple a *vibration* of color that seems to *border* that blue, I do not really see it, I *sense* it. . . . O what *folly* to want to depict the peacock! That blue I claimed to describe is, moreover, *abolished,* the two peacocks have gone on their way, side by side, and only the *green bronze* covers them.[57]

What, then, is that "folly to want to depict" if not the demon of analogy and the opposition that nourishes my words with contrasting vibrations from the world I intuit, a world in which contours, colors, objects, and even I myself are abolished in order to better bring forth the intensity of Being?

The metaphorical writing that characterizes Colette's style flourishes in a genre she makes her own: a mixture of elliptical narration and prose poem. Since there is no established name to define that surprising genre, let us designate it by a generic term, "tendrils of the vine," since the text bearing that title marks a turning point in which style becomes an experience of transubstantiation, a "hooked memory."[58] That genre, a discipline of secrecy, of strikeouts, of rhythm, unites dilation and suspension: "Twenty pages on the colored, tonic, and mysterious ephemera; twenty lines on the notorious and the venerable, whom others have celebrated and will celebrate."[59] Unlike the poetic song in its exaltation, the "tendrils of the vine" entrench themselves in an act of listening to the metaphorical shock between two words: "To sing! O prose writers walled in by your silence, who hold your breath to better hear the timid music of two words set side by side."[60] She pretends not to choose, to accumulate insignificant details: "It is the ordinary that arouses and invigorates me."[61] But that apparent improvisation is played out with a constant concern for avoiding "imposture," which, if we read Colette carefully, is quite simply complaisant narration. "It is therefore to win God's favor that I accumulate these sheets, deprived though they are of the distorting and pleasant touch, of dialogue between imagined characters, of an arbitrary conclusion that slays, marries off, separates. I am falling away from imposture."[62]

TWO NARRATIVE REGISTERS

Apollinaire was the first to hail the "imperious lightness" of *Tendrils of the Vine*, which "will send Colette Willy straight to paradise when the moment comes." The perspicacious poet warned that "people will not immediately grasp what is new about *Tendrils of the Vine* [. . .] it's an arcanum, the study of which is forbidden to most contemporaries!" He advanced the following praise, which anticipates my formulations: "There one finds beauties of the first order that are nothing but *thrilling frissons of the flesh*."[63] In what is the height of audacity in his eyes, the French Colette may be almost American: "I feel she is very French, but she astonishes me the way American women do when I meet them. I tell myself she must be charming, but too independent."[64] All the same, Apollinaire is wrong to think (a kind of misogyny, more or less unconscious, on the part of that sardonic genius?) that this Colettian freedom comes from a relaxed spontaneity, incapable of distinguishing good from evil, as inconsequential as "the dove [that] drops its shit on the passerby, and it is white with a little black-green, like a printed page."[65] Colette did not fail to call these lines of Louise Lalande's "benevolent nastiness."[66] Apollinaire's judgment would later evolve toward greater severity.

In reality, psychologically speaking, the "tendrils of the vine" require a rigorous sobriety. Thus Colette replies to the question, "How do you work?" by saying: "With strictness, that may be the most suitable word."[67] She insists on that draconian craftsmanship: "An artisan, a functionary, that's what we are. [. . .] Three thousand pages spoiled to get two hundred and fifty good cleaned-up ones."[68] But let us not confuse that exigency with formalism, to which Colette takes exception: "To live, don't you see, to live first of all! To get drunk on nature, on everything around you, that's how I work. [. . .] Look around you, soak up the atmosphere of things, that's the purpose of life and the only reason for living."[69] The most concise definition of writing as "tendrils of the vine," however, is found in a text from Colette's later years: "Success is less a matter of thought than of an encounter between words. Sometimes words, signs wandering in the air, when called upon deign to come down, assemble themselves, become fixed. . . . That seems to be how the little miracle I call golden egg, bubble, or flower comes about: a sentence worthy of what it wanted to describe."[70]

The "tendrils of the vine," made in that way, constitute the first version of the alphabet that is Colette's true discovery: a close weave, modest and passionate, between words and desire, recollections and sensations, sense and sound. This writing as balls of blown glass, *sulfures*,[71] is affirmed as an asceticism, in contrast to the inebriation of the earlier romantic plots at which the author distinguished herself. It began at Missy's side and would find its support, its source, and its apogee in the mythic figure of Sido. The "tendrils of the vine" genre—lacunary, antinarrative, extremely reserved and restrained—fragments narrative as it pulverizes time: it scrambles chronology, jumbles time sequences, assembling recollections in a kaleidoscope. It is an expression of the most intimate privacy, of a "sensuality more dispersed than the spasm," "without resolution and without demands,"[72] that is, female sexuality according to Colette. That aspect of Colettian style as "tendrils of the vine" prevails in a series of texts: *Tendrils of the Vine* (1908), *Music-Hall Sidelights* (1913), *Peace Among the Beasts* (1916), which echoes *Dialogues of Beasts* (1904), *The Long Hours* (1917), *In the Crowd* (1918), *The Bright Room* (1920), *Selfish Journey* (1922), *My Mother's House* (1922), *The Hidden Woman* (1924), *Everyday Adventures* (1924), *Break of Day* (1928), *Sido* (1929), *The Pure and the Impure* (1932), *Prisons and Paradises* (1932), *My Apprenticeships* (1936), and even the last gasps of *Fine Seasons* (1945) and *For an Herbarium* (1948).

In counterpoint to that vein Colette develops a novelistic writing that, though it also produces its effects by shattering chronological plotlines, by inserting memory kaleidoscopes and sensorial epiphanies, nevertheless conserves the appearance of a narration devoted to psychological ordeals: *The Innocent Libertine* (1909), *The Vagabond* (1910), *The Shackle* (1913), *Mitsou* (1919), *Chéri* (1920), *The Ripening Seed* (1923), *The End of Chéri* (1926), *The Other One* (1929), and even *Le Toutounier* (1939), *Julie de Carneilhan* (1941), *The Evening Star* (1946), and *The Blue Lantern* (1949). If we often find that complaisant psychology tiresome, let us recall the severity with which Colette herself judged these texts: "loose, rapid, malleable dialogue [. . .] listless and lively language [. . .] my victim [Léopold Marchand] will have learned only one thing from me, but it counts: the art of writing badly."[73] And yet, the "tendrils of the vine" penetrate even the formulaic and gnomic style of *The Blue Lantern*.

In her dual system of writing, the "tendrils of the vine" genre reveals a Colette who excels at intimate description, at the fragment—"selected passages"—which her novels, with their psychological variations, seem designed to prepare us for or to foreground rather than the reverse. Is that because *abridgement* and *condensation,* rather than elaboration,[74] better suit the disorder of the senses, or the fringes of the intolerable, which is precisely what Colette's genius is aiming for? That incisive art of grasping details flourishes as well, and quite particularly, in her portraits, newspaper columns, and other journalistic or theatrical remarks, which offer not a political or aesthetic judgment but a dramatic and generous enticement of the other. For example, Colette, a mediocre Shakespearean, bites into the flesh of the great dramatic author through a mininarrative: she loves Shakespeare's "muscular abridgements, the alternating, jangling sparks of twenty cruel replies."[75] Or, again in the "tendrils of the vine" style, she literally makes love to Madeleine Renaud, describing her as a "butterfly [. . .] that illuminates itself with its own fire. Large eyelids blinking freely seem to veil and unveil her entire face."[76]

Barely shored up by a plot, the narration that allows itself to be contaminated by the "tendrils of the vine" takes on the look of a *short story,* a genre to which Maupassant had brought brilliant distinction in the previous generation. It is both more and less than a short story, however, since Colette cultivates a scaled-down "short story," fragmented, instilled with lyricism, and studded with maxims. It is often difficult to grasp its logical coherence and even more its connection to the other short stories in the same collection: at issue, in fact, is more a unity of *tone* than a common subject. Such is the harmony that confers its unity on the series of texts constituting *Tendrils of the Vine* (1908), *Music-Hall Sidelights* (1913), *The Long Hours* (1914), *In the Crowd* (1918), *Selfish Journey* (1922), *My Mother's House* (1922), *Bella-Vista* (1937), *The Kepi* (1943), and *Gigi* (1944). These short narratives, elliptical little "novels," are also made up of fragments loosely bound together by an often chaotic, nonlinear plot, strewn with lyrical passages, recollections, edifying—or rather unedifying—sequences, leading to the nine "chapters" of *Break of Day* (1928) and the three "volets" of *Sido* (1929). There Colette reaches the pinnacle of her poetic art, but we will find the same thing in *My Apprenticeships* (1936), *The Pure and the Impure* (1932–41), and so on.

Journalistic constraints often imposed that lapidary, hooked, "tendrils of the vine" writing: for example, in the collection *The*

Hidden Woman (1923), every narrative comprises twelve manuscript pages, just what was required to appear in installments in *Le Matin* under the rubric "Tales of a Thousand and One Mornings." These are prose poems about a mystery more instinctual than psychic, sheer drops into uncanniness, on the borderline of the thriller. In fact, the aim of that particular genre, which Colette invented when her writing reached a turning point with *Twelve Dialogues of Beasts* and *Tendrils of the Vine,* is not to recount but to grasp, to seize on, to engrave the *drive* rather then the *soul*—a prepsychic emotion in place of the psyche itself. Its fulguration touches Being through beings and arrives at the animal underside of human psychology. It is an art of subtraction, but it is not dry; the little "short story," intense in its brevity, makes as much use of the poetic metamorphoses of loving couples as of the writer's insights into erotic sadomasochism. If Colette, in that process, does not become a celebrated master of the thriller, it is in the first place because pleasure and sexuality interest her more than the melancholic desolation that guides the pen of her English and North American sisters. Finally and above all, in that inveiglement of jubilation, it is lyrical hyperbole that appeals to the gourmand, who thus eludes the morbidity that delights in long logical inquiries. Even though, beginning in 1930, the writer took pleasure in refining her sentences and, from the start, did not shy away from rococo excess, the essence of her art is that genius for incisiveness, which, even in the novels that conform most closely to the "romance magazine" genre, "slays" with on-target metaphors, marks out a restrained beat, rolls itself up into short narratives: Colette's texts "*pètent sec,*" as Paul Morand had already noted, within the "suffocating atmosphere"[77] of literature in the first decade of the twentieth century.

Without a doubt Colette likes to disparage narration—"It is easy to relate what hardly matters"[78]—and to put forward her own system. "Since then, I have confined myself to stories of love, more or less." More or less. "One speaks of one lover and keeps quiet about the rest."[79] Nevertheless, few of Colette's texts confine themselves solely to the extreme condensation of the nightingale's song she places at the beginning of *Tendrils of the*

Vine. In the collection itself, even after much retouching and tightening over time, two distinct aspects stand out. On one hand she captures psychic states, which cease to be psychic as soon as they are immersed in flora and fauna and can be read as an exquisite or troubling dehumanization, like vibrations of the cosmos. On the other she pursues narrative plots oscillating between vaudeville and the cruelty necessary for a disengagement from love, all of which makes Colette an experienced psychologist of feminine jouissance, perceived as a cosmic solitude, an objectless relationship saturated with elements, a dissemination of self.[80]

That split runs through her entire body of work. In the first place she adds to the "poetic" series composed of "dialogues of beasts," "flora and pomona," the more commercial series detailing "women's adventures," from the *Claudine* books to *The Vagabond* to *Julie de Carneilhan.* In addition, within the poetic memories and meditations themselves, such as *Tendrils of the Vine* or *Sido,* the two aspects coexist and harmonize. These aspects are like the two springs, the destination of her morning strolls, whose complementarity Colette celebrates in *Sido* (1929): one is visible but ephemeral; the other, almost invisible but revealed by the narcissi; one tastes like oak, the other like hyacinth:

I was coming back at the bell for the early mass. But not before eating my fill, not before tracing, in the woods, a large circle like a dog hunting alone, and tasting the water of two lost springs, which I might dream up. One rose from the earth in crystalline convulsions, in a sort of sob, and traced out its own sandy bed. Discouraged as soon as it was born, it dove back underground. The other spring, almost invisible, creased the grass like a snake, displayed itself in secret at the center of a meadow where only narcissi blooming in a circle attested to its presence. The first had the flavor of oak leaves, the second of iron and hyacinth stems. . . . Simply by speaking of them, I want their flavor to fill my mouth as I am ending everything, I want to carry that imaginary mouthful with me.[81]

Colette was thirty-two in 1905, and she knew that, with the fable of the nightingale, she had found her voice. We will never know the exact circumstances of that apprenticeship, which transformed the daring young provincial, the betrayed wife of dear Willy, into a writer of genius. Her belated confessions insinuate that she decided to remain silent about these "jumbled and considerable secrets that she herself [i.e., Colette] did not know very well." They are "part of a woman's true, innermost depths," more than any "romantic catastrophe, its consequences, its phases," which, according to the author, are alien to the female experience. On one hand then, there are the dramas of one's love life of which the public world gets its fill, the novels, the narcissistic exhibition of writers themselves, which Colette also does not refrain from complacently sharing with the public, through her stage appearances and the divulgence of personal or family photos. And on the other, there is the experience, indiscriminately sexual *and* vital, body-soul-and-language, an *other* jouissance that cannot be pegged to any sexual identity and that could be discerned only in the condensed working drawing of the act of writing—since it alone collects "what I know of myself, what I try to hide about it, what I invent about it, and what I guess about it."[82]

THE IMAGINARY AS THE RIGHT TO LIE

The two movements of Colette's writing attempt in vain to approach that inaccessible secret; nevertheless, the author aspires to no authenticity. On the contrary: she advances the paradoxical idea that the unveiling of a woman's secret comes about only at the price of a lie, a feint. Colette prides herself on rejecting logical generalities ("I seek to move beyond the perfidious zone of logic")[83] and speaks ironically of a politician who "wished to expand (I would say: reduce) my life to some grand idea that might have served me almost as a religion, a worthiness (*sic*), an inspiration."[84]

Nevertheless, she does have a "theory," but of the *imaginary as a lie,* a necessary, envied, recommended lie. Willy himself, so stubbornly caricatured as a jailer, is almost thanked for having taught his captive the art of "dissimulating" (in the manuscript, very symptomatically, Colette crosses out the word then decides to keep it) that makes one a writer: "Peace be to that hand, now dead, which did not hesitate to turn the key in the lock. It is to it I owe my most assured art, which is not that of writing, but the domestic art of knowing how to wait, *to dissimulate*, to collect crumbs, reconstruct, glue back together, regild, change the last resort into the first resort, lose and regain in the same instant the frivolous taste for life."[85] Similarly, regarding Adolphe Taillandy, another version of Willy, she supplies this ambiguous praise: "For my part, I knew of no other genius in him than that of lying. [. . .] For him, adultery was only one of the forms—and not the most delectable—of lying."[86]

But the art of lying is professed equally by more sympathetic characters, who are closer to the narrator. For example, Minne erects deception into an art of living: "People who do not lie [. . .] are lazybones who don't even take the trouble to arrange the truth a little, if only out of politeness, or to be intriguing."[87] Claudine herself, confronted with Annie's destructive passion, prefers the ruse to authenticity: "There is a pleasure in attaching ourselves to those who deceive us, who wear lies like a very ornate gown and set them aside only out of a voluptuous desire for nudity. I did not love Renaud less when he was cheating on me, and who knows if the image of Rézi was not more dear to me for what it concealed than for what it yielded?"[88] Paul Masson, called Lemice-Térieux ["Mister Iyus"], was a friend deeply appreciated "for his mania for deception. [. . .] For him, I think, it stood in for vice and art."[89] Homosexuals fascinated her because they were experts at dissimulation: "Next to their art of pretense, everything else seems imperfect. When I had to dissimulate, I had my models before my eyes. I had the daily example of a laborious diplomacy, which served only passion and resentment."[90]

Readers have often expressed astonishment at the memoirist's strange selectiveness and her symptomatic oversights in recounting her beginnings in Paris in *My Apprenticeships*: Colette does not mention the presence of Georgie Raoul-Duval in Bayreuth, does not say that Willy introduced her to Missy, does not breathe a word about the social scandal of two women appearing at the Moulin-Rouge, keeps quiet about Natalie Clifford-Barney and Renée Vivien, and so on. Personal reasons, ranging from a settling of accounts to the discretion due the living, no doubt governed such omissions, which amount to lies. It is nevertheless apparent, if we consider the overall plan for the book, that the "apprenticeship" in question is truly that of literature, which is constructed on the art of dissimulation, artifice, the feint. From the outset, in opposition to the romantic and fatal passion for authenticity, Colette imposed upon herself a discipline of the simulacrum, and she took an interest in people who knew how to make-believe and to abstain, since, in their attitudes defying good common sense, she discerned the seeds of courage and virtuosity that transform someone into an artist. "That is why I was able to give, without love, a place of choice to the young man, for example, whom I saw *pretending* to drink and to smoke opium. Now, it is easier to smoke and drink than to *pretend,* and *abstention,* rare in every domain, reveals an inclination toward defiance and virtuosity."[91]

It matters very little whether that choice was made from the beginning or whether Colette invented it more than thirty years after her debut in literature. Since her "apprenticeships" were in the school of writing, and in it alone—certainly not in a so-called truth to be unveiled about the human or society—it is entirely logical that in *My Apprenticeships* she collects *exclusively* the adventures of those who excel at artifice, from the beautiful Otéro to the deplorable Willy, to Polaire, Mata Hari, and Alexandre Bibesco—and forgets, precisely, the fatal passions. Her homosexual passions, for example, may not be as extinguished as she leads us to believe and, for a thousand reasons, they have to be dissimulated. Literature is a rhetoric, she tells us in substance, it is learned through experiences—often hurtful, alas—which reveal how a role, a star, a couple, a Parisian salon, a sexual difference, or a monstrosity is constructed. In Belle Epoque Paris, people harked back to the century of Louis XIV, lived with no strings attached, aware that the world was only a style, and they were intoxicated with cultivating it. Colette did not escape that cultural context. Moreover, is literature a rhetoric, or is life itself? These friends who accompany me in my pain without sparing their generosity or their irony, and, all in all, my own feverish exploration as I rush between journalism and the music hall, between farce and the sacred: might we not all be "Mister Iyus"?

The imaginary is certainly autobiographical, Colette suggests, but only on the condition that one covers one's tracks, evades the hypothetical truth, deforms the past and the present—in the grip of desire, which, because it roots through the burning past, gives itself the opportunity to project and even program the future of the desiring subject I am. This means that the imaginary is incapable of direct confession, but that falseness in no way prevents it from being prophetic: "In it I called myself Renée Néré, or, in a premonition, I fabricated a Léa."[92] Let us also note the insistence, at the end of the journey, on the author's incapacity to "raise the tone of [her] memories to the level of full-scale confidences."[93]

In blackening Willy's character, Colette neglects to recognize his talents as an editor, as well as the social and sexual education, the cultural formation, he gave her, or the textual discipline he taught her (especially in choosing adjectives, tightening the plot, etc.). Conversely, Colette's attacks make Willy larger than life, make that "widower"—as he described himself following Renaud's death and the murderous criticisms by his wife—an immortal, an ever-desirable target. From the *Claudine* books to *My Apprenticeships,* Willy remains an inexhaustible autobiographical source for Colette's writing. Later, Auguste Hériot provided her with "the flattering, dazzling image of the 'imbecile' "[94] in the character of Max, at Renée Néré's side in *The Vagabond.* Léa, with her "perversity to satisfy an adolescent lover,"[95] and Chéri anticipate Bertrand de Jouvenel, who would be described in *The Ripening Seed.* Henry de Jouvenel and the pregnancy that would result in the birth of Bel-Gazou are in the background of *The Shackle,* but the spiteful settling of accounts at the baron's expense would not come until *Julie de Carneilhan.* In *Break of Day* Vial is certainly an invention, since there is no model, but he has already borrowed some of Goudeket's features—real, or merely desired by the writer?

These supposedly autobiographical works are thus peopled with protagonists who, though inspired by real individuals, are reinvented as the author constructs for herself an "imaginary character" in Valéry's sense, one who "always says more and less than he thinks."[96] The decision to conceal herself at the very moment she shows herself, to distort the theatrical game and what is already a media event to which she complacently lends herself, no doubt demanded that her discourse become fictional, that it deliberately avoid the truth. In addition, and at a deeper level, that true lie-telling is imposed by a crafty logic proper to *experience* itself, which, by internal necessity, can be expressed only in a roundabout way, deformed, on the near side and on the far side of the scorching that constitutes jouissance.[97] Hence the narrator becomes angry with Vial who, as a reader of the *Claudine* books, believes he recognized her in the heroine and seeks to become her accomplice: she does not understand how "one can look for [her] in the flesh between the pages of [her] novels." "Allow me the right to conceal myself there, if only in the manner of the *Purloined Letter*,"[98] she replies, recalling Edgar Allan Poe's famous puzzle. But she admits that her fiction is a truth all the same: "You have detected that in this novel the novel does not exist."[99] Feint or reality? Always both, constantly, since such is the logic of feminine jouissance, of the *other* jouissance, that Colette affirms with a somnambulistic precision that is her share of truth.

THE SOLITUDE OF MUSIC AND OF CRIME

In the labyrinth constructed from the possibility of her writing, the definitive place Colette assigns to man is very revealing. "I don't want to marry anyone anymore, but I still dream I am getting married to a very large cat."[100] Could the cat-man be the woman writer's ideal companion, provided he is accompanied by a flower-man, though one prevented from blooming? "There is no chance that his aspect, his effort to join me, his suffering even suggest to me the agony of the seed underground, the torment of the plant that is nearly torn to pieces by its haste, its duty to blossom. [. . .] That one, however, has already blossomed and lost its blossoms more than once."[101] Maurice Goudeket would be that ideal man who, through his floral distance, like Vial leaving with his young companion, Hélène Clément, in *Break of Day*, lets *the writer* separate from *the woman* she is, in order to devote herself to a single passion: writing, precisely, which is identified with the brightness of day.

Nevertheless, that peace is far from bucolic. The author, without going on at length and with a naturalness worthy of the Roman stoics, slips in two confessions that go to the heart of the serenity finally achieved. She is fifty-five years old. The first is uttered by the woman writer: "It will be necessary to live—and even to die—without my life or my death depending on any love." The other comes from the mouth of a man, the one who will be her "best friend": "I admit that, at certain times, your death might not have displeased me."[102]

Writing is *through* love and is performed *with* the death of the other. As such, it finds its source in a maternal figure named Sido. Colette designates her with a brief, fleeting phrase that places the "heart" and the "letter" on the same level: "In my mother's heart, in her letters. [. . .] I therefore know where to locate the origin of my vocation."[103] In fact, *Break of Day* opens with a letter from Sido announcing to Jouvenel that she cannot "spend a week or so" at her daughter's wedding because the ever-so-rare blossoming of her pink cactus keeps her at home: "It is a very rare plant, which someone gave me, and which, they say, blooms in our climate only once every four years. I am already a very old woman, and, if I went away when my pink cactus was about to bloom, I am sure I would not see it bloom again."[104]

The novel ends with the last letter from the mother who, on the brink of death, addresses her "love," an expression it would be wrong to believe designates her daughter, since it is quite simply, and according to Colette herself, an epistle addressed to the alphabet of the world,[105] in the manner of Lucretius. Colette was inspired by the magnificent letters from her mother; that was demonstrated when she published them, just as it has also been demonstrated that she very subtly altered them. If Colette's writing definitively calls itself "Sido," the question remains: Who is Sido?

The mystery of Sido, an enigmatic figure if ever there was one and a tutelary goddess of the written word, deepens if we connect her to a few of the views of writing proposed by Colette. They are troubling views, which contrast with the author's supposed naïveté about love: they link writing to *solitude,* to *music,* and to *crime.*

When the light of dawn following the night of love is offered as a final metaphor for writing, Colette suggests that writing may *overcome depression.* The rose, a mystical symbol, metamorphoses the woman writer's grieving solitude into floral vitality: "I was now just like the one I've described many a time, you know, that *solitary* and *upstanding* woman, like a *sad rose,* which, in being *defoliated,* has only a *stronger* bearing."[106]

Music, which Colette often presents as a paternal legacy, evokes, like the metaphor of the rose, a storm of virginity and the "release" of happiness as profusion or abandon, a "rectitude" that is not rigidity but a "happy defeat." Nevertheless, to that experience of extreme joy that ordinary language would be unable to render, Colette adds a new constraint, which proposes to reconcile "[her] musical memory, which is alive," with "the living world" itself, by involving in it the pulsing of her own body and mouth:

> I sang within myself, I beat rhythms with my toes and my jaw muscles. [. . .] Musical patterns and sentences are born from the same evasive and immortal couple: the note, rhythm. To write in place of composing is to pursue the same quest, but with a *less visionary trance* and a smaller reward. Had I composed instead of writing, I would have had contempt for what I've been doing for forty years, because the word is hackneyed, and the arabesque of music eternally *virgin.* . . . In consenting, as I finally did, to the fact that every *storm of music*—of beloved music—would be a *happy* defeat, in closing my eyelids on two easy and imminent tears, I did not at first count that *release* as a *progress.*[107]

That search for a "visionary trance" rivaling the "happy defeat" produced by music, which constantly inspires Colette's writing, bursts forth in certain texts, whose meaning, strangely, allows itself to be dominated by an almost autonomous musicality, as if intoxicated with challenging language. The signifier then gives the slip to the meaning developed by the sentence, in order to mark autonomous chords and rhythms, which, from their depths, continue to walk side by side with the sense of the narrative. Hence the convulsions of Colette's sentence, its jerky rhythm, manage to mimic Sido, herself miming Colette's big sister, Juliette, giving birth. That series of reduplications is reminiscent of the nightingale's trills responding in echo to the tendrils of the vine:

> Motionless, her face toward the sky, she was listening, she was waiting. A long, aerial cry, weakened by distance and by fences, reached her at the same time it reached me, and she violently threw her crossed hands against her chest. A second cry, holding the same note like the beginning of a melody, floated in the air, and a third. . . . Then I saw my mother grip her own hips in her hands, and turn about, and pound the earth with her feet, and she began to help, to duplicate, with a low moan, with the oscillation of her tormented body and the embrace of her useless arms, with all her maternal pain and strength, the pain and strength of the ungrateful daughter who, so near and so far from her, was giving birth.[108]

Colette's writing knows how to compose a melody that possesses the movement of the flesh, its contagious toxicity:

> But from the bosom of that silence itself, a sound was imperceptibly born in a woman's throat, a sound that came out hoarse, cleared, acquired its firmness and range by repeating itself, like the full notes the nightingale reiterates and accumulates until they fall away into a roulade. . . . A woman up there was struggling against her invasive

pleasure, was hastening it toward its term and its destruction, in a calm rhythm at first, rushing so harmoniously,
so regularly that I caught myself nodding my head to its
cadence, as perfect as its melody.[109]

In a different way Colette's vocabulary, which unites regionalisms and technical horticultural terms with everyday language,
has the elegance not to be pedantic, technical, or tiresome but
possesses the rare virtue of inscribing meter, nonsense, an appeal
to the emotions and to the invisible.

I remember reading Colette's texts in my native country with a
dictionary in hand, attempting to plumb the exact meaning of
some Burgundian turn of phrase, of ordinary but rare words that
remained opaque to me with my beginner's French. I stumbled
over *aubier,* which is not merely a publisher but a "tender wood,"
over *tartan,* which everyone is supposed to know is "Scottish," over
scille, which concealed a "bulbous plant similar to hyacinth," over
godron, which the well-educated recognize without difficulty as the
decorations trimming a silver service. Like all of you, I couldn't
make head nor tail of the regionalisms for which the author had a
fondness (on Willy's advice?): *acouter* for "wait," *aga* for "look,"
areûiller for "look intently," *flogre* for "overripe," *avoir du goût* for
"to have fun," *regripper* for "to smell astringent odors," and so
many others. Like the Captain, I seek out the technical names of
flowers in books, and I find Colette's page perforated by "am-
pelopsis," "ageratum blossom," the *cuisse-de-nymphe émue* rose,
"carex," "statice," "bouillon blanc," "pink juneberries," "bud-
dleia," "nigella," "lobelia," "convolvulus," "muscari," "Solomon's
seal" "ornithogalum" (known as "star-of-Bethlehem"), "oxalis,"
"helianthus," *vierge du diable,* or *sagesse des chirugiens.* Now that I
cultivate my garden on the shores of the Atlantic and have become
an expert or nearly so, I know much more about them.

But no, Colette's unusual words still surprise me, and I feel all
the humility of the immigrant when faced with her language,
over which she asserts her irrevocable mastery; even more, I feel
my strangeness in relation to that universe itself, which her rare
or obscure words, like the shiny keys of a magician of language,

reflect back at me. Listen again: "marine crisis," "the eupatory," "the aspergillum of *pebreda*," "le lykénée," "the Gothic-ribbed Machaon," "the plaice," "the girthed Girellas," "the large epeira," "the ornithorhynchus." If, as in Colette's case, natural history holds few secrets for you, there you will find plants, birds, fish; for my part, I persistently get lost, find nothing there but music.[110]

That "phonetic intoxication"—Colette's expression, but Roland Barthes might have written it[111]—confuses words with things, both of them off their hinges. Reason runs off, when, for example, a word emptied of its meaning, such as "presbytery," transforms its dreamy syllables into snails or old lilacs and, without alluding to the phallic signifier concealed in it, finally isolates the budding writer from the rest of the world, confines her to a new ministry, which writing would be for her:

> That year, the word "presbytery" had just fallen into my sensitive ear and had wreaked havoc there. [. . .] I had gathered up the mysterious word inside me, as if the beginning of it were embroidered in rough relief, its ending a long and dreamy syllable. [. . .] A little later, the word lost its venom, and I realized that "presbytery" might well be the scientific name for the little yellow and black striped snail. [. . .] Rejecting the debris of the crushed little snail, I picked up the beautiful word, I went back up to my narrow terrace shaded by old lilacs, decorated with polished stones and glass jewels like the nest of a thieving magpie, I baptized it "Presbytery," and became a priest on the wall.[112]

She undoubtedly wanted to generalize that phonetic reverie to the whole world, but Sido intervened to impose the linguistic law, which designates and defines every thing: "I had to [. . .] 'call things by their names.' "[113]

I receive Colette's learned words, along with the neologisms, as so many new variants of the "tendrils of the vine": condensations that concentrate sensations and meanings and eliminate narrative. They reemerge when the narrator's polyphonic body, drunk on sight and touch, describes the magic of fabrics, for example:

Bold neologisms, sounds as rich as an arabesque, as soft as Tibetan wool, you caress the ear with a harmony that is part of the wild chant of the hoax. [. . .] But, when I read the los of the crepellaine, of the bigarella, of the poplaclan, of the djirisirisa, and of the gousselaine—I forget!—a phonetic drunkenness takes hold of me, and I begin to think in pure poplacot dialect.[114]

In *From My Window* (1942) she resumes that wordplay, with the words becoming onomatopoeias to better reveal the mouth of the woman writing, so that no one forgets that is where the words truly originate: "It is cold. *Il fait froid*. You read those two *f*'s in the double puff of breath coming from mouths."[115]

And she becomes intoxicated on learned words that empty the meaning of the sentence and let the flavor of a rhythm, the taste of alliterations, the coolness of a language intermingled with the sap of plants linger on and on. These are rare words, as they are cultivated in Colette's dream by "the scientist, accompanied by a stupefied child":

> He mutters, in ecstasy, botanical litanies: "Ah! It is the *aristolochia labiosa*, it is the *trichopilia tortilis*." I begrudge him only for teaching me Latin words when I would like popular names. But with what familiar names could we coif creatures mad for mimicry, disguised as birds, as Hymnoptera, as wounds and sex organs?[116]

> When, in an amateur's garden, *rhus cotinus* and barren currant bushes are placed up front, who might have supplanted, behind them, the *baguenaudier*[117] all tintinnabulating with vesicular pods, and the purplish-blue althea? What innovator meddled by barring the way to the fritillaria, known as imperial crown, to its heavy orangish capitula, to its odor of bad repute? It attracted to itself a populace of pink and white pyrethrums, corylopsis and physalis veined like lungs, and an abundance of flowers for borders,

white, faintly sweet-smelling, which, in accordance with regional deformations, were called *thlaspi* or *théraspic.*[118]

I will have many other rose window verbena, pipe aris-
tolochias, tufty Spanish grass, cross-shaped Jerusalem crosses,
spiky lupins and insomniac four o'clocks, nebula agrostis,
and vanilla garden pinks. A Saint-James-lily to aid my final
steps as a traveler; the aster to light up my nights.[119]

The feverish young patient's wordplay—hallucination and
charming delirium—transforms into an exotic phantom the expression of the doctor, who diagnoses a *"crise salutaire mais dure,"*
a salutary but severe attack: "He came in, ceremonious, feminine, dressed up for awards night, an *h* on his ear, a *y* on his
blouse: Chryse, Chryse/Chrysis, Chrysis, Saluter. [. . .] Chryse
Saluter-Médure, a young Creole woman from the American
tropics, graceful in her flounced white lingerie."[120]
The senseless words are content to be merely infantile regres-
sions, delighting in the family weakness of sisters huddled together around the memory of their father in the—*toutounier,* a
colloquial expression for a sort of well-worn sofa, a symbol of the
intransmissible family warmth: "My *lolie*! My blue blue *guézézi*!
My little *boudi*!"[121] Critics were scandalized that Colette could
write a book as commonplace as *Le toutounier,* even though she
was offering herself the childlike joy of fetching her clothes from
the *padirac,* of wondering whether the *busette* was still in the
lock, if it was still possible to find *sisibecques*[122] at the tobacco
shop: coded language, nonlanguage, which has idiotically become tenderness, a childish thing.
Let us make no mistake: Colette was not driven by any kind
of formalism. Her rare, unheard-of, incongruous, or learned
words are not the pure play of the signifier. They are rather so
many unknown worlds that pretend to offer themselves to readers, only to better keep us at a distance. They flaunt their defenses and require an initiation: you are not one of us, they say,
try a little harder before achieving our simplicity, because there

is a secret region of the French language that is habitable only by simpletons, the chosen. Unlike Proust, whose *memory* follows the association of sensory recollections, Colette, who lives and feels *language* before anything else, allows herself to be guided by the music of words so that she can put her memory in order. It is when she articulates the consonants and vowels, hears their vibrations, that the other senses awaken in her and finally resuscitate flowers, reality. Hence the *pentstémon* takes on color, and its chromatic orchestration occurs only because I hold it while pronouncing it, while writing it:

> In tending to an image from my memory, I sometimes reconstitute a flower that once intrigued me. Hence we call back from the *abyss the word as it is being swallowed up* and seize it, through a *syllable,* through its *initial,* which we hold up to the light, saturated by mortal darkness . . . I sought that tubular calyx, its scalloped corolla, its cherry color, *its name . . . I hold it.* I won't let go of it, except once and for all, when I reach the end. It is called, bizarrely, *pentstémon.* The *pentstémon,* having come back to me, tamed as it were, very pleasantly plays its part in a violet, red, and mauve orchestration that the city gardener carries off masterfully: red and pink gladioli, pink and red dahlias, the last roses, the pink and purplish-blue altheas, the fiery geraniums, the wooly ageratum that hesitates between blue and lilac, and the *pentstémon.* We'll have them till November, if the autumn is mild.[123]

I have opted for a different reading: perhaps Colette's oddities, though not a *pure music,* also do not call for a supplementary knowledge—while calling for it all the same. Indeed, they are also respirations of sense, equivalents of the exclamations "oh!" and "ah!" with which her prose is studded and that are easily taken for archaisms of her style, for pathetic marks of a bygone age, though they quite simply have the value of ellipses. I therefore propose another version of Colette's "tendrils/trills of the vine": halfway between irony and aberration, the music of the trills prevails over the meaning of the tendril alphabet. Might these rare words that break up the narrative be, in the end, signs of the unrepresentable? There is a senselessness in the world's flesh, say the tendrils/trills, and the sounds of words, which muddle logic, are the feverish or playful sign of that. It brings to mind what is, for some, a divine presence and what for Colette is only a "happy defeat," a "release," even a "hoax," a mockery, which at times, over time, and after the fact, she allows herself to consider "progress."[124]

Finally, this writing, which seeks to name a sensorial enigma, would—with its look of healthy simplicity—take on the appearance of a *police investigation,* of a thriller, to which so many women have brought distinction, from the authors of the English Gothic novel to the queens of the modern whodunit. The excess of sensual pleasure now stands side by side with the excess of cruelty and evil; they are two sides of the same investigation, at the limit of what we believe to be our identities. Hence the fragmentary structure of *Break of Day* (1928), which accumulates scattered signs and attempts to reconstitute a fictive biography, places the narrator and the reader in the presence of a strange genre, a sort of investigation of the genesis of writing, a *poetic detective novel.* The flashes of sensory memory offered by the narrator lead us to reconstitute the puzzle of what was a writer's destiny, with its zones of shadow, the unsaid. And the "purloined letter" is never discovered. The strange collection *Bella-Vista* (1937) is even closer to the detective novel and represents the world of crime: Ruby-Richard threatens to "plug Daste," a serial bird killer; Ahmed gets in a knife fight over Fatima; an incestuous father, old Binard, parades his vices and defies the law in view of a whole village, which knows what is going on and holds its tongue; and an abortionist causes the death of her adorable daughter Gribiche, with the silent complicity of her music hall pals.[125]

Between the "extraordinary story" of a woman writer's evolution and these detective stories, and, in fact, throughout her work, Colette continually illuminates human singularity pushed to the "monstrous." It is a monstrosity with floral and animal charms, which our desires and sensations acquire when they are paroxysmal. That monstrosity may also reveal the death drive, which surpasses jouissance and allies itself with evil. The fact that Colette's writing is also aware of its complicity with horror and that she gives us her—feminine?—version of the inseparable affinity between "literature and evil," to use Georges Bataille's expression, clashes with the official images of our member-of-the-Académie-Française-winner-of-the-Goncourt-prize-and-the-Cross-of-the-Legion-of-Honor, but it will not surprise her attentive readers.

Nevertheless, there is nothing obviously provocative in that journey to the abyss retraced in Colette's writing. Scandal itself is reabsorbed, as is the challenge to morality, and with disconcerting ease. Her sober genius, then, without shocking, but also without feigning the decency exuded by the deeply religious and the deeply perverse, is content to intimidate. "Colette looks around the way one walks when one is alone. It is for herself alone that she looks."[126] The look that returns to the self does not necessarily betray a solitude but, rather, the concentration specific to the act of writing. Colette thought it fitting to give a proper name to that movement of concentration and inveiglement, helix and spiral, attachment and flight, to that wake that encrusts the self in the other and infuses the other in oneself. That name is "Sido." The "tendrils of the vine" are definitively incarnated in a woman, a mother.

APPENDIX

The Tendrils of the Vine[127]

Formerly, the nightingale did not sing at night. It had a gentle wisp of a voice and used it handily from morning till evening, once spring had come. It awoke with its companions in the gray and blue dawn, and they, startled awake, shook the June bugs sleeping on the underside of the lilac leaves.

It went to bed at the stroke of seven, seven thirty, anywhere at all, often in the blossoming vines that smell of reseda, and did nothing but snooze till the next day.

One spring night, the nightingale was sleeping upright on a young bine, its crop in a ball and its head tilted, as if with a graceful stiff neck. During its sleep, the horns of the vine, those brittle and clinging tendrils with the irritating and thirst-quenching tartness of fresh sorrel—the tendrils of the vine, then, grew so thick that night that the nightingale awoke tied down, its feet entangled in forked bonds, its wings powerless.

It thought it was dying, struggled, escaped only with tremendous difficulty, and swore to itself not to sleep all spring so long as the tendrils of the vine were growing.

The very next night, it sang to keep itself awake:

So long as the vine grows, grows, grows,
I will not sleep again!
So long as the vine grows, grows, grows. . . .

It sang variations on its theme, garlanded it with vocalizations, fell in love with its own voice, became the frantic, intoxicated, and gasping singer to which one listens with the unbearable desire to see it sing.

I saw a nightingale singing under the moon, a free nightingale that did not know it was being spied on. It sometimes breaks off, its head cocked, as if to listen within itself for the prolongation of a faint note. . . . Then it resumes with all its might, puffed up, head thrown back, with a look of loving despair. It sings to sing, it sings such beautiful things that it no longer knows what they mean. But I, I still hear in the golden notes, the sounds of grave flutes, the tremulous and crystalline trills, the pure and vigorous cries, I still hear the first naïve and frightened song of the nightingale caught in the tendrils of the vine.

So long as the vine grows, grows, grows. . . .

Brittle and clinging, the tendrils of a bitter vine had bound me, when I, in my springtime, slept a happy, unchallenged sleep. But, in a start of fright, I broke all those twisted strands that already held my flesh, and I fled. . . . When the torpor of a new honeyed night weighed heavy on my eyelids, I feared the tendrils of the vine and I raised up a plaint that revealed my voice to me! . . .

Awake all alone in the night, I watch at present, rising before me, the voluptuous and morose star. . . . To keep myself from falling back into my happy sleep, in the springtime of lies when the hooked vine blossoms, I listen to the sound of my voice. . . . Sometimes, I feverishly cry out what is usually kept quiet, what is whispered very low—then my voice trails off to a murmur because I dare not go on. . . .

I would like to say, say, say, everything I know, everything I think, everything I discern, everything that enchants me and wounds me and astonishes me; but there is always, near the dawn of that sonorous night, a wise cool hand placed over my mouth. . . . And my cry, which was firing up, falls back to moderate verbiage, to the volubility of a child who speaks aloud to reassure himself and to try to forget. . . .

I no longer know happy sleep, but I no longer fear the tendrils of the vine. . . .

WHO IS SIDO?

And you, is it that you've got no hunger,
or that you've got no imagination?

—Colette, screenplay for *Divine* (1934)

The modesty of language is a final arrogance.

—Louis Aragon, "Madame Colette" (August 19, 1954)

A SLOW APPARITION

In the beginning was a motherless child:[1] young Claudine has only a charming and absent-minded father, devoted entirely to what "you have not read, because it will never be finished, his great opus, *The Malacology of Fresnois*"[2]—the science of slugs and snails. His evocation of his late wife is unflattering: "The hundred and fifty thousand francs left you by your mother, a very unpleasant woman."[3] It does not appear that the budding libertine is suffering, and she is not preoccupied with her motherless state, unless, in a psychoanalytic reading, we were to attribute the fervent need the adolescent heroine feels to seek the affection of Mlle Aimée, the teacher's assistant, her painful jealousy of the Sapphic love between Mlle Aimée and the schoolmistress, Mlle Sergent, and her overly intense friendships, as affectionate as they are cruel, with her classmates, from little Luce to gangly Anaïs, precisely to that absence of a mother: "Little Luce also shows some skin, timidly, white and marvelously soft skin; and the gangly Anaïs envies that whiteness so much that she sticks needles in her arm on sewing days."[4]

For the moment let us leave aside the psychoanalytic hypotheses and confine ourselves to the text. Claudine has no mother: in other words, as regards the heroine who represents Colette, the writer eliminates the character of the mother. In addition to that aggressivity underlying the text's roguishness, there is Claudine's criticism of public school; and yet, had not Colette's parents, especially her mother, chosen secular education for their daughter? These attacks, then, are aimed not at Claudine's late mother but at Sidonie Colette, a free spirit and atheist, the author's own mother.

The absence of a mother continues in Colette's other early novels. Hence in *Claudine Takes Off* (1903), Annie has only her father, threatened by blindness and on the brink of death. It will not be until the two *Minne* books (1904–5), reworked into *The Innocent Libertine* (1909), that a mother appears in Colette's writings: she is insignificant but bonded to her daughter because, this time, it is the father who is missing. "All the same, Mama is only thirty-three, and sometimes people in the street notice her modest beauty, lackluster under schoolteacher dresses."[5] "If only we could go on like this to the end of our lives, pressed against each other in a warm and close happiness, how quickly death would be got past, without sin and without pain!"[6] We grasp the intensity of Minne's bond to her mother when we read that, before marrying her cousin Antoine, the young woman dreams only of fleeing with a "notorious murderer" and of suffering from the "burning humiliation of a queen in a valet's embrace" to the point of falling ill: a shameful way of separating from Mama. "'Mama.' Minne would cry out that word only if she feels like she's dying, if terrifying beasts prevail, if her blood, through her slashed throat, spreads like a warm bolt of cloth. . . . That name is the last resort—it must not be taken in vain!"[7] This is an imaginary risk, since, in Colette's early writing, the word is scarcely uttered, to say the least. All the same let us keep in mind the lethal, morbid charge that secret love entails, the pain of jouissance brought on by a love to the death between daughter and mother.

In the following works, *The Vagabond* (1911) and *The Shackle* (1913), the mother is again missing. In the interval an important event had occurred: Colette began living with Missy, and the apogee of their relationship took place between 1906 and 1911. In her letters Sido explicitly recognized the maternal role the marquise de Morny played in relation to her daughter. Was she a dupe? Doubtful. Was she in denial about their sexual relationship or, on the contrary, did Sido demonstrate an extraordinary open-mindedness, "authorizing" a maternal and loving presence at her progeny's side? Both at once. She probably sensed what Colette felt for Missy: "I am content, my love, that you have a friend nearby who cares for you tenderly. You are so used to being spoiled that I wonder what would become of you if you weren't any longer."[8]

In Colette's writings from that period, there is no explicit mention of her mother. But in the three short stories originally dedicated to Missy in *Tendrils of the Vine* (Colette collected these stories into a booklet and published only one copy of it, with the dedication *For Missy*), the I-narrator rediscovers "the love potion that abolishes the years," addressing a *thou* who shares a small garden with her "somewhere in the world, an envied place from which one discovers the whole sky":[9] "I belong to a land I have left."[10] Who is *thou*? Missy, or already Sido? The word "mother" [*mère*] is not used, but its homonym, *mer*, or sea, can be heard: "Leave me. I am ill and wicked, like the *mer*. [. . .] I hate everything, and above all the *mer*! [. . .] Under the leaden wave, I make out the abominable population of footless beasts, flat, slippery, frozen. [. . .] Stay by my side, command the *mer* to depart!"[11]

Mother and daughter thus begin their dialogue, feigning a "strange modesty of feeling."[12] But the image of the mother splits in two: one is peopled with flaccid, "castrated" beasts; the other is protective, powerful. We hear that duality in the invocation, as voluptuous as it is anxious, that Colette, playing the role of the child, addresses to her maternal friend: "You will offer me voluptuousness, leaning over me, your eyes full of a maternal anxiety, you who, in your passionate friend, are looking for the child you did not have."[13] Colette's perception of female homosexuality as a consolation between depressed women, a bitter peace between two similar beings who together protect themselves from heterosexual desire, also dates from that period: "For him, two women embracing will never be anything but a lascivious group, and not the touching and *melancholic image* of *two weaknesses*, perhaps seeking refuge in each other's arms to sleep, to cry, to flee often wicked men, and to taste, better than any pleasure, *the bitter happiness of feeling alike, lowly, forgotten.* . . . What's the use of writing, of pleading, of arguing? . . . My voluptuous friend understands only love."[14]

Although the implicitly maternal haunts the writer's imaginary, the first real mention of Colette's mother dates from August 14, 1909. Published in *La Vie Parisienne*, "A Letter" ungraciously evokes her "charming nutcase of a mother," who challenges her husband by saying: "You're not even related to me." The next two references are warmer: a Christmas story, "The Wooden Shoes" (1909), which Colette never included in any of her collected works,[15] and the article "Let Us Awake,"[16] which mentions "my mother" and her startling way of calling her daughter: "Beauty! . . . my shining sun! . . . My solid-gold jewel!"[17] Two manuscript fragments[18] introduce a young girl by the name of Bel-Gazou and, for the first time, the future Sido, a "plump little lady [. . .] dressed in white" who does not yet have a name.

Sido died on September 26, 1912. Colette de Jouvenel, known as Bel-Gazou, was born on July 3, 1913: big Colette's only child was thus conceived in the month following Sido's death. At forty, she was not a young mother, especially for the time. Whether by virtue of a psychically based infertility or effective contraception, Colette had avoided motherhood up to that point. The biographers have not neglected to insinuate that her pregnancy, nestled in the site of mourning for the mother, may have been an effective strategy for holding on to Henry de Jouvenel. No doubt. Nevertheless, it was a "miraculous" conception, in close proximity to the death of the mother—so cherished, so feared, so envied, so shunned. As a matter of fact, Colette wrote Sido as often as possible: "I was never bored with my sharp-witted companions. As for my chronic need to see Sido again, to live near her, I staved it off by writing her daily letters."[19] The mother did the same, but the daughter rarely went to Châtillon, to the older woman's great regret; in the end, she gave up hoping for the promised visits. So my mother is dead? Long live the mother I am! Colette wrote in 1949: "I have not let go of a character that has gradually imposed itself in the rest of my writings: my mother. It is not done haunting me. [. . .] Since *Sido,* her abridged name has shone radiant in all my memories."[20] Nothing in that declaration is truer than the "gradually." It is time to recall that *Sidonie* was also the first name of Colette herself, who was baptized Sidonie-Gabrielle on August 11, 1873.[21]

Nevertheless, neither Sido's passing nor Colette's motherhood prompted a flood of memories about her mother, who haunted her (she said), and Sido would not crystallize into a major character in her daughter's works for another ten years. The trigger would be *My Mother's House* (1922).

The Child and the Enchantments:
MELANIE KLEIN AND COLETTE

Before Colette actually speaks of Sido in Sido's place, an important stage in that journey can be deciphered in a marginal text, *The Child and the Enchantments,* made famous by Ravel's music. Written in eight days in 1915, delayed by the slow pace specific to the labor of a composer, the libretto for that "lyrical fantasia in two parts" would not be performed until 1925, in Monte Carlo, then in Paris in 1926. By a strange coincidence, Melanie Klein, after reading a review of the performance in Berlin, without seeing the opera or reading Colette's text, presented an analysis of that work before the British Psycho-Analytical Society on May 15, 1929, under the title "Infantile Anxiety Situations Reflected in a Work of Art and in the Creative Impulse."[22] The mother was not yet at the center of Colette's thematics, and only the child's drama held her interest: a recalcitrant boy of six or seven brings the punishment of a strict and frustrating "Mama" upon himself. The observations Colette made of her little Bel-Gazou, as well as the memory of her own childhood and the recollection of her envious cruelty toward the desired and feared maternal body, must have reinforced that oddly incisive psychological vision.

The "lyrical fantasia," then, portrays a little boy "in the midst of an attack of laziness": he does not want to do his homework, stubbornly resists writing (just as Colette did as a child),[23] as well as arithmetic. . . . But the little boy's reluctance to tackle his studies is only the displacement of a profound rage, which turns out to be a secret desire for his mother, as the author subtly suggests; in the development of the plot, she becomes a child psychoanalyst unbeknownst to herself. Nevertheless, it takes Melanie Klein's weighty concepts to evaluate the psychological pertinence of Colette's musical fantasy.

"I want to punish Mama."[24] "I don't love anyone! I am very wicked! Wicked, wicked, wicked!"[25] the little boy declares. The mother's formidable severity certainly seems to justify the child's rage, but is not that image of an uncontrollable mother a product of frustrated desire itself? "Promise us you'll work, Baby!" interrupts Mama, "castrating" her six- or seven-year-old boy, calling him a "baby" and inflicting an oral punishment-frustration on him by putting him on "unsweetened tea and dry bread." If one concedes that the gourmand Minet-Chéri is concealed behind the problem child, one cannot imagine a more unbearable punishment. A violent anger seizes hold of the child, a spectacular aggression, which Melanie Klein would have no difficulty describing as a primordial destructive anxiety and that she would later define as the "schizoparanoid position." Furniture and eating utensils, animals and trees, are all assaulted in turn by the young hero armed with a knife. Nothing calms the little boy in the battle against house and garden, which, in his fantasy, is identified with the mother's body—though a few elements of the father also coexist in them, such as the regularity of the Clock or the Little Old Man teaching arithmetic, both symbols of paternal law.

If the young rebel is Oedipus, he is so in the Kleinian mode, taking as the target of his envious desire not the father but, first of all, the maternal image and all the paternal appendages it contains. Is this Oedipus already a little Orestes? In the course of that "crisis," the child fears he is losing his mind ("Oh! My head! My head!"):[26] Melanie Klein's diagnosis is that, when the young boy becomes fixed in the schizoparanoid position, his ability to think is gravely compromised. It is animal sensoriality, that of cats in their "wordless" nuptial dance—a displaced image of the parents' desired and feared coitus—that seems to give the raging child a different mode of access to the world, reconciling him with the pleasure that up to that time had made him furious, since he felt excluded from it. "'They love each other. . . . They are forgetting me . . . I am alone. . . . ' (*In spite of himself, he calls*): 'Mama!'"[27]

While observing the cat couple, did the child finally recognize that the unconscious cause of his wickedness was nothing but his parents' love, which he envied? Melanie Klein deciphers a violent Oedipus belonging to an archaic and jealous species. She also recognizes Colette's other intuition: the writer was able to point out the importance of what the founder of child psychoanalysis would later call the "depressive position," to which the children we all are accede after the sadism of the schizoparanoid position. In fact, it is in discovering his solitude, in feeling sorrow after the destruction that had earlier mobilized him, that the child transforms himself: he "repairs" (in Klein's terminology) the damaged object, he bandages the squirrel's paw.

At first wounded by the quick-tempered little boy, then bruised by the other beasts, the squirrel is a reflection of the child himself inasmuch as he fuses with the body of a mother from which he cannot separate: by attacking the squirrel, the body attacks itself (by becoming "lazy," unable to learn). Did not Colette describe Claudine as a squirrel in *The Retreat from Love*? "Run faster, pursued by the shadow of shadow, slip on the snow that freezes and screeches like a window pane; run to the haven to which your instinct leads you, to the glowing red door where you stumble, palpitating like a squirrel, and where you sigh, sobered: 'Already!'"[28]

In *Prisons and Paradises*, Pitiriki[29] is an "intrepid" squirrel, which has "the soul of pirates and highwaymen barons"[30] but that agrees to live in the Colettes' garden. In the end it disappears because "the human hand" has fallen upon it, which justifies Colette's hatred of her fellow humans: the writer says definitively she is "wicked toward man."

Like Melanie Klein, Colette thus discovers that the child needs to mistreat the squirrel, a fusional being that handicaps him, only to later make reparations (the "bandaging"): it is through this process that he finally becomes capable of autonomy and culture. When he can *say* "mama," he is no longer in an osmosis of jouissance and rage with his mother: by naming her, he distances his ambivalent desires concerning her. His new personality is henceforth capable of being calmed, he can behave himself and learn. "He cried out a word, a single word: 'Mama!'"[31] the beasts in the garden shout in jubilation, as do the psychoanalysts, and the writer herself.

Marvelously illuminated by Melanie Klein's perspicacity, Colette's genius thus traces the path leading to the transcendence of guilt characteristic of that archaic Oedipus beside an all-powerful mother and transforms violent tendencies, such as personality disorders or mania, and even infantile psychoses, into a *reparation*. But that beneficent evolution comes about if and only if a recognition of Oedipal desire and its ambivalence has taken place. For Klein, that recognition takes on the aspect of a *depressive* experience: I discover that my desire for Mama is a desire to kill her, that Eros is Thanatos. Am I an Oedipus? Perhaps, but I am even more an Orestes. Knowing that, however, makes me free: I agree to lose Mama; my sorrow means that I take responsibility for renouncing my desire for her, and that renunciation is the *via regia* of my autonomy, that is, of my capacity to think, to create, to live.

Colette, for her part, did not insist nearly as much as Klein on that depressivity and on the reparation to which it leads. She does suggest it, of course. "Motherless!"[32] the child laments, while looking at the baby bats he has killed. "I am alone,"[33] he adds, feeling sorry for himself and nothing more. Elsewhere, again in reference to *The Child and the Enchantments*, Colette evokes an emotion that brings a lump to her throat, but the thing that overwhelms her is the admiration she feels for Ravel's music: " 'Amusing, no?' Ravel said. Nevertheless, I got a lump in my throat: the Beasts, with urgent whispers, barely syllabized, were leaning over the Child, reconciled. . . . I had not anticipated that an orchestral wave, constellated with nightingales and fireflies, would lift my modest work so high."[34] In fact Colette did not cry. In all her writings she made the choice not to emphasize discomfort, shortcomings, sorrows: "I who whistle whenever I am sad [. . .] I wish [Sido] had understood that *the supreme offense is pity. My father and I do not accept pity.* Our robustness rejects it. At present, I torment myself because of my father, since I know he had the virtue, better than any seductiveness, of being sad judiciously and of never betraying himself."[35]

Hence Colette would not confront the mother in Melanie Klein's manner, by delving into the "depressive position." In *The Child and the Enchantments,* her self-analytic lucidity led her to a very penetrating lyrical meditation on the mother-child relationship, but only *the child's side is explored.* We witness the release from the guilt of incestuous desire, the emergence of the beneficent image of a mother who is no longer castrating and terrifying but finally "called" with gratitude and affection. Nevertheless the deficiency of this mechanism is that it cannot be approached *from the mother's side,* cannot put into words the memory of that wordless sensuality incarnated in the cat couple, the discovery of which turns out to be decisive in the son's capacity to transform his aggressivity into a call for "Mama." In any case the reader cannot fail to be struck by the extremely condensed nature of this text, practically sketchy and taciturn, despite the obligatory concessions to infantile language. It is not that Colette is unaware of the magic of the sensual style: we have seen her excel at it in various ways, from the *Claudine* books to the *Dialogues of Beasts* and *Tendrils of the Vine.* But she had not yet gone through the "crisis" of individuation, which entailed appropriating not loss-depression-privation as the child experiences them but, on the contrary, *incestuous sensuality itself and in relation to the mother:* she would not do so until *My Mother's House.*

At this stage in her experience, her path diverges from that of Melanie Klein: in doing without the child's and the mother's depressivity (we have just seen that she did not insist on the two protagonists' sorrow at the time of their separation), the writer was moving toward the mother's incestuous desire. In making less of the *depression* side than Klein, Colette makes more of the *perversion* side. When I lose mama, I kill her, but I find her once again in my thoughts, says Melanie in substance, and that thought— Thought—is my new life, a psychic life, a creativity of understanding. I know very well that I am losing Mama, but I am in no hurry to do so, retorts Colette. I want to experience profoundly the pleasure of fusion/destruction that connects us, to feel its charms and its sting, and if, in the end, I must detach myself from it, it will only ever be in saturating—with flavors, scents, and sounds—the memory that contains us and that comes through *our* common language, which has become a sensory word. It is not a Thought that will result from it, but *a*-thought. It is not truly or not exclusively a knowledge; it can be called a sublimation. It includes my sensual memories of Mama's body, of our house, a common, fluid space, geraniums and cats: and I call it "Sido."

It will thus be a matter of turning the *depression* occasioned by the loss of the mother into its opposite, an *incestuous* or *incestual,* and in that sense, *perverse appropriation* of the maternal object. Only on this condition will Colette's exploration not lead— as the "depressive position" would do—purely and simply to an independence of thought and of self, which dissociates itself from the body and installs the subject in an abstraction or in the "general thoughts" Colette mocks and of which she claims to be incapable. The assimilation of the mother and of her desire, that way of "feeding on the mother" ("I alone feed on the mother," asserts the Taoist sage), includes within itself a "surplus of jouissance"—scandalous in terms of the norms of social morality and an exorbitant, monstrous amplification of the ego's drives and sense-making capacities—a surplus that contaminates the reader.

Could Colette's writing be amoral, maniacal, driven by an all-powerful avidity with no respect for prohibitions? Yes, certainly, since the act of writing is in no way a pedagogical journey but, rather, an exploration of limits and transgressions. Leave it to others to interpret that experience, to give it its meaning here and now. Colette, for her part, has no other aim than the *drive to say* that "thing," which is, precisely, the thing that is lost in order for one to speak and is nothing other than *the intense ambivalence of the incestuous bond,* the combination of cruelty and love. Yet, in order to say it, and while saying it, she can only possess that bond, contain it; she even intends to keep it and not lose it, to carry it with her forever. She seems to have acquired the unconscious, somnambulistic certainty that this immersion *before* prohibition and loss, this installation *in what is forbidden* is imperative for her, absolutely necessary to consolidate what she always tried to formulate: the crossing of identities and borders, the dissemination of the ego in the cosmic flux, where, without truly becoming lost, by cultivating the flavors of language, she absorbs the *other side of the subject* she is, that is, her completely other and overwhelming mother, indistinct from the "cardinal points." Above all, do not believe I have lost that mother: I have always possessed her, she is my model. Unless it is the reverse: I have always already found the mother again, a mother who cannot withhold herself, who is not forbidden me, who desires me as I desire her, the incestuous mother into whom I project myself—or rather, the incestuous mother that I, Colette, am. That would be the version of *paradise lost* that, as it stands, will never be lost, since—by cultivating the incest that constitutes it—it is a memory recreated from the osmosis with the other, with Being. Or perhaps it is rather the path the other takes to disappear into Being. Incest with the mother is the condition sine qua non of my marriage to the serenity of Being. Such is Colette's message, not really secret, which takes shape in this last and decisive turning point of her life.

THE INCESTUAL MOTHER WITH "ONE OF [HER] CHILDREN"

Having spent his vacation in Rozven in 1920, Bertrand de Jouvenel returned there in 1921. The love relationship with Colette resumed and plunged them both back into childhood. It was this very young man who suggested to Colette that she let him "know what she had loved. . . . And, in autumn, we went together to Saint-Sauveur-en-Puisaye, to her childhood home." He would confide in 1986: "I believe it was at my insistence that she wrote her book *My Mother's House* in 1922."[36] The galleys of the original edition, dated June 18, 1922, are thus dedicated to her young lover: *To One of My Children.* Given their age difference (Colette was thirty years older than Bertrand), the incestual meaning of their relationship did not escape the writer.

All the same, if one follows the chronological order of the short stories, it is the theme of the rediscovery of childhood that seems to have taken precedence in the writing process. Many secondary characters similar to those in the *Claudine* books people the first stories. Of the thirty short stories that form the original edition, six concentrate on the mother and four mention her in their title.[37] The maternal character, present in the third short story, "Love," then in the sixth, "The Mother and the Beasts," increases in significance. Toward the end of the series, very clearly, the importance of the Sido figure stands out. In addition, when Colette finally chose to inaugurate her collection with the short story "Where Are the Children?" and thus to put the spotlight on Sido, it would seem she was naming her initial theme: the search for the innocence of childhood memory and the depiction of the house of her childhood—and, in doing so, that she was remaining within the tradition of the *Claudine* books.

In reality, an upheaval was under way. In the title of the first story it is the mother's voice that can be heard. As a result, the quest for childhood ("where are the children?") would be read entirely differently: where is that mother who has suddenly begun to speak? What is a mother? And, finally, who is the object of that quest: Claudine or Sido? The book hesitates before masterfully imposing the figure of a new goddess. The critics were unaware of the sexual subtext of that reversal, that is, the role of the incestuous mother assumed by Colette in her affair with the young Jouvenel. In her lifetime it would never be revealed, and only the emergence of that maternal character, replacing the mischievousness of the schoolgirl of Montigny, would hold readers' attention.

In the second short story, "The Savage," the name "Sido" appears and is explained: at the time of the mother's first marriage it was an abbreviation for Sidonie. In the twenty-third story, "My Mother and Morality," it is a friend who calls the mother Sido. It is not until *Break of Day* in 1928 that we read, in the famous "pink cactus" letter, the complete maternal signature: "Sidonie Colette, née Landoy,"[38] which is evoked throughout the novel: "my mother," "she who now inhabits me," and so on.[39] Inspired by Proust, Colette includes the following epigraph: "Do you imagine, in reading me, that I am drawing my portrait? Hold on: it is only my model."[40] Sido would thus be the writer's *model,* but less as a particular woman than as a way of being that embraces Being by transgressing prohibitions: the real itself, the impossible.

From the outset Sido is a hyperbole, set apart from the contingencies of the ordinary: "I remember that, on rainy days, you almost never had mud on your shoes. And I still see that light foot taking a detour to spare a little worm comfortably uncoiled on a warm path. I do not have your blind confidence in delightedly feeling out 'good' and 'evil,' or your art for rebaptizing in your own code old poisoned virtues, and poor sins that for centuries awaited their share of paradise. You fled the stinking austerity of virtue."[41] An immaculate goddess, beyond good and evil, the great figure of Sido assumed her place. Finally the publication of *Sido, or The Cardinal Points* in 1929 and of *Sido* in 1930 forged the definitive myth, with another explanation of the mother's first name, unprecedented until then: "the woman that a single being in the world—my father—called 'Sido.'"[42]

My Mother's House (1922) thus brought about a key reversal. Colette's imaginary, until then centered on *childhood* and the character of the insolent and free *young girl,* the key to the writer's commercial success, now focused on the incantation of *a place:* "the house." That enchanted space rapidly turns out to be *a mother* who stirs her daughter's sensuality. The now totally uninhibited pleasure of close bodily contact between *mother and daughter* replaces the lyrical landscapes of the previous collections or, rather, confers an intimate meaning on them, charges them with an incestual erotics.

Like the universe of Democritus that, had it been smoked, would have come to us through the nose, the character of Sido offers herself through *scents*. Even more than taste, the sense of smell is the narrator's primitive connection to the maternal body; its secret secretions and scents are flushed out, approached in a shameful intimacy. Far removed from the gaze, smell is a diffuse cavity that opens like a full night under the adored mother's cotton dress, then extends outward to the wind, the tobacco plantations, then to the moon. Never was a "transitional object" both so close to the mother's vulva and more detached from it, through that giant and nevertheless discreet expansion of Sido's dress, which is disseminated to the moonbeams caressing a walnut tree. Some of us have tried to replace our Mama with a bit of cloth, a stuffed bear, a handkerchief steeped in her perfume: for her part, Colette brews up an imaginary fabric made of cretonne, smelling of harsh soap, violet, and citronella verbena, and marvelously embroidered in language. Listen:

> I remain in the dark, against Mama's knees. Without falling asleep I close my useless eyes. The linen dress I press against my cheek smells of harsh soap, the wax used to polish irons, and violet. If I move away slightly from that fresh gardener's dress, my head immediately plunges into a zone of perfume that washes over us like a creaseless wave: the white tobacco opens its narrow tubes of scent and its star-shaped corollas to the night. A ray touching the walnut tree wakes it: it ripples, even its lower branches moved by a thin oar of the moon's. On the odor of white tobacco, the wind superimposes the cold bitter odor of the wormy little walnuts that fall onto the lawn.[43]

And further on:

> Mme Saint-Alban shifted a nude with a strong brown smell, the incense of her frizzy hair and golden arms. My

mother smelled of washed cretonne, of the iron heated on the poplar embers, of the leaf of citronella verbena that she rolled in her hands or crumpled in her pocket.[44]

As the reader will later learn, Sido excelled at the "decretal form of observation"[45] that manifests itself in the precise formulation of what she feels, and it is therefore the *voice*—vector of the word—that, from the outset, produces the little girl's fascination with the maternal body the first time she lovingly approaches it. The "house of Claudine"[46] begins therefore with a voice and a scent. "The pretty voice, and how I would cry with pleasure to hear it."[47] It is a ravishing voice: the child, in listening to her mother tell how she brought her into the world, faints. Unless one is a man, like Zola (as Sido reminds us), who sees childbirth as merely "sickly sweet stories," birth is in itself a cataclysm; but it is not so much the event itself that bewitches Minet-Chéri as the music of the maternal voice. She is moved by the "artistic" shock of the suffering and jouissance of a woman giving birth, of the woman-mother against words, a shock resolved in a senseless melody, a deafening buzz, on the near side of thought and of language:

> In vain I wished for the sweet words of exorcism, gathered in haste, to sing to my ears: a silver-toned buzzing deafened me. Other words, under my eyes, painted the quartered flesh, the excrement, the tainted blood. . . . I managed to raise my head, and saw that a bluish garden, walls the color of smoke, vacillated strangely under a sky that had turned yellow. . . . The lawn received me, spread out and soft like one of those little hares that poachers brought freshly killed into the kitchen.[48]

My Mother's House thus clears a path toward Sido through the most secret, the most forbidden byways of the maternal body. The woman spoken about here, or rather the woman speaking— since Sido is supposedly the model for the narrator, as the epigraph indicates—is a woman who has offered her sexual intimacy to a child: and she expresses herself in that "house" without obscenity but also without modesty. The myth of Sido may be modulated later, but it has already found its dwelling place in that flood of scents and voices where the narrator has just set up their imaginary habitat. Indeed, it is not in Saint-Sauveur-en-Puisaye and even less in Châtillon that Claudine's true house is located. It passes through Rozven with Missy and with Bertrand to settle, serene, in the immaterial matter of "washed cretonne" and "poplar embers" of which sensory memory is made. It has become stronger in incest, the two sides of which Colette explores: between daughter and mother and between mother and son. In taking root there, the writer crosses the identity boundaries of beings, strips them of their identity, and transfers them to Being. In psychoanalytic terms, that experience could be called a *sublimation of psychosis.*

In fact, *My Mother's House* (1922) was written between *Chéri* (though published in 1920, the idea for it had been hatching since 1912) and *The Ripening Seed* (1923). Léa, whom Chéri calls Nounoune, is a demimondaine who sexually initiates the son of her friend Charlotte Peloux, "the only women of easy virtue who dared raise her son as the son of a whore."[49] Léa ends up abandoned and depressed by her *chéri,* who is equally defeated: "A gasping old woman replicated her gesture in the oblong mirror, and Léa wondered what she could have in common with that madwoman."[50] In *The Ripening Seed,* the very dignified Mme Camille Dalleray (with an asexual first name and a "sweet virile voice"),[51] known as the Lady in White, with her body "devoted to delicate ravishments, gifted with a genius for spoliation, a passionate implacability, an enchanting and hypocritical pedagogy,"[52] educates young Phil in the ways of the world, all the while preparing him for a happy life with her friend Vinca.

Between the two adventures, the "house of Claudine" is a cosmic pleasure known as Sido. Curled up, as if protected in the arms of parentheses dedicated to incestuous desire (*Chéri, The Ripening Seed*), is an intimacy apparently separate from transgressive love and devoted entirely to purity. Is this, for Colette, simply a matter of removing herself, by writing *My Mother's*

House, from the guilt of the incestuous relationship and of slipping in, between the commercial firebrands intended to seduce and scandalize, an idyllic retreat? Is it a matter of offering herself a noble compensation for this behavior and the writing about it, of which conventional morality disapproves—and that is indirectly called "unworthy" by Colette herself? "House and garden are still alive, I know that, but what does it matter if the magic has left them, if the secret is lost, the one that opened—light, odors, the harmony of trees and birds, the murmur of human voices that death has already cut short—*a world of which I have ceased to be worthy?*"[53] Such a strategy in no way deviates from the logical coherence underlying Colette's writing during that entire period (1919–23) and, in a way, throughout her works— less explicitly to be sure, but very firmly—which is laid out in two different scenes: that of erotic *pleasure* and that of an *other* jouissance. On one side is a vaudevillesque narrative vein with an astonishing psychological acuity; on the other a poetic and fragmentary vein that brings about the narrator's polymorphous perfusion into the elements of the world, with no other "object" than that of writing in unison with the creases of Being. Colette was convinced of the *purity* of that experience, a sort of "purloined letter" of scandalous eroticism. We will return to this question in reference to *The Pure and the Impure.*[54]

For the moment a strange polylogue forms with *My Mother's House,* then *Break of Day,* and finally *Sido.* Composed of lyrical sentences, of little short stories depicting insignificant events and characters, of sensory memories and scattered meditations, this polylogue finally comes together and crystallizes completely in a single "character" named Sido.

The credulous reader attributes the creation of that character either to filial love for a mother who was rather neglected in reality or to the pagan mysticism irrigating the French countryside in the shadow of steeples, to which Colette claims to be the heir. Or the reader may see it as the expression of an animal sensibility, though one subjected to the asceticism of the mot juste. Before determining the logic that drives that "purloined letter" incarnated in Sido, let us see how the character presents herself. *Who* is Sido?[55]

WHAT A CHARACTER!

Sido is certainly a woman. But, above all, she is a figure for the birth of time:

> Burned by fire, cut with a pruning knife, drenched with melted snow or spilled water, she found the means to have already lived her best independent time before the earliest risers had opened their blinds, and could recount to us the awakening of the cats, the work done on nests, the news left her, along with a ration of milk and a loaf of warm bread, by the milkwoman and the bread delivery girl, the news, in short, of the birth of day.[56]

For some, "in the beginning was the Word"; for others, time is a worry that spaces and temporalizes.[57] For Colette, Sido imposes a vision of *time before time,* of the dawn before any temporal duration of works and days. That cosmic burn has nothing in common with the astrophysical hypothesis of the big bang but is immediately incarnated in a human being. Could Colette be a Christian unbeknownst to herself, whose Messiah would be a peasant woman who by dawn saws wood into X's rather than allowing herself to be crucified?

> Dressed for night, but wearing heavy gardener's clogs, her little gray septuagenarian's braid rolled up in a scorpion's tail at the nape of her neck, one foot on the beech X, her back curved in the posture of the practiced pieceworker, rejuvenated by a look of inexpressible delight and guilt, my mother, in defiance of all her vows and of the frozen dew, was sawing logs in her yard.[58]

As the queen of incarnation, this mother extends her body outward to the velvet of flowers, whose color reminds her of the tasty offal of veal and that she tastes with an innocence not devoid of irony: "For in the garden 'Sido' loved the red, the pink, the ruddy daughters of the rosebush, and the Maltese crosses, the hydrangeas, and the Saint-James-lily, and even the physalis-groundcherry, though she accused its flower, veined with red on a pink pulp, of reminding her of a fresh veal lung."[59] A solid countrywoman dedicated to the four cardinal points, as I said, Sido is nevertheless an airy, snowy, windy being: "But in the worst of the din, my mother, her eye on a large magnifying glass encircled with copper, marveled, counting the branched crystals of a handful of snow she had just gathered from the very hands of the West Wind lashing out at our garden."[60] In other words, this woman would be Being in its entirety in its happy splendor, if ancient Greek materialism could be rendered in the feminine form.

After the mother confirmed it to her ("I, atheist"),[61] her daughter was eager to let people know Sido was an unbeliever. Sido railed against the "stupid rot they [the priests] inculcated in those poor kids," all the while offering the priest of her village Jean-Henri Fabre's *Souvenirs entomologiques* [Entomological memories]. In Colette's text Sido allowed her "solid-gold jewel" to go to catechism class but accompanied that permission with unkind and mocking reflections:

Ah! How I dislike that way of asking questions! What is God? What is this? What is that? Those question marks, that madness for investigations and inquisitions, I find incredibly indiscreet! And those commandments, I ask you! Who translated the commandments into such gibberish? Ah! I don't like to see that book in the hands of a child, it is filled with such audacious and complicated things.[62]

She lashes out against confession:

When you raise your hands to heaven! Reveal, confess, and confess some more, exhibit everything you've done wrong! . . . Keep it quiet, punish yourself for it, that's better. That's what they ought to teach. But confession makes the child prone to spewing out streams of words, to delving into his deepest self, which soon becomes more vain pleasure than humility.[63]

With "the insolence of reprobates" Sido goes to services but only to better read in secret. "During mass she was reading from a black leather book, stamped with a cross on both covers; she even became absorbed in it with a piety that seemed strange to the friends of my very dear unbeliever; they could not guess that the book that looked like a prayer book contained, in small type, Corneille's plays."[64] And she lets her dog come with her! She sweeps away the objection of the old priest who protests that mass is not said for the quadruped: "What are you afraid he'll learn, then?" replies our fighter hen.

But the most scandalous, the most exorbitant proof of that atheism, on the scale of a cosmic vibration, is Sido's paradoxical attitude toward the Captain's death: no tears, no sad expression. Her grief as a whole is swallowed up in the fleeting grace of a laugh that Sido allowed to come and that she offered as a gift to her loved ones, to the living:

> And she laughed, my mother in mourning, she laughed her shrill girlish laugh, and clapped her hands in front of the little cat. . . . The flash of memory dried up that shimmering cascade, dried the tears of laughter in my mother's eyes. Nevertheless, she did not apologize for having laughed that day or on those that followed, for she did us the kindness, after losing the one she truly loved, of remaining with us just as she was, accepting her sorrow as she would have accepted the advent of a long lugubrious season, but receiving the passing benediction of joy from all sides—she lived buffeted by shadow and light, hunched over in the storm, resigned, changeable and generous, decked like a foster home with children, flowers, and animals.[65]

Is Sido amoral? She disapproves of the captain's "very simple," even simplistic morality. He prefers not to speak of tiresome things—"and so they cease to exist, huh?"[66] As we have seen, Colette would later depict the humanist generosity of that "heart destined for love": "I am the daughter of a woman who, in a shamefaced, miserly, narrow-minded little region, opened her village home to stray cats, tramps, and pregnant servant girls."[67] Railing against everything and everybody, Sido's "universal contempt" is accompanied by "flashes across her face," which the daughter interprets as "a leap upward, toward a law written by herself alone, for herself alone."[68] But, with *My Mother's House,* Colette insists on her mother's devotion: "Indeed, my mother, who was the loveless and blameless Sido for her first hypochondriac husband, cared for shawl and mortar with loving hands."[69]

Were these labored compliments intended to counter the rumor that the Captain was the father of Achille, the last child of the earlier marriage? Sartre, on visiting Saint-Sauveur, heard that Sido had "quite simply poisoned her husband in order to marry M. Colette"[70]—an accusation dismissed by the justice system.[71] Nevertheless, Sido's judgments were often at variance with conventional morality. For example, she made this judgment of old Binard, the "impure widower," a prolific and incestuous father: "Their house is very well kept. . . . The little one's child [resulting from father-daughter incest] has lashes this long. . . . I saw her the other day, she was nursing her baby on the doorstep, it was delightful. . . . What am I saying? It was abominable when you know what's what, naturally. . . . "[72] The ellipses suggest the truth, but without formulating it. In Sido's eyes, might natural beauty, aesthetics, prevail over social laws?

That would be too simple, since the mother also assumes the role of Superego for Colette. And that great prohibition keeps her from leaving an unfaithful husband, who also holds her captive. More than financial destitution, it is Sido's judgment Colette fears: the thing that prevents the writer from escaping Willy's jail is that she would be subject to humiliation in Mama's eyes. "No, I was not thinking of running away. Where could I go, and how could I live? Always that worry of Sido's. . . . Always that intransigent refusal to return to her, to confess. . . . It must be understood that I possessed nothing of my own."[73]

Was Sido cruel? Certainly, but with a "heavenly cruelty from which wrath was absent."[74] Sido portrays herself to her daughter as a jealous little woman who tortured her half-sister, "my father's daughter," and, as the height of perfidy, she adds that the unfortunate child, whose hands she had crushed, makes her think of—Minet-Chéri herself: "You resemble my father's daughter. [. . .] My father so loved beautiful hands. . . . And I, with the cruelty of children, I immediately molded those soft little fingers, which melted between my own. . . . Yes . . . you see how wicked your mother is."[75] There is a complete confusion of generations and identities here: could the great Colette be the other daughter of "my," of Sido's, father? Or, since she is the Captain's daughter, might the Captain have been like a father to Sido herself? The violence and cruelty of Sido's fantasy are no doubt equal to the childish ferocity that leads her to hurt her half-sister's pretty little hands.

Like mother, like daughter: a same callousness unites them. Taking delight in the account of a fire at her neighbors' house, the mother writes to Minet-Chéri: "What a beautiful fire! Have you inherited my love for cataclysms?"[76] And, when the mother admires the blackbird who tears to shreds the pinkish flesh of cherries,[77] we are reminded of the daughter who goes into raptures about the cruelty of titmice: "They say she's ferocious? But it's man who says that, and how can a man have any idea of what the ferocity of a titmouse is? . . . Ferocious? How pretty she is when she kills! Once she's caught the worm, she pounds on it repeatedly, and takes it apart with the equity of a torturer. Ferocious, yes, no more and no less than mothers."[78] A word to the wise. Colette will not allow herself to be tortured, she has nothing in common with the other daughter of "my father" that Sido remembers. The great Colette is quite simply the daughter of a woman who, when she was in the mood, could be an "overbearing" mother.

And yet maternal savagery could transform itself into a taste for the works of the most sophisticated civilization, without abandoning that passion to devour. Driven by an insatiable curiosity, the very "country" Sido enthusiastically wanders the capital: "As a true provincial, my charming mother, 'Sido,' often had the eyes of her soul fixed on Paris. [. . .] Within a week she had visited the exhumed mummy, the expanded museum, the new store, had listened to the tenor and to the lecture on 'Burmese music.'"[79] Her curiosity leads her to devour numerous books: "Halfway up, Musset, Voltaire, and the four Gospels shone under the russet sheepskin. Littré, Larousse, and Becquerel arched their black tortoise backs. D'Orbigny, ripped to pieces by the irreverent worship of four children, shed its pages blazoned with dahlias, parrots, jellyfish with pink hair, and ornithorhynchuses."[80] That intellectual of the open fields is nevertheless a free spirit and critic who leaves to her daughter the task of discovering her happiness in the library hodgepodge: "What do you expect! Work things out in there, Minet-Chéri. You're intelligent enough to keep to yourself whatever you understand only too well. . . . And maybe there are no bad books."[81] Insubordinate, strained by her "pleasure in struggle, which would abandon my mother only with life itself"[82]—such, in short, is Sido's presence in the world.

To her "solid-gold jewel," Sido gives notice: "Don't touch!"[83] just as she ordered, "Look"—her two mottos. Don't grab butterflies or anything that invites you to touch: the buried seeds waiting to come up—or your body? Perhaps. Or your privates? Surely. You can look, since you will possess only in abstention. The mother who learned "only by getting burned" nevertheless imposed, as the superb frustration, an impassable boundary between looking and touching. Her intervention, "like a Françoise Dolto who had read her Lacan," inflicts symbolic castration through corporeal distance, inciting the child to place herself within the order of the father, the order of language. But is incest really forbidden for that "decretal" mother?

None of the memories related in *Break of Day* suggest so. As in the biblical parable, Sido is a sensualist who enriches herself by giving; she has "the purity of those who squander themselves."[84] She prevents Minet-Chéri from touching, but she herself is intoxicated by plants and beasts and even more by a strange familiarity with her elder son, Achille, which provokes young Colette's bitter jealousy. The beauty of a child's face sows an extremely sensual uneasiness, almost shame, in that perfect mother. Nothing of all that escapes Minet-Chéri, "her masterpiece," and what does it matter if the narrator invents and projects? Sido is truly her creation, it is Colette the writer who invented her mother/ model, on the condition that she appropriate her in that jouissance of proximity that was forbidden her, on the condition that she *touch* the butterflies, the blossoming flowers, the brother, the son, and always from both sides of the couple: touching/touched, man/woman, indistinguishably. Childhood will finally be regained when Colette rejoins the mother in her original, most forbidden passion. And, even in the autumn of her life, Colette will continue to smell, to feel, to taste Sido. Hence the last texts in *The Prime of Life* (1949) evoke her mother, her conception of motherhood and fatherhood and even the beloved dress—the words and the thing—that the writer would like to have us touch: "I had kept Sido's blue dress until then, its little short-waisted bodice all shrunken up and curved by darts in the back, under the breasts, under the arms."[85]

Sido is beloved by the Captain, as we will see, and proud of the conjugal rite, but it is not in that love that Sido thrives: her "two husbands," she says, would have been very surprised to find she was "a great lover."[86] Sido seems to experience passion without being altered by it, even deploring the fact that such "frivolousness" could lead a man to abandon his work and love only his chosen one.[87] "Cumbersome," "complicated," "tyrannical": such is the kind of love whose place Sido "haggles over." She wonders: "There's a lot of fuss, so much love, in these books. . . . My poor Minet-Chéri, people have other fish to fry in life. All those people in love that you see in books, don't they ever have children to bring up or a garden to tend?"[88]

Sido also does not hold the institution of marriage in great esteem: "Your unhappiness begins the moment you agree to be the wife of a dishonest man, your mistake is to hope *he* can give you a home, the same man who put you out of yours";[89] "'It is not so much divorce I blame,' she said, 'as marriage. It seems to me anything would be better than marriage—but it's just not done.' "[90] Colette would repeat Sido's disillusioned opinion of the female condition, elaborating brutally on it: "To her thinking, I had already gone through what she called 'the worst time in a woman's life: the first man.' You only die from that one, after which, conjugal life—or its counterfeit—becomes a career."[91]

Alongside men and in spite of them, children capture her essential desire. The object of her preoccupations and her constant attentions, Sido needs them like the flowers, trees, and beasts of her garden, from which they become indistinguishable. Children, the privileged elements of a hazy space where she finds her bearings only if she finds *them* there, are the landmarks of a disturbing place, an indiscernible "where," where she seeks herself in seeking them. "It was then that, under the old iron arch onto which the wisteria was spilling on the left side, my mother appeared, short and round at a time when age had not yet emaciated her. She examined the massive greenery, raised her head, and shouted into the air: 'The children! Where are the children?'"[92] "Where" emerges from chaotic anxiety and becomes a *place* only if Sido finds the children there.

Sido is attached, with all the force of her seductiveness, less to Minet-Chéri than to her elder son, Achille. During her childhood Colette observed her, in love with the boy who was supposedly the Captain's son, though born a Robineau-Duclos. "'Minet-Chéri. . . . My shining sun. . . . Beauty! . . . ' That last name was not for me, but for the older of my brothers, since an autumn is never pure of passion."[93] Colette accurately deciphered the letters her mother wrote her, her daughter, in which Sido confided at length her jealousy toward Achille's wife, the overly coquettish and fickle (in her eyes) Jane de La Fare.[94] The mother accompanies her "dear big boy" on his errands and sometimes on his house calls, aboard the beautiful automobile of which she seems so proud and that impresses her so much that she begins to learn the secrets of mechanics. The only one of her children to remain close to her, and a doctor on top of it, Achille would watch over the old lady, who found herself very satisfied with him: "One out of four very fortunately, *that* one I could not do without seeing."[95] As yet, she does not add: "In short, I'm no longer afraid because I'm with him, and, if we have to be killed, I'll be with him, which is better."[96] Sido, who proved so indulgent toward the incestuous Binard, seems aware of the love relationship that can occur between a son and his mother: "Like you, I found Mme de Lucenay very sad and changed. Since I know there is no mystery in her own life, I say to myself: 'I'd like you to tell me about Mme Chevreuil, whom I found so changed, so depressed, and so sad! Let's just bet that her son has a mistress, and that the mother is aggrieved and jealous.' "[97]

The envious little girl no doubt noticed very early on the voluptuous benefits a young man derived from such a maternal desire. It was at age thirteen, she believed, that she noted in Maurice, her brother's friend, "the gentle ease of a son who has rarely left his mother's side."[98] She assigns to the dossier of "pure" forms of eroticism the image of Sido trembling with the same desire before a flower's calyx, a chrysalis, or—her elder son, the seducer: "The *purity* of those *who squander themselves!* [. . .] my mother dreamed dramatically of her elder son, the very handsome one, the seducer, throughout his adolescence. At that time, I imagined her wild, full of false gaiety and curses, ordinary, uglier, on the lookout."[99] Later, Colette drew this portrait of her dying mother getting herself dolled up in bed, again to please—or to not displease—Achille: "Listen, listen. . . . It's the car coming up the coast! Minet-Chéri, don't tell your brother I had three attacks last night. In the first place, I forbid you. And, if you don't tell him, I'll give you the bracelet with the three turquoises. . . . You're boring me with your arguments. Yes, it's a matter of honesty! [. . .] But, at my age, there's only one virtue left: not to upset anyone. Quick, the second pillow for my back, let me be sitting up straight when he comes in. The two roses there, in the glass. . . . It doesn't smell like an old lady shut-in in here, does it?"[100]

All her remarks are scattered over the *pure* space that, in Colette's work, contains Sido. At the outer edges of that parenthesis, for social, exoteric purposes, the purity of Sido is replaced by the semiprofessional eroticism of Léa and the more worthy eroticism of the Lady in White. Very symptomatically, Colette begins *Break of Day* by evoking her mother and Sido's two husbands and shows Sido's solicitude toward her, the writer daughter: might a man encourage or, on the contrary, impede the book she was writing? Surreptitiously, the text comes to associate more freely and slips from the *pure* mother to what "pushes the gray-beard toward the tender shoot, and Chéri toward Léa":

> The perversity of satisfying an adolescent lover does not sufficiently devastate a woman. On the contrary. Giving becomes a sort of neurosis, a ferocity, an egoistic frenzy. [. . .] Between the still-young mother and a mature mistress, there is the rivalry of the gift, which poisons two female hearts and creates a yelping hatred, a war of vixens, where the maternal howl is neither the least savage nor the least indiscreet. Overly beloved sons! Buffed by female gazes, nibbled, at her pleasure, by the female who bore you, preferred already from the deepest night of the loins, beautiful coddled young males, you do not pass from one mother to another without betraying her in spite of yourself. You yourself, my dearest, you whom I wanted pure of my ordinary crimes, now I find in your correspondence, set down in careful handwriting, intended—in vain—to hide from me the jarring commotion of the heart, these words: *Yes, like you I found Mme X very changed and sad. I know her private life is without mystery: let's just bet, therefore, that her eldest son has his first mistress.*[101]

Even stranger is this trait described by Sido herself and repeated by her daughter: Sido feels something like an almost sexual arousal around little girls. Is Sido a pedophile? The term is a bit too strong. Nevertheless, a pretty niece makes her stagger with desire like a "great lover" but one unaware of being such. Only the beauty of childhood moves her; her two husbands did not arouse her so much:

> There is something in a very beautiful child that I cannot define and that makes me sad. How can I explain? Your little niece C— is at this moment a ravishing beauty. Not full face, that's nothing as yet; but when she turns her profile in a certain way and her little silvery nose stands out proudly beneath her beautiful lashes, I am struck with an admira-

tion that saddens me somehow. I am assured that great lovers are like that before the object of their passion. Could I therefore be, in my way, a great lover? That's news that would certainly have surprised my two husbands.[102]

There is therefore one Sido who is conscious and another who is not even unconscious—let us say, who is preconscious of her incestuous desires, which would nevertheless be as *pure* (and not to be confused with the excitement of Mmes Chevreuil and Lucenay, whom Sido mocks) as her sensual need for the glossy husks of flowers or tawny cat fur. It is clear Colette only half believes in that maternal purity. She suggests, rather, that desire has two faces: one belonging to Léa-Mme Dalleray; and the other to Sido. They are not by necessity mutually exclusive but can coexist in a single person, or at least in a single text—Colette's, for example.

There will be no cult of Sido, who herself professed no religion: "I don't know where her remoteness from any faith came from";[103] Sido is only (I beg your pardon!) "a great solemn figure," an "oasis" in the desert of love,[104] a "boundless open book,"[105] "the better writer."[106] We feel the effect of the daughter's irony when she describes her mother's nose, for example, a prominent symbol if ever one were needed: "Under that tightly woven bell of spelt, your gray eyes frolic, vagabond, variable, insatiable. On them worry and watchfulness bizarrely impose a diamond shape. No more eyebrows than the Mona Lisa, and a nose, my God, a nose."[107]

Everywhere the closeness of twins and the play of mirrors between two women impose themselves: who is writing whom? Sido's letters, with a beauty as concise as it is spicy, take pleasure in quoting Shakespeare or Molière, but at the same time confine themselves to a circumspect simplicity. By contrast, Colette, in referring to them, intensifies their rhythm, overdoes the spice but scrupulously follows the themes and morals of the maternal discourse. Mother and daughter are peers and rivals, as *My Mother's House* clearly formulates it: "Yes, yes, you love me, but you're a daughter, a female beast, my equal and my rival."[108] Over time the two women nevertheless mark their difference. Colette writes, echoing a letter from her mother of February 16, 1907: "Now that I'm coming undone little by little, now that, in the mirror, I little by little resemble her, I doubt that she, returning, would recognize me as her daughter, despite the resemblance in our features."[109] With more humility and gratitude, she also acknowledges her debt: "Let me reveal to her what I have learned in my turn, to what extent I am her impure relic, her crude image, her faithful servant charged with lowly tasks! She gave birth to me, and gave me the mission to pursue what, as a poet, she grasped and abandoned, the way one seizes the fragment of a melody drifting through space. . . . "[110]

Could the poet be Sido, and also Colette, when she finds no pleasure in long narrations but instead expresses herself in "tendrils of the vine"?

That her mother loved her, Minet-Chéri has no doubt: "My mother let me go, after calling me 'Beauty, Solid-Gold-Jewel'; she watched her work—her 'masterpiece,' she said—running and getting smaller on the slope. I may have been pretty; my mother and my portraits of the time are not always in agreement. . . . I was so because of my age and because of daybreak, because of my blue eyes darkened by the greenery, my blond hair, which would be smoothed down only on my return, and because of my superiority as an awakened child, over the other, sleeping children."[111] The anxious mother is afraid a prowler might abduct her beloved: " 'In Ghent, in my youth,' my mother told me, 'one of our friends, who was only sixteen, was abducted.' "[112] This can be seen as the commonplace fantasy of a mother who fears her daughter's seduction and projects onto the scene of a potential abduction her own sadomasochistic desires, which nevertheless reveals the intensity of the erotic bond between the two of them. And the daughter almost conforms to one of the mother's fantasies by dreaming, first, of *Abduction*: "My innocent reverie caressed the word and the image. [. . .] Two arms, singularly expert at picking up a sleeping body, encircled my back."[113] This was before she allowed herself to be ravished in reality, by Willy and a few others. But how lacking in danger, how reassuring it all is, since Mama had predicted it. "A familiar rhythm, truly, put me to sleep in those ravisher's arms. [. . .] Mama! Come quick! I'm being abducted!"[114]

It is not that Sido is steeped in admiration for everything her daughter does: she does not really appreciate her talents as a mime,[115] as we have seen. Even in childhood the mother's criticism needled her solid-gold jewel: "I don't believe you, but it's a very good imitation. Really, very good, my daughter. You are a miracle of kindness and banality!"[116] This is feigned criticism, in short, an extra goad that could only push "the little one" to develop a hardness without flaw and to seek out the notorious "rule [that] cures everything."[117] Indeed, the mother's complicity never falters, especially not during Colette's marital troubles. As far as Willy is concerned, Sido wishes her daughter would seek revenge: "I would like you to be able to smash him, my treasure, with a work of your own."[118] Even while urging her to reclaim her furniture and silver, she altered her judgment: "Nevertheless, I often tell myself what you tell yourself in vague terms, which is that, if you had not lived with that phenomenon for some time, your talent would not have revealed itself!"[119]

Sido survives, as Colette knows, in her daughter's writing, which took the place of the precious pink cactus, Sido's absolute. The "transitional object" represented by the flora and fauna, savored and cultivated between mother and daughter, transformed itself, over time, into a supple material, Colette's smooth style, elaborate and rich with precise words, but which, fundamentally, turns out itself to be her own body, identified with the pink flower of a prickly plant:

Ah! Is it not my pink cactus that survives me, and which you embrace? How remarkably it has grown and changed! . . . But, in examining your face, my daughter, I recognize it. I recognize it by your fever, by your anticipation, by the devotion of your open hands, by the beating of your heart and the cry you hold back, by the day breaking around you, yes, I recognize, I lay claim to all that. Stay, don't hide, and let both of you be left in peace, you and the one you embrace, for it is really, truly, my pink cactus, which finally wants to flower.[120]

For this Sido, who expresses herself here through her daughter's pen, there is no difference between her cactus and her daughter, just as, for the writer, there is none between herself, her sentences, and the world's flesh. It is that flux of matter and words, that transubstantiation of identities, that Colette calls "Sido." Logically, necessarily, this mother who is indistinguishable from Being brings about the transubstantiation only because she is the Writer. Next to Balzac, whom she admires, and Proust, whom she envies, it is Sido that Colette imitates, refines, rejoins. She likes to reread her letters, to recopy them or claim to do so, and to conclude, after a sentence by the mother printed in italics for us in *Break of Day*: "Between her and me, who, then, is the better writer? Is it not glaringly obvious that she is"?[121]

In the unheard-of experience the daughter imagines with her mother, and that she glorifies, elevating her to a tutelary goddess of writing, what remains of the real model, of the provincial Frenchwoman? A few cinders besmirch her: her retreat to the garden, her confinement to the house, her shopkeeper's concerns sometimes give off an odor of musty nationalism and distill the poison of anti-Semitism. Does not Sido decree, regarding a neighboring family, "They're all very ugly. Badly dressed, Jew faces"?[122] One can immediately find echoes of these very real words, attenuated of course, beginning with the founding text of the Sido myth and repeated by Colette herself: "Adventure? Travel? The arrogance that produces emigrants? [. . .] Minet-Chéri [is] a child of her village, as hostile to the colonist as to the barbarian, one of those who limits her universe to the boundary stone of a field, to the gate of a shop."[123] The acrimony of that shop-and-village nationalism endures until the years of the Occupation.[124] But this musty smell dissipates over time and is so secondary when compared to the exuberant wedding with the world and with beings that Colette continually celebrates, that it is more like an unreflective cliché, a tribute paid to local social rubbish, than the demonstration of a political conviction. Such a conviction is, in fact, lacking in Colette, just as it is alien to the sensory precision that Colette feels the need to call "Sido" in order to anchor her writing in it.

It is not a politics but a cosmogony that Colette embraces as such and deploys with Sido the Voltairean devoted to her garden. Let us turn once more to the mother's letters: "Kisses, how I love you, and greetings to Missy, who is finally happy. Cultivate your garden, that's still the only way to truly live in peace. Write me. Your mother."[125] Finally, we find, written by the mother, this original conception of wealth as a profusion of flowers: "The rent will certainly be lower than for the little house [. . .] but I will no longer have my basket of lilies of the valley or of any flower; and how rested my eyes feel, from all moral and physical ugliness, when I can contemplate the blossoming of a flower of any plant whatever! All in all, it's very tiresome not to be rich."[126] This does not prevent Sido from being proud of herself, no less than her daughter is; but she asserts it with a frankness where irony contends with insolent certainty. "I came to the world three hundred years too early, and it does not understand me, not even my children do."[127]

DEPRESSION, PERVERSION, SUBLIMATION

Truly perverse beings are almost as rare in this world as saints.

—François Mauriac, *La Pharisienne*

We cannot approach the most perverse beings without recognizing them as men. And sympathy for their humanity leads us to tolerate their perversity.

—Marcel Proust, *Jean Santeuil*

FREUD'S WAY: *Père-version* OR *Mère-version*

Of all the advances of psychoanalysis in the exploration of psychic life, the approach to perversion—especially in its relation to sublimation—is one of the most solid but also one of the most complex and most open. In declaring from his early works that the child has a "polymorphously perverse disposition,"[1] Freud takes the guilt out of perversion: we are all perverse by virtue of our infantile past, and, as a result, we remain unconsciously so as adults. All the same he does not efface perversion, either as behavior or as structure: from sadomasochism to voyeurism to exhibitionism, not to mention the various forms of fetishism and homosexuality, symptoms are diagnosed and analyzed as such. But they are also envisioned as potentially inherent in all human sexuality as it appears to the analyst, that is, as essentially perverse in its preliminary pleasures and unconscious fantasies. From there we arrive at paradoxes that others have not neglected to formulate. For example, psychoanalysis claims not only that perversion does not exist but also that we are all perverse.[2] One of the recent indications of that state of affairs is the debate now raging in psychoanalytic societies around the world: Can one be a homosexual and an analyst? And the most difficult thing about this dilemma is defining not who is homosexual but who is an analyst.

In the course of the reflections proposed in this book, we will not enter into the controversies surrounding analytical theory and the practice of perversions. We will confine ourselves to the essential Freudian positions and their contemporary developments, and recall a few fundamental points capable of elucidating Colette's experience.

In *Three Essays on the Theory of Sexuality* (1905), Freud defines perversion as a *transgression* and as *arrested* development: "Perversions are sexual activities which either a) extend, in an anatomical sense, beyond the regions of the body that are designed for sexual union, or b) linger over the intermediate relations to the sexual object which should normally be traversed rapidly on the path towards the final sexual aim."[3] In this view, there is an "overvaluation of the sexual object" that elevates activities relating to zones of the body other than the genitals to the rank of a sexual aim. This behavior, specific to the child, stems from his strong narcissistic investment in the body itself, all of whose erogenous zones (the mouth, the anus, but also the skin and the five senses themselves, which place the baby in contact with the first object, the mother) are taken as objects of satisfaction. If, therefore, the child is for that very reason "polymorphously perverse," the mother is no less so: "A mother's love for the infant satisfies wishful impulses which have long been repressed and which must be called perverse."[4] The father unconsciously takes umbrage at these impulses, especially when they are directed toward a son.

Freudians would later specify that, because of neoteny (that is, the fact that we are born incomplete, in a state of prematurity that requires lengthy maternal and paternal support before we acquire a certain autonomy), the baby possesses a "precocious anxiety" or an "originary phobia," which determines "the appetite for excitation" (*Reizhunger*) and the always uncertain, always substitutive satisfactions. That appetite for excitation, constantly in search of an object of satisfaction, which is itself permanently unsatisfying, is supposedly the inevitable destiny of human drives, the true economy of what Freud identifies as an *original perversion*. And some wonder whether the notion of perversion is not a "counterphobic" concept and whether perversion, or *père-version*, a turning toward the father, does not rather cover up a *mère-version*, a turning toward the mother.[5]

Nevertheless, the founder of psychoanalysis calls the following particularities, in adult life this time, perverse: "first, the disregarding of the barrier of species (the gulf between men and animals), second, the overstepping of the barrier against disgust, third, of that against incest [. . .] fourthly, that against members of one's own sex, and fifthly the transferring of the part played by the genitals to other organs and areas of the body."[6] Perversion is therefore a transgression of "barriers," in other words, of the *prohibitions* articulated by social law inasmuch as it is a law of the father, of prohibitions that channel sexuality toward procreation. In skirting these prohibitions or barriers, the pervert fixes on aims and objects characteristic of infantile sexuality, and that *fixation* denies as a matter of priority the prohibition on incest. For Freud perversion is a fixed passion that returns the pervert to infantile pleasures with the maternal body; this is also because the pervert, even as he denies the prohibition of incest, also denies the mother's castration. Such would be the imaginary mother of the perverse subject: a powerful prosthesis endowed with all the powers of satisfaction because she is a fantasized androgyne, equipped with a penis as well as breasts, lacking nothing. The beautiful analysis of the Leonardo da Vinci "case" allows Freud to demonstrate this hypercathexis in the mother-with-penis, the phallic mother, in the pervert's fantasy. To satisfy infantile omnipotence, the pervert erects the mother in the place of the father's absence or weakness. It is therefore clear why the definition of perversion as the "denial of the mother's castration" is to be understood in terms of that other definition of which it is the corollary: "The abandonment of the reproductive function is the common feature of all perversions."[7]

How does the polymorphously perverse "neoten," that is, the child born incomplete, impotent, dependent on its mother, transform itself into a *perverse subject*? "In the anamnesis of perverts a very early impression of an abnormal instinctual trend or choice of object was quite often found, to which the subject's libido remained attached all through his life."[8] If one admits that that autoerotic fixation comes about, usually as a matter of course, during the fifth or sixth year, one can date the apparition of a perverse structure (different from the polymorphous perversity of the neoten baby), to the beginning of the Oedipus complex.[9] Parental—maternal or paternal—seduction, child sexual abuse, but also a high level of or peculiarity in an innate drive—original predispositions, then—can be the source of such a development. As a result, when the perversion represses normal sexuality—and is not content to accompany it—"if, in short, a perversion has the characteristics of *exclusiveness* and *fixation*—then we shall be justified in regarding it as a pathological symptom."[10]

Very early on Freud posits a certain cultural and historical relativism of perversion: the perversions subtend all the neuroses characteristic of contemporary subjects considered normal, and vestiges of them might be found in certain religious faiths, which would demonstrate the archaic character of this behavior stemming from humanity's childhood. "I have an idea shaping in the mind that in the perversions, of which hysteria is the negative, we may have before us a residue of a primaeval sexual cult which, in the Semitic East (Moloch, Astarte), was once, perhaps still is, a religion."[11] Freud elaborates several times on this idea, grounding the perversions in an infantile sexual predisposition that remains repressed and unconscious in the psychoneuroses, which are themselves defined as "the *negative* of perversions."[12]

It is *regression* that makes perversion emerge, whereas *repression* structures neurosis: "A regression of the libido without repression would never produce a neurosis but would lead to a perversion. [. . .] Repression is the process which is most peculiar to neurosis."[13] Paranoia, for its part, would result from the "forward surge of the auto-erotic current. [. . .] The perversion corresponding to it would be what is known as 'idiopathic insanity.' "[14] Some will say that, in using the perverse tendencies liberated by the foreclosure of the father's role, the paranoid brings about a fusion between his ego and the world, thus creating a grandiose emotional intimacy specific to the pervert: "An 'end of the world' based upon other motives is to be found at the climax of the ecstasy of love [for President Schreber]. [. . .] In this case it is not the ego but the single love-object which absorbs all the cathexes directed upon the external world."[15] In all these approaches the perversion forms *the original sexual backdrop* against which the other behaviors and structures stand out.

IDEALIZATION: LATENCY AND THE SUPEREGO

The complicity between perversion and sublimation is not the least of the complexities or mysteries of this psychoanalytic vision of our psychosexuality. Far from being attributable to the sheer force of the drives or to external agents (seduction, abuse), perversion, by its own logic, *idealizes* the drive from the outset. This amounts to saying that the perversion may be, at its very source, a complex construction mobilizing a large "mental factor": "It is perhaps in connection precisely with the most repulsive perversions that the *mental factor* must be regarded as playing its largest part in the *transformation of the sexual drive.* It is impossible to deny [. . .] in their case [. . .] the equivalent of an *idealization of the drive.*"[16] Could the perversion be an act of creation, a work of art before its time? Freud advances two hypotheses to explain that premature knotting of the *drive* and *idealization* in *perversion,* hypotheses that interest us because of the works of sublimation elaborated in contact with perversion. They concern the role of the *latency* period and that of the *Superego.*

Our capacities for sublimation develop quite particularly during the latency period, which, after the peak of the Oedipus complex, lasts from age five to preadolescence. The attainments of infantile sexuality are repressed at that time, and genital sexuality is not yet developed, so that one can envision latency as a period of "preparatory pleasures." These imply erogenous zones and partial drives that do not lead to their genital realization and, as a result, produce states of displeasure and anxiety, but also, in parallel, opposing mental forces that transform the drives into daydreams, hallucinations, idealizations, sublimations. "It is possible further to form some idea of the mechanism of this process of sublimation. On the one hand, it would seem, the sexual impulses cannot be utilized during these years of childhood, since the reproductive functions have been deferred. [. . .] On the other hand, these impulses would seem in themselves to be perverse—that is, to arise from erotogenic zones and to derive their activity from drives which, in view of the direction of the subject's development, can only arouse unpleasurable feelings. They consequently evoke *opposing mental forces* (reacting impulses) which, in order to suppress this unpleasure effectively, build up the mental dams [. . .] [of] disgust, shame and morality."[17]

This remark by Freud, which links the fate of *sublimation* to that of *latency* and, as a result, to the *partial* satisfaction of *perversions*, suggests that, when the adult attempts to escape genital sexuality, he inevitably runs into the latency period, with its partial pleasures, their tensions and their compensation through sublimation. All the same, beyond latency, sublimation-idealization has its roots in the very origins of psychic development. There is a "primitive creativity," a "primitive sublimation" in relation to the ideal Ego in the very small child, who already constructs a sort of "fetish" levied on his osmotic desire for the mother and on the mother's own desire: this is Donald Woods Winnicott's "transitional object." This object, a piece of cloth or a toy that already *represents* an illusory zone between the child and his desires, protects the subject from the anxiety of separation. With the dawn of sublimation, the latency period engages a complementary process, an "oversublimation" leading to the Ego-ideal (and no longer an ideal Ego), which opens the way to true cultural activities.[18] These different degrees of sublimation are so many "stations" that require the conscious attention of artists in their search for *lost time,* the ideal time of paradisiacal satisfaction: we find them in the themes of writers' works from Colette to Proust, to speak only of the most famous.

Sublimation, a complicated and still enigmatic process, brings about a desexualization and a desintrication of the drives. *Desexualization* means that, in the course of sublimation, the drive changes its aim and its object: instead of seeking the satisfaction of the erogenous zones, the subject's activity procures ideal pleasures, satisfactions connected, for example, to the ideal beauty of beings and things, as well as to an author's own creations composed of words, colors, sounds, which become representative of his narcissism and his ideal Ego. Is that deviation from the genital aim and, more generally, from the sexual aim of the drive toward a desexualized idealization a sort of perversion?[19] Let us rather hypothesize that, in the dynamic of sublimation, what is installed in the place of sexualization is not its repression but a displaced eroticization: this means there is no sexual discharge, but the excitation is maintained, especially through the ideal beauty of beings, objects, creations. A feeling of omnipotence often accompanies such an experience: an omnipotent, maniacal ego constructs a universe that must truly be called imaginary, made up of pleasures that are often maintained only through representations. Moreover, it is *one's* own representations, those created by the subject-author, which depend on no "object" or "other" external to the Ego; and, for that very reason, the imaginary creator experiences them as more powerful than any other pleasure (particularly genital pleasure), and as likely to never fail him, to be imperishable even. Nothing is lacking in that imaginary omnipotence: such a sublimation celebrates the subject's fixation on his infantile omnipotence. As a result, a certain subject is constructed, one who lacks nothing, in fact, except that he lacks a lack.

As for the *desintrication of the drive* internal to sublimation, it means that, when the subject runs away from the external (the object, the other) to withdraw inside (the Ego, narcissism, one's own representations), the usual weave of life drive and death drive comes undone. In sublimatory activity the *erotic* (or *life*) drive no longer has as its aim a sexual object of satisfaction but a *medium* that is either a pole idealizing love (the beauty of another or of self) or a verbal, musical, or pictorial creation, itself highly idealized. As for the *thanatic* (or *death*) drive that is thereby liberated, it has a choice: either to direct itself toward the outside (object, other) on its own and to attack it with a maximum of violence, destructiveness, cruelty; or to deviate toward the Ego in the form of a depreciation, a critical severity, a depressivity, even a suicidal melancholy. As a result of the desintrication of the drive, the apparent narcissistic serenity of the adventure of sublimation actually leaves the subject exposed. He runs the risk of a psychic catastrophe from which only a continuation of sublimatory creativity can save him. That creativity nonetheless entails, in its turn, its own risks of maniacal exaltation and the denial of reality, the underside of its particular delights of extreme and contagious jouissance.[20]

As for the Superego, there is a shift in Freud's thinking as to its role in the search for pleasure and, beyond it, in perversion. Initially, he conceived the pleasure principle in negative terms, as an avoidance of displeasure; but, beginning with "The Ego and the Id" (1923), he sets forth pleasure as a positive principle obtaining under the injunction of the Superego. The Ego represents the external world and the reality principle, in opposition to pleasure, which reigns without restriction in the Id. "The superego stands in contrast to it as the representative of the internal world, of the id."[21] We are now confronted with a new function for the Supergo: far from being an inhibitor of pleasure, as it was in Freud's initial observations, the Superego, which is intimately connected to the Id, is not only a defensive agency but one that pushes the subject toward jouissance; it is a *pousse-à-jouir* (as Lacan would say). It is clear, from the same perspective, that if the Superego is represented by the father, perversion as the transgression of prohibitions is not only a challenge to the father but also a carrying out of his injunction: "The Superego says: 'Jouissance!'" And perversion is a turning [*version*] toward the father [*père*], a submission by the son to the father's desire, a *père-version*. Lacan invites us to conceive of divine authority, at least in monotheism, and of Christ's "redemption" itself as a sado-masochistic submission to the father, a *père-version,* all the while suggesting that the loaded term ought to be abandoned by psychoanalysis: "God is *père*-verse, that is a fact made obvious for the Jew himself. But if we trace things back, we will truly end up—which is not to say that I hope we do—inventing something less stereotypical than perversion. That is actually the only reason I am interested in psychoanalysis, and why I try my hand at giving new life to it."[22] He adds: "Imagining one is the redeemer, in our tradition at least, is the prototype of—it is not for nothing that I write it this way—'*père-version.*' It is insofar as there is a relation between son and father, and has been for a very long time, that the loony idea of redeemer has emerged. All the same, Freud tried to shake off that sadomasochism, the only point at which there is a supposed relation between sadism and masochism—sadism is for the father, masochism is for the son."[23]

Père-version? Or *mère-version?* Both, obviously, in accordance with the various modalities of our difficult, our impossible *independence* as "neotens" from our two parents, and our problematic *freedom* vis-à-vis the indispensable symbolic Law that makes us speaking subjects.

Another experience of pleasure takes shape subsequent to these excavations of psychoanalysis conducted by Freud, an experience defined as a jouissance (Freud uses the term *Genuss* rather than *Lust,* which he reserves for *pleasure*). It designates a state of sexual satisfaction analogous to death, since the expulsion of sexual fluids corresponds to the separation of soma from germ-plasma. "After Eros has been eliminated through the process of satisfaction, the death drive has a free hand for accomplishing its purposes."[24] Jouissance appears as an experience of nonobjective satisfaction, close to primary narcissism according to Freud. One can follow its tracks in the pursuit of the arts, in mysticism, drug addition, and—among women. "In women too we must postulate a somatic sexual excitation and a state in which this excitation becomes a psychical stimulus—libido—and provokes the urge to the specific action to which voluptuous feeling is attached. Where women are concerned, however, we are not in a position to say what the process analogous to the relaxation of tension of the seminal vesicles may be."[25] Lacan amplifies and diversifies that Freudian suggestion by insisting on the difference between *pleasure* and *jouissance*. In the latter, he further distinguishes between the "phallic jouissance" proper to man (and to woman to the extent that, in her fantasy and through the clitoris, a woman identifies with man) and an "*other* jouissance."[26] This means that jouissance divides woman since, through phallic jouissance woman communicates with man, whereas through an "*other* jouissance," which woman feels but does not know how to name or know, she places herself no longer in relation to the Phallus but to the Other. Alone with that *other* jouissance, which remains fundamentally unknown to itself, woman is destined for a structural duplicity.[27]

These psychoanalytic observations will be linked to the split universe of Colette: the "Sido" side and her *other* jouissance, where it is *the object* (the mother, the garden, the "cardinal points") imagined by the Ego that absorbs all the cathexes offered to the external world and that exalts in Being; and the Léa or Lady in White side, with their phallic pleasure or jouissance. Colette nevertheless succeeds in naming that *other* jouissance, which a woman, when she achieves it, manages only to *feel* without knowing how to *say* it: might that not be her ultimate genius?[28]

GENITALITY OR NEOREALITY?

If our pleasures are fundamentally perverse, if our jouissances depend on them, and if all make common cause with our capacities for representation, it is clear that the perversion that attracts us in works of art is that addressed to the *universal logics that inhabit us all*. A separation anxiety presides over our development into supposedly free and autonomous individuals, the anxiety of a "primary disidentification" with the maternal container. The pervert is fixed on that separation anxiety as the father signifies it to him. The paternal prohibition does not necessarily threaten to deprive the son of his organ; more structurally, it represents to the child his incapacity to satisfy the mother genitally. The perverse subject will be the one who denies that paternal or Oedipal prohibition and makes it a denial of genitality. Genitality does not interest me (such would be the pervert's implicit discourse), it does not exist, so long as other pleasures, even more or less sublimatory jouissances, are within my reach. Jouissances provided by whom? For some it will entail spurning the maternal source, fleeing her *abjection*,[29] through the partial pleasures of sadomasochism. Others, on the contrary, will acquire a new-found taste for the Oedipal mother who keeps the child in the role of spouse, the privileged object of her own desires, "my solid-gold jewel," "Minet-Chéri." Whatever the representations, the child does not fail to draw an enormous benefit from that situation of denial: does it not spare him the narcissistic wound that results from the gap separating the child from its parents' generation?

The pervert denies the difference of generations in the same motion that he denies the prohibition of incest and the mother's castration: he fills in the generation gap, effaces the feeling of dereliction that the gap inflicts.[30] "The future pervert has not suffered from a narcissistic deficiency, but from an overfull narcissistic cathexis whose sudden collapse is unbearable to him."[31] To combat that unbearable disidentification, the pervert mobilizes himself in a frenzied, often exhausting quest for paroxystic satisfactions. Within that context, oral satisfaction—the foundation of many drug addictions—may be experienced as the equivalent of an intrauterine and original alimentary satisfaction. Orality is already well developed in utero, before any other activity (at fifteen weeks the fetus sucks its finger; at sixteen it clasps its hands together and explores the uterus).[32]

As a result every perverse act can be interpreted not only as an attack on the procreative couple and as a desire to recover the original mother-child coupling but also as an effort to dominate the genital universe and one's world through the creation of an *other world*. Against the "impure" chaos (to cite Colette's title, *The Pure and the Impure*) of genital sexuality and of all sexuality that encompasses it, a neoreality will be set forth: "my" secret

universe, "my" hidden intimacy, "my work," necessarily dissident, which violates the order of the world and what I perceive
as its intolerable excesses in order to substitute a paradisiacal
serenity. In its megalomaniacal and narcissistic thrust, such creativity, an act of revenge on the mother and father combined,
contains, more or less unconsciously, a hatred of reality.[33] If that
hatred makes common cause with evil, it is because it is propelled
by the hubris of destruction targeting the world of one's parents.
Within that perspective, does not all creativity carry with it a
"perverse," antifamily, asocial value?

With (infantile) creativity set against (parental) creativity, the
issue will be to cathect (the child's) orality and anality more than
(the parents') genitality: anality "idealized" and "sublimated"
into "perfumed paradises," exquisite scents, occupies a central
place in the reconstruction of the new "house of Claudine," and
in many other sublimatory works. It proves to be essential in
every "production" of aesthetic "objects" that pretty up the first
product of our bodies, excrement.

Envisioned that way, perverse reactions can be understood as
a maniacal reaction to a denied depression: rather than accept the
loss of the object and engage in the work of mourning, the subject appropriates—in fantasies and perverse acts—substitute or
ersatz satisfactions, which he hypercathects. Many depressions,
like some cases of mourning, are accompanied by orgiastic abreactions of a perverse nature; in contrast, the treatment of perversions has discovered an underlying painful melancholy that is often impossible to work through.[34]

By fixing the perverse subject in a definitive and scaled-down
structure (some incestuous or fetishistic representation, for example), the stable perversion also assumes the role of protection
against the underlying destructiveness and against the possibility
it will be acted upon: the destruction dwelling within the pervert
is, in fact, tied to a certain sexuality that satisfies him and serves
as an abutment—albeit an excessive, even exhausting, one—pre-
venting the infinite wave of hatred from being unleashed. Anal-
ogously, the creation of aesthetic objects protects anyone under-

taking the desintrication of drives characteristic of the psychic process of sublimation. When these objects are appreciated and enjoy public approbation, the aesthetic activity metabolizes *destructiveness* into the *labor* of creation that, assiduous and scrupulous, can be transformed into a true vocation. Perseverance in creation, the "oof!" of effort, says Colette,[35] her famous "rule [that] cures everything," impose a ferocious discipline on daily existence; but they are laden with supplementary pleasures in that they offer themselves as a safety valve against the destructiveness of the death drive, which exhausts itself like a wave against the jetty.

The crudeness of this psychoanalytic vocabulary regarding the implications of perversion for the drives ought not to mislead us: I wish not to devalorize the work of art by connecting it to pathology but, rather, to indicate the dramatic and no less universal wellspring the artist of genius uses to exalt them and on which her work rests. Those who, for lack of genius, receive works rather than producing them are stirred to their very—inadmissible—core, where similar wellsprings stir. The psychoanalytic hypothesis, in contrast, does not reveal the singular technique particular to each artist, which, built on the logic of her unconscious, transforms them into masterpieces: other specifically literary, stylistic, and semiological investigations examine the arcana of these processes. I have tried to approach a few of them through a close reading of *Tendrils of the Vine*.[36] But the hypothesis proposed by psychoanalysis has enriched our knowledge of the soul, that "psychic apparatus" (according to Freud) with its highs and lows, patiently visited; it allows us to read the formal successes of great artists differently, along with the joy and rage they procure for us. This psychoanalytic archaeology runs the risk of tipping over, of chipping away at, the Colette monument that lovers of belles-lettres and of very French pleasures have been happy to build from her—not without complicity on her part. But perhaps it also offers us the benefit of perceiving more profoundly the impulses that act on her, that assure her a perpetual rebirth and that move us in turn.

SUCCEEDING WHERE THE PERVERT
EXHAUSTS HIMSELF

At one time Apollinaire called Colette "perverse," but he withdrew the adjective, preferring the term "mischievous" ("a soul more mischievous than perverse") and did not hesitate to compare her provocative audacity to the tragic immodesty of early Christian women: "So it was that, delivered from modesty, Roman women martyrs entered the arena." In any case, for the poet it was in vain that this modern woman respected grammar; she squandered herself in too many activities and had far too many ambitions to equal Mme de Sévigné.[37]

Was Colette perverse? Certainly; a little; not at all. She writes where the pervert seeks jouissance: such is her success, well beyond the troubles she complains of and that exhaust the pervert. Perverse acts punctuate her life: from Willy to Missy to Bertrand. But she metamorphosed them: first, by using some of them as a self-analysis, by living-and-meditating on them in her writing, where, in the end, they acquire their definitive reality, a fictive neoreality far from the lying and sublime real. At the core of writing, Colette's "meditation" does not benefit from *interpretations* that, in the course of therapy or self-analysis, manage to stop the subject from acting out by introducing distance; but, from the outset, this meditation is iridescent with sensations and realized in an aesthetic formulation-sublimation from which it becomes indistinguishable. Writing itself thus appears as a substitute for erotic pleasure and the text as a fetish, a sort of perverse but double object, displacing to a second degree the displacement that the fetish in the strict sense brings about. Writing is a displacement of the perverse displacement, a transference of pleasure from the realm of sexuality to all sensations and, simultaneously, to all words.

The *other* jouissance, which Colette calls "Sido," underlies that *reversal of perversion into sublimation,* in such a way that the perversion itself is swallowed up by it and, without disappearing, collects there, but as a purity. In certain circumstances, man as well as woman is capable of that *other* jouissance, and we know of writers who excel at it: Proust, Joyce, Nabokov, each in his own way, to cite only a few modern authors. Or perhaps that femininity, though specific to the *other* jouissance, is also the secret of *all writing*—"purloined letter," as we have said.

In any case, Colette does not especially claim to be a "woman" and even less a "feminist."[38] But, in Colette, a feminine version of separation anxiety (which a man who identifies with his mother might also share) comes to light, through identification and denial. Since we are the "same" (mother and I), I do not lose "her," I experience jouissance by my mother, I am the mother who knows jouissance, hence I am ALL through my sensory text, which remakes the world's flesh. In other words, the woman's relation to the separation anxiety underlying perverse behaviors is such that the *maternal container* (Sido, the garden, the flora and fauna that [ful]fill the mother/nature), inseparable from the *mother tongue,* is refined, possessed. *Mother* and *tongue* are, in the end, carried off to the sublime with a complicitous grace whereby the cruelty of possession is transformed into pacified serenity, achieving the immutable static state of the Eleatics.

The stirrings of the sexual passions are there, but they stand at the edges of the text as it were, ephemeral pretexts of ecstasy. The permanent center, the unmoving axis remains: Sido. Is she a character? A model? An archetype? Or the exquisite border between mother and language? Sido is the designation of *imaginary space itself,* the clearing beyond the perverse acting out, which makes it possible to name the now authorized, avowable, shareable pleasures. "He who loses himself in his passion has lost less than he who loses his passion," wrote Saint Augustine. Colette, lost in her passions, in no way loses herself since, precisely, she has never lost the fundamental passion named Sido. She stands at the very crest where things are elevated into words, where words are affected by things, and vice versa, and that appears to us as the dawn of humanization, the secret of humans. Is it perversion, or sublimation? These terms, and above all their intricateness as revealed by psychoanalysis, are only steps leading us on the adventure of sensory sense, provided we do not confine them to pathology but recognize them as what is specifically human about inexorable sexuality.

This is particularly true in that psychoanalysis—at least in its developments most concerned with truth—is currently abandoning the normativity that taints its fundamental notions (especially perversion) and now considers a number of "perverse" behaviors obligatory rites of passage marking the complex construction of personality.[39] The easing of prohibitions in certain contemporary societies has brought media attention to behaviors that, though perceived as perverse, are neither condemned nor prohibited but increasingly integrated into morality, into legislation itself, and, more generally, into a broader understanding of personal freedom.

Bisexuality, heartily embraced by Colette, is part of that. Several case studies have demonstrated that homosexual relationships occurring in the life of a person who does not necessarily consider herself homosexual, either in the course of analysis through the transference onto her analyst, or independent of it, bring to light a dissociation between the subject's masculine identity and feminine identity, a widespread trait that is nevertheless repressed in most of us. When the genital relationship with a partner of the opposite sex is not accompanied by true emotional abandon, the subject who feels its deficiencies may seek out and attain an "ego orgasm"[40] or an "ego promiscuity"[41] with a person of the same sex. That intense emotional bond, which takes on the appearance of a more or less sublimated homosexuality, in fact leads the dissociated subject from its love for a partner of the same sex to the memory of a primary identification with the infantile love object. As a regressive experience, that attachment may entail the risk of self-dissolution and confusion with the love object. But also, conversely, if these risks are set aside and the ego is strong enough (for example, if it has a strong confidence in or identification with Sido), a paradoxical relationship may occur through that lover's confidence in a homosexual or incestuous partner, a relationship that diverges from instinctual sublimation in Freud's sense. Winnicott calls it an "ego orgasm" assimilable to ecstasy and that grounds "the capacity to be alone." We grasp the difference between a sublimation verging on perversion on one hand, and that "ego orgasm" on the other, if we compare the overexcited play of a child amusing himself to the point of exhaustion (to the point that the parents have to spank him to produce the climax and "calm the play") to another sort of play, this time felicitous, in which the child does not feel threatened by a physical orgasm local in its excitation, and that may be compared to the relaxation experienced during a concert. Certain relationships, apparently perverse because they mobilize bisexuality or incestuous drives, entail that sort of ego ecstasy. Local sexual excitation is often present in such cases; it may remain under the surface or it may be denied. But it may also be completely effaced and may make way for that primary emotional abandon with the other (initially, with the mother). In such situations, an analyst ought to refrain from interpreting these behaviors as homosexual and perverse, at the risk of plunging the patient (who would hear such interpretations as accusations or, on the contrary, as recommendations) into compulsive homosexual or incestuous practices.

Colette's bisexuality, as well as her perverse acting out, can be understood in the same way. She herself suggests it discreetly: in her relations with Willy, the genital act, which was, moreover, accompanied by narcissistic wounds, probably brought her only partial satisfaction. Hence she begins by forcefully denying that "the catastrophe of love, its consequences, its phases" are part of "a woman's intimate life." Moreover, in divulging these erotic "half-lies" (which Colette herself told), a woman "keeps *confused and considerable secrets* from becoming public, secrets she herself does not know very well," buried as they are in "the same *feminine sector, ravaged by bliss and strife,* around which shadows deepen."[42] Those ravages may have been counterbalanced by the possibility of *abandoning oneself emotionally to others* through the detour of perversion (homosexual or incestuous). Thanks to perversion and after it, Colette acquires the capacity to be alone, the capacity for ecstasy in an extreme, though relative, solitude, since the writer constantly solicits her friends, relying on the "best" of them, while never again foundering in a tragic dependence. Whatever may have been its real vigor, the erotic pleasure procured by this acting out (of homosexuality with

Missy, of incestuous sex with Bertrand) proves to be—in hindsight, and through the literary fate Colette was able to give them—less important than the emotional completion they provided. Indeed, the "ego orgasm" characterizing them is experienced as an ecstasy in the sense that the ego rediscovers and recreates the child's direct and silent communication with a reliable mother, a mother-environment. In other words, that relation to the "subjective object," in moving through the perverse act, recreates the uninterrupted presence of the mother who, along with the *capacity for illusion,* grounds the very paradox of the "found"-"created" object, now inseparable from its putting into words. What else is it but "Sido"?

But can we really follow Winnicott when he remarks that, in certain people (he implies: those endowed with a lesser intensity of drives) and in certain (optimal?) family circumstances, instinctual sublimation is simply *replaced* by that ego orgasm, the equivalent of ecstasy? On the contrary, it seems more likely—and Colette's experience attests to this—that sexual satisfaction (that is, the sexual experience of erotic excitation in the act itself) and its sublimation through writing *accompany* the desexualized ego orgasm. Hence that accompaniment, that sexuality/desexualization duet, continues to varying degrees throughout Colette's life, before *pure play* finally takes over. It is only then that the writer, like the ladies of Llangollen in *The Pure and the Impure,* is of no sex because she is of every sex: that of flowers, cats, butterflies.

The term "perversion" and a few allusions to its variants appear very early in Colette's writing, of course: she meditates on them, accepts or rejects them, but only to better eviscerate them.

Psychopathia Sexualis AND MELANCHOLY
ACCORDING TO COLETTE

In *Claudine in Paris* (1901), probably under Willy's influence, Colette refers to Krafft-Ebing, author of the famous *Psychopathia Sexualis* (1886),[43] which influenced Freud's own reflections and is still a bible in the matter. The name of the famous psychiatrist is cited in the mention of an Italian work, *Amicizie di Collegio,* reporting the various types of homosexuality present in secondary schools, which would be discussed in *La Revue* in 1902. "This child spoke to me of an amusing psychological study that one of his compatriots devoted to *amicizie di collegio,* which that transalpine Krafft-Ebing defines, it appears, as 'a mimicry of the passionate instinct'—since, whether Italians, Germans, or Frenchmen, those materialists all manifest the most sickening, pallor-of-death imbecility."[44] Homosexuality was a fashionable theme in literary and artistic circles of the time, and Colette frequented many aficionados of Sodom, who may have influenced the creation of the character of Marcel (in *Claudine in Paris* and *Retreat from Love*): Marcel Boulestin, Jean Lorrain, Edouard de Max, and the marquis of Adelsward-Fersen.[45] She was engaged in removing all the guilt associated with perversion, a tendency that would express itself in *Those Pleasures . . . ,* reprinted in *The Pure and the Impure* (1932): "Can you live on tepidness? No more than on vice, and vice loses nothing thereby."[46]

In addition to homosexuality, it was a secret feminine jouissance with interchangeable objects, frantic with innocence and solitude, that fascinated Colette: she incarnated it, notably, in the character of Irène, the "hidden woman" who flees her husband not to betray him with someone else but to surrender, masked, to a ravaging autoerotic intoxication with various anonymous partners, with "no one."

> He was sure at present that Irène did not know the adolescent intoxicated with dance whom she was kissing, or the hercules; he was sure she was not waiting or looking for anyone and that, abandoning like a grape sucked dry the lips she held under her own, she was going to leave the next instant, to wander on, to pick up some other passerby, to forget him, and to taste, until it was time to feel weary and to go home, only the *monstrous pleasure of being alone,* free, truthful in her *native brutality,* the pleasure of being the stranger, forever alone and shameless, which a little mask

and a hermetic costume had returned to her irremediable solitude and her *dishonest innocence*.[47]

That superb description of the *other* jouissance is provided by a Colette who, through fictive means, walks hand in hand with Freud and Lacan when she does not anticipate them: had not Saint Teresa, in her ecstasy, already discovered that jouissance well before them?

Nevertheless, it is primarily incest that seems to interest the author:[48] after *Chéri* and *The Ripening Seed,* she almost admits it in *Break of Day.* Do we need to recall the backdrop for these texts, as it was reconstituted by Bertrand de Jouvenel himself? "All the same, the climate of scandal surrounding us would finally separate us. Are there good separations? [. . .] The pleasures she gave me were all those procured when the world opens to you, for which I was entirely indebted to her."[49] Their relationship was a scandal, but it opened up the world, in the words of the chief protagonist of that initiation. Is it because Colette took on the role of *author* of that pleasure, a pleasure that is also a deliverance? If she is the incestuous mother, she is nevertheless the one who brought Bertrand and probably herself as well "into the world."

The incestuous fantasy, as I have said, preceded the reality of the relationship between Colette and her husband's son by Claire Boas. The character of Léa is no dupe to the nature of the relationship she is pursuing with Chéri, the "wicked nursling" she had "adopted."[50]

We note that Colette, already the mother of a seven-year-old *girl,* describes in her novels a case of incest with a *boy.* She liked to praise her daughter's masculine features, her robustness rather than her seductiveness, before the presence of Maurice Goudeket gradually separated the two women.[51] It may have been incest/adoption, but, in her eyes, the relationship with Bertrand no doubt constituted an act of revenge that appeased her. Was that also the case for the relationship between Chéri and Léa? "Their long experience with each other made them silent, restored Chéri to inertness and Léa to serenity."[52] According to

Colette, the incestuous adventure revealed the radical strangeness of the two lovers: in transgressing the fundamental taboo, they could, it seems, assimilate their guilt only as "uncanniness." "It's funny," she confided, "at the end of that summer of nineteen-aught-six, in Berthellemy-de-Desséché, there were moments when I believed I was sleeping *with a nigger or a Chinaman*."⁵³ "But no confession rose from the curved mouth, and few words other than sulky or drunken reproaches, along with the name 'Nounoune,' which he had given her when he was little and which he now threw back at her from the depths of his pleasure as a call for help [. . .] and she added: 'I can't explain it to you,' unconcerned and inept at defining the confused and strong impression that she and Chéri *did not speak the same language*."⁵⁴

In the fiction, that identification of the shadow of death floating over the lovers is very self-analytical, except that its obsessive presence is due less to the age difference between the two partners than to the unconscious violence projected by their coupling onto the parental couple, which is condemned to death by the very logic of incest: "Forgive me, Chéri: I loved you as if we were both going to die within the hour. Because I was born twenty-four years before you, I was condemned, and I dragged you along with me."⁵⁵ And, until *The Other One* (1929), Colette remained haunted by that theme of imaginary incest between stepson and stepmother, which persists between the lines of the principal theme of that novel, centered on sublimated homosexual complicity of the "ego orgasm" type, between the two women—the wife, Fanny, and the mistress, Jane—of "Le Grand Farou": "She displayed toward her stepson a benevolence less particular than universal, coddling him as a mysterious emanation of Le Grand Farou."⁵⁶

In the same vein, let us note an article by Colette on a play depicting incest between a father and his (ultimately patricidal) daughter. "In the performance hall at the first intermission, I listened to the Pure in dialogue with the Impure: 'An infinitely distressing Subject. . . . Paternal incest. . . . Frankly, we might have been spared that. . . . ' 'Why? Is it such a serious thing, that a father lusts after his daughter? In nature. . . . ' And I was not bored because I believe that Pure and Impure were both lying."[57] This text came before the character of Old Binard, introduced in 1936[58] as a key piece of evidence in that investigation of the "pure and the impure," which extends well beyond the collection to which it would give its title in 1941. Echoing Sido's opinions, Colette insinuates that, in the animal universe to which "antelopes," that is, the daughters of Old Binard, belong, incest is no crime. But we know that the universe of antelopes was the very human universe that her brother Achille oversaw. It is not serious for a father to lust after his daughter; it is even less so if the lust emanates from the mother, since such is the violence of human desire, its inhuman truth. The writer expresses neither regrets nor remorse. Is Colette monstrous? Or are these disconcerting truths revealed by an unapologetic experimenter?

What remains of the sorrow and latent melancholy, which is still the hidden face of transgressive pleasure when it denies the dramas of disidentification, of separation from the mother? Colette conceals them so well that biographical studies devoted to her generally have nothing to say about them. The most striking, and probably the truest of her representations of the melancholic truth underlying the Krafft-Ebing-style explorations, describes the author at age twenty-nine or thirty (in 1902–1903, therefore, during an acute marital crisis), hardened as if under the effect of "petrifying sources," gnawed at by an internal "hemorrhage," but who has become rigid, like a crab's shell or a triumphant victim who has reached "the age where one no longer dies for anyone, or from anyone." The temptation of suicide is also mentioned, but obliquely, with reference to the woman who managed to divert the death drive. It is truly Sido, the tutelary goddess, who appears to us from the depths of her "other jouissance," Sido, that "purloined letter" of perverse jouissance, who makes suicidal melancholy impossible. Or is it, on the contrary, when one "sets aside" Sido that suicide is no longer a temptation? Colette is ambivalent. "I was far from invulnerable, but I did not imagine dying. With Sido alive, I never imagined voluntary death. Upon setting aside, as I am able, the idea of Sido, upon trying to imagine a youth without Sido,

I believe that suicide and I would never have tempted each other or eyed each other contemptuously."[59]

Nevertheless, suicide is almost announced in the title of another of Colette's novels, but it is that of a man: Fred Peloux, known as the Peloux boy, Léa's lover. In fact, *The End of Chéri* (1926) portrays the new postwar society where the dynamism of Chéri's young wife, Edmée, extinguishes all the desire and all the prospects of the Peloux boy. There is reason to despair in that new social context where young women become passionate about their professional lives, however superficial, rather than allowing themselves to be impressed by the "semi-incestuous collage"[60] of the Colettian hero. Hence Chéri, after attempting to find the shadow of Léa by taking refuge near her "pal," an old friend who cultivates a defaced memory of her, sinks into depression and ends his life: "He got worked up moaning out loud and repeating: 'Nounoune. . . . My Nounoune . . . ' to make himself believe he was out of his head. But he fell silent, ashamed, because he knew very well he did not need to go out of his head to pick up the flat little revolver on the table."[61]

Nevertheless, the new morality is not the only cause of that tragic end, and though it is true that Colette seizes this opportunity to explore a melancholic version of memory by depicting a hero who is overly complacent about a past that kills—in counterpoint to the infantile enthusiasm of *My Mother's House,* which revitalizes—the author's unconscious motives animating *The End of Chéri* may be more complex.

Apart from revenge on the fickle spouse, Colette's pen also targets the young man, morbidly attached to a false mother, excluded from time and, as a result, destined to die; but it is not so much the real figure of the incestuous son at which this settling of accounts (that is, *The End of Chéri*) lashes out. At that date the relationship with Bertrand was over, and Maurice Goudeket had already entered the writer's life. In fact, if we take into consideration Colette's many assertions regarding her virile identifications—for example: "My aim is true mental hermaphroditism, which fills certain highly organized beings. [. . .] 'Why do you not resign yourself to the idea that certain women represent, for certain men, a danger of homosexuality?' "[62]—we can interpret the character of Chéri as a masculine version of herself. Through the relationship with Léa, the narrator of course projects herself into that woman but also into Fred, and this complementary twist she traces in exploring the perverse relationship brings her face to face, in another way, with her phallic aspirations, their impossibility, their necessary failure.

She will be the man who satisfies the mother, granted—but which man? The father, an invalid and failed writer under his outward appearance of a hero/lover? The elder brother, Achille Robineau-Duclos, a courageous doctor who is so inextricably connected to his mother that he dies a year after Sido's death? The younger brother, Léo the "sylph," a charming failed musician, a soul tormented by his childhood memories, which he can share only with his sister and who, as a child, in games with his pals, accepted only "a silent role, that of 'idiot son' "?[63] Although it is likely that Colette was eager to "symbolically kill the son"[64] in writing *The End of Chéri,* he is also the *son she herself is* in her fantasy. Four years passed between *My Mother's House* (1922) and *The End of Chéri* (1926). The "analysis" through writing of the incestuous relationship was conducted without omitting any of the reversible roles in that adventure, and it led to its opposite, transgressive exaltation, its melancholic-suicidal underside. That journey was now complete. *Break of Day* (1928) and *Sido* (1929) could take their place in a reestablished serenity. Pure or impure, what remains of them? Who am I, if I am neither Léa nor Chéri? A torrent named "Sido," which is of no sex because it is of every sex, that of plants and that of beasts, with an inhuman, delicate, or aberrant sexuality. But is it sexuality or sensuality? Its only realization, its sublimated "acting out" in the orgasm of a polyphonic ego, will be writing.

Beyond the seductiveness of the works, Colette's complicity with the various aspects of perversion and the way she passes through them transmit a message to us with a psychoanalytic resonance: there is a suicidal depressivity, she seems to say in *The End of Chéri,* which results from woman's virile identification (I am Chéri) in her incestuous desire for the mother. Through her sexual and writing experience, Colette begins mourning that fantasy but without abandoning her adhesion to the maternal object or her phallic aspiration to dominate the other. But once the self-analysis is abreacted and written down, as we have just seen, her writing can continue to explore that economy while detaching itself from the Oedipal triangle and its substitutes to better posit itself in the world's flesh.

Of course the shadow of depressivity still threatens to fall on many heroines, and it had already cast a gloom over many evocations of the author's own life course, since, according to Colette, woman, "a surprising animal who partakes of the poet, the starling, and the perfect notary,"[65] often brushes against melancholy but does not really succumb to it. Take Minne, for example: "Her idle melancholy is amused, and the blood rises to her pale cheeks. Antoine is content."[66] In addition, it skirts "the real melancholy" of Maugis (Willy).[67] In *The Vagabond* Renée Néré is also not unfamiliar with it: "It seems to me rather that I attract and hold on to melancholics, loners condemned to reclusiveness or to the wandering life, like me. . . . Birds of a feather. . . ."[68] Consider as well Claudine, in conversation with Annie: "As for me, well, love has made me so rich, so filled with pleasures in my flesh, with torment in my soul, with all its irremediable and precious melancholy, that I don't really know how you can live near me without dying of jealousy!"[69] All these women are reflections of a little girl who was never really a child: "I got big, but I was never little. I never changed. I remember myself with a sharpness, a melancholy, that do not deceive me. The same dark and modest heart, the same passionate taste for everything that breathes the free air far from man—tree, flower, timid and meek animal, stealthy water from useless springs—the same gravity, quickly transformed into an exaltation without reason."[70]

Through these novel characters Colette's specific position, which is simultaneously, let us repeat, a psychic behavior *and* a style of writing, takes shape. If the writer Colette forges an art, it is not the art of excavating that pain, of unveiling it or transcending it—as the Scandinavian, English, and Slavic novel do in different ways—or a therapy. No, her heroines, even Julie de

Carneilhan[71] for example, know how to casually mask the sadness they feel. Colette prefers to repress the pain, to kill that killer despair, in order to build on its grave. "I also cry badly, as painfully as a man. But one masters oneself, provided one wants to. As soon as my training took hold, I abstained from crying almost completely. I have friends I've known for thirty years who have never seen a tear on my lashes."[72] *Exeunt* tears, *exeunt* certain pleasures: what matter! A mode of life has constituted itself, inseparable from the writing style, supported by the certainty that she never feels any lack whatever, that she always contains lost time and any eventual loss. There is no mourning; it is possible to possess everything in the style of sensory rememoration. "*What I lack, I do without,* and that's all, don't give me credit for it, no. . . . But once you've known something well by having truly possessed it, you're never wholly deprived of it."[73] The process of getting through depression, which is written about in *The End of Chéri* (1926), thus also includes its stifled denegation. Colette reaches the point of believing that that pain does not merit any consideration:

> It is no more venerable than old age and illness, for which I am acquiring a great repulsion: both will soon want to get a tight grip on me. In advance, I hold my nose. . . . The lovesick, the betrayed, the jealous must give off the same odor. I have a very clear memory of being less beloved of my beasts when I was suffering from a romantic betrayal. They picked up the scent of a major downfall: sorrow.[74]

From these two intersecting movements, the exploration of the slide toward suicide with *The End of Chéri* and the repudiation of that nauseating downfall, there results an unshakable faith in the psychic strength of women. A woman cannot die of sorrow and she knows how to transcend the intrinsic weakness that makes her so vulnerable to love—which Colette fears to the point of nipping it in the bud, and that she calls a "mediocrity":

> And then, I discovered that . . . I was just continuing to live alone. The training was of long date, beginning in my

childhood, and the early years of my marriage had only barely interrupted it: it had resumed, austere, hard to grieve, with the first marital infidelity, and that was the most commonplace part of my story. . . . How many women have experienced that retreat into themselves, that patient withdrawal that follows the outraged tears? I give them a nod while deluding myself: it is almost only in sorrow that a woman is capable of surpassing her mediocrity. [. . .] "She's dying of a broken heart. . . . She died of a broken heart. . . . " When you hear those clichés, shake your head with more skepticism than pity: a woman can hardly die of a broken heart. She is such a solid beast, so hard to kill! You believe sorrow is eating away at her? Not at all. Much more often she, born so ill and weak, acquires thereby hard-wearing nerves, an inflexible pride, an ability to wait, to dissimulate, that makes her grow, and the disdain of those who are happy. In suffering and dissimulation, she exerts herself and becomes supple, as through a daily gymnastics full of risks. . . . For she constantly skirts the most poignant, the sweetest, the most ornate temptation of all attractions: that of taking revenge.[75]

Far from some masochistic complacency toward women's suffering, there is a certainty here that such suffering can continue as such without being devastating. If that "mediocrity" targeted by Colette is truly a fundamental feminine depressivity, she points to the difficulty, even the impossibility, represented by a woman's losing her mother. The proof is that a woman desperately seeks, and in utter futility, her mother in a husband/lover who is "not even related" to her (said Sido). As a result the heterosexual couple is by definition a dubious, unreliable relationship and therefore destined to fail. An—imaginary—solution consists of never separating from that impossible loss, of carrying it like a hidden jewel, a sort of mock distress, by burying it in secret pleasures, *other* jouissances. Of course, over time, that mastery of the pain of separation will evolve, become sharper and more refined, but it is still searingly hot in 1908, when *Tendrils of the Vine* was published:

One goes out without aim, walks without reason, stops without fatigue. . . . One excavates with a foolish avidity the site of recent suffering, without managing to extract the drop of living and fresh blood from it—one picks desperately at a half-healed scar, one misses—I swear to you!—one misses the sharp clean burn. . . . That is the arid period of roving, further embittered by scruples. . . . Of course, scruples! The scruple of having lost the beautiful, passionate, quivering, despotic despair.[76]

Sure of herself and already victorious, having overcome that state of malaise, the Vagabond (from the 1911 novel by that name) is able to retort: "And he'll be able to ask me, in the voice of the master: 'Where are you going?' Female I was, and female I again find myself, to derive suffering and jouissance from it."[77] Then there is this lapidary formula:

You can be sure that a long patience and jealously hidden sorrows have formed, refined, hardened that woman of whom one exclaims:
　"She's made of steel!"
She's "made of woman," simply, and that is enough.[78]

Those Pleasures . . . (1932) portrays a weary and cunning woman: "The veiled face of a bright, disabused woman expert in deception, in delicacy, is well suited for the threshold of this book, which will speak sadly of pleasure."[79] Then Colette hurls this scathing remark at Juan-Damien, who wonders what women have really given him: "What they gave you? Their pain, I think. You're not so badly paid!"[80]

Against that endemic pain, and thanks to the force of the torrent of exaltation called "Sido," a serenity is finally preserved: a petrified sorrow, like a precious treasure, takes shelter there, the mute underside of solar joy; and, in the end, it is forgotten. The memory of the native land, "Sido," swallows up the sorrows of love and even has the magic to transform them into "happy love affairs": "A woman claims as many native lands as she has had happy love affairs. She is born as well under every sky where she recovers from the pain of loving."[81]

A single experience, also internal to the "Sido" torrent and extremely vital, continues to feed on pain and sometimes intensifies it: it is writing itself, perilous and disappointing, an exciting scar: "Again I take up my pen, to begin that perilous and disappointing game, to seize and fix, under the pliant double tip, the shimmering, the fleeting, the exciting adjective. . . . It's only a short crisis, the itching of a scar."[82]

In counterpoint to writing, when Sido's consecration is enunciated as a cult of plants or beasts, a hymn to happiness can finally be heard, even if human happiness is in reality an imposture (we shall return to this).[83] Beyond our passing sadness, and thanks to the subtle perversities at which animals excel, accompanied, naturally, by Colette and Sido, a certain happiness exists, and all the rest is literature: "Animals love happiness almost as much as we do. An attack of tears worries them, they sometimes imitate sobbing, they reflect our sadness for a short while. But they flee unhappiness the way they flee fever, and I believe them capable of banishing it in the long run."[84]

Nevertheless the evidence is crystal clear: the cosmic Sido was the beloved—of the Captain. To love Sido, in the sense of experiencing jouissance with her, of transubstantiating her, of writing her, implies occupying, for a time, the place of Captain Colette. Let us therefore hypothesize as follows: the true "purloined letter" of jouissance, according to the great Colette, is— with Sido and hidden by her—precisely, Jules-Joseph Colette. In fact, if the magic *object* of writing is named Sido, the *subject* of the writing we read, admire, discuss, is, in fact, named Colette, and she signs in capital letters—Colette! That female *first name* is none other than the paternal *patronymic*. That *other* jouissance covers a dark stain. The pain that lurks on the underside of the exaltation proper to writing has remained connected to the father; the name of the father holds the secret trace of it.

PAIN, OR COLETTE THE FATHER

The charming and rather ridiculous papa of the schoolgirl Claudine is a specialist in malacology, more attached to slugs than to his daughter. How could you expect that fanatic to have "a sense of fatherhood from seven o'clock in the morning until nine o'clock at night? He's the best and most tender man between two meals of slugs."[85] Having become a Parisian, Claudine further exclaims: "Because of the noble, rather lunatic father I have, I need a papa, I need a friend, a lover . . . God! A lover!"[86] It is therefore not surprising to learn that the primary mission of her husband, Renaud, is to replace that weird father, not surprising that he poses as a "paternal lover."[87] An ambiguous character as well—soft rather than hard, passive instead of authoritarian—Renaud, in his young wife's eyes, is more feminine than virile. "He loves me, that is beyond doubt, and more than anything. Thank god, I love him, that is also certain. But he's more of a woman than I am! I feel so much simpler, more brutal . . . darker, more passionate. [. . .][88] But he advances toward me with a swarthy face, traversed by a mustache lighter than the skin, softened by a feminine smile, and made so much more beautiful by a paternal love that I dare not. . . . "[89] In any case, the need for a father is felt so strongly that Claudine submits to him like a "beaten child": "Overwhelmed, I obstinately seek, in our past as young marrieds, a memory that can deceive me again, that will give me back the husband I *thought* I had. Nothing, I find nothing . . . except my own submission as a beaten child, and his smile of condescension without kindness."[90]

When Captain Jules-Joseph Colette died on September 17, 1905, Sido wrote to her daughter by her first marriage, Juliette: "I abandon the task of painting for you the immensity of my sorrow. With it I lose all well-being and independence." Colette and Willy, delayed by a flat tire, were not at the church, and Sido worried: "During the ceremony at the church I was absolutely frantic, I saw my children massacred under their automobile."[91] Already an expert at inuring herself to pain, Colette showed no sign of emotion that day: "I brought back with me my share of the paternal legacy: a ribbon from Crimea, a medal from Italy, an officer's rosette from the Legion of Honor, and a photograph";[92] and, from her father's funeral, she would keep only the memory of a "cheerful burial."[93] That same year, 1905, also marked her marriage settlement with Willy.

The Captain's resurrection in his daughter's writings would be slow and would come in the wake of Sido's gradual apparition. An exception is to be noted, however, with the text "A Zouave," published in two parts in Le Matin, on May 27 and June 10, 1915:[94] in the vigor of the portrait and the warmth of filial emotion, it precedes the still uncertain sketch of the maternal features, disseminated here and there,[95] which would crystallize only in My Mother's House (1922). World War I, during which Colette, the young wife of Henry de Jouvenel at the time, was mobilized as a journalist, apparently contributed to that precipitation of the Captain's traits into a war hero. That "soldier in love with battle [. . .] had left behind in Italy his entire left leg, cut off above the thigh, in Melegnano in 1859." He had even received a visit from Napoleon III in the hospital.[96] Colette would resume the account of his war exploits after resuscitating Sido: "Where do you want us to put you, my captain?" his soldiers asked anxiously when he was wounded on the battlefield. "In the middle of the piazza, under the flag!" he replied, deeply in love with his mission and his country. Nevertheless, he was very discreet, and "did not recount to any of his loved ones those words, that hour when he was hoping to die amid the thunder and the love of men."[97]

Thanks to his bravery, the invalid thus made his entry into literature. His resounding laugh pulverized any allusion to his amputation: "'It was at the hospital in Milan, wasn't it, that you got . . . '? 'Yes!' he exclaimed, preferring to designate that tragedy modestly, with the term 'necessary pruning.'" He lacked nothing, no more than his daughter did, and he rejected compassion: "It's not that I have a leg missing, it's that I used to have an extra one."[98] In his daughter's memory only good cheer and Italian songs characterized that cossack-headed zouave: "A singular modesty, or contempt for everything that brings illness and death, recommended the use of diminutives to him."[99] Once the wound had become a tenderness, the zouave would be transformed into a lover, but we will learn this only later: "Were we not worth, he and I, the mutual effort of getting to know each other better?"[100]

The image of the amputee father, even more painful because of its discretion, appears in *My Mother's House*: "I listen to that firm, steady rhythm of two staffs and a single leg, a rhythm that had soothed me throughout my youth, growing more distant.[101] [. . .] I followed in the stairwell his rapid amputee's step, that crow's hop that hoisted him from one stair to the next."[102] In *Sido* Colette reveals the Captain's silent suffering, which the daughter would be the only one to guess and that remained unthinkable for her mother: "[Sido] did not know, when she followed him with her eyes, that that amputee had once been able to run toward every danger."[103] But, above all, Colette makes this poignant confession of her own denied sadness: "It is never too late, since I have fathomed what my youth previously concealed from me: my brilliant, jolly father harbored the profound sadness of amputees. We were almost completely unaware that he was missing, cut off above the thigh, a leg."[104]

If amputation is a brutal symbol for castration, the female first name borne as a patronymic contributes no less, for the unconscious, to that father's feminization. Here is a man called Colette, who is perceived as subjugated to his wife by love and, in addition, who has had a leg amputated. Doctor Freud need not trouble himself, there is enough there to shatter the phallic image of the father who is supposed to incarnate the prohibition and the law. How, then, can we be surprised that Minet-Chéri, as if to intensify and ward off those traits, would develop a passion for a pervert like Willy and would take a great interest in *Psychopathia Sexualis*?

According to the image she wants to leave us of him, however, it is not the father's physical infirmity that sears the daughter most. At least, she manages to compensate for the paternal handicap, as the Captain himself does, by describing him endowed with powerful muscles: "He had great muscular strength, used sparingly and dissimulated in a feline manner, and no doubt he maintained it with a frugality that bewildered our Bas-Bourguignons."[105] That "feline force"[106] (could the Captain be Colette's first "cat-man"?) turns out to be all the more impressive in that it manifests itself through the hand and through anger and because both of these take paper, the writer's privileged tool, as their target. "The little girl" was not unaware of it: "His white hand cannot be lost to me, particularly since I now hold my thumb clumsily, facing outward like his, and since, like that hand, my hands crumple, roll up, annihilate paper with an explosive fury. And then there is anger . . . I shall not speak of my fits of anger, which I got from him. But just go see, in Saint-Sauveur, the state to which my father, with two kicks of his only foot, reduced the mantelpiece of the marble fireplace."[107] The quick-tempered might and Mediterranean fury of Colette-the-father naturally elicited Sido's disapproving fascination: "Italian! . . . Man-with-a-knife!"[108] Conversely, the daughter admires the athletic elegance of that virility, and would constantly seek out his delicate skin in all her lovers and husbands: "He resigned himself to taking a little meat as a remedy after the age of seventy. That southerner, a sedentary man, completely white in his satin skin, never got fat."[109]

The incestuous harmonics with the father accumulate in Colette's pages and impose the image of a seductive Captain, a lover of women, a good singer with a charming bawdiness: "Who, then, could have believed that that baritone, still agile on his crutch and cane, would exhale his sentimental song like a white breath of winter, so that it would turn the attention away from him?"[110]

But, apart from Sido, it is his own daughter that Colette the father carried in his heart, notwithstanding every other female conquest, real or imaginary. Did she really not know that in her early childhood? "As a child, what did I know about him? That he built me delightful 'June bug houses' with windows and glass doors, and also boats. That he sang. That he dispensed—and hid—color crayons, white paper, Brazilian rosewood rulers, gold dust, and thick white bars of sealing wax, which I ate by the handful. That he swam with his only leg faster and better than his four-limbed rivals."[111] Apparently, the daughter was his favorite: "He refused to acknowledge his own carefree musical fancies in his son, 'the lazzarone,' as my mother called him. It was me he granted the most importance. I was still little when my father began to appeal to my critical sense."[112] Was her astonishment feigned when she discovered that attachment? "But now letters from him (I learn twenty years after his death) are full of my name, of the 'little one's' illness."[113] We will remember this when we find her again, tenderly submissive to the "paternal vice" of Willy, a great lover of "tender shoots."

Captain Colette, a poet, city dweller, and fervent lover of Sido, is the exact opposite of his cosmic wife. In the first place, his "scandalous [. . .] sociability [. . .] drew him to politics."[114] The daughter's disapproval of the zouave would only grow after she became the baroness de Jouvenel: Sidi would know something about that. Above all, the Captain did not understand nature. Did he not stubbornly insist on Sunday picnics, even though Sido and her children, who ran wild, did not care for them, immersed as they were, night and day, in the grass, the woods, the flowers. "He loved them in books, told us their scientific names, and outdoors passed by them without recognizing them. . . . He praised any blossoming corolla, bestowing the name 'rose' on it; he pronounced the *o* short, in the Provençal manner, pinching, between his thumb and index finger, an invisible 'roz' . . . [115] [. . .] She added, so as not to hurt him: 'Yes, you see, you hold out your hand to find out if it's raining.'"[116]

That man who kept quiet about his military exploits[117] is passionate about everything written. He displays an ostentatious, boisterous passion for newspapers and books, and collects pens and wax seals, which, over time, would also become a passion for his daughter.[118] In *My Mother's House,* the invalid is associated in the daughter's memory with his library:

My father does not insist, agilely stands up on his only leg, grabs his crutch and cane, and goes upstairs to the library.

Before heading up, he meticulously folds the newspaper *Le Temps,* hides it under the cushion of his wing chair, buries *La Nature* with its azure wrapper in a pocket of his long overcoat. His little Cossack eyes, sparkling under gray flax eyebrows, swipe from the tables every piece of printed provender, which will go straight to the library and will never again see the light of day.[119]

The father's bungling would be unveiled only in *Sido*: Colette slowly lays the foundation for the painful discovery, after her father's death, of a writer without works.

On one of the high shelves of the library, I see again a series of bound tomes with black canvas backs. The nicely sized covers of mottled paper and the rigidity of the binding attested to my father's manual skill.[120] [. . .] Two hundred, three hundred, five hundred pages per volume: beautiful cream laid paper or thick "exercise paper," carefully trimmed, hundreds and hundreds of blank pages. . . . An imaginary work, the mirage of a writing career.[121]

She does not feel pity for him or get a laugh at his expense: she accepts her father's impotence with fraternal understanding— fraternal because bound up with the pain of that impotence and quickly gone—by imposing the failure's name on the pantheon of letters.

In fact, confronted with the chasm of that failure, it is not a shocked woman but a secretly delighted one who contemplates the Captain's blank pages. Sido, for her part, adopts a similar vengeful attitude and gently makes fun of him by covering jars of jam, her own works that she produces for her children and grandchildren, with her husband's useless sheets. Conversely, in these sheets Colette the daughter grounds her determination to persevere in her efforts at writing, first undertaken in Willy's workshop: she will make good on the Captain's dedication, realizing the works he had merely planned as a tribute to Sido and of which he could trace only a few lines:

I too drew from that immaterial legacy when I was starting out. Is it there I acquired the sumptuous taste for writing on smooth sheets, with good tooth, and of not being frugal with them? I dared cover with my large round handwriting the invisible cursive, whose luminous watermark only one person in the world perceived, a watermark that carried off to glory the only lovingly completed and signed page, the dedication page:

> To my dear soul,
> her faithful husband
> JULES-JOSEPH COLETTE[122]

It would be an ingenious accomplishment, but it meant that the daughter preserved within herself the amputee's anxiety and the fear of never succeeding, of never finishing that always exhausting labor[123] of writing, of which, as her friends know, she continually complained: "I advance little, I advance poorly—I advance. But it is terrible to think, as I do, every time I begin a book, that every time I no longer have, or never had, any talent."[124] To the end Colette would be haunted by the specter of the Captain who imposes, on one hand, the "large-limbed" need to write—"I pound into you, I grope toward your presence"— and, on the other, the threat of impotence. She fears she is like him and is wary of that "ultimate indifference, which hardly plucked from my father, Jules-Joseph Colette, anything more than scraps of easy versification, gleaming with banality. [. . .] Yes, he is there. Whatever I do, whatever I undertake and whatever my sly abstentions, he is there."[125]

The discovery of the blank pages left by the Captain is so spectacular, in fact, that we can only imagine the trauma and the compensatory, reparative decision that followed them. Nevertheless, diffuse, ever-present signs were to allow Colette-the-daughter to guess the weakness of Colette-the-father, a would-be writer, as well as the unconscious will and testament he bequeathed: let *it* come to pass! But through whom? Through his first and severe literary critic, his ten-year-old daughter?

The Captain trusted her to read his "oratory prose, or an ode, light verse, sumptuous in their rhythm, their rhyme, sonorous as a mountain storm." He was confidently awaiting the judgment he hoped would be favorable, when, suddenly, the verdict came down from insolent youth: "There's still too many adjectives,"[126] judged Colette-the-daughter. The writer, who at that moment was Colette-the-father, turned bright red with anger and assailed the future great Colette with invectives, "vermin, conceited louse that I was." The scene, however Oedipal—in reverse, since the girl, like a boy, "murdered" papa's writing—was nonetheless formative: the daughter's theatrical love for the father and his true-false anger paved the way for her feeling of guilt toward the amputee, a failed writer and, already, for the little girl's commitment (with the help of the later discovery of his empty records) to the writer's fate. Let us first recall this daughter-father complicity, which Sido does not suspect:

> Unknown, misunderstood. . . . "Your incorrigible good cheer!" exclaimed my mother. It was not a reproach, but astonishment. She believed he was cheerful because he sang. I who whistle whenever I am sad, I who mark the pulsing of fever or the syllables of a devastating name in the endless variations on a theme, I wish she had understood that the supreme offense is pity. My father and I do not accept pity. Our robustness rejects it. At present, I torment myself because of my father, since I know he had the virtue, better than any seductiveness, of being sad judiciously and of never betraying himself.
>
> Apart from the fact that he often made us laugh, that he told stories well, that, carried away by the rhythm, he boldly "embroidered," apart from the melody that rose up from him, did I see him as cheerful? He went about preceded, protected by his song.[127]

Very explicitly, Colette traces her vocation as a writer back to the Captain, suggesting that these first skirmishes with papa around the question of style initiated the actual transmission of the "lyrical" talent for which Willy would reproach her. Yet she would know how to preserve it, all the while refining it in the extreme, forging for herself—thanks more to that condensed lyricism than to the triangular plots of her narratives—the glory for which she was henceforth known.

> From the first moment, we eyed each other as equals, already brothers. It was he, let there be no doubt, it was he who dominated me when music, a dance spectacle—and not words, never words!—brought tears to my eyes. It is he who wanted to come to light, and to live again, when I began, dimly, to write, and who won me the most acerbic conjugal praise—definitely the most useful: "Could I have married the last of the lyric poets?"[128]

Finally, she reunites papa and mama and recognizes her debt to both, together and separately: "My father's lyricism, my mother's humor and spontaneity, all mingled and superimposed: I am wise enough at present, proud enough as well, to sort them out inside me, entirely happy with a split where I don't have to be ashamed of anyone or anything."[129]

After a few very revealing hesitations in her drafts, Colette adds that it is to her father that she owes the nickname (Provençal or Persian?—she wonders dreamily) "Bel-Gazou," which she transmits to her own daughter: a formal anointing, if one were needed, of the Captain as patriarch of the entire line. "Bel-Gazou. Where does that name come from, and why did my father give it to me long ago? It is probably patois and Provençal for beautiful prattle, beautiful language, but it would not be amiss for the hero or heroine of a Persian tale."[130] The two proper names Colette forged, her nom de plume and the term of endearment she gave her daughter, are signifiers attributable to the father Colette. Meanwhile, Sido, who for her part had no difficulty writing, allows herself to be embraced every which way. Moreover, it is after the name "Colette" is mentioned three times in *My Mother's House* (1922),[131] as a designation for both the father and the daughter, that the writer definitively adopts the patronymic Colette as her nom de plume, in 1923 (abandoning "Colette Willy" and "C. de Jouvenel").

In fact, and more insidiously, what sparks that competition and finally transforms the "father's lyricism" into a jewel of French literature under the signature "Colette" is nothing other than jealousy. From Colette-the-father came both the outbursts of anger and the demon of "jealousy, which used to make me so uncomfortable."[132] Or so she believed. Is it the father's jealousy, or the daughter's jealousy of the father *and* of the mother? That man, who once risked his life in battle, now disabled, "remained at 'Sido's' side. Love and nothing else. . . . He had kept only her. Around them, the village, the fields, the woods—desert."[133]

We can believe Colette when she reconstitutes her antecedents in that way. In fact, a love so extreme for mama can only stir, along with jealousy, the girl-boy's fervent desire to conquer that definitive object of paternal love, so ardently desired, but who very obviously maintains her reserve. This is especially true since Sido, according to her daughter, does not neglect to signify her superiority to the Captain: does she not possess her children, whereas he simply wishes to be like them—a child of his wife? "Because you represent what he wanted so much to be on earth. You are precisely what he wished to be. *He* couldn't."[134] But, above all, Sido reaches the point of disavowing that "great love," which nevertheless does honor to her, since she sees it as the very cause of the Captain's failure, the failure of that poor soul who preferred to love a woman rather than construct a body of work: "It is his love for me that annihilated, one by one, all his sharp faculties, which might have pushed him toward literature and the sciences. He preferred to think only of me, to worry about me, and that is what I found inexcusable. Such a great love! What frivolousness!"[135] That's an error not to be committed. At least that is how the daughter interprets it. As a result, it is up to her to live completely differently from the zouave, to write Sido as M. Colette could not have done. That project can transform you into a great woman—the great Colette.

THE METAMORPHIC BODY:
PLANTS, BEASTS, AND MONSTERS

More than to any other vital manifestation, my whole life I have
looked to flowerings. It is in them that, for me, the essential drama lies,
better than in death, which is only a commonplace defeat. [. . .]
The hour never sounds on the end of discoveries. The world is new
to me at my awakening each morning and I will stop flowering
only when I stop living.

—Colette, message to viewers at the evening première of her film
The Ripening Seed (January 20, 1954)

" . . . MY OLD SUBTLE SENSES"

The sexuality deployed in the pages of Colette inhabits the
strange body of that woman, which is born and reborn under the
writer's pen.

Exquisite, inhuman, reckless, maniacal, ferocious, contagious?
Colette's writing imposes a paradoxical body—the metamorphic
body—on our reading and on our desires. Without sexual identity, neither human nor something else but amalgamated to all
identities and setting them all ablaze, it metamorphoses endlessly, permuting roles, desolidifying rifts and barriers, and expanding boundlessly to the dimensions of the cosmos itself. It could
be a cosmic body, in fact, if the cosmos were a transfer of ener-
gies, of elements, of provisional states. What captivates the
Vagabond is never allowed to become fixed, since it is in *passing*

that it finds its rhythm and, in that perpetual slippage, its mode of being: no prohibition arrests that porous shifting from same to other, from normal to deviant, from stage to performance hall, from faun to mummy, from precious stone to water, from glass to grass, from animal to child and from child to adolescent, from man to woman and vice versa. That body, disidentified, transferential, everywhere and nowhere, *exists* because it *is articulated* in a privileged language, that of metaphor: not metaphor as substitution but metaphor as *gesture* of contradiction and tension, as *metamorphosis*.[1] If it is further endowed with an exuberant sexuality, it is only because it accomplishes its dissemination thanks to an extravagant sensoriality. In fact Colette's writing is not focused on the organs, even less on the sexual organs. For her *all the senses are sexual organs,* differing from our ordinary perception only in the respect that, at the very instant she experiences the elements, the elements also experience her: loving/loved, subject/object, she describes a giant orgasm of feeling *and* felt. The barriers among the five senses, like the threshold between intimate perception and external reality that lies behind them, are posited only to be transcended. They are catwalks, never boundaries: "Some part of me suspends itself from everything I pass through—new regions, pure or cloudy skies, seas under rain the color of gray pearl—and clings so passionately to them that it seems to me I am leaving behind a thousand little ghosts in my likeness, rolling on the wave, cradled on the leaf, dispersed in the cloud. . . . But does not a last little ghost, the one most like me, remain seated in my spot by the fireplace, dreamy and quiet, bent over a book it forgets to read?"[2] Similarly, when she prides herself on her lack of literary vocation in her childhood, Colette does not so much deny her destiny as a writer as celebrate her sensory presence of being immersed in a prelanguage. Far removed from the rigors of expression, this is an avidity, a sensual mobility, a harmony with what language is not, but which it absorbs through feeling. "Therefore, I was truly the only one of my species, the only one brought into the world not to write. What sweetness I was able to taste with such a lack of literary vocation! My childhood and my free and solitary adolescence, protected from the worry of expressing myself, were both engaged solely in directing their subtle antennae toward what is contemplated, listened to, touched, and inhaled."[3]

Acting, mime, and dance marvelously suit these intimate pleasures, though they are offered to the gaze of others; they combine narcissistic withdrawal and maximum seductiveness, solitude and omnipotence. In the first place, between 1906 and 1912, there were music hall numbers, of which we know little more than what Colette tells us in *Music-Hall Sidelights* (1913), followed by her performances as a dramatic actress, which ended only in 1926, when for the last time she played the title role in *The Vagabond,* in Monte Carlo, opposite Paul Poiret. Although she later castigated herself as a "music hall failure,"[4] and though some deplored her "sad exhibitions" or called her performance "childish when compared to that of an intelligent career actress," critics praised her "ease, her grace, the suppleness of her movements," and recognized she had "a physical originality of expression." I am inclined to share the enthusiasm of Louis Delluc, who admired her combination of "shamelessness" and "naïveté": "something chaste" and "avidly sensual" must have come through in Colette's body on stage. She hints at this when she claims that *Music-Hall Sidelights* is the book in which she "nowhere needed to tell lies."[5]

When she insists on denouncing the illusion of these displays, which are only cover-ups for her shabby appearance, her aim is not so much to criticize the world of the spectacle as to reveal that the pleasures of her "playful" metamorphic body are inseparable from the "torments" (hunger, thirst, cold, fatigue, sadness) that "prevent you from thinking." But, above all, they expose the actress who is thereby depersonalized to the plasticity of her own body, which is the true subject and object of her writing. Theater brings all these paradoxes together: person, nonperson, body, subject, object, writing. Was it a further challenge to bourgeois morality to represent, in variety shows in the early part of the twentieth century, that "great parade of prostitutes" and to participate in "something like the congress of whoredom"? Or rather, on the contrary, as she contends, countering the rumors that seek to compromise her, was the music hall her very personal way of entering a "modern convent"?[6] I like to think that the stage was the best refuge for the blossoming of her metamorphic body, in the end, since it was disappropriated there—nothing but gestures and roles. In taking the stage, Colette leaves the fixed place of a spectator "grown rigid from fatigue" and "defensive pride" and becomes a Bacchante. "Yes I will dance again on stage, I will dance nude or clothed for the sheer pleasure of dancing, of matching my gestures to the rhythm of the music, of veering, scorched by the light, blinded like a fly in a sunbeam."[7] Had she been "forced" to do pantomime, as Annie lamented in *The Retreat from Love*?[8] In any case, there was nothing "forced" about the autoerotic intoxication of her orgiastic wedding celebration with the public: " 'I did not see the audience,' she said simply. 'They made it dark in the hall. The footlights had a tight grip on my forehead. I heard, felt a warm breath, a movement of invisible beasts, deep in that yawning darkness.' "[9] There she tasted a pleasure that "was not solely physical" but "an imperious pleasure of anxiety and expectation, the pleasure, if I may say so, of a rendez-vous."[10]

Her experience on the stage was apparently a "rendez-vous" with her offered, metamorphic body, as she waited for an indefinite, infinite encounter with a lover, an experience that made visible the profound logic of that other *rendez-vous* Colette never abandoned: writing. Through mime and theater she sought a physical and rhythmic writing and a gesture of meaning also found in her books, which make her savory style something more than mere literature. Did she want to "exhibit herself" when she played a role in *Chéri* after writing it? Certainly—but there are other reasons.

The body deployed in that way is nevertheless neither "hysterical" nor "perverse": in passing through perversion, it takes on the voyeuristic, exhibitionist, or incestuous desires that, when they become entrenched in the unconscious, disable the hysteric's body. Furthermore, for Colette, the metamorphic body's acting out is an obligatory phase leading her from sensations to the most precise words, so that these words can swallow up her members and her sex organs themselves and can finally assume their place. Exhibition is then only a *station* in the journey of sublimation. One of the most dazzling executions of the metamorphic body can be seen in the impressionistic tableau Colette draws of the women's bodies at the music hall:

> These plumes, which may be seaweed, that atmosphere green as pure water, these portraits by masters from which the painted model, suddenly stepping out of the frame, escapes with its life . . . these acrobats who throw, catch in flight, then throw again an airy young woman . . . these blocks, these walls of women veined with red, blue, and white spangles, feminine materials that have no face but are only dazzling volumes, this vast and unctuous play of three colors, each blending into the others, each eating away at the others, each receiving, then returning, its reflection to the others—all this is the very essence of the great music hall.[11]

What a superb metamorphosis of the colors of the French republic into a carnal kaleidoscope! Might there also be, for Colette, a "politics" of the body? A sensual politics, an irony, in short, full of verbal acrobatics?

Narrative does not suit the metamorphic body, which is located beyond the footlights, is without barrier and without prohibition. As for the ordeals that bring narrative plots to their climax, Colette has none left to overcome or describe. In fact, stories and novels illustrate an Oedipal logic, that of forbidden desires and murders that require battles and, as a result, heroes. The metamorphic body, for its part, is not unaware of that logic but, unrepentantly incestuous, it also does not stop there. It has been hypothesized that, in humans, *narrative* is as original as *syntax*: as soon as the infant articulates an echolalia directed at his mother, that incantation may already be a sentence (a particular melody might mean: "I want Mama") but also a fantasy ("I eat Mama"), which betrays a conflict, an ordeal, the pursuit of an aim, a satisfaction, or a frustration. In other words, every sentence is a fantasy, and every fantasy, a narration.[12] Nevertheless, certain subjects prefer to modulate these omnipresent sentences and narratives into dazzling executions of the instant but without becoming fixed in the pose of a poet. More than a *pleasure* with precise objects as its aim, it is the *joy* that overflows and ex-centers them: that ek-static jubilation lies behind a poetics of the fragment in which the union with a torrent and that with a woman, a man, or a cat assume the same importance.

The *ego-source* that writes its polymorphic dissemination is the true object of her exaltation of love: for it, there are no *others,* no inassimilable "different one." Writing traces an avidity that loves itself speaking of love. A voracious *ego* thus asserts itself, pulverized at the four cardinal points, which it appropriates in its metaphorical-metamorphic enunciation. The boundaries between the loving "subject" and the "object" of love blur; love itself is eclipsed in a magnetization, a dispersion-appropriation-formulation that constitutes the metamorphic body and its polymorphous sensations. Colette describes it as a "possession," as "inexorable," and as her "only way" of being while "embracing" beings: "Like the sight of what I love—my friend's beauty, the sweetness of the forests of Fresne—Renaud's desire elicits the same emotion in me, the same hunger for possession and embraces! [. . .] Have I, then, only one way of feeling?"[13] Hypersensitive and possessive, that *ego* is reborn, makes-unmakes-remakes itself in a moiré of ambiguities combining jouissance and suffering, which abolishes the literary and narrative time of ordeals and erects itself into the verticality of the polymorphous instant-space. Its time is sequenced into a series of instants—but instants spaced out ad infinitum, weaving the giant expanse with every transference of identity imaginable. The passage of time, the cycle of the seasons, the round dance of passions that flower and die, allow themselves to be played out in multiple opposing and reciprocal scenes. Cascading perceptions transform the philosopher's "time toward death" into a mosaic of sensory focal points: to the end of her life, Colette described herself as a writer "aided" "by the faithful memory of her brain and of her old subtle senses."[14]

In fact, according to Colette, memory arrests time in places and in phenomena, amplifies it in Claudine's houses and Sido's gardens, in butterflies and herbaria, flora and pomona, dialogues of beasts and other breaks of day. All are objects of her senses and become confused, not under the reign of a single sense but, rather, in her words, which give sense to the senses and where

> a powerful arabesque of flesh, a cipher of tangled members, a symbolic monogram of the Inexorable [frolics]. . . . In that word, the Inexorable, I gather together the cluster of forces which we knew to name only as "senses." The senses? Why not the sense? That would be modest, and sufficient. *The sense*: five other subsenses venture away from it, and it calls them back with a jolt—like the light and stinging ribbons, half-grass, half-arm, delegated by an undersea creature.[15]

Taste, in the literal and figurative sense, dominates Colette's polymorphic body. Her avidity is, in the first place, gourmandise, the pleasures of the mouth: raw garlic, chocolates, legs of lamb and rabbits, simmered dishes, bucolic banquets. Flavors provide a bed for words. Writers may be fundamentally, insatiably oral, and a few great smokers and asthmatics in the pantheon of letters reveal the guilt involved. Conversely, behind the naturalness of a regional cook, Colette embraces oral pleasure with an insolent jubilation: "What is the source of my violent taste for rural wedding suppers? What ancestor bequeathed to me, through such frugal parents, that quasi-religion of sautéed rabbit, of leg of lamb with garlic, of soft-boiled eggs with red wine, all served between the walls of a barn covered with unbleached sheets, on which the red rose of June, fastened to them, glimmers?"[16] Gourmets take pleasure in inventorying Colette's recipes; cookbooks have been inspired by her.[17] Let us mention at least a few of these infinite orgies of the mouth, highlights of the Colettian pilgrimage.

Let us begin with that stupefying child's snack, which would scandalize, or make salivate, more than one modern mother, as well as any writer in love with fresh words and intoxicating rhythms:

A slice of brown bread a foot long, cut straight from the twelve-pound round loaf, its crust peeled off, rolled and crumbled like semolina on the scratched wooden table, then drowned in fresh milk; a big white gherkin marinated for three days in vinegar and a cubic decimeter of pink bacon, without streaks; finally, a pitcher of hard cider with "cinnamon," drawn from the barrel . . . How does that menu strike you? It was one of my snacks as a child. Do you want another?[18]

Let us consider the truffle, a refined food, but, above all, an ecological murderer for Colette: "Bite into the gem of poor soils while imagining—if you have never visited it—its desolate kingdom. For it kills the wild rose, sucks the blood from the oak, and matures under a barren rock."[19] The truffle is to be sampled as follows:

Steeped in very dry good white wine—keep the champagne for banquets, the truffle can easily do without it—not overly salted, tactfully peppered, it will cook in a covered black stew pan. For twenty-five minutes it will dance at a constant boil, dragging along in an eddy and froth—like Tritons playing around a black Amphitrite—about twenty pieces of lardon, half fat, half lean, which give substance to the cooking. No other spices![20]

Let us end with "kicked fish." In this case, you eat a ritual, the fire of hell itself transmuted into paradise:

Prepare your broom, as I call the odorous bouquet of bay leaf, mint, *pebredaï,* thyme, rosemary, and sage, which you have tied together before lighting your fire. So prepare your broom, that is, let it soak in a pot filled with the best olive oil mixed with wine vinegar—here we allow only mild pink vinegar. Garlic—you naïvely thought you could do without it?—crushed to the consistency of cream, enhances the mixture properly. Not much salt, enough pepper.

Careful. Your fire is now almost nothing but embers. [...] That's the moment to give a colossal kick [...] and the whole thing is planted upright, in the midst of hell.[21]

We must be grateful to Colette for revealing the secret source of that oral fixation, which will not let go of her her whole life, threatening to make her fat late in life when other pleasures become dormant. If we are to believe her, it goes back to two women, Sido's seductive stand-ins, but more playful and cruel than she. First, there is Adrienne, a neighbor who was breast-feeding her son when Sido was nursing her daughter: the two women "exchanged their infants one day, for fun." And the great Colette blushed again, haunted by "Adrienne's brown breast and its hard violet nipple."[22] So there is another Mama, Adrienne in the place of Sido, well before Missy. That is not all. The oral pleasures will encompass the full palette only with the "disloyal" Mélie, her nurse:

The guilty, disloyal one, my nurse, Mélie, seated on one of those chairs, opened her blouse and delivered her unrivaled breast, white and blue as milk, pink as the strawberry called *Belle-de-juin*. I came running, agile on my sixteen-month-old legs, and leaned in on my elbows, standing on her knees, disdaining to sit down, since, Mélie assured me, I was nursing "like a grownup." . . . Horrors! She had tainted that breast, that peak visited by the dawn, with mustard! . . .

It was not the burning on my lips that made me cry such a long time. It was because, in the face of my tears, Mélie, my slave, source of my greatest happiness, throwing back her white, beautiful blonde's neck younger than her sunburned face, Mélie, twice a traitor, was laughing.[23]

Nevertheless, since nothing is simple for Colette, Papa, as we have seen, also gets involved in his daughter's orality and gallantly completes the education of her taste buds by having her drink, while she was still very young, cooked wine: "I was very well brought up. As the first piece of evidence for such a categorical affirmation, I will say that I was no more than three years old when my father gave me a full liqueur glass of bronze wine to drink, sent from his native Midi: muscatel de Frontignan. Sunstroke, voluptuous shock, illumination of the brand-new taste buds! That anointing made me forever worthy of wine."[24]

Taste, the most intimate of our senses, begins with a risky advance toward the other: the need to breathe, to drink, to eat; and ends with a retreat into oneself to ferment, to sample, to analyze that booty. Taste, a cannibalistic dependence, of course, is nevertheless at the origin of our discernment; it is even the true embryo of judgment.[25] Taste, apparently an act of approaching the other, an apprenticeship in sharing if ever there was one, is nonetheless, and immediately, devoured by the very intimacy that is initiated with it and continues to distill its joys and its pains in a cannibalistic pleasure. Through taste I appropriate the other, assimilate it. When the archaic oral sense becomes civilized taste, culinary culture, and, even more noble, aesthetic judgment, taste places my intimate cannibalism within the gaze of others but remains no less convinced that it is the transmitting and supreme center of any relationship.

In a civilization of egoists who vie with one another over taste—the French excel at it just as much as the Chinese or the Italians—social life is an ordeal among Narcissuses who pit their singular tastes against each other in long hard battles before extracting a "general spirit" supposed to calm them. The community that results is in fact only an accord of tastes, and people prefer to forget the skirmishes that led to it, in order to celebrate only the shared pleasure, now supposed to be universal. If I write taste, that of my mouth or of my aesthetic preferences, I push its devouring logic to its extreme: I appropriate the shared object that I claim to sample with the reader, I capture it through the creation of a language of my own. Fed on my sensations, this language contaminates the object, assimilates it by confining it in my own sensory experience, before I bind the reader himself within the range of my pleasures, the rhythm of my words, a sovereign trap in which I force my two preys to brew—the world I eat and the reader I devour.

Colette is the superb creator of a language of taste: once the object is swallowed, the reader digested, the ego feeds on its words, and style is only the written face of its eating pleasure—the good breast, mustard included, fully assimilated at last. Hence taste may inevitably punctuate the metaphor of sleepless nights that the writer spends next to Missy. Moving through sight (a butterfly), touch combined with hearing (a breeze brushes against me, but it is already relished like an acid), an avalanche of lime, walnut, and sage leaves, the extended metaphor of sleep finally blossoms into a pungent sap and the taste of citronella:

> Sleep approaches, brushes against me, and flees. . . . I see it! It is like that butterfly of thick velvet I pursued in the garden blazing with iris. . . . You remember? What light, what impatient youth stirred that whole day! . . . An acidic and urgent breeze cast a mist of rapid clouds over the sun, wilted as it passed over the tender leaves of the lime tree, and the flowers of the walnut fell like burnt caterpillars onto our hair, with the mauve blossoms of the Paulownias the color of a rainy Parisian sky. . . . The shoots of the blackcurrant you bruised, wild sorrel forming a rose window in the lawn, the very young, still brown mint, the sage, downy as a hare's ear—everything overflowing with an energetic and pungent sap, which I combined, on my lips, with the taste of alcohol and citronella . . . [. . .] You have given me the defenseless flowers.[26]

Necessarily, naturally, it is on that palate, in my voracious mouth, that the words live: Colette the musician, who continually hears herself writing, is also an eater of her words; she rolls them on her gourmand's tongue. Even though writing entails periods of "mental block," of "annihilation" that offers a "perfect resemblance, I think, to what must be the beginning of a death," it remains a "gourmet" pleasure, attentive to the "noise of erosion that the search for a word produces [. . .] better, and better than better," which offers "fresh word fodder" to the idea.[27]

More airy, more refined than ravenous, and exalted many times over, the *olfactory sense* is, according to Colette, "the most aristocratic of our senses."[28] That judgment does not necessarily contradict her appreciation of taste as "the most uncivilized of [her] senses": "No doubt I did not properly convey my thought, which has not changed, and I meant to say that I perceived the vast autumn, insidiously hatched, issued forth from the long days of June by subtle signs with the aid, above all, of the most un-civilized of my senses, which is the olfactory."[29] She often privi-leged that "olfactory of [her] memory" because it favored the necessary transition between acting body and invisible memory, which is supposedly the camera oscura of our thoughts: "A child's attention obeys the most experienced of her senses. Al-ready mine was smell."[30]

> Legs hanging over a bench, and wobbly with sleep, weary of learning by heart the excerpts, misprints, transposed characters, digressions cut out of newspapers and pinned to the wall, weary of following a half-dream through a haze that moved heavily, in horizontal layers, around the lamp-shades burned by gas and pieced back together with yel-lowed paper, weary of not having had supper, weary of hav-ing had supper, so much weariness fixed the odor, in the olfactory of my memory, of tobacco, thick ink, and the beer brought by a boy, the five "half-pint" handles clasped in one hand.[31]

Shored up by a generalized synesthesia, where the visible is heard, the olfactory touched, sounds tasted, and so on and vice versa, Colette's metamorphic body experiences a season by breathing it in: a night of December is described as "a fresh cemetery scent."[32] And the author takes pleasure in praising the most subtle of judgments, knowing how to distinguish odors, identifying with a dog's sense of smell: "Do you even know how to sort out three or four odors, mingled, woven together, blended: one of a mole, one of a hare who sped by, another of a bird who has gone to sleep?"[33]

Colette was not unaware that that refinement of the olfactory sense stemmed from an equally excessive anal sensitivity, and the writer did not neglect to associate the adjective "excremental" with the perception of scents:

—Kiki-la-Doucette: "Unlike you, I do not have strictly excremental thoughts. The valerian . . . you can't comprehend. . . . I saw her, Her, having emptied a flute of fetid wine that splashed up dangerously, laugh and become delirious the way I do over the valerian . . . The dead frog, so dead it seems to be dried morocco in the shape of a frog, is a sachet permeated with an unusual musk, with which I would like to scent my fur." [34]

This is not a psychoanalyst speaking, just a cat making fun of a dog.

As for the very ritual of writing itself, we have seen how much it owes to the paternal obsessions from which odors, precisely, are far from absent: a "stick of green wax" incarnates that religion of scribes, a symbol no less phallic than odorous. "One day my mother brought me a little stick of sealing wax, and I recognized the piece of green wax, the jewel of my father's desk. . . . No doubt I judged the present disproportionate, since I did not shout for joy. I squeezed the wax in my hand, where, as it warmed up, it gave off a slightly Oriental scent of incense."[35]

Colette, a pianist who meditates before playing,[36] has a keen sense of hearing and grounds *listening* both in the loftiest abstraction and in the most primitive moods. Listening is, in the first place, an intellectual labor: "Listening is an application that ages the face, tires the neck muscles, and stiffens the eyelids by requiring that one hold one's eyes fixed on the person speaking. . . . It is a sort of studious debauchery."[37] As a result the sense of hearing entails, for this musician of the French language, a petrifying wakefulness. Its high degree of symbolism, however, makes it just as capable of electrifying our nerves, the way a cat's fur stands on end:

"But certain musical sounds, certain sly noises, hardly perceptible, send her into a panic, and her entire coat becomes alarmed, ripples with nervous spikes."[38] Noises permeate touch and take on color: "The silky noise of rain caresses the window pane and the neck of the rain pipe sobs like a pigeon."[39] At the same time the nostalgic memory of visible objects settles in sounds: "That fat teardrop the length of a log, that death agony of a very ancient fir tree, which the patient ivy killed."[40] Even the snow offers itself, not to the gaze or to touch (is it because its whiteness and coldness are commonplace?) but to hearing: "[. . .] so that I could listen to the whispering of the snow on the bed of dead leaves. It is a very soft murmur, as if syllabized. I have sought to describe it more than once."[41] Could the model for transfiguration into sound, by means of which every vulgar substance is elevated to a loving caress, be heard in the signifier of the mother's name, Sido, si-do, composed of musical notes,[42] the end of the ascending scale, a source of auditory pleasure? It is finally incarnated in a singer's voice: "Oh! To drink that voice at its source, to feel it spurt up between the polished stones of that gleaming set of teeth, to dam it up for a minute against my own lips, to hear it, to watch it leap, a free torrent, and to burst forth in a long harmonious sheet, which I would crack open with a caress. . . . To be the lover of that woman transfigured by her own voice—and of that voice!"[43]

The gaze, however, at once piercing and turned inward, remains for Colette the most solid anchor in the world's flesh. As a true descendant of the Greeks, who constituted the universe as a visible world, the writer asserts: "For anyone living in the fields and using her eyes, everything becomes miraculous and simple."[44] Truth/unveiling, as uncovering or as discovery, comes about definitively through the eyes, and Sido is the high priestess of that optical anxiety: "She was Anxiety itself, under its variable insignia . . . Other insignia—a pince-nez, two pince-nez, a pair of glasses, a magnifying glass—proclaimed she was also Discovery. Her big word: 'Look!' meant: 'Look at the hairy caterpillar, like a little golden bear!' "[45]

That art of contemplation, which Colette inherits from her mother, develops into an infernal, inhuman acuity: the writer appropriates the witch vision of the cat in order to observe her: "Bluish-gray in the morning, she becomes periwinkle at noon, and iridescent with mauve, pearl gray, silver, and steel gray, like a pigeon in the sun. . . . In the evening, she turns into a shadow, smoke, cloud, she floats impalpable and, like a transparent scarf, throws herself onto the back of an armchair. She slides along the wall like the reflections of a pearly fish."[46] But she never forgets that that optical immersion is mental: "I say 'blue'; but what name are we to give that color that surpasses blue, pushes back the limits of violet, evokes purple in a realm more mental than optical, since, though I call purple a vibration of color that seems to border that blue, I do not really see it, I sense it."[47] For lack of barriers and prohibitions, the metamorphic body uses the visible like a fragile boundary, the condition for identity, the support of fascination, and the threshold of chaos all at once. Although the writer's body positions itself in that way and, by preference, as a spectator, it in no way refrains from moving, "lurching" to join the spectacle itself: "It was a spectator's seat, one of those seats of choice from which the spectator, if he gets drunk, has the right to rush up, duly lurching, to actively play a bit part."[48] That exquisite game, however, runs no risk of collapsing into chaos, since the gaze undertakes to dive into the Styx and writing dares confront sickening abjection and misshapen monstrosity.[49]

But, before reaching that infernal drunkenness, the most intimate things may become soberly visible in Colette: a woman's love often takes the form and color of a landscape that offers itself to view.[50] Hence, when a contrite and obstinate Minne resigns herself to a conjugal love she knows to be disappointing, nothing says so in the narrative except the coloring of the seascape: "The hotel gardens conceal Monte Carlo; there is no longer, above a dark hedge of spindle trees, anything but the moon and the sea. . . . Three nuances—gray, silver, leaden blue—suffice for the cold splendor of the canvas, and Minne hones her gaze to seize the delicate line, the smooth and mysterious pencil mark that, at the very edge of the sea, touches the sky."[51]

To desire is to look. The gaze is the organ of desire for Colette: "But I was not studying Rézi, I was looking at her and desiring her." In contrast, dissimulated eroticism overwhelms her: "[. . .] or else she is on the prowl [. . .] tires me out with an invisible approach."[52] But, still in the Greek manner, it is, in the end, style that does the showing: since words are the best of eyes, colors really do appear to her only if she names them "yellow daffodils" or "violets, violets, violets." "More mauve . . . no, more blue . . . I again see meadows, deep woods, which the first growth of buds covers with an ineffable green haze—cold streams, lost springs, soaked up by the sand as soon as they are born, Easter primroses, yellow daffodils with saffron-colored hearts, violets, violets, violets."[53] The impotence of language in capturing the rainbow is here reversed, through alliteration and repetition, into a victory of the word that, replete with sounds and metaphors, transforms sight into vision.

"O GERANIUMS, O FOXGLOVE . . . "[54]

The metamorphic body is of the land: it lives on land and on the land, and continually makes love to that wife/mother, discovering in the past buried within it the only future possible: "To lift, to penetrate, to tear open the earth is a labor—a pleasure—which proceeds not without an exhilaration that no sterile gymnastics could produce. The underground, once glimpsed, makes all those who live on it attentive and greedy. [. . .] When one breaks ground, even if only the size of a cabbage patch, one always feels like the first, the master, the husband without rivals. The ground one breaks no longer has a past, it relies only on the future."[55] Indeed the Colettian metamorphic body, far from being swallowed up by rocky or volcanic depths, takes pleasure in the living soil, sowed with seeds, blossoming into flora and pomona: Colette's planetary space is a plantation. Is this the vogue for peasantry, a musty Barrésianism from a reactionary exile uprooted from the soil, who revels in suspect, backward-looking evocations to better lash out against the "cosmopolitanism of the cities"? Certainly. Is it also a presentiment of modern ecology and, why not, to stay with ideology, a premonition of the regionalist battles against globalization? In fact Colette's experiment is much more radical and archaic because it is at once corporeal and stylistic.

Every flower is a bouquet of synesthesias: seen, heard, inhaled, eaten, caressed, it invites all the senses to communicate and to contaminate one another at its approach: "I do more than see the tulip come back to its senses: I hear the iris flowering."[56] And all the sensations shore one another up to focus the gaze on the secret of floral rhythm: "Anything that's a lie to rhythm is a lie, almost, to the essence of the creature. The anxiety and pleasure of feeling plants live I have not experienced best at the movies, but through *my feeble but complete senses, shored up by one another,* not by saturating, madly reinforcing, my sight."[57] Even in film, which enlarges the visible, Colette will ask for the restoration of that hyperbolic hearing with which she hears "the din of the plant, increased a thousandfold as well, the thunder of flowerings, the gunfire of burst pods, and the ballistics of seeds."[58] Better than the "extravaganza," only the *shoring up of the senses* may have a chance of capturing that mysterious "drama" of germination: "It's the seed—and not the museum—that is the extravaganza."[59] Did not Sido rush to the aid of all "underground" creatures, to "hearts from which every chance of flowering has been taken away"?[60] Colette too dreams of herself in fertile soil, an expert at rebirth: "Turning over a new leaf, rebuilding, being reborn, has never been beyond my strength"[61]—continually wondering "where flowering [. . .] hatching truly begins."[62] "I am unmoved by the death agony of corollas. But the beginning of a flower's career excites me, as does the beginning of a lepidopteran's longevity. Where is the majesty in what is coming to an end, next to staggering starts, disorders of the dawn?"[63]

Glorified by the essential mystery of new beginnings, the flower, the metaphor of metaphors, more than any other object crystallizes the spark of the imaginary. So it is for the *lily of the valley*: "A whole nation, almost, requires the lily of the valley as bread in the spring."[64] Is it flowers that cover the earth with their bower of vitality and diffuse it in light? Or is it the writer herself who dreams in flowers of her happiness in love?

Apart from a clay horn, apart from a grove of cherry laurels dominated by a Ginkgo biloba—I gave its leaves, shaped like a skate, to my schoolmates, who dried them between the pages of the atlas—the whole hot garden fed on a yellow light with red and violet tremolos, but I could not say whether that red, that violet, resided, still reside in a happiness in love or in an optical glare.[65]

Are these anthropomorphic, and moreover feminine, projections? Perhaps. Colette's flowers are nonetheless cut off from the mob, resistant to human presence: "I believe that the presence of human beings in number tires plants."[66] Nevertheless, and before her sensibility is transformed into superstitions, fascinated as she is by the pythonesses and magicians, her fusion with plants attributes a nervous system, even consciousness, to them: "It is now said they have a complete sensibility, a nervous system, rudimentary eyes.[67] [. . .]. We know that the corolla blossoms only by virtue of efforts that seem to be conscious."[68] The complicity, the continuity of all living things dwells within her.

We will never tire of inhaling, eating, thinking Colette's flowers: even when we believe she is taking the easy way out, that she is playing "Colette in the herbarium" for the umpteenth time, enthroning herself as mistress in a floral tapestry, we are caught by surprise in the recesses of a comparison, an olfactory memory, a provocative paradox. Just consider: the *rose*, the hackneyed queen of rhetoric in every language, wrests metaphors from her that reek of the brazen and shameless woman, but one still pure because cosmic, and then place that woman in the biting frost of current events and verbal music: "It's that the store was gleaming with those roses that have a lip, a cheek, a breast, a navel, a flesh glazed with an indescribable frost, which travel in airplanes, stand erect at the end of a scornful stem, smell like peaches, tea, and even roses."[69] Then there is the *lily*, which allows our provincial lady of letters to make fun—but oh, so respectfully—of Mallarmé and his famous line: *Lys! et l'un de vous tous pour l'ingénuité* (Lily! And just one of you for innocence). What else can be said after that pure white concision? The Montigny innocent nevertheless found the means to sketch the face of the prince of poets, whose contemporary she was—though she did not know him "in person"—as if he were a flower: "No document is worth as much to me as the memory of the human face, the tenacious memory of its color, the incision of the pupil, the radiating wheel of the iris, the forehead, its hair or baldness, the mouth and its successive downfalls, the mouth unable to read its own poem; but it is precisely from such a mouth that I would have liked to hear: 'Lily! And just one of you . . . '" Then she places her own lilies in her "chosen land," which, as we suspected, can only be the vegetable patch, in the company of sorrel, tarragon, and purplish garlic. Their brilliance and their perfume wrest this familiar cry from Sido: "So shut the door to the garden, will you, those lilies are making the parlor uninhabitable!" And she ends with this most pagan and most fervent of homages, which no literature in the world, perhaps, ever offered the Virgin:

> Thus she allowed me to mow them like hay, and to carry them in a sheaf to the altar of Mary at the hour of Benediction. The church was narrow and hot, and the children laden with flowers. The uncompromising odor of the lilies grew thicker and disrupted the hymns. Some of the faithful left hastily, a few bowed their heads and fell asleep, carried off by a strange sleep. But the plaster Virgin standing on the altar brushed with her dangling toes the long caiman jaw that a lily was half-opening at her feet, and smiled at it with indulgence.[70]

Could Colette the florist also be an impenitent humorist? Her discreet laughter adorns itself with flowers to consecrate all that claims to be unamenable to the sensory but also to desanctify idols of every kind.

The flower of flowers, at least for Sido, the ruler of these enchanted plantations, the flower that deserves that every other plant be sacrificed to it, is, in the end, the *baby*, the only being in the world that has the right to harm these living jewels. "She gave him a *cuisse-de-nymphe-émue* rose, which he accepted fitfully, which he brought to his mouth and sucked on; then he kneaded the flower in his powerful little hands, ripped off the petals, rimmed and ruddy in the image of his own lips."[71] Like the young child, the writer eats her fill of cotyledons, foxgloves, and ornithogalums, which she devours with all her senses. The American artist Georgia O'Keeffe (1887–1986) attests in her paintings to the same floral identification, but she glorifies the female genitals[72] specifically rather than engage in this omnipresent sensibility that blossoms in Colette.

As one might expect, it is writing that, according to Colette, is the human experience closest to floral life: an alternation between phallic erection and mysterious flowerings, nativities and repeated resurrections. Does not Colette write like the flower that blossoms in the "fits of erection characteristic of an anemic stalk to which someone has just restored its liquid nourishment?"[73] Does not her memory give birth to an image like a blooming flower? "Hence we call back from the *abyss the word as it is being swallowed up* and seize it, through a *syllable,* through its *initial,* which we hold up to the light, saturated by mortal darkness."[74]

THE ANIMAL, OR AN UNUSED LOVE

In his excellent preface to *Dialogues of Beasts* in 1905, Francis Jammes introduces Mme Colette Willy into French literature and points out the anxiety lurking in her "schoolgirl's laugh": "One does not approach a poodle or a tom cat without a muted anxiety muffling your heart."[75] More to the point of her own sexual truth, Colette adds, in *The Shackle* (1913): "In these sudden hungers of touch, these edgy emotions in contact with a gentle animal, I am well aware it is the force of unused love that overflows; and I believe no one feels them as profoundly as an old maid or a childless woman."[76] Unused love thus seeks an outlet, a refuge, just as the novelistic writing aspires to slip beyond the characters of Claudine, Willy, or Colette herself. The endless banter generated by the ménage à trois would continue to thread its way through her work; but, with *Dialogues of Beasts* she also discovers a way of breathing that will never leave her. Next to plants, beasts will be the sensory focal points of the metamorphic body, its true organs.

Is the love of beasts a sensorial overload, an affective power? Undoubtedly, but it is above all an attention to each moment, a way of *listening*—the most abstract of all the senses—and, moreover, of mental listening: "The mental ears I prick up in the direction of the Beast are still functioning."[77] To belong to the beasts is, in the first place, to rebel against humans, an innocent version of the anarchism cultivated by a Colette disgusted with society: "I would like to leave behind a great renown among the beings that, having retained a trace of my passing on their hide, in their soul, may have hoped, madly, and for a single moment, that I belonged to them."[78] Although not unaware of the cruelty of animals, Colette particularly appreciates their ignorance of war, in contrast to the destructiveness of her fellow humans, of which she is ashamed: "At a time when men are tearing one another to pieces, it seems that a singular compassion draws them to beasts, reopening an earthly paradise that civilization had closed off to them. Only the innocent beast has the right to be ignorant of war."[79] Or again: "A very ordinary little cat, I assure you. But my mother is not of my opinion. She loves him. She admires him. There are no martyred children among the animals."[80] And, if she recoils at the sentimentality of patronesses for whom an affection for beasts replaces true charity, Colette equally despises the indifference of scientists who tyrannize animals in the laboratory:

A terrible thing, a scientist let loose to run free throughout the world. [. . .] What a beautiful nightmare for one of the disciples of the Russian scientist: Doctor Pavlov captured by dogs, chained up, isolated in one of his new tents, harassed by the ticking of metronomes, the sight of food offered and taken away, electrical shocks, the blinking on and off of a red light, the major and minor chords, until he has—O victory of science—salivated at the sight of the letter T.[81]

This means that, without a hint of naïveté, Colette uses the innocence of beasts to wage a true ideological battle against humans: "I
do not believe that any profoundly civilized being charms the
beasts."[82] A yawning abyss separates the two species, human and
animal, an irreconcilable distrust: "But I no longer wish to trace the
portrait, the history of beasts. The abyss, which the centuries have
not filled, is still yawning between them and man."[83] Thus, without hesitation, she places herself in the opposing camp from that of
her fellow humans: "One does not love beasts and men at the same
time. Day by day, I become suspect to my fellows. But, if they were
my fellows, I would not be suspect to them." Jouvenel criticizes her
for this: " 'When I enter a room where you are alone with beasts,'
my second husband told me, 'I have the impression I am being
indiscreet. Some day you will retire to a jungle.' Not wanting to
imagine what insidious—or impatient—suggestion might be concealed behind such a prophesy, not ceasing to nurture the pleasant
tableau of my future it offers me, I will stop there, to remember the
profound, the logical distrust of a very humanized man."[84] It is,
moreover, to be of service to the animal kingdom that Colette
would consider asking for a job, an unusual act: "Only once in my
life did I solicit a position. It was refused me. I asked to direct the
zoological gardens, even though it was abandoned, nothing but rot-
ting stalls, bashed-in glass walls, demolished thatches. [. . .] My
aim, madly, was only to assure the captive beasts a better fate, and
I did not ask for a salary."[85]

Animality, installed in the hearts of men and women, is truly
a monstrosity—Colette does not pursue amoralism so far as not
to acknowledge that: "From the human point of view, it is with
the beast's complicity that monstrosity begins, and the human
point of view is correct."[86]

Yet, without avoiding contradiction, since she considers monstrosity a fascinating human singularity—one that reveals the past
of the species and certain excesses, deplorable to be sure, but that,
in becoming attenuated, in the end banalize normal humans—Colette does not hesitate to place the child and the beast on equal
footing. However scandalous it may be, the comparison is obviously a compliment to the child and allows Colette to contrast it

to the adult, that is, to the writer, and her insipid love life: "Indeed, though I see no drawback in putting in print, and into the hands of the public, distorted fragments of my love life, people would like me to tie together, in secret, very tight in the same sack, everything concerning a *preference* for beasts, and—this is also a question of predilection—the child I brought into the world."[87]

Colette's pages are studded with many resemblances between beast and child, extending to the following assimilation to savagery, in which Bel-Gazou, her own daughter, is confused with the dog Buck: "Between the two attitudes a threatened creature can adopt, she has already *chosen*. Assembling all the weapons of her robust weakness, she lowers her eyelids, her pupils firmly hold the stranger's gaze and, with a hollow sound from the depths of her gullet, she growls."[88]

One of the most productive uses Colette will make of that blurring of the animal and the infantile will be to attribute a human point of view to the beast, which sometimes reveals an ironic distance and sometimes a deeper self, the latter being less that of an unconscious than that of an extravagant sensibility, inhuman in the strict sense. The humor of Kiki-la-Doucette addressing Toby-Chien, is, for example, that of a snob: "But you don't know how to do anything discreetly; your vulgar joy obstructs, your histrionic pain moans. A Southerner, come on!"[89] Toby-Chien, in turn, eyes her with the panicked and envious look of a man jealous of his wife's absolute state of repose: "Are you even alive? You're so flat! You look like an empty catskin!"[90] Or again, Kiki-la-Doucette knows her mistress's secret language as if it were her own, especially when She is humiliated by a depraved husband: "If She were to speak in Four-legged, she would caterwaul. [. . .] Both she and I are usually loath to explain ourselves."[91] Of her collaboration with Ravel in the production of *The Child and the Enchantments,* Colette especially—if not exclusively—remembered Ravel's insistence on the cry of felines.[92] Caterwauling as the immediate code of passion—is this a projection of Kiki-la-Doucette, of Ravel, or of Colette?

Less ironically, it is a journey toward "pure incorporated time" in Proust's sense that Colette's appropriation of animal sensibility sets out for us. If we look at the dates of publication, we must concede that *Dialogues of Beasts* (1904) preceded *In Search of Lost Time* (the first volume of which, *Swann's Way,* appeared only in 1913). That would mean that Kiki-la-Doucette and Toby-Chien are the inventors of the "deeper self" (Colette, for her part, speaks of the "former me" in *Tendrils of the Vine* [1908]) that Proust describes in *Against Sainte-Beuve* (1908–10), and even of "pure incorporated time," which would be set in place over the course of *In Search of Lost Time*.[93] You don't believe me? Read Kiki-la-Doucette:

> Silent, alike, happy, we will listen to the night fall. The odor of lime will become nauseatingly sweet at the very hour when my seer's eyes will grow big, black, and will read mysterious signs in the air. . . . There, behind the sharp-pointed mountain, a calm fire will later light up, a circular haze, frosty pink in the ashen blue of night, a luminous cocoon from which the blinding edge of a sharp moon will hatch and drift by, dissolving the clouds.[94]

Toby-Chien is not far behind:

> Another field, all rosy pink with flowering clover, has just given me another red slap in the eye. . . . The earth is sinking—or else we are rising, I don't exactly know. I see, at the very bottom, very far away, green lawns studded with white daisies—which may be cows.[95]

With the go-between of these two sensibilities, "canine" and "feline," assumed by the writer's "former me," all sensations combine, communicate, and arrange themselves in an unprecedented way. At the juncture of beings and of synesthesias characteristic of the subject of the enunciation, whether it be "cat" or "dog," a new world rises up to engulf sensory time and to enlarge the past, to the point of making it intersect the incommensurable future perfect of the imaginary.

Finally, thanks to that identification with animals, rare and true moments of depersonalization come about, which Colette finally dares confide. Hence, "I dream," "no characters," then "a sad bark." "I" gives a start, designating itself as "Me": "Who's barking?" A dog replies: "Me." Me or you? No, "*She*," the dead dog, *She* [*Elle*] is named *Nell*. Who is "Me"? Who is "You," who is "She"? Finally, "my cry awakens me": could it be the cry of the woman who dreams of *Nell*, of *Elle*? Or the cry of *Elle*, of She, the dog who is another "Me"? If "She" were only my dream, the dream of "Me," am I a dog? "Me"? Who am I?

> SHE: Hush! I haven't got a dress anymore. I'm only a line, a sinuous stroke of phosphorus, a palpitation, a lost moan, a seeker whom death has not put to rest, the moaning re-mainder, finally, of the dog among dogs, of the dog . . .
> ME, *shouting:* Stay! I know! You're . . .
> *But my cry awakens me, dissolves the unfathomable blue and black, the unfinished gardens, creates the dawn and scat-ters, forgotten, the syllables of the name borne on earth, among the ingrates, by the dog who deserved to return, the dog . . .* [96]

Have you really read it? That third person, *Nell/Elle*, the dream dog that I am, the animal noncharacter I invent, makes me—Colette—a dog, perhaps, a nonperson, assuredly, even a mere palpitation: no identifiable representation, not even a name, just a few syllables scattered in the dawn. In this brief text the dog is at the limit of representation, as are all the dialogues of beasts, to which Colette continually makes additions and in-troduces variants—dialogues, in short, with an impossible image of oneself. In the process they initiate an effort at dissolving nov-elistic and human forms under the rustic appearance of a fable, an anecdote, harmless or ridiculous puerility.

Nevertheless, this animalistic philosophy, whose gravity shows through under the cheerful off-handedness of the tale, is revealed in very engaging portraits of real animals, sometimes true idols, who have shared the writer's life: cats, dogs, the faithful com-panions of her existence, but also peacocks, butterflies, elephants, tigers, and on and on.

The cat, a sacred animal in Egypt, is also sacred for Colette. In the many feline variants she composes, the writer best projects her femininity and her art:

> To the Cat species I am indebted in a certain fashion: honorable, dissimulating, with great self-control, a characteristic aversion to harsh sounds, and the need to be quiet for long periods of time.[97]

> I abandoned the cat to her demons and returned to wait for her in the place she did not leave night or day when I was working there, slowly and with difficulty—the table where, assiduous, miraculously mute, but resonating with a dull murmur of bliss, the cat, my model, the cat, my friend, lay, kept watch, or rested under my lamp.[98]

> In associating with cats, one runs the risk only of being enriched. Could it be by calculation that, for half a century, I have been seeking their company? I never had to look far for it: it is born under my steps. A lost cat; a farm cat, hunter and hunted, emaciated by sleeplessness; a bookstore cat fragrant with ink; dairy and butcher shop cats, well fed, but paralyzed, vegetables on the floor tile; wheezy petty bourgeois cats, swollen with calf lung; you happy despotic cats who rule over Claude Farrère, Paul Morand—and me.[99]

Did not Colette, herself a Cat (*Chat?* Or should it be spelled *Shah?*), who describes herself as having "a little cat face with broad temples and pointed chin,"[100] sell her tongue to cats—and also her soul? Never was that wife betrayed by her husbands, that disappointed lover always in search of who knows what, prouder than when she recounted her cat's attachment to her, a cat who, abandoning her kitten, ran for five days and four nights in the snow in search of her mistress. She concludes:

> Since there is no love without damage, I agree to be, in the feline's heart, the favorite, the one who is led through a narrow and fiery passageway to the cat's heart. When I make

my way back, I am sometimes received here as a slightly suspect explorer. Did I not eat my fellow man there? Did I not hatch criminal plots? It may be time for the strictly human race to worry about that . . . In fact, it is worried. On my table a newspaper article bears the grave title: "Does Madame Colette Have a Soul?"[101]

As the height of loving irony Colette likes a cat to eat strawberries—like herself: "How magical and simple everything was among that fauna of the house I was born in . . . So you didn't think a cat would eat strawberries?"[102] Furthermore, not only does Willy bear the feline nickname "Doucette" but, much later, past the midpoint of her life, Madame dreams of marrying into the cat family: "I don't want to marry anyone anymore, but I still dream I am getting married to a very large cat."[103] That cat is very familiar, even familial: if we confine ourselves to odor, there is no difference between Bel-Gazou, the fruit of her womb, and a kitten, for example. "Well licked, well nursed, a kitten smells like hay. Might a good odor, in creatures at the teat, be a function of happiness? Lavender water aside, my daughter, before being weaned, emitted an ineffable odor of threshed wheat."[104]

The *dog*, though just as expert at sensations, is more sorrowful than the cat, often pathetic, sometimes a ridiculous scrap of meat: "Hysterical dog. Sniveling sausage."[105] But what an irreplaceable comrade in distress: "Far be it from me to forget you, hearty dogs, bruised by little, healed by nothing. How could I do without you? I am so necessary to you. . . . You make me feel what I'm worth";[106] "But she comes back afterward, without running, and there are hours when it is hard to bear, in a dog's eyes, the expression of human disappointment."[107] Does not the writer resemble that dog, who listens to the whispers of the world, full of ulterior motives and whom only Colette, her fellow creature, her sister, will know how to render in the right words:

With one ear, [the dog] listens to the whispers of the snow along the closed shutters, with the other she watches for the tinkling of the spoons in the office. Her tapered nose quivers, and her copper-colored eyes, looking straight into the fire, move constantly, right to left, left to right, as if she were reading. . . . I study a bit warily that newcomer, that female and complicated dog who guards well, rarely laughs, behaves like a sensible person and receives orders, reprimands without saying a word, with an impenetrable gaze full of ulterior motives.[108]

No animal, no bug is repugnant to Colette, not even *spiders*: "A beautiful spider from the gardens, goodness, her belly like a clove of garlic, with a historiated cross bendy sinister."[109] And, though wary of *birds*,[110] with which she sometimes claims to be unfamiliar—"I tried to elucidate, in light of my illiterate knowledge, my ignorance about everything having to do with birds"[111]—she is particularly interested in their maliciousness. No doubt it is comic to believe, as Buffon does, that the *titmouse* is "the most ferocious bird,"[112] but *pigeons*, presented as "love birds," nevertheless have "yellow and ferocious eyes"[113]—as Colette certifies.

Many *swallows*, "steel blue with white bellies," people her sky, bright phantoms of our country childhoods: "I know the degree to which the tame swallow surpasses in insolent sociability the most spoiled dog."[114] In their predatory flurries Colette's swallows anticipate the attacks and terror of Hitchcock's *The Birds*: "If they are hunting cries, exclamations of birds worked up by their victory over flies and ephemerae, how can they simultaneously snatch and cry, drink up the insect and expel that almost endless and unrepeated cry, the long breath of powerful winged creatures?"[115] "They'd put out your eye, they'd scalp you with a slash of their big shears, don't you see the steel gleaming in the sun?"[116] "When they want to be, they are almost frightening." But an old lady does not mind being reduced to a "sieve" by the swallows: "Surrounded by birds, the plaintive and blessed old lady, riddled with holes like Saint Sebastian, would not leave her place for anything in the world: she offers herself as a target for the arrows of spring."[117] Of course Colette does fear birds, or is at least wary of them: they are too far away and, even when close, are still out of reach:[118] "I prefer the beast with four feet or paws.

As for birds, which always have their arms crossed behind their backs, and which use them only to fly, they intrigue me, they escape me, they excite me less than quadrupeds."[119] Nevertheless, it is a pair of *sparrows*, nestled away in a fold of her blanket, which extracts from Colette this declaration of love that one would not expect from someone so disenchanted: "To choose, to be chosen, to love: immediately afterward comes worry, the peril of losing, the fear of sowing regret. Such big words about a sparrow? Yes, a sparrow. In love there are no small objects."[120]

Of course, and in earnest, she takes more pleasure in the friendship of wild beasts, the *lioness* for example: the writer and the big cat choose each other and, having exhausted all aggressiveness, eye one another complicitously:

> A poor beautiful lioness recently picked me out from the set of gawkers massed before its bars. Having chosen me, it emerged from its long despair as from a sleep, and, not knowing how to manifest that she had recognized me, that she wanted to confront me, to interrogate me, perhaps to love me enough to accept only me as victim, she menaced, flashed, and roared like a captive fire, threw herself against her bars and suddenly dropped off to sleep, weary, looking at me.[121]

Colette's complicity with the beasts, which appeared in childhood and was cultivated in the most mysterious parts of her writing, has become legendary.[122] Animal trainers were astonished by this woman who slipped her hand into the big cats' cage without getting hurt; writers depict her compassion toward a sick bird, so great that she wrung its neck to help it die.[123] I see that mystery, though it remains intact, as the most eloquent proof of her "metamorphic body," which cannot be translated by words such as "love" and "pity," even less by "vindictive and hardened soul"—as some have liked to caricature her. None of that fits. Colette reveals herself capable of a total osmosis with the most archaic repressed, with the *prepsychic* that inhabits our drives and sensibilities. It lies under the fragile film of words, but her writing has the genius to keep in contact with it, to rehabilitate and transmit it. That prepsychic Colette gives the impression of being a simply physical, floral, animal being, even though she surrenders herself only in words.

It would be tempting to link Colette's osmosis with the animal and plant world to the osmosis behind the art of cave paintings. Hence, in the Chauvet cave (dating from between 26,000–27,000 BP and 30,000–32,000 BP),[124] the prehistoric artist represented, inside and not at the cave entrance, animals he did not hunt and that therefore he did not eat. Without dread, with a majestic empathy, he detailed the dramaturgy of their power and movements. And, in setting down a multitude of "positive" or "negative" imprints of his own hands, he seemed to signify more than a mere possession of the universe he inhabited. According to paleontologists these may be a "transmutation between the categories of living beings: man and animal." "A fusional perception of man and of the animal kingdom," that "zoomorphic representation" seems to me to be undergirded by an *identification* with *strangers*—mammoths, rhinoceroses, bears, or horses—as so many alter egos who "speak the same language and understand one another."[125] The artist projects himself into them and tames the animal figures to create his own figurability. The Chauvet artist fully masters the dramatic richness of that originary figurability, well before he is able to represent the human strictly speaking. In fact, on the cave walls, only the form of a vulva surmounted by an animal head appears, a representation that itself seems in the process of transmutation, as it were, with the cave the artist penetrated so that he could decorate it.

That animal figurability of oneself at the dawn of oneself would thus not be a mere reproduction of the animal cosmos or even its secondary humanization. It is a true shamanistic appropriation of the animal figure with the aim of representing a human interiority that seeks to apprehend itself as such. *That* animal figurability would be nothing other than the originary figurability of human desire.

Colette's plant and animal osmosis appears to stem from the same logic. Could she be a cave artist, more original than even a "primitive" or a "pre-Socratic"? In any case, in her journey between living species her writing intersects a memory much more archaic than that of her Burgundy childhood in Sido's house.

As of 1939 the writer no longer had any domestic animals: "For all property I have only one living beast left, and that is the fire. It is my guest, it is my handiwork."[126] These burning logs install an impersonal animal near Colette, an incandescent nothingness, an intimate monster in which she contemplates her wounds and can feel, with every fiber warmed, the most earthly, the most cosmic of joys, jouissance:

> These agreeable monsters sitting in the back of the fireplace burned for twenty-four hours, perforated with blue wounds, stabbing red spears, comets of sparks, then slowly dozed off under a white ash, haunted by igneous grubs . . .
> To build the fire, light it, stoke the fire, cover the fire: an old science of the savage, the peasant, the vagabond. Why can't I be one or another of them! . . . Following their example I flawlessly administer the fire, with joy, with friendship. And I even exploit it.[127]

Could fire be the ultimate incarnation of Colette's bestiary, her conversion into a friendly and wild fluid? It reveals the secret intention of this body of work, which consumes identities and forms but without dreaming of destroying them, only to stoke the sensorial intensity and thus vie with the light of the sun. "I was now nothing but an irreverent force, strong enough to flout the decisions of solar power, which commands lizards to love and to do battle."[128] That exorbitant claim, in fact, governs the serenity of her writing, her simplicity.

" . . . IF 'MME COLETTE' IS NOT A MONSTER, SHE IS NOTHING" (JEAN COCTEAU)[129]

If the monster is a being "contrary to nature,"[130] either a real animal with "a structure of parts different from that which characterizes the species of animals from which it stems"[131] or a mythological creature (siren, centaur, etc.), then there are no monsters in Colette.[132] Nevertheless, monsters and monstrosity often return in her writings but in a different sense of the word: "From the human point of view, it is at the point of complicity with the beast that monstrosity begins."[133]

In counterpoint to the radiant alphabet, as I have said, there is a monstrous alphabet in Colette.[134] In opposition to the beauty of the metamorphic body diffused in the world's flesh, which she celebrates under the name of Sido, there is its "misshapen, expanding, whirling" underside. It is impossible to flee the terrible depths: "Look," the maternal imperative, also applies to them. Moreover, Colette dissects with an almost scientific obstinacy what now offers itself to view, if not to vision: "I would have liked, prior to the funeral pyre, to have subjected the monster to study, like an anthill under glass."[135] But when the gaze detects the underside of appearances, when the demonstration penetrates the near side of the retina, of propriety, of consciousness, all the senses invade formality and the norm; balance disappears and formlessness swarms into that "study," the text. This foul universe travels through the sonorous, the tactile, the olfactory; it swings toward instinct or drive; a regression pushes us toward abject perceptions and, in mobilizing our disgust, indicates that we are threatened with losing our identity.

On one side, then, is the splendid alphabet that delivers the "play" of the metamorphic body to us. It weaves its "haunted landscape" while dissimulating a "face in the leaves, an arm between two branches, a torso under the knots of rocks,"[136] an alphabet of words, things, and sensations mingling indiscriminately, in which I hear music in the letters.

On the other side is "the solid universe, which capsizes" and unveils "a nauseous chaos without beginning or end," a universe of which, however, "certain arabesques can be like the letters of the alphabet—an O, a U, a big C, a small G—on monstrous motionless cables. [. . .] It stirs, it exacerbates the confusion of its knots, it swells, deforms its monograms and deceives me: the O is a C, the G, a Z. It turns to liquid, runs down the tree, and, moreover, shrinks back, congealed."[137]

What has happened? How does the writing pass from alphabet *play* and enchanted gardens to alphabet *chaos,* which "softens the heart"? A vignette entitled "Snake" recounts the secret of that shift as if it were an optical disturbance. When the writer stops seeing clearly, when the vigilant eye dominating her object (in this case, a snake) is replaced by *imaginary* eyes supposedly belonging to that object itself, then writing takes its leave from the civilized surface of appearances. The author believes she can distinguish, under the "naïveté" of the designs covering the python's skin, a multitude of flat rectangles, diamonds, and trapezoids, which "form a kind of eye, an orb equipped with an almost lifeless gaze, and I recoil."[138] Representation becomes blurred, the watcher, watched, is "terror-stricken" to observe the uncanniness at the site of the *other* facing her: "we are not of the same country or of the same belly."[139] It is only when she understands that these eyes that watched her were not those of *others* but the effect of a blurring of her *own sight* (since the python had "invariable golden eyes" that are truly its own and the troubled vision that frightened the beholder was only her own), that the author can come to her senses: "It is a beast, like you and me."[140] The strangeness is over. It stemmed from a scopic inversion of watcher/watched, subject/object, of a projection of my eyes onto the skin of the other with its unfamiliar monograms.

It is not immaterial to note that that reversal, by virtue of which the looker identifies with the object and believes she sees herself with the eyes of the other, occurs with a snake, a phallic symbol that "moves and goes nowhere," and amid an odor of "unknown excrements." Under these very precise circumstances, devoid of optical defenses, the beholder is led back to her primary sexual revulsion: the python's monstrosity is actually located within oneself, in the observer's unconscious sexuality, rather than residing in the "dreariness of the puddles" facing her. Colette's monstrous animal laboratory is her way of rendering her "uncanniness"—and our own—as an image.

Hallucinations, differently than the observer's gaze, proceed straight to the untenable and are akin to the *dream,* that privileged "process" of exploration "prior to the funeral pyre" that

Colette proposes to undertake to fathom our intrinsic monstrosity. In *The Cat* Alain prefers, to the bridled sensuality of his wife, Camille, a she-cat with which he falls desperately in love. That love against nature, that madness tinged with idyllic serenity (in counterpoint to the ferocious jealousy of Camille, who tries to kill her animal rival), appears monstrous only when the writer enters Alain's dreams. The last of these dreams, of a gazeless gaze, is dominated by "a winged eye that was fluttering";[141] the eye of the Cat, or Alain's eye directed toward his aberration, that of a man in love with a cat? From his very first dreams Alain is confronted with formlessness: "expanding and whirling faces" "equipped with a large eye" evolve into an "underwater change of course" and stare at the sleeper with "the moist gaze of a round monster." Colette defines the dream, "a daily shipwreck," as a scuttling of representation, but one that, by this very fact, depicts the suffering body's passion, its "splintered" breakup "scattering into slightly luminous scraps." "Other times, [Alain's faces] existed only as hand, arm, forehead, eyeball full of thoughts, stardust of nose, chins, and always that bulging eye that, just as it was about to explain, turned and showed nothing but its other, dark side."[142] Like the narrator's hallucination at the sight of the python, Alain's dream is a paradoxical vision that installs us in a different register of representation, more profound and more troubling. The object, here again, is not immaterial to that crisis of the visible: Saha, the adored cat, leads Alain to the very depths of eroticism and will oblige him to leave his wife and seek refuge with his mother. Haunted by the archaic—for Alain, maternal domination; for the observer of the python, an anal and phallic obsession—the subject loses and undoes its identity as well as its stable vision, and the hallucination, like the dream, attests to that unbearable regression.

The terrifying alphabet of Alain's dreams therefore gives us another version of the metamorphic body, the underside of Sido's paradise but continuous with it. Animality and hermaphroditism will take root like the two central figures of monstrosity according to Colette, joined by that of murderers, whom the writer will see in the courtroom and will describe—scandalously—with obvious sympathy. Although it is true that the monstrous appears to her as an uneasy gaze, which accompanies the sexual uneasiness or arousal of the metamorphic body, writing is, in fact, the obligatory element for its flowering. And she cannot consecrate the paradises of sensibility unless she also visits its prisons.

This problematic of monstrosity takes root in the texts written in the late 1920s and the early 1930s: *Everyday Adventures* (1924), *The Hidden Woman* (1924), *The End of Chéri* (1926), *Break of Day* (1928), *Sido* (1929), *Prisons and Paradises* (1932), *The Pure and the Impure* (1932). The same themes are repeated in *The Cat* (1938), *My Apprenticeships* (1936), and *Bella-Vista* (1937), and the murder trials reappear in *My Notebooks* (1941). The period in question follows *My Mother's House* (1922) and *The Ripening Seed* (1923), in which a transgressive sexuality freed from every taboo asserts itself, as does its inversion, in the form of a new exploration of childhood memory: a sort of brutal and no less radical self-analysis, which culminates, as we have seen, in that apotheosis of sublimation itself that Colette glorifies under the name "Sido." In that context the series of "monsters" can be interpreted as a deeper exploration of the tragic, if not the immoral, aspects of the same metamorphic body whose jouissance we have already glimpsed. Accompanied by its monsters, this body reveals itself and triumphs, sure of its imaginary power, pushed to the limits of the self and of the unbearable.

In the early 1930s the triptych of *Prisons and Paradises* (1932), *The Pure and the Impure* (1932), and *The Cat* (1933) repeats, with some distance, the same dialogue and observes the sexual economy of this monstrosity through the prism of a new enigma: superimposed on the opposition normal/monstrous is that of pure/impure. Colette never seems to find a satisfactory definition for these terms, except by invoking an "optical thirst" (once again!) for the "pure" word, which immediately dissolves into a pure signifier, sheer musicality:

Of that word "pure" that *fell* from [a Sapphist's] *mouth,* I listened to the brief tremulo, the plaintive *u,* the *r* of clear ice. It did not awaken anything in me, except the need to hear its unique resonance again, the echo of a drop that falls, breaks free, and joins an invisible body of water. The word "pure" did not reveal its *intelligible* meaning to me. I have only reached the point of quenching an *optical thirst* for purity in the transparencies that evoke it, in the bubbles, the massive water, and the imaginary sites entrenched, out of reach, within a thick crystal.[143]

Or again, on the subject of the two chaste ladies of Llangollen: "Jealous of such an imperturbable tenderness, they will want those two faithful daughters to have fallen short of purity—but what do they understand by purity? [. . .] How difficult respectable men find it to believe in innocence!"[144] Even though all the variants of the monstrous can be understood through the new pair pure/impure, the term "impure" seems reserved for heterosexuality and, more narrowly, for genital sexuality alone, whereas "pure" refers to homosexuality and its sensual variants, sublimated into a ritualized existence, orderly as a work of art. A pure monstrosity would thus stand in contrast to an impure monstrosity: we will return to this after a more detailed reading of loving and sexual relationships according to Colette.[145]

Let us linger for a moment on this "human point of view"— could that be a way of saying that Colette's point of view might be something else, inhuman?—according to which "it is at the point of complicity with the beast that monstrosity begins." Pythons, titmice, blackbirds, and so many other animals therefore absorb the disruptions of human identity and transmute into singular creatures that, in fact, reveal only our shameful shortcomings.

Flowers themselves can become monstrous if we perceive, under the neutrality of the plant, a "complicity" with the beast and with man: hence, the *anemone* is a hedgehog, the *strawberry* has "reddish viscera" and "hairy holes," *pansies* have Henry VIII's head and *lilies of the valley* that of Louis XIV at his most uncouth.[146] But, contrary to the majority of humans, the writer does not complain: there is a strange truth revealed by that contamination of species, identities, and roles—shameful beauty. Certain plants, such as the beautiful *wisteria,* are murderous:

"Sometime it came across the neighboring honeysuckle, the charming honey-sweet honeysuckle with red flowers. At first it seemed not to notice it, then slowly suffocated it the way a snake smothers a bird. I learned, in seeing it do so, what its murderous power was, assisted by a convincing beauty."[147] For others, like the *peony*, their monstrosity lies in their suspect fragrance: "The peony smells like a peony, that is, like a June bug. Through a delicate fetidness, it has the privilege of connecting us to true springtime, carrying suspect odors, the combination of which is well-suited to enchant us."[148] Then there is *tansy*: "Why do the tansy, 'the malodorous tansy,' as the botanists say, and the achillea give my guts heart, why do they give even my heart heart, and why, on the contrary, does the heliotrope, its vomitous vanilla, its mauve half-mourning, disagree with me?"[149] For others, it is their proximity to an old woman's body that is disturbing: "The long strides of that aged and robust woman made the hanging bunches of lily of the valley sway, heads down, twenty, thirty, fifty bunches, each at the end of a twine lasso like poached game."[150] Others, finally, leave the narrator indifferent (she claims) because of the male symbol that, in the center of a cornet of *arum,* plants "a style, phallic and brown [. . .] like a preacher in the pulpit"; "I return, from a lack of sympathy and comprehension, to the other plant that does not touch me and that Western bouquets give a place of honor: the arum [. . .] It does not smell good, that little monk."[151] As for the *orchid,* "a misshapen, charm-filled dream," it seduced a "big-cat hunter in the last century," who in the end preferred it to the jaguar: "I would simply have liked to know whether he had converted out of gratitude to the merciful jaguar, or if the orchid, more powerful in charm than any other game, had forever wounded him in those regions where man, facing two dangers, never fails to choose the worse one."[152] Without going that far, and at first sight, might we not say that flowers are abnormalities, by virtue of the simple fact that their names are "uncommon"?

"You couldn't ask the florist the name of that monster?"
"I did, Mama."

"And what did she tell you?"

"She told me: 'Well I'll be, I'd be at a loss to tell you. But for an uncommon name, it's an uncommon name.'"[153]

The monstrous animality that permeates the plant world is replaced by another, which, "marked with the sign of the Beast" but without referring to it explicitly, reveals its proximity to the depths of ourselves and to our archaism. Hence passionate excesses, some of which will be glorified as *pure*, flirt with the category of the monstrous to better display their unfathomable singularity. The homosexual, for example, like the author herself, is said "to come from afar," driven "to cherish the arbitrary, to lean toward passion rather than kindness, to prefer the battle to discussion,"[154] all features that exclude him from the community of the "Two-legged." Although pure, the lesbian couple, twins and incestuous, are nevertheless monstrous: "It is a time when a life establishes itself as monstrous, laid out like the contemplation before a mirror, a life whose regularity would smother normal love."[155] But it is the artist who is "the authentically wicked one," "the true, the pure," since that hypersensitive person partakes by rights in the monstrous alphabet—even though, "it [is] rare to come across him even once in one's lifetime."[156] Also partaking in that alphabet is the megalomaniac named Pierre Faget, with the omnipotence of a false messiah, who "at least [. . .] will have savored, in that drab republic, all the joys of tyrants and magicians."[157] In that case it is faith that makes someone monstrous, that is, singular and worthy of interest. But is not faith another accommodation of the gaze, a paradoxical vision, without which that false magician would have remained a mere "herbalist"? A zookeeper in charge of the leopards who "handles them like two baby goats" owes his diabolical power to the mysterious complicity he maintains with his captives. In granting him their obedient favor, the big cats become—their jailer's masters. And Colette envies that kept keeper who enters the leopards' cage without fear and for whom their "raucous and choked language softens to a meow."[158] Although she presents herself as a victim of felines,[159] we learn that, on the contrary, at a circus in Germany, Colette's hand, when slipped into their cage, oddly enough pacified the tigers, to the trainers' great amazement.[160]

The list of these traits, monstrous according to Colette, can only be vague and ill defined, because they are so close to covering the infinity of objects likely to contain them. The monstrous, however, results from a fascination that, far from being exclusively optical, changes one's gaze on the world, transforms the body's rhythms and even alters the course of the mind. That fascination leads the subject to modify its being in the world and to confer an unbearable knowledge on it: "Afterward, it is the healthy eye that changes, is aroused, falls in love with the mystery it glimpsed, and continually questions it."[161]

The aberrant surges up everywhere one does not expect it: in the disobedient child, in female ugliness, in the duplicity of heterosexual couples, even in ladies of letters. All "half-mad"? Perhaps, but would it not be better to preserve the brutishness that rises to the surface, in order to avoid other, more insidious monstrosities, like those of banalization and repression? "To convince, whether it be beast or child, is to weaken."[162] Within that logic, it is not incest that makes Chéri blush but a loveless love: "And as he was walking beside Edmée toward the bedroom, which would hear neither reproaches nor kisses, he felt filled with shame, and he blushed at how monstrously well they got along."[163] Benevolence itself can turn out to be criminal, and Sido suspects that the patronesses' hypocrisy dissimulates many heinous deeds: "How I like this letter: *The tea was given in honor of very ugly women. Was it their ugliness that was celebrated? They bring their needlework and work, work with an application that horrifies me. Why does it always seem to me they are doing something bad?* You detected, in disgust, a benevolence capable of more than one crime."[164] Colette enjoys classifying as monstrous the melancholic women whose "dark moods" take the place of sexuality, "even though this was merely latent hysteria, sewing room neurasthenia, the way women penned up far from the other sex arbitrarily and pointlessly manifest it."[165]

Maternal sadism, especially in its violent and lethal component, which attacks the daughter's body—particularly when it bears the fruit of pleasure—holds a prominent place in that series of aberrant behaviors. Obeying the injunctions of her mother, that "old murderess," the unfortunate Gribiche submits to an abortion and dies as a result. The complicity of the women ready to condemn and sacrifice their pregnant friend has little more value: "A certain order of criminality found them judicious, both passive and cautious in face of the peril of giving birth, and they expressed the monstrous in moderate terms."[166]

More comic, entertaining, and frightening are the "half-mad" who haunt the halls of the newspaper, among whom the "ladies of letters" exhibit the marks of madness more visibly than their male counterparts. These female writers, grotesque, "bedecked with the graces and attributes of a second-rate muse," these writers are nevertheless disturbing: "Only black eyes, like bird's eyes that reveal no thought, illuminated that turret with an unstable and mysterious fire."[167]

Colette's amoralism, though it allows her to identify the monstrosity in the human heart, does not spare her from appealing to the norm. It makes her laugh but does not allow her to judge. Similarly, abnormality, another version of monstrosity, having elicited fascination as a way of making its presence known, can only be stigmatized by the writer.

What abnormality is at issue? Mme Ruby, a "boy-woman,"[168] is rejected at the end of one short story, less because of her masculine looks, the sign of an extreme hermaphroditism and of an unintegrated bisexuality, than because she turns out to be—a "disguised muscle man"[169] who knocked up the hotel chambermaid. Is the couple she forms with Mme Suzanne abnormal, then, or are the two innkeepers part of "normal, probably harassed people"?[170] Colette cultivates enigmas and uncertainty: her short story seems to mock the opposition between the "pure" and the "impure" when it does not call into question her book of the same title, saying in substance that, if one attempts to dissimulate the normal behind the abnormal, such secrecy itself, being only too normal, makes the abnormal the ultranormal. Could it be that the abnormal is the overly normal if it is hidden, whereas, conversely, abnormality exposed, if not openly professed, might become normal?

The category of normality, barely posited, is not really abandoned by Colette; but, seen from another angle, it serves to launch anew the inquiry into the diversity of monstrosities. The most troubling, in fact, is the monstrosity that takes on all the appearances of normality, such as the insignificant M. Daste, "the civilized monster rigged out in human guise, lover of the death of birds."[171] Nevertheless, was not that criminal cowering behind the masks of proper society the first to denounce appearances?[172]

Throughout her investigations Colette seeks the signs that would provide sufficient proof of the anomaly. Graphology, phrenology, nothing is overlooked, especially when the author tries to describe true deviants, those who are judged for breaking moral laws. In *In the Crowd,* during the trial of the anarchist terrorist Kilbatchich and his gang,[173] she examines them for revealing signs of deviance. In *My Notebooks* (1941) she includes a chapter titled "Monsters," which brings together portraits of three criminals tried in the 1920s (Marie Becker, Stavisky, and Weidmann): they are "the various kinds of men who take a man's life."[174] Violette Nozière, who had poisoned her father, attracted Colette's attention in 1934.[175] She would go to Morocco in 1938 to follow the trial of Oum el-Hassen, known as Moulay Hassen, accused of homicide and torture, and would wonder about the motives of that adventuress and spy. In the face of that monstrous puzzle the writer hesitates: is it heroism, greed, innocence, or a horrible cold-blooded perversity?[176]

But the distinguishing marks of deviance are lacking. Could they be graphological, as Colette claims in *The Evening Star* (1946), where she examines "the handwriting of the sexually abnormal: passive pederasts, morbid onanists [. . .] and other modest monsters, the friends of darkness, a little murderous, a little suicidal?"[177] Or could it be phrenological: a facial deformity, a suspect detail, as Colette, an admirer of Balzac ("who believed in such things"), does not fail to maintain? "On [the murderer Weidmann] I seek in vain what I sought and found on other criminals: a hideous ear, a sign of prognathism, a gross disproportion between nose and forehead. [. . .] Where, then, is the ineluctable mark, the physical stamp of a failing, of a ferocity?"[178]

The Landru case[179] in particular attracted her attention, and she returned to it several times:[180] in her account published on the front page of *Le Matin* on November 8, 1921 (court session of November 7); in the one for the *Revue de Paris,* December 1, 1921; in "Assassins," *Le Figaro,* Sunday, May 11, 1924, reprinted in *Everyday Adventures* (1924);[181] and in "Landru," reprinted in *Prisons and Paradises* (1932).[182] She mentions him as well in *The End of Chéri* (1926).[183]

From the outset the journalist's tone is a "circumspect" and "deferential" sympathy: "Why, in speaking of him, would I drop my polite tone? [. . .] And I have no desire to fall in line with the statement of charges, which, for four hours by the clock, poured out the most unambiguous epithets on an accused's head: 'Murderer . . . hacker of women . . . sinister fiancé.'"[184] In the *Revue de Paris* on December 1, 1921, she goes so far as to note something that does not appear in the final version of "Landru": "What is inconceivable, a friend told me, is not the curiosity you displayed to see Landru, it is that, having seen him, you have spoken of him with that tone of reserve, of courtesy, almost, indeed, of respect."[185] Having granted Landru the autograph he had requested of her, Colette describes him with a certain indulgence—if not sympathy—detectable in her insistence on comparing him to animals and savages.

In fact, murderers such as Landru or the Englishman Patrick Mahon, are, according to her, the "possessors of an animality elsewhere abolished; they radiate a shadow-filled sweetness awash in the graciousness still falling to the tribes lucky enough to have been spared contact with the Europeans."[186] It is not that Colette "loves" them: with Marcel Schwob, she would more likely say she "does not love" hypocritical sadists, such as bird charmers who are in reality "bloodthirsty sadists." But, unlike the latter, the murderer who concerns her is not a brutish being, who, motivated by fury or alcohol, "takes no pleasure in killing." No, he seems rather to be endowed with the refinement of the pervert, whose eroticism, inseparable from aggressiveness, would make him akin to the animal: "the charity of bestowing death like a caress, of combining it with games that are those of the refined big cats: all cats, all tigers embrace their prey and lick it as much as they pummel it."[187] In Colette's eyes, that "awful innocence" of the murderer cannot be completely blameworthy: it is as if "the ways of the uncivilized jungle" appeared more authentic to him, if not preferable to modern conventions. "He loves with passion, pleases, conquers, grows tired of what he has conquered and gets rid of it through murder."[188]

Nevertheless, and this is an important clinical observation, Colette notes that, if there is atavism in the murderer, it is very suppressed. Disconnected from his passions, isolated by his instincts, Landru is rather a "false self" (as modern psychoanalysts would say) who dissimulates the secrets of his sexuality under "the monochrome pallor" of a respectable, even "ascetic" man:[189] "Around him there was slaughter, bones, cooking; a surviving fiancée got on the witness stand and faltered, suddenly intimidated and submissive yet again under the peaceful, black, unfathomable eyes, which did not seek her out or avoid her, shining like the eyes of birds, like them devoid of language, of pity, and of melancholy."[190] Compared to the "beastly delirium" of the public prosecutor, Landru's coldness makes him a very respectable being. In the same way the public finds the English murderer "sweet" and even "likable."[191]

Colette scoffs at the mob's naïveté and pretends to be taken in by the murderer's innocence only to better fathom his brutishness. In the 1932 portrait, mockery would give way to an insistence on Landru's "serenity."[192] That evolution in the approach to the monstrous is attributable not only to the fact that she was endeavoring to insert the criminal into a series of portraits of high society figures, without making him seem out of place beside the sophistication of Mistinguett and Chanel. Colette's psychological acuity (or could it be the ease women have, according to her, at make-believe, at finding fulfillment in the lie?) leads her to discover that Landru is living with a false personality. During the same period the psychoanalyst Helene Deutsch was describing in detail such "as-if personalities."[193] Compared to the magistrates in court, Landru is, according to Colette, the only one who knows "how to behave," to "be concerned about the proprieties," to assume, if only momentarily, the "greatness our judges lack."[194] He is certainly inhuman, with his very deep-set eyes and, above all, because of that aptitude for simulating life that brings to mind the robot or the wax mannequin: "If that face is frightening, it is because, bony but normal, it seems to be *perfectly imitating humanity,* like those *motionless mannequins* that display men's clothes in shop windows."[195] And Colette identifies in Landru a variant of the "banality of evil" Arendt would later make out in the Nazi Eichmann, equally meticulous, obsessive, and disassociated from his cruelty by virtue of his obedience as a zealous civil servant:[196]

> Landru takes notes, attentive and distant at once, or scans the room without bravado, with the eyes that made so many victims fall in love with him. He makes it clear that the noise bothers him. He calmly blows his nose, folds his handkerchief into a square, smoothes down the little flap of his outside pocket. How *careful* he is!
>
> Did he kill? If he killed, I'd swear it was with that *bureaucratic,* slightly *maniacal,* admirably lucid care he brings to the *organization of his notes,* to the compilation of his dossiers. Did he kill? Then it was while whistling a little tune to himself, wearing an apron around his waist for fear of stains. Is Landru a sadistic madman? No. He is much more impenetrable, at least for me. I can imagine more or less what fury is, lecherous or not, but I remain stunned before the calm and gentle murderer who holds a record book of victims and who may have taken a break from his task, leaning his elbows on the windowsill to offer bread to the birds.[197]

Nevertheless, that insensitivity, which distinguishes the "bureaucratic" and "maniacal" man of obsessions from the pervert hungry for his victims' blood and money and that makes his behavior banal, is, according to Colette, the manifestation of an archaic relic going back, if not to the animal kingdom, then at least to the ancient rites of primitive sacrifices: "Landru seemed to be dreaming above them, *withdrawn from us, returned perhaps to a very ancient world,* to an age when blood was neither more sacred nor more horrible than wine or milk, a time when the sacrificer, seated on the dripping warm stone, lost himself in thought sniffing a flower."[198] Is Colette excusing evil, as some have accused her, or is she grounding it in the recesses of the human condition where anyone might attempt to locate it, to sublimate it?

FROM THE DEATH DRIVE TO DECAPITATION

In Colette's writings abnormal people bear witness to one of her radical intuitions: desire, the life drive, human sexuality, are inextricably mingled with the death drive, a fundamental destructiveness. Avid for a vital flowering, Colette prefers to ignore death, or at least, she is loath to write about it: "But I have no taste for the spectacles and symbols of gracious death."[199] The writer, without any depressive complacency, dealing with the cruelty of capital punishment, chooses a theme that touches on the grotesque and on animal expressionism but also includes remarkable psychological insights.

The image of the "severed head," which recurs in the author's writings, betrays her personal involvement. In that investigation, far from being a neutral observer of the phenomena of zoos, of the courtroom, or of the bedroom, might Colette have run the risk of losing her own head? She speaks ironically about the first decade of the 1900s, smitten, she says, with "blessed decapitations," which she herself prefers to flee with "timid heart," only to plunge into "seaweed and star."[200] And yet Colette does not balk at pursuing the death drive even to the supreme violence of beheading.

Hence, at the exhibition held for the centenary of the death of Géricault (1791–1824), she appreciates four "heads of madmen" and the *Head of a Dead Young Man, Eyes Closed,* which would serve as a model for the man's head lying at the center of *The Raft of the Medusa*—"a captivating head with eyelids invaded by shadow."[201] In painting the horror of a decapitated head, Géricault took delight in the motif of man's eroticized castration. It is not difficult to imagine that Colette, fancying herself a hermaphrodite, was able to second him in that morbid exploration of an always threatened virility.

Here and there, "many a decapitation from ancient works"[202] stirred the writer's imagination, as did "vases from China," whose "silhouette was that of a nude grande dame who, even decapitated, might have held herself upright."[203] Even more formidable, plunging even deeper into the archaic, is the evocation of a decapitated woman, whose tragic fate Colette alleviates by destining her to dance a graceful ballet[204] in an unrealized choreography project. The unfortunate woman is a *sultaness* who, guilty of violently desiring a nomadic fifteen-year-old shepherd (once again, the theme of mother-son incest), and even though there was no physical contact, is decapitated by her husband, the *sultan*. For the unconscious, that punishment of the libidinous mother goes back to a decisive moment in our individuation: when the child gets free of the mother, when it is capable of separating from her without feeling in danger of catastrophe, it loses her in order to be able to conceive of her; and that loss is experienced as an execution, an Orestian matricide, a decapitation. Medusa was the first decapitated woman in Western art.[205]

Who then is the decapitated queen who dances headless in Colette's never-performed ballet? Could it be she herself? The mistress of the young Bertrand? Or the imaginary Léa, Chéri's lover? Let us remember that Colette called her second husband, Henry de Jouvenel, "Sidi" or "the Sultan." Sido, for her part, in describing her daughter's first wedding, asked the groom and his friends: "Don't you think it's better not to compare her to a decapitated woman and a wounded bird?"[206] Or is it Sido herself, the one and only queen whom Colette was to lose, for whose matricide she unconsciously assumed responsibility, so as to give free rein—and only on that condition—to her polymorphous body and her sublimations, including the death drive?[207]

The "extrahuman" Colette describes herself as a "sensor of wellsprings," the deepest of which would be that of the animals that "devoted their brief existence" to her.[208] In thus domesticating the diverse facets of the unbearable, she acquired the conviction that the knowledge that comes of writing about our aberrations—reprehensible or not—is not only an inexhaustible source but the most human, the most honest expression of her metamorphic body: that she is inseparable from it. "O monsters, do not leave me alone. . . . I confide nothing to you, except my fear of being alone, you are the most human, the most reassuring thing I know in the world. . . . If I called you 'monster,' what name would I give to what is inflicted on me as normal?"[209]

FIGURE 2. Colette at five. "I got big, but I was never little. I never changed. I remember myself with a sharpness, a melancholy, that do not deceive me." (*Les Vrilles de la vigne*)

FIGURE 3. Colette in 1900. "When my body thinks [...] everything else falls silent. At those moments, my whole skin has a soul." (*La Retraite sentimentale*)

FIGURE 4. Colette as a little faun in *L'Amour, le Désir et la Chimère* (February 1906). "There is no reality but dance, light, freedom, music.... There is no reality but to mark the rhythm of one's thought, to translate it into beautiful gestures." *(La Vagabonde)*

FIGURE 5. Colette at her desk, seated in the armchair for which she did the tapestry. "So you're there, need to write? You're really there, necessary, large-limbed, typical, you're always there. I pound into you, I grope toward your presence." *(Derniers écrits)*

FIGURE 6. Colette, painting by Jacques-Emile Blanche, 1945,
Barcelona Museum. "From the depths of the severe retreat I created deep
within myself, I'm apt to laugh out loud." *(Les Vrilles de la vigne)*

FIGURE 7. Colette, drawing by Vertès, 1927.

FIGURE 8. Colette, engraving by Dunoyer de Segonzac, 1928.
"An insect's effrontery is inside me. I have the bravery of a soldier ant,
over which danger passes, huge and insignificant." *(La Paix chez les bêtes)*

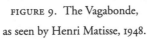

FIGURE 9. The Vagabonde,
as seen by Henri Matisse, 1948.

FIGURE 10. Colette,
drawing by Jean Cocteau, about 1947.

MEN AND WOMEN,
PURE AND IMPURE

*In short, it will have taken me only forty-five years of my career
to be certain that one becomes a great writer—and a great poet as well,
by the way—as much by what one refuses one's pen as by what one
grants it, and that the honor of the writer is renunciation.*

—Colette, "La poésie que j'aime" (1937), in *Paysages et portraits*

*The only virtue on which I pride myself is scruples. Every day
more circumspect with my work, and more uncertain that
I must continue it, only my fear itself reassures me.*

—Colette, *Discours de réception à l'Académie royale de Belgique* (1936)

A NEW MYSTIC?

To write is to reinvent love. In our Western civilization, founded
on Plato's *Symposium* or on the Song of Solomon, from Christian
agape to (post)modern eroticism, relationships with others and
their pleasures have always been written down. Love—consoling,
disappointing, or promising—makes us quiver and live, for better or for worse. Religions and ideology form its ground, modulate and deform it. Aesthetic creations (music, painting, sculpture, literature), which mobilize the sensory experience located at
the intersection of pleasures and relationships, find in the adventure of love their area of choice. In Christianity, because the
Word became flesh and language became Love, literature could
not fail to make love its explicit theme and set forth its consistent

or novel variants. Modern artists, whether they place themselves faithfully in Christianity's wake or seek to steal religion's power, are well aware of that. In the nineteenth century Rimbaud proclaimed himself "an inventor much more deserving than all those who preceded [him]: a musician even, who found something like the key of love" (*Les Illuminations*). And he imagines, in the guise of a key, a visionary paradise that, albeit ephemeral, is nevertheless the kingdom of a vagabond and unshackled jouissance: love is an "irrepressible satisfaction for superior amateurs," an "immense, unquestionable opulence" of "unsuspected finds and terms, immediate possession," "that which will never be sold."

Colette as well might have said she had found that "key of love," but in her own way and in the feminine. Although Rimbaldian sexual opulence is not absent from her writings, she surrounds herself with a halo of an astonishing purity: as we have seen, glowing sensations communicating with one another at every instant challenge and displace sexuality itself. Perfectly lucid as she passes through the "Inexorable," the scandalous Colette embraces her naïveté, pure at the heart of the impure, which she inhabits with an animal innocence on the far side of anxiety.

Colette's genius was able to express with precision woman's *hypersensitive intimacy*, which includes and diffracts *erotic excitation* in a sort of natural "perversity": all the erogenous zones and all the objects in the world are, for her, sources of frustration or satisfaction. In fact, when defensive frigidity is overcome and hysterical erotomania finds its equilibrium, a woman marries not so much a partner as a network of objects or fetishes (with or without him): children, lovers, friends, flora and pomona, activities and various relationships from which she asks for "more." Her mental universe is, as it were, decanted into a pantheism of desires: "It is my body that thinks" and "my whole skin has a soul."[1] Repression and social constraints check that psyche sensitive to the infinite, since, in most cases, only dissatisfaction, a cross between greed and melancholy, remains. Men, perplexed, wonder with Freud: "What does woman want?" What is the unobtainable "object" of female pleasure, which, as a result of that dissemination, makes woman a perpetual Mme Bovary, at worst an impenitent melancholic, at best the "eternal irony of the community" (Hegel)? Psychoanalysis aside (rare are the women who have access to it, and even more rare those who bring it to a successful conclusion), it is writing that offers, for mystical woman saints and for modern "writeresses" [*écrivaines*], a privileged shelter for the mysterious folds and recesses of that hypersensitive intimacy.

Colette brings us a knowledge of the excitability of the female body, a knowledge that, though singular and inimitable, is nevertheless a social fact. This lover who pursues her desires to their culmination stood as a figure of the free woman and was a scandal for conventional morality, which was already rather unsettled at the turn of the twentieth century. Nevertheless, Colette embraced no libertarian cause, not the sociological call for the emancipation of all women (feminism was already under way, with the demands of the suffragettes) nor the sexist cause of a dissident group of feminists (1900 is rightly considered a banner year for Sapphism, particularly in Paris); and, gradually, she detached herself from the ideology of love itself. She replaced it not with resignation but with another variant of Eros, composed of enthusiasm, Dionysian relationships with men, women, plants, beasts, and monsters, and, above all, with their constant metamorphosis into writing.

That metamorphic body whose experiences she details, that body at once wildly excitable and scrupulously submissive to the discipline of writing—never one without the other—seems to have matured, as she herself reconstitutes the true-false memory of it in her autobiographical texts, within the incestuous harmonics of the Colette clan, whose course we have just retraced. In that sense "amorous Colette"[2] was always there, well before Willy's workshops. Nevertheless, the perverse and refined initiation that "unscrupulous" lover of "fresh flesh," that man "past his prime," imposed on her made the gifted student a "prodigy of libertinage, which allows for no disgust."[3] And it is through writing, a superb therapy, a vagabondage without respite, that she follows the hazards of the love relationship, in order to transcend it with a rigorous good cheer. There is no "amorous Colette" other than the stylist Colette, through and beyond the provocative Colette making the news. It is in her writing that the economy of feminine pleasure is continually refined, it is in her texts that the true experience of freedom, simultaneously existential and stylistic, offers itself, because it *is* fundamentally stylistic: a freedom that the reader, with the passing years, receives above all as a reinvention of the lover's discourse, not at all a life plan, as some were too eager to have people believe at the time.

Ever since the Sulamite in the Song of Solomon, women have been inventing the language of love. Although the biblical text admits it only indirectly, by letting a woman in love speak for the first time in the world but attributing her incantation solely to her husband, King Solomon, the long history of Christian mysticism foregrounds women whose amorous fervor is equal to that of men, when it does not surpass it. Saint Teresa of Avila (1515–82) explores the "diamond" of the "castle of the soul," not neglecting to observe that the "knowledge" or "representation" of that space is impenetrable, and her conquest begins at the very bottom, in the company of "reptiles." The negative and annihilating Saint Angela of Foligno (1248–1309) describes herself as "composed of nonlove" and approaches the divine as an "abyss," a "thing that has no name." Saint Hildegard von Bingen (1098–1179) writes her "visions," which stand on the "roof" of words, and does not spare herself wolf heads, leopards, bears, and lions, which penetrate like a scanner into her blood vessels, her brain, her heart, and even her bones. Over time all these women try to find the words for that sensory effervescence, which is addressed not to a partner, to an other, but to that great Other they call "God" and who, passing through the body of Jesus, weds the universe as a whole, not to mention the universe of the loving woman herself. Often disappointed wives or mistresses in the secular world, these women in quest of love, these Christian mystics, transmit truths to us that, even at the start of the twenty-first century, are not fundamentally opaque.

Does love, closer to our own time, still remain a trap that confines the excitability of naïve women devoted to the Other to the point of masochism? Or is it still the experience that allows the most audacious of them to go to the limits of pleasure and self-knowledge? These questions remain open as one passes through the blazing fires of "pure love" according to Jeanne Guyon (1648–1717). How many "women of letters," even now, delight in the role of oblatory mothers in the service of their chosen, and necessarily ingenious, son—a more or less faithful replica of the relations Mme Guyon maintained with the genius Fénelon, who defied Bossuet, a paternal figure if ever there was one? Ready to follow their "great man" without always properly understanding him, these contemporary emulators of Mme Guyon offer themselves as an accommodating spectacle to a society that does not miss the chance to be amused when the taboo of incest is flouted, if only in fantasy: "pure love," already very garrulous at that time, has now become an advertising slot, an eye-catching product of the market, one of many.

Contrary to graphomaniacs such as Mme Guyon, the taciturn Enlightenment libertines let Diderot and Sade do the writing for them. Later, after the storm of romanticism, Mme de Staël and George Sand explored the psychological intricacies of amorous women and timidly lifted the veil on their sexual desires. But it was not until the twentieth century that we would learn more about female eroticism. In the wake of the mystics came Laure's masochistic ecstasy with Georges Bataille. Combining raw desires and obscene language in *Story of O,* Dominique Aury was able to unveil, with disturbing decorum in Jean Paulhan's own words, the violent and no less dominating passivity of feminine jouissance. Subsequent generations dared try their hand at pornography when they did not take up residency there, from Régine Deforges to Virginie Despentes, and, recently, Catherine Millet with her clinical account. From the glorification of male myths in Marguerite Yourcenar to the intoxication of the pain of loving in Marguerite Duras to sexuality neutralized by the irony of tropisms in Nathalie Sarraute, the moderns are anti-Penelopes who continue to weave and unweave the threads that connect them to Eros. And let us not forget those, rarer in France and less famous than their Anglo-Saxon sisters, who prefer to devote themselves to his formidable twin, Thanatos. Women excel, in fact, at accounts of assassinations and cruelty of every kind: for example, Marie Desplechin reserves her dark sarcasm for the brutalities for which a woman knows how to be both the wound and the knife, the deplorable victim and the sinister actress.

I could not mention all of them. Their works, famous or still marginal, constitute the perimeter of this garden of feminine love in whose center Colette holds court. Naïve or lucid, immoderate or seductive, confirmed women writers or still hesitant adventuresses, these women cultivate its edges, do audacious surveys of it. When they manage to create a social or psychological "universe" that distinguishes them from the surrounding literary market, they withdraw back into their experience of love, in the narrow flower bed of their own symptoms. Opposite them, Colette shines in her "mother's house" with *all* the fires of love; she awakens the full rainbow of a feminine sensibility, on the lookout for all other sensibilities. It is not that she went as far as possible in her burning desires: other women may have surpassed her in erotic temerity. Nor is it that she collected experiences of a richness or universality previously unprecedented. But Sido's daughter succeeded in arranging the diversified and often painful specter of her loves in an Eden that is a *language of well-being*. Monstrosity, approached greedily, is itself tamed by Colette, to be restored to us livable and invigorating. Having surveyed even the desert of love, that vagabond flees it, only to better replant it with the "tendrils of the vine." Hence we find, written by her, one of the most supreme sentences in French literature, because it is the most disillusioned: "The vast, but not the desert. To discover there is no desert: that is all I need to prevail over what besieges me."[4]

LOVE EXPRESSES ITSELF ONLY IN METAPHORS . . .

In the double game of her pleasures and her jouissance, that seeker of the exact word understood that love can be expressed only indirectly, through displacement, and incompletely. Her classicism thus distorts modernism, and she can come across as a true postmodern. Colette's language, avoiding both confession and curtness, both lax obscenity and tyrannical mastery, is fundamentally free because it follows the path of metaphors.

So jouissance cannot be expressed? Naturally, Saint Teresa; perfectly right, Angela of Foligno! I agree with you one hundred percent. Since the mists of time all those who have tried their hand at it have wasted their breath. And yet now it can finally be expressed: infinitely, indefinitely, when a woman weds her senses, as Sido does, to the "four cardinal points" and celebrates with each metaphor a union of love with Being. Her writing then becomes a torrent, a current: not a current of consciousness, or even of the unconscious, but a current discharging the self, by virtue of which the Self joins the world's flesh, the torrent of love and of phenomena. There is no other way of being *au courant*, in the know, about one's own ecstasy, one's misfortunes, one's narcissism, one's perversions, one's couplings and their downfall, than this metaphorical-metamorphic current that writes them.

The writing of such a deluge of metaphors is not the "language" of love, *it is love* as such, that is, a voluptuousness accompanied by words, reaching toward the impossible and the inevitable. Colette manages to make it contagious. Beyond "love" and "happiness," whose impostures she mocks, she communicates not enthusiasm—the Greek *entheos* means "inspired by a god," and nothing is less inspired than the "plump bee" Colette—but an *acquiescence to the world*, in which her "Ego" slips away and is lost. She communicates an acknowledgment of Being, which swallows her up; a sense of belonging to a world without death, where rebirth is expected. "Nothing withers, it is I who move away, let us be reassured."[5]

In effect, let us be reassured: beyond time and changing mores—our own are freer, as everyone knows—Colette's images of love make the false peasant, the indefatigable stylist, "our Colette." That expression was used, in a sort of republican fervor, during the final years of her life. In repeating the expression, I would like to give it a transversal meaning that could link national pride to Colette's appetite for Being. In hindsight we discover she is not simply a French writer and that, though her writing may call for the plural ("our"), it is not the plural of a community—it is not the "we" of the Burgundians, or people of native French stock, or citizens of the interwar period, or anything else. It is a "we" that is au courant about the pure and the impure, a "we" of transfusion, of contagion, of feeling/felt: a paradoxical space of "chiasmus," explains Merleau-Ponty, an interface of inside and outside, subject and object, a polytopy of decanting and communion beyond the fractures, the cruelty, the war between the sexes and the isolation of different species. It is a certain way of being outside oneself, of expressing a disseminated, disidentified, inhuman self, a self au courant about the world's flesh. It is a way of being in love, obviously, but in Colette's pure and impure sense; she is au courant about every kind of love and fixes on none.

. . . OR, HOW TO WREST ONESELF AWAY FROM LOVE

"Love, bread of my pen and of my life!"[6] she exclaimed until her twilight years. And yet, that obstinate, amorous woman continually rid herself of love, made fun of it, and was wary of it: is it not that estrangement that allowed her to develop, in writing *Retreat from Love,* what she called "forces that have nothing to do with literature"[7] but that, in transforming her relation to others and to the world, also and above all changed her way of writing? The word "love" itself appeared grotesque to her: already, Claudine lamented, in approaching Rézi, that "that unnuanced word is inadequate for me."[8] Colette replaces it fourteen times with "desires," seven times with "arousal," six times with "tenderness."[9] And she laughs at writers who, like a transpyrenean aesthete she knew who used a single pejorative, "pig," exclusively, have "only one word to say 'love,' it's just as ridiculous."[10] From the start Colette sought, with Minne, "a love different from Love [that] could bloom in the very shadow of Love." Could that be possible if Maugis desires and renounces her, since "something in me is [. . .] more valuable [. . .] than my beauty"?[11] Love, of which Sido often disapproves ("one of the last letters from my mother: 'Love is not an honorable feeling' "),[12] may be even more harshly devalorized by the daughter: "Any love at all, if one relies on it, tends to arrange itself like a digestive tube."[13]

Motherhood and marriage are two "banalities"[14] of love that conceal the variety of the world. But they are banalities one misses, all the same, as Fanny did, thinking of the imminent departure of the "other one," her rival who had become like a sister: "Tomorrow, dreamed Fanny, tomorrow, if she goes away, I will be like this, alone beside this fire, like a woman who is finished with a big part of love."[15]

Beginning with Claudine, feminine passion is bittersweet and expresses itself in oxymorons: "Voluptuousness appeared to me like a staggering and almost somber wonder. [. . .] Pleasure [. . .] overwhelms me, crushes me in a mysterious despair that I seek and fear."[16] Of that passionate love, Renée Néré restores the keen pleasures before opting to wait for absence and, if not for renunciation, at least for the necessary displacement of love called writing—a true vagabondage and the only one. Flower, fruit, and animal metaphors then unite with carnal details and portray the physiology of the kiss according to Colette, who avoids vulgarity as much as lyricism, restoring sexual pleasure in its plenitude, albeit unsatisfied. She devotes precise attention to the organs, to the rhythms of the partners, and shows the sweet irony of woman's defeat in an ultimately shared jouissance:

> There is almost no space left, almost no air left between our two faces, and I breathe abruptly, as if I saw myself with a start, in order to free myself. [. . .] Yes, the lips that kiss me, sweet, fresh, impersonal, are truly the same as yesterday, and their ineffectualness irritates me. . . . Suddenly they change, and I no longer recognize the kiss, which takes on life, becomes insistent, shuts down, and resumes, moves about, rhythmic, then stops as if to await a response that does not come. . . .
>
> I move my head imperceptibly, because of the mustache that brushes against my nostrils, with a fragrance of vanilla and honeyed tobacco. . . . Oh! . . . all of a sudden, in spite of myself, my mouth has opened of itself, has opened

as irresistibly as a ripe plum split open in the sun. . . . From my lips to my flanks to my knees, that insistent pain, that swelling of a wound that wants to reopen and pour out—forgotten voluptuousness—is now reborn and propagates.

[. . .] Nothing is urgent, except for that kiss to begin again. We have all the time . [. . .] His mouth has the taste of my own at present, and the slight odor of my face powder. . . . It wants to become new, that knowing mouth, and to further vary its caress, but already I dare indicate my preference for an almost motionless, long, drowsy kiss—the slow crushing, one against the other, of two flowers, where only the palpitation of two coupled pistils quivers. . . .

Now we rest [. . .] my submissive dog eyes, slightly sheepish, slightly beaten, very coddled, accepting everything, the leash, the collar, the place at her master's feet.[17]

Further on, she confesses a masochistic submission: "Female I was, and female I again find myself, to derive suffering and jouissance from it."[18]

Nevertheless, in spite of that sincerity, which obliges her to describe herself as an "obstinate pleasure brute," a "gluttonous beast," an "abandoned child that trembles in me, weak, highstrung, quick to hold out her arms, to implore: 'Don't leave me alone,' " Colette discovers a new imperative. That "voluptuous body with closed eyes, deliberately blind, stretched out, ready to perish rather than leave the site of its joy," also contains the paradoxical desire of a woman seeking her independence. The fear of betrayal and the jealousy toward the inevitable rival overtly feed that desire to flee. More secretly, feminine love, according to Colette, is always an anxiety, alongside and beyond voluptuousness. It was wrong for some to say that the floral Colette is without a soul: it is the *boundless unknown* she dreads, because she proposes to seek it, but alone—escaping through writing. Consider:

If I had only to give myself! But there is not just voluptuousness. . . . Voluptuousness holds, in the boundless desert of love, an ardent and very small place, blazing so bright that at first one sees only it: I am not a brand-new girl, to be blinded by its brilliance. Around that inconstant hearth, it is the unknown, it is danger. . . . What do I know of the man I love and who wants me? When we have risen from a brief embrace, or even from a long night, we will have to begin to live next to each other, through each other. He will bravely hide the first disappointments that come from me, and I will keep quiet about mine, out of pride, modesty, pity, and especially because I will have expected, dreaded, them, *because I will recognize them.* [. . .] What to do [. . .] to write, briefly, since time is running short, and to tell lies.[19]

These confessions are striking for their naturalness: neither dully naturalistic nor pathetically seductive or scabrous, their simplicity would have been commonplace without the intensity of the voluptuousness and of the anxiety, without the concern for sensual detail, without the phrasing that follows the climax of pleasure and accompanies it in its fall. There is an astonishing health to Colette's eroticism, which she attempts to make admissible through the word "pure." Only a few metaphors hint at the monstrous anomaly of that sexuality, so natural in appearance: do those "coupled pistils" evoke the male-female couple or, rather, the coupling of two males within the heterosexual embrace itself? Does the vagabond in love with independence always remain a "dog"? Behind the conventional idyll, a style laden with allusive descriptions raises the specter of prison and of wounds:

I escape, but I am not rid of you yet, I know that. Vagabond and free, I will sometimes wish for the shadow of your walls. . . . How many times will I return to you, dear support where I rest and wound myself? How many times will I call for what you could give me, a long, suspended, stoked, renewed voluptuousness . . . the winged fall, the fainting spell where forces are reborn from their death itself . . . the musical murmur of crazed blood . . . the odor of burned sandalwood and of trampled grass. . . . Ah! For a long time yet you will be one of the cravings along my path![20]

These apprehensions lead suggestively to the image of the sadistic lash: "There is no longer in me, above, below me, anything but the lashed sea, the crumbling stone, the panting cloud."[21]

It would therefore be wrong to believe that Renée-Colette is making plans for a narcissistic retreat, a naïve protection against the risks eroticism makes us take in relation to the other, to better confine herself within a cocoon of mirrors destined for possible glory. Beyond that defensive or counterphobic strategy—which is not alien to writing, a solitary act and a self-affirmation—Colette will expose herself to new loves, which will spare her neither the surprises of voluptuousness nor the ordeals of the encounter. After Willy, through Missy, Jouvenel, or the transgression with Bertrand, and even with her "best friend" Goudeket, she immerses herself in a polyphony of love, hungry to penetrate—beyond any coupling—the intimate secret of beings and things: of marginals by preference, whose "purity" she likes, plants and beasts quite naturally, with which she continues to take her jouissance in a bacchic delirium. But she is less the Bacchante who, according to the Greek legend, runs tormented by a destructive madness, than a sovereign female and jubilatory Dionysus:

Her initial contact with things came about through all the senses. She was not satisfied to look at them, she had to sniff them, she had to taste them. When she'd go into an unfamiliar garden, I'd tell her: "You're going to eat it again!" and it was extraordinary to see her set to work. She went about it hastily and greedily. [. . .] She pulled off the flower petals, examined them, sniffed them for a long time, she crumpled the leaves, chewed them, licked the poisonous berries, the toadstools, intensely reflecting on what she had smelled, tasted. [. . .] Finally, she left the garden, gath-

ered up her scarf, hat, shoes, stockings, dog, and husband,
which had been abandoned one after the other. Her nose
and forehead stained with yellow pollen, her hair mussed
with twigs sticking out of it, a bump here, a scratch there,
her face unpowdered and her neck moist, staggering, short
of breath, she was just like a Bacchante after libations.[22]

Hence, when she wrested herself from "that good fat love,"[23]
that "surface foam,"[24] from its "decorative layout in the cul-de-
sac style of those harbors,"[25] since "all love tends to create a dead-
end atmosphere,"[26] she accompanied that act with a search for
other variants of passionate relationships.

It is folly to believe that the periods devoid of love are
"blanks" in a woman's existence. On the contrary. What
remains, in the telling, of a passionate attachment? Perfect
love can be recounted in three lines: "He loved me, I loved
Him, His presence abolished every other presence; we were
happy, then He stopped loving me and I suffered. . . . "
Honestly, the rest is oratory, or verbiage. With love gone,
there comes a lull that revives friends, passersby, as many
episodes as a well-populated dream entails, normal feelings
such as fear, cheerfulness, boredom, an awareness of time
and of its fleetingness.[27]

In counterpoint to love, friendship is lauded as a "counselor
more powerful than love . . . with an exquisite essence, slow to
develop, easily suppressed, [which] quibbles, sulks, and withdraws, whereas love, that good fat love, presses on and moves the
obstacle."[28]

In *Break of Day* Vial is supposed to be the "perfect lover" capable of "descending to take his place in the depths, where love [...]
does not always have access."[29] Could these abyssal zones be those
of indifference? Colette objects: "But I am not dead, far from it, or
unfeeling. I can be hurt."[30]

Without regret, the narrator is animated by a new fervor when
she observes, in her mature years, "that it is going to be necessary

to live—or even to die—without [her] life or death depending on love."[31] In admitting she "is born as well under every sky where she recovers from the pain of loving,"[32] Colette considers the interludes between two passions, the "blanks" in her life, definitively more romantic than love itself. As a result one is left to "draw them from the shadows, where the shameless obligation to speak of love in my own name relegated them."[33] The "contacts" as well as the "relationships" turn out to be "cheerful, varied, multiple," and lead her to discover that life is possible in spite of loneliness: the short trip on the Claridge hotel elevator puts her "in contact, by itself, with a varied humanity,"[34] and the friendship with Hélène Picard expands "to become a relationship that separation strains without breaking, which proves its strength in absence and forms its judgments with a disdainful freedom."[35] Everything strengthens her in that opening to the world.

FROM THE WOMAN-OBJECT TO OBJECTLESS LOVE

Illusion, fantasy, dream—the writer tends to mourn love by linking it to the past: "Only my dreams are left to resuscitate, from time to time, a love."[36] "Some day, I will see myself breathing in the love from my past, and I will admire the great agitations, the wars, the celebrations, the loneliness."[37] Indeed, there is another pleasure, "not keen but honorable, of not speaking about love,"[38] especially since true possession (but is that not already a variant of love?) is possible only in abstention, as Sido did not neglect to teach her. "There can be no doubt about it, my mother knew, she who never learned anything, as she said, 'except by getting burned,' she knew that one possesses in abstention, and only in abstention."[39]

Colette was perhaps one of the first to focus on the role of the *woman-object*, played especially by Vinca for Phil at the beginning of *The Ripening Seed*: "He had no more desire to caress her than to beat her, but he wanted her trusting, devoted to him alone, and available like the treasures that made him blush—dried petals, agate marbles, shells and seeds, pictures, a little silver watch."[40] At the end of that novel, and in many declarations scattered throughout her works, Colette asserts that the role of slave may be inevitable. All the same, it does not take the vagabond long to transfigure the shackled woman. But it is a cat, Kiki-la-Doucette, to whom, in 1908, Colette entrusts the task of articulating a new version of *objectless love,* the incommensurable love of an ecstatic ego that, because it is free of its objects, can remake its world to fit its excitement: "As for me, I love! I love everything I love so much! If you knew how I embellish everything I love, and what pleasure I give myself in loving!"[41] Our female Dionysus dreams of herself as a feline.

The palette of love is divided up in a thousand and one ways. Love as game: "Yes, I am still playing, now and then, with my little wool merchant. Nothing has changed, except that now I'm the one who's playing less well than he, and who's losing."[42] Love as "contentment" and "surprise": waking and sleeping alternate, "as new as love, but less restricted, and free of sex. He sleeps, I stay awake. He sleeps, I stay awake."[43] Love as flightiness: "One must never ask even a single question. [. . .] The true name of love, which represses and condemns everything around it, is 'flightiness.' "[44] Against "general ideas," especially those concerning love, "I live on the capital of frivolity, which comes to sustain long lives."[45] Colette, because she is not unscrupulous, does not fail to judge that frivolity "crude": "But what strange resignation! A kiss, and everything becomes simple, tasty, superficial, and with a slightly crude ingenuousness."[46] That flightiness is no doubt devastating, since "everything that is loved strips you bare";[47] but is it not preferable to the sticky ungainliness of the "serious attachment"?[48] "You claim you love me, which means that I bear, at every hour, the weight of your worry, of your canine attention, and of your suspicion."[49] Love as absence and waiting, which can be the mark of a detestable submission: "I am ashamed of myself, I who *wait.* [. . .] I detest myself, and I detest Jean."[50] It can also be seen as the sign of an animal wisdom: is not the Beauce dog an expert in the art of waiting for her mistress?[51] But that patience is also and very naturally akin to the true aristocracy of the heart: "Waiting, waiting. . . . It's learned at the good schools, where highly elegant ways, the supreme knack for knowing-how-to-decline are also taught."[52]

Combining "old wives' tales" and the subtle lessons of independence in that puzzle of love psychology, Colette was able to lavish a true sentimental education on women of her time. But it would be wrong to believe that women readers of today, half a century after the writer's death, no longer need it. Every day the women's magazines and novels vaunted by the media bore us silly with that "sexual liberation" and even "hard-core sex," whose protagonists have in no way surpassed the Colettian character of the "amorous woman, fatalistic, verging on childishness, gourmandise, and kindness, lazy like those whom the weight of a serious attachment makes weary by midday."[53] The new version of love, in contrast, if it exists, is obliged always to begin, as Colette wishes, with that minimal declaration Renée Néré addresses to her partner and that initiates her independence: "I am not of your opinion."[54] It is only then that a "circumspect respiration" opens, something Colette continues to call a "love" but that gives the slip to "that bungler, avidity." That vagabondage of love, though not truly a libertinage, does not reject "what I am most unfamiliar with: the brief encounter"[55] protected by silence: "It is our silence as superior animals that enhances somewhat our swift adventure."[56] In reply to Jean, for whom "it is a question of voluptuousness, voluptuousness, and more voluptuousness," Renée says: "Why couldn't delicacy have almost as great a share as cynicism in our attitude?"[57] There is delicacy, cynicism, but also ambivalence: woman, according to Colette, feels a "fraternal ease" with man. And though she is never "vanquished" in pleasure, though she has "never known *that,* the intelligent joy of the flesh that immediately recognizes and adopts its master and that is eager for him, becomes easy, docile, generous. . . . It is so beautiful, so simple, it doesn't resemble love"[58]—does she not necessarily place her partner in "danger of homosexuality"?[59] "I am proud he owes me as much as I owe him."[60]

For Colette, love, confused with voluptuousness and yet stretched into ideal self-affirmation, at times rises to the pinnacle of the Western spiritual tradition and allows itself to be celebrated like a Janus, with love/illusion and love/cruelty as its two faces. Alongside her never-refuted fidelity to the original Eden, the only "complete image of love" the writer celebrates is that of her parents: "It was good for me to know, and to remind myself at times, of that complete image of love: a man's head, already old, engulfed in a kiss to a little housewife's hand, graceful and wrinkled."[61] It is that family garden, or that fantasy of parents reunited, that feeds her own stubbornness in loving, the same stubbornness that she reads as specific to all women and that Mitsou describes, with a laconic perspicacity, as a stubborn persistence in illusion: "Nevertheless, a woman [. . .] flowers, knows how to adopt a bearing, a color, to create an illusion for the most delicate ones. My love, I am going to try to become your illusion."[62] The fierce Armande, an inverted replica of the delicate Mitsou, opens her heart to Maxime only when she sees him hurt, almost dying: "She descended and gave him her hand. Then she synchronized her step with that of the stretcher-bearers and walked downcast, covered with stains and disheveled, as if she were emerging from the very hands of love."[63]

Could love, according to Colette, be at its extreme a love of the impossible, intoxicated by the threat of castration and, in the end, a love to the death? "To suffer from absence, to suffer from waiting, to suffer from love, it's all the same."[64] It is nevertheless, and perhaps for that very reason, a terrifying cosmic force, love beyond the sexes, a reckless freedom that cuts us off from social ties: "And always we place 'fear' where we ought sometimes to have 'love,' love in complete freedom, subtle complicity with unknown forces, mad palpitation of an extraordinary but not unique heart, reckless regression toward what sociability took away from us."[65]

Mourning the object of love, however, does not plunge Colette and her heroines into the melancholy of an "unused love."[66] Even while recognizing the loneliness of lovers—since pleasure is incommunicable in "our lives as voluptuous strangers"[67]—she also immediately falls back on an avid sampling of the autoerotic side of love, which she calls a *voluptuousness*. And the "brute giddy on pleasure"[68] auscultates that "cyst one carries within oneself": "I swear to you it is scarcely mental."[69] Once the connection to the other has been compromised, not thrust aside but held at a distance, all her attention comes to bear on her own senses: "Senses? Yes, I have them . . . I had them at a time when Adolphe Taillandy deigned concern himself with them. Timid, routine senses happy with the usual caress that satisfied them, fearful of any libertine effort or complications . . . slow to get aroused, but slow to subside, healthy senses, in short."[70] The partner turns out to be less a person than "fresh flesh" of which the "old Bacchante"[71] gets her fill, on the lookout for the "demons of a silent sabbath agitat[ing]" her.[72]

Her sex is everywhere and nowhere, as mental as it is cutaneous: "My body [. . .] is more intelligent than my brain. It feels more acutely, more completely than my brain. When my body thinks [. . .] everything else falls silent. At those moments, my whole skin has a soul."[73] But her pleasure is above all oral:

Dazzled by the sudden shade, I made out, on the table, the four o'clock bread, the loaf still warm, and I broke open the fragrant crust to empty it of its soft dough and to pour raspberry jelly on it. . . . The afternoon snack! My favorite little gobbler's meal, a varied bite I could take out on the main branch of the walnut tree, or into the barn, or to the afternoon recess, an eventful time when we found a way to eat while running, laughing, playing hopscotch, without any of us choking to death.[74]

The celebratory body prepares its whole self to dance to the world's rhythm:

You came across me when I was little and playful, dancing on the road and chasing my blue shadow ahead of me. I veered like a bee, and the gold dust pollen powdered my feet and hair the color of the road. . . . You saw me coming back from the fountain, cradling the amphora in the hollow of my hip, as the water, to the rhythm of my step, leapt onto my tunic in round tears, in silver snakes, in short curly rockets that rose, frozen, up to my cheek.[75]

Yet no kindness softens that infinite sensuality, which can be experienced as a threatening, unfathomable excitement: "O pleasure, ram that cracks one's forehead and begins again!" "It may be only displaced curiosity, which persists in knowing, on this side of death, a little of what there is beyond life."[76] But it is also feared, like a routine that allows mental laziness to set in, and runs the risk of abolishing the lover's creative capacities: "Like all those who never used their vigor to its limit, I am hostile to people who are consumed. Voluntary consumption always seems like a sort of alibi to me. I'm afraid there is not enough difference between the habit of voluptuousness and, for example, the cigarette habit."[77]

With an ironic tenderness, Colette mocks the emulators of Bovaryism, tormented by an eternal aspiration on the part of female desire for grandeur, necessarily impossible to find and disappointing by definition: "Always that mania for something grand. [. . .] What do I call grand? Well, I have no idea, Madame, since I haven't got it! If I had had it even once, I guarantee you I would surely have recognized immediately that it was grand!"[78] An interminable consumption of the other, the slow— never total—eclipse of the partner in favor of the flowering of Being, takes shape in such a pursuit of love.

Jealousy—violently felt, then abandoned—marks the stages of that quasi-dissolution of the other. First the amorous woman wants to possess the lover to the point of wishing to kill her rival, "to the point of understanding that there are only two kinds of human beings: those who have killed, and those who have not killed."[79] "It is only the homicidal wish that teaches jealousy a lesson."[80] Then that desire for death acknowledges itself as a desire for the other woman and, even more radically, as a desire to possess the image of oneself, the rival being the ideal mirror, the supreme narcissistic version of the amorous self, with whom a pact will be sealed against the man: "With that beautiful blonde woman, with a sweet brunette whose hair was similar to mine—with another, and yet another, I stopped exchanging, I will never again exchange, over a man, through a man, that intense threat, these reflections of one mirror in another, that indefatigable emanation, which wronged the lover himself."[81] Only then will jealousy, "the curiosity of an incurable man who finds amusement in his illness,"[82] stop tormenting Colette. The writer will rush to leave her "abode," which was not as unbearable as she had made it out to be: "I had the opportunity to descend to the depths of jealousy, to settle there and to dream of it at length. It is not a suffocating abode, and if, in writing, I used to compare it to hell like everyone else, I beg you to ascribe the word to my lyricism."[83]

Cannibalistic mourning of the other thus leads Colette to a conception of love that disassociates itself from happiness to become a pure quest for the mot juste and to culminate in extreme voluptuousness, which is nothing other than the voluptuousness of naming. In fact, love, strained if not broken, is by essence the opposite of happiness: "One learns to live, then? Yes, if only without happiness. Bliss teaches nothing. To live without happiness, and not to waste away from it, that is an occupation, almost a profession."[84] Indeed, happy love is not content to be sterile: "Happiness? Well, I don't want it. [. . .] It's a terrible sterility, happiness is. It's just material for a book."[85] It devours you raw: "Is not receiving happiness from a being—yes, we have to use that word 'happiness,' which I don't understand—choosing the sauce with which we want to be eaten?"[86] "Here I'm returning to a time when I lived in a peculiar state of dissimulated banishment and unhappiness."[87]

That dual aspiration for complete voluptuousness and independence in relation to the male partner can be reinforced only in female homosexuality, itself founded on bisexuality, which Colette from the outset claims for herself.

A QUEEN OF BISEXUALITY

The writer asserts that, as an adolescent, she imagined herself "queen of the earth," endowed with a "boy's square brow."[88] "I was twelve years old, with the language and manner of an intelligent boy, a bit gruff, but my strange appearance was not mannish, because of a body already femininely shaped, and above all two long braids, whistling like whips around me."[89] She proclaims: " 'I'll be a sailor!' [. . .] because she sometimes dreams of being a boy and of wearing blue trousers and a beret."[90] And she attributes that conviction of being both girl and boy to her milieu, to a natural and liberal upbringing in which seduction has nothing to do with gender: "I come from a milieu where male and female beauty are equally valued. [. . .] the little frequenting I did, in my past life, of a world without epithets made it easy for me to find out that the ways of pleasing are the same in men as in women, and hardly more discreet."[91]

That androgyny suits equally well the ambiguity of her husbands and partners: the "threefold" Renaud, for example, composed of "childish rage, amusement, and feminine modesty," drives Colette to play the role of his "violated ship's boy."[92] In her early days Colette, a "masculine" woman, "self-assured in the company of men," said she was "hostile toward the idea of associating with women." She feared their "sumptuousness, which required both caution and a certain distrust."[93] But, when that fear was promptly and valiantly overcome, as we know, the writer declared peremptorily: "My aim is true mental hermaphroditism, which charges certain highly organized beings."[94] Her friend Marguerite Moreno imputed to Colette's dual nature the fear the writer inspired in men and the separations that resulted: Might it not be such virility, such psychic bisexuality, that leads man to pit himself, in Colette's company, not against a woman but against another man? "Why do you not resign yourself to thinking that certain women represent, for certain men, a danger of homosexuality?"[95] What to do then? What being in the world could recognize and accept without fear that "mental hermaphroditism" so powerfully embraced by Colette? "But, if you're telling the truth, who will take us for women?—Women. Only women are neither offended nor fooled by our virile wit."[96] Very subtly Colette traces an often vague line of demarcation between, on one hand, her bisexuality, which she believes common to all women, and, on the other, Sapphic libertinage, which itself has several versions.

Endogenous female homosexuality is itself presented in Colette's writing as a voluptuousness between daughter and mother. Missy was the source of that discovery: "You will offer me voluptuousness, leaning over me, your eyes full of a maternal anxiety, you who, in your passionate friend, are looking for the child you did not have."[97] A healing relic of the original bond, it cannot be confused, according to Colette, with what a man or some other stranger imagines as a "vice," even a Gomorrhean "love": the two women seek refuge with each other to console each other for the harshness of life and, above all, for the troubles attributable to heterosexuality.[98] Since the female couple is, as a result, "such a fragile creation, and threatened by everything,"[99] the two women lovers cannot imagine or dread separation: "*twin* bodies, *similarly* afflicted, devoted to the *same* concerns, to the *same* fateful chastity. . . . A woman is amazed, moved to resemble a beloved woman, and feels pity . . . [. . .] it is not from passion that the fidelity of two women blossoms, but thanks to a sort of *kinship*."[100] In that version of female homosexuality, which Colette perceives as "parental," the wedding of sameness cements a "delicate solidarity that lives only on incessant and shared concerns."[101] And here is the idyllic portrait of that paradise, where time suspends its flight in "a day of sweetly enjoyed retirement":

It is that sensuality without resolution and without demands, happy with the exchanged gaze, the arm on the shoulder, moved by the odor of warm wheat that has sought shelter in a head of hair, it is these delights of constant presence and habit that engender and excuse fidelity. A marvelous brevity of days, like a lamp reflected in a series of mirrors! Perhaps that love, which is called an outrage to love, eludes the seasons, the waning of love, provided it is governed with an invisible severity, that it is nourished by little, that it lives groping and aimless, and that its sole flower is a trust that the other sort of love cannot fathom or understand but can only envy—the way that, by virtue of its grace, half a century passes like a day of sweetly enjoyed retirement.[102]

Does such an idealization resist the conflicts and hostilities of everyday life? Colette enjoys cultivating the paradisiacal tone of female homosexuality as the "pure," negative stand-in for dangerous voluptuousness: "I wrote 'kinship' when I perhaps ought to have written 'similarity.' Close resemblance heartens even voluptuousness."[103] It is easy to imagine that it is sublimation, the act of writing, that is proposed as the ultimately successful and lasting realization of that version of love, of which only Sido, the imaginary mother, could be the goddess. Does not Colette describe the communication between lesbians as an excessively economical cipher, a staggering alphabet with mute trills, "tendrils of the vine" of an exemplary swiftness? "I took pleasure with admirable swiftness in the mute language, in the exchange of threats, of promises, as if, once the *slow male was thrust aside, every message from woman to woman became clear,* staggering, limited to a small, infallible number of signs."[104]

Nevertheless, she will have to develop that "mute language" in novels and short stories, to extract the pair of female homosexuals from the "dead-end atmosphere" in which it gets bogged down, like any love. Another flaw affects that parental osmosis: the sensorial presence of the twin body, its tangible reality, is indispensable. Otherwise, the Gomorrhean relationship breaks up: "A woman is not faithful to a woman who is not there."[105]

Hence we learn of the extreme economy underlying Colette's elliptical style: in short, would it entail *translating, as close as possible to what is felt,* these lightning flashes, the immediate intuitive sense of belonging that links the two women in love? The more virile of them might therefore not be the one who looks the part, but the one who, her senses fixed on that quasi-mute osmosis of love between two women, manages to transpose the succinct signs into that tight and hypersensitive enunciation I have called "tendrils of the vine."[106]

The Sapphic experiences that attract Colette's desire and attention stem from her "mental hermaphroditism," without, nonetheless, being confused with it. They are revealed in the *Claudine* books, with the teachers and students of Montigny, then, more explicitly, with Rézi. The Gomorrah of 1900 finds an echo in Colette's works with the evocations of Missy, Natalie Barney—the "pope of Lesbos"—and her friends, in particular the poetess Renée Vivien (pseudonym of Pauline Tarn). Contradictory feelings permeated that milieu of "castes": distrust between Colette and Natalie Barney; Colette's fascination with Renée Vivien's melancholic writing; but also her disavowal of Renée's "puerility" and erotic consumption, which is suspected of being "less than sincere."[107] And, above all, a deep ambivalence runs through her affair with Mathilde de Morny, alias Missy. The latter, divorced from the marquis de Belbeuf in 1903, shared Colette's life from 1906 to 1911.

Missy lent her features to Margot in *The Vagabond* and *The Shackle,* and can be made out in *Tendrils of the Vine* ("Sleepless Night," "Gray Day," "The Last Fire") and in *The Pure and the Impure.* "The Lady Knight" mortified the marquise, who had been abandoned by Colette. In a letter to Marguerite Moreno, the writer would call Missy an "incomplete being,"[108] shortly after her suicide in 1944. After being inhibited for a long time by Proust's vast Gomorrhean fresco, Colette finally portrayed Sapphism in *The Pure and the Impure.* Far removed from the narrative subtleties and the accumulation of psychological details characteristic of the various characters in *In Search of Lost Time,* it is, on the contrary, a lapidary text. With that "decretal gift of observation" she attributed to Sido[109] and that she possessed to a remarkable degree, Colette sketched Gomorrah as mininarratives incrusted in a tightly written essay, which depicts an idyllic Sapphism alongside another, rather ridiculous one.

Driven by a sharp skeptical tenderness, the writer hails the emotional devotion, the pure quest for love and solidarity impossible to find elsewhere, that she observed in female homosexuals: "Over and above an anxious and weak courtship, her square white forehead, her anxious eyes, nearly black, sought what [the Lady Knight] never found: a calm emotional climate."[110] "Among those women both free and frightened, who loved sleepless nights, semidarkness, idleness, play, I almost never encountered cynicism."[111] Comparable to aristocrats who have lost their standing, certain Gomorrheans fascinated Colette. In their underclass eroticism,

she emphasizes the timid dignity with which they allow themselves to be mistreated by voracious young people who take advantage of their (masochistic?) need to give:

> It was different with their protégées. A brutal, cunning, of-
> ten greedy group of young people pressed around these
> women, who, from their origins no less than from their
> childhood, had a taste for the vulgar accomplice and the
> comrade in livery, because of an incurable timidity, which
> they dissimulated the best they could. The pride of giving
> pleasure lifted the weight of any other dignity from them,
> they tolerated a young mouth using the familiar *tu* form
> with them, and they rediscovered, behind the insult, the
> trembling and secret diversion of dinners from their child-
> hood at the table in the servants' hall.[112]

Nevertheless, disapproval bursts out without warning: "Sapphic libertinage is the only unacceptable one."[113] That had to be
expected: if lesbian love is of a parental nature and functions as
an antidepressant, it is not erotic. In the cozy cocoon, which is
only a "creation of the mind," "feverish pleasure," according to
Colette, has only a "small part," whereas the intervention of the
drives of men, who "like to be lusted after as something superfluous," can easily annihilate the peacefulness of that "incubator." "The most ordinary invasion can mortally change the
steady incubator atmosphere, within which two women devote
themselves to a creation of their minds."[114]

The writer reserves her most acerbic criticism, however, for
those of her sisters who mimic men: an Amazon is only a "rat
that has lost its tail." "Seated on the beautiful back of a bony
purebred, elevated by the cleft base of a chestnut croup on which
two ellipses of creamy light were dancing, they were freed from
a clumsiness that afflicted their gait, the clumsiness of a rat that
had lost its tail."[115] In her eyes there is nothing more distressing
than a woman who imagines she is a man: "You understand, a
woman who remains a woman is a complete being. She lacks
nothing, even beside her 'friend.' But if she gets it into her head

that she wants to be a man, she's grotesque. What is more ridiculous, and sadder, than a simulated . . . man?"[116] Colette shares the view of a certain Loulou, who says to her masculine woman friend: "Well, as for me, it humiliates me to be with a man who can't pee against a wall."[117]

By contrast, the male homosexual seems to be accepted without reservation: "I have it in me to recognize a kind of legitimacy in pederasty and to acknowledge its eternal character."[118] "There is a powerful seductiveness that emanates from a being of uncertain or dissimulated sex."[119]

Conscious of her male component, Colette discovers, with a scarcely ironic regret, that a male homosexual is more of a woman than the women-objects in imagery throughout the world: "O graces of a sleeping man, again I see you! From brow to mouth, he was, behind his closed eyelids, only smiles, nonchalance, and the malice of a sultaness in the moucharaby, . . . And I, the fool who would have 'very much liked' to be fully a woman, I contemplated him with a male regret, he who had such a pretty laugh and was moved by a beautiful line of poetry or a landscape."[120] But she quickly takes stock of the androgyne's tragic incompleteness: although he believes he lacks nothing because he has combined the two sexes, the androgyne knows he is doomed never to be able to attain—the feminine: "Fashioned for the use and enmity of woman, he nevertheless recognizes from afar, in a man, his species, his own pleasant peril as subgenus; he rapidly ruins his fellow if he is obliged to confront him, but by preference he stands apart. Indeed, he knows he is doomed as soon as a woman, in speaking of him, says 'them,' instead of 'He.' "[121] In the "cold friendship" of male homosexuals, Colette takes stock of a forgetfulness of the other sex, that strange amputation she takes for wisdom: "They taught me not only that man is amorously content with man, but also that one sex can do away with the other by forgetting it."[122] Might that be the ultimate end of the war between the sexes, which this so-called amorous woman did not forget throughout her life?

Colette does not trace so much the image of a virile homosexuality, composed of grandeur and wickedness "in the manner of the baron de Charlus," as that of the androgynous man, of whom she delivers the most poignant portrait in French literature: that of a wanderer in quest of maternal adoption. He obtains it, in fact, in these lines by Colette: "Anxious and veiled, never nude, the androgyne wanders, is astonished, begs under his breath. . . . His half-match, man, is quick to be frightened, and abandons him. He still has his half-match, woman. Above all, he still has the right, even the duty, never to be happy. If jovial, he's a monster. But he incurably hauls around his seraphim misery, his gleam of a tear, among us. He goes from tender propensity to maternal adoption."[123]

Having thus explored in herself and in others that rainbow of sexual postures and identities, Colette arrives at a certainty, not the least seductive of the discoveries of her genius: there is a sexual and psychological maturity of women that takes on the appearance of a youthful delicacy.

PRECOCIOUS MATURITY, OR DELICACY ACCORDING TO MITSOU AND GIGI

Although she never acknowledged the cubists or the surrealists, Colette proposes a portrait of woman composed of superimpositions of contradictory and often incompatible images, in a complex and polytopic vision evoking Picasso's paintings.

In the first place, there is the *tender shoot*, in whom one recognizes the young Colette herself, awakened to passion by a "paternal vice" that she very quickly transcends, like Claudine, who will continue on as Louisette, the insolent little peasant girl, "avid the way children are criminal, with grace, with majesty."[124] Colette then adds the *mature mistress* who loves "fresh flesh" (Colette can also be recognized in her): Léa, Camille Dalleray, or, in a more drab, if not tragicomic, manner, Marco. The latter is abandoned by her young lieutenant after having unluckily put on his kepi. Does that headgear give her an overly virile, somewhat transvestite look, thus revealing a lover's unconscious fantasy that his conscious mind cannot, alas, bear? But, in that comedy—it's a long way from *Chéri*—the abandoned woman emerges cheerfully, since she manages to be paid for her work as a ghostwriter, no longer one penny per line but two.[125]

Superimposed on these two figures, the tender shoot and the mature mistress, is the *greedy* and *mystical woman* who devours her objects, such as Annie, Renée, or the "hidden woman." But their rebellion will be counterbalanced by the careful class distinction of Julie de Carneilhan. A woman who is unfortunately incapable of sensuality is a true scandal in Maxime's (and hence Colette's) eyes: before Armande awakens to pleasure, he deplores the fact that she "never misses an opportunity to push away from her whatever is savored, touched, inhaled."[126]

Femininity—plural, complex, and multifaceted—is experienced as a process of infinite rebirth: "A feminine creature begins several times over to blossom anew."[127] What explanation is there for that mystery in woman? Her capacity to easily return to childhood and to deprive herself of one particular being to better see her reflection in Being. Every woman, then, has her "house of Claudine," her secret garden where the resources for her successive rebounds are lurking. And, as for Alice, every woman has that gift of communion with nature where erotic passion—always somewhat frustrating—obtains the cosmic plenitude that no "object," no partner can procure for her: "She abruptly opened the window, received on her overheated face a lashing of cold rain, a puff of wind carrying the odor of flooded humus, and closed the shutters again. Michel had not moved, and, seeing him motionless, she felt ashamed."[128]

To man's great displeasure, woman for Colette forms a duo only with the landscape:

> She moved back toward the window to throw out, with one of those movements men call masculine, her consumed cigarette, returned to light another, and sat down comfortably in the armchair next to the desk table. She kept a close watch on her own gestures and their freedom, to the point of choosing the cane armchair, the table's armrest, the light from the lamp on her face, and of abandoning to Michel,

in feigned generosity, the couch and the shade. The cres-
cent moon was filling the long curtainless window with a
powdery bright blue, and the pinkish beam cast by the
lamp reached the closest stars of the syringa.[129]

That puzzle of femininity is enriched with a vision in which it
reaches its peak and seems to be that of the ideal creature: the
characters of Mitsou and Gigi permeate all the other feminine
images that abound in Colette's works and offer us a purified
transcendence of them. Indeed, these "women" are artists of a
subtle sensibility, which transcends humans and the world
around them. Mirages of an ideal and affectionately ironic femininity, they stem less from a social reality—to which, however,
they are not alien—than directly from Colette's own writing,
whose sublimatory alchemy they share.

We know how emotional Proust became, weeping as he read
the letter Mitsou sent to the lieutenant.[130] Like him, I love that
true, simple girl, with her furniture in bad taste, and who espous-
es Colette's truth, writing in her own way with an "impregnable
innocence."[131] The response to the question the text poses—
"Mitsou, or, How Wit Comes to Girls"—is performative: it is entirely given by the context and style of the short story. There is no
doubt: wit comes to girls through writing.

The war, the little actress's very French and modern beauty,
as well as the "sidelights of the music hall" Colette knows perfectly well, a mixture of cynicism and simplicity, favor adventure as much as renunciation. Hence the social and historical
circumstances that determine the theme of the story are set in
place. The rest is simply magic, and it lies in the power of the
discourse. Colette, a master of the art of abridgement, here deploys another variant of the "tendrils of the vine" of which she
is fond: the narrative becomes obscured under the incisive *dialogues* and the exchanged *letters*. The passion between Mitsou
and the lieutenant, not in any respect narrative, would thus be
theatrical and epistolary.

The crystallization of love is inseparable from a rhetorical revelation: wit comes to the young girl only if it is indiscriminately

an art of living and an art of naming. We are alerted from the outset to that close mix between the reality of love and the art of words, if only by the strange name "Mitsou." Is it Persian as well? Not at all! Those shrill tones are rather a sarcastic echo of the mechanization taking place at the time ("It's a name made from the initials [. . .] of two organizations, one called Minoteries Italo-Tarbaises [Flour Mills of Italy and Tarbes] and the other Scieries Orléanaise Unifiées [Unified Sawmills of Orléans]. That produced M.I.T.S.O.U.: Mitsou"),[132] to which the aforementioned Mitsou, by her wit, is destined to give the lie.

Indeed, the little actress turns out to be a perfectible lover inasmuch as she forges a style for herself and excels at expressing a passion that is a dispossession. The lieutenant is well-educated and richer than she, but in vain: it is Mitsou who prevails in taste and delicacy, because she prevails in style. Let us not be too hasty to impute her renunciation merely to female masochism, which would make her humbly efface herself so as not to have to cry over cruel defeats. An extreme psychological delicacy, a subtle acceptance of the impossible reinforced by the fear of social misalliance, and the frustrations imposed by war combine with a self-mastery that is acquired only through the mastery of language—and that raises this apparent feminine misery to one of the summits of French literature. Lieutenant Robert, whose life as a soldier "is imprinted with a character of religious intensity and exertion," lets himself be unsettled by Mitsou to the point of seeing her as the prefiguration of the woman he will love[133] but only to better leave her. "Is she stupid? Not really. One is not stupid with refined senses, and with such an aptitude for feeling what is not reasoned out. Her great crime is [. . .] precisely that she obliges one to think of her."[134] Yet Mitsou, even more refined than he supposes her, surpasses Robert in the art of dispossession, which, completely alien to indifference, reaches its climax when the young woman understands—and writes—that supreme love, the one she managed to bring into being between the two of them, is only the capacity to "create an illusion for the most delicate ones." What is at issue, if not an aptitude for the imaginary, the very one the writer cultivates and that Mitsou grounds in a woman's ability to physically desire another body but also to get free of it and love only its ideal representation—unless the latter precedes the former?

As for love, Mitsou begins her last epistle by remarking on a difference between the sexes: he does not love her ideally, even though he desires her, whereas she herself can only idealize him, in order, subsequently, to desire him. "My dearest, the difficult thing for you was not to be loved by me. The almost impossible thing for me is to be loved by you."[135] Courteous, delicate, and respectful of her lover, she attributes to him—and to him alone—that rhetorical awakening that came about in herself during their relationship: "You found me on the edge of a stage where I was singing three couplets, and I did not have as many ideas as couplets in my head. What pleased you about me, you're the one who put it there."[136] Then she acknowledges that "what pleased," that "suppressed budding," had in fact come about in *herself*, in both her body and her mind. She then abandons the humility of *ça* in favor of a final *I*—Mitsou, disenchanted, articulates with a disturbing pride the disillusioned *I* that sings the eternal wonders of illusion. Listen, Her Majesty Mitsou is speaking to you. A young woman asserts with grace, and with a few grammatical mistakes, the triumph of the imaginary: "You have only to ask. Would I of preferred a walk in the daytime instead of our next night? I don't hesitate, I would of preferred the night. My love, the night is less awkward, it's less intimate. I'll always be almost your equal, so long as I'm completely naked in your arms and in bed. The most terrible thing is that we has to get up, and then I tremble before you. [. . .] Nevertheless, a woman who is stubborn about love, *ça* grows fast. *Ça* flowers, *ça* knows how to adopt a bearing, a color, to create an illusion for the most delicate ones. My love, My love, *I* am going to try to become your illusion."[137]

In a register closer to vaudeville than to the idyll, since the presence of the two prostitutes overcharges the short story with sociological naturalism, Gigi imposes on Colette's readers the nobility of a youthful maturity that is in all respects the equal of Mitsou's. The short story is inspired by incidents in which the age difference between Colette and Willy is replicated: Gigi is sixteen and Gaston thirty-three. As if to make fun of her own romantic naïveté, she first called it "The Backward Girl."[138] But it is now the Occupation and Colette is seventy. Like other writers and filmmakers who, out of denial, caution, or the desire to forget the atrocities of the war, created works that take their distance from them, that old woman dreams of disobedient youth: Gigi, or the freshness of a resistance? Did Colette also imagine her ordeal as a counterpoint to the political reality of the time? *Gigi*, first published in 1942 and ultimately in a bound volume by Ferenczi in 1945, has a "pure heart" that seems to echo this letter to the Petites Fermières of June 9, 1945: "The authentic accounts of the torture camps create a suffocating atmosphere. What imagination will ever equal that of the tormentors? Tell me about yourselves, pure hearts."[139]

In order to seduce Gaston Lachaille of "Lachaille Sugar," a ladies' man whose scandalous love affairs have been in the news, Aunt Alicia and Mme Alvarez (who, "from her past life [. . .] kept the honorable habits of women without honor, and taught them to her daughter and to her daughter's daughter")[140] vie with each other to give advice to little Gilberte: "The face you can put off to the next morning if need be, in an emergency or when traveling. Whereas attentions to the body's nether regions are a woman's dignity."[141] Or again: "A pretty set of weaknesses and a fear of spiders, that's our indispensable baggage with men [. . .] because nine out of ten men are superstitious, nineteen out of twenty believe in the evil eye, and ninety-eight out of a hundred are afraid of spiders. They forgive us . . . many things, but not for being free of what disturbs them."[142] Without overlooking the crafty advice of her grandmother and aunt, Gigi understands instinctively that, in love, one must forgo. The poignant melodrama uses every trick in the book to wring tears from the simple folk. "Get out of here!" the little one dares yell at the head of prestigious Lachaille Sugar, against the desires of the two matrons.

> She was blinding herself with her two fists, which she
> slammed into her eyes. Gaston had joined her and was

seeking, on that well-defended face, the place for a kiss. But he found for his lips only the ridge of a little chin covered with tears. At the sound of sobbing, Mme Alvarez came running. Pale and circumspect, she stood, hesitant, at the kitchen door:

"My God, Gaston," she said, "what's the matter with her?"

"Eh," said Lachaille, "the matter is she doesn't want to!"[143]

The clearly happy ending, with the eternal marriage, places that analysis of female psychology in the category of popular entertainment, and it would take all of Audrey Hepburn's discerning elegance for Gigi's distinctiveness to mark itself off from melodrama and to light up Broadway in 1951. Indeed, the virtuosity of that short story lies in an art situated at the opposite extreme from that of Mitsou. Playing with stereotypes, caricaturing the clichés of the demimonde and of pulp fiction femininity, Gigi touches the "nerve,"[144] as Colette herself would say, of the light comedy imaginary so cherished by the French public. Whereas the Mitsou story is rhetorical bravura and makes an extreme taste in love coincide with the virtuosity of a letter, *Gigi* is merely sensation, intuition, all acts without words. Does not Gigi make do with a "So . . . there it is. Hello. . . . Hello, Gaston"?[145]—platitudes that would sound farcical if they did not stand in sharp contrast to the duplicity of the seductive ploys calculated by the two panders.

In fact, that ellipsis in Gigi's language is not even a disavowal of vaudeville. It expresses the generous humor of the author, who wagers on a youthful innocence whose maturity proves to be more pragmatic than the cunning of the old courtesans. What if that got to the heart of "perversion" in Colette? Standing against the cynicism of the professional women is a perversity of unconscious calculation that Gigi acts out. It is neither manipulation nor naïveté that make Gaston budge, it is "abstention" (as Sido would say) and frustration, which reinforce desire and put the lovers' truth to the test.

Nevertheless, the comic side of that idyll and its "perverse" charm lie in the fact that Mamita's and Alicia's scheming is in no way shown to be foiled by some absolute purity on Gigi's part. On the contrary. The unconscious strategy of the young heroine, another version of the "tender shoot," halfway between the innocent and the tramp, succeeds much better than the plan hatched by her educators, even while standing in opposition to it: Gigi will not be just another mistress of "Lachaille Sugar," and Gaston marries her in the end. Without thinking about it, but also without remaining deaf to the two women's intentions, Gigi realizes their desires as prostitutes who dream, finally, only of marriage and respectability. Beyond their explicit designs, the young girl manages to arrive via an indirect, apparently opposite, but finally complicitous and much more efficient route. We are in the realm of the unsaid, and rarely has one of Colette's texts been so faithful to the primary calling of her writing, which is to show the *budding* of a passion and of a style rather than its *unfolding*. Here, flowering is indicated in the negative, by substraction, both in the modesty of Gigi's and Gaston's feelings and in the lacunae of the narrative. The young woman's attractive maturity can be discerned in the vaudeville blanks: Colette's ellipses abruptly precipitate the action and inundate the matrimonial business in a mixture of pathos and irony that assures the success of popular art.

" . . . THOSE MEN THAT OTHER MEN CALL GREAT "

Mature jouissance and psychic bisexuality do not, one suspects, favor the cult of the great man, or of man in general in Colette: "During my life, I have hardly gotten close to those men that other men call great. They have not sought me out."[146]

All the same, let us not hasten to decide that Colette is homophobic or that she distrusts men, she who, though she never shared the rage of antiphallocratic feminists, might have wanted to keep phallic power for herself alone. "Colette-culotte"— "Colette wears the trousers"—the experts have not refrained from snickering.[147] Yet the vitriolic landscape she constructs of the world of men also does not spare that of women: the same blistering cruelty on the lookout for weaknesses and monstrosities drives that Dionysian writing, that writing "by knifepoint." Who, in fact, is that Colettian man from whom a "gulf" separates the heroine after an "indignant pleasure" extracted from "high combat"[148] and who poorly dissimulates his anxiety in a feverish accumulation of conquests? "If you only knew the women I could run into around a lover! . . . It's horrible. The word is not too strong."[149] "For a lover, could the obsession with power equal the obsession with impotence?"[150]

Since the lovers' "we" is impossible and fidelity itself does not suffice to "foster confidence,"[151] the feminine "I" finally rebels against "my humiliation at belonging [to someone] more than I owned [him]."[152] "To own" or to "moor oneself": between these two poles Colette's heroines hesitate. Renée will express, very submissively, that wavering with which her sisters are also familiar: "I believe that many women, like me, wander at first, before again taking their place, which is *on the near side* of man."[153] The result of that ambivalence is not a pure and simple rejection of man: "There is no company so good that one does not part ways; but I am undertaking to take my leave courteously. No, you did not kill me, perhaps you never wished me any harm. . . . Farewell, dear man, and also welcome."[154]

The issue, rather, is to reject the belief in the absolute couple and attempt to construct a sexual freedom: "Don't you see that chance might have made me one of those women restricted to one man, to such a point that, sterile or not, they carry the crystallized innocence of old maids to their graves? . . . In imagining such a fate, my carnal double, tanned like leather by sun and water, whom I see leaning forward in the mirror, would tremble from it, if she could still tremble from a retrospective peril."[155] That freedom, by virtue of the risks assumed and the proper distance finally found, calms tensions and turns playful: "Between the man and me, a long period of recreation begins. . . . Man, my friend, will you come breathe together?"[156]

As Colette works to get free of men, the act of separating herself from Willy, which looks like a posthumous settling of accounts, no doubt occupies the foremost place. After Colette puts her first husband in the *Claudine* series, then kills him off (Renaud in *Retreat from Love*), after she makes many allusions to the deadlocks involved in being a couple (Renée Néré in *The Shackle* and *The Vagabond*), she draws a portrait of Willy in *My Apprenticeships* (1936) that would be caricature if it did not verge on the tragic.

She omits neither the psychiatric diagnosis of "pathology"—a "neurosis" revealed by a "tic," "intoxication," "feverishness" "an imbalance," "a photographic frenzy"—nor graphological interpretations of the secretive person he is,[157] nor even a phrenological description: "The powerful skull, the eyes flush with the forehead, the abbreviated nose with no defined bridge between the low cheekbones, all his features joined forces to form a curve."[158] Colette, who does not dare write a "novel" about Willy ("The impediment is that no being knew him intimately"),[159] who cuts short the complete revelation she initially proposed to make,[160] nevertheless braves self-censorship, proceeding through passionate strokes that make her deceased husband a true hero, a "gambler"[161]—a "living dead man," some have said. Although the writer-wife spends her time denying the character's key importance, the text, conversely, confirms it.

Her scathing comments hit the mark and the caricature distills her venom: "an agility strange in an obese man, and the hardness of an eiderdown quilt stuffed with pebbles;"[162] "he resembled Queen Victoria above all"[163]—no compliment to his virility, pace the powerful monarch. The depraved Willy has every flaw, the most unforgivable of which is his baldness. "My bad start, which had planted between me and all young men a man past his prime. [. . .] I who had never—for good reason—lovingly touched a man's head of hair."[164]

Henri Gauthier-Villars reacted to the attacks formulated during his lifetime by calling Colette "my widow" and making fun of her claim to the *Claudine* books, which he considered their joint project—"If Mme Colette and I had had a child, she would say she had made it all alone." But it was futile: Colette won the deciding match, especially when she targeted Willy's failure as a writer: a critic, perhaps; a writer, certainly not! Was he tormented by inhibitions? "Between the desire, the need to produce a commodity in print and the possibility of writing, there arose in that strange author an obstacle, whose shape and nature, perhaps terrifying, I could never make out."[165]

With poisonous generosity she recognized he had certain talents: "And was it not simpler for a man with an ear for music, able to accompany himself on the piano and to sing in a soft and agreeably husky tenor voice, was it really not easier to write? No. Everything seemed easy for him, everything seemed permitted him, except the writer's task."[166] "I persist in believing that this critic, who borrowed even his critical arguments from others, was a born censor, incisive, quick to strike the weak spot, to awaken, with a slightly cruel jab, one's dormant self-respect." But he lacked perseverance and humility: "He must have frequently believed back then that he was about to write, that he was going to write, that he was writing. . . . Once his pen was held in his fingers, a slackening, a syncope of the will took his illusion from him."[167] And Colette wholeheartedly devotes herself to a commentary on the term *déflocquement*—Old French, if you please—which she borrows from Balzac (and Rabelais) to designate his collapse into drug addiction. It is a "horrible phenomenon that seems to dissolve the bones, to undermine all the resources of the will. Were these the abdications that many addicts experience when effort is required?"[168] The vengeful wife feigns objectivity by slipping in a few compliments, but it is in vain: the insult has been hurled. This man, with whom she had allowed herself to be photographed seated as he stood upright, with her wearing an "expression at once submissive, impassive, half-nice, half-condemned," now made her "rather ashamed."[169] The book was published in 1936, and the settling of accounts with Willy (he had died in 1931) seemed complete. The settling of accounts with Jouvenel remained.

Between the baron and his future wife, everything began with an intense complicity, apparently as existential as it was sexual. The circumstances of World War I took Colette to the front, where, in her job as a journalist, she acquired a knowledge of the war that was altogether extraordinary for a woman of that time. The war also strengthened the relationship between the two lovers; and the vagabond did not hesitate to once again delight in assuming the role of a shackled women, this time in a harem (as she wrote in a letter to Annie de Pène).[170] Later, when Germaine Patat entered Jouvenel's life (in 1920) and the couple's troubles became obvious (in 1923), Colette made friends with her rival; and it is in *The Other One* that she gives her version of that friendship between women. This transposition of the threesome inspired by the reality of the Jouvenel marriage is exaggerated, however, and verges on vengeful caricature in the imaginary depiction of a drab man, poor Farou, dominated by "his" two women. He is far removed from the fascinating Henry de Jouvenel, who enjoyed squandering his nobility in journalism (according to his friend Anatole de Monzie). And yet. . . . The model can be made out more easily in the character of Herbert d'Espivant, ex-husband of Julie de Carneilhan, whom he left for Marianne, a Jewish woman, a character that allows Colette to take her revenge on Germaine Sarah Hément and Claire Boas. Herbert d'Espivant—not the usual man-object of the Colettian gallery—though always seductive, even to the point of dragging the elegant Julie into shady business transactions, does not shine when compared to Julie de Carneilhan and her noble panache: "Always that credit available to sensuality, she thought, pleasure-blackmail, pleasure-panacea, pleasure-lethal blow. So that's all he knows?"[171]

An autumnal light, which makes the "ideal lover" "her best friend," bathes the portrait of men in the later texts. In them the reader recognizes Colette's third husband, Maurice Goudeket. We have already pointed out the passion that joined the couple and that certain of Colette's declarations may have overlooked or even dissimulated. To confine ourselves to the written statements, consider this confidence to the Petit Corsaire: "What connects me to Maurice, what attaches him to me? It's my virility."[172] It is clear why Goudeket suppressed that passage—but what truth and frankness on Colette's part in her perception of the couple's bisexuality, which the writer no longer fears. Trust and respect can be read in another portrait of a man, that of Vial in *Break of Day* (some believe they also recognize Goudeket in it). The narrator can tell him of her emotional independence, since she has gotten free of him[173] and no longer fears solitude.

The mutual solicitude was reinforced by World War II: Maurice was imprisoned at the Compiègne camp; Colette made every effort to get him freed and sent him provisions. It was also reinforced by old age: the pythoness of the Palais-Royal, having become impotent, needed the support, without pity, of her "best friend." Consider these sentences, written by the gourmand Colette, which condense, in the tragic days of the Occupation, her love for her husband, transformed into an indestructible friendship: "I have held onto those lines, the first to come from the Compiègne camp, and which signified exchanges, life, the resumption of hope. I have also kept a list that reached me later. [. . .] A list, or rather a litany, that petitioned, if I could entrust them to a safe route—thank you, Dr. Breitmann—for butter, jam, sugar, and, above all, like an ardent refrain, above all, 'bread, in heaven's name, bread!' "[174]

Such a final rehabilitation of her trust in men cannot erase the recurring image that takes shape in Colette's writings: the "virile walk-on," often a "man-object,"[175] is drab. Apart from Chéri, who has already been mentioned, Maxime in *The Vagabond* and Jean in *The Shackle,* among others, fit that description. Chéri, diminished, "mysterious as a courtesan,"[176] is loved by Léa only because he is "submissive, poorly tamed, incapable of being free."[177] He is a poor man, always floored, timid, inept at responding to the circumstances of life, however uncomplicated, like the loss of love, for example, which a woman, on the contrary, does not fear to face. "How stupid a man looks when someone reminds him of something about a love that no longer exists! You little imbecile, for my part, it doesn't bother me to remember that."[178] Chéri is not so different from Farou, caught between his two women: "A man in that situation? . . . There's not one in a hundred who would turn it to his advantage, if not to his honor."[179] "I found him worse than useless, really worse than useless! Why was he worse than useless?"[180] The four sisters, devastated by impossible loves, having found refuge in their father's home, subscribe to Hermine's verdict, which denounces male "childishness": "Have you ever seen a man make a gesture at the precise moment you were expecting him to make it?"[181] Weak, wounded by the unfaithful woman, the man despairs and commits suicide in earnest. The title character of "The Photographer's Lady,"[182] the only female character to make a suicide attempt, botches it. After Chéri, it is Michel who confirms that tragic fate: disappointed by Alice's infidelity, or simply by her independence, he drowns himself.[183]

As for the opposite of this melancholic, the one we would now call a phallocrat, "He" is merely pretentious, a false master, wholly satisfied to rule over inferior woman and, for that very reason, ridiculously idealized: "He needs—for the women expect it!— the Woman-of-the-World with blotchy skin who's interested in music and who makes spelling mistakes, the mature virgin who writes him, in a calm bookkeeper's hand, a 'tousand' horrors."[184] Or again: "He, weak, He, fickle, and in love with the love He inspires, He, who savors the game of feeling entangled in a hundred little hooked women's fingers. [. . .] So. . . . Farewell to everything! Farewell . . . to almost everything. I leave Him to them. Perhaps some day He'll see them as I see them, with their little gluttonous sow faces. He will flee, frightened, trembling, disgusted by a pointless vice."[185]

All the same, the compassionate acknowledgment of male weakness shows through beneath the caricature. It is as if Colette let herself get carried away by an identification, not with the power attributed to the man's phallus but with the fragility of male castration and its latent melancholy: "O skittish, recurrent, and delicate modesty of man."[186] In the same way, she deplores that modern invention, the shirking of the paternal function: "But for a mother, the absence of protection, passive paternity, is an exhausting regime."[187]

Her projection onto male sexuality leads Colette to superb insights, which no other woman had written before her, about the androgynous man. Mme Dalleray contemplates, "disillusioned, the features that might no doubt later be those of a brown-haired man of rather ordinary attractiveness, but which his seventeen years, for a short time yet, kept short of virility."[188] Even in Vinca's arms Phil will not be free of his feminine passivity: "Philippe abandoned himself to a careless and recent habit of passivity, acquired in soft arms; but though he sought, with a barely tolerable bitterness, the resinous perfume, the accessible bosom, at least he was moaning effortlessly the name 'Vinca darling . . . Vinca darling.' "[189] The feminine man is, in the end, only a manchild: "But neither Camille Dalleray nor Vinca, in her dream, wanted to remember that Philippe was only a tender little boy, eager only to place his head on someone's shoulder, a little boy of ten."[190]

In closely examining his "plaintive features, less like those of a man than like those of a battered young girl,"[191] Colette disappears into the pain of a man confronting his virile power as well as his castration. "He was hiding, the best he could, a pain he did not understand. What had he thus conquered the night before, in the perfumed shadow, in jealous arms, that could make him a man and victorious? The right to suffer? The right to faint from weakness before an innocent and harsh child? The right to tremble inexplicably before the delicate life of beasts and the blood escaping from its source?"[192] She enjoys discreetly naming the tumescence and detumescence—the "flight" and "fall"—of the male organ: "He lowered his head, saw passing before him two or three incoherent, ineluctable, images, in flight the way one flies in a dream, falling as one falls in diving, at the instant the undulations of the wave are about to join the turned-up face— then, without enthusiasm, with a reflective slowness, with a calculated courage, he placed his bare arm once again in the open hand."[193] She detects the ruses: "Something of the charm of unfaithful husbands slipped into him and made him suspect."[194] But these rather rare marks of complicity contrast sharply with the predominant tone of annoyance: what good were men after all? "It's not such a serious thing, a man, it's not eternal! A man is . . . no more than a man."[195]

In the end, for Colette, man is always defeated, even and above all in a ménage à trois: "A cold observer of mores, not without lucidity, confirmed that in a voluptuous trio there was always one betrayed person, and often two. I like to think that the most constantly deceived is the patriarch behind closed doors, the clandestine Mormon. He has really deserved it, as a traditional provocateur, a miniature pasha."[196] That disabused detachment may explain the lack of consistency in Colette's male characters, which she was the first to remark on, recognizing that it was only with Farou in *The Other One* that she felt "on somewhat more solid ground": "Cozily wedged between his wife and his mistress, Farou leans on them, borrows a little life from two women rivals who do not hate each other."[197] Not content simply to deprive him of a first name and to dub him "Farou"—a name one gives to "herd dogs in my native region," though his self-satisfaction inevitably brings to mind the assonant *faraud,* "swaggerer"—Colette also mocks that imaginary "monarch" full of "his favorite, Muslim species of happiness"[198] and presents him as a stereotypical seducer, molded of cunning and cowardice.

Nevertheless, is Farou not a man, the only one in Colette's writings to excel at a career, an artistic career moreover, since that unfaithful husband is a famous comic author? Don't believe a word of it. Colette's wickedness reaches one of the heights of perfidy when she demolishes that *scribbler* of plays incapable of feeling, taking from him even the qualification of man of the theater, seeing his work only as a feminine caprice, easy work: "Very unhappy. . . . Can he be very unhappy? Or even sad? In any case, he is not wicked. But no one has ever had the opportunity to say, or to hear it said, that he is good. Or cheerful, moreover. How little like a man of the theater he seems! Yet he loves the theater. . . . No, he does not love the theater, he loves to write plays. Why am I made in such a way that I assimilate his profession, his art, to capricious woman's work? No, not altogether woman's work, but an easy profession."[199]

In short, this Farou is an empty center around whom the affectionate solidarity of Fanny and Jane, his wife and mistress, respectively, is constructed. In any case Farou the antihero "leaves the text before the end of the story,"[200] making way not for the conformist message that marriage must necessarily be saved, which Colette supposedly attempted to convey in this text, but for the disabused idea of the impossibility of the couple, against which only the wisdom of female solidarity prevails.

We are nonetheless still troubled by an unexpected, even underhanded, perhaps unconscious kinship between this man and the writer: Farou is the only one of her characters to have no first name, and that is also the case for Colette the author herself. She has only a last name, which was initially a first name. Feminine, masculine, last name, first name: her settling of accounts is infinite, with man, my fellow, my brother, my father.

THE FEMININE IDEAL INCLUDES ITS NEGATIVE

Corresponding to the drab men are formidable women: Colette's "ogre" eye[201] pulverizes appearances and portrays, with and beyond voluptuousness, the protagonists in a true war between the sexes.

The plan to write a book entitled *Women* for Grasset in 1936 never came to fruition of course,[202] but her body of work as a whole traces the complex image of a second sex for which Colette spares neither her enthusiasm, as we have already seen in detail, nor the pitiless revelations of female psychology. Endowed with an invincible force, woman—with the exception of the "photographer's lady"—never lets herself be beaten down; in psychoanalytic language one would say she knows nothing of castration and wants to know nothing about death. Sido explains to her daughter: "As for me, I risk less, you understand. I'm only a woman. Past a certain age, a woman almost never dies by her own hand."[203]

Colette nevertheless looks at the attraction of suicide: was it to free herself from the specter of depression dating from when she was with Willy? Or from the recurrent depression of her old age? "The Photographer's Lady," a "new nightmare" when it is not "barf," long and painful to write, was published in *Les Oeuvres Libres* in 1944, next to a report on the Compiègne camp, where Goudeket was interned.[204] It relates the destiny of a woman who survived a suicide attempt. Much more than a disavowal of her death-seeking period, in it Colette celebrates the resistance of the second sex: might woman, along with "the child and the old man," be "equal in endurance"?[205] "Fairly often . . . I stop to think about those men, those women, who do not have the courage to wait for death. I dream of their end, I who, out of indifference, think so little of my own. [. . .] They are headed toward an invisible goal. That idea of departure, irreconcilable with the idea of complete death, though it may mitigate voluntary immolations, may be guilty of facilitating them to an equal degree."[206] There will be no "voluntary immolation," then, since death "can wait" and is "complete": the Colettian hero has no doubt about that. Even better, one might say, a woman is potentially criminal and not neurotic about her criminality: "A woman knows everything about the crime she may perpetrate."[207]

Nevertheless, with her "maniacal daydream" in which "every day she deceives [herself] about [her] wisdom," woman is "fragile." It is the reverse side of her hardness, bound up with it. She "likes being a female" who desires only "to serve some purpose with respect to love."[208] That taste for service and submission verges on slavery and masochism: "Dignity is a male flaw. I should rather have written that 'disgust is not a feminine frailty'";[209] "The spirit of contradiction is as strong in woman as the instinct for proprieties. If her only possession is bad luck, she clings to her bad luck";[210] "I am waiting for an end, knowing it is not I who will put a stop to my cowardice, but the man who first used me."[211] The character of the young Vinca is one of her most naïve and most "original" incarnations: "Maybe next year she'll fall at his feet and will say women's words to him: 'Phil! Don't be mean . . . I love you, Phil, do with me what you will. . . . Talk to me, Phil.'"[212] A morose narcissism lies at the core of the female soul, which delights in the "often poignant spectacle" of another woman's pain, "designed to produce the selfish and striking fear called presentiment. It is almost always herself that a woman takes aim at in a woman's sorrow."[213]

Is a call for revolt hidden in these observations of a painful condition, as the feminists who discovered Colette believed? Or, on the contrary, is it the disenchanted diagnosis of a dead end, a nature that cannot be transcended except perhaps by sacrificing femininity to "mental hermaphroditism"? "Yes, woman keeps, deep within herself, a trust directed at the ravisher."[214] Even the superb Julie de Carneilhan is a dominated dominatrix: "From Becker to Coco Vatard, in front of how many men had she humiliated herself in a domineering tone?"[215]

Passionate about the face,[216] especially the female face, Colette continually examines it and loves it, and that "landscape of choice,"[217] sometimes "frightened, declining," gives her the desire to exclaim to women: "Go out and please, go out and love, go out and destroy—go out and play!"[218] Even though she harbors a deep compassion for that "mysterious plurality, the imposing Freemasonry of women, whom the world hypnotizes, overworks, and disciplines,"[219] she despises the universe of appearances in which women become alienated, constantly preoccupied, like Valentine, with the tyrannical "What do they look like?" Although a complicity can be established between unhappy women on the basis of that profound distress, Colette has no illusions about the solidity of such solidarity, "constantly disintegrated by man, constantly reforming at man's expense."[220] Indeed, violent aggressiveness and a "peculiarly feminine and strong, and, consequently, creative, malevolence"[221] constitute the other face of that voluntary servitude. Colette amuses herself describing Léa and Charlotte, those "two old enemy women,"[222] like "two dogs [that] come upon the slipper they used to tear apart."[223] Or again, there is this more cunning assessment: "There, thought Léa cheerfully. Two women a little older than last year, the usual nasty and routine words, the weak-willed distrust, meals in common."[224]

Man always lets himself be dominated by "the other woman," who is not the more charming one, as some might have naively believed, but the more intractable, the more authoritarian. He submits to "that malcontent, that difficult, that superior one."[225] The modern woman, like the young Edmée, who marries Chéri, is an out-and-out castrator who awakens a mixture of fear and fascination in Colette: "Equipped with patience, often subtle, Edmée did not pay attention to the fact that the female appetite to possess tends to emasculate every living conquest and can reduce a male, magnificent and inferior, to the function of a courtesan."[226] She adds: "And work, and activity, and duty, and women who serve the country. . . . Are you kidding, and who are crazy about dough. . . . They're businesswomen, to the point of making you sick of business. They're hardworking to the point of making you loathe work."[227]

Above all, however, it is with old age—a reflection of maternal power—that a woman turns definitively into a witch: "She liked those old knowing ladies, full of claws, satanic, and as maternal as fiends in a hell for the convalescing damned."[228] This prevents Colette, however, from becoming emotional about her own aging: "You watch a castaway emerge from a tangled heap of feminine effects, still weighed down as if by algae—though the head is safe, the rest is struggling, its salvation is not assured— you watch your sister, your comrade emerge, a woman who has slipped past the age of being a woman."[229] She does not neglect to emphasize the nasty little remarks that old women exchange: " 'The nose of Marie Antoinette!' asserted Chéri's mother, who never forgot to add: 'and, in two years, that dear Léa will have the chin of Louis XVI.' "[230] Chéri does not omit to turn that perfidy to his own account when he looks at Léa: "Chéri saw the lower part of her face, similar to that of Louis XVI, dance for a brief time."[231] It is, in fact, pointless to wait until old age to describe an infernal femininity: a singer's mouth looks like a gaping monstrosity, which does not even save—since it enhances— the singer's genius. "I calculated the vast opening she would soon expose, the quality of sounds that cavern would bellow. . . . A fine gob!"[232]

Yet these women's ferocious demonism is only an appearance. At bottom—but there is no bottom—it is only lies, dissimulation, and falsehood: "During those furtive seasons of drought, she sought to put herself to shame, but a savvier Alice was not unaware that a woman is ashamed only of what she lets show, not of what she feels."[233] Like Julie a woman is ready for the "wonderful havoc of truth, of trust."[234] In short, the "female genius" is "occupied with tender imposture, with circumspection, with abnegation."[235] Colette arrives at a condensation of the tu-multuous face of the hysteric, tormented by her duplicity and her fear of others: "Morose, weak, then well-behaved and secretive, trusting in her face, which, full and soft like that of children, be-trayed little more than the major tumults, she wavered between a tedious pain and the fear of everything that is external disorder, cries, confessions, the convulsion of faces and bodies."[236]

This sorcery, which eats away at itself, can either "do without man's presence, his existence"[237]—does not Colette describe her-self as "more or less a widow"?[238]—or can temporarily retreat to the background, to better prepare itself for the passionate and in-terminable war with the other sex. It is "a harsh retreat where a female passion confines itself, a voluptuous training period, a rig-orous induction, without which, the duc de Morny asserted, a woman remains in the state of a rough sketch."[239]

The figure of the mother, the original and maleficent power, crystallizes and shores up that vision of a redoubtable femininity that permeates the pages of Colette's writings.

MOTHER AND CHILD

Lurking in Sido's cosmic and protective shadow, a ravaging motherhood threatens the daughters in Colette's pages. Are not a mother and a daughter, alike and rivals, destined to hate each other, like Marie-Laure and Edmée, for example, with the daugh-ter developing in a minor key what the mother vulgarly applies: "Exactly what Marie-Laure needed, though she must hate her all the same."[240]

Gribiche's mother is the commonplace and frightening expres-sion of that suppressed maternal paranoia, that "monstrous in moderate terms." The "old murderess" deals ruthlessly in a "cer-tain order of criminality," since she is ready to let her daughter perish by giving her an abortion rather than face "the peril of giv-ing birth."[241] Louise's mother joins her in a different order of monstrosity: furious at catching her "tender shoot" daughter in the arms of an older man, she would have stoned the guilty party had she been able. In the meantime, and before conspiring with her daughter to drive off the intruder, her violence toward the girl evokes the bloody image of the guillotine: "With one hand thrust into her daughter's hair, she turned the girl's face toward me. She grasped her by her hair as she would have brandished a severed head, so hard that the child's eyes were slanted."[242]

As if ravaged by that violence of motherhood, Colette's heroines, such as Claudine or Renée Néré, doubt their own capacities as mothers: "A child, me! Which end do you hold it by? Surely, if I gave birth to something, it would be a baby beast, hairy, striped, with soft paws and already hard claws, upright ears and horizontal eyes, like its mother."[243] "So now I've spent thirty-three years without imagining the possibility of being a mother. Am I a monster?"[244] As for herself, Colette repeats the words of one of her colleagues at *Le Matin,* who said she had "a man's pregnancy,"[245] and even admitted she had lived through "a pseudomotherhood that was never easy for [her]."[246]

In the first place, the world of children somewhat saddens her. That image of depressing, even repulsive childhood may be interpreted as a projection of the old melancholy that tormented the young body in its latency and adolescent period, a body not yet exposed to sensuality; the "acting out" of the adult, culminating in the incestuous act, will allow Colette to alleviate that melancholy in *My Mother's House.* Nevertheless,

> children, children. . . . Kids, tots, bambinos, nippers, brats. . . . Slang is inadequate, there are too many of them! By chance, returning to my isolated and distant villa, I come across, in that frog pond, in that warm basin the sea fills and leaves alone every day . . . red jerseys, blue jerseys, rolled-up trousers, sandals; straw hats, berets, linen bonnets; pails, spades, folding chairs, forts. . . . Everything that ought to be charming inspires melancholy in me. In the first place, there are too many of them![247]

Turning to the canine world, she can express her rejection of childbirth with even more candor: "That's what I prefer, of the ten breeds that have my respect, those to whom the opportunity for motherhood is barred."[248]

Her own pregnancy, however, would seem to her in hindsight altogether comparable to the "bliss of pregnant female animals," "a long party." "It must have made me complete, since I have not forgotten it, and I think of it at a time when life cannot bring me any more plenitude."[249] It is a completely different matter for the mother she was able to be: "The late child—I was forty years old—I remember welcoming the certainty of her presence with a reflective distrust, keeping it quiet. It was myself I distrusted. It was not a question of physical apprehension. I had fears about my age, my possible ineptitude at loving, at understanding, at immersing myself. Love—I believed this—had already done me a great deal of harm by monopolizing me for twenty years in its exclusive service."[250] "But the meticulous admiration I devoted to my daughter, I did not call it—I did not feel it was—love."[251] "Was I putting enough love into my contemplation? I dare not make that claim."[252]

These doubts do not necessarily show Colette to be a bad mother, a mother incapable of giving herself to her daughter. Without setting aside that suspicion—which "little Colette" confirms, deploring the lack of attention her mother granted her—Colette's texts approach motherhood in minute detail but unsparingly. The same vigilance, ready to swing over to cruelty, guides her pen when she examines her emotions or her incapacity to understand that new and singular being, whom she attempted, however—how many mothers are capable of it?—to respect in her strangeness. Let us reread what she says and recognize that very few texts by writers, men or women, from Saint Augustine and Rousseau to the moderns, have attempted as hers did to seize the mystery of the child in its difference without assimilating it to the adult.

The uncanniness of that new arrival is necessarily expressed in terms of wildness; her strangeness—like that of men and women, and perhaps even more than theirs—is akin to the monstrous. " 'To look is to learn.' Granted. But, in general, we accuse it—our concern, our abyss, the impregnable fortress, the savage, the unknown, the child—of looking little and poorly."[253] She examines the loneliness of the child who, instead of obeying us, prefers to surrender to the "great masters," natural spaces and the sea [mer] (oh, yes!), to be precise:

> Just so, we point out to him what he did not wish to see, and his fruitless obedience tires him; he shuts down, shrinks up, and irritates us. His refuge is in the image, unless, privileged, he surrenders entirely to the greatest masters: the forest, the fields, and the sea. . . .
>
> I saw, I respected the solitude of a child, entrusted in summertime to the sea, in autumn and winter to a landscape of hills and chestnut groves. The sea and the landscape so satisfied all her needs that I was a little jealous of the sea, especially the sea . . . she seized hold of brand-new beings, they adopted her as if they recognized her.[254]

An image of the child without fixed contours, immersed in space and sensations, stands out in these texts, which resonate with the infantile according to Colette, the same infantile she mobilizes to write the world's flesh and the sensual flowering of self. "Every time a child, a marvel both of dissimulation and of spontaneity, believes itself safe from our penetration, it abandons itself and shows itself as it is, without mental age, full of passion, jealous, perfect."[255] That childhood, wild and destructive, is often confused with animal life, as we have seen: "Crawling toward me is my little swaddled larva, which someone had set down on my bed for a moment. The perfection of an animal!"[256] The enduring vagabond in Colette seeks out (perhaps favors?) that savagery of infantile madness, precisely, making it a sign of authenticity, of difference: "Resignation is not a virtue of early childhood, and knowing how long it takes them to learn to be good, we would prefer to find our children a little mad."[257] She observes the child with interest, but the mother in her is no dupe regarding the cruelty of her own demands, or about the shrewdness with which her young victim is capable of trapping her:

My primary victim was bursting with health and even with beauty, despite my cruelty. Enlightened at a very young age about my impassiveness, she had quickly accepted the bargain we offer to apartment pets: be crazy outdoors and good at home. If it is not very difficult to establish maternal authority, it is less easy to consolidate it, since the fresh, subtle instinct, the varied ruses of children are constantly on the alert. It is up to us—did I not speak of them as of so many adversaries?—to thwart them.[258]

And, with a Kleinian prescience, Colette detects the destructiveness of the child's young "ego": "A child is never altogether its own dupe. After the first shock has passed, ruining a dream pleases its instinct, which is less to build than to devastate."[259] She adds: "Harmfulness is instinctive in the child and terribly ingenious. Its hunger for destruction—that is, for invention—finds satisfaction wherever it can."[260] That destructiveness, if it were truly well received, would be transformed into creativity: "A child seeks, goes astray, trembles at a hundred hidden poems, gets frightened and discouraged."[261]

Armed with a gift for observation as ruthless as it is complicitous, Colette can become a child-care consultant. Is not the modern age, she observes, that of "the child who has no childhood"? "Contemplating the childhood of today is a generation of discouraged parents."[262] Today (or always?), boys are more excitable, little girls more poetic.[263] That mother-consultant does not prove to be very modern, however, when, preferring madly vagabond children to good little ones, she goes so far as to ban the wearing of glasses: "A myopic child who can play, get around, run without corrective lenses, is a normal and happy child until the day, in accustoming him to glasses, we make him an official weakling."[264]

The most pertinent remark Colette makes about childhood is provided in the little anecdote that describes the dog Nonoche, who no longer responds to her puppy's calls but joins the rutting males. It is only when the *mother* manages to be a *lover* as well and imposes that optimal distance between the child and herself, that the very condition for thought, for her child, and for a life for both of them, is fulfilled. Such, in fact, is the model of the "good mother" that the voluptuous Colette bequeaths to us and that she places in the eyes of the puppy, staring at that mother who is leaving him: "His head buzzing, powdered with sand, Nonoche's son gets back on his feet, so astonished he dares not ask why or follow the one who will never again be his wet nurse, and who is walking away with great dignity along the little black path, toward the haunted wood."[265] Against convention, heeding her desires, the courageous Colette discovers, like a sleepwalker, the psychic demands of a healthy motherhood.

All that did not help her be an ideal mother. Far from it. "Whatever you do, Madam, it will be a mistake!" Freud supposedly told a woman seeking advice on how to bring up her children. If motherhood is an impossible vocation for all women, it is even more gravely so for Colette who, in the exaltation of writing, projects herself into the other, captures him and reduces him, willy-nilly, to the mere object of a game, to a sign among signs swept up in the whirlwind of an indomitable avidity.

Twice Colette names her daughter after herself: "Colette" for the public records, "Bel-Gazou" for family and friends. These signifiers, both of them linked to the Captain, weld daughter and mother together in a single twin identity under the sway of the zouave. Far from recognizing the new woman, her daughter, that way of naming her is already itself (like the body of work written by "big Colette") an unconscious attempt at reparation at the site of the failed writer, the amputated Captain. Two fragments Colette sent to Germaine Patat, probably dating from 1912, and an article in *Le Matin* the same year, all of them linked to the genesis of *My Mother's House,* describe a child nicknamed "Bel-Gazou" who climbs trees and a low wall.[266] Clearly, they can only be about herself, so nicknamed by the Captain. In giving the exact same nickname to her own daughter, who would be born a year later, in 1913, did the writer imagine she was being reborn in that infant? She projects herself into her to the point of absorbing her through the signifier: first name, last name, and nickname would be shared between them.

So it is with the maternal unconscious, the most formidable of all. Consciously, the little girl is approached with all the precautions due a stranger: "I know that, for her faithful nurse, my Bel-Gazou is by turns the center of the world, a perfect masterpiece, the possessed monster from which one must extirpate the demon at every moment, a champion runner, a dizzying abyss of perversity, a 'dear little one' and a little lamb. . . . But who will tell me what my daughter is for herself?"[267] Such discretion touches on the sustained attention Colette brings to her child and that commentators have refrained from discussing, preferring the image of a great egoist to it.

She is alarmed that the little girl, reflecting the difficult circumstances of the war, "speaks coolly of requisitioning Little Red Riding Hood's cake";[268] "My little rubicund drudge, my still lisping farmer, my graceful Eros-with-wheelbarrow, I feel uneasy at seeing a 'child of the war' growing up in you."[269] Like every mother, she immerses herself in a musical reverie as she listens to her progeny's echolalia: "And alone in her dark bedroom, without a night-light, [her daughter] launches the imperious song of a nightingale in the shadows."[270] She adds: "O cascades of silver on white gravel, o ascending rockets lit up at the instant they fall back to earth, musical scales whose shrillest note is like a firebrand, sequins, yarns about a crystal with a thousand sparkles—there, behind the door, in that dark room, is my last treasure of light: the voice, the laughter of Bel-Gazou."[271] Maternal tenderness blossoms when the writer observes the "passing hypnosis" of the little girl who believes she too is writing but to a nonexistent brother—perhaps, already, her masculine, fantasized double?—which resonates with the "mental hermaphroditism" of Mama, who abandons her in order to write:

She opens an intangible desk whose cover says: "Creak!" like the one in the library, and she writes. She writes without paper, without ink or pen; she writes, her mouth pursed, with pauses, hesitant nibbles on her little finger, strikeouts, a perfect imitation of the writer, she who does not know, or barely knows, how to write. . . . Ah, what is she writing? And

to whom? I can't stand it any longer. [. . .] Bel-Gazou
does not wake to reality and replies from the depths of
her dream:
"I'm writing to my brother."
"To your brother!!! You have a brother?"
A little contemptuous smile.[272]

In addition, wondering about the conjunction between father
and daughter, their mutual love and identities, she notes: " 'She
is ravishing at this moment': that is because, on the little girl's
tender face, the moment superimposes the striking double of a
man's face."[273] The examples could be multiplied. In the first
half of the twentieth century, in French (and world) literature,
Colette was no doubt the only one to have explored motherhood
in that way, with a contagious naturalness, a psychological subtlety free from romantic hyperbole and religious mawkishness.[274]

Within the context of Colette and Henry de Jouvenel's troubled marriage, the utterly dedicated writer's dominating personality and her bisexuality, which sparked the affection and rivalry
of the other woman—not to mention the unconscious cruelty
entailed simply in the act of *writing about others*—could only
make the situation of "little Colette" very uncomfortable. Only
time and the death of her mother allowed the daughter to overcome her bitterness and to formulate this expression of filial gratitude marked by appeasement: "In what was not her profession,
my mother was a dilettante, and it is no one's fault if that dilettante was as versed in botany as in cooking, in music as in theater, in animals as in children, in friendship as in love."[275]

THE WAR BETWEEN THE SEXES

Men and women being what they are, the couple is a painful
hypothesis whose truth erupts into the war between the sexes. "So
it is with the routine of suffering, so it is with the habit of blun-
dering love, so it is with the duty to poison, innocently, every life
lived as a couple."[276] *Duo* notes the incompatibility between Alice

and Michel, due less to a personality clash than to a structural fact. Instinctively, Maria the maid knows it:

> "He's revenging himself."
> "For what?"
> "For the fact that he's my man and I'm his woman. That's quite enough. Madame doesn't believe it?"[277]

Where so many writers have depicted the feminine jouissance that seduces man but also transfixes or excludes him, could Colette be the first to reveal the solitude of the woman shocked in turn by man's jouissance? "She did not dare show how much the excesses of virile abandon, its jerky sobs and stammering, left her cold and scandalized."[278] As they age, the two sexes become farther and farther apart: the woman dwells on the expression of her "gratitude," forgetting the "cruelty of the giver, his baseness, and his mastery," while "the man harbors a bitterness that time does not extinguish."[279]

Voluptuousness itself is built on a total lack of communication, summed up in this inescapably disenchanted sentence: "But I am beginning to believe that a man and a woman can do anything together with impunity, anything except hold a conversation."[280]

Since communication between the sexes is impossible, sadomasochism will become a wave propelling a certain relationship between them: if the couple exists, it holds itself together only through the war between the sexes. In the first place, there is almost no "duo" for Colette that is not at least a "trio": Claudine, Renaud, and Rézi in *Claudine Married*; "me," Jean, and May in *The Shackle*; Chéri, Léa, and Edmée in *Chéri* and *The End of Chéri*; Phil, Vinca, and the Lady in White in *The Ripening Seed*; and so on. This last narrative provides the formula for the triangular tension necessary to the sexual relationship, according to Colette, where the loving body finds itself torn between two forms of domination: "What was there in common between that body, between the use love might make of it, between its inevitable ends, and the fate of another woman's body destined for delicate ravishment, gifted with a genius for despoiling, with a passionate implacability, with an enchanting and hypocritical pedagogy?"[281] Furthermore, on every side, and even in an apparently more conformist relationship, eroticism implies a play between dominant and dominated, a power struggle. The tender camaraderie of the "tall and masculine" Vinca is only the visible face of her "masculine games" and her "athletic rivalry"[282] with Phil: "She struck him suddenly in the face with a fist so unexpected and so masculine that he almost leapt on top of her and beat her soundly."[283]

In his passion for the young woman Phil dreams of himself as the "master" who "possesses" her to the point of being able to inflict death: "On that sloping rock, he dreamed of possession the way a timid adolescent may dream, but also like a demanding man, an heir bitterly resolved to enjoy the property that time and human laws destined to him. He was, for the first time, the only one to decide their fate as a couple, entirely free to abandon her to the waves or to clutch at her on the jutting rock, like the stubborn seed that, with little nourishment, thrived there."[284] This would not prevent him—on the contrary—from abandoning himself in a wholly feminine way to Mme Dalleray and from leaving to the woman/mother the role of "master": "He was also wary of the strong and resinous perfume that permeated Ker-Anna and the body, nude or veiled, of the one he named in a whisper, with the pride of a libertine little boy or the melancholic remorse of a spouse who had cheated on a beloved woman, his mistress one moment and his 'master' the next."[285] Later he finds in Vinca herself the power of a mean-spirited rebel who knows how to subdue her man: "A new Vinca, full of voluptuous insolence, persisted under his closed eyelids, a coquettish Vinca, well armed, suddenly enhanced by embonpoint, Vinca mean-spirited and rebellious at will."[286]

If "a pleasure poorly given, poorly received, is a perfectible work,"[287] its perfectibility lies in the sadomasochistic realm of the desire in question and requires from the Colettian couple an art of jouissance through suffering. "I will tell him: 'It is a premature dream, a delirium, a torment during which you bit your hand, poor little companion, courageous assistant in my cruel task.'"[288] For him jouissance is related to death, with a sound "low and muffled like the cry of a creature whose throat is being cut." For her it is even more epileptic: "a song that came, a feeble echo, from the depths where life is a terrible convulsion."[289] Similarly, Léa, who "submits" to "serve" the pleasure of her young lover as a "good mistress," "saw with a sort of terror the instant of her own defeat approaching; she endured Chéri like a torment, pushed him away with her powerless hands and held him between her powerful knees. Finally, she seized his arm, cried out weakly, and sank into that abyss from which love returns pale, taciturn, and full of a yearning for death."[290]

Could this be, for Colette, the attenuated and nevertheless very audible echo of the "divine marquis"? We are reminded of him when we see her seeking a "pure" eroticism, in opposition to the "impure"; or when she believes she finds in beasts a way out of war, that of soldiers and that between the sexes, which, Colette is sure, human beings cannot do without. "I gathered together beasts in this book, as in an enclosure where, it is my wish, 'there shall be no war.' "[291]

"THOSE PLEASURES THOUGHTLESSLY CALLED PHYSICAL . . ."

In 1931–32, the line "those pleasures thoughtlessly called physical," which Colette mistakenly attributes to *Break of Day* (1928),[292] provided her with the first title, *Those Pleasures . . . ,* in *Le Gringoire* and with the publisher Ferenczi, for what would become, in 1941, *The Pure and the Impure,* published by Editions Calmann-Lévy. Colette explains herself on the title page: "If I had to justify this change, I would find only a keen taste for crystalline sounds, a certain antipathy for ellipses ending an incomplete title—reasons, in short, of very little importance."[293] One seeks in vain, in the text itself, a less formal, more reasonable explanation. The notions of purity and impurity, though they run through this kaleidoscopic book—composed of portraits and impressions that coincide with or contradict each other, of complicitous or ironic echoes, of sensual confessions and fleeting meditations—nevertheless remain beyond reach. Is it the dialogical style of the text[294] that dictates this lack of precision, or a hypnotic uneasiness awakened by the experiences shared? The definition of the word "pure" is constantly dodged, and the book ends with a pirouette, a reverie on sounds and sensations. In alluding to the lesbian couple known as the "ladies of Llangollen," Colette reports the feeling of a lesbian who sees that union not as a variant of motherhood or a relationship between lovers but as a communion "in spite of the man, in a profound and progressive indifference toward that man. Our infinity was so pure that I had not even thought about death." And, as if touched to the quick by the clarity of this confession (could the pure be the absence of man, the "space between" women?), the writer takes refuge in a denegation ("it awakened nothing in me") composed of metaphorical associations relating to the sound of the word "pure."[295] A note in *The Black Opera Glass,* dated October 20, 1935, is a bit more explicit: " 'Nothing,' says Balzac, 'consoles us for having lost what appeared to be infinite to us.' Nothing reassures those who have skirted the edge of the precipice where human morality collapses, have brushed against the fragile line that separates the pure from the impure."[296] Does the infinitely pure open up when moral prohibitions recede?

The history of that book attests to its central place in Colette's writings and invites us not to confine ourselves to the magic of words, which she uses to better inspire us to dream of the secrets contained in these pages. From her very first literary writings she was interested in homosexuality, in Lesbos, even in Krafft-Ebing, as attested by the *Claudine* books. Then came a proposal for a play about Don Juan, between 1908 and 1910. Already a confirmed writer, Colette enthusiastically welcomed Proust's *Sodom and Gomorrah* and sent him this letter in July 1921: "*No one in the world* has written pages like that one on the Invert—no one! That is proud praise I offer you, since, if I once wanted to write a study on the Invert for the *Mercure de France,* it was *that one* I was carrying inside me, along with the incapacity and laziness that kept me from bringing it out."[297] Let us add that she drafted part of *The Pure and the Impure* on the well-named yacht *L'Eros,* on which she and Goudeket took a cruise from July 10 to August 9, 1930. The publisher Calmann-Lévy, who reprinted the "definitive" version in 1941, was not wrong when he pointed out in his introduction that "it is clear that Colette felt a preference [for this text]. 'Some day people may notice,' she was wont to say, 'that this is my best book.' "298

Composed of fragments that echo or stand in counterpoint to one another, *The Pure and the Impure* has led commentators to take a greater interest in the rhetorical effects than in the deep motivations behind the text, which, at a turning point in a literary career that was now fully recognized, took on a testamentary value. In fact, the Sapphic idyll of the ladies of Llangollen contrasts with the sexual obsession of Renée Vivien; and the poet with his distinguished little peasant seems to defy the wild homosexuals that provoke Colette's black humor, such as the unfortunate Pepe, or the underground lesbian culture whose bad taste the writer mocks. Charlotte and Damien, "Madame How-Many-Times" and Don Juan, the Lady Knight and Sarah Ponsonby stand opposed, but they also call to one another; perhaps some of them have even met each other. But what do they have in common?

At the risk of tearing away the diaphanous veil that protects Colette's thoughts, namely, the way she plays with the sounds of words, we may identify certain constants: *purity* is on the side of the homosexual couple, provided it manages to rid itself of the violence of the flesh and unite with the infinite. The variants of that infiniteness are as likely to be platonic love as a feminine "mental hermaphroditism," which, for man, represents a "danger of homosexuality." But, in the end, all are rooted in the infantile sensual innocence that coincides with the original perversity of the human being,299 the same human being that assumes every gender and every posture with the exception of genitality and the Oedipus complex, which establish the norm of the heterosexual couple and procreation. On the contrary, *impurity* is on the side of the war between the sexes, which Colette calls an "enmity" and that she assumes is stronger on the part of a man who believes his mistresses "have sensually exploited him."[300] That enmity can be discerned both in the excesses of heterosexual desire (the Don Juans, the "gobs," the "Madame How-Many-Times," the "consumed," all sorts of lunatic and inauthentic behaviors driven by tyrannical violence) but also in the excesses of homosexual relationships when they ignore "the celestial paths of Llangollen" and run aground in transvestism, the "melee of the sexes," when not in female caricatures envious of virility, whom Colette likes to mock. In short, the impure is that "routine of the abyss,"[301] where, in the excesses of desire, the most conformist bourgeois sexuality and the most marginal transgressions, which mimic the latter's logic, meet.

In a draft from the early pages of *The Pure and the Impure* that was not kept in the final version, Colette reveals that the secret of purity lies in wresting the heterosexual away from normative sexuality and that such purity aspires to reconnect with autoerotic infiniteness in an ocean of opium. Although she begins by saying she has "always had trouble admitting that love, and even pleasure, is a couple's business," the author abandons that token of sexual orthodoxy and borrows a procession of painful confessions that drive her toward an avowal. At certain hours "in a woman's life," which "are never happy times" but are certainly times of "knowledge," provided she is not led there by the traps of "snobbishness" or a "spirit of bravado," by a "hopeless" "eccentricity," the following occurs: "One evening the woman goes away by herself, thus taking her unselfconsciousness with her." She then joins "friends" and goes to "opium dens." The fact that Colette frequented opium addicts such as Claude Farrère, Schwob, Toulet, and perhaps Masson,[302] and that Sido herself alluded to her presence in the dens,[303] is, for our purposes, less interesting than the place occupied by drug addiction in the experience of pleasure according to Colette and, above all, the use she makes of it in her writing.

Charlotte is the first protagonist who indulges in that pure pleasure: in the dark rooms of the den, she is content to mimic jouissance with her voice in order to reassure her young lover about his virility and the love they share. It is in the struggle between the flesh, which remains insensitive, and the melody of the "merciful lie" that the first figure of purity takes shape. If Charlotte fascinates Colette, it may be less by virtue of the enigma of hysterical frigidity than by the miracle of the feint. In fact, Charlotte performs an imaginary act par excellence, which does not fail to appear as a double for the act of sublimation itself, the act of writing in particular. Is it not detached from a real orgasm, whether experienced or brushed aside, only a contagious and convincing representation of it? Could the voice of the opium addict be an equivalent of writing and Charlotte an emulator of Colette?

> From the bosom of that silence itself, a sound was imperceptibly born in a woman's throat, a sound that came out hoarse, cleared, acquired its firmness and range by repeating itself, like the full notes the nightingale reiterates and accumulates until they fall away into a roulade. . . . A woman up there was struggling against her invasive pleasure, was hastening it toward its term and its destruction, in a calm rhythm at first, rushing so harmoniously, so regularly that I caught myself nodding my head to its cadence, as perfect as its melody.[304]

She adds:

> But I was thinking of the *romantic reward* she granted the young lover, of the almost public pleasure, of the lament of the nightingale, the full notes, reiterated, identical, one extending into the other, racing to the breaking point of their trembling equilibrium at the height of a torrential sob. . . . Therein lay the secret, no doubt, of Charlotte's *melodious and merciful lie*. I thought the young lover's happiness was great, if I measured it by the *perfection of the deceit* of the woman who delicately worked to give a touchy and weak boy the loftiest idea a man can have of himself.
> A female genius, occupied with tender imposture, with consideration, with abnegation, thus dwelt within that tangible Charlotte, the reassuring friend of men.[305]

Let us also emphasize that, if Charlotte's purity exists, it is inseparable from its object, the man-child, her partner. A glorified version of Chéri, the counterpart of Phil in *The Ripening Seed,* the young man remains anonymous here. Lurking in the unsaid of the narrative, he yields all the space to the generous maturity of the faker Charlotte. Exit the hero: this story is that of the heroine who devotes herself to the man-child. That nonhero is an ambiguous character: as a man, he completes her and fills her with his phallic presence; as a child greedy for loving recognition and narcissistic jouissance, he reveals his dependence and a feminine passivity beyond his castration. An amphibious being for whom Charlotte destines her gratifying lie, that other "little faun," the nameless adolescent at the beginning of *The Pure and the Impure,* reflects back to his benefactress the inverted image of her bisexuality. It is their double bisexuality, their two forms of polymorphism that appease each other in that wedding of purity according to Charlotte—in the simulacrum.

Opposite it, and in contradistinction to the purity of that "female genius,"[306] lies the territory of the Impure. "Then, pell-mell [. . .] flesh, more flesh, mysteries, treachery of the flesh, failures of the flesh, surprises of the flesh."[307] Charlotte expresses the tension between the two, setting the body in opposition to the heart, the "Inexorable" to the "mental," "the senses" to "sense," which seems "more modest" and introduces "the peaceful night tamed by opium." "In my heart, I am completely devoted to that child. But what is the heart, Madame? It is worth less than it is reputed to be. It's very easygoing, it accepts anything. One stocks it with what one has, it's so undemanding. . . . The body, for its part. . . . All right, fine! It has, as they say, discerning tastes, it knows what it wants. A heart does not choose. One always loves in the end. I'm certainly proof of that."[308]

Nevertheless, once that opposition is established, purity is not simply of the "heart" nor impurity essentially of the "body," since "who can fix your unstable borders?" It is in the *infinity of wresting away* that purity resides, in the "arbitrary limit" between the two empires, even in the extravagant experience that "holds them in check," without ever fixing them as such or excluding

one in favor of the other. "*Senses, intractable lords,* ignorant like
the princes of former times who learned only the indispensable:
to dissimulate, to hate, to command. . . . It is you, however,
whom Charlotte, lying in the peaceful night tamed by opium,
held in check, assigning arbitrary limits to your empire; but who,
then, if only Charlotte, can fix your unstable boundaries?"[309]
How can we not read, once again, in that auscultation of purity
according to Charlotte, an image of sublimation, acted out as an
interminable journey by a diffuse hypersensitivity in search of its
representation: a journey between the felt and the said, the real
and the symbolic, the Inexorable and Grace? Senses or sense?

Alongside that tension/purity according to Charlotte, which
places us in proximity of the drive *and* of the imagination, another face of purity imposes itself: pure is characterized as whatever excludes the other sex. If the inexorably impure is truly heterosexuality, that is, "normal" libido, it is on the basis of "the
antipathy of one sex for the other" that the territory of the pure
has a chance to open. "The antipathy of one sex for the other
exists apart from neuropathy. Since then, I have not observed,
in changing my environment, that the opinion of 'normal people' is very different."[310] A monstrous purity may exclude women: "Off by myself with my former 'monsters,' I named 'pure'
and loved the atmosphere that banished women. But, on that
count, I would also have liked the purity of the desert, and that
of the prison. The prison and the desert are not within everyone's reach."[311] Symmetrically, the ideal case of perfect purity,
the "tenderness" between the ladies of Llangollen, excludes
men: the elder one, Lady Eleanor Butler, and her young companion, Sarah Ponsonby, go into exile from the world and
spend their whole life in a solitude for two, populated only by
their mutual affection, their daily tasks, and the contemplation
of nature. "They went for walks in front of their cottage for
fifty-one years."[312] Naturally, contemporaries disapproved: was
not that the very epitome of anomaly, of the impure? "Jealous
of such an imperturbable tenderness, they will want those two
faithful girls to have fallen short of purity—but what do they
understand by purity?"[313]

There is, according to Colette, an artificial morality, that of the family order, which, in condemning "a disorderly and pure flame"—let us understand: a humanity prior to the prohibition, original and innocent—transforms that flame into an abnormal, impure phenomenon to be outlawed. And, for purity to burst forth again, that family order, or that official morality, has only to weaken: "When, finally, the two families, overwhelmed, not making 'head nor tail' of that madness, of that disorderly and pure flame, yield, the two young girls become once again sweet as pet doves."[314]

Does Colette truly believe in the idyll of an "us" that would be safe from the abuses of power, without psychic or physical "penetration" ("Penetration, the voluptuous gift for wounding!")?[315] Her amoralism does not really seem to be a dupe to that utopia exempt from order and domination, since she notes that Lady Eleanor, "the writer" of the Llangollen couple, does not mention the name of her companion, who thus quite simply disappears into the pleasantness of that paradise. "She is no longer Sarah Ponsonby, but a part of that double person named 'us.' She loses even her name, which Lady Eleanor almost never writes in keeping her journal."[316] This subtly demonstrates that purity will never be simple, much less absolute, but that it always comes from an in-finite transcendence of the norm, and from an equally in-finite taking flight of the Inexorable, in an attempt to rejoin the peace of "sense" in the singular. As elsewhere, in that universe of sensual serenity there will always be the conquerors and the conquered, the authors and the anonymous.

In that gallery of the pure, the Lady Knight, with her unexpected counterpart Don Juan, are clearly the most ambiguous figures, the most inseparable from the impure.

I have already mentioned[317] the caricatural vision of transvestite homosexuality that Colette attacks: the Lady Knight combines a touching "clumsiness" and the "male love smell of a horse."[318] In fact, "what cross-dressing women have the most difficulty imitating is a man's stride."[319] Her attractiveness borders on the impure: Missy verges on the ridiculousness of "modest monsters" when she wears giant shoes to imitate men. But im-

purity—or is it a monstrous purity?—bursts out above all in the
Lady Knight's alter ego, another reflection of Missy, the character of the baroness de La Berche, an "old lady with a man's face,"
a failed being with an "aborted femininity," who becomes
Chéri's ideal companion at the end of his life. "A woman charged
with sexual monstrosity carries it not without bravura, not without a certain grandeur characteristic of the condemned
woman."[320] Later on, however, Colette contrasts that ambivalence to the open disgust that unsuccessful cross-dressing men,
decked out in women's underclothes, inspire in her. The writer
rises up against "those little crimes against nature [. . .] those
poor figures of false men, those anatomies of women to be cast
off, those aborted efforts at a forehead, a chin, a skull."[321] Could
she be the only one to incarnate the purity of hermaphroditism?
The Evening Star suggests as much, evoking not the cross-
dressing of the young Colette, but the writer she is, with her
"woman's eyes" bent over a pen held by a "short hard [male] gardener's hand."[322]

Purity, the enemy of the Inexorable, can reside both in melancholy and in platonic love. The androgyne has the "obligation
never to be happy. If jovial, he/she is a monster."[323] Like the
yearning for the incestuous couple, it is the androgyne's sadness
and "grandeur of a condemned person" that guarantee his/her purity. As a result, and despite its impurities, the aristocratic soul of
the Lady Knight, who allows herself to be woefully exploited by
the women she loves, nevertheless maintains its purity, since hers
is a platonic love: of her mistresses, it is the eyes her "timid heart"
prefers, "silently excited and perpetually adolescent," ready to
"blissfully lose her life between algae and the stars." "'What more
is needed than a pair of eyes?' asked the Lady Knight."[324] Nevertheless, is it in purity or in its opposite that the Lady Knight is engulfed when Colette discovers some affinities between her and
Don Juan, since they both constantly accumulate female conquests? Like the insatiable Damien, the Lady Knight finds that
women "go too far," and that the gluttony for pleasure is "somehow a little sad, a little repulsive." Fascinated by the female orgasm and hungry to be able to procure it for her lovers, the Lady

Knight—that cross-dressing Don Juan—nevertheless feels something like a remoteness from eroticism, if not a disapproval of it. At least she expresses a certain uneasiness by taking on the role, which she wants to be as insignificant as possible, of a medieval "donor" unworthy of appearing in the painting: "I am of the opinion," she says, "that in the old Nativities, the portrait of the 'donor' occupies much too much space in the painting."[325]

In the end her purity stems from her passion, which no object satisfies. Implicitly, the Lady Knight considers every libidinal object impure ("revolting," she says), and she has a keen awareness that there is no solution to the "lack" that defines her: "I am neither this nor that, nor, alas! something else . . . , said the Lady Knight, letting go of the impure little hand. What *I lack cannot be found* by looking."[326]

Colette's Don Juan, inspired by the actor Edouard de Max and by many illustrious works—Mozart's *Don Giovanni* is not mentioned, however, and Molière's *Don Juan* is neglected ("Molière [. . .] knows even less about it than I")[327]—is the image not of machismo but of the "terrible trauma of virile pleasure."[328] Returning to the "enmity" between the sexes, Colette recognizes an overabundant jouissance in women: as "man's storehouse of plenty," she "knows she is nearly inexhaustible." In contrast, man, a victim of what Colette does not call "castration" but that greatly resembles it, and especially the man who "faces" a "great number of women," experiences "possession" as "a bolt of lightning," which "creat[es] for him a particular state of misery, the neurasthenia of a Danaïd." Equipped with a desire resembling a leaky jar, the ladies' man is therefore only a cursed Danaïd, whose secret wish would be "that a woman finally love him enough to refuse herself."[329] The impurity of the libidinous collector would thus conceal the purity of the man whose unconscious desire is, in a word, *outside sex*.

There is, however, nothing angelic about that Don Juan variant of purity: it conceals an incomprehension of women, even a profound aversion to them. "You wouldn't really want me to devote myself to their happiness the first day I was sure about them? In any case, I would not be a ladies' man if I had made love a great deal."[330] More envious than nostalgic, Don Juan judges that feminine pleasures "go too far,"[331] that women "don't know how to turn back."[332] By glorying in the role of educator of the second sex ("I taught them well"), he expects a reward and sulkily regrets not receiving a great deal in exchange. Impervious to complicity, or even to psychology, he does not understand the narrator's sharp digs: "What they gave you? Their pain, I think. You're not so poorly paid!"[333] In fact, doesn't he complain of being incapable of jouissance—like a woman? Don Juan the frigid? A feminine pleasure "equal" to his own seems like a vexation to him, which he cannot allow himself to "forgive," since his jouissance comes only from *his* mastery, *his* domination: "To be their master in pleasure, but never their equal. . . . That is what I do not forgive them."[334] At an even deeper level, that misogynous Don Juan is a misanthrope. But could the reason he defends himself so passionately against the company of humans be that he fears men and, more crudely, men's sexuality? Don Juan the misanthrope, or Don Juan the homophobe? "I have nothing to exchange, I have never had anything to exchange with men. In the little time I have frequented them, their conversation in general has made me ill, and furthermore, they bore me. 'I believe,' he said, hesitating, 'I believe I don't understand them.' "[335]

What if Colette's Don Juan were only an inflexible phobic? A man without truth? A "false self"? "Is it only victory you love? Or, on the contrary, don't you set any store in that victory?"[336] Under the heaping pile of his masks and behind a pretence of indifference ("I mean he does not make—or very rarely makes—love.—Bravo! Is making love indispensable? Making it is all well and good, but let it be with insignificant persons"),[337] Don Juan conceals an irremediable fear of his emotions, of "anger," "disorder," the "illogical," of his own "femininity." "I wanted him to give in to anger, to a disorder of any sort that would have revealed him to me as illogical, weak, and feminine, as every woman demands, at least once, of any man."[338]

Purity is finally achieved through its incarnation in the two "virgins of Llangollen" and shifts toward a celebration of the infantile. From the start Colette recognizes she is entering a territory that, for her, is clearly untouchable, sacred: "How it displeases me to coldly examine such a fragile creation threatened by everything: a pair of women in love!"[339] There is a female homosexual relationship—a "noble" passion, "a fiery and chaste marriage engagement"—that is not that of androgynes or transvestites. Its profound logic is that of the *mirror*: the life of such a *duo* is "laid out like the contemplation before a mirror,"[340] a "series of mirrors."[341] Its "origin" is not erotic and has nothing to do with voluptuousness, which, as we have seen, is impure. It is rather a question of a hypersensitivity Colette calls nonsensual and that she describes as a "kinship," a "similarity": "By living together in love, two women can finally discover that the origin of their reciprocal penchant is not sensual—is never sensual. Poor childish and misguided cynicism of Renée!"[342] Sisterhood, a reduplication of the mother-child relationship, creates between two such women in love a "delicate solidarity that lives only on endless and shared tasks."[343]

We are at the zero point in time of the differentiation of beings and sexes. In fact, no temporality—the time of worry and history—seems to interfere with that paradise "outside time, beyond reach." The American and French Revolutions occurred, but, like so many other political events, in vain: for Lady Eleanor and Sarah Ponsonby time has stopped, they live for half a century in the finally regained pure time of perfumed paradises, "a day of sweetly enjoyed retirement."[344] Colette, captivated by "the reciprocal faith" of these "two stubborn friends," rejects the wariness of Mme de Genlis who, though respectful of such polite and cultivated noble ladies, deplores their "dangerous exaltation." As in a child's dream, she reads Lady Eleanor's journal complicitously and goes along, with a barely ironic affection, with its "sweet solitude" peopled with readings (Mme de Sévigné, Rousseau, Mme de Maintenon), with teas, currants, hair rolled up in papers, visits to Margaret the cow, amazement at a calf or a rabbit. "Read. Wrote. Drew. Beautiful sunrise, azure sky."[345] Without being altogether the dupe of that idyll, in which Lady Eleanor assumes the role of a "cautious jailer—the male,"[346] in which she conceals and abolishes (the consenting?) Sarah under the tender anonymous names she constantly lavishes on her ("Beloved, My Better Half, Darling")—Colette's approval nevertheless remains total. Could that be because she deciphers, in that monastic enclosure, a kinship with her personal pantheism rooted in "the house of Claudine," in "Sido," in the perpetuation of childhood memory? "Childish adventures, fantasies full of love. . . . If only [Eleanor] dared say it all!"[347]

A piece of Colette's personality is revealed here, in the confession of the writer's identification with female homosexuality, which she seems to consider endogenous, inevitable, and not culpable. The little girl's archaic connection to the mother's breast may be its inescapable foundation. And she indulges in this praise of the breast, the secret of that original female homosexuality whose innocence she wants to have us admit: "I have a bone to pick with those who believe it is not unseemly to stroke a young cheek, warm and fresh as a peach under its velvet, but that, if the palm of the hand cups, squeezes, or gently weighs the breast, pink as a peach and with a navel like it, one has to blush, raise the alarm, cast a slur on the assailant."[348]

Is Colette a Freudian? That unveiling of the desire between daughter and mother was written by her at almost the same moment that the Viennese doctor was devoting himself, more than usual, to female sexuality, discovering that "the bisexuality [. . .] in the innate disposition of human beings, comes to the fore much more clearly in women than in men," and that it can be traced back to the archaic relationship between two "likes," daughter and mother. The founder of psychoanalysis compares that phase of psychic development situated before the Oedipus complex to the "Minoan-Mycenean civilization behind the civilization of Greece."[349] Colette nowhere mentions Freud: did she even notice the issue of the literary review *Le Disque Vert*,[350] which considers writers' perspectives on Freudian theories?

More significant is what she takes from Sarah Ponsonby who, after the death of her friend Eleanor, which does not seem to afflict her very much, says of her garden: "A friend brought me sixteen geraniums this morning, of which fully fourteen are new to me, though I already possess eight varieties of them, I think. I will send you the list. For, children that they are, they can be parents by next spring, and their descendants will not be unworthy of your own in that season. I thank you for the seeds of Heartsease, I'm just afraid they'll be difficult to grow in this unfavorable climate."[351] Such words might very well have been uttered by Colette or by Sido.

THE INFANTILE REVISITED FROM THE DIRECTION OF THE IMPURE

Kinship, similarity, the cult of flowering: what difference is there between the themes that attract the virgins of Llangollen and those that haunt Colette-Sido? None, since the same "purity," the same dual and cosmic hypersensitivity permeate them. And yet, from that sensorial *reality,* which she grounds in endogenous, because archaic, female homosexuality and with which she is not unfamiliar, Colette constructs an *imaginary* world. For her the infantile is remade, revisited, recreated as style. To reach that point she had to pass through the perversion of the Sapphists and a few others to recover in her imagination and in writing that idyll of the infantile she reconstitutes in the Llangollen couple and that may be only the artifact of sublimation, the realist fallout from the Colettian infantile—unreal, imaginary, recreated.

She had to wrest herself away from the norm, flout the law, familiarize herself with the impure, and only then reconcile herself with the "polymorphously perverse" in herself, that is, with the imaginary child, that storehouse of plenty, that mirage of all possibilities. Colette, who often uses, if only in quotation marks, the adjective "normal," deals with all the sexual anomalies with "respect" and "keenness," in the words of Maurice Goudeket.[352] The infantile thus revisited—in counterpoint to the enmity between the sexes and in the wake of the rehabilitation of homosexuality—escapes mere "neuropathy," and the "monster" acquires "a kind of legitimacy."[353]

As a result the representation of childhood in Colette can be perplexing: it is neither Rousseauist innocence, nor the crude ambiguity of Gyp's Petit Bob, nor the corruption of Rachilde's *L'animale* [The female animal] (to cite only two of her contemporaries). Of course, from the *Claudine* novels to *Sido,* from the little girls of Montigny to the narrator's two "savage" brothers, Colette's childhood universe lacks neither puerile Sapphism nor daring mischief, nor even erotic persecutions and vices. Nevertheless, the time of desire expands in Colette's childhood and marks a pause in a space where the sadomasochistic violence is toned down. Rooted in that erotic *spacing of time* is the idealized image, beyond its ambiguities, of the parental couple and of her birthplace itself. House, garden, village, peasants, the heroicomic evocation of rural France is part of childhood according to Colette. The writer's province is part of time regained, the imaginary time that is openly called *infantile* and not civic, political, or ideological.

Moreover, the childhood past imposes itself as the center of Colette's imaginary, less by these *themes* than by virtue of the *means* of childhood the writer uses to approach them. Infantile memories are recovered using rhetorical methods that seem to remain faithful to the logic of childhood. The *avidity* of latency, which is called hyperesthesia, underlies the avalanche of sensorial metaphors, whether of sight, taste, smell, touch, or hearing. The *reversible sensations* of the child—who is a subject with uncertain boundaries, whose repression is problematic—can be made out in Colette's more than "Baudelairean" synesthesia. Infantile *indifferentiation,* which does not yet respect the boundary between subject and object, same and other, can be deciphered in the figures of doubles, the mixtures, in sexual ambiguity and other Colettian "monstrosities." The *timelessness* of the unconscious, which contaminates childhood, colors the dislocated temporality of her narratives. Infantile "Cratylism," the tendency to "motivate" the arbitrary signifier of language by giving a meaning to sounds apart from the sense of the words, becomes for her a way of thinking. Is not her reverie on the word "presbytery" similar to her claim to "define" the *pure* and the *impure* on the basis of the impression the vowels and consonants in those two words make on her?

Like the duc de Morny, who thinks that "a woman remains in the state of a rough sketch" if she has not known the love of another woman,[354] Colette convinces us that a writer remains in the state of a rough sketch unless she offers herself "mental hermaphroditism" and incest as "a voluptuous training period" or "a rigorous induction," in order to test, as in a laboratory, the psychosexual polymorphism characteristic of childhood, the abnormal sensuality that constitutes us at a profound level and that the childhood memory in fact crystallizes. If one moves backward from that laboratory, defined as the passage through perverse sexuality, it is possible to reach the infantile. Let us rather say it is not so much *regained* as *recreated,* in a tone midway between scandal and innocence. And that betweenness, that back-and-forth motion, seems to be both at the foundation of the logic of sublimation and at the heart of the Colettian idea of "purity."

To write that experience, the very term "pure" cannot and must not ever be definitively fixed. But, fragile as a spider's web, it remains barely discernible, held "in between." And, since the pure/impure pair thus elaborated swallows up the classic dichotomies of normality/abnormality and morality/immorality, there is not, for Colette, an "amoralism" in Gide's sense. The perverse experience is not an aim in itself nor the major source of pleasures. The writer's desire passes through it, first intersecting the childhood hearth from which the pure radiates and subsequently recovering the equivalent of that logic of hyperesthesia, of synesthesia, of timelessness, of the indifferentiation and fragmentation characteristic of childhood, in that savory and simple way of naming that characterizes Colette's writing. As a result, in unison with the infantile, language will hold itself between words and things in the pure impurity of the sensual word, of nameable sensitivity. "Moi, le petit faune au regard farouche / L'âme des forêts vit entre mes dents / Et le dieu du rhythme habite ma bouche" [I, the little faun with ferocious gaze / The soul of forests lives between my teeth / And the god of rhythm dwells within my mouth],writes Renée Vivien, in the poetic portrait she draws of Colette.[355] The "little faun" is truly the Colette who has reconnected with the sexual amphibian she was as a child and who, strengthened by that ambiguity, assimilates the forest and accompanies in her language the rhythm of the world: inside and outside, woman and beast, language and being, mouth and soul. Unlike the child who separates itself from the bosom of nature in order to learn to speak, Colette grounds the French language in the sensory maternal space she uses to steady herself and that is named Sido. Both the child and Colette are miracles in the flowering of sense and the sensory, one at one end, one at the other: two faces of that *purity* of the *imaginary* itself as creativity, as apparition-revelation, and that could not be reached without crossing through the "Inexorable," the "impure," the "monogram of flesh." Thus it is not surprising to read, written in Colette's hand, that it is her work devoted to *incestuous fantasies*— namely, *Chéri* (1920)—that she grants the greatest literary value in her twilight years, though she judged, somewhat earlier, that *The Pure and the Impure* was her "best book." "For the first time in my life I felt sure, deep down, that I had written a novel that would not make me blush or doubt."[356] Does not that text, which she calls "symphonic" because of a harmony between the "loquacious Chéri" and the "laughing Chéri"—though it is dominated by silence ("his mutism")[357]—"regain altitude," as she believes, because it shows a glimpse, precisely through the door of the impure, of the paradises of childhood now inaccessible to the pragmatic postwar society and to any society?

Because she has known the pure and the impure, Colette imposes, with an incomparable certainty, the imaginary as a new version of the sacred. A scandalous innocence, some will say. Her pagan texts attest to a diffuse, total, and obstinate spirituality, which permeates the flower and the monster, writing and sex. It irradiates the place where Colette situates herself, in the infantile regained, with perversity, between sense and the sensory. Such is the crossroads of original sublimation that makes the polymorphously perverse child, the fierce faun, a speaking being.

That unbeliever, who fancies herself an atheist like Sido, has convinced herself and convinces us that we have no transcendence other than the purity of sublimation, if and only if it wrests itself from the inexorable flesh to which it nevertheless belongs and within which it flowers. "It seems to me that a need to escape everything and everyone, a leap upward, toward a law written by [Sido] herself, for herself, was setting them ablaze."[358] That "leap upward," toward a "law written by her," is performed by Colette herself in a gesture at once sensual and mental that connects the infantile itself to its formulation. The writing that results, and whose purity seduces us, is not unfamiliar with any aspect of the impure; and, if it has nothing to do with an auto-erotic egotism, that is because the "law" it formulates is that of a subject disseminated in the world's flesh. The infantile ceases to be synonymous with narcissism and articulates the facts, and a subjectivity pushed to the extreme expresses the most natural objectivity. Never has a writer succeeded with such immediate simplicity—without the metaphysical refinement of the sarcastic Proust or the touchy passion of the Southerner Faulkner—at a reformulation, not of the divine but of the immanence of the sacred at the very heart of our shortcomings, our childishness, our simple presence in the world, and of the world itself. That sacred is presented in Colette's language through the "red petunia" or the "white lilacs obliged to bloom in winter," whose purity incites the lieutenant in love with Mitsou to confuse it with his mistress's body: "I remember that, because of the red petunia of your cheeks, under the harsh light, your arms and the groove on your back looked green, green as the white lilacs obliged to bloom in winter."[359]

What is at issue? An erotic act? A rustic bouquet? A cooing of Ronsardian language, full of alliterations, *r, j, l,* and *v,* liquid as a kiss? Love is the inexorable, which is purified through sensory words to encompass a polymorphous body in the presence of the world. Skeptical of happiness, Colette passes through perversion and enhances the time of childhood. Her writing thus diffuses a modern version of faith incarnate: the reverse side of illusion, useless consolation, imaginary enthusiasm, all fleeting, fragile, but in the end possible. That version of the sacred may well be the very unconscious of the Catholic faith: of its cult of passion, of *père-version*, of their maternal and infantile underside. Colette did not expect it—except perhaps at the end of her life, when she solicited a missal from Mauriac, motivated no doubt by worldly, political and historical, factors but not solely by them. The Catholic hierarchy was there, obviously, uncomprehending. That spirituality and its unconscious resonance connected with the memory of a people, extending beyond the atheists who identified with "our Colette." And if her profound logic is that of sublimation, as I believe I have depicted her grasping and formulating it, then this woman's writing has every chance of connecting with other forms of spirituality throughout the world.

WHICH COUPLE? OR, THE TRIUMPH OF THE IMAGINARY

Beyond its Greek, Jewish, and Christian antecedents, the modern couple was established by so-called enlightened bourgeois ideology as it was forged with the help of the Enlightenment philosophers. We are indebted to Rousseau (1712–78) for its outlines and its values. *The New Heloise* (1761) describes a society and a moral system in decomposition, of which Roxane and Saint-Preux are the victims. *Emile* (1762), in response to that debacle, invents a new reality: a couple for whom the sexual relationship, because founded in nature, is declared possible.

To properly assess the sexual meaning and the social import of that invention, one must place it within the perspective of the reflections conducted in earlier centuries on morals on the one hand and on their relation to despotic power on the other. Rousseau is to be read in the light of La Boétie (1530–63) and his *Discours de la servitude volontaire* [Discourse on voluntary servitude], and in relation to the *Lettres persanes* [Persian letters] and *L'esprit des lois* [The spirit of laws] by Montesquieu (1689–1755). Within that perspective the Rousseauist couple seems to propose an alternative both to the sensual jouissance in which the polygamous Oriental ruler abolishes himself and to its parallel, the decline of monarchical power.

Beginning in the sixteenth century, and particularly in the seventeenth and eighteenth centuries, there was a very keen interest in seraglios among French authors and the French public.[360] The master of the harem seems to be less a man than a "manlet" [*hommeau*], even a "dead man" [*homme mort*], wedged between tyrannical mothers and obsequious eunuchs, with a soft body and a supposed phallic power that is only a power by default, both amid his multitude of wives and within the political realm. Travelers and philosophers referred smugly to that foreign set-up, since in it they glimpsed the archaeology—if not the essence itself—of what was unfolding before their eyes in French society: the bankruptcy of political power, the deficiency of sexual relations. Geographical peculiarities, historical facts, structural dead ends? In the official report on the phantasmatic impossibility of sexual relations and the crises of despotic power, the *new couple* would be, in other words, the miraculous formula destined to found a subject with two faces, the guarantee both of the relation between parent and children and that between state and citizens. We already know—and Rousseau's texts show this—that this formula is not tenable. "But it can be contested only in the mode of debauchery, perversion, crime." The "new harmony" that the couple reinvented very quickly came to look like a "sham mechanism" that "conceals a hell of debauchery and perversion."[361]

Built on the "enmity" between the sexes, with men-objects or effeminate men sometimes dominated by "mental hermaphrodite" women, Colette's universe of love seems to stem directly from that past, its reality and its ideology. Nevertheless, the version of the love relation she proposes, though neither philosophical nor political, attests to a *radical change* in the angle of approach, not only because it is a woman writing but because her existential project entails navigating the couple. It does not, however, find excitement in the realm of criminal transgression or by retreating to a more archaic model, such as wagering on a consoling transcendence granted by a Great Other. Neither metaphysical nor sociopolitical, the way of *being in the world* specific to Colette, which culminates in the writing *of* and *in* the world's flesh, implies a consideration of the impasses as well as the fertility of the love relationship, with its homo- and heterosexual valences. It attests to a *profound modification* of the *conception of the couple,* which feminists have not been wrong to see as a courageous beginning of women's freedom. But her essential message nevertheless still consists of inspiring a transformation of *subjectivity* itself, of the risky balance that constitutes it, between sense and sensation, law and passion, purity and impurity. Neither the imperative to reproduce the species nor that of social stability—both guaranteed by the couple—guides Colette's thought. There is nothing but a constant concern for the emancipation of the subject, with a priority given to the woman subject who wishes to achieve her sensual freedom in order to maintain her curiosity and creativity in a plurality of relationships.

Is not Colette's journey through love the journey of religion? Recall her rage against the Eternal City: "The basilicas make me gag. I hate Saint-Peter's and Santa Maria Maggiore, and if Saint John of Lateran did not have its cloister. . . . "362 "Scenes of what I call Catholic savagery: holy staircases climbed on one's knees, paving stones full of spittle and dirt and garbage, which tongues lick in the shape of a cross (it's horrible!), confessionals every ten paces in Saint Peter's basilica. [. . .] Annie, the Middle Ages are a curious era! [. . .] Despicable priests—two ten a hundred—who speak loudly and pace the flagstones with a big-soled stride—it is clear God is their familiar carpet."363 That fury calmed with time.364 We follow the profound meaning of her atheistic conviction by pursuing the infinite, but always passionate, detachment from the love relationship that she proposes and for which she substitutes a friendly, floral, animal passion for Being in language. Neither illusions nor zealotry are abolished in the proximity—never achieved in French—between imaginary effervescence and the stylistic labor that replaces them. But in Colette's writing no absolute object, no redemptive pole, no reference point alien to passion endures. Passion remains, but it clings only to the mere *adjustment between the felt and the said,* the lived and the represented, the loved and the said. Colette's sublimity and monstrosity reside in that total resorption of any transcendence by the arabesque, the alphabet, embroidery, the monogram, in that permeability between the world's flesh and the French language, in her style.

To believe in God implies a belief in an absolute alterity, as redemptive as it is apocalyptic. If alterity is abolished in the delirium of an omnipotence fanning the pleasures of a tyrannical ego, what remains is solipsism. Yet writing—and particularly Colette's writing, full of transubstantiation, which installs the felt into words and words into sensations—leaves nothing out but does not erect itself into an imaginary mastery. An infinite and heterogeneous passion (sense/sensations), it is consumed at the very moment it engenders itself and vice versa. Fire and flowering, it sets only itself in motion again. It is an endless dynamic, which death alone consumes, since writing ceases, only to write anew.[365] Death itself does not put an end to that bacchanalia, since it opens the time of unpredictable readings, undecidable appropriations, unwarranted or legitimate interpretations, like my own.

That anamorphosis of the love relationship, which is the foundation of the individual in the Western tradition, is rich with anarchistic vertigo, with elation as much as personal anguish, and does not fail to trigger scandals in a society with whose norms it collides even today. We read it, however, as a libertarian promise; our deepest, most secret self shares it in the solitude of reading, and our acts of love as well as our social behaviors coincide more and more openly with it as the third millennium begins. Indeed, we now know that Colette's solitary path, her imaginary solution, is one of the most radical and, for that very reason, perhaps one of the only ones possible: before building new models or existential structures between the sexes, for the family and in view of a new type of nation or federation, it is on the *imaginary* capacity, on its possible flowering—or, on the contrary, on its stifling in Technology and the Spectacle—that our aptitude for sexual jouissance and, as a result, for life itself depends. Colette's writing attests to that defense and illustration of imaginary experience—in the transversal and constitutive aspect of any relationship to the other, the couple, or the group—with a force unexpected in her own time and contagious even today.

I saw a singer on the stage whose body metamorphosed itself when she "entered" her voice. More exactly, it was the voice that, resonating in her mouth, her throat, her lungs, her digestive tube, her skull, her eyes, her hair, her breasts, her skin, and her bones, created another woman, an understudy for the one who had just come onstage, and who held herself taut as a bow under the prima donna's visible appearance. That act of doubling was identifiable only in the first instants of the concert, since we were subsequently carried away by the internal woman alone and by the many masks she then imposed on her character in the profane world. It was a *possession*, but controlled, unfolding before our eyes, dominated by vocal technique and by an exquisite intelligence that shaped a *new subject,* reborn with every note, completely artificial and nevertheless with a power superior to that of the visible body. That possession made the artist even more alive than the woman but animated with a new, vocal, mental, inhuman, deceitful, monstrous, and nevertheless shareable life, which resonated with the listeners.

The experience of writing for Colette, that pure and impure modulation of the love relationship that she invented with such brio, contains the same power of possession that transfigured the prima donna. The act of writing creates a double of the naughty little Burgundian girl and of the pythoness of the Palais-Royal as a cosmic power—sometimes approaching the extravagance of a sideshow freak—with a contagious generosity. You cannot see her imaginary, stretched taut like the strings of a lute or like the vocal chords of my baroque singer; but you hear it while reading these dense and graceful sentences in which Colette endures her sorrows, shivers at the hard winters, and is consumed in the burning-hot summers.

Before arriving at possession, before revealing the heart of the "self," Colette locked herself away in a long inner silence: "Months passed, and years, during which, offering myself as a spectacle here and there, I exercised the right to keep quiet about myself."[366] With the passing days, this became a "bureaucratic courage": "Returning to Paris, I took to my work with that slow and stubborn, bureaucratic, courage, which has not left me."[367]

But, as time went on, that distance was accompanied by an icy humor at her own expense: "For a woman who was induced to be reborn from her ashes more than once, or simply to emerge without help from the tiles, flooring, and plaster that fell on her head, there is, after more than thirty years, neither passion nor venom, but a sort of cool pity and laughter, without kindness I grant you, that resonates at my own expense and at the expense of my character who occupies the foreground."[368]

The "self" cannot be found in that detachment from love, of which Colette became the first woman explorer, without immolating herself in melancholy. According to that friend of the beasts, "possession" is merely a continual emancipation. The imaginary that prevails in her journey is a way of making love to Being with her entire body transferred into words. Beasts, plants, all of you, nobody, what is that? A galloping breakaway, through language, toward the break of day and until nightfall. Indeed, Colette continues to *dare*—and what more might one dare, what more will you dare?

> Yes, already I so loved the dawn that my mother granted it to me as a reward. I got her to wake me at three thirty, and I went out, an empty basket on each arm, toward the truck garden tucked away in the narrow bend of the river, toward the strawberries, the blackcurrants, and the bearded redcurrants.[369]

> If I follow it, a fragrant dust censes me, warm leather, sweaty beast, a bit of Her perfume. . . . The road unwinds beneath me like a ribbon being pulled, marked out by horse turd eggs. O what a joy to be so little and so quick in a great galloping shadow![370]

> What if I were now going to be less gentle, to myself and others, until the end of the fine season in Provence, constellated with sparkling geraniums, with white dresses, with half-open watermelons showing their igneous hearts like exploded planets?[371]

The cool of evening is accompanied here, for me, by a shiver resembling a laugh, a new air gown on my free skin, a mildness that hugs me more tightly as the night closes in. If I trusted that leniency, that instant would be the instant for me to grow up, to brave, to dare, to die. . . . But I regularly escape it. Grow up . . . For whom? Dare. . . . What more could I dare?[372]

A LITTLE POLITICS
ALL THE SAME

In politics, Mme Colette does not need to be whitened

because she is white. She felt as much repugnance for black as the

impressionists, to whom she is akin, though she was never involved

with their group and was probably blind and indifferent to their work.

She is alone. Alone she was. Alone she remains.

—Jean Cocteau, "Colette," *Discours de réception à l'Académie royale de Belgique*
(October 1, 1955)

That refusal to lay out a metaphysics that ignorance of commitment.

—Léon-Paul Fargue, "Colette et la sensibilité féminine française" (1947),
in *Portraits de famille*

Regardless of whether one judges her blind, regardless of the fact that she herself declares she was averse to politics, that innocent took on at least three issues currently at the core of political pre-occupations: women, the war, images. She expressed personal positions, stemming more from a sensory approach than from an intellectual judgment and that reveal her daring as much as her errors. She was a free woman but opposed to feminism; outraged by the Occupation but a contributor to *Gringoire*. She was a magician of the French language but equally fond of "media attention" before that term was even current: she loved to appear onstage, allowed her books to be illustrated in all sorts of ways, and was a fervent fan of cinema, one of the first French writers to be involved with it in its early days. In all her contradictions she participated to excess in "politics" in the most modern, the most open, and the most uncomfortable sense of that word.

AN ANTIFEMINIST

Even though, in the freedom of her moral conduct, in her demand for financial and emotional independence, and in her self-assurance as an author, the "Vagabond" opened the way for women's emancipation, "Mme Colette" remained an obstinate antifeminist. It is not that she was insensitive to what is conventionally called "women's issues": in *Paris-Soir* she even had an occasional column about women's lives. And, on November 28, 1938, she called on her women readers to write to her, introducing herself as "a woman among women." The mail flooded in immediately, and all the individual stories passionately interested her. In *Marie-Claire,* she replied to a certain "Desperate Denise,"[1] and that was only the beginning. But, though personal case histories attracted her, politics did not interest her. She did not understand it, especially the politics of politicians: at the time of the Munich accords, her article in *Paris-Soir* was titled "The Dove Has Returned," which attests to a good dose of naïveté, which, in any case, was shared by the editors and readers. The idea of tackling the female condition from a social or political angle she found absurd, even in her early days as a writer. Nevertheless, she was able to make strides in her literary career only after many battles and painful "apprenticeships."

"Are you a feminist?" asked *Paris-Théâtre* on January 22, 1910.

"I, a feminist?"

"Yes . . . from the . . . social perspective, naturally."

"Oh, no! The suffragettes disgust me. And since a few women in France have taken it upon themselves to imitate them, I hope they'll be made to understand that such ways will not do in France. Do you know what those suffragettes deserve? The lash and the harem."[2]

It is easier to tolerate these words of disgust if one knows they were counterbalanced in Colette by an equally violent rejection of the conventional image of woman prevailing at the time and, alas, even today: that of the foolishly amorous woman or the "mature and soft" bourgeois woman:

> It seems to me I see, some ten years from now, an argumentative, curt old Colette with the hair of a Russian university girl and reformist dress, championing free love, proud separatism, and blah-blah-blah, a heap of nonsense! Brr! But what demon shows me, even more terrible, the image of a Colette in her forties, burning with a new love, mature and soft under my makeup, combative and desperate! I push away the two ghosts with both arms.[3]

There is no doubt that Colette attacks her passionately political sisters, who, in her eyes, are caricatures of women, mimics of men. There is nothing less feminine, nothing more distressing, nothing emptier than a woman moved by political ambitions: "They don't do anything, and they don't appear to be idle. A long period of training seems to have taught them to replace action with vivacity, and thought with conversation."[4] "Boredom gives them the illusion of a serious role, which raises them almost to the level of that glum man over there, on the rostrum, shaking a bell." What do these ladies lack, then? "It's . . . something else [. . .] a charm they disdain, yet a very feminine one, which is made up of incompetence, confusion, silence."[5]

In that rejection of feminism, I hear not so much a denial of emancipation as an awareness of the frustrations and "harm" that the women of that generation had to endure to make any headway, especially in politics. Does not Colette reject above all that excessive burden the emancipated woman inflicts on herself in the process of becoming an overexploited proletarian, if not already an exhausted and depressive "superwoman"? In traditionalist accents, it is "charm" Colette attempts to save—against the overproductive consumer society. "The great change for women, a quarter century ago, was that they adopted a way of life where, to begin with, *everything did them harm*."[6] She adds:

> The humming of a factory, the reverberations of a build-

ing's catwalks, the dry harpsichord of the typewriters, it is clear that, to the sound of this disagreeable music, the active woman is overworked. But she would not know to exhaust herself without the violent passion for necessary profit and emulation. She acquires and augments her value there, at the expense of her personality.

In what women, in what young girls do we find a *charm* that speaks of secrecy, of an agreeable past, of modesty, if not in those whose profession confines them to the solitude of a laboratory assistant, a relatively untroubled silence, an *internal colloquy?*[7]

The apocalyptic vision of "hardened working girls" who have no "solitude" is a very Chaplinesque version of *Modern Times*, but in the feminine. The writer denigrates the "destructive life" of work on the assembly line:

Admire what she has obtained on her own in so few years! Hardened, yes, she is. But she no longer knows what hard-working solitude or silence is. To live as part of a team if not in a crowd is an all-powerful adaptation, and however much a hard-working woman may complain about it, she cannot imagine escaping it. Edgar Allan Poe did not write a companion piece to *The Man in the Crowd*. Work in common, which the times have imposed, has led woman to pleasures in common, leisure in common, and she has demanded them. The factory smock leads to two identical plus fours, two twin pullovers, two tandem bicycle seats.

Rivals at work, accomplices at pleasure; it must truly be admitted that is a destructive life for a woman.[8]

Nevertheless, Colette, still in love with women, admires the working girls' dexterity, their capacity for adaptation, and their professional competence: "Women's hands are better at it than men's."[9] Sensitive to the influence of history and technology on the evolution of mores, she observes that World War I virilized women, whereas World War II, though not abandoning that tendency to make women hard, favored a commodity femininity more than a seduction femininity: "The war virilized them, dressed them in scanty Old Testament tunics, shaved their heads into a banister knob, plastered down their hair as on male Argentinian dancers. . . . One of the peculiarities of the current war is the exclusively, dangerously feminine look that has been imposed on women."[10]

She is not afraid to address those modern young girls, disrespectful of limits, immodest in their provocative dress: "We wish to say, to those little girls who never grow up, who are disheveled and uncovered: 'Hush . . . we are not alone.' "[11]

Is this an old woman overtaken by events expressing herself in these sensible reports, or is it the Colette we have run into in her literary texts, enemy of the vulgar, passionate about the good taste and purity at the very heart of the Inexorable?

There was nothing like the troubled period of the Occupation to bring to light, sometimes dangerously, all this author's ambiguities.

THE OCCUPATION, OR THE POLITICS OF THE GOURMAND OSTRICH

None of the major events of the late nineteenth and early twentieth centuries, whether the Dreyfus affair or the Universal Exposition, for example, held the young woman's attention.[12] During World War I the journalist Colette would prove to be more sensitive to human dramas than to the geopolitical balance of power. Whereas Henry de Jouvenel excelled at diplomacy, his second wife, baroness Colette, was bored at the dinners where public figures gathered. But her correspondence from the front, which she always held in contempt ("paltry journalistic things," is how she dedicated *The Long Hours* [1917], to which she made severe cuts for the Fleuron edition), was judged innovative at the time. Colette invented a new kind of interview article: "lyric journalism—lyric is not a synonym for fanatic—based on everyday encounters with historical events by a woman, a mother, a traveler, an artist."[13]

Before World War I her articles were published in *Le Matin* under the rubric "Tales of a Thousand and One Mornings." They would give rise to the volume entitled *In the Crowd* (1918). In it she tackled both political problems and social events, ranging from the Bonnot gang to the Tour de France to dirigibles. Always seeking out passions, the writer Colette reveals her own in these portraits of mores, of celebrities or of crowds "sketched" on her blue paper, victims of the fever caused by the various events or of the sessions of modern exorcism offered by sports. Collective life in its resemblance to a novel is foregrounded, and Colette knew how to push the ordinariness of social life, everyday existence, to the center of the dominant political preoccupations. If reevaluating the politics of politicians in terms of the *politics of the personal* has been a significant contribution of modern journalism, we need to recognize that "apolitical" Colette participated more actively than many other writers of her time in that upheaval, imperceptible at the time and whose scope can be measured only today.

Nevertheless, she cannot always avoid the dreary, specifically political subjects; for example, she wrote a short article on the People's University. Created in 1898 following the moral crisis precipitated by the Dreyfus affair, intended to link the intellectual elites to the masses, and hailed from the start by Péguy as "an infinite hope, an infinite illusion as well," in February 1914 these universities seem to have appealed to Colette, who noticed the sharpness of the studious working-class women she chose to highlight:

> It is truly the intelligent elite of a people that gathers here, respectful of the texts read to them, courteous to the point of holding back their coughs and their applause until the curtain falls. Almost all who come to spend the evening here sacrifice a few hours of their sleep. They are still carrying on them, men and women alike, bits of string, flakes of smelted metal, spots of varnish or acid. Most of the women and young girls belong to the delicate Paris race, which has small hands and sharp eyes. Sunday evening, amid the

crowd that thronged into the hall and rose up the walls like water that has been forced back, there was not a single man who had had "one too many." And the People's University must be a unique place, where the zeal of the machinist comrades, the bit part comrades, the theater director comrades, is so contagious that, on that same Sunday it was possible to recognize, under the somewhat powdery appearance of an improvised prop man bravely carrying a ladder, M. Simyan, former state minister.[14]

But, as has already been pointed out, it was her activity as a journalist on the eve of and during World War II that raised questions. Without precise convictions Colette contributed to weeklies with opposing political positions. Her principal contributions were to *Le Petit Parisien,* a Pétainist and collaborationist paper.[15] On the far right of the political chessboard was *Gringoire,* founded in 1928 and run by Horace de Carbuccia, who would compromise himself with the German authorities during the Occupation; he would publish *Julie de Carneilhan* in 1941. More toward the center right was *Candide,* the organ of the Librarie Arthème Fayard, which, since its founding in 1924, had diffused the opinions of Action Française; Fayard would publish *The Kepi* in 1943. In February 1934, when Léon Blum came to power, both publications flaunted an antidemocratic ideology and often hatred. On the center left was *Marianne,* run by Emmanuel Berl. Colette wrote for all three papers, not concerning herself with the moral backing she thus gave to each of them. Until Goudeket's arrest on December 12, 1941, she does not seem to have been aware of the reality of the Occupation. She participated in the intense literary activity of the capital and frequented collaborationist social circles. In a letter to Hélène Jourdan-Morhange (Moune) in July 1941, the writer mentions a luncheon at the home of the famous American patron of the arts Florence Gould, in the company of an American, a Russian, four French people, the Carbuccias, and a German.[16]

The texts of that period, collected in *Backward-Looking Journal* (1941), *From My Window* (1942), and *Fine Seasons* (1945), reveal the secret face of that worldly Colette: a worried, wounded woman who withdrew into herself to wait and to remember the past. She suffered for the starving, the deported, the persecuted—simple human compassion, without political interpretation:

> There were also—to our deep terror, agitation in our hearts—the shouts, the calls, one night when, bureaucratically, the enemy abducted the Jewish children of the neighborhood and their mothers, separated Jewish husbands from their wives, and caged up the men in one van, the women and children, selected out, in two other vans. . . . Shall I compare my own nightmare of absence to those separations? I shan't dare, since my own ended the very hour my own missing person, liberated, walking shakily on the ice-glazed road, approached the Compiègne train station. [. . .] Apart from the emaciation, I had not yet seen extrahuman colors on a man, the greenish white cheeks and forehead, the orange along the edges of his eyelids, the gray of his lips.[17]

Published in 1946, these sentences are a summing up: they benefit from the hindsight and judgment that followed the defeat of Nazi Germany and the advent of Liberation. During the Occupation, Colette's attitude was much less clear: incapable of taking a position—assuming she even had one—she made it impossible for herself to openly express her views—assuming she adopted any. Indeed, from the moment she chose to continue to write for the collaborationist press, she had to confine herself to "half-lies, half-silence, half-evasions."[18] In so doing, she nevertheless developed a sort of resistance of taste, the Colettian version, in sum, of national pride: she tried to lift the spirits of the rationed and underfed French people by appealing to the French culinary tradition and its peasant astuteness. Colette's position was simple, and it was her heroine Julie de Carneilhan who declares it: "I do not argue about the war. That is not a woman's business, to argue about the war."[19]

Once that deficiency of judgment was set out and embraced as it were, the writer was left to depict the anguish that over-

took the French during the German occupation. It is called a
"danger":

> Thus [an old peasant woman] conveys to us the perception
> of a danger that the acacia wastes its time pointing out: the
> danger of forgetting, of being outside the world, the danger
> of no longer suffering, of no longer loving, of being kept
> safe in spite of ourselves from what harms us. We who,
> since September, have seen Paris and its suburbs change, we
> grow old with waiting, we would never have believed that,
> at the heart of a spared village, dreamy, far from the times
> and its dramas, the most profound sadness awaited us.
> DANGER. . . . Let us not omit the danger that comes
> from solitude, from the lack of work . [. . .] The danger of
> perceiving we have gotten old, smart, sad, strangers to the
> serenity that surrounds us.[20]

Occupied France is a castle in ruins: "Every time we go out,
every time we come home, the worm-eaten poster warns us,
pointlessly. Nonetheless, the enormous remains of the twin castles continue to disintegrate. In the hours of great nocturnal silence, the ruins shift."[21] Only her daughter's "green thumb" inspires some hope in this writer/mother surrounded and
depressed by a disintegrated world: "We lay claim to exhuming,
from the ruins and collapses, a garden, of retracing rows," since
"my daughter's 'good hand' cares for and calls forth flowers."[22]

Despair becomes restrained: "A little of the serenity of those
who have lost everything slips into us."[23] Colette, aged sixty-
seven in 1940 and ill, felt herself growing old but refused to let
herself be beaten down. She does not say, "Let us resist" but, "Let
us defend ourselves! Anything rather than yield, dissolve into
confessions, sit down on these ruins, on our ruins, take our heads
in our hands, call out to the missing, cry the names of dispersed
friends and lost cities."[24] Lovingly, she contemplates a resigned
France, but—who knows?—one no less eternal in "defeat," in
the figure of the old peasant woman peeling potatoes: "Very old,
faded, her mind far away, she is one of the old women who, for

three-quarters of a century, have never failed to sit on her doorstep every day at the same hour to peel a few potatoes, to call the roving chickens, to shell the peas, to slice the gray bread. What does she know of invasion, of defeat?"[25] She praises (in *Flowers and Fruit*, reprinted in *Gigi* in 1944) the "defensive" grace of the French garden: "In all times the Frenchman, living by thrift on his land, decided that the cultivation of flowers and the care they demand are wastes of time and money. [. . .] Inhospitable by nature, the Frenchman cares *in a defensive manner* for his immediate boundaries, surrounds himself with wild rose, blackthorn, and juniper; he puts barbed wire around his garden if need be, and his first imaginary debauchery is the fence."[26]

It is truly among these "people of the land" that Colette seeks refuge to survive, that is, "to write, to describe":

> All the sights elicit the same duty, which may be only a temptation: to write, to describe. Of this war, I have not seen any of the violent acts under incendiary flashes. To every writer falls the task that her faculties, chance, the state of decline or the vigor of her age designate for her. I have found my resting place among the people of the land, those who, with the hazards of wars, saw invaders disguised by their armor march over their plowed fields.[27]

Within that context, the article "My Burgundy," published in *La Gerbe* in 1942,[28] and the dictée for the schoolchildren of France are somewhat easier to explain. Though objectively scandalous, these texts may have represented subjectively, for Colette, a defensive withdrawal—though one closer to Pétain than to De Gaulle, there's no denying that.

Does the historical meaning of the Occupation really escape her? In any case, she does not see its true shape; the container of history eludes her. "I am waiting—oh, so patiently—for our age to have given birth to its own vase."[29] The carving up of France into two zones inspires only a simplistic judgment: in the north there is confusion; in the south, retreat into peaceful contemplation. "Up there, in the north, electoral violence, great worries about solidarity, and the enmity of nations are raging, up there everything is in an uproar, pierced by individual cries, then falling back again into the full and confused sound of a deceptive unanimity. But here, we are very far from the north."[30] And when that retreat turns out to be illusory, when the gourmand must face the privations of the northern zone, her "defense" takes the form, rudimentary to say the least, of an alimentary resistance. In 1944, Colette (seventy-one years old) was already physically disabled. Did she experience the "fear of want" specific to the aged and the powerless? Or did she add, to that natural anxiety, a calculated naïveté that allowed her to laugh in the occupier's face: all the same, the inventors of good French cuisine would not allow themselves to be intimidated by those foreigners so idiotically lacking in taste!

For Colette, as, in fact, for many of her contemporaries, the Occupation could be summed up as a scarcity of food. In fact "all around there is nothing—almost nothing. The hard peach seems to be unaware it's July. Let's not even mention the walnuts and hazelnuts. Apples and pears are saved for later. No meat except, twice a week, 'white veal,' which, from its birth to its death, has known only the darkness of a pit where it is supplied with milk, veal as pale as its name, the sight of which turns our stomachs."[31] As the height of misery, "garlic, which is in short supply, has never been more necessary."[32] Even worse: "Have you got any champagne? No? Don't look away, I know you're lying. I lie too. I too have champagne. It's just that I'm like you, I don't dare drink such precious bottles. [. . .] Our joy, around a table capped with friends, will not be long enough or deep enough this year for us to noisily top it off with a good year wine."[33] And she remembers that Sido, during World War I, had buried her wine to protect it from those "gray men," the Germans:

> And for a moment I had the impression that the German army had to be composed only of gray men like that one, gray clothes, gray face, gray hair, like images on newsprint.
> "What did you do?"
> "I went home and buried the good wine," replied Sido,

not without pride. "The wine dating back to my first husband."[34]

Like her, Colette would carry "her worries inside, and a smile on her face."[35]

Since the word "impossible" is not French, food scarcity is not French either. Aren't there treats to be found in Paris pastry shops? "I suggest to the ingenious proprietress that she introduce, as an open-face sandwich, a thick layer of beans cooked in red wine on square rusk. That's the favorite snack of the children from my region."[36] Even better, let's make *flognarde*! And Colette launches into the story of the succulent treat before giving the details of the recipe, since a *flognarde* is made for next to nothing and filled with beautiful memories of the region: "The *flognarde* entrusted me, through the authorized go-between of the priest of Flogny (Yonne), with its letters patent and its certificates of origin, which are not without interest. The *flognarde* was born in Flogny and is at least a centenarian. M. Flogny of Flogny, the postmaster, once ran an inn and a posthouse."[37]

Let us be thankful to her, all the same: if Colette likes good food, she is no less a gourmand of literature. "The true privation is the absence of books."[38] And how proud she is to belong to a people who, in those difficult times, did not forget to improve themselves. "But let us believe that a very sure instinct predisposes a harshly punished people, ignorant of its future form, to question their past, to want to know the foundations that have assured their greatness and might still answer for their future. Three thousand copies of Montaigne sell every month. Would anyone dare say that the French reader delivers the solid majority of its votes to the easy authors?"[39]

In the end a true cult of France awakens in Colette, to which she attempts to give shape in her texts: "I devote a cult, dormant within myself, to my country."[40] It takes the form of a hymn to the "underfed girls" of Paris: "One is tempted to say, since they have so much mordancy and grace, that the worst life conditions sharpen and refine the character of their Parisian beauty."[41] This

tribute extends to old Paris, gleaming with—the inevitably tri-
color—hyacinth:

> Recently, you served noble designs: during the bad springs of
> the Occupation, Paris, swelling with hope, embittered by a
> profound resentment, sold bulbs at florist shops—three
> bulbs to a pot—that found a way to be seditious: "A pretty
> pot of tulips, Madame, for apartment cultivation?" March
> came, the awakened mother-of-pearl bulb split open its dry
> envelope, which, in the place of tulips, let out three gallantly
> chauvinistic hyacinths—one blue, one white, one red.[42]

The capital is wise as well, knowing how to survive on little:
"The ideas of Paris, the fantasy of Paris. . . . Yes, but also the wisdom of Paris. Paris draws on itself for its wisdom and moderation. There is measure only from Paris."[43] "A proverb says:
'Where there is nothing, the king loses his rights.' The king perhaps, but not *taste, the invention of Paris*. We have seen in the last
few months what Paris knows how to make from 'nothing.' "[44]
Because she herself is a provincial, a "stranger" to the capital, Colette is an admirer of the acerbic banter and the courage of the
cheeky Parisian urchins:

> Perhaps a native of the provinces draws a particular faith
> from Paris, in the light of which it is easier to endure the
> foreign menace, to receive and transmit the imponderables
> of a besieged capital, to adapt herself to the nights of bomb-
> ing, to assimilate a war-charged atmosphere, darkened, cor-
> rupted by war, to admire the child, the man, the woman of
> Paris standing in mockery in front of the crude propagan-
> da posters.[45]

The modern reader is still surprised, if not scandalized, by
the following praise of French levity in the face of the bloody
horror of the Occupation. "These are light, innocent moments.
Our difficult and troubled life needs serene images more than
ever. More than ever we love a certain kind of science fiction,

represented, on the pages of the beautiful entomology books, with all the appeal of an enchanting truth."[46] That cult of happiness serves only to reveal a culpable blindness to the historical issues. For our political innocent, it is a magical way of staving off unhappiness, of consolidating the forces of hope. Of all Colette's works, only two love stories end happily: "Armande"[47] and "Gigi," both written under the Occupation. It is as if it were absolutely necessary that things go well, that there be no reason for despair. That seems to be the message. A citizen of the imaginary, Colette dreams of rebirth: under the defeat she examines bulbs, listens to the birds announcing the fine season, watches for the revival of plants. "A few of them have already improvised a little arabesque of song, a budding melody, by which they promise the world an end to winter and dare anticipate the season of love."[48] In hindsight she will be convinced that she cultivated a kind of opposition: "So it is that, in its courteous, sly, stubborn way, the Palais-Royal began its resistance and prepared itself to sustain it. What 'resistance,' what war would I speak of, if not of the ones I have seen? I can hardly leave this spot at the window anymore, smack dab in the middle of Paris. It is only from there that I saw Paris plunge into sorrow, grow black with grief and humiliation, but also refuse itself more every day."[49]

Even if we indulgently grant her that fantasy, let us note it is a very peculiar rebellion, which Colette knows is very French, weaving together a resistance to melancholy and a rejection of the dishonorable reality.

> "*Melancholisch*," [that's what the occupiers are]. . . . The unanimous refusal, emanating from every stone, every passerby, every woman seated near a baby carriage, pushed them outside. An intense, compact refusal, a blind and deaf refusal, mute as well, a refusal to perceive the invader's presence, to read Paul Chack's poster and the other dishonorable billboards, a mental regurgitation opposing the propaganda thrust at them by the newspapers and the airwaves. . . . A refusal to smile, to be seduced, to be terrorized.[50]

This does not prevent the writer from expressing a certain shame at having remained silent (about the compromises? the deportations?), of having abandoned herself to "passivity"; but she quickly tempers that uneasiness with the pride at having been able to break her silence and sustain a contagious optimism:

> The life of a Jew during the Occupation depended on a sort of insane, complicated bureaucracy, on violet emblems printed with a stamp, on star-shaped insignia applied on the left side, on brutality worthy of Doctor Tar and Professor Feather, on methodical interference always heavy with threats. During the last eighteen months, the man I call my best friend left our own home every evening to go sleep here, there, anywhere, his peaceful condemned man's sleep.
>
> I am surprised to be giving written form to the memories triggered by the tinkling of a doorbell. *It's because one tires of everything, even of keeping quiet.* I do not like anything about what the war years bequeathed to me. Not even the *difficult passivity,* consumed less with deceiving the occupier than with *inspiring optimism in the occupied,* since optimism is a matter of contagion.[51]

A few characters in the novels and short stories of that period, secret nodal points par excellence, betray, at best, Colette's ambiguity, torn as she was between, on one hand, her hypersensitivity in tune with human suffering and, on the other, her political blind spots.

Julie de Carneilhan (Fayard, 1941), which Colette herself called a "damned venomous disgusting novel,"[52] does not just reveal the persistent rancor Colette felt for her ex-husband Henry de Jouvenel, alias Herbert d'Espivant. Marianne, the second Madame d'Espivant, is a beautiful Jewish woman who, of course, stirred the jealousy due a rival, but Colette's animosity was also directed at her fortune, necessarily suspect, and, moreover, managed with an implacable coldness. Marianne bears the brunt of Colette's suppressed anti-Semitism, of her tenacious resentment of the first baroness de Jouvenel, Claire Boas, and, above all, of her no less keen jealousy of Henry's third wife, the very rich Germaine Sarah Hément, the widow of Charles Louis-Dreyfus. Conversely, in the character of Julie de Carneilhan, Colette probably transposed traits she admired in Isabelle de Comminges, a superb horsewoman and the mother of Renaud de Jouvenel; the latter would marry Arlette Louis-Dreyfus, the daughter of his father's third wife.

Nevertheless, in the novel Herbert d'Espivant marries Marianne, supposedly to use her fortune to get elected to office. The rich "American wife–style" heiress does not hand over any "dowry" to him; at very most, she is content to place "all her possessions" at her husband's disposal, which quite simply means that "she pays, she does not give."[53] To take some little advantage of that godsend, the poor d'Espivant drags Julie into a despicable transaction: she gives him a fake IOU for a million francs. D'Espivant's health is compromised by it; Marianne, finally moved, allots her husband a sum for his personal use; meanwhile, Julie, as compensation for her "forgery," obtains 10 percent of Marianne's gift. It is a dark scheme that does not make anyone look good, especially not the cynic d'Espivant. By virtue of it Marianne becomes nothing but a dupe. "Those people" she represents are greedy, they know how to count, but in vain; they always find people more cynical than they. That seems to be the novel's moral. Julie's proud retreat to her land suggests, in contrast, that there is a world composed of other values, noble and rooted in national time and space, which holds in contempt the vulgar and cosmopolitan world dominated by the money of "those people." That banal anti-Semitism, which Colette shares with many of her contemporaries,[54] does not so much latch onto her rival's Jewishness as express a cliché, that of the hatred/fascination for "foreign" Jewish capital:

> Marianne's fortune is . . . it's a huge foreign body, capricious, enormous, secretive, which speaks every language, which is always hurting somewhere [. . .] it's not "money." It's a bureaucracy. It's a labyrinth. Ultimately, at the end of

a passage, you bump into a little old man named Saillard, who's asthmatic and bears no title. [. . .] "It didn't work out, Saillard doesn't want to." [. . .] Doesn't want to set aside four million for a state acquisition, doesn't want to advance eighteen hundred thousand francs for the purchase of a ravishing little Fragonard, a unique opportunity![55]

Marianne's money ought to be, is everybody's. . . . It's sad, mysterious money with a somber Mexican mug, which makes the noise of metals held prisoner underground.[56]

In fact, it is in the sexual assessment of her rival done by Julie that the truly feminine and racial perfidy slips in: "Avidly, she sought the 'pinkish wax statue' described by Espivant, did not discover it immediately, and took for a slightly Jewish pallor what was carnation without transparency, flesh with the texture and opacity of marble."[57] The beautiful Marianne, then, is made like a statuette, "with nothing but unusual materials, jade, aventurine, ivory, amethyst"; she is a "magnificent creature, who has not the slightest idea what becomes her";[58] "perfectly beautiful," she has "something inexpressibly ordinary," a "plebeian naïveté"; she "lacks class."[59] Even when upset Julie does not forget to be mordant: "That may be what is most touching about [Marianne], that vague sadness, that widowed look, that apathy of a hot-blooded woman."[60] And, if she allows herself to be mortified to tears before the rich Marianne, is it not to make her fall all the more easily into the trap set by d'Espivant?

Nevertheless, Colette's sympathy overlays the caricature when she depicts another character, M. Tigri-Cohen, in "The Photographer's Lady":[61] "The disgraced figure of Tigri-Cohen steps into the small arena of light. His ugliness was sometimes ironic and cheerful, sometimes pleading and sad, like certain overly intelligent apes that have cause simultaneously to cherish man's gifts and to tremble in fear of them. I have always thought Tigri-Cohen took a great deal of trouble to look crafty, venturesome, and unscrupulous."[62] A dealer in pearls (like Goudeket?), which he appreciates more as an amateur than as a merchant,[63] this ugly man goes too far: "He gambled with his whole face, the face of an ugly and passionate mime, always, always too rich with too much expression, with too much laughter, with too much pain."[64]

The narrator admits her words, though half-truths, are inspired by "friendship" and stem from the sensible compromise she has imposed on herself, in order not to directly contradict the peremptory judgment of the jeweler made by her husband:

> But at home I did not speak either of the nice little fetish or of Tigri, since my then-husband had got such a rectangular and inflexible idea of the jeweler, a conception of the "trafficker" so banally false that I would have been unable to plead the man's cause or correct my husband's error. Did I have a real attachment to the little hand hewer? *Did I feel friendship for the misunderstood Tigri-Cohen?* I don't know. The instinct to dissimulate did not carve out a very large space in my different lives. What mattered to me, as to many women, was to escape the judgment of certain beings who I knew were prone to error and who leaned toward a certainty proclaimed in a tone marked by indulgence. Such treatment pushes us women to separate ourselves from the simple truth as from a flat and unmodulated melody, to take our pleasure deep within *half-lies, half-silence, and half-evasions.*[65]

A short text, "Gone,"[66] evokes, without naming it, the exodus of Jews who fled the persecution and the laws of Vichy. It is a most ambiguous text, and emphasizes the uneasiness of those forced into exile: "They're gone. Fear, or pride, took them away from us, wrenching a confession from them that would never have come out had there not been war, this war, and peace, this peace."[67] But who constitutes the "us" that suspects the exodus is the "distinguishing mark of an easy life"? And what, conversely, is the "truth" that is supposedly "elsewhere," and about which "I think"? Torn between "us" and "I," the writer wants to know "if they miss us." Is it that she feared, on the part of the persecuted, a disavowal of France, feared a condemnation that was exaggerated, unacceptable in her eyes? "For it is more comfortable for us to believe that the 'departed' are going away with their habits, their everyday playthings, the distinguishing marks of an easy life. I think the truth lies elsewhere. A terrible blow between the shoulders made them spit up a truth, bright red, that left them short of breath, and, unburdened, they've gone."[68]

More pathological, faithful to the state of stupor and aberration that Colette feels has fallen on France during the Occupation ("everything's mixed up in it!"), is the image of the backward "poet," the young Tonin. While everyone is complaining about the armistice and believes the young Tonin impervious, he goes out into the fields by himself and imitates the voice on the radio but only to proclaim the opposite of defeat, to deny the penury and announce the free sale of chocolate: "He had to defend himself one morning against the blows of children who launched an attack for fun, and he was mimicking his mother, Mme Tonin, crying: 'He don't know there's an armistice, do he? He don't know it's awrful, do he?' I recognized that, though Tonin lacked verbal arguments, he was by all means reacting, both with brief words rich in meaning and sound, and with a few punches and a few kicks with his espadrilles."[69] Like Colette, who strives to offer clever recipes to her readers of women's magazines during the Occupation, the village idiot persists in diffusing messages of encouragement to the population: "'Radio-Corrèze here,' said the voice. 'By the decree dated we bring to the attention of your listeners the knowledge that the armistice is not real, and that, on the contrary, everything is going very well.'"[70]

Like an admission of powerlessness, an ironic criticism of her own attitude, the similarity between Colette and the backward boy is pointed out in these last lines: "Lonely, wild, Tonin gave himself up entirely to the poet's mission: to forget reality, to promise the world miracles, to celebrate victories in song, and to deny death."[71]

Again through the metaphor of pathology, "The Sick Child"[72] allowed Colette to draw a painful picture of childhood, in counterpoint to the images left us by the paradise of Montigny or the child's closeness to animals. She thus explores the sick body, an unusual theme that now becomes hers; but that "sick child" may very well also represent—in the context she created it—France itself suffering under the Occupation. It is a poignant image of a regression, a quasi-death, but also, in the end, of a recovery, a rebirth. Indeed, we discern that the child had been allowing himself to die ("So he did not cry out. In addition, many anonymous, fabulous strangers were already beginning their abduction") and that health returned to him only when he recovered in earnest the desire to fight against death ("a small, hard, trembling force"), the desire to live. "There is a time that urges one to apply oneself to living. There comes a time to renounce dying in mid-flight."[73] Colette, in sum, had no other form of resistance to barbarism than to "promise the world miracles" and to "renounce dying in mid-flight."

LIVING THE IMAGE: FROM ILLUSTRATION . . .

Sido's lesson, "Look," which inspired so much aesthetic jouissance in Colette, seems equally to have destined the writer for the society of the image taking shape, which, though no one knew it at the time, would become the "society of the spectacle." With a keen nose for the secret trends of her age, this poor excuse for a politician nevertheless felt at ease with the unfurling of images that was beginning and that was to characterize the twentieth century, from the illustrated book to the cinema. Nevertheless, beyond her aptitude and her obvious comfort with the vogue for "advertising" and display,[74] which Willy had had no trouble stimulating in his overly gifted student, Colette proposed, in that culture of *appearances* that became a culture of the image, an *other* gaze.

Shored up by all the senses experienced in passion, the *image written* by Colette is the opposite of the "spectacle," in which "the pictorial arts" in the strict sense easily bog down, and constitutes a true counterweight, a contradiction of their voguish universe. The result was on one hand a Colette who was the friend and accomplice of her illustrators, a great writer who used her talent to hail the beginnings of French cinema, a woman who favored everything that could make her writings "seen" by the greatest number of people. On the other hand, the reverse shot, was a Colette whose texts eluded every "illustration" and every "film," all of which looked like drab travesties when compared to her incisive and carnal style. Even more surprising is how she wandered into the most exigent currents of avant-garde cinema, whose legacy would be developed by the "New Wave," which would seem to be diametrically opposed to her art.

Some 180 artists played a role in illustrating Colette's works.[75] Among the most frequently illustrated texts, it is not surprising to find, in first place, the *Claudine* novels, with fifteen different versions; then *The Vagabond*, with eleven; *Dialogues of Beasts*, with nine; followed by *The Ripening Seed* and *Gigi*, with six versions, including some of the most important.

During the first half of the twentieth century, up to the 1950s, the illustrated book, now losing ground to the domination of graphic novels and threatened with being swallowed up by the power of the Internet, was a new "mixed genre" favoring the conjunction of writing and image, as well as a popular phenomenon without equivalent up to that time. Stemming from romanticism, which had extracted the "beautiful books" from rich collectors' private rooms to diffuse them to a broader public, the illustrated book, in enlisting lithography, established a dialogue between painters and writers. Subsequently the democratization of publishing was to overcome the reluctance of bibliophiles, bring in a clientele of art lovers, and finally offer "semideluxe" publications likely to seduce the middle classes receptive to "advertising." Colette was born within that context and took it to her bosom along with husband Willy. A host of illustrators flocked to her texts, encouraged by the publishers and by the author herself. Posterity has remembered the work of Dunoyer de Segonzac, who engraved a series of etchings for *La treille muscate*,[76] but also her friends Mariette Lydis and Grau Sala, and finally, designers such as Christian Bérard, to whom we are indebted for the playful illustrations for *Gigi*—and whose abstract theater sets were appreciated by Colette.

Colette rarely went to museums and took no notice of painting: "Since my ignorance gives me no guide, I simply flee instinctively the peace of museums, whose serenity weighs heavy on me, as well as the gold-ceilinged emptiness of basilica."[77] Years later the artistic wealth of Rome had no greater appeal for her. She took away only the flavor of a few new dishes: "Since I did not speak the language of the country, I did not do a good job of visiting the Eternal City, and even less its museums, from which I emerged shattered and timid, beaten black and blue with masterpieces. I ate at fairly modest restaurants, and the one at the Basilica Ulipi always had what was required to satisfy me, as long as it had available, in addition to the plate of pasta, a daily mound of new little artichokes, sealed in boiling oil and stiff as fried roses."[78] Even the French paintings of her time, especially if they dared meddle with the "gardens of our France," repelled her because of their "long premeditation" and "applied reverie." She blamed Claude Monet for his "artistic tyranny" and his "disciplined flowers."[79] Although some painters found grace in her eyes, it was for the good and simple reason that their works had the good luck to appear edible to her, like some "caramelized Monticelli"[80] or the paintings of Luc-Albert Moreau, "a lover of consistency, of a slightly thick color."[81] In contrast, in the case of those that appealed to her—Cézanne, Van Gogh, and sometimes Matisse, whose "vigilant brain" knew how to transform dancing girls into a choreography of petals, paradoxes, and tentacles before fixing them in music, in "eternal equilibrium"[82]—she preferred (or claimed) not to understand. Resisting knowledge, she got gratification from spending time with their canvases only through an immediate sensorial jouissance: "Another great contentment rewarded my ignorance of painting: I will never know, will never need to know 'how it's done,' for example, that impalpable, that perfect and mysterious resemblance to breathable air that bathes and divides the branches of Cézanne's green tree. Nor why I relish in the extreme that canvas where everything is prickly, hostile, burned with dust, Van Gogh's *Thistles*. Nor why, left cold by Matisse's human figures, I am won over by his *Trees*, sparse against a silver sky."[83] And until the end of her life she persisted in that admission of indifference to art: "Apart from the art concealed in painted color, a beloved text, a sound, a form, art has governed my life very little."[84]

These lacunae or this coquettishness about pictorial art can be better understood if we recall that Colette, who is proud she knows how to look, in reality never looks only with her eyes but with *all her senses*. Her sight is a vision of the flesh as a whole, moved by the vibrations of desire; and her written images are movement, "rhythms" that reveal "the essence of objects" in order to reinforce, but "madly," the optical grasp. "Anything that's a lie to rhythm is a lie, almost, to the essence of the creature. The anxiety and pleasure of feeling plants live I have not experienced best at the movies, but through *my feeble but complete senses, shored up by one another,* not by saturating, madly reinforcing, my sight."[85] That vision "shored up by all the senses" mobilizes synesthesias in which the "gaze" meets not only sight but smell and touch as well, so that the eye allows itself to be invaded by the diversity of perceptions and brings life itself to life:

> All of us shudder when a rose, coming apart in a warm room, abandons one of its conch-shaped petals, sends it sailing, reflected, across a smooth marble floor. The sound of its fall, very slight, distinct, is like a syllable of silence and is enough to move a poet. The peony loses its blossoms all at once, releases a wheel of petals at the foot of the vase. But I have no taste for the spectacles and symbols of a gracious death. Speak to me rather of the victorious sight of the irises at work, of the arum that squeaks as it unfurls its cornet, of the large scarlet poppy that forces open its slightly shaggy green sepals with a little "click," then hastens to stretch out its red silk, pushed by the seed-bearing capsule hairy with blue stamens.[86]

The painter and draftsman let themselves be seduced by that orgy, which is nevertheless only *partly scopic,* but they fall short of translating its profusion solely with the means of a visual art, especially if they persist in being flatly realistic, or seductive and submissive "to fashion." Indeed, that "shoring up" of representation by "all the senses," though it may have reached its apogee in the writings about plants and landscapes, is not absent from those on the beasts or from the human portraits.

Hence Mitsou, Gigi, Chéri, and Colette herself did not allow themselves to be fixed by any "illustration" or "portrait," not even that of a master. The essence of those creatures of writing is not in sight but in the polyphony of a mysterious style where meaning embraces the rhythm of desires and perceptions. The superiority of Colette's style can thus be measured by comparing it to a few of the *portraits* of her—to mention only them—that adorn her illustrated editions. The portrait by Jacques-Emile Blanche (reproduced at the beginning of the 1905 edition of *Dialogues of Beasts*) reveals a perverse innocent with a sharp profile (fig. 6). But where is the woman who depicts herself as follows (speaking of the dog): "An insect's effrontery is inside me. I have the bravery of a soldier ant, over which danger passes, huge and insignificant"?[87] Matisse's lithography (for *The Vagabond* in 1948) flattens her out more than it refines her (fig. 9), even though one might have expected that master of femininity to capture the following self-portrait: "If, from my childhood, I am left with an unusual mastery of my tears, I have also kept the gift of being moved, with an intensity barely diminished by time, at certain hours, and not only those that gather into an irresistible bouquet the sound of a perfect orchestra, moonlight reflected in the glistening box trees and laurels, and the smells of soil where summer and storms are brewing."[88] The Vertès drawings depict a worried, persecuted woman (fig. 7). Perhaps only the complicitly tender and vigorous pencil belonging to Dunoyer de Segonzac, a regular visitor to La Treille Muscate, reveals a Colette whose dark side arcs toward her tragic serenity (fig. 8): "Among other earthly goods, I hankered for the license he would give me to savor my sadness: 'Oh! When everything's going well, I'll treat myself to boiled-down tears. . . . ' That's what they say!"[89] As for the portrait executed by Jean Cocteau, it displays the cruelty of true friends who love us for our monstrosity (fig. 10).

But let us return to Gigi.[90] Mariette Lydis and Grau Sala, latching onto *Gigi,* used drypoint in an attempt to translate the universe of panders that is transcended by the loving delicacy of

Claudine's young antithesis. The fifteen plates by Mariette Lydis (1948) no doubt give the most flagrant misinterpretation: a close-up of Gigi as frontispiece, presented as a stereotypically flighty adolescent girl, with a little nose, a round neck, permanented hair. Nearby, in the same dimensions, Gaston Lachaille is represented as a smooth operator: a long nose over the inevitable mustache, his hair in a crew cut. Mariette Lydis, a careful draftsman, takes an interest in the hands—to make the portraits look true and sensual? She's out of luck: Colette never speaks of her characters' hands in the short story.[91] In contrast the thirty illustrations by Grau Sala (1950) contain a small portrait of Gigi, surrounded by an oval garland, inviting us to see it not as the reality of the character but as a representation of past time. Gigi dressed as a bride, on the frontispiece and in the final image, bears the signature: "Grau Sala, photographer." In addition there are elements of the Parisian landscape, fin-de-siècle playlets that underscore the documentary choice of that illustrative style. But, in the end, the typographical overload (newspaper titles, shop signs) isolates the images from the novel and disrupts our reading of them. Opposite Colette's works or, rather, against them, a dated imaginary is set up, and that rivalry causes confusion about how the text is to be received. Nevertheless, it is the text that defies time, at the expense of the autonomous and now, alas, obsolete illustrations.

Christian Bérard's art is completely different. He uses a lithography technique applied to inks and gouaches. Complicated whorls, elongated strokes, suggestions rather than documents: the pen has its fun and the color alternates between blue-green dots and pink bows in the heroine's hair or at her belt. The page makeup integrates the illustrations into the text, and often the movement of the lithography seems to pulse to the rhythm of the sentence. Even while appealing to the tastes of the time, with elegant women in hats, clowns, and skaters, and exaggerating with rococo effects the hairstyles or other very Belle Epoque distinguishing marks, Bérard manages to confine himself to allusion. Hence Bérard sums up the famous shoe that Gigi, surprised by Gaston, keeps in her hand, with a high heel and an angry eyebrow under a lock of hair.[92] Nevertheless, the illustrated magazine borders on a caricature of mores and retains none of the lyricism of laconic maturity that Colette's writing knows how to inflect on the invisibility of emotions. Bérard's art does not capture the defiance of loving silence that Colette's irony tenderly launches at the social world of the spectacle, the very same world the illustrators move in, along with Lachaille the seducer, but which Gigi, as we have seen, may be the first literary character to haughtily ignore.

We will never know what Colette thought of these illustrations, which she solicited and encouraged. Perhaps she judged them useful, both socially and commercially and, in that sense, politically as well. She remained very stingy with compliments for the artists. Hence, for his *Treille muscate*, Dunoyer de Segonzac received only this very succinct tribute: "For that occasion, the great Dédé did an admirable set of light, airy drawings, into which he put a great deal of skill and art. He drew [. . .] my house very plain, did it a great deal of honor, and it will be his glory."[93] Luc-Albert Moreau did not merit any greater effusiveness: "Those shimmering blacks, those beautiful drawings, more beautiful than on noble paper, I continue to discover, in looking slowly at them, new reasons to like them."[94] Really? What reasons?

I find it significant that the only enthusiastic praise we find from her is of the theater sets done by Bérard, who had a passion for abstraction. Was this a way of suggesting what was missing from the illustrations of her own texts? Colette certainly did not value abstraction, and we know she did not like modern art. She cavalierly dismisses the cubists as "far too occupied [. . .] with driving the air from their paintings, with forgetting that mysterious, slightly divine thing called perspective, the miracle that, all of a sudden, four centuries ago [. . .] filled the portraits of trees and mountains with a necessary breath and suddenly pushed the cloud, the rolling plain, and the sea waves back to the far end of the sky."[95] But she seems to pay attention to abstraction perceived as a rhythm of forms and colors that transcends appearances and tends to follow, through the play of contrasts and juxtapositions, the creation and defeat of figures and passions, places and times, the very same ones that preoccupy her own writing. In Christian Bérard she points to "the raw, fresh, and generous taste [. . .] that loves the very white whites, makes light blues collide with a barely ripe red, lovingly marries blue to violet and mauve, surprises and quenches our thirst."[96] Notice to amateurs: let them therefore produce the "illustrated" Colette with Christian Bérard's abstract technique. Could that be the writer's secret wish? She would like to convey her texts through a clash of colors and volumes more than through the relentless realism or the feverish imagery of local color and worldly details. Might there be, behind the classical Colette, the populist Colette, an avantgardist unbeknownst to herself? Without forcing the matter, that is what her preference for Christian Bérard suggests, while at the same time making it impossible to move any closer to the modernists. In any case, her experiences with film are not far from confirming my (audacious?) hypothesis.

. . . TO CINEMA: IN PRAISE OF THE IMAGINARY

Since it was a rhythm that Colette was seeking in the visible, film quite naturally excited her. Though she was never a movie actress or director, she was involved in various aspects of cinema: criticism, subtitling, dialogue, screenplays. Several of her works were adapted for the screen: *The Innocent Libertine,* which became *Minne,* with Musidora as producer and in the lead role (1916); *The Vagabond* and *The Hidden Flame,* also with Musidora (1917 and 1918); *Gigi* and *Mitsou,* produced by Jacqueline Audry (1948 and 1956), with Danièle Delorme in the title role; then *The Cat,* which constituted the second episode, *Envy,* in Roberto Rossellini's *The Seven Deadly Sins* (1952); *The Ripening Seed,* directed by Claude Autant-Lara (1954), with Edwige Feuillère; and finally, *Gigi,* the American version, produced by Vincente Minelli (1958) after Colette's death, starring Leslie Caron. That is only a few of them, all unavailable now, or nearly so. Furthermore, Colette also wrote the subtitles for Léontine Sagan's *Jeunes filles en uniformes* [Young girls in uniform] (1932), dialogue for

Marc Allégret's *Ladies Lake* (1933), and the screenplay for Max Ophuls's *Divine* (1935).

From a taste for the art of cinematography, a fascination with the social phenomenon it immediately became, and also no doubt from a need to earn her living (though she complained "there is no money" in cinema, meaning not as much as she had hoped), Colette was one of the first French writers to write *about* cinema, to refer to the new vision of the world that a movie camera produces, to inquire into the influence on the public of the "seventh muse," on that way of being together and on the strange perception of reality it inaugurated. In reading her 1914–17 columns in *Excelsior, Le Film,* and *Filma,* we find that she appreciated both the novelty of cinematographic language and its social impact: it is as if, like an unexpected foretaste of Roland Barthes's "mythologies," she perceived that it is the particularity of a "language" that crystallizes a social phenomenon and that, as a result, an event profoundly marks social life only if it is a semiotic event. In 1916, at a time when refined people still considered cinema a "diversion of maidservants" (in the words of Simone de Beauvoir, evoking the reaction of her own parents) and well before the surrealists (Aragon and Breton expressed their nostalgia for the marvelous and for burlesque cinema in 1929), Colette admired the achievements of the movie camera, which opened a new age of the imaginary by braving dangers and defying physical laws.[97] The specialists are agreed in recognizing her "key role" in the formation of that "aesthetic turn" constituted by the introduction of film into French habits.[98]

Nevertheless, with a few rare exceptions (including "The Other Side of Cinema" in *Landscapes and Portraits*), she did not collect her writings on film for the Fleuron edition, which she oversaw in 1948, and it would not be until Alain Virmaux and Odette Virmaux's work[99] that it would be possible to read her film columns, as well as the subtitles to *Jeunes filles en uniformes* (1932), the dialogue for *Ladies Lake* (1933), and her screenplay of *Divine* (1935). Shortly before her death she undoubtedly judged it was more important to highlight her properly literary writing. It is also very possible that the film *industry,* which began to take root at the expense of cinematographic *art,* discouraged her from including her work with film in the prestigious *Complete Works* undertaken by Fleuron, which were to sanctify the "Colette monument."

Three periods stand out in Colette's relationship to cinema: her beginnings as a columnist from 1914 to 1917, culminating in the "Roman period" with her participation in the shooting of *The Vagabond* and Musidora's leading role; the period between 1931 and 1935, when she became more directly involved in film production proper, with subtitling, dialogue writing, and screenplays; and finally, that between 1947 and 1953, with the appearance of new adaptations of her works as well as Colette's transformation into a screen star.

Dating from that last period were, on one hand, her keen sense of the importance of film as a communication tool useful for her own fame but also as a medium of social information and the forming of public opinion; and on the other her equally keen judgment of the weaknesses of the medium, when compared to her increased awareness of her own art and of literature in general. Not only did the writer authorize various adaptations of her books and allow herself to be filmed, not only did she like to go to the movies in her wheelchair but, as Goudeket explained, she also set aside, "at the expense of books," a place in her room at the Palais-Royal for a television set, at a time (a few years before 1954) when few French people owned that now commonplace household object. And she eagerly followed its broadcasts. This did not prevent her from expressing this, at the very least skeptical, view: "I have to invent cinema from time to time, I see one film a year, or two. That is not enough. It suffices, given the time to rehabituate myself to the rhythm, to the black and white of the screen, to make me astonished at the rudimentary, majestic, inadmissible naïveté remaining in cinematographic images and invention."[100] Furthermore, that astonishment at "the inadmissible naïveté" of film is as much a compliment as a charge against the new art, since it is truly its popular freshness, as well as the magic it exerted on the crowd's emotions, that attracted her to film in the early part of the twentieth century.

The reader accustomed to the clichés about a conservative and populist Colette would be surprised, however, to discover that she praised the strictly formal pursuits of cinema. Hence, in 1917 she became excited by the style of Abel Gance's *Mater Dolorosa,* which married the taste for the exemplary prop to a ghostly atmosphere: "I applaud a new use of the still life, the emotional prop. Watch as the veil falls onto the wood floor. There we attain the meaningful set, the furnishings full of ulterior motives. . . . The action unfolds among lights of a rare richness, gilded whites, great deep blacks; I also remember certain dark foregrounds where Mme Emmy Lymm's speaking and imploring head floats on the surface like a decapitated flower."[101] She expressed her preference for silent black-and-white films, which supposedly best realized cinema's ambition for true artistic pursuits and saved it from psychological repercussions and photographic illustration: "The white, the black, their infinite combinations and contrasts demonstrate every day that they admirably accept arbitrariness, that is, the intervention of human art."[102]

But it was the documentary that, with a cautious enthusiasm, Colette welcomed for its "miracle freshness," seeing it both as an invitation to the most acute observation and as an equivalent to description. For this woman for whom writing, as we have said, was less a personal fantasy than an existential immersion in the world's flesh, the emotional film image possessed the incommensurable advantage of being able to seize the natural writing inherent in the world itself. Far superior to any work of the imagination and its "sentimental banality," cinematographic language may be in its way a sort of "alphabet," a "monogram" or "arabesque" capable of expressing "the extravagance of reality, the unbridled fantasy of nature."[103] And she admired the "slow motion" and "fast motion" of an "educational film" that made children and the writer herself pensive:

The first time, a "slow motion" lifted a seagull off the ground, held it motionless in the air, then rocked it, propped it up on the wind. The waving and banking of the wing quills, the mechanism of the tail feathers—the tail's rudders—the whole secret of flight, the whole simple mystery of aviation revealed in an instant, dazzled us and brought tears to our eyes. A little later, the "fast motion" recorded the germination of a bean, the birth of its boring radicels, the avid yawn of its cotyledons, from which the first stalk, hurling out its snake's head, shot forth.[104]

This passage attests to Colette's infatuation with the documentary. The writer was, in fact, the first to predict the current regimen of teaching with televised images and the Internet when she wrote: "I know one must not seek, cinematographically, enchantment, marvels, indisputable miracles, anywhere but in what is called the educational film."[105] But this can also be read as praise for her personal style—the exact opposite of that of the "illustrators" who had such difficulty grasping the sensory sense of her texts. In fact, Colette's writing enriches the image by making the world accede to the visible only after transmuting both world and visibility into the precision of a vocabulary, the passion of metaphors, the lucid rhythm of a sentence on the watch.

Furthermore, even though her film columns were commissioned at random, for showings of sometimes mediocre films and for the needs of the newspapers, Colette was the person who revealed American documentary film to the French public. Hence, in 1914 she reviewed *The Scott Expedition to the South Pole* and in 1916 *The Cheat*. The great documentary on the Scott expedition led her to discover a "cinematographer [who] has ceased to be a good implement of vaudeville with its grotesque imbroglio. Some day there will undoubtedly be no other method besides film for teaching children and young people."[106] Note that these lines are not taken from *Le Monde de l'Education* in the third millennium but from the pages of *Le Matin* on June 4, 1914.

Within that same discovery of American film, Cecil B. De Mille was indebted to Colette (and to Louis Delluc and Cocteau) for the fulsome praise with which he was showered in France. In *The Cheat* the future author of *Chéri* appreciated, beyond the melodrama of high society, the creation of a true cinematographic code that dared distance itself from the excesses of theater; she also praised the enigmatic masked performance of the Japanese actor Sessue Hayakawa. Without knowing Griffith, Chaplin, Mack Sennett, or Max Linder, Colette nevertheless hailed American cinema as such, capable of cultivating in its conservatories the art of film as an autonomous expression, of paying particular attention to tableaux and crowd scenes, and, as a result, of anticipating French cinema by a great deal. "French commerce, French art, French fortunes will have reason to worry and to suffer."[107]

Let us add to these subtle observations her real political concern for the cinematographic profession. Colette was interested in the "film actor," in the "dark side of cinema,"[108] and in the public that chose the "movies" to unwind from an exhausting daily life and to temporarily restore their good cheer. Here is a Colette attentive to film as to a new political bond, a public performance of private life destined for a mass audience, and, already, for advertising, for better and for worse. Sadoul and Mitry would not miss a chance to praise Colette's reliable taste, even her "commitment" in film matters.

Apollinaire, who, like Colette, contributed to *Excelsior,* was the only one to write, not on but *for* film: the visionary author of *Les calligrammes* created a dramatic film in 1917, *La Bréhatine,* with André Billy; after that, one had to wait until 1930 for Cocteau's *Le sang d'un poète* [A poet's blood] to appear. Here again, Colette was a pioneer.

Let us point out, among the cases of direct participation in cinema, her dialogue for Marc Allégret's *Ladies Lake,* based on the novel by Vicki Baum. Colette recognized the heroine, Puck, as her own Vinca from *The Ripening Seed* and managed to impose a very personal mixture of styles, playing on social comedy and fantasy. She was involved in *The Hidden Flame,* shot in 1918 with Musidora, and she even encroached on the screenwriter's role, suggesting production elements and atmosphere (close-ups, photographic elements, etc.) for a film that is now lost, like the text she wrote for it.

But a few scattered remarks by Colette suggest that what she sought in film was a mode of expression different from literary narration, not only because her own mode was already a condensation of the "tendrils of the vine" style and because silence onstage (with which she was well acquainted as a mime) required that she take into account silence on the screen; but also because she maintained that film, as a specific art, ought to circumvent narration.[109] And she attacked certain French films, "vaudeville drawn from the Young Adult Library,"[110] that distorted the essence of this new art. Colette the mime seemed to remember that the word is a "crude obstacle separating us from silence,"[111] when she extracted from *Music-Hall Sidelights* the screenplay for Ophuls's *Divine,* produced by Simone Berriau, who also played the title role.

Colette's aim, like Ophuls's, was a cinematographic spectacle deprived of novel plots: "No narration, good god! Detached touches of color, and no need for a *conclusion*."[112] The film that resulted, still considered "very modern," was in its time a total commercial failure. That did not prevent its producer, without any regret, from rejoicing at having made it: "What filled me with enthusiasm was the way Colette composed the screenplay, exactly with cinematographic titles in mind. Short scenes, limited dialogue, a central motif and all around it characters, bits of sentences, rapid visions of a world that at the time gave the story all its meaning, that situated the atmosphere."[113] Woven around a little peasant girl who has a brief experience in the music hall before returning to her home in the countryside, *Divine* used fragments of *Shooting Notes, Music-Hall Sidelights,* and *The Vagabond.* The film displays more interest in the set than in the action and only allows a third of the sound track to be heard distinctly, "as in life," a delighted François Truffaut exclaimed.[114] In addition there was the accumulation of fleeting elements that required an increased attention from the viewer, a proliferation of details (like the ring of the diva who will not tolerate displaying herself naked, rolling down the stairs in close-up; a mysterious black sack that the women pass from hand to hand, before someone discovers a newborn inside, etc.), a combination of reality and image (a real snake, instead of an artificial animal, provoked "live" fear in Simone Berriau), tracking shots, spiral staircases, the movie camera whirling around objects. All that is enough to make *Divine,* again in Truffaut's words, a "master-

piece of verve and health." The New Wave would see Ophuls—
and implicitly Colette, who inspired him and went along with
him in his aesthetic choices for that work—as a true precursor.

As for the screen adaptations of Colette's works, let us recall
the event—or the indecent assault—constituted by Claude
Autant-Lara's film based on *The Ripening Seed* in 1954. Then
there were the two versions of *Gigi:* the French (in 1948) by
Jacqueline Audry, with Danielle Delorme playing a very Romantic, if not mournful, Gigi; and the one in which Vincente Minelli, with Leslie Caron (in 1958) accentuating French flightiness and
the cinemascope effects of Belle Epoque tableaux, transformed
the tradition of the French music hall into an authentically American musical comedy. Maurice Chevalier as Gaston Lachaille, as
well as Minelli's style itself, preserve Colette's own rapid and allusive style, but it is song and dance that replace dialogue. The
American-style comedy overwhelms the delicacy of the Colettian
ellipsis; her Gigi, full of subtlety, is effaced in the labored elegance
of the mischievous Caron. "It's Colette's story made to suit international tastes," Chevalier explained, by way of justification.
"There's nothing pejorative about that for me, on the contrary;
one must often adjust, transpose, typically French things so that
the other countries understand us."[115] When the film was shown
in Paris in 1959, Colette was no longer alive. Some deplored the
"operetta"; others were pleased to see the Americans improve the
moral climate of the amoral Colette. Some believed there was
more of Willy in it than of his illustrious wife.

Colette might have found no reason for complaint in that ex-
ploitation of the imaginary: Had she not already lent herself to it
in a thousand and one ways? It is as if, having foreseen the inevitable inflation of the spectacular in which our civilization of
visible passion—a "representable" passion—is reaching its completion and bogging down, she could only go along with the
movement. A mime and actress with illustrated books and
films—by all means. *Look,* let people look: make it so that everything is visible, and then let them get on with it. But, at the same
time, she breathed into the images—when she was able, as a
writer of dialogue or as a screenwriter—condensations, silences,

"tendrils of the vine," even New Wave–style allusions. She did so on the condition, as in the short film Yannick Bellon devoted to her in 1950, that she pretend to indulge in her daily and no less labored—artificial—gaiety, even while concealing herself on-screen, showing herself from the back, playing the comedy flirt, placing herself off camera and speaking in voiceover. Everything is visible, and everything is somewhere else: look and read. In short, Colette complements the reign of images with the cooing of her words, the silence of her writings, and that other, passion-ate, inexpressible silence of the sensations she feels and immedi-ately transmits like a contagious fever to the reader-viewer-experimenter, who has become in turn a polyphonic body, a Rameau's Nephew, a one-(wo)man band.

It may seem strange, even scandalous, to bring together with-in a single *political* perspective Colette's choices concerning im-ages and feminism and her defensive, even ingenuous attitudes during the Occupation. It is not simply the primacy she gave to the imaginary experience that makes us adopt that perspective: the imaginary, it is true, is predominant for her and, in follow-ing its logic, we remain faithful to what was essential to her throughout her life and in the multiplicity of her attitudes and experiences. In so doing, we nevertheless touch on something key in and for our civilization.

We are a culture of representable passion—that is truly what Sido and Colette say with their maxim, "Look." What they suggest thereby is that there is no other way to be passionate, just as there is no other way to drain the passion from the passions except to represent them—not in order to muffle them but to recognize them, make them breathe and live in words and images, imagine them closest to their sensory and monstrous truth. In other words, to sublimate them by transmuting them into signs. It is on the condition that we *represent* ourselves as vagabond or as shackled that we have a chance to acquire our freedom. Since freedom is, by definition, the foremost political issue, this amounts to saying that the representation of passions—what is called the *imaginary*—is in no way an insignificant backdrop but, rather, an *integral part of the political*. The rights of man and, recently, of woman, include in that sense and necessarily the rights to imaginary passions: that is where their purities and impurities are distilled, their dignity and freedom acquired. This microcosm, this imaginary laboratory that art and literature explore, does not possess the pragmatism and efficacy of a "position" within which we are in the habit of confining the "political act." They are not even "acts": they prepare the way for them and indefinitely contest them by rehabilitating without respite the concern for the singular, the attention granted to the incommensurable in every person, at the risk of errors, blindness, errancy. And they move deeper into that third way, which opened with the origin of language and the representations that accompanied sacrificial rituals, which is neither the truth of fields of knowledge nor a "political rattle."[116]

In the face of the misery and the unleashing of passions that are currently wreaking havoc throughout the world, it is embarrassing to insist on the dimension of human experience known as the *imaginary*, whose importance, absolute because specific to each person, we can finally appreciate thanks to the development of democracies. In fact, however, once certain urgent needs have been satisfied, certain identity struggles mollified, the politics of freedom necessarily becomes a politics of the personal. And it requires the maximum attention to everything that makes representing the necessarily singular passions possible to make them viable and shareable. All the same, politics cannot be reduced to a politics of images, as happens, alas, when it tries to manipulate the opinions of voters, who have fallen into the role of mere spectators. But the politics that misunderstands the sublimation of conflicts of sexuality, identity, and the passions—ignoring, in short, the "tendrils of the vine"—is only an administration that runs the risk of being quickly overrun by ethnic and religious clashes. And the ingenuous Colette—the one who, nevertheless, knew how to give a fine popular resonance to the personal's pact with the imaginary—laughed in the face of politicians, made fun of their knowledge, which the writer did not possess, and sneered at their short-sightedness, which her "alphabets," shored up by all the senses, often managed to transcend in premonitory visions.

STILL WRITING, BETWEEN
BALZAC AND PROUST

Writing is a drawing, often a portrait, almost always a revelation.

—Colette, *L'étoile Vesper* (1946)

Success is less a matter of thought than of an encounter between words. Sometimes words, signs wandering in the air, when called upon deign come down, assemble themselves, become fixed. . . . That seems to be how the little miracle I call golden egg, bubble, or flower comes about: a sentence worthy of what it wanted to describe.

—Colette, "Fleurs" (1939), in *Mélanges*

"BALZAC, DIFFICULT? HE? MY CRADLE, MY FOREST, MY JOURNEY?"

My Mother's House evokes the family library, "a room built of books," in which the "black Balzac" belonging to Sido, an avid reader, occupied a privileged place between a "mottled Voltaire" and an "olive Shakespeare."[1] The Houssiaux edition of Balzac's works, which the family possessed, and which it was not forbidden to go nosing about in, became for the little glutton an "inexhaustible jungle."[2] Colette replaced it with a Houssiaux II after her first marriage, followed by a Houssiaux III, which accompanied her to the end of her life. To those who were surprised she could quote Balzac from memory, Colette replied: "You have to start when you're very little,"[3] alluding to the section of *Claudine in Paris* where the heroine likes to "warm up to the familiar titles of books, and to reopen Balzac from time to time,"[4] nostalgic for the volumes that "hide snack crumbs between their pages."[5] In *Claudine Married* the author recounts being regaled with "bitter peaches, after [she] tasted, lying flat on her belly under the great fir, an old Balzac spread out between [her] elbows."[6] One could not find a better illustration of the feeling that links Colette to the author of *The Human Comedy*: she associates the joy of reading to pleasures of the mouth—one of the most archaic pleasures, a maternal connection if ever there was one—which she appreciates more than anything else. To Balzac, and to him alone, she devotes not *one* but *four* substantial studies.[7] Throughout her works she mentions no fewer than fifty-five Balzacian characters.[8]

Let us recall, in 1910, this labored affectation on the part of the Vagabond, after a long passage on the act of writing: "It takes too much time to write! And then, I'm not Balzac."[9] And, in 1947, at the end of her life, witness the humble submissiveness of Colette, who, in fact, was rising to the pinnacle of fame: "I have long had the habit of believing Balzac at his word, of going along with him everywhere it pleased him to lead me."[10] Between these two dates a "Balzacian genius for lying" possesses Renée's husband, Taillandy,[11] a character in *The Vagabond* who is a transposition of Willy. And a confession made by Bertrand de Jouvenel recalls that their love affair in Rozven, during the summer of 1921, unfolded around Balzac, especially his novella *The Unknown Masterpiece*.[12] From one end of her life's journey to the other, Colette acknowledged only one master, without explaining in detail that choice. But she allows us to make out, against the background of that journeyman relationship, the secret ambitions of her body of work.

What did she admire in Balzac? Spontaneously, she liked his sense of "detail," flattering herself that she had borrowed it from him: the description of a flower, or the curve of a shoulder, the notation of a bloodred color (which also appealed to her in the works of her painter friend Christian Bérard), the precise evocation of twelve bracelets, or even that "French fidelity, with its passion for precious and durable woods, deep carvings, silks."

With the aid of "details," an era lives again, a city with its topography, a body with its passions. Nevertheless, with and beyond them, Colette contemplates the ideal beauty of the senses. Although the young Colette made fun of a Balzac who sometimes wrote "badly,"[13] at the end of her life the proven writer paid a rousing tribute to the master's magical realism:

> O details, as ingenious as they are childish, no one will make me blush at you, accommodations, feminine in the extreme, and you, clock and vases! A jewel following the curve of a shoulder, a sparkling monogram hidden in the rosette of a garter, a camellia pinned to the collar, repeated at the waist, then at mid-skirt, then at the hem, a camellia without which the gown would have no meaning. . . . "There, now," exclaims Balzac, "here are Sancho's three hundred goats!" He's making fun, but refrains from eliminating the flower. He counts, on the amber-colored flesh of Josépha Mirah, twelve pearl bracelets on each arm. I count them with him, and I relish the serenity, the lucidity transmitted by a writer who was never afraid, in describing the delicate and even the slight, of diminishing himself.[14]

She adds:

> When he brings us into the bedroom where the Girl with the Golden Eyes will die, guilty of having loved there, we cannot fail to cry out: "Now here's a fine lair to shut up two lovers and a crime!" Crimson, white, poppy red with black tufts, here and there gold, the flame of waxes, on the walls an Indian muslin that turns pink as it slips over a red wall hanging: Christian Bérard loves nothing today so much as those bloody colors. I loved them before he did, and if fate were to give me—one more time, only one—the chance to move out of my house, to savor the pleasure of moving in, would I not go take the advice, from my old Hossiaux edition, of Grindot, the boldest of the architect-decorators of eighteen hundred and forty-seven?[15]

As in a hallucination, that taste for textual detail takes on substance in a cult of the *real object*—which then becomes a *fetish*—when it does not veer toward the worship of some knickknack that had belonged to the great man. Hence the reader Colette doubles as a collector who likes to recount how her godmother, wife of General Désandré, had bequeathed "Balzac's tiepin" to her. That gift, which was passed down via her godmother's love for Sido and via the military careers of her godfather and Captain Colette, was, very symbolically, lost upon the death of the amputee. "A malignant sort of disorder" had entered the Colettes' house when the father died; and, as if by chance, at the very moment it was discovered that he had written nothing, someone noticed Balzac's tiepin had vanished into thin air.[16]

Papa disappears with Balzac's tiepin. Colette's literary experience has often been linked to the father's failure, which the daughter felt the obligation to erase. Now we know that a second challenge is added to it, more gigantic and inseparable from the first: to recover Balzac's tiepin. Would Balzacian writing, relished until that time as a maternal snack, be transformed under the dual paternity of the Captain and Balzac as chief authorities, absent and needing to be restored? In any case, Balzac provides the atheist Colette with the sole opportunity to embrace the "religion of [her] adolescence, the guide of [her] early education."[17] In their third Houssiaux edition, Balzac's works play the role of a Sido-style "Bible" for her. A guarantee of literary good taste and a remedy against discomfort, it awakens the memory of appetizing snacks and of a few flowers stepping straight out of Time: "A Houssiaux tailor-made for me, mottled black and red [. . .] excellent against fever, supreme against certain novels that 'have just come out,' against those vying for a prize. At home it is unharmed by bread crumbs and Gruyère rinds, but not always safe from an old rose petal or a stiff dry pansy resembling Henry VIII."[18]

Nevertheless, Balzac's maximum seductiveness lies, according to Colette, in the admiration the writer devotes to the human creature, "whether charged with a crime or, by his grace, innocent of everything."[19] With the "details," by slipping into them, Colette is drawn much more to the coexistence of contrasts in human beings and the mad violence of their passions than to the portrait of social struggles and the fierce dramas of the capital city, at which the author of *The Human Comedy* supposedly excels. To persuade ourselves of this, we need only cite, among the fifty-five Balzacian heroes she mentions—aside from her favorite, Valérie Marneffe, who earns the right to a special article—those she mentions at least four times: Lucien de Rubempré, the baron de Hulot, Philomène de Watteville, and Paquita Valdès. But we also find Doctor Rouget, the duchesse de Langeais, Colonel Chabert, cousin Pons, and Zambinella-Sarrasine.[20]

These characters, as diverse as one could imagine, hold the attention of Sido's daughter because they are "vigorous creatures, full of vitality, of pathetic verisimilitude."[21] No mention is made of Père Goriot or of Eugénie Grandet, who usually appealed to the popular imaginary. Colette prefers Lucien de Rubempré, not so much for his social ascent as because "that handsome young man [. . .] fancied himself a poet as well"[22] and because she dreams "of the four lines that were to save [him]" (they are contained in the first letter, "smelling like balsam," which Marie-Louis-Anaïs [Naïs] de Nègrepelisse sends to Lucien in reply to his long epistle). Not surprisingly, a revealing piece of writing on the passion of love elicited by the former Lucien Chardon, son of the pharmacist of Angoulême, seizes the author's attention. Similarly, Baron Hulot, a "solid and defaced ruin,"[23] impresses her only as a plaything for female lovers. As for Vautrin, he is in her eyes an expert at masquerades—sometimes a false abbot, Carlos Herrera with a greasy paper under his wig,[24] sometimes a formidable bandit like Jacques Colin who "kills, plunders, then joins the police force the way one becomes a monk."[25]

But it is Balzac's women who, through their sly eroticism and an implacable cruelty, captivate the author of *The Cat*. Through them Colette reads *The Human Comedy* as an exploration of monstrous—particularly female—sexuality, which may be as much the true driving force behind bourgeois ascension as the sophisticated rites of the aristocrats.

The proper names of these passionate women seem to matter more and in a different way than the brief descriptions with which she surrounds them: they appear in her writings like emblems, summations that are universally transparent, hence pointless to develop for the uninitiated. From the often bloody histories Balzac attributes to them, Colette confines herself to extracting, once more, only a few apparently harmless, very French details, which all reveal, however, a merciless death drive she calls a "perdition." Philomène de Watteville is a young seamstress, an embroiderer (like Colette?) who lives in the shadow of her mother (the baroness de Watteville, pious and despotic, imposes a severe religious upbringing on her daughter) but conceals under her frail appearance an "iron character" and "more than one Beelzebub under the skin." The good girl becomes infatuated with the lawyer Albert Savarus and burns with an infernal jealousy for the female main character in a short story of which Savarus is supposedly the author, "Ambitious out of Love." Of all these imbroglios, which weave a "novel within the novel," Colette retains only the repressed [*sic*] passion of the embroiderer Philomène for an imaginary heroine, and her criminally relentless annoyance at the (male) author of the short story: "All *repressed women,* all troublemakers, were and still are great seamstresses. Philomène de Watteville tirelessly embroidered slippers."[26] "Sinister nineteenth-century girls, *smothered in the maternal shadow* and pulling their needles . . . Balzac is watching you." " 'What are you thinking about, Philomène? You're almost over the line. . . . ' Three stitches too many on the line of the slipper she was making for her father, and Philomène de Watteville will reveal her profound and criminal preoccupation. . . . But she undoes the three stitches that go over the line, and begins again to hatch, in invisibility and peril, the ruin of Albert Savarus."[27]

Mme Marneffe, for her part, is described as a "chubby and very French little beauty," "all charm and perdition."[28] Colette delights in the details of "eighteen hundred and forty-seven" dress and furnishings styles, whose opulence resonates like a fatal metaphor and suggests (but only to readers of *Cousin Bette*) the diabolical charms and scheming of the "Laïs of Paris,"[29] who, in Balzac, incarnates the "married courtesan" type. There is no allusion in Colette to the vicious stratagems of the "false respectable lady," Cousin Bette's accomplice in her revenge against the Hulots and particularly against her excessively beautiful cousin, Adélaïde Hulot. Colette's interest is directed less toward the fall of the Hulot house or to the downfall of Hector Hulot, debauched father and overly lavish lover, than to his young mistress, Valérie Marneffe—and that interest is full of admiration. There is no detachment, no condemnation of Valérie, a flower of evil on the Parisian pavement, whose perverse seduction drives the revenge plot. With her miserable office worker husband, whose death she awaits, her Brazilian lover, from whom she accepts "every demand," and Père Hulot, whom she destroys, Valérie Marneffe is, for Balzac, "a devil in a skirt." For her part Colette retains only Valérie's elegant taste as an artist in seduction. To achieve her aim, Mme Marneffe does not need Machiavellian weapons; a rose between her breasts is enough to "make any man under thirty-five lower his eyes."[30] According to Colette (the character), Valérie Marneffe's perversity is resolved in the prowess of (the author Balzac's) writing. And, of that fit of passion, Colette mentions only the art of the stylist, who knows how to charge a visual detail with the psychological unsaid—which she herself chooses precisely to spare us.

The Girl with the Golden Eyes prompts Colette to reveal slightly more of the crime: briefly she recalls the affair between Paquita and Henri de Marsay and especially the love-to-the-death that attaches him to his half-sister, the marquise de San-Réal. She overlooks the secret society that fascinated Balzac, that of the Thirteen Men, "strong enough to place themselves above the law," and passes over the sadism of the love between Paquita Valdès and Marsay. It is the lethal voluptuousness between the two women she evokes with an extraordinary, precise economy and in a passionately intense pitch: "I picture the struggle in which the marquise de San-Réal tears to pieces the marvelous body of Paquita, the girl with the golden eyes."[31] "The Girl with the Golden Eyes marks with her bloody hands the poppy red silk, the white muslin in a love nest no man had ever entered."[32] Because she knows whereof she speaks, and her language is perfectly adapted to that red and white "nest" between two women that no man has ever visited, Colette knows she is just as precise as Balzac and more concise than he. But did he not have to precede her so that, of all the fires blazing with that Dantesque sensuality in the heart of bourgeois France, Colette could extract a few burning coals, a few flaming "tendrils of the vine," of those she knew how to weave?

Succinctly, accompanied by lapidary vignettes, the *names* of Balzacian characters intervened in Colette's writing, as if to open, beneath the apparent classicism and modesty of her own texts, the abyss of passions that her works suggest in condensed form but that Balzac's genius had explored in abundance. We must reclaim Balzac as an "intertext," evoke in anticipation Valérie Marneffe's and Paquita Valdès's complexity, so that the "tendrils of the vine" characteristic of Colette's art will deploy all the monstrosity they never fail to transmit to the reader but distilled and camouflaged behind an overly restrained decency. Balzac's works, embraced less as stylistic support (despite the shared taste for detail) than as a kinship in the descent into hell, play the role of a "red lantern" beside the "blue lantern." Colette waves her Balzac like a sign of acknowledgment addressed to her readers, the bold explorers of the intolerable—under a light-hearted appearance. Included are those who do not know they are explorers but take themselves for bucolic country people or emulators of the depraved Willy, to whose brotherhood she also belongs, behind the masks of hearty eater, excellent gardener, or innocent libertine.

It is therefore not astonishing that, at the end of her life, Colette investigated the mystery of the man Balzac and the enigma of the beautiful. While admiring the power of the author—a genius for detail, a master of love's hell—the young woman reader had overlooked the context of "the hunted writer's painful prolificacy, his setbacks as financier, printer, and pineapple grower." Belatedly, Colette wanted to discover the man and his life: "At present, it is that man I seek, his bursts of laughter, his jutting lip. [. . .] Tell me how Balzac was hounded, betrayed, unloved."[33] She accepts everything from him: the dressing gown stained with ink and coffee, the intoxication that "furrows the body of a man who had been sitting for too long"—everything but—the supreme sign of their love—Mme Hanska: "I separate the great man from that Slavic lady."[34]

No doubt more mature by virtue of her own literary career, she recognizes Balzac as the one who knew how to go along with and depict men in the grip of their passions while avoiding the divine solitude of a pure desert, which he replaced with a human—necessarily human—comedy. And Colette underscores, to Balzac's glory, these words written by the master: "The desert is God without men."[35]

Then, having discovered, in her third Houssiaux edition purchased from a second-hand bookseller, the annotations of a previous reader, Colette is astonished to find a question mark inscribed next to this short sentence in *Splendeurs et misères*: "The senses have their ideal beauty." Is it not precisely the beauty of all these monsters—Lucien, Paquita, Vautrin, Coralie, Louise de Bargeton, and others—that Balzac's *Comedy* illuminates for us? It is truly because human deviance is sublime that humanity is ridiculous: but it takes Balzac to capture, in a detail, the *ideal beauty* of the *infernal senses*. When Colette follows in the footsteps of the master in mapping these perditions, does she not seek to do the same thing? Does she not claim she possesses Balzac "cadastrally"? "I may have sold farms, changed houses, lost my money: Balzac is my inalienable property."[36] Is it more "inalienable," therefore, than Sido's house, which, for its part, was lost, sold, transformed? For Colette, who compressed time into sensory space, that humble, that pretentious cadastral fidelity to the ideal Balzac, to that Balzac in the impossible desert, is the most personal confession of her literary credo. Beyond Sido's garden, it is the topography of Balzac that magnetizes Colette's writing.

Although *The Unknown Masterpiece* is, to my knowledge, never mentioned by Colette, it occupies a place in the cult she devotes to the writer, all the more revealing given that this programmatic text resonates with the novelist's own aesthetic. It was during her relationship with Bertrand de Jouvenel, whose role we observed in the crystallization that was to lead Colette's genius to

Sido,[37] that the two lovers read Balzac's text: "It was at this time [1921] that Balzac became a subject of conversation between us, and such an important one! It was she [Colette] who had me sample that phenomenal short story: *The Unknown Masterpiece,* an extraordinary lesson on the self-destruction of a work of art when it is too often taken back to the drawing board."[38]

The self-destruction that Bertrand de Jouvenel, as part of his own story, chose to privilege in the short story is not its only theme. Balzac develops above all an aesthetic of the living form, influenced by Hoffmann, Diderot, Delacroix, and Théophile Gautier, which represents the rivalry between *life* and *works*. Not only does that preoccupation, as we have seen, underlie Colette's writing as a whole; it is also found at the heart of her biographical and novelistic experiences in the early 1920s. How can we fail to imagine that the coalescence sought by Colette between verbal expression *and* sensory world, between literature *and* the world's flesh, does not find a vibrant echo in the digressions of Frenhofer who, in *The Unknown Masterpiece,* calls for shattering "first appearance" in order to "descend" into the "intimacy of form" and to seize the "nothing" that is the "flower of life"?[39] The old master is so in love with his painting *La Belle Noiseuse* that he forbids anyone else to see it. Disregarding his love for Gillette, the young Nicolas Poussin offers her to Frenhofer as his model, obtaining in exchange the right to see the masterpiece. Balzac thus sets up an opposition between real eroticism (Nicolas Poussin with Gillette) and aesthetic enthusiasm (which Frenhofer feels only for his portrait of Catherine Lescault, known as the Belle Noiseuse)—like Colette herself, who oscillates between her real relationship with Bertrand de Jouvenel on one hand and the imaginary world of *Chéri* and *The Ripening Seed* on the other. Between the real person or the imaginary creature, which should prevail? Nicolas Poussin (like Colette?) seems to want to reconcile the two: he nevertheless yields to the fervor of the old artist, privileging jouissance of the work, before perceiving that Frenhofer's aesthetic vertigo is destructive: of the so-called masterpiece, all that endures is a chaos of colors from which only "a delicious foot, a living foot" stands out.[40] In the end might not the perfect work of art, the work of art itself, be a lovable and ridiculous fetish—like this woman's foot—that floats over a "slow and gradual destruction"?[41] Might it be a forever unknown, illusory jouissance, an illusion that only Gillette's simplicity and Poussin's very French moderation can elude, by counterbalancing the demoniacal convulsions of genius with erotic pleasure?

That is the Balzacian dilemma into which Colette cast the young Bertrand, attributing to herself, of course, the male role of the artists and making her husband's son play the role of Gillette or the Belle Noiseuse, whichever he chose. In the end Frenhofer burns his canvas before taking his own life. Very remote from such an absolutist metaphysics of creation, Colette—who ought rather to be identified with Nicolas Poussin as seen by Balzac—reserves for herself the right to make her life itself a work and, to an equal degree, to breath the flesh of life into her work.

Finally, it is also in Balzac that Colette discovers the character of Antonia Chocardelle, "a still likable and unlucky woman," who runs a "reading room [. . .] a trade befitting a single lady," a practice Colette recommends reviving during the Occupation.[42] Is this a "political" approach that proposes reading—and, preferably, reading Balzac—as the sole remedy against national despair or a discreet confession of the metamorphosis that was to lead "amorous Colette" to her cosmic solitude, though inhabited, in a Balzacian manner, by the "love of reading," which leads to the "love of the book," the only one that's worthwhile?

PROUST? "AS IN BALZAC, I'M AWASH IN IT . . .
IT'S DELICIOUS . . . "

Colette venerates Balzac but, even more explicitly, it is her contemporary Marcel Proust to whom she devotes her greatest admiration: a lovely acknowledgment of proximity, if not of complicity.[43] Childhood, memory, sensory time, and many writings dedicated to the author of *In Search of Lost Time* allowed me to discern, beyond the glaring differences between Colette and "little Marcel," a kind of mysterious twinship, which seems to raise Proust to Balzac's level in the Colettian pantheon. Then I discovered, belatedly, that this connection had been made by Colette herself. During a lecture by M. Paul Reboux[44] on the theme "How They Write: From Marcel Proust to Jean Cocteau," the critic turns to Colette and asks her to speak of her colleagues. After a few hesitations (Colette is reluctant to fall into the role of critic, that "chopper of heads," as she said), she agrees to express her views on Proust:

> *Colette:* I have a kind of passion for everything Marcel Proust wrote, for almost everything he wrote. . . . As in Balzac, I'm awash in it. . . . It's delicious . . . (*Long applause*).
>
> *Paul Reboux:* But doesn't the length of his sentences bother you?
>
> *Colette:* No. Why would they trouble me? It is a particular wave. Sometimes you have to be a good swimmer. . . . But it's up to readers to go to Proust and not for Proust to go to the readers. . . . They'll certainly come . . . (*More applause*).[45]

This enthusiasm, which became stronger as the years went by, was far from immediate. Colette met Proust in the salon of Mme Arman de Caillavet (née Léontine Lippmann) and very quickly found herself mixed up in various worldly intrigues, which, moreover, almost caused a rift with the writer. In effect, Anatole France, Mme de Caillavet's lover, was not insensitive to Colette's charms, while Willy, for his part, attempted to seduce Jeanne Pouquet, their hostess's daughter-in-law. Mme Caillavet alerted Colette to this. As was his habit, Willy made a joke of it, declaring that the revelation ran the risk of making his wife lose her sight. Proust proposed she see an oculist. Shortly after Colette's serious illness, Mme de Caillavet broke things off with the Gauthier-Villars. A first letter from Colette to Proust dates from that period (about May 1895?). The young woman was clearly writing under Willy's dictation: she criticized Proust, who had read excerpts of his "Portraits of Painters" at the home of Made-laine Lemaire ("One must not harm them as you do, by speak-ing ill of them, it's bad luck"), praised the young man for having detected in Willy a talent that, in reality, was nothing but a ge-nius belonging to Proust alone ("[you] had seen so clearly that, for [Willy], the word is not a representation, but a living thing"), and ended with this sentence laden with homosexual and bisex-ual insinuations: "Indeed, it seems to me we have a number of tastes in common—for Willy, among others."[46]

The first—anonymous—mention of Proust by the writer Co-lette can be discerned without difficulty in *Claudine Married*: the young heroine meets, at the home of "Mère Barmann" (Mme Arman de Caillavet) a "young and pretty boy of letters." Colette had first called him a "young Yid of letters," an expression that Willy, more cautious, had felt it his duty to correct.[47] As a novice writer Proust lavishes Claudine/Colette with clumsy compli-ments, loaded with allusions to the hermaphroditic muses, and praises her soul of Narcissus, "filled with voluptuousness and bit-terness." " 'Sir', I told him firmly, 'you're raving. My soul is filled only with red beans and little slabs of smoked bacon.' He fell silent, thunderstruck."[48]

Colette's frank irony, which does not fail to betray her veiled hostility, dimmed over the years: common themes and characters appeared in Colette's and Proust's writings, even as each of the two writers put forward a unique poetics, but in complicity with each other, and attested to their mutual admiration.

1901: *Claudine in Paris.* The heroine discovers she has a cousin named Marcel—no relation to Proust the writer, except that said cousin is homosexual and fascinates the young woman as if he were her double. One might also think of her friend Marcel Boulestin. Marcel would accompany her until *The Retreat from Love* (1907).

1902: Colette makes fun of Mme Arman de Caillavet, alias Mme Barmann, in *Claudine Married*—she can be found in the guise of Mme Irène Chaulieu in *The Innocent Libertine* in 1909. Proust, for his part, was inspired by Anatole France's famous Egeria to create the character of Mme Verdurin in 1908. In fact, the Verdurin "clan" defined itself from the outset by *excluding* the nuisances, which cannot fail to recall the "rifts" between Mme de Caillavet and the Gauthier-Villars, and with Proust himself.

1903: Rose-Chou, a character from *Claudine Takes Off,* may be inspired by Jeanne Pouquet, Mme de Caillavet's daughter-in-law. Proust would use her as well to create Gilberte.

1904: Colette publishes the first *Dialogue of Beasts* in the Mercure de France. Under the mask of animals she "exudes" "drop by drop,"[49] she says, a profound sensibility, more personal than that of the *Claudine* books, and explores a "keen, honorable" "pleasure," a "duty toward [oneself]" "not to speak of love." Proust would call that sensory being, at the crossroads between childhood and animality, a "profound self" in *Against Sainte-Beuve,* which he would undertake between 1908 and 1910 and would never complete (the volume would be published only in 1954).

1908: *Tendrils of the Vine* mentions, in a cove of the Somme, the forest of Crécy—"at the first breath" of these woods, "my heart swelled," "*a former me* rose up."[50] Could this be the same "profound self" sketched out in Proust's unpublished notes of the same year? He would invent the noble line of the Crécys[51] and the character of Odette de Crécy in 1910–11.

1913: *Swann's Way* is published on November 14. In a letter dated the 28th, Proust wrote Louis de Robert: "As for Mme de Jouvenel [. . .] I have the greatest admiration for her." And at the end of the same month she waxed enthusiastic: "I find he has an immense talent."[52]

1917–18: Colette publishes *The Long Hours,* in which she reveals her impressions of her travels to Venice and Rome (in 1915). Proust, who had discovered Italy with Ruskin and had visited Venice with his mother in 1900, writes Colette a laudatory letter.

Are these simply chance encounters, or echoes, handled differently by the two authors but that are commonplaces of a single society, a single culture? To be sure, it is impossible to identify which of the two had priority for one invention or another, since their paths were very much parallel, though each was traced in its inimitable developments by a specific and noble genius. All the same, the dates seem to indicate that Colette had a clear lead in the plunge into the sensorial and the infantile she began with the *Claudine* books. Proust, for his part, exhibited, detailed, and meditated on involuntary memory with a broader cultural background, gasping for breath, less concerned with cosmic dignity than with the surrender of identity. Moreover, whereas the author of *Sodom and Gomorrah* flushed out the infantile like a hidden, often obscene, secret that revealed itself only "involuntarily" (to the point that some have, quite wrongly, compared it to the Freudian unconscious), Colette, for her part, apparently never left the childhood paradise and was continuously awash in its supposedly comforting purity.

We may nevertheless wonder about that immediate presence of childhood in Colette: is it truly as "natural" to her as she asserts? Or is it only a discovery that came at a particular point in her own "search," in the face of ordeals in a conjugal life whose eroticism was no bed of roses. This is especially the case since the universe of Montigny, the house of Claudine and of Sido, was gradually being elaborated to preserve that past happiness as an "other scene," diametrically opposed and in counterpoint to Parisian life. I have already indicated that this myth of writing/childhood, under the aegis of the goddess Sido, was elaborated thanks to an exploration of incestual fantasies, then of an incestual reality. For Colette the unconscious does not remain repressed, it is often abreacted in a perverse act that does not become fixed in passion but, on the contrary, favors sublimation. Nevertheless, if Colette's childhood is also the object of a "search," it is neither culpable nor transgressive, and it is that innocence (pagan, utopian, feminine), that removal from the Law but not from "scruples," that distinguish it from Marcel's always somewhat "accursed" memory.

It was in 1919, when *Mitsou* came out, that the already well-known author of *Sodom and Gomorrah*—who would win the Prix Goncourt the same year for *Within a Budding Grove*—wrote his now-famous missive to Colette, in which he admitted he had wept "in reading Mitsou's letter."[53] Until the end of his life, ill, admiring, and ironic as usual, he would maintain contact with her by letter, regretting that he was unable to cultivate social relations with the "baroness."

"Beginning with *Mitsou*" (1919), Colette said, the two writers exchanged their books. Colette's letters were also laudatory, though less effusive, in keeping with the style and character of Sido's daughter. "Ah! If only I was lucky enough to have someone bring a Marcel Proust out for my vacation."[54] Proust answered in kind: "It is I who am proud to be decorated[55] alongside the author of the ingenious *Chéri*.[. . .] You are well aware that I am the admirer, and you the admired." But he also spoke ironically of Mme de Jouvenel's worldly concerns: "When you've finished with all your castles in Brittany, in Corrèze, everywhere. . . . "[56] Colette reclaimed the advantage: in early July 1921 she read *Guermantes' Way II*, followed by *Sodom and Gomorrah*; and "every night Jouvenel, who has grown accustomed to it, gently removes from beneath me your book and my glasses. 'I'm jealous, but resigned,' he says.[. . .] No one in the world has written pages like that one on the Invert—no one!" A confession follows that makes Proust a rival, no longer of Sido but of Colette herself, and far superior: "This is proud praise I offer you, since, if I once wanted to write a study on the Invert for the *Mercure de France*, it was *that one* I was carrying inside me, along with the incapacity and laziness that kept me from bringing it out."[57] Finally, the letter reveals Colette's admiration for Proust's style; he knew how to write sex as "plant" and as "animal" (as Colette herself did, in a completely different way). "Who, after you, would dare touch the lepidopteron, vegetal, ornithological awakening of Jupien approaching Charlus?"

In reading that exchange more closely, the analyst might decipher the supreme infidelity Colette inflicted on her husband: Sidi was joking, not suspecting he was right to be jealous of Marcel Proust, of his writing, of his world of inverts. Colette in fact "slept" with the text of *Sodom and Gomorrah* and sought the female version of the "accursed race."

Let us go one step further: has anyone noticed that the relationship with her stepson Bertrand de Jouvenel came after that reading of *Guermantes' Way* and *Sodom and Gomorrah*? The infidelity to Henry de Jouvenel/Sidi "committed" with Proust thus preceded the one she would consummate with Bertrand and that would lead her to *My Mother's House,* then to *Sido.* Colette suggested the existence of Bertrand to her fellow writer—as if to excuse herself for being a mother or, on the contrary, to suggest that, having read *Sodom and Gomorrah,* she too was preparing to inhabit regions equally dangerous and transgressive, though in a completely different way. "I leave on the 12th with a motley family of Jouvenel children, a daughter I produced, two others that come to me from somewhere else and who are charming."[58] Had not Proust taken some of her flowers to describe homosexuals? It was now her turn to close in on the accursed races, to dare as he dared, but in her womanly, motherly way.

This is only a hypothesis, but that may have been the fantasy, no doubt unconscious, that took root with *Mitsou, Chéri, Sodom and Gomorrah, The Ripening Seed,* and *My Mother's House:* a mirror of resemblances and differences, of reciprocal models, of competition and liberties. Homosexuality in one author corresponded to mother-son incest in the other. Until the end of her life, well after Proust's death, Colette would continue to root around the names of his flowers, believing she found his botanical knowledge deficient (even though it was she who, for once, was wrong about the "eupatory agrimony"), but admiring—yet again!—her accomplice's style: "'Fleur-de-lis in tatters,' that's full of grace."[59]

We might therefore attribute to a Proustian influence the flowering of the maternal figure, Sido, in Colette's late works: her analogue in Proust's work would be the grandmother who comes to haunt the narrator.[60] It is true Colette reread the letters of her mother, Sidonie Colette, to "extract a few jewels from them" and to write *Break of Day.* It is also true that the first epigraph of that book is taken from Proust: "the 'I' who is me and who may not be me."[61] Then Colette replaces it with another, independent of Proust and that, like Stendhal's, is completely invented: "Do you imagine, in reading me, that I am doing my portrait? Hold on: it is only my model." In spite of the debt that linked her to the "young boy of letters," did she know that she too had regained her own lost time? She did so in her personal way, without formulating it as Proust would have done, that is, in both philosophical and dreamy turns of phrase. Rather, for her there is a sudden chill that remains lucid in the very midst of sensory intensity: sober, clear-sighted, even premonitory? It begins with the childlike and bucolic effusiveness of the *Claudine* books and the profound perception of *Dialogues of Beasts*, then continues with the "former me" of *Tendrils of the Vine,* which already lined up "the golden instants of that slow and pure fine day,"[62] instants that give a foretaste of the "pure incorporated time" Proust would not articulate until *Time Regained.*

Sido's flowering thus came about through a transgressive movement appropriating the infantile, which also passed through the experience of incest.[63] Colette's letter to the author of *Sodom and Gomorrah,* written in July 1921, suggests that reading Proust encouraged that sexual audacity. But the writer's later work would demonstrate that her own path toward that infantile in touch with perversion is entirely different, characteristically feminine, and specifically Colettian. She had already written it in *Chéri* (1920), which preceded her affair with Bertrand and that Proust found "ingenious." She would act it out, since such was the necessity of her unconscious logic, of her personal journey, after she was moved by the reading of *Sodom and Gomorrah* and became engaged in a competition with "little Marcel." Alongside the incestuous maternal figures such as Léa (1920) and Mme Dalleray (1923) who cleared the way, the woman who purifies and sublimates them—namely, Sido (1929)—takes shape. The maternal figure for Colette would then take on a dignity and presence that she would never acquire in the sarcastic Proust. On the basis of that confrontation with *Sodom and Gomorrah,* childhood memory, which was always the secret driving force of Colette's writing, would claim a new place, visible, to be meditated on, centered around Sido.

Two logics of unconscious memory henceforth take shape, at work in the two authors, who are both similar and irreconcilable. Beginning with *The Pure and the Impure,* Colette's remarks, assembled as always into "tendrils of the vine," illuminate them with admirable honesty.

Ten years after her letter of homage to Proust's "invert," she returned to the subject in *The Pure and the Impure* (1932). Though apparently abandoning the theme of memory, she continued to explore it with the intuition specific to her calm genius, which I would sum up this way: *the path of perversion is only a road toward the infantile.* And, even though the "impure" relentlessly refuse to take that journey, Colette remained persuaded— she did not make it explicit but let it be read between the lines in the mininarratives of *The Pure and the Impure*—that perversion necessarily, inevitably, leads to the infantile, the memory of which (the archaic face) was situated in mother-child incest and whose purity (the sublime face) led finally to an immersion in Being. That was the only means to bathe her writing in the world's flesh.

In so doing, she gave the master of Sodom his due, since he had traced the same path on the male side; but, at the same time, she situates herself as a better explorer of Gomorrah than he: "Since Proust illuminated Sodom, we feel respect for what he wrote. After him, we would not dare touch those hounded beings, who are careful to cover their tracks and produce their own cloud with every step, the way sepia does."[64] The respectful Colette did not, as we know,[65] recognize herself in the "unfathomable and precious girls" of Proust's Gomorrah, in their "bad angel frenzy." The image of Gomorrah did not have the "staggering truth" of Sodom and seemed to her, at the very most, entertaining. Then the verdict comes down: "The fact is, pace the imagination or error of Marcel Proust, there is no Gomorrah." Female homosexuality for her is composed of solitude and prisons, of aberrations and snobbery; it feeds on puberty and the community of secondary schools; but these "scant training grounds [are] insufficient to engender and fuel a widespread, well-established vice and its indispensable solidarity. Intact, enormous, eternal, Sodom contemplates from above its puny imitation."[66]

It would be easy to reproach Colette, in that admiring rivalry with Proust, for her desire to vie for his aura as an expert on "accursed races." No doubt she was wrong about the complexity of female homosexuality. Personal experience and her literary vision of it led her, as I said, to make it an obligatory stage—but only a stage—on the way to the capturing of childhood memory and in no way an exploration of a form of sexuality in itself. It is at that precise point that the two authors diverge, and that is why we will have to return to their respective approaches toward memory regained: blasphematory transgression for one, serene dignity for the other.

In the midst of a meditation on memory, Colette is naturally led to evoke Proust. Significantly, it is a memory that now finds itself relieved of the weight of a privileged love relationship (no longer a couple, the male or female partner is henceforth secondary), to curl up in flowers and words or, rather, in that gap where flowers and words blossom together, "saturated with mortal darkness."[67] Like Proust, who dreams about a "patch of yellow wall," Colette says she is subject to "the temptation of the past" rather than to the "vehement thirst for knowing the future." "The break with the present, the return back to the past, and, abruptly, the apparition of a patch [sic] of the fresh, unprecedented past, whether they are given me by chance or by patience, are accompanied by a collision with which nothing compares, and of which I could not give any sensible definition." After the evocation of that "patch of fresh past," Proust's name crops up to confirm that "it is hardly the role of writers, of their abilities, to love the future."[68]

Finally the time comes when Proust transforms himself into one of Colette's characters. A flower among flowers, an emblem of France, of its taste and its arts, Proust—his hair, his mouth—is described in *Flowers and Fruit*.[69] Colette recalls his eighteenth year and the "wholly Oriental absence of expression" of his big eyes; she also recalls the portrait painted by Jacques-Emile Blanche and her meetings with Proust at the Ritz. With firm strokes she draws the writer's vitality and weakness: "Illness, work, and talent reshaped that lineless face, those soft pale and Persian cheeks, tousled the hair that was not silky and fine but thick, with a frightening vitality, dense as the black and blue beard that, scarcely shaven off, broke through the skin again."[70] She portrays the impenitent of genius: "Quite to the contrary, I was expecting to see appear, ravaged but powerful, the sinner who, with his weight of genius, was making the frail young man in tails unsteady on his feet."[71] And she remains nonplussed in the face of a decidedly inaccessible Proust: "No one protects himself better than a being who seems to abandon himself to everyone. Behind his first line of defense breached by brandy, Marcel Proust, taking up posts more remote and more difficult to storm, was spying on us."[72]

My Notebooks (1945) provides a series of portraits wherein Proust precedes Balzac. Colette insists on his "tired freshness," on his "agitation and pallor [that] seemed the result of a terrible force," on his assiduous politeness. She notes the mixture on him of "marks of death" and "extreme youth" and comments on the nocturnal energy of these "exceptionally fragile beings" who awaken at hours when other people grow weary. Then she returns in detail to their meeting at the Ritz during World War I. Like "a drunk best man," Proust had offered to accompany her back to Auteuil, since no cab driver wanted to take her there in the middle of the night. Colette then "recounted" to him that she had the habit of taking off her shoes under the streetlamps of the Concorde and, shoes and stockings in bundles, of returning home barefoot. "He took a great deal of pleasure in my little story," and left the then-vagabond with the memory of an astonished and young smile and of the "shadow [that] filled the black oval of his mouth, open to get some air."[73]

A last round of memories reintroduces Proust in Colette's *Line by Line* (1949). And once again the man imposes himself with his mystery rather than with the writing that bears its traces: a Proust whose notorious "youth" Colette diagnoses as more than feminine. "It's that he seemed singularly young, younger than all the men, younger than all the young women."[74] She likes his mouth, tragic under the air raids on the Ritz:

Yes. I remember that, under a blue streetlamp, Marcel Proust was choking from asthma, was tilting back a mauve face furrowed with shadows and invaded by an eager beard. We could read on his features, in that open mouth that drank up the darkness speckled with blue violet, that he would soon die. He still had the strength to admire the night and its war periwinkles. At the same moment, an air raid occurred and I had to seek shelter with Proust in the Ritz Hotel. When the warning had passed, he rushed up, gasping but animated by a worldly grace, and spoke of sending around a cab for me, as if there were any cabs in Paris at two o'clock in the morning.[75]

Colette, who lays claim to the right to flee the dying, lingers with fascinated pen on the dandy in the grip of a "furious wind" and already inhabited by death:

An everyday gala uniform, in short, but disturbed as if by a furious wind that, beating the hat down onto his neck, crumpling his linen and the flapping ends of his tie, filling with black ash the furrows of his cheeks, the cavities of his eye sockets, and his gasping mouth, had pursued that tottering young man, aged fifty, even unto death.[76]

MEMORY AND WORTHINESS

The search for "lost time" mobilized an "involuntary memory" in Proust that awakened delicious sensations and forbidden desires. The most anodyne and apparently idyllic reminiscences, like those produced by the taste of a madeleine dipped in tea, trigger in the narrator of *In Search of Lost Time* a cascade of memories that are so many profanations. The appropriation of the mother, which underlies the appropriation of childhood memory, presupposes an incestuous relationship experienced as a transgression. What follows is, first, the desire to keep a Mama destined for Papa—or for M. Swann—to himself; then the blasphemy addressed to a secondary maternal figure, Tante Léonie; and finally, the profanation of her sofa, sold to a madam and experienced like the "violation of a dead woman." That procession ends with the impossible act of wresting oneself away from the desired grip of the other. It is a grip represented/experienced through self-suffocation in an asthma attack or, perhaps, in the masochism scene in which the baron de Charlus has himself whipped while chained to a bed in a homosexual bordello. In Proust the search for lost sensation is always a search for the infantile, even though it remains a more or less distant horizon, whereas the space of his adventures, at once desired and threatening, sources of infinite sadomasochistic pleasures, is deployed in the scandalous relationships of the "accursed race." Sodom and Gomorrah are the truth of the madeleine: the dramas of desire eclipse the idylls of regressive infantile satisfactions, and it is social history with its wars and intrigues that in the end dominates the sensual poetry of time regained.[77]

Colette's itinerary is different. Granted, the act of tethering writing to childhood memory, which Proust for his part continually illustrates and theorizes, is primary for her. Indeed, it was with *Claudine at School* (1900), after the first sexual revelations and the conjugal wounds that accompanied them, in the crucible of that initiation and renunciation characteristic of her psychic maturation, that Colette gave written expression to her time regained. For her it is from the outset a seizing of the infantile: "My name is Claudine, I live in Montigny; I was born there in 1884; I will probably not die there." The setting is laid out in a few strokes, and it takes only one page for the past to be articulated as sensory and musical duration: "Just the requisite number of red roofs to set off the velvety green of the woods. Dear woods!"[78] The wager of the unconscious is made in all the *Claudine* books: diametrically opposed to the heroine's love life, its escapades and disappointments, is a serenity of childhood memory as refuge, stand-in, worthiness. The heroine will take the time to clarify the logic and the paths of her sense of being rooted, through the finally recovered figure of the mother (a projection of herself or a premonitory model? Who can say?). Immediately, Colettian recollection is rapture: a staggering grasp of the felt object and a lifting of the ego. Unlike Proust, who advances on paths of profanation as sinuous as his breath and syntax, Colette proceeds through serene captures, in a staggering adequation between the felt and the said, shored up by the certainty—which she believes is her right—not of appropriating the mother by some blasphemy but of sharing with the mother a mutual osmosis in the alphabet of the world. Thus her quest for memory abandons the path of guilt, which is the path of a narration; she progresses, on the contrary, through incisive assertions of a pride sure of itself, adopting the poetic aspect of a series of condensations.

Colette's awareness that her writing is an act of installing herself in childhood memory, diametrically opposed to the tempestuousness of love, seems to take hold in *The Retreat from Love* (1907), then in *Tendrils of the Vine* (1908). Proust, for his part, abandoned the drafts of *Jean Santeuil,* and it is the *Cahier de 1908,* long unknown to the public, that contained all the seeds for *In Search of Lost Time.* Colette may therefore be the pioneer of time regained, but the way she clears the path to the memory Proust calls "involuntary" is different. Although it does not seem unjustified to say it was she who *invented* "the search for lost time," it must immediately be added that what she found there was an "impregnable innocence,"[79] the exact opposite of Proust.

1907. To write is to reconnect with a childhood wisdom; to write is to stop time in full instants; to write is to find a "secret voice" as well as an "animal" who becomes my double; to write is to relive the time incorporated in "such a blond sun, such a lilac, blue by virtue of being mauve":

> When I was little, a great precocious wisdom sent me, at my moments of greatest joy, several melancholic warnings, with a full-flavored bitterness beyond my years. It said to me. . . . What? You're thinking of a beautiful lady in white with a diadem, who appeared to me amid the dark foliage of the old walnut tree? Not at all. It was simply, trivially, the "secret voice," an almost painful immobilization of my thought, of the whole little healthy, excited, and satiated animal, a half-open door that, for children of my age, usually remained closed. . . . It told me: "See, stop, this instant is beautiful! Is there anywhere else, in your whole life rushing by, such a blond sun, such a lilac, blue by virtue of be-

ing mauve, such an exciting book, such a piece of fruit streaming with sweet flavors, a bed so fresh with coarse white sheets? Will you ever again see more beautifully the shape of those hills? How long will you remain this child intoxicated solely with your life, merely with the pulsing of your happy arteries? Everything is so fresh in you that you don't imagine you have members, teeth, eyes, a soft and perishable mouth. Where will you feel the first sting, the first fall? . . . Oh! Wish you could stop time, wish you could remain a little longer like yourself: do not grow up, do not think, do not suffer! Wish it so hard that a god somewhere feels moved by it and grants it you![80]

1908. Memory is an abandoned space: "I belong to a country I have left";[81] the "form of the years" is like a ribbon incrusted with crystals:

> The form of the years has changed for me—during which time I myself was changing. The year is no longer that undulating road, that unrolling ribbon that, since January, had climbed toward spring, climbed, climbed toward summer, to blossom as a calm plain, as a burning meadow interrupted by blue shadows, dotted with dazzling geraniums—then descended toward a fragrant, misty autumn smelling of the marsh, of ripe fruit and game—then sank toward a dry, sonorous winter glistening with frozen ponds, with snow pink under the sun. . . . Then the undulating ribbon rushed down, dizzy, until it broke off sharply before a marvelous, isolated date, suspended between the two years like a hoar frost blossom: New Year's Day.[82]

Writing is an antidepressant that dries one's tears by transplanting "goodness" and "justice" into the memory: "Move away slowly, slowly, without tears; don't forget anything! Take with you your health, your good cheer, your coquetry, the little bit of goodness and justice that has made life less bitter for you; do not forget!"[83]

As a result, the idea Proust developed of a two-faced recollection surfaces between the lines. Every recollection encloses a past sensation paired with a sensation experienced and written in the present: "I am [. . .] hypersensitive, and I have only to recall certain keen emotions to experience them anew."[84]

The Vagabond (1910) deploys that split specific to recollection by evoking Colette as a little girl who, since childhood, has watched the narrator pass: "Standing on the edge of the wood, a child was watching us pass, a little girl of twelve, whose resemblance to me I found striking. [. . .] Yes, standing at the edge of the thicket, my fierce childhood watched me pass, dazzled by the rising sun."[85] And, again in *Three . . . Six . . . Nine . . .* (1944), recollection is as it were suspended in a motionless duration, nonexistent as temporal flow, fixed forever between a "we," planted in the present, and "our child eyes" riveted to the past: "The home we are born in, even if beloved, never exists altogether in reality, since we see it with our child eyes, vast and distorting."[86]

A late text, "The Past,"[87] sums up the role Colette attributes to the childhood past: to offer a compensation to the disappointment of the adult's love life and, as a result, to be a focal point for the imaginary. "O solitude of my childhood, you my refuge, you my remedy, citadel of my young pride, with what force I loved you, and how I feared, already, to lose you!" Just before that confidence, she places childhood in the absolute but inaccessible false bottom of the novel: "The novel of my childhood . . . I would like to write it and I fear, in trying to do so, that I shall fail. How easy and petty a love story seems therefore, next to that of an adolescence where the idea of love, tarnished by rival passions, appears not as the aim and fate of a life but as an uncertain pinnacle, as formidable as the perilous and fragile capital of a column, as the sparkling and superfluous arabesque." Indeed, when the time of childhood is regained, temporality is abolished: nothing is lost and nothing passes or comes to pass. Dazzled space remains.

For Colette, to remember is, above all, to feel. Recollections belong to the eyes, the nostrils, and the mouth, constituting the timeless essence of words: "You protest, you shake your head with your grave laughter, the green of the new grass discolors the bronze water of your gaze. . . . More mauve . . . no, more blue. . . . Stop that teasing! Rather bring to your nostrils the invariable fragrance of those changeable violets and look, while inhaling the philter that abolishes the years, look as I do at the springtimes of your childhood coming back to life and growing before you."[88]

A violet, perceived and named *today*, is also immediately a *memory* of violets: "O violets of my childhood! You rise before me, all of you, you lattice the milky sky of April, and the palpitation of your countless little faces intoxicates me."[89]

Thus arranged in pairs, recollection is a safe haven, a happy solitude: "Oh! I was sure of it! Claudine never resists evoking the past. At the mere words: 'Do you remember?' she relaxes, confides, opens up entirely. . . . At the mere words: 'Do you remember?' she nods her head, her eyes alert, her ears pricked as if toward a murmuring of invisible fountains."[90]

It is in *The Vagabond* (1910) that the internal "kingdom" of memory, a space of sensory solitude as well as of writing, becomes clearer, more explicit: the character of Renée Néré discovers it in response to her inner drama, which is an always exhausting (feminine, hysterical?) desire that knows no satisfaction. When Max's thoughts become a "torment," the heroine takes refuge in "one of her perfect moments," where she tastes the "wonders of the earth" and that she calls a "kingdom."[91] That retreat, less solitary than the runaway claims, requires the voluptuous discipline of *feeling* in view of *naming*—and, on that sole condition, the world becomes her true kingdom. Renée Néré "remembers" having found refuge in the act of writing—she is the author of two works, *Next to Love* and *The Forest of Birds*: "For myself, a particular word is enough to recreate the smell, the color, of the hours lived, it is as sonorous and full and mysterious as a shell in which the sea is singing."[92]

When eroticism has been finally—but never definitively—passed through, writing takes root in Colette as a refuge memory that requires the word "worthiness."[93] The concern for "honorable silence," the aversion toward "indiscreet poetry," are present from the young woman's first writings, when she discovers she has been deceived: "Who then dared murmur, too close to my irritable ear, the words 'downfall,' 'debasement'? . . . Toby-Chien, Dog of common sense, heed me well: I never felt more worthy of myself! From the depths of the severe retreat I created deep within myself, I'm apt to laugh out loud."[94] Later Colette would insinuate, through Sido, that she herself was not a great lover (she quotes an invented letter from her mother in *Break of Day:* "Could I therefore be, in my way, a great lover? That's news that would certainly have surprised my two husbands!").[95] She nevertheless asserts that, at the beginning, she was certain of being loved. By Captain Colette? By Sido? Before Willy?

It may be in that image of a parental loving Superego that what she would call a "scruple" is rooted, that is, the imperative of our consciousness to conform to the ideal left by our parents. Nevertheless, that scruple sometimes transforms itself into a persecutor, into a threat of "flunking the oral," and cuts short even dreams of love, like "Him," "the highest common factor," "He, when he spied on me through the window, to know whether I had cheated on him [. . .] because, to dream, then to return to reality, is only to change the place and gravity of a scruple."[96]

Paradoxically, logically, Colette returns to that imperative for worthiness after having violated the parental prohibition on incest. "Scruples" assert themselves more clearly after her affair with Bertrand de Jouvenel: it is after *Chéri* and *The Ripening Seed,* in *My Mother's House,* that this clarification of childhood memory as a capture by rights—a happy capture—of the mother occurs. There again the ambiguous regret of not being "worthy" of it takes shape (ambiguous because it calls for a denial and seems so sure of obtaining it). The idea of a transgression of prohibitions fades, since it is subsumed by a cosmic serenity: "House and garden live again, I know it, but what does it matter if the magic has left us, if we have lost the secret that opened a world—light, smells, harmony of trees and birds, murmur of human voices that death has already cut off—of which I have ceased to be worthy?"[97]

I said it is Sido to whom Colette traces the certainty of that worthiness. This is because her mother possessed the "decretal" gift of "observation" and did not give in to complacency of any kind—not to religion, not even to the sacrificial love of her husband—and because she was the daughter of her grandmother, Mme Eugène Landoy, whose stolen medallion Colette was to recover. "'My children,' I recited, 'never forget your *worthy and virtuous mother.*' It's signed Eugène Landoy."[98] It is also because the love between a mother and her daughter appears self-evident to the writer but on the condition, let us repeat, that the hatred is passed through, set aside, forgotten, or analyzed (which is not ruled out)—in the acting out as incest, rewritten in *Chéri* and *The Ripening Seed*, which introduces ambiguous female figures, despicable or enviable.

Short of or beyond any perversity, this ultimately regained relationship between the daughter and her mother may participate in a *time other* than the *time of desire,* the latter being, as Proust clearly saw, the time of war and death. Cast, on the contrary, into the time of flowering, Colette celebrates, with her own time regained, the other caesura, that of beginning, of eternally beginning anew. It is a necessarily ecstatic, necessarily cyclical time, condensed into happy instants and into "tendrils of the vine," bittersweet, bitter, drunk. Living.

No breaking and entering, no curse, no dishonor, no phallic penetration sullies her—nothing but the maternal time of *beginning*. Colette thrives in that paradoxical time that continues to produce flowerings, just as Sido is moved as she stands and waits in front of a flower still in the bud: "There was never in her life the memory of a dishonored wing, and if she trembled with desire around a closed calyx, around a chrysalis still rolled up in its glossy husk, at least she waited, respectful, for the hour. . . . The purity of those who have never been guilty of breaking and entering!"[99] That introjection of flowering cannot be recounted at length; it is inscribed in a concise gesture that is both flavor and sense, taste and symbol. "Christmas everywhere has fed on symbols. We will make like Christmas this year, and to the symbols we will add this bittersweet dessert: the poignant, imperishable flavor of recollection."[100] The plots become sketchy, what remains is the condensed resonances: "Still it is a fidelity, I shall say, of resonance."[101]

There is no question of childishness or of a complacency toward a past that kept us prisoner, the way Léo, the younger of

Colette's brothers, was kept, lost in his dream of an unfaithful reality. Unlike that unhappy sylph, Colette will fancy herself an "invulnerable child."[102]

A pure solitude accompanying the accumulated stress sums up the internal state of memory thus regained as "tendrils of the vine": Colette is a cruel woman who softens in times of stress. "To reach out toward the perfect is to return to one's starting point. The truly adventurous do not return there; but there is nothing of the true adventuress in me."[103]

Sleep itself becomes a memory without history for her, a replica of a pacifying maternal presence, a pure image of visual and tactile beauty, soft and vibrant as a butterfly. "Sleep approaches, brushes against me, and flees. . . . I see it! It is like that butterfly of thick velvet I pursued in the garden blazing with iris. . . . You remember?"[104]

Like that enveloping sleep, writing in search of flowering examines birth and suspends time because it absorbs evil in the elation of a departure without history:

> I had returned to the beginning of my life. Such a long way to come back to myself here! I call to the vanished sleep, the dark curtain that sheltered me and which has just gone away from me, leaving me shivering and naked as it were. . . . Patients who believe themselves cured are acquainted with these relapses of the illness; but such relapses find them childishly surprised and complaining. "But I thought it was over!" It would take little to make me moan out loud, like them. . . .
>
> Fatal sleep, too sweet, which abolishes the memory of myself in less than an hour![105]

What does it matter if in the beginning was the pain, when the will to live persists and with it the will to bring memory, extending to one's own birth, back to life: "Through the force of cries and pain, my mother drove me from her loins, but, since I came out blue and mute, no one thought it useful to concern themselves with me."[106] She adds: "Another fifteen January 28s passed without changing a thing, over that room where I was born half suffocated, displaying a personal will to live, and even, to live a long time, since I have just had my seventy-fifth birthday, which my friends around me stubbornly call 'a fine day.'"[107]

Against that background of celebrating the instant, the settling of accounts continues nonetheless, and worse than ever. Willy would come in for his share in *My Apprenticeships*[108] and Jouvenel for his in *Julie de Carneilhan*.[109] Two recollection regimes would thus sustain Colette's own writing: the erotic regime of revenge; and the bucolic regime of a female Dionysus reconciled with the original mother and free to abandon herself in a serene intoxication. Since there is no time, there is no History for Colette: for her the dismissal of politics is structural, not a mere innocent's thoughtlessness.

As for Colette's dreams, we will not learn a great deal about them. The logic of the dream immediately runs up against "the insinuation, the spitefulness of the real." "The give and take of love, the blissfulness of the gallop" itself, which attempts to restore to the dreamer "what had long since been taken from [her]," are swept away by the "overly judicious observation" of her hurt leg: "I couldn't get back into the saddle. [. . .] I woke up."[110] "Periwinkle lions" or "an English sprig": that is almost all she consents to reveal to us, surrealist figures of a cruelty subdued, of an animality calmed to the point of becoming plantlike. Even the archaic (maternal) threat, the guerilla warfare between females, is turned around into bucolic irony. Could that worthiness, that innocence of time regained à la Colette be the sign of a lack of imagination, of which people have accused her or, on the contrary, as for Mallarmé, is it a retreat of the imaginary via recollection toward what Freud calls "the navel of the dream" and Colette the "bottom of the dream"? Is it a final point, on the borderline of unrepresentable sensation, where the imaginary folds back against itself, where it refuses to "soar on a daily basis," only to better name the single instant that deserves to endure, the instant of acquiescence to the world, the instant of beginning, of rebirth? "One of my colleagues, and not the most insignificant of them, has asserted I have no imagination. That, if it is true, is a very good thing. But what would he say of Mallarmé, as quoted by Henri Mondor? 'Perhaps the imagination struggles at the bottom of the dream, in those people who refuse to let it soar on a daily basis.'"[111]

Even if Colette was that "forgetful woman who [would] leave the maternal home without looking back,"[112] as she accused herself of doing, in reality she continued to rely on the fleeting instant of memory regained. Memory, I hold on to you, she says in substance; I have no need to seek you. It is important simply, naturally, to begin anew to adapt sense to the sensory. That is called writing.

With the precision that comes of a friendly rivalry, Anna de Noailles revealed a Colette composed of "solitude," "pride," and "contempt," who drew her originality from "the feeling for a human geography." She noted that *there is,* strictly speaking, *no time in Colette,* except that of the pure instants that fill the "land" the writer created, composed indiscriminately "of soul and bodies," with no gap between the components, no journey except within her proud solitude, her "impregnable innocence."[113]

It is now clear to us how that absorption of the *time* and *space* of birth is shored up for Colette by a reconciliation with the infantile that required a phase of *mère-version.*[114] Colettian *mère-version,* a writing of perversion stripped of guilt, stands as the necessary logic that bends the movement of time into an Eden, a space of jouissance. It is a space outside time, apolitical, asocial, an imaginary place, therefore, and in that sense a nonplace: is it not *u-topia* itself? Utopia as a reconciliation with *mère-version* underlies the dynamic of sublimation in Colette. The imaginary inhabits that utopia where *I is the mother.* Whereas psychoanalysis tries to elaborate the violence of desire and of perversion itself by relying on a subject conscious of "castration" (according to Freud), of the "depressive position" (according to Klein), of "lack" (according to Lacan), *the experience of sublimation diverges from that path.* It creates a u-topia, in the sense of an imaginary, asocial place of ec-stasy, which suspends the limits between "subject" and "object" and immerses the ego in Being. It is an enigmatic, scandalous, radiant sublimation: it brings to mind the jouissance that floods the face of the god Mithra. "In spite of the halo of light surrounding his form, the youthful Persian god remains obscure to us."[115] So admits Freud, turned toward the father. If only we could approach that light by reading the ecstatic Colette, who passed through the "house of Claudine" to recreate Sido, her model and her double.

I see Colette's "impregnable innocence" as the source of the honesty of judgment that governs her pen when she writes about Artaud, for example. There is nothing so remote in appearance from the bucolic woman of Burgundy as the infernal Artaud. But when a hostile press lashed out after the performance of *Les cenci,* Colette devoted two articles to Artaud's art, oddly linking her monstrous purity to the "theater of cruelty."[116] Far from easy on the actor-poet, visibly shocked by his violence, she was nevertheless complicitous with his Nietzschean truth: "M. Antonin Artaud is an execrable actor. And yet, with his absurd violence, his wild eyes, and his barely feigned fury, he takes us along with him, beyond good and evil, into a desert where we burn with the thirst for blood."[117] But it is the second article that encourages Artaud and recommends his show to the public: "'If you stay till the end,' she writes, 'having hated, high-hatted, hooted at the play, acknowledge that an experiment like Artaud's serves the theater better than the nice little comedy that believes itself deft because it has risked nothing.' Then she concludes: "Go this week to the new bad play, before going to hear the others."[118] Artaud understood: "Is it not Colette who, in *Le Journal,* gave *Le Journal's* public opinion, and who, in a separate and free paper, gave her personal opinion, which is pure enthusiasm?"[119] Colette, not at all involved with modern art as Artaud was, never officially reprinted her article from *Sélection de la Vie Artistique:* nevertheless, in her "impregnable innocence," she wrote it in the heat of the battle, always listening to the "Inexorable."

The sensual Colette thus brings us face to face with a most enigmatic experience, sublimation, which indissolubly weaves together the real *and* the symbolic, flesh *and* words, and that, in the end, governed—a rare feat—her entire being. She does not refrain from commenting on it, in fact, even while claiming to be averse to "generalities."

"BECAUSE WRITING LEADS ONLY TO WRITING"

From her claim that she lacked a literary vocation[120] to the confession of a "large-limbed" need to write,[121] Colette sprinkles her works with scattered notes on writing, which, over time, takes root as an absolute experience: with and against love, with and against history. It is writing alone that inflects a woman's character; writing too that inflicts its specific space and time on the reality of existence itself, thus inspiring a "premonitory" logic on the progress of life.

Colette, resembling neither her father, the Captain, who left only a legacy of blank pages, nor Sido, who, on the contrary, "seated at a table anywhere at all [. . .] wrote,"[122] reveals that, far from being light-hearted, her own story as a "writer who did not want to write" turned out to be "a melancholic adventure."[123] She smiles compassionately at the poets who sing at night under her windows at the Palais-Royal: "Yes, the timid human creature needs to 'say something to someone,' if only in crude terms."[124] But she mocks the preciosity of admirers of the grand style: "Style is almost always the bad taste of our predecessors, dating from the day it becomes agreeable to us."[125] This is another way of denying her own participation in literature. All the same, the French language, manipulated in "high style," excited the woman of Burgundy: "But with each jewel of beautiful language gathered, glistening in the white Provençal dust, I admire the fact that a syntax in high style forces back the alluvium of slang, of sports jargon, of pretentious humor flooding in from all sides."[126] In the midst of the World War II debacle, Colette lent an ear to the antiquated words of popular language, which revived, without knowing it, the century of Louis XIV: "Such a beautiful sentence, which carries a whiff of the seventeenth century, nevertheless blossoms here on illiterate lips."[127] Or she ensures the timelessness of Latin terms, like the peasant woman who, "caring for a swallow lashed by the wind, which had taken shelter under gadrooned tiles," expressed herself this way: "'Leave it,' she said, 'by tomorrow it will have recovered its virtues.'"[128]

In the last years of her life, writing imposed itself on Colette as a formal concern, but, from the outset, it was experienced as a singular experiment, even as the proof par excellence of singularity: "'*Shows imagination; but one senses a conscious effort to set oneself apart.*' That note, written in red ink in the margin of a French composition, sticks in my mind."[129] The aim of that self-affirmation, which collides with academic conformism, is to reckon with the scars—it being understood that a scar is not a birthmark but a very singular "acquisition."[130] Nevertheless, Colette does not list her sorrows and she celebrates joy, which she will always prefer to laments: "I was very right to trust in what I knew least, my peers, human solicitude.[. . .] If some day I were to write my memories of 'the other side,' it seems to me that, by contrast, the 'oof' of effort, the cry of pain, would come forth in a sound of celebration, and I could complain about it only with a happy face."[131]

This is a deceptive hedonism if ever there was one, since, against all expectations, it is the pain of writing that this woman discreetly reveals. But only her faithful readers root out the "crises" via the detours of her sentences, beneath the scarred images: "Again I take up my pen, to begin that perilous and disappointing game, to seize and fix, under the pliant double tip, the shimmering, the fleeting, the exciting adjective. . . . It's only a short crisis, the itching of a scar."[132]

Colette's concern for the mot juste is built on her fascination, from childhood, with *sound,* which propels her toward reveries, jostles conventional meanings, overloads strange melodies with bizarre ideas, finally managing to make language tip toward the world's flesh, where it becomes equal to a "venom" or a "crushed snail." And, as we have seen, the author, a "realist," reveals the very "surrealist" alchemy of her style by detailing her childlike reverie on the word "presbytery."[133] Contrary to what a scientistic mind would believe, it is not by censoring the reverie but by letting it resonate that the writer seizes the chance to add sound to the sense and to the thing.

For the little provincial girl, does the "big event" consist of her engagement to be married or of the writing of letters to her future husband? "The big event of our engagement, for me, had been our correspondence, the letters I freely received and wrote."[134] With her Paris debut Colette slips into the role of a woman of the world, and writing then becomes her secret "kingdom," her protective citadel: a splitting in two. Even marked with Willy's seal, writing develops, like an *exile,* against the "prison" that he supposedly imposed on Colette, to give birth to the *Claudine* books. Later, her writing, becoming more than the spontaneous means of defense it was initially, asserts itself through the anti-*Claudines,* the texts belonging to the "tendrils of the vine" genre, and programs a new poetics. Writing, defined as Claudine's "double" that "mirrors" her "choice of indifference" and her "fortress of solitude," carves out a true "retreat" that "defies the invader." On one side is the "ironic" and "sweet" Claudine. On the other the one who says: "Leave me my share of uncertainty, of love, of sterile activity, of full-flavored laziness, leave me my poor little human share, which has its price!"[135]

From that moment on, the country girl Colette begins a happy meditation on her exile in the land of sublimation. Renée the Vagabond is the author of an unsuccessful book that nevertheless installs her in that other "kingdom," where words create things: "For myself, a particular word is enough to recreate the smell, the color, of the hours lived, it is as sonorous and full and mysterious as a shell in which the sea is singing."[136] Like Sido, who knows "that one possesses in abstention, and only in abstention,"[137] Colette's heroine suggests that, after the raw, naïve suffering ("My God! How young I was, and how I loved that man! And how I suffered!") comes the time of a second suffering "with an intractable pride and obstinacy," which immediately precedes the act of "making literature."[138] Far from being reduced to a simple *defense* of the wounded woman in love, the act of writing blossoms in that movement of *dispersion of the ego,* which "suspends" itself from everything it passes through, then separates from the author overseeing that immersion:

A Vagabond, granted, but one who resigns herself to turn about in circles, in place, like them, my companions, my brothers. . . . Partings sadden and intoxicate me, it's true, and some part of me suspends itself from everything I pass through—new regions, pure or cloudy skies, seas under rain the color of gray pearl—and clings so passionately to them that it seems to me I am leaving behind a thousand little ghosts in my likeness, rolling on the wave, cradled on the leaf, dispersed in the cloud. . . . But does not a last little ghost, the one most like me, remain seated in my spot by the fireplace, dreamy and quiet, bent over a book it forgets to read?[139]

Writing is a *greediness* that stands in for all the lacks it creates: "My voracious wish creates what it lacks and eats its fill."[140] But it is also a *fever*. Colette describes the splitting in two that takes hold of her under the effect of illness, and she reminds us of certain states of depersonalization from her early childhood. She believes she sees a straight-haired twin who vies with her for Sido's love. "As I was growing up, growing old, she had the luck to remain a little girl. She dates from long ago. In hours of fever my mother, Sido, bent over me: 'Do you want something to drink, Minet-Chéri?' I wanted above all for her not to perceive my suspect twin, the little straight-haired girl whom she might have loved."[141] Nevertheless, that hallucinatory process is at the heart of the literary experience itself, which, though better mastered than a high fever, shapes the narrator's true personality: Was Colette born of Sido and of the Captain, or of the loss and reshaping of self that is writing itself? Like fever, fiction "is the beginning of what one does not name";[142] and, like a wild child, it "scour[s] the coppice and the soaked meadows, like an independent dog who answers to no one."[143]

The self-assured mistress of the "fever" and of the "independent dog" that drive her, Colette nevertheless remains her own privileged theme, barely dissimulated behind her fictive characters. As the fruits of her self-duplications and self-dispersions, merciless portraits of the narrator done by herself reproduce for us, in place of the author—of the woman and, more broadly, of humans—a dizzying *polytope*. Is Colette fascinating? "Then try!

If I were a man and knew me thoroughly, I would not like me very much: unsociable, in a lather, and rebellious at first sight, a nose that claims to be infallible and makes no concessions, maniacal, falsely bohemian, very 'proprietary' deep down, jealous, sincere out of laziness and a liar out of shame . . . I may say that today, but tomorrow I'll find myself charming."[144]

The aim of her writing is to track a whirlwind of identities: "woman" will be the imaginary creation that best attests to that polymorphic body, a restless "acrobat" without boundaries, priceless:

> How quickly everything changes! . . . Women especial-
> ly. . . . This one, in a few months, will lose almost all her
> mordancy, her natural and unconscious pathos. Will the sly
> atavism of concierges, of money-grubbing little merchants,
> come to light in this foolish eighteen-year-old Jadin, so lav-
> ish with herself and her scanty moolah? Why, facing her,
> did I think of the Bells, German acrobats with an English
> name whom Brague and I knew in Brussels? Incomparable
> in strength and grace in cherry-red leotards that made their
> blond skin look pale, all five of them lived in two unfur-
> nished rooms, where they cooked for themselves on a small
> cast-iron stove. And all day long—the impresario told us—
> it was mysterious palavers, meditations on financial jour-
> nals, savage arguments about gold mines, Sosnowiec and
> Crédit d'Egypte! Money, money, money. . . . [145]

Try to pin her down, her features slip away: beautiful or ugly? "Wearing hair twisted Alsatian-style, two little ribbons fluttering at the ends of my two braids, the part down the middle of my head, looking very ugly with my temples uncovered and my ears too far from my nose, I sometimes went up to the house of my long-haired sister."[146] She is surely wounded as much by the gratification as by the ordeals: "At random and anonymously, I asked for compensation, which they sometimes handed over a little like a coconut tree does its nuts—bam! right on the head."[147] Like Proust's, her exhibitionism conceals a mystery that obstinately eludes us: "One does not penetrate the privacy of a caryatid, one contemplates it."[148] Added to the contradictory facets that time deposits in Colettian space is the kaleidoscope of the narrator's identifications and projections: Is "Sido" Sido or once more Colette? Model or copy? Recall the epigraph to *Break of Day*: "Do you imagine, in reading me, that I am doing my portrait? Hold on: it is only my model."[149]

The force of desire then comes along to definitively blur her features. Moved by an impetuous fantasy, desire constructs a "premonitory" reality, that is, an imaginary so imperative that the real body is obliged to carry out what writing had already programmed, before leaving in its turn the last word to the imaginary: first Léa and Chéri, then Colette and Bertrand, and finally *The Ripening Seed*.

In that interlacing of identities Colette—who hates generalities, she says—nevertheless meditates with dazzling precision on the "ephemeral," the privileged target of her writing, and underscores the imbalance characterizing the rhythms of her narratives. Neither the "notorious" nor the "venerable" merit that the author linger on them; only the commonplace or the "hackneyed" has value. Understand: she celebrates only the everyday made astonishing once more, revealed in its invigorating details, which require the grip of a "tendrils of the vine" writing. "Twenty pages on the colored, tonic, and mysterious ephemera; twenty lines on the notorious and the venerable, whom others have celebrated and will celebrate; astonishment at the hackneyed, here and there a propensity to sleep out of boredom at the sound of the great 'ahs!' that the world expels before a marvel, a messiah, or a catastrophe—that is, I think, my rhythm."[150]

Writing, the organizing center of her entire existence, never becomes a fetish activity for Colette. She joyously makes fun of the rituals that surround the cult of writing and her fellow writers: "We are not pretty when we write. One purses his mouth, another sucks on her tongue, shrugs a shoulder; how many chew the inside of their cheek, drone on like Sunday mass, rub their tibia bone with their heel?"[151] Displaying a supreme disdain for the "creative process," she prefers to keep secret the feverish pleasure that accompanies her discovery of the mot juste and complains that she suffers when that grace is slow in coming. There is no need for "notes," "mumbo-jumbo," or other "reference points" to write. Rather, she places sexuality and writing, capital punishment and the portrait side by side, suggesting that a particular character favored the "literary puberty" of the narrator, who sets herself up, through the act of writing itself, as a "praying mantis" for her heroes and objects:

> Among my notes. . . . What notes? You'll not find one behind me. Oh, I tried. Everything I noted became sad as a dead frog's skin, sad as the plan for a novel. Putting my faith in writers who take notes, I had made notes on a piece of paper, and I lost the paper. I therefore purchased a notebook, already American, and I lost the notebook, after which I felt free, forgetful and responsible for my forgetfulness.
>
> Not a note, not a notebook, not the slightest little mumbo-jumbo of reference points. Where, then, have my heroes without footprints come from? The first of them all, Renaud, whom Claudine married, is inconsistency itself.[. . .] I had no sooner created him than I took a dislike to him, and as soon as he left himself open, I killed him. With his death, I had the impression I was completing a sort of literary puberty, had the foretaste of the pleasures the praying mantis allows itself.[152]

Might writing be, all things considered, embroidery? By that amused wink at the popular crafts, even at female masturbation, more or less happy or revanchist— recall the perverse Philomène de Watteville[153]—Colette persists in desanctifying the very French religion of belles lettres. Nevertheless, in her attachment to embroidery, she is once more searching for the immersion of the mental act in the gesture of the living body and in the world's flesh. In the first place, while embroidering one can sing, which the "scribbler" does not usually allow herself to do: is that a way of saying that she, Colette, unlike so many others, sings while writing and that this is heard in her sentences? "'We scribblers,' said Carco, 'we're the only ones who can't sing while working.' My new work sings. It sings *Bolero* like everyone else. It sings: *'Believing I had found a woodcock down in the meadows. . . .'* It sings: *'When I was in my father's house—Little pug-nose.'* Unlearning to write must not require a great deal of time."[154]

In reality, embroidery hardly makes her "unlearn writing," since it intersects "cerebral labor," "falls into rhythm," then "out of rhythm" with it: "I pierce and pierce again. The *équille*—the needle—shines between two threads, tugging at its woolen tail. My memoirs are written in blue greenery, in pink lilacs, in multicolored Anthemes."[155] Pen and needle, mind and hand, tongue and fingers go together: "Consider how much time was wasted before someone inscribed, among the virtues that tapestry work engenders, that of regulating the pace of cerebral labor? Just as the trotting of two horses harnessed together falls into rhythm on an echoing road, then out of rhythm, only to fall in again, the need to do tapestry work and literary invention form a friendship, then part ways, then reconcile."[156]

And here is a last version of the alphabet according to Colette: it is "the cross-stitch, called the tapestry stitch," which, along with the wool and its threads in every color, intersects the glossy skin of blackcurrants and cherries.

> After some fifty years occupied with the duty to write black on white, I find it sweet to do tapestry work. The needle sparkles in my fingers, I pierce and repierce a canvas with thick threads, I guide the wool, prisoner of the oblong eye, I decide that the greenery is blue, the lilac pink, the marguerite multicolored; I consider it natural that a bough befitting the blackcurrant bears huge cherries as its fruit, each marked, on its scarlet equator, with four white stitches representing the glistening of a glossy epidermis. . . .
>
> Cross-stitch, called the tapestry stitch, has counted me among its practitioners for a few years, but the ill—or the good—comes from much further back.[157]

Furtively, the lovers of cross-stitch, of which I am one, will agree to leap for joy at the sight of an extraordinary capital M encircled with roses, of a number 2 that sits up and begs, of a Q on its tail, of a little fruit dish holding six apples in the shape of a pyramid, of a knock-kneed stork.[158]

In short, whether or not it is embroidery or tapestry, writing for Colette is a physical act, a gesture of the hands and of the whole body. That leads her to "hear" the bees, the guinea fowl, and the sows, when she does not make writing travel through a "mental hole," "a perfect likeness" to death, before becoming once again quite simply a path, an amusing, endless passage:

> I leave, I dash onto a path that used to be familiar, at my old pace; I aim toward the old gnarled oak, the poor farm where cider and butter on bread were generously meted out to me. Here is the bifurcation of the yellow path, the creamy white elderberries, surrounded by bees in such numbers that one hears, at twenty paces, their wheat thresher sound. . . . I hear the guinea fowl sobbing, the sow grumbling. . . . That's it, my working method. . . . Then suddenly a *mental block,* a void, annihilation, a *perfect resemblance,* I think, to what must be the beginning of a death, the road lost, blocked, erased. . . . No matter, I'll have had great fun along the way.[159]

Glass balls or, as she prefers to call them, *sulfures,* are the other craft that seems to offer Colette an analogy with the act of writing. In blowing a dahlia, a pansy, the two-colored crown of Saint Louis, or the profile of Queen Elizabeth, the glassblower immortalizes a living (generally floral) presence, entrusting it to the transparence of crystal. Without being affected by the collector's craze, Colette nevertheless likes to roam the boutiques and to welcome specialists on the subject, to surround herself with the most beautiful objects. I imagine her pythoness's lair at the Palais-Royal, smelling of jasmine and cat odors, decorated with *sulfures,* butterflies from Brazil, multicolored necklaces, her writing case strewn with sheets of her famous blue paper, with her pens and her rectangular magnifying glass, illuminated by her "blue lantern"—everything there is artifice and writing, the paper-weights and the mask of the officiant, its face with a malicious smile, powdered white, thin mouth painted red and eyes under-lined with a stroke of kohl. Objects and author exert the same ascendancy over flowering: it is a matter of capturing the freshest of presences and of making the slender charm of a "sphere of tamed water" last. Like Bel-Gazou, I like to imagine that these "balls" crystallize Colette's writing as much as "the ponds and springs of her native province."[160]

Writing, lived and conceived in that way, is not unaware of death—how could it be?—but empties it of its burden of anguish ("The grave is nothing but an empty box") and transforms the timeline (necessarily lost) into a *duration of intermittences,* of flowerings. The past unfolds, first, as recollections of sensory instants (a perfumed handkerchief, an intonation), while the future is measured by the timelessness of a "poignant writing":

> It is with a constrained and cold heart that I care for [Renaud's grave]. Nothing saddens me there, nothing holds me there. Nothing remains, underneath, of the one I love, the one of whom I still speak, in my heart, saying: "he *says* this. . . . He prefers that. . . . " A grave is nothing but an empty box. The one I love endures wholly in my memory, in a still-perfumed handkerchief I unfold, in an intonation I suddenly recall and to which I listen for a long instant, head bent.[161]

She adds:

> A memory, an image, the unforgettable sound of a voice, of a poignant writing: only there, there and nowhere else, the one who is no longer maintains a secret warmth, there only he lives again, at the hours of tender worship and despair. But the tomb? Is its overpowering stone door and its crude ornamentation of glass jewels, porcelain, and stucco

the dwelling of a soul? Nothing calls to me or keeps me on the mound, on the slab, which nevertheless bears two beloved names.[162]

For this pagan woman who is reborn in the rite of writing, death as a concern with the hereafter is only an illusion that immediately evaporates; a calcinated toad or a petrified ossuary, it "does not interest" her.

> Someone found one dead the other day—an old man. All dried up like an expired toad that the midday sun calcinates before a bird of prey has the time to eviscerate it. Death, thus deprived of a large share of decomposition, is more decent in our living eyes. A friable and light body, hollow bones, a great devouring sun above it all: will that be my final lot? I sometimes make a serious effort to think about it, to make myself believe that the second half of my life has brought me a little gravity, a little worry about what comes *after*. . . . That's a brief illusion. Death does not interest me—not even my own.[163]

In fact, when the "oneself" is so indissolubly coiled in writing, itself the "alphabet" of the world's flesh, the "monogram of the Inexorable," can one truly imagine an end to "oneself"? Can one imagine putting an end to oneself? "How difficult it is to put an end to oneself. . . . If one has only to try, it is said, I try."[164] That question of Colette's is not only the expression of an old lady's anxiety nor simply a relic of her overcome melancholy, which surfaces at times, a black twin, though one subdued by her writing: "There is always a moment in the life of young persons when dying is just as normal and seductive to them as living, and I was hesitating."[165] Later she writes: "But I abdicate in the face of boredom, which makes me a wretched being, ferocious if need be. Its approach and its capricious presence, which affects the muscles of my jaw, dances in the pit of my stomach, sings a refrain to which my toes mark time. I do more than dread them, I flee them."[166] At issue is an inquiry into the *renunciation of writ-*

ing, a renunciation Colette, the least religious person in the world, may have dreamt of in order to preserve her vagabond freedom, detached from any shackle, including the compulsion to write. Nevertheless, she concludes "with humility"—but what pride there is in that submissiveness—that she is going to "still write": "There is no other fate for me."

Writing, as pain, brutality, or insurrection, will continue to flower within her so long as her hand is able to guide the pen on the blue paper: "Yet, if I am immobile this evening, I am not without a plan, since moving within me—in addition to that twisted pain, like a huge wine press screw—is a *brutality* much less familiar than *pain,* an *insurrection* that, in the course of my long life, I have several times denied, then foiled, and finally accepted, because writing leads only to writing."[167]

Beyond that certification of vital perseverance, it is Colette's specific spirituality that surfaces, sudden and discreet, in a requiem: unlike other labors, which end once the tool has been set down, there is a joy of writing that lies in the very duration of the sublimating adventure and destines it for the infinite. Is a piece of writing completed? Rather, it is "to be continued" if it inscribes the "Inexorable." And what if, in the "alphabet" of dead "sand" the writer leaves behind her, a rereading could begin that would bring back to life, through the reader or interpreter, once again and interminably, the "monogram," the only "precious" thing, of the world's flesh? "I once thought that the task of writing was like other chores: once the tool was set down, you exclaimed for joy: 'Done!' and you clapped your hands, from which the grains of sand you thought precious rained down. . . . It is then that, in the figures that the grains of sand write, you read the words: 'To be continued. . . . '"[168]

For my part, I have tried to make the grains of sand of Colette's writing live, a writing chiseled by the temporality of beginning, of rebirth, of astonishment. When it is approached in that way, it is clear it does not allow itself to be "done." Indeed, it is the very rhythm of flowering that it transmits to us.

10

IS THERE A FEMININE GENIUS?

To Simone de Beauvoir

For a long time the works of Hannah Arendt, Melanie Klein, and Colette have illuminated and sustained my work and my existence, in rhythm with the contingencies and necessities of the intellectual life. The years I have devoted to writing this triptych, and the years prior, have entailed a constant association with them; as I conclude, I have the impression I have truly shared these women's lives. All the years of research have established close ties among us, composed of a sisterly proximity in which affection vies with unconscious projection, betraying an erotic contagion. These ties are composed as well of irritating differences and critical dismissals. Nevertheless, it is my admiration for these three women that dominates my reading, and the feeling of benevolent agreement prevails in considering their meandering adventures. Some around me have said that the interpretations proposed here are a token of generosity. If readers were to confirm that impression, that would be the best gift Arendt, Klein, and Colette could have offered me, by revealing what the harshness of life does not always allow one to display.

The provocative hyperbole of "genius" has been the guiding thread helping me to decipher, in the works of these three twentieth-century women, how they transcended their respective fields (political philosophy, psychoanalysis, literature), inviting everyone to attempt a similar self-transcendence by following the battles and advances of Arendt, Klein, and Colette, and by bringing new energy to his or her own. Indeed, I am persuaded that the ultimate result of the rights of man and of woman is nothing other than the Scottist ideal, which our age now has the means to realize: attention directed at the *ecceitas,* care granted to the flowering of our singularity, concern for the advent of the "who" within the "anything whatever"—with "genius" being the most complex, the most seductive, the most fertile version of singularity at a given historical moment, and solely on these conditions, inscribed in duration and in the universal.

SIMONE DE BEAUVOIR: "SITUATION" AND "INDIVIDUAL OPPORTUNITIES"

Thus, emphasizing the singularity realized in exemplary works (especially in my own field, the "humanities") is also a way of disassociating myself from feminism as a mass movement. Women's struggles for emancipation have passed through three phases in modern times: the demand for *political rights* by the suffragettes; the assertion of an ontological *equality* with men (as opposed to an "equality in difference"), which led Simone de Beauvoir in *The Second Sex* (1949) to demonstrate and prophesize a "fraternity" between man and woman beyond their natural specificities; and finally, in the wake of May '68 and psychoanalysis, the search for the *difference* between the two sexes, which supposedly entails an original creativity on the part of women, both in the experience of sexuality and across the entire range of social practices, from politics to writing. In each of these phases the aim was the liberation of women as a whole: in that respect the feminists did not depart from the totalizing ambitions of the libertarian movements stemming from Enlightenment philosophy and before it, from the dissolution of the religious continent, which those movements set their hearts on realizing here on earth, with rebellious negativity, paradisiacal teleology. We are only too aware today of the impasses entailed by these total and totalitarian promises. Feminism itself, whatever its various currents in Europe and America, has not escaped from these aims and, in the end, this tendency has rigidified into a short-lived militantism, which, ignoring the singularity of subjects, believes it can encompass all women, like all proletarians or the entire Third World, with demands as relentless as they are desperate.

Nevertheless, we need to acknowledge that the most illustrious of its inspirational women, Simone de Beauvoir, was far from underestimating the "subject" in woman or the "individual" who "experiences an indefinite need to transcend herself." Philosophy, faithful to a perspective stemming from existentialist morality and putting Marxism to use in its own way, has endeavored to emancipate woman from her minority status, which obliges her to be the Other of man, who has neither the right nor the opportunity to constitute himself as Other in turn. Deprived of the possibility of plans and transcendence, woman, so constituted by the history of a society dominated by men, would thus be doomed to immanence, frozen into an object, "since her transcendence [is] perpetually transcended by another essential and sovereign consciousness."[1] Even while struggling against women's reduction to biology alone—"one is not born a woman: one becomes one"[2]—Simone de Beauvoir was in reality still fuming against metaphysics, since it confined woman within the *other*, in order to posit her as *facticity* and *immanence* and to refuse her access to true humanity, the humanity of autonomy and freedom.

But in setting aside the problematic of difference in favor of equality, Beauvoir did not allow herself to go any further with the existentialist project (though she anticipated the move), which ought to have led her to meditate, on the basis of the condition of women in the plural, on the opportunities for freedom on the part of each one as singular human being: "The drama of woman is the *conflict* between the fundamental demand of every *subject,* which always posits itself as essential, and the imperatives of a *situation,* which constitutes her as inessential. How, in the *female condition,* can a *human being* be realized in full? [. . .] This means that, in taking an interest in *individual opportunities,* we will not define these opportunities in terms of happiness, but in terms of freedom."[3] In fact, even though de Beauvoir's reflections drew broadly from the accomplishments of women "subjects" or "individuals," all as exemplary in their genius as Saint Teresa, Mlle de Gournay, Théroigne de Méricourt, and Colette, *The Second Sex* is devoted less to the "human being," to "individual opportunities," than to the "female condition" as a whole. Indeed, it is from the transformation of that condition that the author expected a possible individual autonomy and feminine creativity, "opportunities" of the singular being, whose liberation, according to her, is the principal historical objective.

The author of *The Second Sex* undoubtedly lived too soon to defend female singularity, when so many sexual and economic "conditions" still obstructed women's emancipation. Her philosophical journalism, expounded in a tone of intense commitment combined with a vast pedagogical erudition and tinged with an irony as clear-sighted as it is elegant, was to assure her book a never-surpassed success. Furthermore, her issues remain relevant today, given how molded by conservatism and archaism the *global age* that is dawning after *modern times* is proving to be. All the same, it is not certain that the "conflict" between the *condition of all women* and the *free realization of every woman*—a conflict that, according to the philosopher, is at the foundation of female suffering—would be settled if one were *simply* concerned with the "condition" and underestimated the "subject." In her reflections Beauvoir herself, privileging the transformation of the female "condition," contributed toward a dismissal of the essential issue, which is that of singular initiative, and toward a consignment to the shadows of the undecidable opportunity of the *ecceitas.* Arendt, Klein, Colette—and so many others—did not wait for the "female condition" to evolve in order to realize their freedom: is not "genius" precisely that breach through and beyond the "situation"?

To appeal to the genius of every woman, of every man or woman, is a way, not of underestimating the weight of History—these three women, better and to a greater extent than others, confronted it and jostled it, courageously and realistically—but of attempting to free the female condition, like the human condition in general, from biological, social, or fateful constraints by emphasizing the conscious or unconscious initiative of the subject against the weightiness of its program, dictated by these various forms of determinism.

Might not the singular initiative be, in the end, that intimate, infinitesimal, but ultimate force on which the deconstruction of any "condition" depends? My inquiry, in investigating the irreducible subjectivity of these three women, their creative singularity, has addressed their "individual opportunities" in terms of freedom—in Beauvoir's vocabulary. Hence, beyond our differences, I am convinced that I have taken up and developed an essential idea from *The Second Sex,* which, under the constraints of History on one hand and of her own existentialist choice on the other, Beauvoir had to leave in abeyance: *How, through the female condition, can a woman's being be fulfilled, that is, her individual opportunity in terms of freedom, which is the modern sense of happiness?* It is obvious that in formulating my study in this way, I wish to express as well as I can my debt to Simone de Beauvoir, a pioneer too often and unfairly criticized or underestimated, and to dedicate this triptych to her memory.

It would be pointless to compose a list of traits supposedly shared by Arendt, Klein, and Colette, in order to define a would-be catalogue of what constitutes the female genius. Singularity in itself is without common measure: it is not repeated in identical form from one individual to the other. Nevertheless, the reader may identify certain significant points of intersection in the specific trajectories of these three authors, and I will return to them by way of conclusion. But before that, and rather than writing a true treatise on female sexuality, I owe it to the reader to supply a few remarks on the second term in my title, whose definition I have intentionally put off until now, hoping that its meaning would be clarified empirically through the concrete experiences of the three geniuses: What is "female"? Or rather, what is the "feminine"? Can one define, not Woman or *All* Women, but a *feminine specificity* that is declined differently in each sex (the feminine of woman, the feminine of man) and in a singular manner for each subject, without confining that subject within the "other" or the "unrepresentable"?

Without proposing a systematic thesis, I have, in my previous psychoanalytic writings, attempted to respond to that question by approaching the *feminine* from the angle of the various psychic symptoms or structures I was able to analyze in the treatment of my female and male patients. Against that background of reflection, the existential and cultural experiences of Arendt, Klein, and Colette took shape and contributed toward refining, even modifying it. I will present succinctly my own hypothesis of the *feminine,* the fruit of my familiarity with the history and the current state of psychoanalysis (the sources of which I cannot give in toto here) as well as my own experience as a therapist, in order to uncover what, in the lives and writings of these three geniuses, might fall to the *feminine.*

THE TWO-FACED OEDIPUS

A woman's psychosexual development encompasses two versions of the Oedipus complex: several authors, along with Freud, have noticed this and I, for my part, have proposed a new interpretation of it.[4]

Let us call *Oedipus prime* the most archaic period, from birth to the so-called phallic phase, situated between the ages of three and six years. In his conclusive studies of female sexuality,[5] Freud insists on what is conventionally called "phallic monism": the primary characteristic of "infantile genital organization [. . .] consists in the fact that, for both sexes, only one genital, namely the male one, comes into account. What is present, therefore, is not a primacy of the genitals, but a primacy of the *phallus.*" In other words, for the psyche, the child is originally masculine, whatever its anatomical sex—"the little girl is a little man." That axiom, initially considered characteristic of infantile (and not adult) sexuality, or a fantasy, in the end took root in Freud's writings as a given sine qua non of all sexuality.

Nevertheless, in his last writings Freud discovered a particular relation between the little girl and her mother, adhesive and intense, not easily accessible in analysis because encysted in preverbal sensorial experience. The founder of psychoanalysis compares it to the "Minoan-Mycenean civilization behind the civilization of Greece." That would at the origin of psychic bisexuality, which "comes to the fore much more clearly in women than in men." Lacan, for his part, who forcefully underscores the "primacy of the phallus" shoring up the "symbolic function" and the Name of the Father in the organization of subjects of both sexes, remarks, without insisting on it, that the "maternal instinct" may be a part of female sexuality irreducible to analysis because it escapes the influence of phallic primacy.[6]

Finally, contemporary clinical observation has led a number of psychoanalysts to suggest that, at the origins of infantile sexuality, the neoteny (prematurity) of humans exposes the *infans* to the adult's and, in particular, the mother's, intrusion. Although protective, parental support is seductive: from the outset infantile sexuality is formed under the effect of these parental, and especially maternal, "enigmatic signifiers."[7] These signifiers imprint, on the child's erogenous zones, the mother's unconscious, which carries the erotic connection that attaches the mother to the father and to the paternal unconscious itself. That initial coexcitation between mother and baby seems, all things considered, very far from the idyllic models of the "Minoan-Mycenean" according to Freud, or of a serenity of "being" before a drive-based "doing," according to Winnicott. Infantile sexuality, which is not that of the *instincts* but that of *drives* understood as psychosomatic constructions, always already biology-and-sense, is thus formed, from the origin, through the newborn's interaction with both its parents and under the influence of maternal seduction. It is the mother who provides care and thus becomes the agent of unconscious intrusion; nevertheless, through her womanly desire for the father (the child's father or her own) and through the acting out and discourse of the child's own father, it is the father who intervenes from the outset as subject of that original marking, for the girl and for the boy, and differently depending on the child's sex.

The child, who allows herself to be seduced and who seduces with her skin and her five senses, opens herself up, in fact, via her orifices: the mouth, anus, and vagina for the little girl. Usually the female sexual organ is not aroused, but it is difficult to imagine that it is covered merely with an insensitive mucous membrane—it is a "harder wood," Freud proposes, bizarrely and incautiously,[8] unless that supposed insensitivity is defensive. Rightly, the founder of psychoanalysis observes in both sexes the absence of an *unconscious representation* of the vagina, other than as "lacunary" or *cloacal,* taken "on lease" from the anus, in Lou Andreas-Salomé's expression.[9] But, in not being visual, is not the *representancy* of cavernous excitation—vaginal or cloacal in particular—by that very fact more unfathomable and troubling for the subject's future unity?

The seduced, orificial child has experienced a breaking and entering: at the origin of Minoan-Mycenean sexuality, we find a sexual being, "polymorphously perverse," an anticipation of the woman's penetrated being. Throughout that first period of psychic sexuation, the sexuality of *Oedipus prime,* open to maternal-paternal seduction, is, though passive, nonetheless reactive and active: the emission of stools and vocal and gestural expressions aggressively mark it. For the boy, penile excitation (later reinforced by the phallic phase) superimposes itself on the complex range of reactions due to that original breaking-and-entering/seduction that provide the underlying structure of the male subject's "feminine position." That position will persist in male sexuality, especially through the desire to possess the father's penis orally and anally, to destroy it in the maternal breast, which is fantasized as containing that penis, and so on.

For the little girl *Oedipus prime* entails more complex ambiguities. On one hand, the "skin-ego,"[10] the orificial ego,[11] and all the little girl's sensoriality offer themselves to seduction-passivation, which sets in motion narcissism as well as masochism and sadistic abreactions: to devour the breast along with the penis, to bombard with feces, to capture/be captured by the five senses, etc. Clitoral excitability, which varies with the subject and is supposedly of lesser intensity than penile excitability, nevertheless also remains mobilized, pushing the girl to actively possess the first object, the unconscious seductive mother. But that erectile activity seems to a great extent covered up, even dominated, by orificial excitation, by the erotic participation of the oral-anal-vaginal cavernous body in the hypersensitive connection with the mother. Whereas Karl Abraham, then Melanie Klein and the English School insist on that early role of a vaginal/anal femininity in the Oedipus complex, particularly that of the girl, Freud points to it only rarely, above all in the Dora case history (1905).[12] As Jacques André has noted, that text is, significantly, contemporary with Freud's analysis of his own daughter Anna. This was an extraordinary opportunity for a male analyst and father to encounter the little girl's early genital seduction—by her father. The little girl's intense vaginal/cloacal mobilization, as well as her clitoral excitation, structures her original sexuality as a psychic bisexuality: both passive *and* active. Thus bisexuality is more pronounced in the girl than it is in the boy.

Moreover, seen from this angle, which the treatment of adult women confirms if only by identifying defensive symptoms, *Oedipus prime* appears not to be dominated by a simple passivation but, alongside and beyond it, by a setting in place of an *interactive subjectivity* that cannot be interpreted in terms of a simple active/passive dichotomy. The orificial breaking and entering is offset not only by clitoral excitation but also by *the early elaboration of a relationship of introjection/identification* with the loving-and-intrusive object, the mother (inasmuch as she also relays the father's desire).

Through introjection, the girl installs the loving object within: the excited *cavity* of the internal body is transmuted into an internal *representation*. Thus begins a slow and lasting work of psychization, which will be accentuated by *Oedipus double prime*, in which one finds the female tendency to privilege the psychic and the hypersensitive representation/idealization of love, in counterpoint to the erotic excitation characteristic of the drives. That feminine psychization nevertheless gets into difficulties because of the identification with the agent of parental seduction—a projective identification favored by the resemblance between daughter and mother and by the projection of maternal narcissism and depressivity onto the daughter.

For the girl the result is on one hand an early *psychization* of the object of love, which the young ego introjects even while identifying with it; and on the other, because of the projective identification with the intrusive mother, the creation of a *real relationship* of possession of and dependence on that same object. The little girl's cavernous and sensorial excitability and the psychic interiority that accompanies it become stabilized when she latches onto the real external object. This means that the sensorial reality of the object, the mother's (and later, the lover's) real presence, are required as compensation for the breaking and entering of the cavernous body and for the psychic introjection constantly at work. And that *real need for connection* is posited as the place of the cloacal underside, laying claim to an insatiable imaginary premium for the oral, anal, and vaginal pleasures to which the little girl submits (more than she actively seeks them). The little girl's relationship to her maternal object is mirrored in the mother's symmetrical attachment to her daughter-infant: the female parent does not so much erect her daughter as a phallic prosthesis, as she does with the boy as a general rule, as project her own narcissistic fantasies and her latent sadomasochism or depressivity onto her, in response to the little girl's orificial and sensorial jouissances.

Breaking and entering of the orificial body by the other; oral, anal, and clitoral aggression and possession of the other; and finally, repression of excitability and compensation through psychic and sensorial hypercathexis of the object, which early on creates an *interiority* dependent on the object: that economy of *Oedipus prime* proves to be more pronounced in the little girl than it is in the little boy's monovalent *Oedipus*. Because of the anatomical difference between the sexes and, to an equal degree, for historical and cultural reasons that determine the ambivalence of the parental seduction directed at the "second sex," the girl's *Oedipus prime* exposes her to a later development that is both more fragile and more complex than the boy's.

The girl is more exposed to passivation, since clitoral excitation does not erase orificial jouissance, as it does in the little man, for whom phallicism supposedly dominates, if it does not abolish, oral/anal receptivity. Nevertheless the little girl henceforth presents herself as better defended by the constitution of a *precocious interiority*, where the introjection of the other (of the mother as mediator of the father), conveyed by the daughter/mother identification, transforms that maternal other into an indispensable object, as the vital copresence of a connection to others, experienced like a *need*, always already there, a stand-in for *desire*, to be cultivated and maintained in external reality. That copresence will endure as an absolute necessity for female psychosexuality.

In other words the little girl's dependence on her mother's love paves the way from the outset for the status of the woman's erotic object. That object will only rarely be a "partner" in desire but will rather be, more exclusively, a "lover." The woman will demand that he understand her, as if he were—an imaginary mother. The psychic and hypersensitive connection the female lover demands of the male is not likely to be mutual, and that dissymmetry inexorably determines the misunderstandings between the sexes. As for a woman's potential fulfillment in an exclusively erotic quest, she will need a very strong phallic identification to be able to conceal the broken-and-entered interiority and the need for psychic connection, as well as to be satisfied with the *mile e tre* objects *petit a*, which fail to secure fetishistic satisfaction for Don Juan himself.

Beyond the pitfalls of narcissism and passivating masochism, the complexity of *Oedipus prime* therefore constitutes the little girl as a *psychic* being of *connectedness*. The emergence of the little girl's sexuality marks the dawn of love and sociality. Of course that economy, to varying degrees, also governs the feminine side of man, which remains repressed by victorious phallicism when it is not, a contrario, abreacted by homosexual acts.

My observations on the little girl's *Oedipus prime* do not call into question the structuring role played in psychic life by phallic agency and the castration anxiety to which it leads. I confine myself to assigning these functions to their place as organizers of the unconscious but without forgetting that they intervene in the child's psyche through the mediation of parental seduction, combined with the seduced child's reactive excitability.

Post-Freudian therapy, in fact, maintains that, in participating in the repression of excessive infantile excitation, the *structuring* phallic component is accompanied by an *other libido,* which is not exclusively passive but that works itself through by shoring itself up in a *stable objectal relationship,* the foundation of psychic interiority and of relationships to others. We thus posit a bisexuality from the psyche's beginnings, formulating the hypothesis that the *feminine position* in both sexes, and more intensely for the little girl, from the outset accompanies the phallic agency in *Oedipus prime.* Is it not precisely that feminine position taking shape with *Oedipus prime,* more violently than castration anxiety in the strict sense (which would make its appearance in the phallic phase), that supports the fact that the feminine is "more inaccessible," in Freud's words, and in both sexes?[13] There is a fear of passivation, a fear of narcissistic and masochistic regression, a fear of losing the visible reference points of identity through a sensorial engulfment that runs the risk of dispersing the subject into an endogenous, even a pathological autism. The *feminine* is the first elaboration of these phobias of the *infans* and will be repressed through the subsequent accession to the phallic.

In woman, however, the *polymorphously feminine* of *Oedipus prime* remains a barely repressed continent. More exactly, it will be masked by reactional *femininity* and its displays of beautification or narcissistic reparation, by which woman's later phallicism reacts to the castration complex. It is during the phallic phase, which, between the ages of three and five, installs the subject in Oedipal triangulation, that the woman subject will effect another psychic shift, by means of which the choice of sexual identity will be definitively completed.

The widespread opinion that psychoanalysis is a "biologiza-tion of man's essence" is so easily believed that it is not superflu-ous, at this point in our journey, to recall that the psychoanalyt-ic theory of sexuality is a theory of the *copresence of sexuality and thought*. Optimal frustration, the mother/child separation, the depressive position, lack, primary identification, sublimation, idealization, the acquisition of the Ego-Ideal and of the Superego are only a few well-known stages in the positioning of the sub-ject in that web of energy *and* sense, excitability *and* law that characterizes human sexuality from the analytical perspective. The phallic phase constitutes the exemplary experience of it, which, for that very reason, I have called a "phallic *kairos*" (the Greek term *kairos* evokes a mythic "encounter" or a fateful "cut"). How is that encounter arranged?

Subsequent to neurobiological maturation and optimal expe-riences of separation from the object, the phallic stage becomes the central organizer of the copresence of sexuality and thought in both sexes. The child, who has already developed language and thought, is not satisfied to cathect his or her sex organs and their excitability but, rather, links the cognitive operations he applies to the external world to the internal movements of his drive excitations. An equivalence is therefore established be-tween the pleasure of the phallic organ on one hand and access to language, to the function of speech and thought on the oth-er. At this stage in his development the male subject in forma-tion is able to take note of the fact that the father is not only the one he wants to kill in order to appropriate the mother; hence-forth he perceives what must truly be called the father's separa-bility. The father, a third party, the regulator of the sensorial mother/child dyad, becomes a *symbolic father,* the agency of *pro-hibition* and of the *law*. The little boy, bearer of the penis, cathects that organ of pleasure, particularly since it is first and above all that of the father, whose organizing role within his fa-milial and psychic world the child is henceforth capable of rec-ognizing. Many authors have pointed out the particularities that destine the *penis* to be cathected by both sexes, in order to be-come the *phallus,* that is, the signifier of privation, of a lack of being, but also of desire, including the desire to signify—all these components make the phallus the signifier of symbolic law. The penis, visible and narcissistically recognized; erectile and charged with a strong erotogenic sensitivity; detachable, hence "culpable/cuttable," susceptible to being lost—is, as a result, apt to become the support of difference, the privileged actor in the binary system (0/1) that founds any system of meaning (marked/unmarked), the organic factor (hence real and imaginary) of our psychosexual computer.

For the little girl as well, a decisive encounter (the *kairos*) takes place between the mastery of signs and sexual excitation, welding together her being as a thinking and desiring subject. No longer oral or anal excitation but, with or without the perception of the vagina, clitoral excitation dominates in this period we call *Oedipus double prime* and where, unlike the boy, the little girl *changes object*: the father replaces the mother as the aim of desire.

At present, let us delineate the ambiguity of that change.

On one hand, like the boy, like any subject of speech, thought, and the law, the daughter *identifies with the phallus* and with the father who is its representative: without that "phallic assumption," she could not maintain her role in the universality of the human condition, a condition that makes her a speaking being according to the law. Within that phallic position, however, the girl, when compared to the boy, is disadvantaged. Lacking a penis, devalorized by that fact in every known culture that is patriarchal and patrilinear, she adheres to the phallic order while bearing the unconscious trace of *Oedipus prime*, of its polymorphous sensoriality, pledged to the desire for the mother, which impresses the indelible mark of an endogenous female homosexuality on her. As a result the girl gains full access to the phallic order—which is erected against the background of the "dark continent" or the "Minoan-Mycenean"—in accord with the modality of "as if," the illusory, "I play the game, but I know very well I *am* not part of it, because I do not *have* it." As a result, if she does not fix her phallic position in the virago's pose, this position constitutes the female subject in the register of *radical strangeness,* constitutive exclusion, irreparable solitude.

In addition, as if that necessary but artificial phallicism were not already sufficiently conflictual and difficult to assume, it must be modulated by a new psychic posture, for which *Oedipus prime* had already paved the way but that is completed only during *Oedipus double prime*: even while being a phallic subject of speech, thought, and the law, the girl withdraws, not into the passive position, as it is customarily said, but into the receptive position, to become *the object of the father*. As a speaking being, she is a phallic subject of the social symbolic order; but, as a woman, she nevertheless desires to receive the penis and obtain a child from the father, from the place of the mother with whom she continues to settle the matter of original coexcitation with *Oedipus prime*.

In following the twists that her accession to *Oedipus double prime* demands of the woman subject, we can understand the irreducible strangeness a woman experiences in the phallic/symbolic order and whose symptoms the hysteric exhibits as anxiety or conversion when she becomes fixed in a denial of the phallus and of castration. At best that strangeness takes on the aspect of an antiestablishment discontent, incomprehensible in terms of social rationality. "What does woman want?"—that is truly the burning question, which Freud was not the only one to formulate. But that strangeness can be purged in revolt or insubordination, which Hegel hailed in woman as the "eternal irony of the community." If by chance that constitutive exile of woman in the phallic/symbolic universe turns out to be more irreconcilable, it may reach the point of deviating into chronic depressivity or even intractable melancholy. Or it may be failure, with the suicidal repercussions of the "rejection of the feminine" (that of *Oedipus prime*, over which the rejection of castration, the hysteric reaction to *Oedipus double prime*, stumbles) entailed by anorexia and bulimia: all are morbid symptoms in which the gaping excitability of the cavernous (passively eroticized) body of *Oedipus prime* insistently manifests itself, incapable of defending itself against the intrusion of maternal-paternal seduction in any way other than by force-feeding or sealing off the erogenous zones.

In contrast, when the female subject manages to get through the complicated turnstile that *Oedipus prime* and *Oedipus double prime* impose on her, she may have the opportunity to acquire that strange maturity that man often lacks, bandied about as he is between the phallic pose of the "macho" and the infantile regression of the "impossible Mr. Baby." Endowed with that maturity, a mother can welcome her child not as a phallic or narcissistic prosthesis (as it most often is) but as the real presence of the other: perhaps the first, if not the only one possible other, with which civilization, as a set of relationships based no longer on Eros but on its sublimation into Agape, begins.[14]

Freud, who thought that only a "small minority" of human beings "are enabled by their displacing what they mainly value from being loved onto loving," interpreted that sublimation as a defense against the loss of the object, without deciphering it as a working-through of narcissistic love, as the biblical or gospel prescription suggests: "Love thy neighbor as thyself." He wanted to admit that the mystics, like Saint Francis of Assisi, had gone "furthest" toward an "inner feeling" created by such means, but he emphasized that that *interiority* with "inhibited aim," that "evenly suspended, steadfast, affectionate feeling" did not have "much external resemblance."[15] Could he have forgotten to consider motherhood in his argument? In fact, the founder of psychoanalysis separates the "work of civilization," that is, the "disposition toward universal love," from the "interests of the family" to which women dedicate themselves; and he reproaches women—though he acknowledges they "laid the foundations of civilization by the claims of their love"—for being incapable of a "work of civilization" because ill-suited to the sublimation of their instincts.[16] When the mother manages to transcend her domination of the child as phallic prosthesis and to remove the passion from her relationships to others, what opens for her, in a certain serenity, is the cyclical time of generations, of new beginnings, and of rebirths—beyond the time of desire, which is the time of death.

As a result, this woman is no longer participating in the game of masquerade, however amusing and seductive, in which femininity is constructed as a cosmetics to disguise the feminine. She has metabolized the cavernous and hypersensitive receptivity of

Oedipus prime into a psychic depth: that is the *feminine*. All the same, she is not unfamiliar with *femininity,* which knows how to make believe in order to defend itself from the feminine, by excelling in seduction and even in virile competition. What we perceive as a harmonious feminine personality succeeds in making the feminine coexist with femininity, receptivity with seduction, welcome with performance: a "mental hermaphrodite" is how Colette diagnosed it. That polyphony of supple relationships stripped of passion confers on the original lacunary feminine a calmed social and historical existence. This means, in effect, that *Woman* does not exist, in the sense that there are a plurality of female versions, and that the community of women is never anything but singular woman*s*.

Once female sexuality has been analyzed in that way, how do the works of female geniuses take it into account or, on the contrary, how do they detach themselves from it, get free of it?

INTERSECTIONS

Beyond the incommensurable differences and originality of the three bodies of work we have visited, we are struck by a few common traits:

1) Although concerned to defend the singularity of "who" threatened by totalitarianism, Arendt does not take refuge in solipsistic incantation. Against the isolation of philosophers, whose "melancholic tribe" she mocks (From Plato to Kant and, finally, to Heidegger) and against the anonymity of the crowds where all individual "ones" are dissolved, our "political journalist," as she liked to define herself, appeals to a political life capable of assuring the originality of every individual in memory relationships and in narrative relationships destined for others. That realization of "who" in the "relationship" is a distinctive mark of Arendt's political thought, which is both intensely libertarian and eminently social. This attracts to her the paradoxical adherence of the most atypical anarchists and of the most conservative minds. It is not a simple reversal of idealist philosophy on the platform of

sociology, nor simply a tribute to Aristotle in counterpoint to Plato, that can be deciphered in that transvaluation of the political *relationship*. It is above all the conviction, as ontological as it is existential, that the "who" "remains hidden" in the "ego alone" and "appears so sharply, so clearly, [only] to others."

Melanie Klein, for her part, radically transforms the Freudian hypothesis of an original narcissism and posits, from the start of the baby's psychic life, an "ego" capable of "object relationships," albeit partial (the breast), before the child can construct an objectal relation to the "total object" subsequent to the depressive position. For this psychoanalyst psychism is nonexistent and unthinkable from the outset without an "ego," which she immediately posits with its correlate, the relationship with the "object."

"Amorous Colette" is continually betrayed—and continually betrays—in her love relationships. She declares herself beyond the passion of love: "One of the great banalities of existence, love, is withdrawing from mine.[. . .] Having escaped from it, we perceive that all the rest is cheerful, varied, multiple." Don't be fooled, don't see that as the beginning of a melancholic remark: thanks to the friendship she offers others, and through the discipline of writing that immerses her in Being, this woman never abandons her participation in the plurality of the world, which she celebrates as a pagan mysticism involving the fulfillment of the ego through a multitude of cosmic relationships. That is truly the amorous sense of "all the rest is cheerful, varied, multiple."

In these affirmations of the *ego inseparable from the variety of its relationships*—political, psychic, sensorial, amorous, written— I would be tempted to read a constant of female psychosexuality. A woman is less isolated in erotic pleasure and more dependent on the other—whether that other is an imaginary psychic support or a need for real presence, as we have seen in briefly considering the genesis of female sexuality. Might a woman be more inclined than a man to seek and cultivate, in the *relationship,* what has to do with the blossoming of the singular, rather than stigmatizing what, in that relationship to others, restricts and bullies pleasure? And, even while rebelling against shackles, constraints, prisons, camps, and other social concentrations that "banalize" us, women would never stop seeking, all the same and forever, in the *relationship with the object*—"cheerful, varied, multiple," and constantly open to reinvention—the conditions necessary for psychic and political freedom.

2) In diagnosing totalitarianism as a radical evil that dared declare "the superfluity of human life," Arendt made herself the defender of life, on the condition that *that life possess a sense:* life not as *zoe* but as *bios,* inaugurating a biography for the memory of the Commonwealth. In the intricacies of *wanting, thinking,* and *judging,* philosophy seeks to elucidate the sense of that life coextensive with thought, which the two forms of twentieth-century totalitarianism began by destroying, in order to annihilate—along with thought—life itself. Arendt, scandalized, but without abandoning her sense of humor, can even make fun of Eichmann, who "banalizes evil" not by engaging in banal crimes (as some accuse her of having insinuated) but because he is "incapable of distinguishing good from evil," because he possesses the "sad gift of consoling himself with clichés," which is "closely related to his incapacity to *think*—to think especially from the perspective of others." Arendt made her political struggle against totalitarianism a philosophical battle for thought: not calculation-thought but inquiry-thought, taste-thought, forgiveness-thought.

In inaugurating the psychoanalysis of children, Melanie Klein did not exchange *eroticism,* which Freud placed at the foundation of psychic life, for the *pain* of the newborn, whom she assumes to be schizoparanoid, then depressive, as that "ingenious tripe butcher" (in Lacan's expression) has so often been accused of doing. In focusing on troubled childhood, and especially on infantile psychosis, which handicaps the cognitive faculty, Klein was the first to make psychoanalysis an art of tending to the capacity for thought. Bion, Winnicott, and many others after her and in discussion with her, continued to innovate in their analytical practice, making it increasingly attentive to the conditions that make the human mind possible, that lead it to an optimal creativity.

It was not only coquetry that made Colette declare herself averse to literary art. Did she refuse to let herself be confined to the fetish of the book, to the rituals of a milieu? Without a doubt. But she was far from escaping these aesthetic and social traps, whose perversities did not displease her at all. Nevertheless, this woman exercised the art of words not as a rhetoric, as a pure form, even less as a message of ideas. If she thought while writing, it was because that written thought was immediately a new life that procured her, beyond a new ego and a new body, a true osmosis with Being. Her sensual, gustatory, sonorous, fragrant, and tactile writing is a thought become flesh: Colette did not invent a literary form, she constructed an alphabet of the sensory world by embroidering the fabric, by eating the tissue of the French language. Is she a novelist, a writer? Of course, but with, as a bonus, an indomitable appetite that never wearies of remaking the world's flesh in Sido's language.

In different ways none of these three women is content to place thought, or sublimation, at the heart of life: all three identify life and thought with each other, to the point of achieving that extreme bliss where *to live is to think-sublimate-write*. The metaphysical dichotomy between "abstract" and "concrete," "meaning" and "matter," "being" and "existence," dissolves in their experiences and in their reflections. Could it be an echo of Christian incarnationism that I hear in these modern adventures, which, nevertheless, claim to be resolutely secular? Or is there not a new resonance with the female psychosexuality I sketched above, which is loath to isolate itself in the obsessive palaces of "pure thought," in superegotistical abstraction or phallic mastery of logical calculation (though many women are capable of such abstract performances—reputed to be masculine—precisely through virile identification)? Does not the feminine, on the contrary, prefer these so-called poetic regions of thought, where sense takes root in the sensory, where representations of words stand side by side with representations of things, and where ideas yield their place to drives?

3) In her philosophy of freedom, Arendt, without having had the experience of motherhood, ascribes a nodal function to the time of birth: it is because men *are born* "strangers" and "ephemeral" that freedom—which is the very capacity to begin

anew—has an ontological foundation. "That freedom [. . .] is identical to the fact that men are because they are born, that each of them is a new beginning, that each begins, in a sense, a new world." By contrast, the Reign of Terror eliminated "the very source of freedom birth confers on man, and which resides in the capacity man has to be a new beginning." To the time of worry, the time for death, whose original importance in the formation of thought she does not deny, Arendt adds a meditation inspired by Saint Augustine and Nietzsche, enriched by her own experience of twentieth-century politics, and that relies on a different temporality: that of the new beginning, of history as renewal.

Thanks to her analysis under Ferenczi and Abraham, the depressive Melanie Klein managed to be reborn and to become an analyst. Furthermore, in wresting herself from the German language and drawing a new theoretical inspiration from English within the context of British psychoanalysis, she reinforced the analyst's countertransferential involvement in the treatment, one of her most fruitful discoveries. Were these suggestions, acts of violence, intrusions on her young analysands' malleable psyches? There has been no dearth of criticism from her adversaries, and it is not always unjustified. But, in reality, through her new technique of interpretive intervention, Melanie, in her infantile fantasies, opened herself to the child who had come to consult her. Thanks to that projection of her unconscious, but always attentive to the patient's privacy, she managed to name the unspeakable trauma of the other, to have it named with the child's words. Freud practiced transference and countertransference without making them explicit, and it is Klein's female disciples, not Melanie herself, who theorized the analyst's countertransference. But it is truly Melanie who made clear the need for that projection at the origin of interpretation: in bringing back to life the child in the analyst, she made it possible to bring out the infantile in everyone. It was then Winnicott, another of Klein's attentive dissidents, who formulated analytic treatment itself as a perpetual rebirth of the subject: beyond biological destiny and the familial burden, being reborn is therefore possible for each of us. Freud bequeathed to us a vision of the timeless, *zeitlos* unconscious. Through the play of transference/countertransference, Klein and the post-Kleinians invite us to conceive of the temporality of analysis as that of a new beginning, a rebirth.

Colette avoided lingering on the inevitability of death and preferred, with Sido, to wax ecstatic about flowering: "More than to any other vital manifestation, my whole life I have looked to flowerings. It is in them that, for me, the essential drama lies, better than in death, which is only a commonplace defeat." The flowering of the "pink cactus," the blooming of plants and the birth of children: this woman, who was not an ideal mother herself—far from it—would rediscover in writing as well, in writing above all, that rhythm of her own, which is always that of the infinite, the new beginning. "Turning over a new leaf, rebuilding, being reborn, has never been beyond my strength."

That temporality, whether or not it is based on the experience of menstrual cycles and motherhood, which interrupts linear time and the course of desire-to-death, also seems to resonate with female psychosexuality. From *Oedipus prime* to *Oedipus double prime,* we have recalled, a woman completes a complex journey, changing positions and objects: passivation, receptivity, aggression, possession. She goes from the mother to the father, from the sensory to the signifiable, from the cloacal and the vaginal to the phallic, from the internal object to the external object, and back to that perpetual Oedipus, which never seems completed in the female subject, never closed, but that is appeased when love is stripped of its passion in motherhood, friendships, cosmic relationships. Could the two-faced Oedipus, interminable, always beginning again, be the source of this insistence on the rhythm of renewal, against the linear time of fated completion?

Let us recapitulate these few traits shared by our three geniuses: the permanence of relationships and of the object; the concern to safeguard the life of thought, because thought is life; and the insistence on the time of flowering and rebirth. Others, more or less convincingly, could certainly be added. The fact that they can be linked to constants of female psychosexuality, according to the psychoanalytic view, does not prevent us from encountering them as well in the works of a large number of male authors—since psychic bisexuality is shared by both sexes. Furthermore, in the course of the investigation conducted on each of our three women of genius, we noted to what degree they owed their accomplishments to their "mental hermaphroditism," to repeat Colette's expression, and to what extent, without phallic assertiveness, it would have been impossible, by all appearance, for them to realize their singularity.

I have linked a few distinguishing features of their works to female sexuality in order to underscore that phallic assertiveness did not occur as a defensive revendication against the feminine, as a mimicking of male power, which would have led our authors to be only pale epigones of the masters in their time or in their field. Rather, it served as a way for them to carve out, on the "dark continent" of the feminine, essential elements of the female experience that correspond to their psychosexual difference, thus falling into step with the deepest levels of the female unconscious and contributing to the realization of a body of work, which we, as a result, receive as authentic, since the passion for unconscious truth is the indelible mark of both the man and the woman of genius.

All the same, beyond these intersections, but also in them, what interested me as I lived with Hannah Arendt, Melanie Klein, and Colette, was, I repeat, not to note how they are like all women but how each of them, against the background of that common condition, modulated an original and unprecedented advance. Is the permanent need for a relationship with the object specific to the feminine? No doubt: but Arendt, Klein, and Colette, each in her own way, provide fruitful developments of that need and make innovations in politics, psychoanalysis, or literature. Might thought incarnated as life be more easily identifiable in a woman, with her latent hysteria, than in obsessive man? Certainly: but what counts is the specific impact of thought on life in politics, psychoanalysis, and writing, which we find in the adventure of Arendt, in a different way in Klein, and again, in a still different way in Colette. Might the rhythm of the new beginning be a counterweight to the phallic temporality of the desire-to-death, finding its foundation in female fertility and in a woman's psychic plasticity? Perhaps: but it is the incomparable version Arendt gives in politics, Klein through her projective interpretations, and Colette in her cult of plant blossomings and of writing that make their writings works of genius(es).

Attentive to sexual difference, our investigation on the female genius has led us, in short, to transcend the dichotomy of the sexes, to take our distance from the initial presupposition that posits a binary sexual system. That transcendence came about not only because psychic bisexuality appeared to us as a given, characteristic of both sexes, with dominant traits differing from one sexual identity to another and from one individual to another; not only because every sexual identity specific to a given subject is, as a result, constructed as a variation on a dominant trait; but, finally and above all, because creativity pursued to its full blossoming in genius pushes that variation to the limit, to the point of a maximum singularity, which can nevertheless still be shared. Within the risky solitude of innovation that burned each of them, Arendt, Klein, and Colette nevertheless inaugurate the possibility of a necessarily public opinion and—why not?—of a school, at best of a seduction that entices a communion of readings, a community of readers.

With their sexual, social, and political liberation, women have taken the stage in the various fields of knowledge and skill in the modern Commonwealth, which has raised the question of their equality with or difference from men. Such was the major inquiry of the twentieth century. By contrast, the third millennium will be that of individual opportunities, or it will be nothing at all. I have wanted with this triptych to aid in the move through the now old inquiry anxious to fix sexual identity. And, beyond the sexual polymorphism that is already taking shape in the global era—to the point of calling into question both the identity of each of us and the very possibility of the couple and of natural procreation—I would like to think that every subject invents in its private life a specific sex. It is there that one's genius resides, which is quite simply one's creativity.

Is there a feminine genius, then? The genius of women from the last century has invited us not to elude the question and to consider this: concerns about the feminine have been the communitarian path that has allowed our civilization to reveal, in a new way, the incommensurability of the singular. Although it took root in sexual experience, that incommensurability of genius is realized in the risks that each person is capable of taking, by calling into question thought, language, one's time, and any identity that finds shelter in them.

NOTES

1. WHY COLETTE? SHE INVENTED AN ALPHABET

1. Colette, *Ces plaisirs . . .* (1932), reissued under the title *Le pur et l'impur* (1941) and *Le blé en herbe* (1923), Pl 2:1238; see below, 297, n. 292.
2. Colette, *La naissance du jour*, Pl 3:371.
3. Ibid.
4. Colette, *Douze dialogues de bêtes*, Pl 2:40.
5. Colette, "Serpents," in *Prisons et paradis*, Pl 3:658–59.
6. Colette, *Le pur et l'impur*, Pl 3:617.
7. Ibid., 565.
8. Colette, *La Vagabonde*, Pl 1:1084.
9. Ibid., 1074, my emphasis.
10. Colette, *Le voyage égoïste*, Pl 2:1099.
11. Colette, "Fièvre," in *Journal à rebours*, Pl 4:136.
12. Colette, "Provence," ibid., 202.

13. Colette, "Le poisson au coup de pied," in *Prisons et paradis*, Pl 3:696. On that "materiality of writing" according to Colette, see G. Ducrey, *L'abécédaire de Colette* (Flammarion, 2000), 7–21.

14. Colette, *Le pur et l'impur*, Pl 3:589.

15. Colette, *Mes apprentissages*, Pl 3:1039.

16. C. Pichois and A. Brunet, *Colette* (Ed. de Fallois, 1999), 193.

17. Colette, "Provence," in *Journal à rebours*, Pl 4:203.

18. Colette, "La Chaufferette," ibid., 176.

19. Colette, "Lettre à un ami" (probably to Claude Farrère), in Sido, *Lettres à sa fille 1905–1912*, preceded by *Lettres de Colette* (Des femmes-Antoinette Fouque, "Ecrits d'hier," 1984), 25.

20. Freud discovered the importance of women's bisexuality some time after Colette. In 1931 he wrote, "Bisexuality [. . .] comes to the fore much more clearly in women than in men." S. Freud, "Female Sexuality," in *The Standard Edition of the Complete Psychological Works of Sigmund Freud*, trans. J. Strachey (London: Hogarth, 1953), 21:227–28.

21. Colette, interview in *Nouvelles Littéraires* (November 13, 1937), Pl 3:1822; cf. also "La Chaufferette," in *Journal à rebours*, Pl 4:174–75.

22. Colette, *Discours de réception à l'Académie royale de Belgique*, Pl 3:1079.

23. Quoted by J. Chalon, *Colette, l'éternelle apprentie* (Flammarion, 1998), 223, my emphasis.

24. Colette, *Sido*, Pl 3:505.

25. Colette, *La naissance du jour*, Pl 3:278.

26. Colette, *Sido*, Pl 3:503.

27. Ibid., 504.

28. Colette, *Le pur et l'impur* (1932), Pl 3:551–653.

29. Colette, *Sido*, Pl 3:517.

30. Colette, *L'ingénue libertine*, Pl 1:799.

31. Colette, *La naissance du jour*, Pl 3:282.

32. Ibid., 368.

33. Ibid., 285.

34. Sido, *Lettres à sa fille 1905–1912*, letters of February 19 and August 18, 1909, 255 and 295.

2. LIFE OR WORKS?

1. " 'You will measure only later,' Mendès told me shortly before his death, 'the power of the literary type you have created.' If only I

had created, free from any masculine suggestion, one that, in its simplicity, and even in its likeness, better deserved to endure!" Colette, *La naissance du jour,* Pl 3:316.

2. A vigilant Catulle Mendès warned her of the danger: "In twenty or thirty years, it will be known. Then you'll see what it is to have created a type in literature. You don't realize—a power, certainly, yes, certainly! But also a sort of punishment, an error that follows you around, sticks to your skin, an unbearable reward you gag on" (Colette, *Mes apprentissages,* Pl 3:1013).

3. A. Gide, *Journal,* vol. 2 (1926–50; Gallimard, "Bibliothèque de la Pléiade," 1997), 751 (February 11, 1941). And, regarding *Mes apprentissages,* on February 19, 1936: "There is much more than giftedness: a sort of *genius, very particularly feminine,* and a great intelligence." Ibid., 525, my emphasis.

4. Michèle Sarde, unfairly decried by masculist criticism, took the initiative in rehabilitating Colette's genius in the light of the women's movement of the 1970s but without confusing it with the latter: see *Colette, libre et entravée* (Stock, 1978; coll. "Points," 1984). Claude Pichois and Alain Brunet provide the most scrupulously documented biography, *Colette.* In the United States Judith Thurman produced an analytical biography whose exemplary lucidity considerably enriches French criticism: *Secrets of the Flesh: A Life of Colette* (New York: Alfred A. Knopf, 1999, forthcoming in French translation from Editions Calmann-Lévy). Let us also note Herbert Lottman, *Colette* (Fayard, 1990); Nicole Ferrier-Caverivière, *Colette l'authentique* (PUF, 1997); Claude Francis and Fernande Gontier, *Colette* (Perrin, 1997); Jean Chalon, *Colette, l'éternelle apprentie*; Michel del Castillo, *Colette, une certaine France* (Stock, 1999).

5. See G. Beaumont and A. Parinaud, *Colette* (Seuil, coll. "Ecrivains de toujours," 1951), 8.

6. Colette, *La naissance du jour,* Pl 3:316.

7. Colette, *L'étoile Vesper,* Pl 4:850.

8. Colette, "Mes idées sur le roman," in *Le Figaro* (October 30, 1937); Pl 3:1831–32.

9. Colette, *L'ingénue libertine,* Pl 1:744.

10. Colette, *La retraite sentimentale,* Pl 1:843.

11. Colette, *L'étoile Vesper,* Pl 4:814.

12. *L'Express,* November 19, 1959.

13. Has it not been noted, with the sort of irony that makes fascina-

tion bearable, that Saint Theresa of Lisieux, born on January 2, 1873, was the exact contemporary of Colette, born on January 28 of the same year? See Chalon, *Colette, l'éternelle apprentie,* 41.

14. J.-M. G. Le Clézio, *Le Monde,* January 25, 1973, quoted in Castillo, *Colette, une certaine France,* 316.

15. See below, chap. 4, "The Incestual Mother with 'One of [Her] Children,'" 133; and chap. 5, "Idealization: Latency and the Superego," 159.

16. *Nini-pattes-en-l'air:* the name for a loose woman or prostitute; literally, "Nini with her paws in the air"—trans.

17. Literally, "farts dry"; the expression describes a precise, decisive, implacably controlled style that is nevertheless nonconformist and scandalous—trans.

18. P. Morand, *1900* (Les Editions de France, 1931), 189.

19. Sido, *Lettres à sa fille 1905–1912,* letter of September 12, 1907, 117.

20. See Pichois and Brunet, *Colette,* 8: "Colette's family is like a small number of French families that do not practice village, canton, and region endogamy."

21. Francis and Gontier (*Colette*) demonstrate that the Landoy family, originally from the region of Rheims, immigrated in the fifth generation to Charleville, where Colette's grandfather Henry was born. They had gone to the West Indies and had settled there for some time, before finally returning to France. That would explain the "mixed blood" in the Landoy descendancy.

22. See Pichois and Brunet, *Colette,* 16.

23. Sido, *Lettres à sa fille 1905–1912,* letter of February 13, 1909, 254–55; letter of February 24, 1909, 259.

24. Colette, *La maison de Claudine,* Pl 2:968.

25. Ibid., 980.

26. Ibid., 1013.

27. Ibid., 1014.

28. He would not sell it until 1925, to F. Ducharne, a Colette admirer, who donated it in usufruct to the writer in 1950; Colette, with M. and Mme Ducharne, sold the residence to Docteur and Mme P. Muesser, whose descendants, Docteur and Mme Y. Muesser, are the current owners. See Pichois and Brunet, *Colette,* 46.

29. The exact relationship between the two men has not really been established. See Pichois and Brunet, *Colette,* 31 and 55: were they members of scientific societies, or did they meet as soldiers during the Crimean and Italian campaigns?

30. Ibid., 51.
31. Ibid., 55.
32. See Willy, *Indiscrétions et commentaires sur les "Claudine"* (Pro amicis, 1962), 19; episode rewritten by Colette in *Claudine à Paris,* Pl 1:354ff.
33. Colette, *Mes apprentissages,* Pl 3:998.
34. See Pichois and Brunet, *Colette,* 6off. ["Tender shoot," the conventional translation of *Le tendron,* one of Colette's novels, also means "sweet young thing"—trans.]
35. Colette, *Mes apprentissages,* Pl 3:1003.
36. Ibid., 1011.
37. Ibid., 1005.
38. Ibid., 1007.
39. Ibid.
40. Ibid., 1023.
41. See Pichois and Brunet, *Colette,* 69.
42. Colette, *Mes apprentissages,* Pl 3:1023.
43. See Chalon, *Colette, l'éternelle apprentie,* 88.
44. Quoted in Pichois and Brunet, *Colette,* 113.
45. This "poetic" and unfinished novel by Proust was written between 1895 and 1900 and published in 1952 (Gallimard, coll. "Bibliothèque de la Pléiade," 1971), 399; see below, chap. 9, "Proust? 'As in Balzac, I'm Awash in It . . . '" 368.
46. See Pichois and Brunet, *Colette,* 80.
47. F. Jammes, preface to *Douze dialogues de bêtes,* Pl 2:5–6.
48. See Colette, *Sido,* Pl 3:495–549. *Sido ou les points cardinaux* was published by Krâ in 1929; the completed and definitive text, *Sido,* by Ferenczi in 1930.
49. I will return to this idea in chap. 7: "Men and Women, Pure and Impure," 241.
50. "[1910] . . . the Colette comet thinks she can rival Halley's in brilliance!" in Chalon, *Colette, l'éternelle apprentie,* 152.
51. See Pichois and Brunet, *Colette,* 129ff.
52. See below, chap. 7, "The Infantile Revisited from the Direction of the Impure," 310.
53. Quoted by Pichois and Brunet (*Colette,* 133), who add this commentary, with which I can only agree: "One must admire Colette for demanding her right to freedom in a tone that no Frenchwoman, with the exception perhaps of Rachilde, would have had the courage to adopt publicly."

54. See Pichois and Brunet, *Colette,* 142.

55. Colette, *Mes apprentissages,* Pl 3:1024.

56. Colette, *En tournée* (Ed. Persona, 1984).

57. Sido, *Lettres à sa fille 1905–1912,* letter of February 16, 1907, 73; it was written in the context of the *Egyptian Dream* scandal in January.

58. Ibid., letter of March 16, 1907, 82.

59. Ibid., letter of July 20, 1909, 286.

60. Ibid., letter of April 3, 1909, 263.

61. Ibid., letter of February 26, 1907, 77.

62. *Le Figaro,* March 2, 1940, reprinted in F. Mauriac, "La rencontre avec Barrès," *Oeuvres autobiographiques* (Gallimard, coll. "Bibliothèque de la Pléiade," 1990), 179.

63. The play was performed in New York in 1908 at the Manhattan Opera House, without Colette and with Christine Kerf as the only French actress in the cast.

64. See Pichois and Brunet, *Colette,* 201.

65. Colette, "Les Sauvages," in *Sido,* Pl 3:547.

66. See Pichois and Brunet, *Colette,* 275.

67. See Y. Resch, "notice," in Colette, Pl 4:1156.

68. Colette, letter of September 27, 1912, to Léon Hamel, in *Lettres de la Vagabonde,* OCC 15:72.

69. Colette, *Sido,* Pl 3:533–49.

70. Colette, *Les heures longues* (1917), Pl 2:525–34 and 581–90.

71. Colette, "Un taube sur Venise," in *Les heures longues,* Pl 2:534–38: "Venice, fragile on the edge of a threatened sea, Venice, which hides under the sand like the flatfish when the gulls pass over."

72. Quoted in Pichois and Brunet, *Colette,* 231.

73. See below, chap. 7, "Mother and Child," 287.

74. See Colette, *Lettres à ses pairs,* letter from Marcel Proust to Colette (May? 1919), text established and annotated by C. Pichois and R. Forlain, OCC 16:135–36; see also below, chap. 7, "Precocious Maturity, or Delicacy according to Mitsou and Gigi," 267.

75. According to *L'étoile Vesper,* Pl 4:843.

76. See below, chap. 5, "Depression, Perversion, Sublimation," 155.

77. Colette, *Le pur et l'impur,* Pl 3:645.

78. "On the edge of a desk, with the window behind me, my elbow askew and my knees twisted, I wrote with application and indifference. [. . .] I took to my work with that slow and stubborn, bureaucratic, courage, which has not left me." Colette, *Mes apprentissages,* Pl 3:995–1029.

79. B. de Jouvenel, "La vérité sur *Chéri*," in Colette, Pl 2:lv.

80. Ibid., lvi.

81. See Pichois and Brunet, *Colette*, 533n. 55.

82. Freud maintained that the "psychical reality" of the dream and the fantasy is a resistant field, the only truly "real" one, compared with other psychic phenomena. See Freud, *The Interpretation of Dreams,* in *The Standard Edition,* 5:613.

83. De Jouvenel, "La vérité sur *Chéri*," lvii.

84. Colette, letter from early August 1921, in *Lettres à Marguerite Moreno,* OCC 14:228.

85. De Jouvenel, "La vérité sur *Chéri*," lvii.

86. Colette, *Mes apprentissages,* Pl 3:1024.

87. Colette, *La maison de Claudine,* Pl 2:968.

88. See below, chap. 4, "Who Is Sido?" 123.

89. "She's a filthy thing," she would tell Cocteau, later calling her "vulgar by birth" in her journal. See Pichois and Brunet, *Colette,* 277.

90. Colette, letter of June 23, 1925, in *Lettres à Marguerite Moreno,* OCC 14:278.

91. See Chalon, *Colette, l'éternelle apprentie,* 244–45, 262, 269, 272–73.

92. See below, chap. 6, "The Metamorphic Body: Plants, Beasts, and Monsters," 194: chap. 6, " . . . My Old Subtle Senses," 194; chap. 6, "O Geraniums, O Foxglove . . . ," 209; chap. 6, "The Animal, or An Unused Love," 213.

93. "Upon arriving, Cocteau showed us a sick bird he had found on the Champs-Elysées. Colette took it, examined it, and wrung its neck in the garden." In J. Green, *Oeuvres complètes* (Gallimard, coll. "Bibliothèque de la Pléiade," 1975), 4:48, *Journal,* May 25, 1929, quoted by Pichois and Brunet, *Colette,* 311.

94. See below, chap. 7, "Mother and Child," 287.

95. Colette de Jouvenel, in S. Chardin, *Ils parlent de leur mère* (Hachette, 1979), 104–5: "A child cannot bear sharing his mother . . . To put it bluntly, he is *cuckolded.*[. . .] I wanted to be Jewish because I had many Jewish friends at high school whose families fussed over them. I dreamed of regular visits, of sweets, of fine clothes."

96. See Pichois, "notice," in Colette, Pl 1:1593.

97. Colette, letter to Misz Marchand, July 1933, in *Lettres de la Vagabonde,* OCC 15:210. [The grammatical error consists of taking

argent (money) for a feminine noun, when it is grammatically masculine in French. The mistake may have been made under the influence of the common expression *gagner la vie,* to earn one's living; *vie* is a feminine noun—trans.] The *Robert* dictionary indicates that *argent* can appear in the feminine in folk expressions (*de la bonne argent,* good money, for *du bon argent*).

98. See *Journal de Renée Hamon,* September 1938, reprinted in Colette, *Lettres au Petit Corsaire,* OCC 16:47.

99. See Pichois and Brunet, preface, in Colette, Pl 4:x.

100. See Pichois and Brunet, *Colette,* 441.

101. The weekly columns for *Le Petit Parisien* would be collected in *From My Window,* which became *Paris from My Window;* see Colette, Pl 4:xi.

102. See below, chap. 8, "A Little Politics All the Same," 322.

103. H. Lottman, *Colette,* 379–80.

104. In December 1942.

105. See Colette, preface, Pl 4:xiv.

106. L. Aragon, "Madame Colette," *Les Lettres Françaises,* August 12–19, 1954, reprinted in *Cahiers Colette* 16 (1994): 123–29: "Une odeur d'innocence envahit les chemins [. . .]. Mélange singulier de mémoire et d'oubli [. . .]. Etrangère à l'histoire et partout asservie [. . .]. Une aile va manquer au murmure français." ["An odor of innocence invades the roads.[. . .] A singular mixture of memory and forgetting.[. . .] A stranger to history and everywhere enslaved.[. . .] A wing will be missing from the rustling of French."]

107. See below, chap. 8, "A Little Politics All the Same," 322.

108. M. Goudeket, *Près de Colette* (Flammarion, 1956), 197.

109. *Le Cri du Peuple,* March 4, 1942.

110. See below, 65–66.

111. See below, chap. 9, 359, n. 7.

112. The work is cited as one of "the major political and social studies," next to those of Charles Maurras, Léon Daudet, Joseph de Maistre, and Napoleon. See Thurman, *Secrets of the Flesh,* 437.

113. Bertrand, at first fascinated by National Socialism, later joined the Allies and worked for them, taking advantage of the Germans' trust. See below, chap. 8, "The Occupation, or the Politics of the Gourmand Ostrich," 326.

114. Lottman, *Colette,* 262–63.

115. Thurman, *Secrets of the Flesh,* 472 and 475.

116. See R. de Jouvenel, *Confidences d'un ancien sous-marin du PCF* (Julliard, 1980); M. Mercier, "Colette et Renaud de Jouvenel," in *Cahiers Colette* 22 (2000): 9–54.

117. See B. de Jouvenel, *Un voyageur dans le siècle* (Robert Laffont, 1979), 250–56.

118. Colette, letter to Germaine Beaumont of 1942, in *Lettres à Annie de Pène et Germaine Beaumont* (Flammarion, 1995), 210.

119. Colette, *Lettres aux Petites Fermières* (Le Castor Astral, 1992), 90.

120. Colette, letter of April 4, 1944, in *Lettres à Marguerite Moreno*, OCC 14:436.

121. Ibid., letter of June 7, 1944, 444.

122. Céline, letter to Jean Paulhan of June 5, 1950, in *Lettres à la NRF* (Gallimard, 1991), 106. My thanks to Henri Godard for pointing out Céline's outbursts against Colette.

123. Thurman, *Secrets of the Flesh,* 470.

124. Aragon, "Madame Colette," see above n. 106.

125. S. de Beauvoir, *Lettres à Nelson Algren* (Gallimard, 1997), letter of March 7, 1948, 189.

126. Ibid.

127. See S. de Beauvoir, *La force des choses* (Gallimard, coll. "Folio,") 2:490; and E. Lecarme-Tabone, "Simone de Beauvoir et Colette," in *Cahiers Colette* 20 (1989): 119–25.

128. S. de Beauvoir, *Le deuxième sexe,* vol. 2: *L'expérience vécue* (Gallimard, coll. "Folio Essais," 1989), 48, 121, 140, 174, 188, 196, 208, 210, 256, 286, 338, 358, 379, 410, 413, 421, 446, 465, 562, 574–78, 580, 629, 630, 636.

129. Despite what Thurman says (*Secrets of the Flesh,* 451–54); see also below, chap. 8, "A Little Politics All the Same," 322.

130. In her will of July 17, 1945, Colette disowned her daughter, on a suggestion from Goudeket; see Colette, Pl 4: xiv. It was only at the end of her life, when she had succeeded in recuperating the rights to her mother's works after lengthy litigations with Goudeket, nicknamed the "Crocodile," that Colette de Jouvenel rediscovered the tenderness she felt toward Colette and came to consider herself the "priestess" of that "Bible." (See Castillo, *Colette, une certaine France,* 293). Colette de Jouvenel died on September 16, 1981.

131. See below, chap. 9, "Still Writing, Between Balzac and Proust," 358.

132. Manuscript quoted in Lottman, *Colette,* 431.

133. See Pichois and Brunet, preface, in Colette, Pl 4:xv.
134. Ibid., xvii–xxii.
135. See A. Virmaux and O. Virmaux, *Colette au cinéma* (Flammarion, 1975).
136. See below, chap. 8, "Living the Image: From Illustration . . . ," 341; and chap. 8, " . . . To Cinema: In Praise of the Imaginary," 348.
137. Colette, letter to Gérard d'Houville, late April 1931 (pseudonym of Marie de Régnier), in *Lettres à ses pairs,* OCC 16:350.

3. WRITING: *Tendrils of the Vine*

1. Colette, "La Chaufferette," in *Journal à rebours,* Pl 4:174–75.
2. Colette, *Discours de réception à l'Académie royale de Belgique,* Pl 3:1079. "The source of humility lies in the awareness of an unworthiness—and sometimes as well in the dazzling awareness of a holiness. Where in my career could I have drawn on anything but astonishment?" (ibid.).
3. Colette, interview in *Nouvelles Littéraires,* November 13, 1937, Pl 3:1822. "I have no other dark clouds in my life. Money worries—you get out of them. But this forced labor. [. . .] I'm so content, so content when I'm not writing that I see clearly that I ought not to write. It's an open-and-shut case. To reestablish my good name, I always try to do what I do as well as I can. That's also a consolation. The blue paper as well, that's to console me" (ibid.).
4. Colette, letter of November 1931 to Lucie Delarue-Mardrus, in *Lettres à ses pairs,* OCC 16:253.
5. Colette, *Mes apprentissages,* Pl 3:1041, my emphasis.
6. Colette, *Le fanal bleu,* Pl 4:1060.
7. Colette, *Belles saisons,* OCC 11:45.
8. Colette, "Gîte d'écrivain," in *Derniers écrits,* OCC 14:61.
9. Colette, *Mes apprentissages,* Pl 3:1041, my emphasis.
10. See P. D'Hollander, *Colette: Ses apprentissages* (Klincksieck, 1989), 178ff; and M. Mercier, "notice," in Colette, Pl 1:1530–44.
11. Colette, *Mes apprentissages,* Pl 3:1041.
12. See below, chap. 6, "O Geraniums, O Foxglove . . . ," 209; and chap. 6, "The Animal, or an Unused Love," 213.
13. Issue 1 (May 15, 1905); 2 (June 1), 3 (June 15); 5 (July 15); 11 (October 15); then 1 (January 1, 1906).
14. See S. Freud, "On Psychotherapy," in *The Standard Edition,* 7:260.

15. Colette, *Paysages et portraits,* OCC 8:439.
16. As she would describe it herself in *Mes apprentissages,* PL 3:1065.
17. *Rigadon:* a traditional French dance—trans.
18. Colette, *Claudine à l'école,* Pl 1:7–8.
19. Ibid., 8.
20. Ibid., 155.
21. Colette, *Claudine à Paris,* Pl 1:278.
22. Colette, *Claudine en ménage,* Pl 1:514.
23. Ibid., 517.
24. Ibid., 524.
25. Colette, *La retraite sentimentale,* Pl 1:953.
26. Colette, *Lettre de Claudine à Renaud,* appendix, Pl 1:527–29, my emphasis.
27. See J. Kristeva, *Le temps sensible: Proust et l'expérience littéraire* (Gallimard, 1994), 211–26.
28. *Le Mercure Musical,* May 15, 1905.
29. Colette, *Les vrilles de la vigne ,* Pl 1:959–61. See below, 120–22.
30. Colette, *Douze dialogues de bêtes,* Pl 2:8–10. See below, chap. 6, "The Metamorphic Body: Plants, Beasts, and Monsters," 194.
31. *Ecorché:* an anatomical figure or manikin showing the muscles and bones that are visible with the skin removed (*Webster's Third International Dictionary*)—trans.
32. Colette, "Les Paons," in *Prisons et paradis,* Pl 3:659–60.
33. Colette, *Bella-Vista,* Pl 3:1144–45.
34. In Colette, *Aventures quotidiennes* (1924) and *Prisons et paradis* (1932); see below, chap. 6, "If 'Mme Colette' Is Not a Monster . . . ," 224.
35. Colette, "Assassins," *Le Figaro,* May 11, 1924; reprinted in *Aventures quotidiennes,* Pl 3:85.
36. Colette, *Le pur et l'impur,* Pl 3:561. See also the allusion to "Mme Odenowska's tame nightingale," which, though Polish, betrays its owner for an instant and falls asleep on the writer's shoulder; in Colette, *L'étoile Vesper,* Pl 4:877–78.
37. See Colette, "Papillons," *Akademos,* March 15, 1909, reprinted in *La paix chez les bêtes* (1916), (Pl 2:126–37); "Papillons" (1923), "Journal intermittent," in *En pays connu* (OCC 11:350); *Splendeur des papillons* (1937, Plon); "Papillons," in *Journal à rebours* (1941), Pl 4:184–87; and Vladimir Nabokov, *Nabokov's Butterflies,* ed. Brian Boyd and Robert Michael Pyle (Boston: Beacon Press, 2000).

38. Colette, "Fièvre," in *Journal à rebours,* Pl 4:138.
39. Colette, *Mes apprentissages,* Pl 3:1008.
40. Colette, *Claudine s'en va,* Pl 1:544–633, and "notice," ibid., 1533.
41. See below, chap. 4, "The Incestual Mother with 'One of [Her] Children,'" 133; and chap. 7, "A Queen of Bisexuality," 260.
42. Colette, *Claudine en ménage,* Pl 1:441, 475, 488.
43. Colette, *Mes apprentissages,* Pl 3:1021.
44. Colette, "Propagande," in *La maison de Claudine,* Pl 2:995.
45. Colette, "Vins," "La treille muscate," in *Prisons et paradis,* Pl 3:691.
46. Ibid., 692.
47. Carnaval is the Mardi Gras celebration lasting from the Feast of Kings (Epiphany) until Ash Wednesday—trans.
48. "Nuit blanche," "Jour gris," and "Le dernier feu" are preceded by the dedication *For M.,* which will disappear when Colette distances herself from her lover. That effacement may attest less to a settling of accounts with Missy than to a station on the way to sublimation, which for Colette is a detachment from any love relationship: "one of the great banalities of existence, love" (Colette, *La naissance du jour* [1928], Pl 3:285).
49. See below, chap. 7, "A Queen of Bisexuality," 260.
50. C. Baudelaire, *Paradis artificiels* (Gallimard, coll. "Bibliothèque de la Pléiade," 1975), 419–20 and 398.
51. Colette, "Fleurs," "La treille muscate," in *Prisons et paradis,* Pl 3:699, my emphasis.
52. "Truth will begin only at the moment the writer takes *two different objects,* posits their *relationship,* analogous in the art world to the unique relationship of the law of causality in the world of science, and encloses them in the *necessary rings of a beautiful style.* And even, like life, when bringing together a quality common to two sensations, he will extract their common essence by reuniting one with the other to draw them away from the contingencies of time, in a *metaphor.*" M. Proust, *A la recherche du temps perdu* (Gallimard, coll. "Bibliothèque de la Pléiade"), 4:468, my emphasis.
53. L. Aragon, *Le traité du style* (Gallimard, NRF, 1928), 209.
54. R. Barthes writes: "It is not the diversity of opinions that astonishes and excites; it is their exact oppositeness; it is enough to make you exclaim: *that's too much!* That may be a structural, or tragic, jouissance strictly speaking." *R. Barthes par R. Barthes* (Seuil, 1975), 66, quoted in D. Deltel, "Le paradoxe dans l'écriture de Colette," in *Colette, Nouvelles approches critiques,* proceed-

ings of the Sarrrebrück colloquium, June 22–23, 1984 (Nizet, 1986), 160.

55. Colette, "Fleurs," "La treille muscate," in *Prisons et paradis*, Pl 3:699.

56. See J. Kristeva, *Sens et non-sens de la révolte* (Fayard, 1996), 259 and 287.

57. Colette, "Les paons," "Paradis terrestres," in *Prisons et paradis*, Pl 3:661, my emphasis.

58. Colette, *Le fanal bleu*, Pl 4:1010.

59. Colette, *Mes apprentissages*, Pl 3:987.

60. Colette, *La jumelle noire*, OCC 12:63.

61. Colette, *Le fanal bleu*, Pl 4:966.

62. Colette, *L'étoile Vesper*, Pl 4:859.

63. G. Apollinaire, "Sur la littérature féminine" (columns published under the pseudonym "Louise Lalanne" in the review *Les marges* [1909]), in *Oeuvres en prose complètes* (Gallimard, 1991), 2:923.

64. Ibid., 921.

65. Ibid., 924.

66. Ibid., 1671.

67. Interview with Colette by F. Lefèvre, *Nouvelles Littéraires,* March 24, 1926.

68. Reported by C. Chauvière, *Colette* (Firmin-Didot, 1931), 210.

69. Interview with G. de Sissant and P. Darius, *Gringoire,* December 4, 1931, quoted in J. Dupont, *Colette* (Hachette, 1995), 145.

70. Colette, "Fleurs," in *Mélanges,* OCC 14:11.

71. See below, chap. 9, "Memory and Worthiness," 379.

72. Colette, *Le pur et l'impur,* Pl 3:617.

73. Colette, "Léopold Marchand par Colette," *Journal de Monaco,* December 9, 1924, in *Lettres de la Vagabonde,* OCC 15:264.

74. Which follows the logic of "secondary processes" specific to consciousness, according to Freud.

75. Colette, *La jumelle noire,* OCC 12:51.

76. Ibid., 151.

77. P. Morand, *1900,* 189: "A few simple, dense, tight styles *pètent sec* in that suffocating, vulgarly elegant atmosphere—that is Colette."

78. Colette, *Gigi,* Pl 4:520.

79. Colette, *L'étoile Vesper,* Pl 4:814.

80. See below, chap. 5, "Idealization: Latency and the Superego," 159; and chap. 6, "The Metamorphic Body: Plants, Beasts, and Monsters," 194.

81. Colette, *Sido*, Pl 3:502.
82. Colette, *La naissance du jour*, Pl 3:315.
83. Colette, "Un suicidé," in *Paysages et portraits*, OCC 13:393.
84. Colette, *Le fanal bleu*, Pl 4:968.
85. Colette, *Mes apprentissages*, Pl 3:1030, my emphasis.
86. Colette, *La Vagabonde*, Pl 1:1082.
87. Colette, *L'ingénue libertine*, Pl 1:744.
88. Colette, *La retraite sentimentale*, Pl 1:843.
89. Colette, *Mes apprentissages*, Pl 3:1009.
90. Colette, *Le pur et l'impur*, Pl 3:642.
91. Colette, *Mes apprentissages*, Pl 3:984, my emphasis.
92. Colette, *La naissance du jour*, Pl 3:286.
93. Colette, *L'étoile Vesper*, Pl 4:814.
94. Colette, *La naissance du jour*, Pl 3:293.
95. Ibid., 295.
96. P. Valéry, *Tel Quel*, in *Oeuvres* (Gallimard, coll. "Bibliothèque de la Pléiade," 1960), 2:569.
97. See below, chap. 5, "Idealization: Latency and the Superego," 159.
98. Colette, *La naissance du jour*, Pl 3:341.
99. Letter to André Billy, between April 18 and April 24, 1928, regarding *Break of Day*, in *Lettres à ses pairs*, OCC 16:270.
100. Colette, *La naissance du jour* (1928), Pl 3:304.
101. Ibid., 348.
102. Ibid., 349–50.
103. Ibid., 304.
104. Colette, *La naissance du jour*, Pl 3:277. In reality Sido accepted her son-in-law's invitation, adding that she was obliged to abandon her cat, a sedum, and a gloxinia for the pleasure of visiting her daughter. See Colette, Pl 2:1397.
105. See above, chap. 1, "Why Colette?", 1–3.
106. Colette, *La naissance du jour*, Pl 3:365, my emphasis.
107. Colette, *Mes apprentissages*, Pl 3:1069, my emphasis.
108. Colette, *La maison de Claudine*, Pl 2:1020–21.
109. Colette, *Le pur et l'impur*, Pl 3:556.
110. See N. Houssa, *Le souci de l'expression chez Colette* (Ed. du Palais de l'Académie, 1958), 159–64.
111. See R. Barthes, who mentions an "out-loud writing" in *Le plaisir du texte* (Seuil, 1973), 104, and the excellent commentary by Y. Resch in Colette, Pl 2:1672.
112. Colette, *La maison de Claudine*, Pl 2:986–87.

113. Ibid., 986.
114. Colette, "Nouveautés" (1924), in *Le voyage égoïste*, Pl 2:1160.
115. Colette, *Paris de ma fenêtre*, Pl 4:598.
116. Colette, "Flore et pomone," in *Gigi*, Pl 4:533.
117. *Baguenaudier:* a Mediterranean shrub of the legumenosae family—trans.
118. Ibid., 556.
119. Ibid., 558.
120. Colette, "L'enfant malade," in *Gigi*, Pl 4:490.
121. Colette, *Le toutounier*, Pl 3:1257.
122. Ibid., 1227–28.
123. Colette, "Flore et pomone," in *Gigi*, Pl 4:548–49.
124. Colette, *Mes apprentissages*, Pl 3:1069, already quoted above, 112.
125. See M.-C. Bellosta, "notice," in Colette, Pl 3:1825.
126. R. Gignoux, "Colette," in *Les Cahiers d'Aujourd'hui* 8 (December 1913): 413, reprinted in Pl 2: xxii.
127. All extracts in this appendix are taken from Colette, Pl 1:959–61.

4. WHO IS SIDO?

1. See M. Delcroix, "notice," in Colette, Pl 2:1612–16.
2. Colette, *Claudine à l'école*, Pl 1:27.
3. Colette, *Claudine à Paris*, Pl 1:349.
4. Colette, *Claudine à l'école*, Pl 1:122.
5. Colette, *L'ingénue libertine*, Pl 1:675.
6. Ibid., 676.
7. Ibid., 728.
8. Sido, letter of February 26, 1907, 76.
9. Colette, "Le dernier feu," in *Les vrilles de la vigne*, Pl 1:978–79.
10. Ibid., 974.
11. Ibid., 973–74.
12. Colette, "Nuit blanche," in *Les vrilles de la vigne*, Pl 1:971.
13. Ibid., 972.
14. Colette, *La Vagabonde*, Pl 1:1207, my emphasis.
15. Colette, "notice," "Les sabots," in *Les vrilles de la vigne*, Pl 1:1545–46.
16. *Le Matin*, September 28, 1911, reprinted in *Dans la foule* (1913), Pl 2:642.
17. Ibid., 643.

18. Discovered by Claude Pichois, and which Colette dates to 1912, "if I am not mistaken"; see Pl 2:1085–87 and 1611.

19. Colette, *Mes apprentissages*, Pl 3:1006.

20. Colette, preface, in *La maison de Claudine*, OCC 6:11.

21. See above, chap. 2, "Life or Works?" 26.

22. See M. Klein, *The Writings of Melanie Klein*, vol. 3: *Love, Guilt, and Reparation, and Other Works, 1921–1945* (Delacorte/Seymour Lawrence, 1975), 214; and J. Kristeva, *Female Genius*, vol. 2, *Melanie Klein* (Columbia University Press, 2001), 186–87. See also Colette, Pl 3:149–70, and C. Milner's "notice," 133–40, as well as her "Melanie Klein et les sortilèges de Colette," in *Cahiers Colette* nos. 3–4 (1993): 36–44.

23. Colette, "La Chaufferette," in *Journal à rebours*, Pl 4:174: " . . . when at six I knew how to read, but did not want to learn to write. No, I did not want to write. When one can enter the enchanted kingdom of reading, why write?"

24. Colette, *L'enfant et les sortilèges*, Pl 3:151.

25. Ibid., 153.

26. Ibid., 162.

27. Ibid., 167.

28. Colette, *La retraite sentimentale*, Pl 1:914.

29. It is reminiscent of the squirrel Rikki-Tikki-Tavi in Kipling's *Jungle Book*, which Colette and Sido adored.

30. Colette, "Ecureuil," in *Prisons et paradis*, Pl 3:662–66 and 1603.

31. Colette, *L'enfant et les sortilèges*, Pl 3:168–69.

32. Ibid., 165.

33. Ibid., 167.

34. Colette, "Un salon en 1900," in *Journal à rebours*, Pl 4:167.

35. Colette, "Le Capitaine," in *Sido*, Pl 3:519, my emphasis.

36. De Jouvenel, "La vérité sur Chéri," lvii.

37. See M. Delcroix, "notice," Pl 2:1614.

38. Colette, *La naissance du jour*, Pl 3:277.

39. See M. Delcroix, "notice," Pl 2:1617.

40. Ibid., 275.

41. Ibid., 318.

42. Colette, *Sido*, Pl 3:505.

43. Colette, *La maison de Claudine*, Pl 2:996.

44. Ibid., 1046.

45. Colette, *Sido*, Pl 3:496.

46. ["The House of Claudine" is the French title of *My Mother's House*—trans.]

47. Colette, *La maison de Claudine,* Pl 2:970.

48. Ibid., 991–92.

49. Colette, *Chéri,* Pl 2:732.

50. Ibid., 828.

51. Colette, *Le blé en herbe* Pl 2:1213.

52. Ibid., 1224.

53. Colette, *La maison de Claudine,* Pl 2:968, my emphasis.

54. See below, chap. 7, "Those Pleasures . . . ," 297; and chap. 7, "The Infantile Revisited . . . ," 310.

55. For a view different from my own, see the very fine study by M.-F. Berthu-Courtivron, *Mère et fille, l'enjeu du pouvoir: Essai sur les écrits autobiographiques de Colette* (Geneva: Droz, 1993).

56. Colette, *La maison de Claudine,* Pl 2:1056.

57. In Heidegger's usage of the term *Zeitgen,* "temporalize" has the sense of "mature." See Martin Heidegger, *Being and Time,* trans. J. Macquarrie and E. Robinson (Oxford: Basil Blackwall, 1962), 411.

58. Colette, *La maison de Claudine,* Pl 2:1057.

59. Colette, *Sido,* Pl 3:501.

60. Ibid.

61. Sido, letter of March 29, 1907, 86; and also, shortly before her death, the letter of May 27, 1912, ibid., 504.

62. Colette, *La maison de Claudine,* Pl 2:1042.

63. Ibid., 1042.

64. Ibid., 1044.

65. Ibid., 1043.

66. Ibid., 1051.

67. Colette, *La naissance du jour,* Pl 3:278.

68. Colette, *Sido,* Pl 3:509.

69. Colette, *La maison de Claudine,* Pl 2:973.

70. J.-P. Sartre, *Lettres au Castor* (Gallimard, 1983), 227 (July 1939).

71. Colette, *La maison de Claudine,* notes and variants, Pl 2:1632.

72. Colette, *Bella-Vista* (1937), Pl 3:1214.

73. Colette, *Mes apprentissages,* Pl 3:1064.

74. Colette, *La naissance du jour,* Pl 3:292.

75. Colette, *La maison de Claudine,* Pl 2:1006–7.

76. Colette, *La naissance du jour,* Pl 3:319.

77. Colette, *Sido*, Pl 3:509.
78. Colette, "Mésanges," in *Aventures quotidiennes*, Pl 3:111–12.
79. Colette, *Sido*, Pl 3:496.
80. Colette, *La maison de Claudine*, Pl 2:987.
81. Ibid., 990.
82. Ibid., 1056.
83. Colette, *La naissance du jour*, Pl 3:289; then *Sido*, Pl 3:506.
84. Colette, *La naissance du jour*, Pl 3:290.
85. Colette, *L'étoile Vesper* (1946), Pl 4:813.
86. Colette, *La naissance du jour*, Pl 3:289.
87. Ibid., 360.
88. Colette, *La maison de Claudine*, Pl 2:989.
89. Ibid., 1048.
90. Colette, *La naissance du jour*, Pl 3:292.
91. Ibid., 294.
92. Colette, *La maison de Claudine*, Pl 2:968.
93. Colette, "Automne," in *Journal à rebours*, Pl 4:164.
94. Sido, undated letter of 1907, 109ff.
95. Ibid., letter of March 10, 1908, 161.
96. Ibid., letter of July 8, 1910, 367.
97. Ibid., letter of November 6, 1907, 126. This passage, "Let's just bet that her son has a mistress," is designated as a "jewel" by Colette when she cites it in her letter of July 9, 1927, to Marguerite Moreno, in Colette, *Lettres à Marguerite Moreno*, OCC 14:312. Colette was completing *Break of Day* (1928) at the time.
98. Colette, *La maison de Claudine*, Pl 2:1036.
99. Colette, *La naissance du jour*, Pl 3:290, my emphasis.
100. Colette, *La maison de Claudine*, Pl 2:1053–54.
101. Colette, *La naissance du jour*, Pl 3:295–96.
102. Ibid., 289.
103. Colette, *Sido*, Pl 3:508.
104. Colette, *La naissance du jour*, Pl 3:371.
105. Ibid.
106. Ibid., 370.
107. Ibid., 335.
108. Colette, *La maison de Claudine*, Pl 2:1053.
109. Colette, *La naissance du jour*, Pl 3:278.
110. Ibid., 290.
111. Colette, *Sido*, Pl 3:502.
112. Colette, *La maison de Claudine*, Pl 2:983.

113. Ibid., 984.

114. Ibid.

115. Sido, letter of February 16, 1907, 73.

116. Colette, *Sido,* Pl 3:512.

117. Colette, *Mes apprentissages,* Pl 3:1039.

118. Sido, letter of July 20, 1909, 286.

119. Sido, letter of February 4, 1911, 409.

120. Colette, *La naissance du jour,* Pl 3:278.

121. Ibid., 370.

122. Sido, letter of April 1, 1907, 89.

123. Colette, *La maison de Claudine,* Pl 2:981.

124. See below, chap. 8, "The Occupation, or the Politics of the Gourmand Ostrich," 326.

125. Sido, undated letter of 1911, 414.

126. Ibid., letter of April 16, 1907, 89.

127. Ibid., letter of July 24, 1909, 288.

5. DEPRESSION, PERVERSION, SUBLIMATION

1. S. Freud, *Three Essays on the Theory of Sexuality,* in *The Standard Edition,* 7:191.

2. See R.-J. Stoller, *La perversion, forme érotique de la haine* (Payot, 197); I. Barande and R. Barande, "Antinomie du concept de perversion et épigenèse de l'appétit d'excitation," in *Revue Française de Psychanalyse* 47, 1 (1983): 208.

3. Freud, *Three Essays,* 7:150.

4. S. Freud, "Leonardo da Vinci and a Memory of His Childhood," in *The Standard Edition,* 11:117.

5. Barande and Barande, "Antinomie du concept de perversion," 205–9.

6. S. Freud, *Introductory Lectures on Psycho-Analysis,* in *The Standard Edition,* 15:208 [translation slightly modified—trans.].

7. Ibid., 16:316.

8. Ibid., 16:348.

9. S. Freud, "A Child Is Being Beaten" (1919), in *The Standard Edition,* 17:177–265.

10. Freud, *Three Essays,* 7:161.

11. S. Freud, *Extracts from the Fliess Papers* (1897–1902), in *The Standard Edition,* 1:243.

12. S. Freud, "Fragment of an Analysis of a Case of Hysteria," (1900),

in *The Standard Edition*, 7:50; see also S. Freud, *Three Essays*, 7:166ff.

13. Freud, *Introductory Lectures*, 16:344.

14. Freud, *Extracts from the Fliess Papers*, 1:280.

15. S. Freud, "Psycho-Analytic Notes on an Autobiographical Account of a Case of Paranoia (Dementia Paranoides)" (1911), in *The Standard Edition*, 12:69n. 1.

16. Freud, *Three Essays*, 7:161, my emphasis [translation slightly modified; the Strachey translation has "instinct" for "drive"—trans.].

17. Ibid., 7:178, my emphasis [translation slightly modified—trans.].

18. See A. Green, "L'idéal: Mesure et démesure" (1983), in *La folie privée: Psychanalyse des cas limites* (Gallimard, 1990), 255–92.

19. See M. Gitnacht, "Perversion, sublimation et répétition transférentielle," in *Revue Française de Psychanalyse* 62 (1992): 1802.

20. On sublimation and its relation to narcissism and the desintrication of the drives, see S. Freud, "The Ego and the Id" (1923), in *The Standard Edition*, 19:46: "The transformation [of erotic libido] into ego-libido [. . .] involves an abandonment of sexual aims, a desexualization.[. . .] By thus getting hold of the libido from the object-cathexes, setting itself up as sole love-object, and desexualizing or sublimating the libido of the id, the ego is working in opposition to the purposes of Eros and placing itself at the service of the opposing impulses of the drives."

21. Freud, "The Ego and the Id," 19:36.

22. J. Lacan, *Le Séminaire RSI* (1974–75), session of April 8, 1975, in *Ornicar*, no. 5, 43, text established by J.-A. Miller.

23. J. Lacan, *Le Séminaire, Le sinthomme* (1975–76), session of February 10, 1976, in *Ornicar*, no. 8, 11, text established by J.-A. Miller.

24. Freud, "The Ego and the Id," 19:46 [translation slightly modified—trans.].

25. S. Freud, "On the Grounds for Detaching a Particular Syndrome from Neurasthenia under the Description 'Anxiety Neurosis' " (1895), in *Standard Edition*, 3:109.

26. "There is a jouissance [. . .] *beyond the phallus*. . . . There is a jouissance proper to her, of which she may know nothing, except that she feels it—that, *ça*, she knows. She knows it, of course, when *ça* happens. *Ça* does not happen to all of them." in J. Lacan, *Le Séminaire*, book 20, *Encore* (1972–73) (Seuil, 1975), 69 [*ça* is also the French term for "id"—trans.]. What follows is this ar-

gument, which will interest lovers of a mystical Colette: "And why not interpret a face of the Other, the God face, as supported by a feminine jouissance?" Ibid., 71. And, further on: "The Other is not simply the place where truth stammers. It deserves to represent that to which woman has the fundamental relation." Ibid., 75.

27. See J. Lacan, "L'étourdit," in *Scilicet*, 4 (1973): 23. The jouissance man has of woman "divides her, making solitude her partner, while union remains on the threshold." See also C. Millot, "Les deux sources," in *La vocation de l'écrivain* (Gallimard, coll. "L'Infini," 1991), 81.

28. See above, chap. 3, "Metaphors? No, Metamorphoses," 95, and chap. 3, "The Solitude of Music and of Crime," 110.

29. See J. Kristeva, *Pouvoirs de l'horreur: Essai sur l'abjection* (Seuil, 1980), 43–66.

30. See J. Chasseguet, "Introduction à la discussion du rapport de Massimo Tomasini," in *Revue Française de Psychanalyse* 56 (1992): 1618.

31. Ibid., 1620.

32. See M. Tomasini, "Désidentification primaire, angoisse de séparation et formation de structure perverse," in *Revue Française de Psychanalyse* 56 (1992): 1559.

33. See Chasseguet, "Introduction à la discussion," 1622–63.

34. See J. McDougall, "De la douleur psychique et du psychosoma," in *Plaidoyer pour une certaine anormalité* (Gallimard, 1978), 184–203: "Identifications, Neoneeds and Neosexualities," in *International Journal of Psychoanalysis* 67 (1986): 19–31; "Déviation sexuelle et survie psychique," in *Eros aux mille visages* (Gallimard, 1996), 250–68.

35. See Colette, *Mes apprentissages*, Pl 3:1076.

36. See above, chap. 3, "Writing: *Tendrils of the Vine*," 74.

37. See G. Apollinaire, "La littérature féminine," 923.

38. See below, chap. 8, "An Antifeminist," 323.

39. Joyce McDougall, carefully following the experience of perversion, argues for the recognition of neosexualities. See her "De la douleur psychique et du psychosoma," 184–202, and "Déviation sexuelle et survie psychique," 250–68.

40. In the expression of D. W. Winnicott; see "The Capacity to Be Alone," in *The Maturational Processes and the Facilitating Environment: Studies in the Theory of Emotional Development* (New York: International Universities Press), 34–35.

41. See M. Khan, "Orgasme du moi dans l'amour bisexuel," in *Figures de la perversion* (Gallimard, 1979), 239.

42. Colette, *La naissance du jour,* Pl 3:315–16, my emphasis.

43. His book *Legal Medicine of the Mentally Ill* was translated into French in 1900.

44. Colette, *Claudine à Paris,* Pl 1:301.

45. Colette, *Le pur et l'impur,* "notice," Pl 3:1503.

46. Ibid., 652.

47. Colette, *La femme cachée* (1924), Pl 3:6, my emphasis.

48. See J. Malige, *Colette, qui êtes-vous?* (Lyon: La Manufacture, 1987).

49. De Jouvenel, *Un voyageur dans le siècle,* 58.

50. "In which respect, she half lied, proud of an affair—she sometimes said: an adoption, out of a propensity for sincerity—that had lasted six years." In Colette, *Chéri,* Pl 2:722; "With a fierce arm Léa protected him from the bad dream, and rocked him so that he would remain, for a long time—without eyes, without memories, and without plans—like the 'wicked nursling' to whom she had been unable to give birth." Ibid., 817.

51. See Pichois, preface, in Colette, Pl 2:l.

52. Colette, *Chéri,* Pl 2:730.

53. Ibid., 739, my emphasis.

54. Ibid., 744, my emphasis.

55. Ibid., 827.

56. Colette, *La seconde,* Pl 3:398.

57. Colette, M.-C. Bellosta, "notice," in "Le Sieur Binard," in *Bella-Vista,* Pl 3:1901–1902.

58. Colette, "Le Sieur Binard," in *Bella-Vista,* Pl 3:1208–14.

59. Colette, *Mes apprentissages,* Pl 3:1052.

60. Colette, *La naissance du jour,* Pl 3:285.

61. Colette, *La fin de Chéri,* Pl 3:273.

62. Colette, *Le pur et l'impur,* Pl 3:586 and 587.

63. Ibid., 534.

64. As Pichois notes in Colette, Pl 3:1348.

65. Colette, "Les joyaux menacés," in *Le voyage égoïste* (1922), Pl 2:1135.

66. Colette, *L'ingénue libertine* (1909), Pl 1:779.

67. Ibid., 792.

68. Colette, *La Vagabonde* (1910), Pl 1:1107.

69. Colette, *La retraite sentimentale* (1907), Pl 1:864.

70. Colette, "Le miroir," in *Les vrilles de la vigne* (1908), Pl 1:1032.

71. Colette, *Julie de Carneilhan* (1941), Pl 4:261: "a sadness to whose bottom she forbade herself to descend."

72. Colette, *Mes apprentissages* (1936), Pl 3:1000.

73. Colette, *Le pur et l'impur* (1932–41), Pl 3:565, my emphasis.

74. Colette, *La naissance du jour* (1928), Pl 3:287.

75. Colette, *La Vagabonde*, Pl 1:1087.

76. Colette, "La guérison," in *Les vrilles de la vigne*, Pl 1:1027.

77. Colette, *La Vagabonde*, Pl 1:1184.

78. Ibid., 1087–88.

79. Colette, *Le pur et l'impur*, Pl 3:566.

80. Ibid., 581.

81. Colette, *La naissance du jour*, Pl 3:282.

82. Colette, *La Vagabonde*, Pl 1:1074.

83. See below, chap. 7, " . . . Or How to Wrest Oneself Away from Love," 248.

84. Colette, *La naissance du jour*, Pl 3:287.

85. Colette, *Claudine à l'école*, Pl 1:27.

86. Colette, *Claudine à Paris,* Pl 1:362.

87. Colette, *Claudine en ménage*, Pl 1:411.

88. Ibid., 414.

89. Ibid., 472.

90. Colette, *Claudine s'en va*, Pl 1:585.

91. Pichois, preface, in Colette, Pl 1:lxxxiv.

92. Colette, *Lettre à Natalie Barney,* Pl 1:lxxxiv.

93. Colette, "Un zouave" (1915), in *Les heures longues* (1922), Pl 2:524, and "Le rire," in *La maison de Claudine*, Pl 2:1049–51.

94. Colette, "Un zouave," in *Les heures longues*, Pl 2:521–24.

95. See above, chap. 4, "A Slow Apparition," 123.

96. Colette, "Un zouave," in *Les heures longues*, Pl 2:524.

97. Colette, "Le Capitaine," in *Sido* (1929), Pl 3:521.

98. Colette, "Un zouave," in *Les heures longues*, Pl 2:522.

99. Ibid.

100. Colette, "Le Capitaine," in *Sido*, Pl 3:521.

101. Colette, *La maison de Claudine*, Pl 2:976.

102. Ibid., 1035.

103. Colette, "Le Capitaine," in *Sido*, Pl 3:525.

104. Ibid., 524.

105. Ibid., 518.

106. Ibid.

107. Ibid.

108. Ibid., 519.

109. Ibid., 518.

110. Ibid., 520.

111. Ibid., 516.

112. Ibid., 517.

113. Ibid., 521.

114. Ibid.

115. Ibid., 523.

116. Ibid., 525.

117. Ibid., 521: "Strange silence of a man who spoke easily: he did not recount his feats of arms."

118. See Colette, "La cire verte," in *Le képi,* Pl 4:384–96.

119. Colette, *La maison de Claudine,* Pl 2:975–76.

120. Colette, "Le Capitaine," in *Sido,* Pl 3:531.

121. Ibid., 531–32.

122. Ibid., 532.

123. "Man is not made to labor, and the proof is that it tires him." Colette, *Le pur et l'impur,* Pl 3:645.

124. Colette, letter to Francis Carco of March 1924 (perhaps regarding *The End of Chéri*), in *Lettres à ses pairs,* OCC 16:298.

125. Colette, "Gîte d'écrivain," in *Derniers écrits,* OCC 14:61.

126. Colette, "Le Capitaine," in *Sido,* Pl 3:517.

127. Ibid., 519.

128. Ibid., 517.

129. Ibid.

130. Colette, *La maison de Claudine,* Pl 2:985.

131. Ibid., 997, 1049, 1073.

132. Colette, *La naissance du jour,* Pl 3:364.

133. Colette, "Le Capitaine," in *Sido,* Pl 3:525.

134. Ibid., 530.

135. Colette, *La Naissance du jour,* Pl 3:360.

6. THE METAMORPHIC BODY:
PLANTS, BEAST, AND MONSTERS

1. See above, chap. 3, "Metaphors? No, Metamorphoses," 95.

2. Colette, *La Vagabonde,* Pl 1:1119.

3. Colette, "La Chaufferette," in *Journal à rebours,* Pl 4:175.

4. Colette, *L'envers du music-hall,* "notice," Pl 2:1349.

5. Colette, preface to the 1937 edition, Pl 2:324.

6. Colette, *L'envers du music-hall*, "notice," Pl 2:1350.

7. Colette, "Toby-Chien parle," in *Les vrilles de la vigne*, Pl 1:997.

8. Colette, *La retraite sentimentale*, Pl 1:889.

9. Ibid., 894.

10. Colette, *L'entrave*, Pl 2:338.

11. Colette, *La jumelle noire*, OCC 12:170.

12. See J. Kristeva, *Female Genius*, vol. 2, *Melanie Klein* (Columbia University Press, 2001), 98–100, 163.

13. Colette, *Claudine en ménage*, Pl 1:463.

14. Colette, *Le fanal bleu*, Pl 4:996.

15. Colette, *Le pur et l'impur*, Pl 3:565.

16. Colette, *La maison de Claudine*, Pl 2:1010.

17. See M.-C. Clément and D. Clément, *Colette gourmande* (Albin Michel, 1990); this work reconstitutes Colette's "recipes" on the basis of her texts and various statements.

18. Colette, "Puériculture," in *Prisons et paradis*, Pl 3:728.

19. Colette, "Rites," in *Prisons et paradis*, Pl 3:732.

20. Ibid., 732.

21. Colette, "Le poisson au coup de pied," "La treille muscate," in *Prisons et paradis*, Pl 3:696.

22. Colette, *Sido*, Pl 3:514.

23. Colette, "Puériculture," in *Prisons et paradis*, Pl 3:730.

24. Colette, "Vins," in *Prisons et paradis*, Pl 3:691.

25. See J. Kristeva, *Female Genius;* vol. 1, *Hannah Arendt* (Columbia University Press, 1999), 223–29.

26. Colette, "Nuit blanche," in *Les vrilles de la vigne*, Pl 1:970–71.

27. Colette, *L'étoile Vesper*, Pl 4:881.

28. Colette, *Le pur et l'impur*, Pl 3:585.

29. Colette, "Automne," in *Journal à rebours*, Pl 4:156.

30. Colette, "Sido et moi," ibid., 169.

31. Colette, *Mes apprentissages*, Pl 3:1012.

32. Colette, "Le Matou," in *La paix chez les bêtes*, Pl 2:95.

33. Colette, "Le dîner est en retard," in *Douze dialogues de bêtes*, Pl 2:25.

34. Ibid., 23.

35. Colette, "La cire verte," in *Le képi*, Pl 4:387.

36. See G. Beaumont, who mentions Colette's "musical infallibility": "Perhaps it is also the pursuit of an inner cadence, the resumption of a phrase as obsessive as that of Vinteuil's sonata, that some-

times holds Colette in a deep state of rest, eyelids closed, a state that is not sleep." Beaumont and Parinaud, *Colette*, 19.

37. Colette, *Le pur et l'impur*, Pl 3:579–80.
38. Colette, "La Shâh," in *La paix chez les bêtes*, Pl 2:91.
39. Colette, "Le premier feu," in *Dialogues des bêtes*, Pl 2:36.
40. Ibid., 35.
41. Colette, *L'étoile Vesper*, Pl 4:767.
42. *Si* is the French name for the musical note *ti.*—trans.
43. Colette, "La dame qui chante," in *Les vrilles de la vigne*, Pl 1:1036.
44. Colette, *La maison de Claudine*, Pl 2:1000.
45. Colette, "Sido et moi," in *Journal à rebours*, Pl 4:172.
46. Colette, "La Shâh," in *La paix chez les bêtes*, Pl 2:91.
47. Colette, "Les paons," in *Prisons et paradis*, Pl 3:661.
48. Colette, *Le pur et l'impur*, Pl 3:589.
49. See below, chap. 6, "If 'Mme Colette' Is Not a Monster . . . " 224ff.
50. See Y. Resch, *Corps féminin-corps textuel: Essai sur le personnage féminin dans l'oeuvre de Colette* (Klincksieck, 1973), 49–64.
51. Colette, *L'ingénue libertine*, Pl 1:817.
52. Colette, *La retraite sentimentale*, Pl 1:897.
53. Colette, "Le dernier feu," in *Les vrilles de la vigne*, Pl 1:978.
54. Colette, *Sido*, Pl 3:501.
55. Colette, *La naissance du jour*, Pl 3:326.
56. Colette, "Fleurs," in *Aventures quotidiennes*, Pl 3:95.
57. Colette, "Flore et pomone," in *Gigi*, Pl 4:527.
58. Ibid., 528.
59. Colette, "Camélia rouge," in *Pour un herbier*, Pl 4:906.
60. Colette, *La naissance du jour*, Pl 3:363.
61. Ibid., 349.
62. Colette, *Prisons et paradis*, appendices, "Luxe," Pl 3:801.
63. Colette, "Flore et pomone," in *Pour un herbier*, Pl 4:529.
64. Colette, "La treille muscate," in *Prisons et paradis*, Pl 3:698.
65. Colette, *Sido*, Pl 3:501.
66. Colette, *La naissance du jour*, Pl 3:301.
67. Colette, "Fleurs," "La treille muscate," in *Prisons et paradis*, Pl 3: 697.
68. Ibid.
69. Colette, "La rose," in *Pour un herbier*, Pl 4:885.
70. Colette, "Lys," in *Pour un herbier*, Pl 4:889.
71. Colette, *Sido*, Pl 3:508.

72. See J. Kristeva, "Georgia O'Keeffe: La forme inévitable," introductory essay in *Georgia O'Keeffe* (Adam Biro, 1989), 7–16.

73. Colette, "Flore et pomone," in *Gigi*, Pl 4:529.

74. Ibid., 548.

75. F. Jammes, preface, in Colette, *Douze dialogues de bêtes*, Pl 2:5–6.

76. Colette, *L'entrave*, Pl 2:367.

77. Colette, *La naissance du jour*, Pl 3:304.

78. Ibid.

79. Colette, *La paix chez les bêtes*, Pl 2:73.

80. Colette, "Le petit chat retrouvé," in *Journal à rebours*, Pl 4:183.

81. Colette, *La paix chez les bêtes*, Pl 2:147–48.

82. Colette, "Assassins," in *Aventures quotidiennes*, Pl 3:86.

83. Colette, *La naissance du jour*, Pl 3:303.

84. Ibid.

85. Colette, "Amertume," in *En pays connu*, OCC 11:276.

86. Colette, "Assassins," in *Aventures quotidiennes*, Pl 3:86.

87. Colette, *La naissance du jour*, Pl 3:303.

88. Colette, *La paix chez les bêtes*, Pl 2:152.

89. Colette, *Douze dialogues de bêtes*, Pl 2:8.

90. Ibid., 7.

91. Colette, "Toby-Chien parle," in *Les vrilles de la vigne*, Pl 1:996–98.

92. Ravel, writes Colette, "did not treat me like a privileged person, did not consent to give me any commentary, any preview of the music. He seemed to be worried only about the 'caterwauled duet' between the two Cats, and asked me gravely if I saw any disadvantage to his replacing 'meow' with 'mrrreow,' or vice versa." Colette, "Un salon de 1900," in *Journal à rebours*, Pl 4:167.

93. I shall return to this. See chap. 9, "Proust? . . . ," 368.

94. Colette, *Douze dialogues de bêtes*, Pl 2:15.

95. Ibid., 18.

96. Colette, "Un rêve," in *Les vrilles de la vigne*, Pl 1:986–87. On Colette and depersonalization in the dream, see below, 226–27.

97. Colette, "Amours," in *Les vrilles de la vigne*, Pl 1:983.

98. Ibid., 984.

99. Ibid., 981–82.

100. Ibid., "Sido et moi," in *Journal à rebours*, Pl 4:172.

101. Colette, "Le coeur des bêtes," ibid., 4:182.

102. Colette, *La maison de Claudine*, Pl 2:1000.

103. Colette, *La naissance du jour*, Pl 3:304.

104. Colette, "Le coeur des bêtes," in *Journal à rebours*, Pl 4:180.

105. Colette, "Toby-Chien parle," in *Les vrilles de la vigne*, Pl 1:998.

106. Colette, "Amours," ibid., 982.

107. Colette, *Les bêtes et l'absence*, Pl 2:899.

108. Colette, "Rêverie du Nouvel An," in *Les vrilles de la vigne*, Pl 1:963.

109. Colette, *La maison de Claudine*, Pl 2:1001.

110. See above, chap. 3, "Writing: *Tendrils of the Vine*," 74.

111. Colette, "Flore et pomone," in *Gigi*, Pl 4:539.

112. Ibid., 540.

113. Colette, "1915," in *En pays connu*, OCC 11:342.

114. Colette, *La maison de Claudine*, Pl 2:1000.

115. Colette, "Hirondelles," in *Journal à rebours*, Pl 4:123.

116. Ibid., 124.

117. Colette, "Hirondelles," in *En pays connu*, OCC 11:267.

118. Colette, "Les paons," in *Prisons et paradis*, Pl 3:659–60.

119. Ibid.

120. Colette, *Le fanal bleu*, Pl 4:976.

121. Colette, *La naissance du jour*, Pl 3:304.

122. On Colette's corporeal complicity with plants and beasts, see the "dictionary" of Régine Detambel, *Colette: Comme une flore, comme un zoo,* a catalogue of images of the body (Stock, 1997).

123. See Pichois and Brunet, *Colette,* 311.

124. BP (Before Present): the carbon-14 dating method provides the absolute age of an organic material in years elapsed since the death of the organism. It is often expressed in relation to the present time.

125. J. Robert-Lamblin, "Un regard anthropologique," in *La grotte Chauvet: L'art des origines* (Seuil, 2001), 204–7.

126. Colette, *Le fanal bleu*, Pl 4:1058.

127. Colette, "Au coin du feu," in *En pays connu*, OCC 11:285.

128. Colette, "Hirondelles," in *En pays connu*, OCC 11:268.

129. *Discours de réception à l'Académie royale de Belgique* (Grasset, 1955), 27.

130. See Aristotle, *De generatione animalium,* 4.2–3.

131. *Encyclopédie* (1765), vol. 10, s.v. "Monstres."

132. See V. Leys, *Les monstres de Colette,* DEA thesis, Université Denis-Diderot (Paris-VII), personal communication; and B. Brayn, "Colette et les bêtes dans leurs prisons-paradis," in *Cahiers Colette* 15 (1993), colloquium at the Sorbonne and the INRP, June 1–2, 1992, 115–26.

133. Colette, *La naissance du jour,* Pl 3:303.

134. See above, chap. 1, "Why Colette?" 1.

135. Colette, "Monstres," in *Mes cahiers* (1941), OCC 14:172.

136. Colette, *La naissance du jour,* Pl 3:371. Cited above, chap. 1.

137. Colette, "Serpents," in *Prisons et paradis,* Pl 3:658–59.

138. Ibid., 657.

139. Ibid., 658.

140. Ibid., 659.

141. Colette, *La chatte* (1933), Pl 3:882.

142. Ibid., 818–19.

143. Colette, *Le pur et l'impur,* Pl 3:653.

144. Colette, *Prisons et paradis,* Pl 3:625, my emphasis.

145. See below, chap. 7, "Those Pleasures . . . ," 297, and "The Infantile Revisited . . . ," 310.

146. Colette, *Pour un herbier* (1948), Pl 4:885–920.

147. Colette, "Moeurs de la glycine," in *Pour un herbier,* Pl 4:893.

148. Colette, "Fétidité," ibid., 897.

149. Ibid., 898.

150. Colette, "Muguet," ibid., 904.

151. Colette, "L'Arum pied-de-veau," ibid., 917–18.

152. Colette, "Orchidée," ibid., 892.

153. Ibid., 891.

154. Colette, *Le pur et l'impur,* Pl 3:646.

155. Ibid., 616.

156. Colette, *La naissance du jour,* Pl 3:286.

157. Colette, "Pierre Faget, sorcier," in *Prisons et paradis,* Pl 3:749.

158. Colette, "Léopards," in *Prisons et paradis,* Pl 3:682.

159. Ibid.

160. See Pichois and Brunet, *Colette,* 311.

161. Colette, *Le pur et l'impur,* Pl 3:603.

162. Ibid., 643.

163. Colette, *La fin de Chéri,* Pl 3:247.

164. Colette, *La naissance du jour,* Pl 3:318.

165. Colette, *Bella-Vista,* Pl 3:1149.

166. Ibid., Pl 3:1172.

167. Colette, "Demi-fous," in *La femme cachée,* Pl 3:56.

168. Colette, *Bella-Vista,* Pl 3:1101, 1112, 1119, and passim.

169. Ibid., 1142.

170. Ibid., 1143.

171. Ibid., Pl 3:1144–45.

172. Ibid., 1110: "What are appearances, Madame, what are appearances?"

173. Colette, "La bande" (1913), in *Dans la foule*, Pl 2:614–17.

174. Colette, "Monstres," in *Mes cahiers*, OCC 14:170–80.

175. Colette, "1934," in *Journal intermittent*, OCC 11:356–67; and "Le drame et le procès," in *A portée de la main*, OCC 11:452–54.

176. Colette, "Oum el-Hassen," in *Journal à rebours*, Pl 4:146–56.

177. Colette, *L'étoile Vesper*, Pl 4:806.

178. Colette, "Monstres," in *Mes cahiers*, OCC 14:179.

179. Désiré-Henri Landru (1869–1922) was sentenced to death for the murder of ten women and the son of one of them, and was guillotined on February 22, 1922.

180. See M.-C. Bellosta, "notices" and notes, in Colette, Pl 3:1298–1332ff.; and M. Mercier, ibid., 1583–1628.

181. Colette, Pl 3:84–87.

182. Colette, Pl 3:746–49.

183. Colette, Pl 3:210: "Landru doesn't count. [. . .] He's normal, Landru is."

184. Colette, "Landru," in *Prisons et paradis*, Pl 3:746.

185. Ibid., notes and variants, 1616.

186. Colette, "Assassins," in *Aventures quotidiennes*, Pl 3:86.

187. Ibid.

188. Ibid., 86–87.

189. Ibid., 85.

190. Ibid.

191. Ibid.

192. See "Landru," in *Prisons et paradis*, Pl 3:748, in which Colette reprints, with a few cuts and edits, the 1921 article, shifting the initial sympathy for the monster's brutishness to an attention to his capacity for simulation.

193. See Kristeva, *Female Genius*, vol. 1: *Hannah Arendt*, 58 and 248–49n. 102.

194. Colette, "Landru," in *Prisons et paradis*, Pl 3:746–47.

195. Ibid., 747, my emphasis.

196. See Kristeva, *Female Genius*, vol. 1: *Hannah Arendt*, 144–49.

197. Colette, "Landru," in *Prisons et paradis*, Pl 3:748, my emphasis.

198. Ibid., 748, my emphasis.

199. Colette, "Flore et pomone," in *Gigi*, Pl 4:529.

200. Colette, *Le pur et l'impur*, Pl 3:596.

201. Colette, "Assassins," *Le Figaro* of May 11, 1924, reprinted in *Aventures quotidiennes,* Pl 3:84; see also notes and variants, 1311.

202. Colette, "Nudité," Pl 4:418.

203. Colette, "Tulipe," in *Pour un herbier,* Pl 4:895.

204. Colette, *La décapitée,* OCC 13:291–308.

205. See J. Kristeva, *Visions capitales,* exhibition and catalogue (Ed. de la Réunion des Musées Nationaux, 1998).

206. Colette, "Noces," in *Gigi,* Pl 4:564.

207. On the monstrous mother in Colette, see chap. 7, "Mother and Child," 287.

208. Colette, *Le pur et l'impur,* Pl 3:643.

209. Ibid., 638–39.

7. Men and Women, Pure and Impure

1. Colette, *La retraite sentimentale,* Pl 1:896–97.

2. To borrow Geneviève Dormann's term in *Amoureuse Colette* (Herscher, 1984).

3. Colette, *Mes apprentissages,* Pl 3:1015 and 1020.

4. Colette, *Le fanal bleu,* Pl 6:965.

5. Ibid.

6. Colette, *L'étoile Vesper,* Pl 4:863.

7. Colette, *Mes apprentissages,* Pl 3:1041.

8. Colette, *Claudine en ménage,* Pl 1:468.

9. Ibid., "notice," 1352.

10. Ibid., 432.

11. Colette, *L'ingénue libertine,* Pl 1:799.

12. Colette, *La naissance du jour,* Pl 3:288.

13. Ibid., 294.

14. Ibid., 285. Let us recall that dispassionate good cheer: "One of the great banalities of existence, love, is withdrawing from mine. The maternal instinct is another great banality. Having escaped it, we perceive that all the rest is cheerful, varied, multiple."

15. Colette, *La seconde,* Pl 3:489.

16. Colette, *Claudine en ménage,* Pl 1:387.

17. Colette, *La Vagabonde,* Pl 1:1159–60.

18. Ibid., 1184.

19. Ibid., 1211–12.

20. Ibid., 1232.

21. Colette, *L'entrave*, Pl 2:443.
22. Goudeket, *Près de Colette*, 23.
23. Colette, *Mes apprentissages*, Pl 3:1053.
24. Colette, *La naissance du jour*, Pl 3:368.
25. Colette, *Le pur et l'impur*, Pl 3:598.
26. Ibid., 597.
27. Colette, *Bella-Vista*, Pl 3:1097.
28. Colette, *Mes apprentissages*, Pl 3:1053.
29. Colette, *La naissance du jour* (chap. 9), Pl 3:368.
30. Ibid., 350.
31. Ibid., 349. It is 1928. Colette is fifty-five.
32. Ibid., 282.
33. Colette, *Bella-Vista*, Pl 3:1097.
34. Colette, *Trois . . . Six . . . Neuf . . .* , Pl 4:730.
35. Colette, *L'étoile Vesper*, Pl 4:830.
36. Colette, *La naissance du jour*, Pl 3:281.
37. Ibid., 367.
38. Colette, *Mes apprentissages*, Pl 3:1041.
39. Colette, *La naissance du jour*, Pl 3:290.
40. Colette, *Le blé en herbe*, Pl 2:1186.
41. Colette, "Toby-Chien parle," in *Les vrilles de la vigne*, Pl 1:996.
42. Colette, *La naissance du jour*, Pl 3:369.
43. Colette, *Bella-Vista*, Pl 3:1207.
44. Colette, *La naissance du jour*, Pl 3:364.
45. Colette, *L'étoile Vesper*, Pl 4:838.
46. Colette, *L'entrave*, Pl 2:395.
47. Colette, *Bella-Vista*, Pl 3:1128.
48. Colette, *La seconde*, Pl 3:399.
49. Colette, *L'entrave*, Pl 2:427.
50. Ibid., 393.
51. Colette, *Les bêtes et l'absence*, Pl 2:899.
52. Colette, *La naissance du jour*, Pl 3:370–71.
53. Colette, *La seconde*, Pl 3:399.
54. Colette, *L'entrave*, Pl 2:440.
55. Ibid., 395.
56. Ibid., 396.
57. Ibid., 395.
58. Ibid., 406–7.
59. Colette, *Le pur et l'impur*, Pl 3:587.
60. Colette, *L'entrave*, Pl 2:407.

61. Colette, "Le Capitaine," in *Sido*, Pl 3:527.

62. Colette, *Mitsou*, Pl 2:716.

63. Colette, "Armande," in *Le képi*, Pl 4:410.

64. Colette, "Souci," in *Pour un herbier*, Pl 4:899.

65. Colette, "Plein air," in *Journal à rebours*, Pl 4:188.

66. To borrow André Gide's expression in *Romans* (Gallimard, coll. "Bibliothèque de la Pléiade," 1958), 471.

67. Colette, *L'entrave*, Pl 2:410.

68. Colette, *La Vagabonde*, Pl 1:1217.

69. Colette, *La retraite sentimentale*, Pl 1:844.

70. Colette, *La Vagabonde*, Pl 1:1110.

71. Colette, *La retraite sentimentale*, Pl 1:904.

72. Colette, *L'entrave*, Pl 2:427.

73. Colette, *La retraite sentimentale*, Pl 1:896–97.

74. Ibid., 911.

75. Colette, "Chanson de la danseuse," in *Les vrilles de la vigne*, Pl 1:967.

76. Colette, *Le pur et l'impur*, Pl 3:609.

77. Ibid.

78. Colette, "La dame du photographe," in *Gigi*, Pl 4:523.

79. Colette, *Le pur et l'impur*, Pl 3:648.

80. Ibid., 649.

81. Ibid., 651.

82. Colette, *L'entrave*, Pl 2:444.

83. Colette, *Le pur et l'impur*, Pl 3:648.

84. Colette, *Mes apprentissages*, Pl 3:1041.

85. Colette, interview after a series of lectures in April 1931, in Pl 3:xxx, preface.

86. Colette, *Le pur et l'impur*, Pl 3:643.

87. Ibid., 629.

88. Colette, "Le miroir," in *Les vrilles de la vigne*, Pl 1:1033.

89. Colette, *La maison de Claudine*, Pl 2:1013.

90. Ibid., 980.

91. Colette, *L'entrave*, Pl 2:389–90.

92. Colette, *La retraite sentimentale*, Pl 1:926.

93. Colette, *Mes apprentissages*, Pl 3:1054.

94. Colette, *Le pur et l'impur*, Pl 3:586.

95. Ibid., 587.

96. Ibid.

97. Colette, "Nuit blanche," in *Les vrilles de la vigne*, Pl 1:972.

98. Colette, *La Vagabonde*, Pl 1:1207: "For him, two women embracing will never be anything but a lascivious group, and not the touching and melancholic image of two weaknesses, perhaps seeking refuge in each other's arms to sleep, to cry, to flee often wicked men, and to taste, better than any pleasure, the bitter happiness of feeling alike, lowly, forgotten. . . . What's the use of writing, of pleading, of arguing? . . . My voluptuous friend understands only love."

99. Colette, *Le pur et l'impur*, Pl 3:615.

100. Ibid., 616, my emphasis.

101. Ibid., 617.

102. Ibid., 617–18.

103. Ibid., 616.

104. Ibid., 597, my emphasis.

105. Ibid., 615.

106. See above, chap. 3, "Writing: *Tendrils of the Vine*," 74.

107. Colette, *Le pur et l'impur*, Pl 3:598.

108. Colette, letter of June 7, 1944, in *Lettres à Marguerite Moreno*, OCC 14:445.

109. Colette, *Sido*, Pl 3:496.

110. Colette, *Le pur et l'impur*, Pl 3:594.

111. Ibid., 592.

112. Ibid.

113. Ibid., 617.

114. Ibid.

115. Ibid., 594.

116. Ibid., 611–12.

117. Ibid., 613.

118. Ibid., 638.

119. Ibid., 596.

120. Ibid., 588.

121. Ibid., 589.

122. Ibid., 632–33.

123. Ibid., 596.

124. Colette, "Le tendron," in *Le képi*, Pl 4:370.

125. Colette, "Le képi," ibid., 317–53.

126. Colette, "Armande," ibid., 398.

127. Colette, "La cire verte," ibid., 388.

128. Colette, *Duo*, Pl 3:971.

129. Ibid., 923.

130. See the letter from Marcel Proust to Colette, May 1919, in Colette, *Lettres à ses pairs,* OCC 16:135–36.

131. See below, chap. 9, "Memory and Worthiness," 379.

132. Colette, *Mitsou,* Pl 2:669.

133. Ibid., 709–10.

134. Ibid., 708.

135. Ibid., 715.

136. Ibid., 715–16.

137. Ibid., 715–16, my emphasis [*Ça,* the demonstrative pronoun "that," and also the psychoanalytic "id," can be used informally to mean "they"—trans.].

138. See M. Mercier, "notice," in Colette, Pl 4:1225.

139. Quoted in Colette, Pl 4:1216.

140. Colette, *Gigi,* Pl 4:451.

141. Ibid., 449.

142. Ibid., 460.

143. Ibid., 472.

144. See *Le Figaro* of February 19, 1954, quoted by Pichois and Brunet, *Colette,* 450: "It is necessary to recognize that, with Gigi, I must have 'touched a nerve,' as the dentists say."

145. Colette, *Gigi,* Pl 4:476.

146. Colette, *Mes apprentissages,* Pl 3:983.

147. See Pichois and Brunet, *Colette,* 80.

148. Colette, *L'entrave,* Pl 2:448.

149. Colette, *La seconde,* Pl 3:477.

150. Colette, *Le pur et l'impur,* Pl 3:585.

151. Colette, *L'entrave,* Pl 2:442.

152. Ibid., 443.

153. Ibid., 461.

154. Colette, *La naissance du jour,* Pl 3:288.

155. Ibid., 286.

156. Ibid., 285.

157. Colette, *Mes apprentissages,* Pl 3:1035: "The art of dissimulating to such a point that the handwriting, delicate at the beginning of the letters, becomes, with no deformation, so small that it is a challenge even under the magnifying glass, like those manuscript feats on which one reads—if one can—the entire Credo on the back of a postage stamp."

158. Ibid., 1019–20.

159. Ibid., 993.

160. Colette, letter to Germaine Beaumont, January–April 1936 (private collection), Pl 3:1693, "notice."
161. Colette, *Mes apprentissages,* Pl 3:992.
162. Ibid., 1021.
163. Ibid., 1020.
164. Ibid., 1015.
165. Ibid., 1032.
166. Ibid., 1034.
167. Ibid., 1036.
168. Ibid., 1036–37.
169. Ibid., 1025.
170. Colette, letter to Annie de Pène, May 1915, in *Lettres à Annie de Pène et Germaine Beaumont,* 41.
171. Colette, *Julie de Carneilhan,* Pl 4:272. See also below, chap. 8, "The Occupation, or the Politics of the Gourmand Ostrich," 326.
172. See Renée Hamon's journal, housed in the Bibliothèque Nationale, quoted in Pichois and Brunet, *Colette,* 419.
173. Colette, *La naissance du jour,* Pl 3:349.
174. Colette, *L'étoile Vesper,* Pl 4:818.
175. See M. Biolley-Godino, *L'homme-objet chez Colette* (Klincksieck, 1972).
176. Colette, *Chéri,* Pl 2:744.
177. Ibid.
178. Colette, *La fin de Chéri,* Pl 3:217.
179. Colette, *La seconde,* Pl 3:487.
180. Ibid.
181. Colette, *Le toutounier,* Pl 3:1249.
182. Colette, "La dame du photographe," in *Gigi,* Pl 4:499–526.
183. Colette, *Duo,* Pl, 3:975–76. "He held himself very erect, his jaws tightly clenched, and savored the license finally to enter, without witnesses, a new, somewhat resistant element, in dark, rather brown and reddish tones, where he felt assured he would not run into anyone."
184. Colette, "Toby-Chien parle," in *Les vrilles de la vigne,* Pl 1:995.
185. Ibid.
186. Colette, *Nudité,* Pl 4:427.
187. Colette, *A portée de la main,* OCC 11:458.
188. Colette, *Le blé en herbe,* Pl 2:1257–58.
189. Ibid., 1256.
190. Ibid., 1263.

191. Ibid., 1225.
192. Ibid., 1228.
193. Ibid., 1221.
194. Ibid., 1220.
195. Colette, *La seconde*, Pl 3:477.
196. Colette, *Le pur et l'impur*, Pl 3:652–53.
197. Colette, *L'étoile Vesper*, Pl 4:840.
198. Colette, *La seconde*, Pl 3:489.
199. Ibid., 409.
200. Y. Resch, "notice," in Colette, Pl 3:1430.
201. Arlette Louis-Dreyfus, who married Renaud de Jouvenel, describes her this way: "She liked what was fresh. She looked at us as at beautiful pieces of fruit. That was not the attraction of elderly people to youth. There was an 'ogre' side to her gaze." See the interview in *Cahiers Colette* 16 (1994):100.
202. C. Pichois (with A. Brunet), preface, in *Colette*, Pl 3:xi.
203. Colette, "Le Capitaine," in *Sido*, Pl 3:527.
204. Colette, Pl 4:1227.
205. Colette, *L'étoile Vesper*, Pl 4:765–66.
206. Colette, "Faits divers," *La République*, January 23, 1934, quoted in Pl 4:1222.
207. Colette, *Le pur et l'impur*, Pl 3:648.
208. Colette, *L'entrave*, Pl 2:328.
209. Colette, *Mes apprentissages*, Pl 3:1020.
210. Ibid., 1074.
211. Ibid., 1075.
212. Colette, *Le blé en herbe*, Pl 2:1186.
213. Colette, *L'entrave*, Pl 2:350.
214. Colette, "L'impasse," in *La femme cachée*, Pl 3:17.
215. Colette, *Julie de Carneilhan*, Pl 4:258.
216. Colette, *Belles saisons*, OCC 11:20: "Remove the human face from my reach and everything is changed."
217. Colette, "Cheveux en quatre," in *Belles saisons*, OCC 11:56.
218. Colette, *Avatars*, appendix, Pl 3:xxxiii.
219. Colette, "De quoi est-ce qu'on a l'air?" in *Les vrilles de la vigne*, Pl 1:1020.
220. Colette, *La seconde*, Pl 3:490.
221. That is what the narrator feels for Clouk, Chéri's twin, but Colette does not keep that sentence in the published text. See Colette, Pl 2:liii, preface.

222. Colette, *Chéri*, Pl 2:798.

223. Ibid., 803.

224. Ibid., 798.

225. Colette, "L'autre femme," in *La femme cachée*, Pl 3:33.

226. Colette, *La fin de Chéri*, Pl 3:240.

227. Ibid., 190.

228. Colette, *La seconde*, Pl 3:447.

229. Colette, *La naissance du jour*, Pl 3:285.

230. Colette, *Chéri*, Pl 2:723.

231. Colette, *La fin de Chéri*, Pl 3:216.

232. Colette, "La dame qui chante," in *Les vrilles de la vigne*, Pl 1:1035.

233. Colette, *Le toutounier*, Pl 3:1245.

234. Colette, *Julie de Carneilhan*, Pl 4:264.

235. Colette, *Le pur et l'impur*, Pl 3:562.

236. Colette, *La seconde*, Pl 3:444.

237. Ibid., 490.

238. Colette, *La naissance du jour*, Pl 3:335.

239. Colette, *Le pur et l'impur*, Pl 3:612.

240. Colette, *Chéri*, Pl 2:729.

241. Colette, "Gribiche," in *Bella-Vista*, Pl 3:1172–75.

242. Colette, "Le tendron," in *Le képi*, Pl 4:380.

243. Colette, *La retraite sentimentale*, Pl 1:873.

244. Colette, *La Vagabonde*, Pl 1:1179.

245. Colette, *L'étoile Vesper*, Pl 4:871.

246. Colette, *Le fanal bleu*, Pl 4:984.

247. Colette, "En baie de Somme,"in *Les vrilles de la vigne*, Pl 1:1042.

248. Colette, "Amours," ibid., 982.

249. Colette, *L'étoile Vesper*, Pl 4:872.

250. Ibid., 871.

251. Ibid., 875–76.

252. Ibid., 875.

253. Colette, "Regarde," in *Autre bêtes*, Pl 2:194.

254. Ibid., 195.

255. Colette, *De ma fenêtre*, Pl 4:671.

256. Colette, *L'étoile Vesper*, Pl 4:875.

257. Colette, *Paris de ma fenêtre*, Pl 4:672.

258. Ibid., 611.

259. Colette, *Belles saisons*, OCC 11:38.

260. Colette, *Le fanal bleu*, Pl 4:984.

261. Colette, "Regarde," in *Autres bêtes*, Pl 2:195.

262. Colette, *Le fanal bleu,* Pl 4:984.

263. Colette, *Paris de ma fenêtre,* Pl 4:672.

264. Colette, *Journal intermittent,* OCC 11:350.

265. Colette, "Nonoche," in *Les vrilles de la vigne,* Pl 1:992.

266. Colette, Pl 2:1085–89.

267. Colette, *La maison de Claudine,* Pl 2:985–86.

268. Colette, "Bel-Gazou et la vie chère," in *Les heures longues,* Pl 2:574.

269. Ibid., 573.

270. Colette, *La chambre éclairée,* Pl 2:887.

271. Ibid.

272. Colette, "Fantômes," in *La chambre éclairée,* Pl 2:889.

273. Colette, *La maison de Claudine,* Pl 2:985.

274. Even today, the famous correspondence between Mme de Sévigné (1616–96) and her daughter, Mme de Grignan, remains an unmatched masterpiece, which, directly and especially indirectly, reveals a mother's ravaging passion for her daughter. Anna de Noailles (1876–1933), after giving birth to a son on September 18, 1900, confides the experience of that happy event in her correspondence (see E. Hugonnet-Dugna, in *Anna de Noailles, Biographie/Correspondance* [Michel de Maule, 1989], 41–47) and later mentions her child in her poems (see, among others, *La course dans l'azur* in Anna de Noailles, *Choix de poésies* [Grasset, 1930–63], 105). In a less personal register, close to Zola's pathetic naturalism, in 1908 Lucie Delarue-Mardrus (1880–1945) published *Marie fille-mère,* a novel that depicts the horrors of childbirth, with descriptions based on statements she collected in maternity wards. The author of many poems for children, she also published *Roman de six petites filles* (1909). In Italy in 1906, Sibilla Aleramo wrote *Une femme,* a novel that would be published in Italian only in 1950 (reprinted in French by Edition des Femmes in 1974). This text retraces her emancipation against a background of psychological and family crises: she decides to leave her husband, as well as her son, to whom, however, she is very attached. The popular novelist Raymonde Machard (1889–1971) in 1919 published *Tu enfanteras . . . ,* a novel that was recognized by the Académie Française, which glories in the joys of motherhood (but the day the book came out, her little girl died). Much later Anaïs Nin (1903–77) devoted dramatic pages in her journal, written in French, to her difficult labor, which ended in the birth of

a stillborn daughter (August 1934) (see Anaïs Nin, *Journal, 1931–1934* [Livre de Poche, 1998], 477–91).

These rare examples illustrate how incompatible women's writing was with motherhood, when it was not imagined as a necessary escape from it, destined to liberate women from the burden of tradition and allow them more noble achievements. The feminist movement itself, with Simone de Beauvoir in the lead, and even the feminists of the 1970s followed the same line of reasoning. It would not be until the second wave of the latter movement that women's works that freely and unneurotically deal with the maternal vocation would appear in France and elsewhere, though that tendency still encounters various forms of resistance.

275. C. de Jouvenel, "Colette et le presse-papiers," in *Cahiers Colette* 16 (1994):95.

276. Colette, *La naissance du jour,* Pl 3:281.

277. Colette, *Duo,* Pl 3:965.

278. Ibid., 918.

279. Colette, *Le pur et l'impur,* Pl 3:566–67.

280. Colette, *Duo,* Pl 3:958.

281. Colette, *Le blé en herbe,* Pl 2:1224.

282. Ibid., 1189, 1219.

283. Ibid., 1253.

284. Ibid., 1202.

285. Ibid., 1240.

286. Ibid., 1191.

287. Ibid., 1268.

288. Ibid., 1269.

289. Ibid., 1233.

290. Colette, *Chéri,* Pl 2:814–15.

291. Colette, *La paix chez les bêtes,* Pl 2:73.

292. E. Harris, *L'approfondissement de la sensualité dans l'oeuvre romanasque de Colette* (Nizet, 1973), 18. It is actually found in the short story "La comparaison": "The world of emotions thoughtlessly called physical"; see *Le Matin,* March 31, 1923, 4; and Colette, *Le blé en herbe* (1923), Pl 2:1238.

293. Colette, *Le pur et l'impur,* Pl 3:551.

294. As Jacques Dupont insightfully notes in Colette, Pl 3:1507, "notice."

295. Colette, *Le pur et l'impur,* Pl 3:653: "Of that word 'pure' that fell from her mouth, I listened to the brief tremulo, the plaintive *u,*

the *r* of clear ice. It did not awaken anything in me, except the need to hear its unique resonance again, the echo of a drop that falls, breaks off, and joins an invisible body of water. The word 'pure' did not reveal its intelligible meaning to me. I have only reached the point of quenching an optical thirst for purity in the transparencies that evoke it, in the bubbles, the massive water, and the imaginary sites entrenched, out of reach, within a thick crystal."

296. Colette, *La jumelle noire,* OCC 12:246.

297. Colette, *Lettre à ses pairs,* early July 1921, OCC 16:140, see below, chap. 9, "Proust? . . . " 369.

298. Colette, *Le pur et l'impur,* note on the text, Pl 3:1515.

299. See above, chap. 5, "Depression, Perversion, Sublimation," 155.

300. Colette, *Le pur et l'impur,* Pl 3:567.

301. Ibid., 609.

302. Ibid., notes and variants, 1517–18.

303. See Sido, *Lettres à sa fille 1905–1912,* letter of January 8, 1911, 405.

304. Colette, *Le pur et l'impur,* Pl 3:556.

305. Ibid., 561–62, my emphasis.

306. Ibid., 562.

307. Ibid.

308. Ibid., 564.

309. Ibid., 566, my emphasis.

310. Ibid., 638.

311. Ibid.

312. Ibid., 622.

313. Ibid., 625.

314. Ibid., 620.

315. Ibid., 643.

316. Ibid., 621.

317. See chap. 7, "A Queen of Bisexuality," 260.

318. Colette, *Le pur et l'impur,* Pl 3:594.

319. Ibid.

320. Colette, *La fin de Chéri,* Pl 3:198.

321. Colette, *L'étoile Vesper,* Pl 4:807.

322. Colette, *Le pur et l'impur,* Pl 3:589.

323. Ibid., 596.

324. Ibid.

325. Ibid., 595.

326. Ibid., 596, my emphasis.

327. Colette, *Le fanal bleu*, Pl 4:990.
328. Colette, *Le pur et l'impur*, Pl 3:567.
329. Ibid., 567.
330. Ibid., 578.
331. Ibid., 580.
332. Ibid., 581.
333. Ibid.
334. Ibid., 580.
335. Ibid., 582.
336. Ibid., 579.
337. Ibid., 574.
338. Ibid., 579.
339. Ibid., 615.
340. Ibid., 616.
341. Ibid., 618.
342. Ibid., 616.
343. Ibid.
344. Ibid., 618.
345. Ibid., 621.
346. Ibid., 625.
347. Ibid., 623.
348. Ibid., 625.
349. S. Freud, "Female Sexuality," in *The Standard Edition*, 21:226; see also S. Freud, "Some Psychical Consequences of the Anatomical Distinction between the Sexes," in *The Standard Edition*, 19:248–58; and S. Freud, "Femininity," in *The Standard Edition*, 22:112–35.
350. *Le Disque Vert*, special issue, "Freud et la psychanalyse" (Paris and Brussels, 1924).
351. Colette, *Le pur et l'impur*, Pl 3:627.
352. See M. Goudeket, p. 86: "[*The Pure and the Impure*] approaches the question of sexual anomalies with assurance, leaving nothing in the shadow.[. . .] Colette had granted them the same keenness of observation and the same respect as the other vital manifestations."
353. Colette, *Le pur et l'impur*, Pl 3:638.
354. Ibid., 612.
355. See R. Vivien, "La flûte qui s'est tue," *Oeuvres poétiques complètes, 1877–1899* (Ed. Régine Deforges, 1986), 316.
356. Colette, *L'étoile Vesper* (1946), Pl 4:843.

357. Ibid., 841.
358. Colette, *Sido*, Pl 3:509.
359. Colette, *Mitsou*, Pl 3:683.
360. See A. Grosrichard, *Structure du sérail: La fiction du despotisme asiatique dans l'Occident classique* (Seuil, 1979).
361. Ibid., 221–23.
362. Colette, letters to Léon Hamel, Rome, June 28, 1915, in *Lettres de la Vagabonde*, OCC 15:106.
363. Colette, letter to Annie de Pène, Rome, April 1917, in *Lettres à Annie de Pène et Germaine Beaumont*, 94.
364. See chap. 2, "The Idol Cornered by History," 62.
365. See chap. 9, "Because Writing Leads only to Writing," 391.
366. Colette, *Bella-Vista*, Pl 3:1175.
367. Colette, *Mes apprentissages*, Pl 3:1029.
368. Ibid., 1034.
369. Colette, *Sido*, Pl 3:501–502.
370. Colette, "Elle est malade," in *Douze dialogues*, Pl 2:39.
371. Colette, *La naissance du jour*, Pl 3:317.
372. Ibid., 308.

8. A Little Politics All the Same

1. Colette, preface, Pl 3:xii.
2. Quoted in Colette, preface, Pl 2:x.
3. Colette, article in *La Vie Parisienne*, August 14, 1909, quoted in Pl 1:1589.
4. Colette, "Les femmes au congrès," in *Dans la foule*, Pl 2:601.
5. Ibid., 602.
6. Colette, *De ma fenêtre*, Pl 4:582, my emphasis.
7. Ibid., 583, my emphasis.
8. Ibid.
9. Colette, "Ruines," in *Journal à rebours*, Pl 4:134.
10. Colette, *De ma fenêtre*, Pl 4:692.
11. Ibid.
12. The expression *pratiquer la politique de l'autruche*, literally, "to practice the policy [or politics] of the ostrich" is the French equivalent of the English expression "to bury one's head in the sand"—trans.
13. According to A. Billy, quoted in Colette, Pl 2:1430.
14. "A l'Université populaire," in *Dans la foule*, Pl 2:636–37.

15. See Pichois and Brunet, *Colette*, 436.

16. See Colette, letter to Mme Moreau of July 28, 1941, in Colette, *Lettres à Moune et au Toutounet* (Des femmes-Antoinette Fouque, coll. "Correspondance," 1985), 209; and above, chap. 2, "The Idol Cornered by History," 62.

17. Colette, *L'étoile Vesper*, Pl 4:774.

18. Colette, "La dame du photographe," in *Gigi*, Pl 4:512.

19. Colette, *Julie de Carneilhan*, Pl 4:265.

20. Colette, "Danger," in *Journal à rebours*, Pl 4:127–29.

21. Ibid., 126.

22. Ibid., 129.

23. Colette, "Ruines," in *Journal à rebours*, Pl 4:131.

24. Colette, "Danger," ibid, 129–30.

25. Ibid., 127.

26. Colette, "Flore et pomone," in *Gigi*, Pl 4:536–37, my emphasis.

27. Colette, "Fin juin 40," in *Journal à rebours*, Pl 4:110.

28. See above, chap. 2, "The Idol Cornered by History," 62.

29. Colette, *Paris de ma fenêtre*, Pl 4:629.

30. Colette, "Provence," in *Journal à rebours*, Pl 4:191.

31. Colette, "La Providence," in *Journal à rebours*, Pl 4:115–16.

32. Colette, *Paris de ma fenêtre*, Pl 4:625.

33. Colette, "Les rois," in *Belles saisons*, OCC 11:50.

34. Colette, "Fin juin 40," in *Journal à rebours*, Pl 4:111–12.

35. Ibid., 117.

36. Colette, *Paris de ma fenêtre*, Pl 4:616.

37. Ibid., 625.

38. Colette, "Ruines," in *Journal à rebours*, Pl 4:132.

39. Colette, *Paris de ma fenêtre*, Pl 4:604.

40. Ibid., 579.

41. Ibid., 638.

42. Colette, "Tulipe," in *Pour un herbier*, Pl 4:895.

43. Colette, "Paris," in *Belles saisons*, OCC 11:55.

44. Ibid., 54, my emphasis.

45. Colette, *L'étoile Vesper*, Pl 4:779.

46. Colette, "Papillons," in *Journal à rebours*, Pl 4:187.

47. Colette, *Le képi*, Bouquins, "notice," 3:278.

48. Colette, *Belles saisons*, OCC 11:12.

49. Colette, *L'étoile Vesper*, Pl 4:777.

50. Ibid., 778.

51. Colette, *L'étoile Vesper*, Pl 4:783–84, my emphasis.

52. Colette, letter to the Petites Fermières of February 4, 1941, quoted in Pl 4:1155.
53. Colette, *Julie de Carneilhan*, Pl 4:243.
54. Hence, to depict the 1900s, Paul Morand drops this remark: "Gyp, called to the High Court to testify, when asked his profession, replied, 'anti-Semite'" (*1900*, 23).
55. Colette, *Julie de Carneilhan*, Pl 4:245–46.
56. Ibid., 271.
57. Ibid., 299.
58. Ibid., 299–300.
59. Ibid., 301.
60. Ibid.
61. See Colette, *Gigi*, collection published in 1944 (Lausanne: La Guilde du Livre).
62. Colette, "La dame du photographe," in *Gigi*, Pl 4:504–5.
63. Ibid.; "His taste for the beautiful pearl has always seemed to me more sensual than commercial."
64. Ibid., 506.
65. Ibid., 511–12, my emphasis.
66. Colette, "Partis . . . ," in *Journal à rebours*, Pl 4:144–46.
67. Ibid., 144.
68. Ibid., 145.
69. Colette, "Le poète," ibid., 122.
70. Ibid.
71. Ibid., 123.
72. Text included in *Gigi*, 1944 edition.
73. Colette, "L'enfant malade," in *Gigi*, Pl 4:498.
74. Willy the voyeur was a pioneer of what would become the "illustrated novel," publishing in 1904 a work that presented itself as a "modern" attempt to include in the novel many "photographic illustrations," in which the author himself can be recognized as well as his friends, male and female. See Willy, *En bombe: Roman moderne*, photographic illustrations (Librarie Wilson, 1905).
75. In what follows, I am indebted to A.-M. Christin's study, "Colette et ses illustrateurs," delivered at the Colloque de Cérisy, 1988, and published in *Cahiers Colette* 11 (1989): 171–90.
76. Colette, *La treille muscate*, published on April 15, 1932, by the presses of Aimé Jourde in Paris; engravings by André Dunoyer de Segonzac, printed by Jacques Frélaut on the presses of Roger Lacourière in Paris; published courtesy of Segonzac.

77. Colette, "Impressions d'Italie" (1915), in *Les heures longues,* Pl 2:530.

78. Colette, "Flore et pomone," in *Gigi* (1944), Pl 4:541.

79. Ibid., 538.

80. Colette, *Paysages et portraits,* OCC 13:374.

81. Colette, *Trait pour trait,* Pl 4:942–43.

82. Colette, *Paysages et portraits,* OCC 13:402–4.

83. Ibid., 374–75.

84. Colette, *L'étoile Vesper,* Pl 4:812.

85. Colette, "Flore et pomone," in *Gigi,* Pl 4:527, my emphasis.

86. Ibid., 529.

87. Colette, "La chienne trop petite," in *La paix chez les bêtes,* Pl 2:102.

88. Colette, *L'entrave,* Pl 2:388.

89. Colette, *L'étoile Vesper,* Pl 4:784.

90. See above, chap. 7, "Precocious Maturity, or Delicacy according to Mitsou and Gigi," 267.

91. See Christin, "Colette et ses illustrateurs," 185.

92. Ibid.

93. Quoted in R. Bienvenu, "*La Treille Muscate* de Colette et son illustration par Dunoyer de Segonzac," in *Iconographie et littérature,* ed. A. Niderst (PUF, 1983), 161.

94. Colette, letter to M. Luc-Albert Moreau of December 28, 1933, in *Lettres à Moune et au Toutounet,* 82–83.

95. Quoted by Bienvenu, "*La Treille Muscate* de Colette," 162.

96. Colette, *La jumelle noire,* OCC 12:270.

97. See Virmaux and Virmaux, *Colette au cinéma,* 10.

98. Ibid., 17.

99. Virmaux and Virmaux, *Colette au cinéma.*

100. Colette, *Le fanal bleu* (1949), Pl 4:998.

101. Colette, "*Mater Dolorosa,* " in *Le Film,* June 4, 1917, quoted by Virmaux and Virmaux, *Colette au cinéma,* 43. On Colette and decapitation, see above, chap. 6, "From the Death Drive to Decapitation," 238.

102. Colette, "Noir et blanc," November 10, 1935, in *La jumelle noire,* OCC 12:257.

103. Colette, "Cinéma," June 15, 1924, in *Aventures quotidiennes,* Pl 3:104.

104. Ibid., 103–4.

105. Ibid., 102.

106. Colette, "L'expédition Scott au cinématographe," in Virmaux and Virmaux, *Colette au cinéma*, 32.

107. Colette, "*Forfaiture*," in *Excelsior*, August 7, 1916, quoted by Virmaux and Virmaux, *Colette au cinéma*, 37; "La critique des films," *Le Film*, May 28, 1917, in ibid., 41.

108. Colette, "L'envers du cinéma," in *Paysages et portraits*, OCC 13:420–29, quoted in Virmaux and Virmaux, *Colette au cinéma*, 279–87.

109. See J.-C. Bonnet, "Colette et le cinéma," in *Cahiers Colette* 11 (1988): 195.

110. Colette, "*Mater Dolorosa*," quoted in Virmaux and Virmaux, *Colette au cinéma*, 46.

111. Colette, *L'envers du music-hall*, Pl 2:232.

112. Colette, letter of mid-September 1924, in *Lettres à Marguerite Moreno*, OCC 14:261.

113. See C. Beylie, *Max Ophuls* (Seghers, 1963), 45.

114. Quoted in Bonnet, "Colette et le cinéma," 197.

115. M. Chevalier, *Les Lettres Françaises*, January 8, 1959.

116. Colette, "Propagande," in *La maison de Claudine*, Pl 2:993: "the word 'political' obsessed the ear [of Colette's father] with a pernicious rattle."

9. Still Writing, Between Balzac and Proust

1. Colette, "Ma mère et les livres," in *La maison de Claudine*, Pl 2:988. The title of this section is taken from Colette, "La cire verte," in *Le képi*, Pl 4:393.

2. Colette, "Fragrance," in *Mélanges*, OCC 14:37.

3. Colette, "Souvenirs balzaciens," in *Balzac: Le livre du centenaire* (Flammarion, 1953), 17.

4. Colette, *Claudine à Paris*, Pl 1:233.

5. Ibid., 281.

6. Colette, *Claudine en ménage*, Pl 1:518.

7. Colette, "La Rabouilleuse," October 8, 1936, in *La jumelle noire*, OCC 12:328–31; "Lectures," initially published in *De Jeanne d'Arc à Pétain* (1944), under the aegis of Sacha Guitry, now in *Mélanges*, OCC 14:18–22; "A propos de Madame Marneffe," in *Trait pour trait*, Pl 4:953–57; and "Souvenirs balzaciens," tribute read at the Sorbonne by Pierre Fresnay, in *Balzac: Le livre du centenaire*, 16–18.

8. See N. Houssa, "Balzac et Colette," in *Revue d'Histoire Littéraire de France* (January–March 1960): 18–46; and M. Hecquet, "Colette lectrice de Balzac," presented at the Colloque de Cerisy, 1988, in *Cahiers Colette* 11 (1989): 157–69.

9. Colette, *La Vagabonde*, Pl 1:1074.

10. Colette, "A propos de Madame Marneffe," in *Trait pour trait*, Pl 4:954.

11. Colette, *La Vagabonde*, Pl 1:1083.

12. De Jouvenel, in *Un voyageur dans le siècle*, 57.

13. Colette, "Lectures," in *Mélanges*, OCC 14:20.

14. Colette, "A propos de Madame Marneffe," in *Trait pour trait*, Pl 4:954.

15. Ibid., 955.

16. Colette, "Souvenirs balzaciens," 16.

17. Ibid.

18. Ibid., 17.

19. Ibid.

20. See Houssa, "Colette et Balzac."

21. Colette, "Lectures," in *Mélanges*, OCC 14:19.

22. Colette, "Tulipes," in *Pour un herbier*, Pl 4:894.

23. Colette, "Lectures," in *Mélanges*, OCC 14:20.

24. Colette, *L'étoile Vesper*, Pl 4:818.

25. Colette, "Lectures," in *Mélanges*, OCC 14:22.

26. Colette, "Frénésie, de Charles de Peyret-Chappuis," in *La jumelle noire*, OCC 12:454, my emphasis.

27. Colette, *L'étoile Vesper*, Pl 4:879, my emphasis.

28. Colette, "A propos de Mme Marneffe," in *Trait pour trait*, Pl 4:953–54.

29. Laïs: Greek courtesan, friend of Alcibiades—trans.

30. Ibid., 954.

31. Colette, *La jumelle noire*, OCC 12:329.

32. Colette, "Lectures," in *Mélanges*, OCC 14:22.

33. Ibid., 21.

34. Colette, "Souvenirs balzaciens," 18.

35. Colette, "Lectures," in *Mélanges*, OCC 14:22.

36. Ibid., 19–20.

37. See above, chap. 4, "The Incestual Mother . . . ," 133; chap. 5, "Genitality or Neoreality?" 164; and chap. 5, "Succeeding Where the Pervert Exhausts Himself," 168.

38. De Jouvenel, *Un voyageur dans le siècle*, 57.

39. H. de Balzac, *Le chef-d'oeuvre inconnu* (Flammarion, 1981), 49–50.

40. Ibid., 69.

41. Ibid.

42. Colette, *Paris de ma fenêtre*, Pl 4:604.

43. The title for this section is taken from Colette, in *Conferencia, Journal des Université des Annales*, April 1, 1926, 378. My thanks to Mme Marie-Françoise de Courtivron for bringing my attention to this source.

44. Published in *Conferencia*, 368–78.

45. Ibid., 378.

46. Colette, letter to Marcel Proust, May 1895, in *Lettres à ses pairs*, OCC 16:134.

47. Colette, *Claudine en ménage*, Pl 1:427; and note of D'Hollander, 1350.

48. Ibid., 428.

49. Colette, *Mes apprentissages*, Pl 3:1041.

50. Colette, *Les vrilles de la vigne*, Pl 1:1043, my emphasis.

51. National memory preserves a bitter recollection of the "battle of Crécy": the first major battle of the Hundred Years' War, during which the army of Philippe VI had been cut to pieces by the English archers of Edward III, did, in fact, take place near Crécy in 1346.

52. *Correspondance de Marcel Proust*, edited by P. Kold, 21 vols. (Plon, 1970–93), 12:337 and 353.

53. Ibid., to Mme Colette de Jouvenel, early March 1919, 18:118–19; see above, chap. 7, "Precocious Maturity . . . ," 267.

54. Colette to Marcel Proust, letter of June 1920, in *Lettres à ses pairs*, OCC 16:137.

55. They were both awarded the rank of chevalier of the Legion of Honor.

56. Marcel Proust to Colette, letter of November 1920, in *Lettres à ses pairs*, OCC 16:138.

57. Colette, in fact, never wrote on the invert in the *Mercure* but would deal with the subject in *Those Pleasures . . .* (*The Pure and the Impure*).

58. Colette to Marcel Proust, early July 1921, in *Lettres à ses pairs*, OCC 16:140.

59. Ibid., letter to Henri Mondor (1951), 395.

60. See Mercier, "notice," in Colette, Pl 3:1387.

61. She "translates" these words, which Proust formulated as follows: "Already, in this first volume, you will see the character who recounts, who says 'I' and who is not me, discover, all of a sudden, years, gardens, forgotten beings, in the taste of a mouthful of tea in which he dipped a bite of madeleine." In M. Proust, *Essais et articles: Contre Sainte-Beuve* (Gallimard, coll. "Bibliothèque de la Pléiade"), 558.

62. Colette, "Dialogues de bêtes," in *Les vrilles de la vigne*, Pl 1:1004.

63. See above, chap. 4, "The Incestual Mother . . . ," 133.

64. Colette, *Le pur et l'impur*, Pl 3:628.

65. See above, chap. 7, "The Infantile Revisited from the Direction of the Impure," 297.

66. Colette, *Le pur et l'impur*, Pl 3:628.

67. Colette, "Flore et pomone," in *Gigi*, Pl 4:548.

68. Colette, "La lune de pluie," in *Chambre d'hôtel* (1940), Pl 4:66–67.

69. Colette, "Flore et pomone," in *Gigi* (1945), Pl 4:550.

70. Ibid.

71. Ibid.

72. Ibid., 551.

73. Colette, "Proust," in *Mes cahiers*, OCC 14:144–47.

74. Colette, "Marcel Proust," in *Trait pour trait*, Pl 4:924.

75. Colette, "Lumières bleues," in *En pays connu*, OCC 11:364.

76. Colette, "Marcel Proust," in *Trait pour trait*, Pl 4:925.

77. See J. Kristeva, *Le temps sensible*: "Equilibre du blasphème," 32; "Voir l'étouffement: une flagellation," 295; "L'écriture comme thérapie de la caverne sensorielle," 296; "L'interprétation entre mots-signes et mots-fétiches: Une beauté," 301.

78. Colette, *Claudine à l'école*, Pl 1:7–8.

79. See M. Mercier, "La solitude, inexpugnable innocence," in "Colette," special issue of the review *Europe* (November––December 1981): 3–12.

80. Colette, *La retraite sentimentale*, Pl 1:886–87.

81. Colette, "Jour gris," in *Les vrilles de la vigne*, Pl 1:974.

82. Colette, "Rêverie de Nouvel An," in *Les vrilles de la vigne*, Pl 1:963–64.

83. Ibid., 966.

84. Colette, "Toby-Chien" (appendices), in *Les vrilles de la vigne*, Pl 1:1058.

85. Colette, *La Vagabonde*, Pl 1:1132.

86. Colette, *Trois . . . Six . . . Neuf . . .* , Pl 4:714.

87. Colette, "Le passé," in *Paysages et portraits* (1909–53), OCC 13:313–15.

88. Colette, "Le dernier feu," in *Les vrilles de la vigne*, Pl 1:978.

89. Ibid.

90. Colette, "Le miroir," in *Les vrilles de la vigne*, Pl 1:1032.

91. Colette, *La Vagabonde*, Pl 1:1221.

92. Ibid., 1084; see also "notice," ibid., 1591–92.

93. See Françoise Mallet-Joris, "Une vocation féminine," in *Cahiers Colette* 1 (1977): 51: "I was struck during an attentive rereading by how often the word 'worthiness,' that concern for good behavior, recurred in Colette's writing."

94. Colette, "Toby-Chien parle," in *Les vrilles de la vigne*, Pl 1:997.

95. Colette, *La naissance du jour*, Pl 3:289.

96. Ibid., 282.

97. Colette, *La maison de Claudine*, Pl 2:968.

98. Colette, *L'étoile Vesper*, Pl 4:816, my emphasis.

99. Colette, *La naissance du jour*, Pl 3:290.

100. Colette, "Noël," in *Belles saisons*, OCC 11:71.

101. Colette, *Belles saisons*, OCC 11:23.

102. Colette, "Les sauvages," in *Sido*, Pl 3:538.

103. Colette, *Discours de réception*, Pl 3:1083.

104. Colette, "Nuit blanche," in *Les vrilles de la vigne*, Pl 1:970.

105. Colette, *La Vagabonde*, Pl 1:1154.

106. Colette, *Le fanal bleu*, Pl 4:1003.

107. Ibid., 860.

108. See above, chap. 7, " . . . Those Men That Other Men Call Great," 274–78.

109. Ibid., 371.

110. Colette, *L'étoile Vesper*, Pl 4:849.

111. Ibid., 850.

112. Colette, *La maison de Claudine*, Pl 2:984.

113. Letter from Anna de Noailles to Colette of February 13, 1928, in *Lettres à ses pairs*, OCC 16:172.

114. See above, chap. 5, "Freud's Way: *Père-version* or *Mère-version*," 155.

115. S. Freud, *Totem and Taboo* (1912–13), in *The Standard Edition*, 13:153.

116. The first article, in *Le Journal* of May 12, 1935, was reprinted in *La jumelle noire*, OCC 12:225–29. The second, long unlocatable,

was discovered by Alain Virmaux in *Sélection de la Vie Artistique* of May 18, 1935, and published by him in "Colette et Antonin Artaud," in *Cahiers Colette* 19: 193–204.

117. Quoted in Virmaux, "Colette et Antonin Artaud," 198.

118. Ibid., 200.

119. See Antonin Artaud, *Oeuvres complètes* (Gallimard, 1979), 5:45.

120. See, among other writings, Colette, *Discours de réception* (1936), Pl 3:1079–80; and "La Chaufferette," in *Journal à rebours* (1941), Pl 4:174. The title of this section is taken from Colette, *Le fanal bleu,* Pl 4:1060.

121. Colette, "Gîte d'écrivains," in *Derniers écrits* (1953), OCC 14:61.

122. Colette, "La cire verte," in *Le képi,* Pl 4:386.

123. Colette, "La Chaufferette," in *Journal à rebours,* Pl 4:175.

124. Colette, *L'étoile Vesper,* Pl 4:817.

125. Colette, "Flore et pomone," in *Gigi,* Pl 4:555.

126. Colette, *Journal à rebours,* Pl 4:201.

127. Ibid., 200.

128. Ibid., 201.

129. Ibid., 156.

130. Colette, *La naissance du jour,* Pl 3:297.

131. Colette, *Mes apprentissages,* Pl 3:1075–76.

132. Colette, *La Vagabonde,* Pl 1:1074.

133. Colette, *La maison de Claudine,* Pl 2: 986; see above chap. 3, "The Solitude of Music and of Crime," 115.

134. Colette, "Noces," in *Gigi,* Pl 4:561.

135. Colette, "Le miroir," in *Les vrilles de la vigne,* Pl 1:1031.

136. M. Mercier, "La vagabonde et le royaume," "notice," in Colette, *La Vagabonde,* Pl 1:1592.

137. Colette, *La naissance du jour,* Pl 3:290.

138. Colette, *La Vagabonde,* Pl 1:1083–84.

139. Ibid., 119.

140. Colette, "Le dernier feu," in *Les vrilles de la vigne,* Pl 1:979.

141. Colette, "Fièvre," in *Journal à rebours,* Pl 4:142.

142. Colette, "Elle est malade," in *Douze dialogues de bêtes,* Pl 2:40.

143. Colette, *La maison de Claudine,* Pl 2:969.

144. Colette, *La retraite sentimentale,* Pl 1:882.

145. Colette, *La Vagabonde,* Pl 1:1133.

146. Colette, "Ma soeur aux longs cheveux," in *La maison de Claudine,* Pl 2:1014.

147. Colette, *Mes apprentissages,* Pl 3:987.

148. Ibid., 988.
149. Colette, *La naissance du jour*, Pl 3:297.
150. Colette, *Mes apprentissages*, Pl 3:987.
151. Colette, *Trois . . . Six . . . Neuf . . .* , Pl 4:709.
152. Colette, *L'étoile Vesper*, Pl 4:840.
153. See above, chap. 9, "Balzac Difficult? . . . " 358.
154. Colette, *L'étoile Vesper*, Pl 4:880.
155. Ibid.
156. Colette, *Belles saisons*, OCC 11:45.
157. Ibid., 41.
158. Ibid., 42–43.
159. Colette, *L'étoile Vesper*, Pl 4:769–70, my emphasis.
160. See C. de Jouvenel, "Colette et le presse-papiers," 96; and G. Ingold, "Mme Colette et ses boules de cristal," *Cahiers Colette* 16 (1994): 87–93. See also T. Capote, "The White Rose," in *The Dogs Bark* (New York: New American Library, 1951). Capote reports the words of Colette, who in 1948 offered him a Baccarat crystal *sulfure* called *the white rose*: "Peaceful. Yes, that's very true. I've often thought I would like to carry them with me in my coffin, like a pharoah" (15). And the American writer became in turn a collector of *sulfures*.
161. Colette, *La retraite sentimentale*, Pl 1:944.
162. Colette, "Le tombeau rouvert," in *En pays connu*, OCC 11:348.
163. Colette, *La naissance du jour*, Pl 3:307.
164. Colette, *L'étoile Vesper*, Pl 4:881.
165. Colette, *Mes apprentissages*, Pl 3:1007.
166. Colette, "La dame du photographe," in *Gigi*, Pl 4:518–19.
167. Colette, *Le fanal bleu*, Pl 4:1060.
168. Ibid.

10. Is There a Feminine Genius?

1. S. de Beauvoir, *Le deuxième sexe* (Gallimard, 1949), 1:31.
2. Ibid., 2:13.
3. Ibid., 1:31, my emphasis.
4. See J. Kristeva, "Encore l'Oedipe, ou le monisme phallique"; and "De l'étrangeté du phallus ou le féminin entre illusion et désillusion," in *Sens et non-sens de la révolte*, 141–223.
5. See S. Freud, "The Infantile Genital Organization," in *The Standard Edition*, 19:142; "Some Psychical Consequences of the Ana-

tomical Distinction between the Sexes," in *The Standard Edition,* 19:248–58; "Female Sexuality," in *The Standard Edition,* 21:225–43; "Femininity," in *The Standard Edition,* 21:225–43; and *Outline of Psychoanalysis,* in *The Standard Edition,* 23:144–207.

6. "Why not posit here: the fact that everything that is analyzable is sexual does not mean that everything that is sexual is accessible to analysis?" What is "undrained" by phallic mediation would be, above all, "the entire current of the maternal instinct"; See J. Lacan, "Propos directifs pour un Congrès sur la sexualité féminine," in *Ecrits* (Seuil, 1966), 730.

7. J. Laplanche, *Nouveaux fondements pour la psychanalyse: La séduction originaire* (PUF, 1987), 125.

8. See Freud, *Three Essays,* 7:221.

9. See L. Andreas-Salomé, *L'amour du narcisisme* (Gallimard, 1980), 107.

10. Didier Anizeu, *Le Moi-Peau* (Paris, 1985).

11. See Jacques André's comments and developments in *Aux origines féminines de la sexualité* (PUF, 1995).

12. See S. Freud, "Fragment of an Analysis of a Case of Hysteria," in *The Standard Edition,* 7:7–122; and "A Child Is Being Beaten," in *The Standard Edition,* 17:177–205.

13. See S. Freud, "Analysis Terminable and Interminable," in *The Standard Edition,* 23:252.

14. See J. Kristeva, "De la passion selon la maternité," in *La vie amoureuse,* presented at the Colloque de la Société Psychanalytique de Paris, November 2000, published in *Revue Française de Psychanalyse* (July 2001): 105–20.

15. See S. Freud, *Civilization and Its Discontents,* in *The Standard Edition,* 21:101–102.

16. Ibid., 103.

BIBLIOGRAPHY

ORIGINAL EDITIONS OF COLETTE'S WORKS

Claudine à l'école. Ollendorff, 1900, under Willy's name.

Claudine à Paris. Ollendorff, 1901, under Willy's name.

Claudine en ménage. Ollendorff, 1902, under Willy's name and with the title *Claudine amoureuse.*

Claudine s'en va. Ollendorff, 1903, under Willy's name.

Douze dialogues de bêtes. Mercure de France, 1904, under the name "Colette Willy."

La retraite sentimentale. Mercure de France, 1907, under the name "Colette Willy."

Les vrilles de la vigne. Ed. de *La vie parisienne,* 1908, under the name "Colette Willy."

L'ingénue libertine. Ollendorff, 1909, under the name "Colette Willy" (composed of *Minne* [Ollendorff, 1904, under Willy's name] and *Les égarements de Minne* [Ollendorff, 1905, under Willy's name]).

La Vagabonde. Ollendorff, 1910, under the name "Colette Willy."

L'entrave. Librairie des Lettres, 1913, under the name "Colette (Colette Willy)."

L'envers du music-hall. Flammarion, 1913, under the name "Colette (Colette Willy)."

La paix chez les bêtes. Georges Crès et Cie, 1916.

Les heures longues. Fayard, 1917, under the name "Colette (Colette Willy)."

Dans la foule. Georges Crès et Cie, 1918, under the name "Colette (Colette Willy)."

Mitsou: Ou comment l'esprit vient aux filles. Fayard, 1919, under the name "Colette (Colette Willy)."

La chambre éclairée. Edouard Joseph, 1920, under the name "Colette (Colette Willy)."

Chéri. Fayard, 1920, under the name "Colette (Colette Willy)."

Le voyage égoïste. Edouard Pelletan, 1922, under the name "Colette (Colette Willy)."

La maison de Claudine. Ferenczi, 1922, under the name "Colette (Colette Willy)."

Le blé en herbe. Flammarion, 1923, under Colette's name.

La femme cachée. Flammarion, 1924.

Aventures quotidiennes. Flammarion, 1924.

L'enfant et les sortilèges. A. Durand et fils, 1925.

La fin de Chéri. Flammarion, 1926.

La naissance du jour. Flammarion, 1928.

La seconde. Ferenczi, 1929.

Sido. Krâ, 1929; Ferenczi, 1930.

Le pur et l'impur. Ferenczi, 1932, under the title *Ces plaisirs . . .* ; reissued in 1941 by "Armes de France" with the new title.

Prisons et paradis. Ferenczi, 1932.

La chatte. Grasset, 1933.

La jumelle noire. Ferenczi, 1934–38.

Duo. Ferenczi, 1934.

Mes apprentissages. Ferenczi, 1936.

Discours de réception à l'Académie royale belge de langue et de littérature françaises. Grasset, 1936.

Bella-Vista. Ferenczi, 1937.

Le toutounier. Ferenczi, 1939.

Chambre d'hôtel. Fayard, 1940.

Julie de Carneilhan. Fayard, 1941.

Journal à rebours. Fayard, 1941.

Mes cahiers. "Armes de France," 1941.

De ma fenêtre. "Armes de France," 1942.

Le képi. Fayard, 1943 ("Le képi," "Le tendron," "La cire verte," "Armande").

Nudité. Ed. de la Mappemonde, 1943.

Trois . . . Six . . . Neuf . . . Corrêa, 1944.

Gigi. Lausanne: La Guilde du Livre, 1944; the text published by Ferenczi in 1945 comprises "Gigi," "L'enfant malade," "La dame du photographe," and "Flore et pomone."

Belles saisons. Ed. de la Galerie Charpentier, 1945.

L'étoile Vesper. Geneva: Ed. du Milieu du Monde, 1946, 175–333.

Pour un herbier. Lausanne: Mermod, 1949.

Le fanal bleu. Ferenczi, 1949.

Trait pour trait. Le Fleuron, 1949.

Journal intermittent. Le Fleuron, 1949.

La fleur de l'âge. Le Fleuron, 1949.

En pays connu. Manuel Bruker, 1949.

A portée de la main. Mélanges. 1950. *Oeuvres complètes.* Le Fleuron.

COLLECTIVE EDITIONS

Four editions are currently available:

Oeuvres complètes, in fifteen volumes. Flammarion, 1948–50. Known as the Fleuron edition, edited by Maurice Goudeket with Colette's participation.

Oeuvres complètes, in sixteen volumes: Flammarion, 1973–76. Known as the Centenaire edition; augmented version of the Fleuron edition, posthumous collections assembled by Maurice Goudeket: *Paysages et portraits, Contes des mille et un matins* (vol. 13); *Derniers écrits* (vol. 14); and three volumes of correspondence edited by Claude Pichois: *Lettres à Marguerite Moreno* (vol. 14); *Lettres de la Vagabonde, Lettres à Hélène Picard* (vol. 15); *Lettres au Petit Corsaire;* and *Lettres à ses pairs* (vol. 16).

A bound version of this edition was published at the same time by Le Club de L'Honnête Homme.

Romans. Récits. Souvenirs. In three volumes. Robbert Laffont, coll. "Bouquins," 1989, edited by Françoise Burgaud.

Oeuvres, in four volumes. Gallimard, coll. "Bibliothèque de la Pléiade," 1984, 1986, 1991, 2001, edited by Claude Pichois.

VARIOUS PUBLICATIONS NOT APPEARING IN
THE PREVIOUSLY CITED EDITIONS

Les Cahiers Colette publishes newly discovered or little known texts: see esp. nos. 2 (1979), 12 (1990), 13 (1991), and 14 (1992).

Alain Virmaux and Odette Virmaux. *Au cinéma* (criticism and columns, film dialogue). Flammarion, 1975. Additional texts by the same authors in *Europe* (Nov.–Dec. 1981): 119–86.

Alain Galliari. *Au concert* (music and theater columns, signed "Claudine" in 1903). Bordeaux, Le Castor astral, coll. "Les Inattendus," 1992.

Une amitié inattendue. Correspondence between Colette and Francis Jammes, introduction and notes by Robert Mallet. Ed. Emile-Paul Frères, 1945.

En tournée . . . Cartes postales à Sido, edited by Michel Remy-Bieth, with a preface by Michel del Castillo. Persona, 1984.

Lettres à Annie de Pène et Germaine Beaumont, edited by Francine Dugast. Flammarion, 1995.

Sido, *Lettres à sa fille 1905–1912,* preceded by *Lettres de Colette,* preface by Bertrand de Jouvenel, Jeannie Malige, Michèle Sarde. Des femmes-Antoinette Fouque, 1984.

Colette, *Lettres à Moune et au Toutounet* (Hélène Jourdan-Morange and Luc Albert-Moreau), text established and edited by Bernard Villaret. Des femmes-Antoinette Fouque, coll. "Correspondance," 1985.

Lettres aux Petites Fermières, edition established and edited by Thérèse Colléaux-Chaurang. Bordeaux: Le Castor astral, 1992.

Entretiens radiophoniques with Colette, by André Parinaud (1949), distributed since 1991 by Audivis (four Radio-France cassettes, ref. K-5040).

See Also:

Claude Pichois and Alain Brunet. *Colette.* Ed. de Fallois, 1999.

Jacques Dupont. *Colette.* Hachette, 1995.

Donna M. Norell. *Colette: An Annotated Primary and Secondary Bibliography.* New York and London: Garland, 1993.

Cahiers Colette, publication of the Société des Amis de Colette, 89520 Marie de Saint-Sauveur-en-Puisaye (France).

EDITIONS CITED IN THIS BOOK

Pl 1; Pl 2; Pl 3; Pl 4: *Oeuvres complètes,* vols. 1, 2, 3, 4. Gallimard, coll. "Bibliothèque de la Pléiade," 1984, 1986, 1991, 2001.

OCC: *Oeuvres complètes.* Flammarion, 1973. Centenaire edition.

Index

285; hardening of, 324–26; hypersensitive intimacy of, 242–43; Jewish, 278; jouissance of, 11, 15, 105, 110, 163–64, 169, 173, 274, 295, 306, 307, 449n26; and love, 208, 242–46, 250, 251, 256, 262, 284, 424; maturity of, 418; modern, 256, 285–86, 324–26; music-hall, 198; as objects, 254–60, 266, 405, 417; and the other, 164, 244, 420; pain of, 284, 307; in politics, 58–59; public *vs.* inner lives of, 106; singularity of, 404–8; as slaves, 255; stereotypes of, 323–24; strength of, 180–81, 284; suicides of, 44, 264, 283–84; as tender shoots or mature mistresses, 267–74; and thrillers, 119; transvestite, 265–66, 300, 304–5, 324; ugly, 232; working, 177, 324–26; working-class, 327; as writers, 468n274. *See also* the feminine; feminism; homosexuality, female; sexuality: female
Women (unpublished; Colette), 283
"The Wooden Shoes" (Colette), 126
Woolf, Virginia, 10
words: and animals, 222–24; botanical, 114–18; Colette on, 358; and female homosexuality, 298; and film, 356; and the gaze, 209; and love, 248, 270; and metamorphoses, 98; "phonetic intoxication" of, 115, 116; and Proust *vs.* Colette, 377; sensory referents of, 99, 393; sounds of, 87, 89, 93, 94, 97, 100, 101, 115, 117–18, 299, 311–12, 392; and

sublimation, 390; and taste, 3, 200, 204; and thought, 422; unusual, 114–17
world's flesh, 18, 81, 83, 290, 314, 318, 376; and the couple, 316; domestication of, 96; and embroidery, 397; and the gaze, 207; and jouissance, 169; and monstrosity, 225; and the mother, 153, 179; and self, 247; writing as, 57, 248, 351, 367, 392, 401, 402, 422
World War I, 46–48, 185, 277–78, 293, 325, 326, 332–33
World War II, 5, 7, 47, 62–67, 329, 391, 436n113; Colette in, 62, 66–67, 328; collaborators in, 62, 64, 66, 70; and women, 325–26
worthiness, 384–90
the writer: the Captain as, 189–91; and monstrosity, 231, 233; and painter, 342; and reader, 24; Sido as, 153, 192; Willy as, 277
writing, 9, 391–402; abridgement in, 102–3, 104–5, 269; and alphabet, 101, 119, 401, 402; and animals, 37–38, 213, 222–24; and Balzac, 359, 364; and Being, 76, 81, 83, 85, 139, 247; and Bel-Gazou, 293–94; and the body, 196, 398–99; and childhood, 23–24, 394; Colette on, 13, 74–75, 128, 190, 358, 420, 444n23; cult of, 396–97; and depression, 382; and drugs, 300; and ego orgasm, 172; and embroidery, 397–99; and the father, 183; and feigned orgasm, 301; and female homosexuality, 263; and film, 351; and flowers, 110–11, 112, 213;

EUROPEAN PERSPECTIVES

A Series in Social Thought and Cultural Criticism
Lawrence D. Kritzman, Editor